The **Rough Guide** to

Sydney

written and researched by

Margo Daly

with additional contributions by

Alison Cowan and Adrian Proszenko

W9-CBU-737

ROUGH GUIDES

NEW YORK • LONDON • DELHI

www.roughguides.com

Introduction to
Sydney

It might seem surprising that Sydney, established in 1788, is not Australia's capital. Despite the creation of Canberra in 1927 – intended to stem the intense rivalry between Sydney and Melbourne – many Sydneysiders still view their city as the true capital of Australia, and certainly in many ways it feels like it. The city has a tangible sense of history in the old stone walls and well-worn steps in the backstreets around The Rocks, while the sandstone cliffs, rocks and caves amongst the bushlined harbour still contain Aboriginal rock carvings, evocative reminders of a more ancient past.

Flying into Sydney provides a thrilling close-up snapshot of the city as you swoop alongside cliffs and golden beaches, revealing toy-sized images of the Harbour Bridge and the Opera House tilting in a glittering expanse of blue water. Towards Mascot airport the red-tiled roofs of suburban bungalows stretch ever southwards, blue squares of swimming pools shimmering from grassy back yards. The night views are nearly as spectacular, with skyscrapers topped by colourful neon lights and the illuminated white shells of the Opera House reflecting on the dark water as ferries crisscross to Circular Quay.

Sydney has all the vigour of a **world-class city**, and a population approaching five million people; yet on the ground you'll find it still possesses a seductive, small-town, easy-going charm. The furious **development** in preparation for the year 2000 Olympics, heralded as being Sydney's

Spring and summer outdoor festivals and events

From rock concerts on the Opera House steps to film festivals under the stars, Sydney really takes advantage of its climate and setting to host some wonderful outdoor festivals and events in the warmer months between September and April.

Spring is heralded in September by the glorious **Festival of the Winds** (see p.251) when colourful kites overtake Bondi Beach. By early October, locals have begun to tentatively take to the water, and the **Manly International Jazz Festival** (see p.134 and p.251), with many free, outdoor, beachside stages, gets under way over the Labour Day long weekend. Sydney beaches are again celebrated in November, when the fortnight-long **Sculpture By the Sea** (see p.252) sets up the ultimate sculpture park on the coastal walk between Bondi and Tamarama.

In early December, summer is kicked off with the first of Sydney's outdoor rock concerts, **Homebake** (see box p.210), a celebration of Australian talent held in the green space of The Domain. There's a huge **Christmas party** on Bondi Beach (see p.253), popular with backpackers, while the **Sydney to Hobart Yacht Race** (see p.252), ploughing through

coming-of-age ceremony, alarmed many locals, who loved their city just the way it was. But the development brought a greatly improved transport infrastructure, and the $200 million budget improved and beautified the city streets and parks and resulted in a rash of luxury hotels and apartments which are still adding themselves, often contentiously, to the beloved harbour foreshore. The city's **setting** is one that perhaps only Rio de Janeiro can rival: the water is what makes it so special, and no introduction to Sydney would be complete without paying tribute to one of the world's great harbours. Port Jackson is a sunken valley which twists inland to meet the fresh water of the Parramatta River; in the process it washes into a hundred coves and bays, winds around rocky points, flows past the small harbour islands, slips under bridges and laps at the foot of the Opera House.

the harbour's heads on Boxing Day (December 26), provides a colourful post-Christmas spectacle. The year ends – and begins – with a spectacular fireworks display on **New Year's Eve**. The midnight fireworks go off over the Sydney Harbour Bridge and the themed pyrotechnical extravaganza is choreographed to music.

A few days after New Year, the **Sydney Festival** begins, running through most of January. Highlights include several free night-time outdoor concerts in The Domain, featuring opera, jazz and classical music, and film screenings at the very scenic outdoor cinema at Mrs Macquaries Chair (see p.249). The concurrent **Sydney Fringe Festival**, based at Bondi Beach, is more irreverant (see p.250), and the **Flickerfest International Short Film Festival** (see p.218), at the same time, shows films under the stars at the Bondi Pavilion. The **Australia Day** celebrations on January 26 focus attention on the harbour, as Sydney ferries, tall ships and yachts compete in a variety of races, and a fireworks display at Darling Harbour completes the mainstream activities. As an alternative, there's Australia's biggest indigenous music concert, **Survival** (see p.250), at Waverly Oval. The **Big Day Out** (see p.210), Sydney's best outdoor rock event, takes place around Australia Day at Sydney Olympic Park. January ends on a chill-out note with the city's biggest outdoor, beachside dance-music festival, **Vibes on a Summer's Day** (see p.210).

February is overtaken by **Gay + Lesbian Mardi Gras** events (see p.221), which culminate in the huge parade on Oxford Street at the end of February or beginning of March, with the Dykes on Bikes leading the wonderfully decked out floats and outrageously dressed drag queens. The party season either ends with the Mardi Gras parade or with the short-film festival **Tropfest's** outdoor screening, which packs out The Domain and closes Victoria Street in Darlinghurst at the end of February.

Taken together with its surrounds, Sydney is in many ways a microcosm of Australia as a whole – if only in its ability to defy your expectations and prejudices as often as it confirms them. A thrusting, high-rise commercial centre in the **Central Business District (CBD)**, a high-profile gay community in **Darlinghurst**, inner-city deprivation of unexpected harshness, with the highest Aboriginal population of any Australian city, and the dreary traffic-fumed and flat suburban sprawl of the **western suburbs**, are as much part of the scene as the beaches, the bodies, the sparkling harbour, the booming real estate and the world-class restaurant scene. The sophistication, cosmopolitan population and exuberant nightlife of Sydney are a long way from the Outback, and yet fires are a constant threat to the bush-surrounded city.

But all in all, Sydney seems to have the best of both worlds – if it's seen at its gleaming best from the deck of a harbour ferry, especially at weekends when the harbour's jagged jaws fill with a flotilla of small vessels, racing yachts and cabin cruisers, it's at its most varied in its **neighbourhoods**, with their lively café and restaurant scenes. Getting away from the city centre and exploring them is an essential part of Sydney's pleasures. A short ferry trip across to the leafy and affluent North Shore accesses tracts of largely intact bushland, with bushwalking and native animals and birds right on the doorstep. In the summer the city's hot offices are abandoned for the remarkably unspoilt ocean and harbour **beaches** strung around the eastern and northern suburbs, and day-trips away offer a taste of virtually everything you'll find in the rest of Australia.

What to see

Port Jackson, more commonly known as **Sydney Harbour**, carves Sydney in two halves, linked only by the **Sydney Harbour Bridge** and Harbour Tunnel. The south shore is the hub of activity, and it's here that you'll find the **city centre** and most of the things to see and do. Many of the classic images of Sydney are within sight of **Circular Quay**, making this busy waterfront area on Sydney Cove a good point to start discovering the city, with the **Opera**

△ Monorail, Darling Harbour

House and the expanse of the Royal Botanic Gardens to the east of Sydney Cove. It's also near the historic area of **The Rocks** to the west, and prominent museums and art galleries. From Circular Quay south as far as King Street is the **CBD**, with pedestrianized Martin Place at its centre. Just east of Martin Place, **Macquarie Street** is Sydney's civic streetscape, lined with fine colonial sandstone buildings including the New South Wales Parliament House. Beyond Macquarie Street the open space of **The Domain** stretches to the Art Gallery of New South Wales. To the south of the Domain, **Hyde Park** is very much the formal city park, overlooked by churches and the Australian Museum, and with a solemn war memorial.

Park Street divides Hyde Park into two; heading west along it you reach the ornate Town Hall, around which Sydney's shopping heart is focused, including the glorious Queen Victoria Building. Watching over it all is the Sydney Tower, with 360-degree views from the top. The city's two main thoroughfares of George and Pitt streets stretch downtown to the increasingly down-at-heel Central Station and the area known as **Haymarket**, where a vibrant Chinatown sits beside the entertainment area of **Darling Harbour**, with its major museums and attractions.

East of the city centre, following William Street uphill past Hyde Park, is **Kings Cross**, Sydney's red-light district and major travellers' centre, full of accommodation, strip joints and late-night cafés. The adjacent waterfront area of **Woolloomooloo** is home to a busy naval dockyard and some lively pubs. North and east of "the Cross" you move gradually upmarket, with the **eastern suburbs** stretching along the harbour to Watsons Bay, meeting the open sea at South Head. Running south from the head are the popular and populous **eastern beaches**, from Bondi through Coogee to Maroubra ending at La Perouse and the expanse of Botany Bay. Further south brings you to surf territory at Cronulla and the **Royal National Park** across Port Hacking, and a stunning coastal drive down the south coast to Thirroul.

From the southeast corner of Hyde Park, Oxford Street steams through the gay, restaurant, club and bar strip of **Darlinghurst**, becoming increasingly upmarket through gentrified **Paddington**, which has Centennial Park as its playground. South of Oxford Street, opposite Paddington, **Surry Hills** is another up-and-coming area, with plenty of action on Crown Street. The nearby Sydney Cricket Ground and Fox Studios are twin focal points at Moore Park. On the western side of Surry Hills is Central Station; heading west brings you to Sydney University, surrounded by the café-packed and youthful areas of **Newtown** and **Glebe**. West of Glebe, ugly Parramatta Road heads to Italian-dominated **Leichhardt** and **Haberfield** while the nearby harbour suburb of **Balmain**, once a working-class dock area, has been long gentrified, but its big old pubs still make for a great pub crawl. Further west, **Sydney Olympic Park** at Homebush Bay, the focus of the 2000 Olympics, is really Sydney's geographical heart, and beyond the great sprawl of the western suburbs, the World Heritage-listed **Blue Mountains** offer tea rooms, scenic viewpoints and isolated bushwalking.

△ Roof of the Opera House

The bushclad **North Shore** of the harbour is very much where the old money is. There are some wonderful spots to reach by ferry, from Taronga Zoo to Manly. North of Manly the **northern beaches** stretch up to glamorous **Palm Beach**, which looks across to several national parks, including **Ku-Ring-Gai Chase**. Flowing towards Pittwater and Broken Bay is the sandstone-lined **Hawkesbury River**, along which are historic colonial towns. North of here, the **Central Coast** is a weekend beach playground for Sydneysiders, while inland to the northwest is the **Hunter Valley**, Australia's oldest and possibly best-known wine-growing region, set amongst pastoral scenery.

When to go

Since Sydney has such wonderful beaches, the **best time** to come is **between early October and Easter**, the official swimming season, when the beaches are patrolled, and outdoor swimming pools reopen.

The sunny **springtime** months of September and October are when the wild flowers are in bloom, and the smell of blossoms such as jasmine fill the warming city streets, while the bush is alive with critters not yet reduced to summer torpidity. The sweltering hot **summer months** are mid-December, January and February; Christmas can often see 40°C in the shade, though it's been known to be cool and overcast; average summer temperatures are 25°C. Sydney is subtropical, with high and very oppressive humidity in summer building up to sporadic torrential rainstorms (dubbed "southerly busters" by the locals). This is party time, combining high summer with Christmas and New Year festivities, as well as the city's many other festivals and events (see box on pp.iv–v).

April, when the Royal Agricultural Show hits town, is anecdotally – and actually – the rainiest month. May is a contrastingly glorious time when you can bet on dry sunny weather and blue skies as Sydney heads for its mild **winter months** of June, July and August. Don't expect bare trees and grey skies – native trees are evergreen and the skies are usually a less intense blue. Temperatures are rarely less than 10°C, colder during the night, and decidedly chilly the further you go west, with frost on the plains heading to the Blue Mountains – where there are rare light snow-falls. Bring a coat, scarf, gloves and woolly hat if you want to go to the mountains in winter; it gets cool at night in summer too. A jumper and jacket should keep you warm enough in the city, where the cafés continue with their outdoor seating, with braziers to radiate some heat.

▽ Café, Darling Harbour

	Jan	Feb	Mar	Apr	May	Jun	Jul	Aug	Sep	Oct	Nov	Dec
Max. temp. (°F°)	78	78	76	71	66	61	60	63	67	71	74	77
Min. temp. (°F°)	65	65	63	58	52	48	46	48	51	56	60	63
Max. temp. (°C°)	26	26	24	22	19	19	16	17	19	22	23	25
Min. temp. (°C°)	18	18	17	14	11	9	8	9	11	13	16	17
Rainfall (inches)	3.5	4.0	5.0	5.3	5.0	4.6	4.6	3.0	2.9	2.8	2.9	2.9
Rainfall (mm)	89	102	127	135	127	117	117	76	74	71	74	74

things not to miss

It's not possible to see everything Sydney has to offer on a short trip – and we don't suggest you try. What follows is a selective taste of the city's highlights: outstanding museums, beautiful beaches, exciting festivals and fantastic excursions beyond the city – all arranged in colour-coded categories to help you find the very best things to see and experience. All entries have a page reference to take you straight into the guide, where you can find out more.

01 **The Rocks** Page **47** • The heart of historic Sydney, The Rocks also offers great shopping and interesting pubs.

02 Royal Botanical Gardens Page **62** • A picnic in the beautiful Botanical Gardens, with spectacular views of the city and harbour, is a real treat.

03 Sydney pubs Page **195** • From ultra-chic designer bars to historic watering holes – there's a wealth of places for a great night out in Sydney.

04 Taronga Zoo Page **121** • With a superb hilltop position overlooking the city, surrounded by natural bush, this is a fantastic spot to see Australian critters as well as those from further afield.

05 Hunter Valley wineries Page **281** • One of Australia's most famous wine-growing regions.

06 Manly Page **133** • The ferry trip out to Manly, a lively beach suburb, with its unbeatable views of the harbour, is a must.

07 The Queen Victoria Building Page **73** • Built in 1898, this beautifully restored arcade combines an exquisite historic interior with shops selling the latest fashions.

08 Bondi Beach Page **125** • One of the best-known beaches in the world, big, brash Bondi is synonymous with Australian beach culture.

09 **Paddington** Page **93** • With its gorgeous colonial-style houses, Paddington is best explored on Saturday, when the famous market is in full swing.

10 **Opera House perform-ance** Page **58** • Admire the stunning exterior of this Australian icon, or, better still, take in a performance.

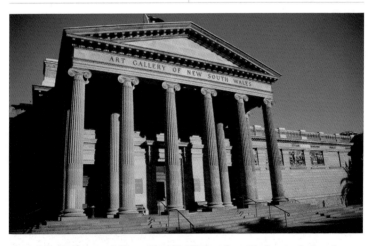

11 **Art Gallery of New South Wales** Page **67** • A vast collection of Australian and European art in an imposing Neoclassical building.

13 **Blue Mountains** Page **288** • The World Heritage-listed Blue Mountains make a great weekend break from Sydney.

12 **Oxford Street** Page **91** • Crammed with bars, clubs, restaurants, shops and cinemas, Oxford Street is worth a visit in the day and especially at night.

14 **Cruising on the Hawkesbury River** Page **273** • The best way to explore the pretty Hawkesbury River is to take a leisurely cruise.

15 Watsons Bay Page 116 •
After admiring the harbour bay, check out the treacherous cliffs of The Gap, and then sample some of *Doyles'* famous fish.

16 Fish Market Page 83 •
Offering an enormous variety of fish, this frenetic early-morning market is a real spectacle – with opportunities for a water-side picnic too.

17 Climbing Sydney Harbour Bridge Page 46 •
Climb the famous coathanger for great harbour views, or simply walk across and save $150.

18 Gay + Lesbian Mardi Gras
Page 221 • The biggest celebration of gay and lesbian culture in the world.

Contents

Using this Rough Guide

We've tried to make this Rough Guide a good read and easy to use. The book is divided into eight main sections, and you should be able to find whatever you want in one of them.

Front section

The front **colour section** offers a quick tour of Sydney. The **introduction** aims to give you a feel for the place, with suggestions on where to head for and when to go. Next, the author rounds up her favourite aspects of Sydney in the **things not to miss** section – whether it's exciting festivals, amazing sights or a great market. Right after this comes a full **contents** list.

Basics

The Basics section covers all the pre-departure nitty-gritty to help you plan your trip. This is where to find out how to get there, about money and costs, Internet access, transport and local media – in fact just about every piece of **general practical information** you might need.

The City

This is the heart of the Rough Guide, divided into user-friendly chapters, each of which covers a city district. Every chapter starts with an **introduction** that helps you to decide where to go, followed by an extensive tour of the sights.

Listings

This section contains all the consumer information you need to make the most of your stay, with chapters on **accommodation**, places to **eat** and **drink**, **nightlife**, **shopping**, **festivals**, and more.

Beyond the city

These chapters describe attractions **further out of the city**, with all the accommodation, eating and practical details you'll need for both day-trips and longer stays.

Contexts

Read Contexts to get a deeper understanding of what makes Sydney tick. We include a brief **history** and a detailed further reading section that reviews dozens of **books** relating to the city.

Index + small print

Apart from a **full index**, which includes maps as well as places, this section covers publishing information, credits and acknowledgements, and also has our contact details in case you want to send in updates and corrections to the book – or suggestions as to how we might improve it.

Colour maps

The **back colour section** contains detailed maps and plans to give you an overview of the city and help you explore.

Map and chapter list

Contents

Front section

Basics

The City

Listings

Beyond the city

Contexts

Index + small print

Colour maps

1. Around Sydney
2. Sydney suburbs
3. Sydney Harbour
4. Central Sydney

5. State Transit Sydney ferries
6. CityRail network
7. Useful bus routes from the city

Map symbols

Maps are listed in the full index using coloured text.

▬▬	Expressway	⌂	Hut
═══	Main road	Λ̇	Campsite
───	Minor road	◉	Accommodation
▭▭	Pedestrianized street	▣	Restaurant
▥▥	Steps	⊠	Post office
- - - - -	Path	ⓘ	Information office
▬▬	Railway	⊞	Hospital
───	Metro Monorail	⊛	CityRail station
- - - - -	Metro Light Rail	Ⓜ	Monorail station
— —	Ferry route	●	Metro Light Rail station
───	Waterway	Ω	Sydney ferries
⌂⌂	Mountains	▣	Parking
▲	Peak	⊠	Gate
ʌʌʌ	Rocks	⍦	Fountain
◠	Cave	⌇	Golf course
✈	Airport	▮	Building
♦	Place of interest	⊞	Church
●	Museum	⬭	Stadium
⍢	Lighthouse	▨	Park
⚐	Lookout	⊡	Christian cemetery
▲	Temple	▨	Beach
⛩	Buddist temple		

Basics

Basics

Getting there

Few will be surprised to learn that flying is the main way of getting to Sydney. You can fly pretty much every day from Europe, North America and Southeast Asia. Air fares depend on the season, with the highest being the two weeks either side of Christmas, although you can get a low-season bargain if you fly on Christmas Day itself. Fares drop during the "shoulder" seasons – mid-January to March and mid-August to November – and you'll get the best prices during the low season, April to August. Because of the distance from most popular departure points, flying at weekends does not alter the price.

However, you can certainly cut costs by going through a **specialist flight agent** – either a consolidator, who buys up blocks of tickets from the airlines and sells them at a discount, or a **discount agent**, who in addition to dealing with discounted flights may also offer special student and youth fares and a range of other travel-related services such as travel insurance, rail passes, car rental, tours and the like. Some agents specialize in **charter flights**, which may be cheaper than anything available on a scheduled flight, but again departure dates are fixed and withdrawal penalties are high. One possibility is to see if you can arrange a courier flight, although you'll need a flexible schedule, and preferably be travelling alone with very little luggage. In return for shepherding a parcel through customs, you can expect to get a deeply discounted ticket. You'll probably also be restricted in the duration of your stay.

If Sydney is only one stop on a longer journey, you might want to consider buying a **Round-the-World** (RTW) ticket. Some travel agents can sell you an "off-the-shelf" ticket that will have you touching down in about half a dozen cities – Sydney is frequently part of the regular eastbound RTW loop from Europe. Figure on £850/US$1300 for a RTW ticket including Australia.

Many airlines and discount travel websites offer you the opportunity to book your tickets **online**, cutting out the costs of agents and middlemen. Good deals can often be found through discount or auction sites, as well as through the airlines' own websites.

From Britain and Ireland

The market for flights between Britain and Australia is one of the most competitive in the world and prices have never been lower. Qantas, British Airways, Singapore and Malaysia Airlines offer **direct flights** to Sydney in 22–23 hours. Other airlines involve a change of plane for connecting flights, and potentially long waits in between, which can make the journey last up to 36 hours. However, it often costs no more to break the journey in such **stopover** points as Southeast Asia, New Zealand or North America, or even Argentina, South Africa or Japan, so that it need not be a tedious, seat-bound slog. Some airlines usually have great **special deals** as well that include discounted or free flights en route or in Australia itself. All direct scheduled flights to Australia depart from London's two main airports, Gatwick and Heathrow, though Singapore Airlines has daily flights from Manchester to Singapore that connect with onward flights to Sydney. There are no direct flights from Ireland.

Of course, you can still take a **boat** to Sydney from the UK, cruising with P&O (☎020/7800 2222, ⓦwww.pocruises.com); their once-yearly 39-night "Boomerang" cruise to Sydney on the *Aurora* leaves Southampton in early January and goes via the Carribean, the Panama Canal, Mexico, San Francisco, Honolulu, Fiji and New Zealand. P&O's own price is £4395 on the *Aurora*, but you can get a cheaper price from a travel agent.

Fares and flights

Most of the discount and specialist agents listed opposite can quote fares on scheduled flights. For the latest prices and special deals, check out the ads in the travel pages of the weekend newspapers, London's listing magazine *Time Out,* the free listings magazine *TNT*, but especially the **websites** of travel agents and the airlines themselves for "online specials" available via Internet auctions; also check out the discount travel websites listed on p.12. However, **booking ahead** as far as possible is still the best way to secure the most reasonable prices, and unless it's an Internet special, it is almost invariably cheaper to buy tickets through **agents** rather than through airlines themselves. Note that all the fares quoted below are exclusive of airport tax – this is usually a hefty £60–80, depending on the airline, route and ticket price.

High season differs slightly from airline to airline, but the most expensive time to travel to Sydney is always the two weeks before **Christmas** until mid-January. **Shoulder seasons** are mid-January to March and mid-August, to November, while the **low season** runs from April to the middle of August, with prices rising a little and reduced availability from the beginning of July to the middle of August, coinciding with the peak European holiday times.

Return **fares** to Sydney for a non-direct flight on one of the less prestigious airlines can start as low as £550 in the low season, with special offers occasionally dropping the price to around £450; some of the cheapest deals are with Korean Air. Off-peak return fares for a direct flight on one of the better airlines usually start at around £650, going up to about £800 but can drop as low as £500. In the two weeks before Christmas, all the airlines have similar rates: you can find fares for £800 but these sell fast and you would be lucky to find anything for less than £1000 return. However, if you don't mind flying on Christmas Day itself you may find a much cheaper deal. To stand a chance of getting one of the cheaper peak-season tickets, book at least six months in advance. In the shoulder seasons, you should expect to pay at least £660–700 (or around £800 with a prestigious airline).

Also, between mid-November and mid-January, European Airlines offer once-weekly direct **charter flights** from London Gatwick to Sydney, with fares from £499 from mid-November to early December, rising to £899 and £999 in the two weeks before Christmas and dropping down to £649 after Christmas. The cheaper prices come with restrictions including limited departure dates and options of two-, three- or four-week stays only. There are pricier Business Class tickets (from £1499) or you can upgrade for £100 to a the better-staffed, quieter (no infants) Upper Deck; bookings are through Austravel (see opposite).

With Qantas you can fly from **regional airports** at Aberdeen, Belfast, Edinburgh, Glasgow, Manchester or Newcastle to connect with your international flight at Heathrow. There is no extra charge from Manchester, but you'll pay a **supplement** of £25 each way from the others.

An excellent alternative to a long direct flight is a **multi-stopover ticket**, which can cost the same or just a little more than the price of an ordinary return; breaking your journey at the airline's stopover points, most commonly in Southeast Asia or in the US. Unusual routes are inevitably more expensive, but it's possible to fly **via South America** with Aerolineas Argentinas, which offers stops in Buenos Aires and Auckland – at least £925 return – or there are good deals **via Japan** on All Nippon Airlines and Japan Airlines.

Another option is a **Round-the-World** (RTW) ticket. A good agent such as Trailfinders (see opposite) can piece together sector fares from various airlines: providing you keep your itinerary down to three continents prices range from around £850 for a simple London–Bangkok–Sydney–LA–London deal to well over £1000 for more complicated routeings.

Although most of the cheaper routeings **from Ireland** involve a stopover in London and transfer to one of the airlines listed opposite, there are often good deals on Olympic Airways (℡01/608 0090) **from Dublin** via Greece. Singapore Airlines (℡01/671 0722) has flights ticketed through from Dublin, Shannon or Cork via London to Singapore and Sydney, while Malaysia Airlines (☏ 01/676 1561) also goes from all three Irish airports via Kuala Lumpur. The three airports are also served by the affiliated British Airways and Qantas (both ☏ 01/874 7747); all their flights to Sydney have a Dublin–London add-on included in the price. Malaysia Airlines fares start from around IR£770 for an open one-year return in low season, up to IR£1300 in the Christmas period, while a Singapore Airlines ticket would cost around IR£910 in the shoulder season. A low-season, fare **from Belfast** with British Airways starts at £610, going up to £720 in the shoulder season. In high season, fares average at around £1000. For youth and student discount fares, the best first stop is Usit (see p.12).

Packages are a good option for those worried about spiralling costs or those who want to enjoy quality hotels at a cheaper price. There are plenty of more flexible tours which combine Sydney with other areas of Australia; Travel Bag offers some good tour options, plus some action and eco-oriented trips including the Great Barrier Reef. As well as flights, the Australian expert Qantas also offers quality city packages.

Airlines

Aerolineas Argentinas ☏ 020/7494 1001, ⓦ www.aerolineas.com.ar.
Air China ☏ 020/7630 0919 or 7630 7678, ⓦ www.air-china.co.uk.
Air New Zealand ☏ 020/8741 2299, ⓦ www.airnz.co.uk.
Alitalia ☏ 0870/5448 259, Republic of Ireland ☏ 01/677 5171, ⓦ www.alitalia.it.
All Nippon Airways (ANA) ☏ 020/7224 8866, ⓦ www.ana.co.jp.
Austrian Airlines ☏ 0845/601 0948, ⓦ www.aua.com.
British Airways ☏ 0845/773 3377, ⓦ www.britishairways.com.
Emirates Airlines ☏ 0870/243 2222, ⓦ www.emirates.com.
Eva Airways ☏ 020/7380 8300, ⓦ www.evaair.com.tw.
Garuda Indonesia ☏ 020/7467 8600, ⓦ www.garuda-indonesia.co.uk.
Japan Airlines ☏ 020/7408 1000, ⓦ www.jal.co.jp.

KLM Royal Dutch Airlines ☏ 0870/507 4074, ⓦ www.klmuk.com.
Korean Air ☏ 0800/0656 2001, Republic of Ireland ☏ 01/799 7990, ⓦ www.koreanair.eu.com.
Malaysia Airlines ☏ 0870/607 9090, ⓦ www.malaysia-airlines.com/uk.
Olympic Airways ☏ 0870/606 0460, ⓦ www.olympic-airways.co.uk.
Qantas ☏ 0845/774 7767, ⓦ www.qantas.co.uk.
Singapore Airlines ☏ 0870/608 8886, in Manchester ☏ 0161/830 8888; Republic of Ireland ☏ 01/671 0722; ⓦ www.singaporeair.com.
South African Airways ☏ 020/7312 5000, ⓦ www.flysaa.com.
Thai Airways ☏ 0870/606 0911, ⓦ www.thaiair.com.
United Airlines ☏ 0845/844 4777, ⓦ www.unitedairlines.co.uk.
Virgin Atlantic ☏ 01293/747 747, ⓦ www.virgin-atlantic.com.

Discount travel agents

Austravel ☏ 0870/166 2020, ⓦ www.austravel.net. Specialists for flights and tours to Australia; agent for European Airlines charter flights to Sydney (see p.10). Issues ETAs and traditional visas for an administration fee of £16.
Bridge the World ☏ 020/7911 0990, ⓦ www.bridgetheworld.com. Specialists in RTW tickets.
Flightbookers ☏ 0870/010 7000, ⓦ www.ebookers.com. A major online travel agent with a range of low-fare flights to Sydney; also Flightbookers offices in central London and at Gatwick.
Flynow.com ☏ 0870/444 0045, ⓦ www.flynow.com. Large range of discounted tickets.
Lees Travel ☏ 020 7262 2665, ⓦ www.leestravel.com. Good deals on Korean Air flights as well as other airlines.
North South Travel ☏ 01245/608 291, ⓦ www.northsouthtravel.co.uk. Friendly, competitive travel agency, offering discounted fares – profits are used to support projects in the developing world, especially the promotion of sustainable tourism.
Quest Worldwide ☏ 0870/442 2699 or 020/8547 3322, ⓦ www.questtravel.com. Specialists in RTW and Australian discount fares.
STA Travel ☏ 0870/1600 599, ⓦ www.statravel.co.uk. Worldwide specialists in low-cost flights and tours for students and under-26s, though other customers welcome. Also has offices in Sydney.
Trailfinders ☏ 020/7628 7628, ⓦ www.trailfinders.com. Excellent for multi-stop

and RTW tickets, including some unusual routeings via South Africa, the Pacific and the US – their very useful quarterly magazine is worth scrutinizing for RTW routes. Well informed and efficient – visa service available at the Kensington High Street branch. Also has a branch in Sydney.

Travel Bag ☎0870/890 1456, ⊛www.travelbag.co.uk. Well-established long-haul travel agent with a good reputation for Australian coverage. Direct and RTW flights on all the best airlines such as Qantas, British Airways and Singapore, plus packages.

Discount travel websites

⊛**www.cheapflights.co.uk** Flight deals, travel agents, plus links to other travel sites.
⊛**www.dialaflight.co.uk** Useful for tracking down bargains, plus telephone sales for scheduled flights (☎0870/333 4488).
⊛**www.ebookers.com** See p.11.
⊛**www.etn.nl/discount.htm** A hub of 750 worldwide consolidator and discount agent Web links, maintained by the non-profit European Travel Network.
⊛**www.expedia.co.uk** Microsoft's venture into the Internet travel market, offering special fares and an online booking service.
⊛**www.flightline.co.uk** A telephone-based outfit (☎0800/036 0777) also offering online searches for cheap scheduled flights.
⊛**www.lastminute.com** Offers good last-minute holiday package and flight-only deals.
⊛**www.priceline.co.uk** Name-your-own-price website that has deals at around forty percent off standard fares. You cannot specify flight times (although you do specify dates) and the tickets are non-refundable, non-transferable and non-changeable.
⊛**www.opodo.co.uk** User-friendly, UK-only booking site – owned by major airlines such as BA and Air France – with good deals on flights and packages.
⊛**www.travelocity.co.uk** Destination guides and the best deals for car rental, accommodation and lodging as well as fares – monitors fares on over seven hundred airlines worldwide to track the best prices.

Irish flight agents and operators

Australia Travel Centre ☎01/804 7188. Specialists in long-haul flights.
Thomas Cook ⊛www.tcsignature.com; Dublin ☎01/677 1721; Belfast ☎028/9055 0232. Mainstream package-holiday and flight agent with occasional discount offers.

Trailfinders Dublin ☎01/677 7888, ⊛www.trailfinders.ie. One of the best-informed and most efficient agents for independent travellers; produce a very useful quarterly magazine worth scrutinizing for RTW routes.
Travel Care 35 Belmont Rd, Belfast 4 ☎028/9047 1717, ⓕ9047 1339, ⊛www.travelcare.ie. Discount flight specialists.
Unijet Parkwood House, Newforge Lane, Belfast BT9 5NW ☎028/9031 4656, ⊛www.unijet.com. Discount scheduled fares; the best agent to contact for Malaysia Airlines ticket deals.
Usit Now Dublin ☎01/602 1600, ⊛www .usitnow.ie. Student and youth specialists for flights and trains.

From the US and Canada

From Los Angeles it's possible to fly nonstop to Sydney in fourteen and a half hours. Qantas, United, Air Canada and Air New Zealand all operate **direct flights**. Flying on an Asian airline will most likely involve a stop in their capital city (Singapore, Tokyo, Hong Kong etc) and if you're travelling from the West Coast of North America you'll probably find their fares on the Pacific route somewhat higher than their American or Australasian competitors.

Many of the major airlines offer deals with **stopovers** either at **Pacific Rim** destinations such as Tokyo with Japan Airlines, Honolulu with Air Canada or Kuala Lumpur with Malaysia Airlines or at a number of exotic South Pacific locations with Air New Zealand. Either there will be a flat surcharge on your ticket or they may offer you a higher-priced ticket allowing you to make several stops over a fixed period of time. But the best deal will probably be a Circle Pacific or **Round-the-World** (RTW) ticket from a discount outfit such as Travel Avenue.

Fares and flights

Most of the consolidators and discount agents listed opposite can quote and offer the best fares on scheduled flights, though you can go direct through airlines. It's also worth checking airline **websites** for "online specials" available via **Internet auctions**, the latest way to sell last-minute seats, or try specialist discount travel and auction websites such as Hotwire or Skyauction. If you travel a lot, **discount travel clubs** are another option – the annual membership fee may be worth the benefits, such as cut-price air tickets and car rental. Many airlines offer youth or student fares to **under-26s**.

However, **booking ahead** as far as possible is still the best way to secure the most reasonable prices. Fares vary significantly according to season – generally **high season** is December–February, **low season** April–August, and other times are **shoulder**. The highest prices are over Christmas and New Year; booking as far in advance as possible at these times is highly recommended.

Sample lowest standard **scheduled fares** for low/high seasons are: from Chicago or New York (US$1200/$1900), LA or San Francisco (US$900/$1500); Montreal or Toronto (CDN$1900/$2500) and Vancouver ($1800/$2000). To see more of the world, a sample **RTW ticket** LA–Sydney–Bangkok–Delhi–Mumbai–London–LA costs around US$2500.

Airlines

Air Canada ☏1-888/247-2262, ⊛www.aircanada.ca.
Air New Zealand US ☏1-800/262-1234; Canada ☏1-800/663-5494; ⊛www.airnz.com.
Cathay Pacific ☏1-800/233-2742, ⊛www.cathay-usa.com.
Malaysia Airlines ☏1-800/552-9264, ⊛www.malaysiaairlines.com.
Qantas ☏1-800/227-4500, ⊛www.qantas.com.
Singapore Airlines ☏1-800/742-3333, ⊛www.singaporeair.com.
United Airlines ☏1-800/538-2929, ⊛www.ual.com.

Discount flight agents, travel clubs, courier brokers and consolidators

Air Brokers International ☏1-800/883-3273, ⊛www.airbrokers.com. Consolidator and specialist in RTW and Circle Pacific tickets.
Airtech ☏212/219-7000, ⊛www.airtech.com. Stand-by seat broker; also deals in consolidator fares and courier flights.
Airtreks.com ☏1-877-AIRTREKS or 415/912-5600, ⊛www.airtreks.com. Circle Pacific and RTW tickets. The website features an interactive database that lets you build and price your own RTW itinerary.
Council Travel ☏1-800/2COUNCIL, ⊛www.counciltravel.com. Nationwide organization that mostly specializes in student/budget travel.

Flights from the US only. Owned by STA Travel.
Educational Travel Center ☏1-800/747-5551 or 608/256-5551, ⊛www.edtrav.com. Student/youth discount agent.
International Association of Air Travel Couriers ☏308/632-3273, ⊛www.courier.org. Courier flight broker with membership fee of $45/yr.
Skylink US ☏1-800/247-6659 or 212/573-8980, Canada ☏1-800/759-5465, ⊛www.skylinkus.com. Consolidator.
STA Travel ☏1-800/781-4040, ⊛www.sta-travel.com. Worldwide specialists in independent travel; also provide student IDs, travel insurance, car rental, rail passes, etc.
TFI Tours ☏1-800/745-8000 or 212/736-1140, ⊛www.lowestairprice.com. Consolidator.
Travel Avenue ☏1-800/333-3335, ⊛www.travelavenue.com. Full-service travel agent that offers discounts in the form of rebates.
Travel Cuts Canada ☏1-800/667-2887, US ☏1-866/246-9762, ⊛www.travelcuts.com. Canadian student-travel organization.
Travelers Advantage ☏1-877/259-2691, ⊛www.travelersadvantage.com. Discount travel club; annual membership fee required (currently $1 for 3 months' trial).
Worldtek Travel ☏1-800/243-1723, ⊛www.worldtek.com. Discount travel agency for worldwide travel.

Online booking agents

⊛**www.etn.nl/discount.htm** A hub of 750 worldwide consolidator and discount agent Web links, maintained by the non-profit European Travel Network.
⊛**www.expedia.com** Discount air fares, all-airline search engine and daily deals.
⊛**www.flyaow.com** Online air travel info and reservations site.
⊛**www.hotwire.com** Bookings from the US only. Last-minute savings of up to forty percent on regular published fares. Travellers must be at least 18 and there are no refunds, transfers or changes allowed. Log-in required.
⊛**www.priceline.com** Name-your-own-price website that has deals at around forty percent off standard fares. You cannot specify flight times (although you do specify dates) and the tickets are non-refundable, non-transferable and non-changeable.
⊛**www.skyauction.com** Bookings from the US only. Auctions tickets and travel packages using a "second bid" scheme. The best strategy is to bid the maximum you're willing to pay, since if you win you'll pay just enough to beat the runner-up regardless of your maximum bid.

@ **www.travelocity.com** Destination guides, hot Web fares and best deals for car rental, accommodation and lodging as well as fares. Monitors fares on over seven hundred airlines worldwide to track the best deals on fares for you. Provides access to the travel agent system SABRE, the most comprehensive central reservations system in the US.

Packages and tours

Several of the operators below, such as United Vacations, offer **city stopovers**, providing, for example, two nights' accommodation and perhaps a day-tour, starting at around US$180 on top of your ticket. Organized tours of Australia, which inevitably take in Sydney, cost from US$3500 for a typical two-week tour – such as those offered by Adventures Abroad – taking in the usual cultural/historical/natural sights.

Tour operators

AAT Kings ☎ 1-800/353 4525,
@ www.aatkings.com.
Abercrombie and Kent ☎ 1-800/323-7308,
@ www.abercrombiekent.com.
Adventure Center ☎ 1-800/227-8747,
@ www.adventure-center.com.
Adventures Abroad ☎ 1-800/665-3998,
@ www.adventures-abroad.com.
ATS Tours ☎ 1-800/423-2880,
@ www.atstours.com.
Australian Pacific Tours ☎ 1-800/290-8687,
@ www.aptours.com.
Goway Travel ☎ 1-800/387-8850,
@ www.goway.com.
International Gay and Lesbian Travel Association ☎ 1-800/448-8550,
@ www.iglta.org.
Qantas Vacations US ☎ 1-800/252-4162;
Canada ☎ 1-800/268-7525;
@ www.quantasvacations.com.
Swain Australia Tours ☎ 1-800/227-9246,
@ www.swainaustralia.com.
United Vacations ☎ 1-800/917-9246,
@ www.unitedvacations.com.

From New Zealand

New Zealand–Australia routes are busy and competition is fierce, resulting in an ever-changing range of deals and special offers; your best bet is to check the latest with a specialist travel agent or the relevant airlines'

websites. Flying time from Auckland to Sydney is around three and a half hours.

Ultimately, the price you pay for your flight will depend on how much flexibility you want; many of the cheapest deals are hedged with restrictions – typically a maximum stay of thirty days and a fourteen-day advance-purchase requirement. However, there are few restrictions on the new Web-based New Zealand airline, Freedom Air. It specializes in no-frills, low-cost trans-Tasman air travel, with flights from Auckland, Christchurch, Dunedin, Palmerston North and Wellington to Sydney. There are few restrictions on how long tickets stay open and advance purchase has little effect on ticket prices, which cost around $NZ590 return.

Only Qantas, Air New Zealand, Freedom Air and Aerolineas Argentineas have tickets that stay open for one year, while Polynesian and Malaysia Airlines offer tickets open for up to six months; there are also ninety-day tickets that fall between the two extremes in price. The cheapest thirty-day return **fare from Auckland** to Sydney is usually with Aerolineas Argentineas or Polynesian Airlines for $NZ475–550, but flights tend to be heavily booked. Polynesian's six-month ticket is the cheapest long-stay ticket at $985. Qantas and Air New Zealand each have similarly priced daily direct flights to Sydney (NZ$699–799). Whether you fly from **Wellington** or **Christchurch** generally makes no difference to the fare.

Prices peak primarily from December to mid-January. Outside **peak season**, when the airlines often have surplus capacity, they may offer promotional fares, which can bring down prices to as low as NZ$535 for a thirty-day return from Auckland to Sydney.

There's a huge variety of **packages** to Sydney available; call or check the websites of any of the travel agents listed opposite. The holiday subsidiaries of airlines such as Air New Zealand and Qantas offer short **city-breaks** (flight and accommodation) and **fly-drive** deals for little more than the cost of the regular air fare.

Airlines

Aerolineas Argentinas ☎ 09/379 3675,
@ www.aerolineas.com.au.

Air New Zealand ☎09/357 3000,
Ⓦwww.airnz.co.nz.
Freedom Air ☎0800 600 500,
Ⓦwww.freedom.co.nz.
Malaysia Airlines ☎09/373 2741,
Ⓦwww.malaysiaairlines.co.nz.
Polynesian Airlines ☎09/309 5396;
Ⓦwww.polynesianairlines.co.nz.
Qantas ☎09/357 8900, Ⓦwww.qantas.com.au.
Thai Airways ☎1300/651 960,
Ⓦwww.thaiair.com.

Specialist travel agents

Flight Centres 350 Queen St, Auckland ☎09/358 4310, Ⓦwww.flightcentre.co.nz, plus branches nationwide. Competitive discounts on air fares and a wide range of package holidays and adventure tours.

Holiday Shoppe 27–35 Victoria St West, Auckland, plus 79 other branches around the country ☎09/379 2099,
Ⓦwww.holidayshoppe.co.nz. Long-established Budget Travel has now merged with Holiday Shoppe to form one of New Zealand's largest travel agencies. Still good for budget air fares and accommodation packages
STA Travel Shop 2B, 187 High St, Auckland ☎09/309 0458, fastfare telesales ☎09/366 6673 or ☎0508/782 872, Ⓦwww.statravel.co.nz, plus branches nationwide. Fare discounts for students and those under 26, as well as visas, student cards and travel insurance.
Student Union Travel 5 Victoria St East, Auckland plus branches in Hamilton and Christchurch ☎09/379 4224 or ☎0508/639 932,
Ⓦwww.sut.com.au. Student/youth travel specialists.

Red tape and visas

All visitors to Australia, except New Zealanders, require a visa or an Electronic Travel Authority (ETA). Visa application forms are obtained from the Australian High Commissions, embassies or consulates listed on p.16; citizens of the US can also get them from the embassy Internet sites.

Three-month tourist visas, valid for multiple entry over one year, are issued free and processed over the counter, or are returned in three weeks by mail. However, the computerized system, Electronic Travel Authority (ETA), can speed things up for nationals of the UK, Ireland, the US, Canada, Malaysia, Singapore, Japan and most European countries. Applied for online, the ETA replaces the visa stamp in your passport (ETAs are computerized) and saves the hassle of queuing or sending off your passport. ETAs can be applied for on the Web with a credit card for A\$20 (see the Australian government websites on p.16 or go directly to Ⓦwww.eta.immi.gov.au) or are available from travel agents and airlines at the same time as you book your flight. In this case an additional fee is levied on top of the cost of your ETA – in the UK around £16.

Entry requirements do change, so if in doubt, check with your nearest embassy or consulate before leaving.

Longer visas, working visas and extensions

Visits from three to six months incur a fee (A\$65 or the equivalent in your country). If you think you might stay more than three months, it's best to get the longer visa before departure, because once you get to Australia visa extensions cost A\$160. If you need to extend your visa while in Sydney, contact the Department of Immigration, 26 Lee St, near Central Station (☎13 18 81). You may also be asked to prove you have adequate funds to support yourself – at least A\$1000 a month. If you're visiting immediate family who live in Australia, apply for a Sponsored Family Visitor Visa, (A\$165), which has fewer restrictions.

Twelve-month **working holiday visas** – with the stress on casual employment – are easily available to British, Irish, Canadian, Dutch, German, Japanese and Korean single people aged 18–30, though exceptions are made for young married couples without children. You must arrange the visa before you arrive in Australia, and several months in advance; the processing fee is A$160. Young US citizens (18–30) can join the Special Youth Program combining a four-month holiday with short-term work (membership US$495; contact BUNAC ☎1-800/GO BUNAC or 203/264 0901, ⓦwww.bunac.com).

Australian embassies and consulates

You may be already living and travelling outside your own country when you decide to visit Sydney. For a full list of **Australian embassies and consulates**, consult the Australian Department of Foreign Affairs and Trade website (ⓦwww.dfat.gov.au/missions/index.html).

UK Australian High Commission, Australia House, Strand, London WC2B 4LA ☎020/7379 4334, ⓕ7240 5333. For addresses of Honorary Consuls in Manchester and Edinburgh, see ⓦwww.australia.org.uk.

Ireland Australian Embassy, Fitzwilton House, Wilton Terrace, Dublin 2 ☎01/664 5300, ⓕ662 3566, ⓦwww.australianembassy.ie.

US Australian Embassy, 1601 Massachusetts Ave NW, Washington, DC 20036 ☎202/797-3000, ⓕ797-3168; Australian Consulate-General International Building,150 E 42nd St, 34th floor, New York, NY 10117-5612 ☎212/351-6500, ⓕ351-6501. For Consulate-General addresses in Atlanta, Honolulu, LA, Chicago and San Francisco see ⓦwww.austemb.org.

Canada Australian High Commission, Suite 710, 50 O'Connor St, Ottawa, Ontario K1P 6L2 ☎613/236-0841, ⓕ236-4376. For Australian Consulate office addresses in Toronto and Vancouver, see ⓦwww.ahc-ottawa.org.

New Zealand Australian Consulate-General, 8th floor, Union House, 132–138 Quay St, Auckland 1 ☎09/303 2429, ⓕ377 0798; Australian High Commission, 72–78 Hobson St, Thorndon, Wellington ☎04/473 6411, ⓕ498 7135, ⓦwww.australia.org.nz.

Customs and quarantine

The **duty-free allowance** on entry is one litre of alcohol and 250 cigarettes or 250g of tobacco. Australia has strict quarantine laws that apply to fruit, vegetables, fresh and packaged food, seed and some animal products, among other things. Expect to be welcomed into the country with the ritual on-board pesticide spray.

Insurance

The national healthcare scheme in Australia, Medicare, offers a reciprocal arrangement – free essential healthcare – for citizens of the UK, Ireland, New Zealand, Italy, Malta, Finland, the Netherlands and Sweden. This free treatment is limited to public hospitals and casualty departments (though the ambulance ride to get you there isn't covered); at GPs you pay upfront (about $40 minimum) with two-thirds of your fee reimbursed by Medicare (does not apply to citizens of New Zealand and Ireland). If you are entitled to free emergency healthcare from Medicare, you may feel that the need for the health element of travel insurance is reduced. In any case, some form of travel insurance can help plug the gaps and will cover you in the event of losing your baggage, missing a plane and the like.

A typical travel insurance policy usually provides cover for the loss of baggage, tickets and – up to a certain limit – cash or cheques, as well as cancellation or curtailment of your journey. Most of them exclude **"high-risk" activities** unless an extra premium is paid: depending on the insurer, these can include water sports (especially diving), skiing or even just hiking; check carefully that any policy you are considering will cover you in case of an accident. Many policies can be chopped and changed to exclude coverage you don't need – for example, sickness and accident benefits can often be excluded or included at will. If you do take medical coverage, ascertain whether benefits will be paid as treatment proceeds or only after return home, and whether there is a 24-hour medical emergency number. When securing baggage cover, make sure that the per-article limit – typically under £500 – will cover your most valuable possession. If you need to make a claim, you should keep receipts for medicines and medical treatment, and in the event you have anything stolen, you must obtain an official statement from the police.

Before spending money on a new policy it's worth checking whether you are already covered: some all-risks **home insurance** policies, for example, may cover your possessions against loss or theft when overseas, and many private medical schemes such as BUPA or PPP include cover when abroad, including baggage loss, cancellation or curtailment and cash replacement as well as sickness or accident. Bank and credit

Rough Guides Travel Insurance

Rough Guides offers its own low-cost travel insurance, especially customized for our statistically low-risk readers by a leading British broker, provided by the American International Group (AIG) and registered with the British regulatory body, GISC (the General Insurance Standards Council). There are five main Rough Guides insurance plans: No Frills for the bare minimum for secure travel; Essential, which provides decent all-round cover; Premier for comprehensive cover with a wide range of benefits; Extended Stay for cover lasting two months to a year; and Annual Multi-Trip, a cost-effective way of getting Premier cover if you travel more than once a year. **Premier, Annual Multi-Trip** and Extended Stay policies can be supplemented by a "Hazardous Pursuits Extension" if you plan to indulge in sports considered dangerous, such as scuba-diving or trekking. For a policy quote, call the Rough Guides Insurance Line: toll-free in the UK ☎0800/015 09 06 or ☎+44 1392 314 665 from elsewhere. Alternatively, get an online quote at www.roughguides.com/insurance

cards often have certain levels of medical or other insurance included and you may automatically get travel insurance if you use a major credit card to pay for your trip (check the small print on this, though, as it may not be of much use).

In Canada, provincial health plans usually provide partial cover for medical mishaps overseas, while holders of official student/teacher/youth cards in **Canada and the US** are entitled to meagre accident coverage and hospital inpatient benefits. Students will often find that their student health coverage extends during the vacations and for one term beyond the date of last enrolment.

Information, websites and maps

Information on Sydney is easy to get hold of, either from Australian Tourist Commission offices, via the Internet, or, after arrival, from any of the city's tourist offices.

If you want to do a bit of **general research** on your trip before arriving in Sydney, you should contact the Australian Tourist Commission, who have offices or helplines in the UK, the US and New Zealand (see below); they can post out their annual publication, the glossy *Australia, A Traveller's Guide*, which has a detailed section on Sydney, and has a useful directory of addresses. You can also get information at the Tourist Commission's website (ⓦwww.australia.com). Also check out the website for Tourism New South Wales in the list of useful websites opposite. Once in Sydney, there's no shortage of places offering information, but the two major tourist offices, the Sydney Visitor Centres, are at the international airport – grab hold of some free information booklets and maps when you arrive – and at one of the major tourist centres, The Rocks.

Australian Tourist Commission offices abroad

United Kingdom Gemini House, 10–18 Putney Hill, Putney, London SW15 6AA ("Aussie Helpline" charged at 50p a minute: ☎0990/022000, or check their website which has a UK edition ⓦwww.australia.com.

US Visitors should contact the "Aussie Helpline" for tour information (☎805/775-2000), or check

out the tourist commission's website, ⓦwww.australia.com, which has a US edition. **New Zealand** Level 13, 44–48 Emily Place, Auckland 1 ☎09/379 9594, or check out the tourist commission's website, ⓦwww.australia.com, which has a NZ edition.

Tourist information offices

The **Sydney Visitor Centre** on the ground floor (arrivals) of the international airport terminal (daily 5am until last arrival; ☎02/9667 6050), offers the most comprehensive tourist information service. Staff can arrange car rental and onward travel – it's licensed to sell train and bus tickets – and book hotels (but not hostels) anywhere in Sydney and New South Wales free of charge. The **accommodation bookings** here are at stand-by rates, so it's possible to get a good deal. Most hostels advertise on an adjacent notice board; there's a free phone line for reservations.

The main central tourist office is the other **Sydney Visitor Centre** in The Rocks at 106 George St near Circular Quay (daily 9am–6pm; ☎02/9255 1788, ⓦwww.sydneyvisitorcentre.com; see also p.47), offering a similar range of literature (see opposite); they have a self-service budget accommodation booking board with free phones directly linked to the listed hotels. Otherwise tourist information is supplied by the **Darling Harbour Visitor Information Centre** (daily 9.30am–5.30pm; ☎02/9281 0788, Ⓦwww.darlingharbour.com.au), next to the IMAX cinema; the three green **City Host information kiosks** at Circular Quay, Martin Place and Town Hall (all daily 9am–5pm; no phone); and the **Manly Visitor Information Centre** (Mon–Fri 9am–5pm, Sat & Sun 10am–4pm; ☎02/9977 1088, Ⓦwww .manlyweb.com.au), by the Manly ferry wharf, which also has lockers for valuables ($2).

National park information

For information on Sydney Harbour National Park, the series of bush-covered foreshore and islands around the harbour, the **National Parks and Wildlife Service** (NPWS) have an information centre and bookshop at Cadman's Cottage, 110 George St, The Rocks (daily 9am–5pm; ☎02/9247 8861, Ⓦwww.npws.nsw.gov.au). They produce a very handy detailed free fold-out map, *Sydney Harbour National Park,* which provides excellent detail of the harbour, showing all the main sites, ferry routes and bushwalks.

For information on other national parks around Sydney, such as the Royal National Park, and camping permits, go to the National Parks Centre, nearby at 102 George St, The Rocks (☎02/9253 4600). The Sydney Map Shop, part of the Surveyor-General's Department, 23–33 Bridge St, City (☎02/9228 6111) sells detailed national park and bushwalking maps.

Publications

Ask at the tourist offices for *Sydney: The Official Guide*, a free booklet with excellent maps of Sydney and the surrounding areas, plus a CityRail and ferry plan. The *Hip Guide to Sydney* is also handy. Several free monthly **listings magazines** are worth picking up at tourist offices: the weekly *Where Magazine* is probably the best for general information, while *This Month in Sydney* is also worth consulting. Sydney Council distributes a basic photocopied guide, *City Life*, every Wednesday to all visitor centres and information booths, and also publishes the bi-monthly *Official Sydney Events Guide* (free

from the Town Hall, $3.25 from newsagents); similar information is available on their website (see below). To get under the skin of Sydney, read Friday's *Sydney Morning Herald* for its "Metro" listings supplement.

TNT Magazine is the best of an array of publications aimed at **backpackers**, while **hostel notice boards** themselves act as an informal network, advertising everything from cars to camping gear; you can pick them up at travellers' centres such as Backpackers World Travel, with several offices including one near Central Station at 482 Pitt St (☎02/9282 9711; for other locations check Ⓦwww.backpackers-world.com.au), and Backpackers Travel Centre, also with an office near Central at 488 Pitt St (☎02/9215 2400; for other locations check Ⓦwww.backpackerstravel.net.au).

Useful websites

Though we give relevant websites throughout the guide, some general sites on Sydney are listed below. For information on Internet access in Sydney see p.34.

Ⓦ**www.sydney.citysearch.com.au** The ultimate Sydney online guide to arts and entertainment, music, movies, eating, shopping and even the local weather, with links to tourist attractions and accommodation.

Ⓦ**www.smh.com.au** Read selected daily news pages of the *Sydney Morning Herald*, and check the classifieds for jobs, cars, rental properties and share and holiday accommodation.

Ⓦ**www.cityofsydney.nsw.gov.au** Website with a useful list of festivals and events; produced by the City of Sydney council.

Ⓦ**www.mardigras.org.au** The official Sydney Gay & Lesbian Mardi Gras site, with links to other gay and lesbian sites.

Ⓦ**www.sydneyvisitorcentre.com** The website of Sydney's tourism bureau has useful listings and links for accommodation, tours, cruises, attractions and car rental.

Ⓦ**www.viewsydney.com** Rooftop cameras in The Rocks quarter show a slice of life in real time.

Ⓦ**www.tourism.nsw.gov.au** The official site for Tourism New South Wales focuses on Sydney plus the surrounding state, with info on tours, events and accommodation.

Maps

For wandering around the centre of Sydney, the maps in this book should be sufficient, but if you crave greater detail, or are staying by the beach or in the inner or outer suburbs, or are driving, you might like to buy something more comprehensive. The best place to **buy maps** in Sydney is the Map Shop, 371 Pitt St (☎02/9261 3601, ⊛www.mapworld .net.au; Mon–Wed & Fri 8.30am–5.30pm, Thurs 8.30am–6.30pm, Sat 10am–3.30pm). The two best maps to buy are HEMA's *Sydney and Region* map ($5.95; ⊛www .hemamaps.com) which gives an overview of the area around Sydney, showing major roads and freeways, and detailed coverage of the metropolitan area as well as an inset map of the CBD; UBD's Sydney Suburban Map (no. 262; $6.95; ⊛www.ubd-online .com) gives comprehensive street detail of the CBD and the surrounding suburbs within a 10km radius. If you've rented a car, make sure the rental company has provided a Sydney street directory before you head off. For longer stays, the best street directory to buy is the latest edition of Gregory's *Compact Sydney* street directory ($16.95; ⊛www.gregorys-online.com) with all the detail but in a paperback book size that can easily fit into a handbag or daypack and at around half the price of the larger-sized directories. For getting out of Sydney, a New South Wales state map doesn't provide enough detail on the areas we've included in our "Beyond Sydney" chapters, though it will show freeways and major roads. It's better to buy a copy of Gregory's *200 kilometres around Sydney* map for more detail and coverage of all the major tourist drives ($5.95). See also p.19 for details of free national park maps.

New South Wales's motoring organization, the NRMA, 74–76 King St, City (☎13 21 32, ⊛www.nrma.com.au), publish **road maps** of New South Wales, and a useful map of Sydney. The maps are free to members of associated overseas motoring organizations.

Specialist book and map suppliers

UK and Ireland

Blackwell's Map and Travel Shop 50 Broad St, Oxford OX1 3BQ ☎01865/793 550, ⊛maps.blackwell.co.uk.
Easons Bookshop 40 O'Connell St, Dublin 1 ☎01/858 3881, ⊛www.eason.ie.

Heffers Map and Travel 20 Trinity St, Cambridge CB2 1TJ ☎01865/333 536, ⊛www.heffers.co.uk.
Hodges Figgis Bookshop 56–58 Dawson St, Dublin 2 ☎01/677 4754, ⊛www.hodgesfiggis.com.
The Map Shop 30A Belvoir St, Leicester LE1 6QH ☎0116/247 1400, ⊛www.mapshopleicester.co.uk.
National Map Centre 22–24 Caxton St, London SW1H 0QU ☎020/7222 2466, ⊛www.mapsnmc.co.uk.
Newcastle Map Centre 55 Grey St, Newcastle-upon-Tyne, NE1 6EF ☎0191/261 5622.
Ordnance Survey Ireland Phoenix Park, Dublin 8 ☎01/802 5300, ⊛www.osi.ie.
Ordnance Survey of Northern Ireland Colby House, Stranmillis Ct, Belfast BT9 5BJ ☎028/9025 5755, ⊛www.osni.gov.uk.
Stanfords 12–14 Long Acre, WC2E 9LP ☎020/7836 1321, ⊛www.stanfords.co.uk.
The Travel Bookshop 13–15 Blenheim Crescent, W11 2EE ☎020/7229 5260, ⊛www.thetravelbookshop.co.uk.

US and Canada

Adventuroustraveler.com US ☎1-800/282-3963, ⊛adventuroustraveler.com.
Book Passage 51 Tamal Vista Blvd, Corte Madera, CA 94925 ☎1-800/999-7909, ⊛www.bookpassage.com.
Distant Lands 56 S Raymond Ave, Pasadena, CA 91105 ☎1-800/310-3220, ⊛www.distantlands.com.
Elliot Bay Book Company 101 S Main St, Seattle, WA 98104 ☎1-800/962-5311, ⊛www.elliotbaybook.com.
Globe Corner Bookstore 28 Church St, Cambridge, MA 02138 ☎1-800/358-6013, ⊛www.globecorner.com.
Map Link 30 S La Patera Lane, Unit 5, Santa Barbara, CA 93117 ☎1-800/962-1394, ⊛www.maplink.com.
Rand McNally US ☎1-800/333-0136, ⊛www.randmcnally.com. Around thirty stores across the US; dial ext 2111 or check the website for the nearest location.
The Travel Bug Bookstore 2667 W Broadway, Vancouver V6K 2G2 ☎604/737-1122, ⊛www.swifty.com/tbug.
World of Maps 1235 Wellington St, Ottawa, Ontario K1Y 3A3 ☎1-800/214-8524, ⊛www.worldofmaps.com.

New Zealand

Specialty Maps 58 Albert St, Auckland ☎09/307 2217.

Costs, money and banks

If you've stopped over from Southeast Asia you'll obviously find Sydney, with its high Western standard of living, expensive on a day-to-day basis. Fresh from Europe or the US you'll find prices comparable and often cheaper, particularly for accommodation and eating out, and especially taking into account the very favourable exchange rate. Australia is well set up for independent travellers, and with a student, YHA or a backpackers' card (see below) you can get discounts on a wide range of travel and entertainment in Sydney.

Currency

Australia's currency is the Australian dollar, or "buck", divided into 100 cents and shown on currency tables as AU$. Colourful plastic notes with forgery-proof clear windows come in $100, $50, $20, $10 and $5 denominations, along with $2, $1, 50¢, 20¢, 10¢ and 5¢ coins. There are no longer 1¢ or 2¢ coins, but prices are regularly advertised at $1.99 etc and an irregular bill will be rounded up or down to the closest denomination, which can be confusing at first.

Exchange rates fluctuate around an over-the-counter rate of A$2.50 for £1; A$1.50 for US$1; A$1.15 for C$1 and A$0.90 for NZ$1. For the most current exchange rates, consult the useful currency converter website ⓦ www.oanda.com.

Costs

The absolute minimum **daily budget** for food, accommodation and transport alone is $65 if you stay in a hostel, eat in the cheapest cafés and restaurants and travel by public transport. Add on sightseeing admissions and a minimal social life and you're looking at least $110. Staying in decent hotels, eating at moderate restaurants, and paying for tours and nightlife, extend your budget to at least $160–220 per day.

Hostel **accommodation** will set you back $18–30 per person, while a double room in a moderate hotel costs costs $80–120. **Food**, on the whole, is good value: counter meals in hotels and cafés often start from $12; restaurants cost upwards of $30 for a reasonable three-course feed, and many let you BYO (bring your own) wine or beer.

Drinking out will set you back around $3 for a small glass of draught beer, $4–6 for a bottled brew, and local wine by the glass starts at $4 for an ordinary drop but expect to pay at least $7 for something choicer. Beer is good value bought in bulk from a "bottle shop" – a "slab" of beer (24 cans) costs around $30; a decent bottle of wine will set you back from $14, with *vin ordinaire* from as little as $8.

Renting a car costs around $65 a day; the longer you rent for, the cheaper the price. Fuel, with substantial local variations, averages 88–98¢ a litre; cheaper than in the UK, dearer than the US, but vast distances see it used up fast.

Youth and student discounts

Once obtained, various official and quasi-official **youth/student ID cards** soon pay for themselves in savings. Full-time students are eligible for the International Student ID Card (ISIC, ⓦ www.isiccard.com), which entitles the bearer to special air, rail and bus fares and discounts at museums, theatres and other attractions. For Americans there's also a health benefit, providing up to US$3000 in emergency medical coverage and US$100 a day for sixty days in hospital, plus a 24-hour hotline to call in the event of a medical, legal or financial emergency. The card costs US$22 for Americans; C$16 for Canadians; NZ$21 for New Zealanders; and £7 in the UK. If you're no longer a student, but are 26 or younger, you still qualify for the International Youth Travel Card, which costs the same price and carries the same benefits, while teachers qualify for the

See Sydney & Beyond Smartvisit Card

All of Sydney's tourist offices sell the **See Sydney & Beyond Smartvisit Card** (☏131 661 711; ⓦwww.seesydneycard.com) which comes in one-, two-, three- or seven-day versions, with or without a transport option (a Daytripper or Travelpass – see p.28) and including admission to forty attractions in Sydney and the Blue Mountains – from the National Maritime Museum to a guided tour of the Opera House. You would have to be a fast worker to give the pricey pass much added-value but since it can be bought in advance on the Internet, a seven-day version in particular would make a good present; rates (with/without transport) are one-day $75/$59, two-day $130/$99, three-day $175/$129, and seven-day $255/$189.

International Teacher Card (same price and benefits). All these cards are available from your local student travel agent in the US, Canada, the UK and New Zealand, and in Australia itself, or you can download an application from the website. Once you are in Australia, purchasing either an **International YHA Card** or **Backpacker Resorts VIP Card** will give you discounts on not just the relevant hostel accommodation, but a host of transport, tours, services, entry fees and even meals; they're worth getting even if you're not planning to stay in hostels.

Travellers' cheques

Although they are the traditional way to carry funds, **travellers' cheques**, such as those sold by American Express and Thomas Cook, are no longer the cheapest nor the most convenient way to bring your funds into Australia – credit or debit cards or Visa TravelMoney are more simple options (see opposite). However, travellers' cheques offer more security as they can be replaced if lost or stolen (remember to keep a list of the serial numbers separate from the cheques). Australian dollar travellers' cheques are ideal as theoretically they're valid as cash and so shouldn't attract exchange fees; smaller businesses may be unwilling to take them, but you can always change them for free at the local offices – American Express have more outlets and agencies in Australia than Thomas Cook. Travellers' cheques in US dollars and pounds sterling are also widely accepted, and banks should be able to handle all major currencies. It's worth checking both the rate and the commission when you change your cheques (as well as when

you buy them), as these can vary quite widely – many places charge a set amount for every cheque, in which case you're better off changing relatively large denominations. You'll need your passport with you to cash travellers' cheques.

The usual fee **to buy travellers' cheques** is one or two percent, though this fee may be waived if you buy the cheques through a bank where you have an account. Make sure to keep the purchase agreement and a record of cheque serial numbers safe and separate from the cheques themselves. In the event that cheques are lost or stolen, the issuing company will expect you to report the loss forthwith to their head office in Australia (for numbers, see opposite); most companies claim to replace lost or stolen cheques within 24 hours.

Credit and debit cards

Credit cards are a very handy source of funds, and can be used either in ATMs or over the counter. MasterCard and Visa are the most widely recognized; you can also use American Express, Bankcard and Diners Club. Remember that all cash advances are treated as loans, with interest accruing daily from the date of withdrawal; there may be a transaction fee on top of this. However, you may be able to make withdrawals from ATMs in Australia displaying the Cirrus-Maestro symbol and be able to pay for goods via EFTPOS (see opposite), using your debit card, which is not liable to interest payments, and the flat transaction fee is usually quite small – your bank will able to advise on this. Make sure you have a personal identification number (PIN) that's designed to work overseas.

Visa TravelMoney

A compromise between travellers' cheques and plastic is Visa TravelMoney, a disposable prepaid debit card with a PIN which works in all ATMs that take Visa cards. You load up your account with funds before leaving home, and when they run out, you simply throw the card away. You can buy up to nine cards to access the same funds – useful for couples or families travelling together – and it's a good idea to buy at least one extra as a backup in case of loss or theft. There is also a 24-hour Australia-wide toll-free customer assistance number (☎1800 125 440). The card is available in most countries from branches of Thomas Cook and Citicorp. For more information, check the Visa TravelMoney website at ⓦwww.usa.visa.com/personal/cards/visa_travel_money.html.

Banks and foreign exchange

The major banks, with branches countrywide, are Westpac (ⓦwww.westpac.com.au), ANZ (ⓦwww.anz.com.au), the Commonwealth (ⓦwww.commbank.com.au) and National Australia (ⓦwww.national.com.au) banks; their head branches, all with foreign currency counters, are in the CBD, on and around Martin Place (see p.70); you can search their websites for suburban and out-of-town branch locations. **Banking hours** are Monday to Thursday 9.30am to 4pm and Friday 9.30am to 5pm (and at the time of writing a change in the law has made Saturday opening legal, though not yet fully in practice). Automatic Teller Machines (**ATMs**) are usually located outside banks but sometimes in front of ordinary shops in shopping strips. **Bureaux de change** are found in both the domestic and international airport terminals, and around Central Station and through the city centre; only a few in the city are open at the weekend, and solely the ones at the airport late at night, so try to exchange your currency during the week.

Foreign exchange offices

American Express Outlets include Level 1, 124–130 Pitt St (Mon–Fri 8.30am–5.30pm; ☎1300 139 060); Shop 4, Quay Grand Hotel, Circular Quay East (Mon–Fri 9am–5pm, Sat & Sun 11am–4pm) and within the Travel Bookshop, Shop 3, 175 Liverpool St (Mon–Fri 9am–5pm, Sat 10am–1pm). Lost or stolen travellers' cheques ☎1800 251 902. **Singapore Money Exchange** Shop 10 Eddy Ave, Central Station (Mon–Fri 8am–5.30pm; ☎02/9281 4118). **Thomas Cook** 175 Pitt St (Mon–Fri 9am–5.30pm,

Sat 10am–2pm; ☎02/9231 2901) with longer weekend hours at Shop 64, Lower Ground Floor, Queen Victoria Building, corner of George and Market streets (Mon–Fri 9am–6pm, Sat 10am–3pm). **Travelex Australia** 37–49 Pitt St, near Central Station ☎9241 5722 (Mon–Fri 9am–5.15pm, Sat 10am–2.45pm).

Opening and using a bank account

If you're spending some time in Sydney, and plan to work, it makes life a great deal easier if you **open a bank account**. To do this you'll need to take along every piece of ID documentation you own (a passport may not be enough, though a letter from your bank manager at home may help), but it's otherwise a fairly straightforward process. The Commonwealth Bank and Westpac are the most widespread options, and their **keycards** give you access not only to ATM machines but also anywhere that offers **EFTPOS** facilities (Electronic Funds Transfer at Point of Sale). This includes most shops, service stations and supermarkets, where you can use your card to pay directly for goods; some of them will also give you cash (ask for "cash back"). However, bear in mind that **bank fees and charges** are exorbitant in Australia; most banks allow only a few free withdrawal transactions per month (depending on who you bank with – it's well worth shopping around before you open an account), and there are even bigger charges for using a competitor's ATM machine, as well as monthly fees.

Wiring money

Having **money wired from home** is never convenient or cheap, and should be considered a last resort. It's also possible to have money wired directly from a bank in your home country to a bank in Australia, although this is somewhat less reliable because it involves two separate institutions. If you go down this route, your home bank will need the address of the branch bank where you want to pick up the money and the address and telex number of the head office, which will act as the clearing house; money wired this way normally takes two working days to arrive, and costs around £25/US$40 per transaction. Otherwise, to have money wired from home fast, arrangements can be made with TravelersExpress MoneyGram (☉www.moneygram.com) through Thomas Cook foreign exchange outlets, and Western Union (☉www.westernunion.com) through American Express; see outlet addresses on p.23. There is also a Western Union office within Travelex, 37–49 Pitt St, near Central Station (☎02/9241 5722).

Arrival

The classic way to arrive in Sydney is, of course, by ship (see p.9), cruising near the great coathanger of the Harbour Bridge to tie up at the Overseas Passenger Terminal (see p.56) alongside Circular Quay. Unfortunately you're more likely to be arriving by air, train or bus, and the reality of the functional airport, train and bus stations is a good deal less romantic.

By air

Sydney's **Kingsford Smith Airport**, referred to as "Mascot" after the suburb where it's located, near Botany Bay, is 8km south of the city (international flight times ☎13 12 23). Domestic and international terminals are linked by a free shuttle bus (every 30min), or you can take the Airport Express bus for $3.

See box opposite for **buses** into the city. You can take a **train** right into the centre: the Airport Link underground railway connects the airport to the City Circle train line (15min; every 15min; one-way $10.60) However, as it is a suburban commuter service it can be crowded at peak hours, there is no dedicated space for luggage and it is more expensive than Airport Express buses, which will drop you off near your hotel. With three or more of you it can be cheaper to share a **taxi**, which will cost $30 to $35 from the airport to the city centre or Kings Cross.

Bureaux de change at both terminals are open daily from 5am until last arrival at rates comparable to major banks. On the ground floor (arrivals) of the international terminal, the **Sydney Visitor Centre** (daily 5am until last arrival; ☎02/9667 6050) can arrange car rental and onward travel – it's licensed to sell train and bus tickets – and can **book hotels** anywhere in Sydney and New South Wales free of charge and at stand-by rates. Most hostels advertise on an adjacent notice board; there's a freephone line for reservations, and many of them will refund your bus fare; a few also do free airport pick-ups.

By train and bus

All local and interstate **trains** arrive at **Central Station** on Eddy Avenue, just south of the city centre; long-distance and interstate trains arrive at what is known as the Country Trains terminal. There is left luggage by the main entrance to the country trains terminal off Pitt Street ($8/$6/$4 per 24hr depending on size) and showers at the volunteer-run **Travellers' Aid** (Mon–Sat 7.30am–2pm; shower $3, with towel $5) near Platform 1. From Central Station, and neighbouring **Railway Square** you can hop

Airport buses

State Transit

Airport Express buses (#300; green and yellow) run to Kings Cross via Central Station, the city centre, The Rocks and Circular Quay (daily 5am–11pm; every 10min; $7, $12 return valid two months; ⓣ13 15 00), picking up and setting down at various stops, including hotels and hostels. Tickets can be bought on board and at the Sydney Visitor Centre in the international terminal (see p.24), where you can also buy tourist bus passes – the Sydney Pass (see p.28) includes return airport–city transfer so it's best to buy it here.

State Transit also has a daily commuter route: the **Metroline** #400 goes frequently to Bondi Junction via Maroubra and Randwick in one direction, and to Burwood in the other (tickets cost a maximum of $4.70).

Shuttle services - Sydney area

Eastern Suburbs Airport Shuttle minibus service has a quick call-out service to and from the eastern beaches – Bondi, Coogee, Randwick, Clovelly and Bronte – and drops off at all hostels, motels and hotels ($12 one-way; bookings ⓣ0500 881 113, ⓦwww.supershuttle.com.au).

Kingsford Smith Transport/Sydney Airporter offers a private bus service dropping off at hotels or hostels in the area bounded by Kings Cross and Darling Harbour ($8 one-way, $13 return; ⓣ02/9667 3221 or 9666 9988 3hr before to book an accommodation pick-up; ⓦwww.kst.com.au). The service leaves when the bus is full.

surfacetoair minibus service to the city and the northern beaches – including Manly, Whale Beach and Palm Beach – drops off at accommodation (ⓣ02/9913 9912, ⓦwww.surfacetoair.com.au). Book in advance by phone or email giving the day, time and flight and they will designate a waiting point. Manly $30, Palm Beach $49 (cheaper rates for couples and groups).

Coach and shuttle services - central coast and south coast

Bennetts Airport Shuttle runs a pre-booked door-to-door service to accommodation anywhere on the Central Coast ($47, cheaper rates for couples and groups; ⓣ1300 130 557, ⓦwww.ben-air.com.au).

onto nearly every major bus route, and from within Central Station you can take a CityRail train to any city or suburban station (see "City transport" on p.23).

All **buses** to Sydney arrive and depart from Eddy Avenue and Pitt Street, bordering Central Station. The area is well set up with decent cafés, a 24-hour police station and a huge YHA hostel (see p.166), as well as the **Sydney Coach Terminal** (daily 6am–10pm), which also has luggage lockers ($6–9 per 24hr depending on size) and oversize luggage storage (backpacks $10, bikes $14 per 24hr). The **Travellers' Information Service** (ⓣ02/9281 9366) in the coach terminal can make hotel **accommodation bookings** at stand-by rates while a range of hostels advertise on an adjacent notice board with free phones for direct reservations; many of them provide free pick-ups (usually from Bay 14). You can purchase coach tickets and passes from the Information Service as well as Sydney Passes (see p.28), and arrange harbour cruises and other tours.

City transport

Sydney's public transport network is reasonably good, though the system relies heavily on buses, and traffic jams can be a problem. There are buses, trains, ferries, a light rail system and the city monorail to choose from, plus plenty of licensed taxis.

Trains stop running around midnight, as do most regular buses, though several services towards the eastern and northern beaches, such as the #380 to Bondi Beach, the #372 and #373 to Coogee and the #151 to Manly, run through the night. Otherwise a pretty good network of **Nightride buses** follow the train routes to the suburbs, departing from Town Hall Station (outside the Energy Australia Building on George Street) and stopping at train stations (where taxis wait at designated ranks); return train tickets, Railpasses and Travelpasses can be used, or buy a ticket from the driver. For stays of more than a few days, a weekly **Travelpass** is a worthwhile investment (see box on p.28). For public transport information, routes and timetables call ☏13 15 00 (daily 6am–10pm; ⓦwww.131500.com.au).

Buses

Within the central area, **buses**, hailed from yellow-signed bus stops, are the most convenient, widespread mode of transport, and cover more of the city than the trains. With few exceptions buses radiate from the centre with major interchanges at Railway Square near Central Station (especially southwest routes), at Circular Quay (range of routes), from York and Carrington streets outside Wynyard Station (North Shore), and Bondi Junction Station (eastern suburbs and beaches). **Tickets** can be bought on board from the driver and cost from $1.50 for up to two distance-measured sections, rising to $4.70; $2.60 (up to five sections) is the most typical fare. Substantial discounts are available with TravelTen tickets and other travel passes (see box on pp.28–29); these must be validated in the ticket reader by the front door. Bus **information** – including route maps, **timetables** and **passes** – is available

from handy booths at Carrington Street, Wynyard; at Circular Quay on the corner of Loftus and Alfred streets; at the Queen Victoria Building on York Street; at Bondi Junction bus interchange; and at Manly Wharf. For detailed timetables and route maps see Sydney Buses' website ⓦwww.sydneybuses.nsw.gov.au.

Trains

Trains, operated by **CityRail** (see colour map), will get you where you're going faster than buses, especially at rush hour and when heading out to the suburbs, but you need to transfer to a bus or ferry to get to most harbourside or beach destinations. There are six train lines, mostly overground, each of which stops at Central and Town Hall stations. Trains run from around 5am to midnight, with **tickets** starting at around $2.20 single on the City Loop and for short hops; buying off-peak returns (after 9am and all weekend) means you can save up to forty percent.

Automatic **ticket machines** (which give change) and barriers (insert magnetic tickets, otherwise show ticket at the gate) have been introduced just about everywhere. Fines for fare evasion exceed $150. All platforms are painted with designated "nightsafe" waiting areas and all but two or three train carriages are closed after about 8pm, enforcing a cattle-like safety in numbers. Security guards also patrol trains at night. At other times, if the train is deserted, sit in the carriage nearest the guard, marked by a blue light.

Ferries and cruises

Sydney's distinctive green-and-yellow **ferries** are the fastest means of transport from Circular Quay to the North Shore, and indeed to most places around the harbour.

Even if you don't want to go anywhere, a ferry ride is a must, a chance to get out on the water and see the city from the harbour. There's also a speedy **hydrofoil**, the JetCat, which reaches Manly in half the time the ferry takes, but with less charm.

There are ferries going off in various directions from the wharves at Circular Quay including cruises (see colour map). The last ferry service from Circular Quay to Manly is at 7pm after which time the faster JetCats operate until midnight, 11pm on Saturdays. Other ferry routes, such as those to Parramatta and Pyrmont Bay, also operate only until early evening, while ferries to locations including Neutral Bay and Balmain continue to around 11.30pm. Except for the Manly Ferry, services on Sunday are greatly reduced and often finish earlier. Timetables for each route are available at Circular Quay or on the Sydney Ferries website (www.sydneyferries.nsw.gov.au).

One-way **fares** are $4.30 ($5.40 for the Manly Ferry); return fares are doubled. The pricier JetCat to Manly and RiverCat to Parramatta are $6.70 and $6.40 respectively. Once again, the various Travelpasses and FerryTen tickets can be a good deal – see box on pp.28–29 for details.

Harbour cruises

There's a wide choice of **harbour cruises**, almost all of them leaving from Jetty 6, Circular Quay and the rest from Darling Harbour. Before you part with your cash, however, bear in mind that apart from the running commentary (which can be rather annoying), most offer nothing that you won't get on a regular harbour **ferry** for a lot less. The best of the ordinary harbour ferry trips is the thirty-minute ride to **Manly**, but there's a ferry going somewhere at almost any time throughout the day. If you really want to splash out, you could take a **water taxi** ride – Circular Quay to Watsons Bay, for example, costs $52 for the first passenger and then an additional $7 for each extra person. Pick-ups are available from any wharf if booked in advance (try Water Taxis Combined on 02/9555 8888; www.harbourtaxis.com.au). One water taxi company, **Watertours**, located on Cockle Bay

Wharf in Darling Harbour (02/9211 7730, www.watertours.com.au), even offers tours on their latest-model, bright yellow taxis, which look like New York cabs on the water, from $10 for a speedy ten-minute one-way spin under the Harbour Bridge, past The Rocks and ending up at the Opera House (every 15min). There's also a fifty-minute cruise which takes in Fort Denison and the yacht marina in RushcuttersBay as well as some pricey waterfront real estate (every 15min; $20), and a one-hour sunset cruise (sunset nightly; $25).

The **Australian Travel Specialists** (ATS) at Jetties 2 and 6, Circular Quay, the Harbourside Shopping Centre at Darling Harbour and Manly Wharf (02/9211 3192; www.atstravel.com.au) book all cruises. Those offered by State Transit – **Harboursights Cruises** (13 15 00; www.sydneyferries.nsw.gov.au) – are the best value: choose between the Morning Harbour Cruise (daily 10.30am; 1hr; $15), the recommended Afternoon Harbour Cruise to Middle Harbour and back (Mon–Fri 1pm, Sat & Sun 12.30pm; 2hr 30min; $22), and the Evening Harbour Cruise (Mon–Sat 8pm; 1hr 30min; $19).You can buy tickets at the Sydney Ferry ticket offices at Circular Quay. The STA cruises are also included in a Sydney Pass – see box, pp.28–29.

Captain Cook Cruises at Jetty 6, Circular Quay (02/9206 1111, www.captaincook.com.au), the big commercial operator, offers a vast range of cruises on their very large boats, including morning and afternoon "Coffee" Cruises into Middle Harbour (daily 10am & 2.15pm; 2hr 20min; $39), a lunch cruise (daily 12.30pm; 1hr 30min; buffet $52, two- or three-course $56–$66), a range of dinner cruises including the two-course Sunset Dinner (includes a drink; daily 5pm; 1hr 35min; $69) and Opera Afloat with opera singers accompanying a four-course dinner (daily 7pm; 2hr 30min; $99). Also available are a Harbour Highlights Cruise (daily 9.30am, 11am, 12.45am, 2.30pm, 4pm; 1hr 15min; $20; option of getting off at Darling Harbour on the 11am, 2.30pm and 4pm trips) and a hop-on-hop-off five-stop Sydney Harbour Explorer (daily from Circular Quay 9.30am, 11.30am, 1.30pm & 3.30pm; $22; combined ticket with the zoo or the

Travel passes

In addition to single-journey tickets, there's a vast array of **travel passes** available. The most useful for visitors are outlined below; for more **information** on the full range of tickets and timetables, phone the Transport Infoline or check out their website (daily 6am–10pm; ☎13 15 00, ⓦwww.131500.com.au).

Passes are sold at most **newsagents** and at **train stations**; the more tourist-oriented Sydney Passes and Sydney Explorer Passes can be bought on board the Explorer buses, at the airport (from the Sydney Visitor Centre and the STA booth in the international terminal and from State Transit ground staff in the domestic), at State Transit Info booths, from the Sydney Visitor Centre in The Rocks (see p.18) and at some Countrylink offices as well as at train stations.

Tourist passes

Sydney Explorer Pass (one-day $30) comes with a map and description of the sights, and includes free travel on any State Transit bus within the same zones as the Explorer routes. The red **Sydney Explorer** (from Circular Quay daily 8.40am–5.22pm; every 18min) takes in all the important sights in the city and inner suburbs, via 26 hop-on-hop-off stops. The blue **Bondi Explorer** (daily from Circular Quay 9.15am–4.15pm; every 30min) covers the waterside eastern suburbs (19 stops include Kings Cross, Paddington, Double Bay, Vaucluse, Bondi, Bronte, Clovelly and Coogee). A **two-day ticket** ($50) allows use of both bus services over two days in a seven-day period.

Sydney Pass (three-, five- or seven-day passes within a seven-day period; $90/$120/$140) is valid for all buses and ferries including the above Explorer services, the ferry and JetCat to Manly, the RiverCat to Parramatta and a return trip to the airport valid for two months with the Airport Express bus (buy it at the airport on arrival). It also includes four narrated harbour cruises, one of them in the evening, and travel on trains within a central area.

Buses, trains and ferries

Travelpasses allow unlimited use of buses, trains and ferries and can begin on any day of the week. Most useful are the **Red Travelpass** ($30 a week), valid for

aquarium is $39) circuiting between Circular Quay, the Man O' War Jetty at the Opera House, Watsons Bay, Taronga Zoo and Darling Harbour.

Matilda Cruises, based in Darling Harbour (Aquarium Wharf, Pier 26; ☎02/9264 7377, ⓦwww.matilda.com.au), offer various smaller-scale cruises on sailing catamarans (engines mostly used), with big foredecks providing great views. Departures are from Darling Harbour (either at the Aquarium or King Street wharves) with pick-ups from Circular Quay twenty minutes later. Morning and afternoon cruises include tea, coffee and biscuits (10am, 12.15pm & 3.05pm from King St Wharf; 1hr 30min; $27); there's a buffet on the Lunch Cruise (12.15pm; 2hr; $56.20), while the pricey Dinner Cruise allows you to dine on the foredeck (King St Wharf 7.30pm, Circular Quay 8pm; 3hr 30min;

$94.50). They also offer the **Rocket Harbour Express Cruise**, a one-hour trip stopping at the Aquarium Wharf at Darling Harbour, Man O' War Jetty at the Opera House, Commissioners Steps at Circular Quay West, Taronga Zoo and Watsons Bay; you can get off at the stops and rejoin later cruises (9.30am–4.30pm; every hour; $20.50 includes refreshment; ticket lasts all day but for one complete circuit only). There is also a straight Matilda Ferry service, the Rocket Express, shuttling between Darling Harbour, the Star City Casino and Circular Quay ($4.50 one-way, $7.50 return) and they also have a weekday Lane Cove River ferry ($4.50 one-way, $7.50 return; see p.150) and a commuter service to Homebush Bay $4.50 one-way, $7.50 return (see p.145).

If you're feeling romantically inclined, or mutinous, you might fancy sailing with the

the city and inner suburbs, and inner harbour ferries (not the Manly Ferry or the RiverCat beyond Meadowbank); and the **Green Travelpass** ($38), which allows use of all ferries – except JetCats before 7pm. Passes covering a wider area cost between $42 and $52 a week, and monthly passes are also available.

DayTripper tickets ($13.40) are also available for unlimited travel on all services offered by CityRail, Sydney Buses and Sydney Ferries.

Buses and ferries

The **Blue Travelpass** ($27 a week) gives unlimited travel on buses in the inner-city area and on inner-harbour ferries but cannot be used for Manly or beyond Meadowbank; the **Orange Travelpass** ($34 a week) gets you further on the buses and is valid on all ferries; and the **Pittwater Travelpass** ($47 a week) gives unlimited travel on all buses and ferries. These travelpasses start with first use rather than on the day of purchase.

Buses

TravelTen tickets represent a 45 percent saving over single fares by buying ten trips at once; they can be used over a space of time and for more than one person. The tickets are colour-coded according to how many sections they cover; the Brown TravelTen ($18.90), for example, is the choice for trips from Leichhardt to the city, while the the the Red TravelTen ($23.50) is the one to buy if you're staying at Bondi.

Ferries

FerryTen tickets, valid for ten single trips, start at $26.50 for Inner Harbour Services, go up to $39.30 for the Manly Ferry, and peak at $55.80 for the JetCat services.

Trains

Seven Day RailPass tickets allow unlimited travel between any two nominated stations and those in between, with savings of about twenty percent on the price of five return trips.

Bounty (office at 29 George St, The Rocks, ☎02/9247 1789, ⓦwww.thebounty.com), a replica of Captain Bligh's ship made for the film starring Mel Gibson. It normally embarks at Campbells Cove, The Rocks, for various cruises daily. The ship was unavailable for cruises at the time of writing; call or see the website for details. You can instead sail on an authentic old sailing ship, Sydney's oldest, the **James Craig**, an 1874 three-masted iron barque, which is part of the Sydney Heritage Fleet, based at Wharf 7, Pirrama Rd, Pyrmont, near Star City Casino. The beautifully restored square rigger does cruises on Saturdays (9.30am–4pm; $190; over-12s only; morning and afternoon tea and lunch provided). A similar sailing experience is offered by **Svanen Charters** (☎02/9698 4456, ⓦwww.svanen.com.au), moored at Campbells Cove next to the *Bounty*: this sail-ing ship, built in 1922, offers day-sails on the harbour for $93.50, including morning tea and lunch, or longer overnight sails to Broken Bay or Port Hacking ($275).

With **Sydney by Sail** (☎02/9280 1110, ⓦwww.sydneybysail.com), you can enjoy the harbour from on board a luxury Beneteau yacht. Groups are small (from six up to 20) and if you're interested the skipper will even show you some sailing techniques. The popular three-hour Port Jackson Explorer cruise sails Sydney Harbour and surrounding inlets (daily 1–4pm; $120). Departures are from the National Maritime Museum at Darling Harbour, with free entry to the museum thrown in on the day (so buy your ticket in the morning and check out the museum before the afternoon sail). The yachts are also available for charter (see p.259).

For something completely different, **Aussie Duck** (☎13 10 07, ⓦwww.aussieduck.com) combines a land and a sea tour in an amphibious vehicle (Mon 2.30pm, Thurs & Fri 12.00 & 2.30pm, Sat & Sun 10.30am, 12.30pm & 2.30pm; 1hr 30min; $60). The fifty-seater brightly painted "coach" departs from Clocktower Square in The Rocks and spends 45 minutes touring around the city centre until a startling "splash-down" into Walsh Bay, when it's transformed into a jet-powered boat zooming around Darling Harbour and the Opera House. This is strictly a "fun" tour, with everyone given duck quackers and pumping themed music accompanying the different sights. Another alternative to the sedate cruises listed above is offered by **Ocean Extreme** (☎0414 800 046 or 0418 213 145, ⓦwww.oceanextreme .com.au) on *Extreme 1*, an RIB (Rigid Inflatable Boat), with small groups of ten passengers taken on a hair-raising forty-minute "Adrenaline Tour" (daily 11am & 1pm; $70; bookings necessary) at speeds of more than 100km an hour; most of the harbour scenery is a blur but it's great fun. More thrills can be had with **Harbour Jet** (☎1300 887 373, ⓦwww.harbourjet.com) on the 35-minute "Jet Blast" (daily except Tues noon, 1.45pm, & 4.15pm; $50) that departs from the Convention Jetty, Darling Harbour; with speeds of 75km an hour, including a 270-degree spin, and accompanied by blasting music, it's not for the faint-hearted and is loathed by the locals – New South Wales Premier Bob Carr wants to ban the boats.

There are also a number of water-based cruises leaving from **Manly** Wharf (see p.135).

Monorail and Light Rail

The **Metro Monorail** (☎02/9285 5600, ⓦwww.metromonorail.com.au) is essentially a tourist shuttle designed to loop around Darling Harbour every three to five minutes, connecting it with the city centre. Thundering along tracks set above the older city streets, the "monster rail" – as many locals know it – doesn't exactly blend in with its surroundings. Still, the elevated view of the city, particularly from Pyrmont Bridge, makes it worth investing $4 (day-pass $8) and ten minutes to do the whole circuit with its eight stops (Mon–Wed 7am–10pm, Thurs–Sat 7am–midnight, Sun 8am–10pm).

Metro Light Rail (☎02/9285 5600, ⓦwww.metrolightrail.com.au) runs from Central Station to the Pyrmont peninsula and on to Lilyfield in the inner west. There are fourteen stops on the route, which links Central Station with Chinatown, Darling Harbour, Star City Casino, the fish markets at Pyrmont, Wentworth Park's greyhound racecourse, Glebe (with stops near Pyrmont Bridge Road, at Jubilee Park and Rozelle Bay by Bicentennial Park) and Lilyfield, not far from Darling Street, Rozelle. The air-conditioned light rail vehicles can carry two hundred passengers, and are fully accessible to disabled commuters. The service operates 24 hours to the casino (every 10–15min 6am–midnight; every 30min midnight–6am) with reduced hours for stops beyond to Lilyfield (Mon–Thurs & Sun 6am–11pm, Fri & Sat 6am–midnight; every 10–15min). There are two zones: zone 1 stations are Central to Convention in Darling Harbour, and zone 2 is from Pyrmont Bay to Lilyfield. Tickets can be purchased at vending machines by the stops; singles cost $2.60/$3.60 for zone 1/zone 2, returns $3.90/$4.90, a day-pass costs $8 and a weekly one $28, which includes the monorail. A TramLink ticket, available from any CityRail station, combines a rail ticket to Central Station with an MLR ticket.

Taxis

Taxis are vacant if the rooftop light is on, though they are notoriously difficult to find at 3pm, when the shifts change over. The four major city cab ranks are outside the *Regent Hotel* on George Street, The Rocks; on Park Street outside Woolworths, opposite the Town Hall; outside David Jones department store on Market Street; and at the Pitt Street entrance to Central Station. Drivers never expect a tip but often need directions – try to have some idea of where you're going. Check the correct tariff rate is displayed: tariff 2 (10pm–6am) is twenty percent more than tariff 1 (6am–10pm). To book a taxi, call ABC (☎13 25 22); Legion (☎13 14 51); Premier (☎13 10 17); RSL (☎13 15 81); St George (☎13 21 66) or Taxis Combined (☎02/8332 8888). For harbour water taxis call Taxis Afloat (☎02/9955 3222).

Driving and vehicle rental

Renting **your own vehicle** really allows you to explore Sydney's more far-flung beaches and national parks and other day-trip areas.

Most foreign **licences** are valid for a year in Australia. An International Driving Permit (available from national motoring organizations) may be useful if you come from a non-English-speaking country. **Fuel prices** start at around 90¢ per litre unleaded, with diesel slightly cheaper. The **rules of the road** are similar to those in the US and UK. Most importantly, **drive on the left** (as in the UK), remember that seatbelts are compulsory for all, and that the **speed limit** in all built-up areas is 50kph (or 60kph if signposted; 40kph in school zones during school hours). Outside built-up areas, maximums are between 80kph and 110kph. All changes in speed limits are frequently and obviously signed. Whatever else you do in a vehicle, don't **drink alcohol** to excess; random breath tests are common even in rural areas, especially during the Christmas season and on Friday and Saturday nights. One rule that might catch you out in town is that **roadside parking** must be in the same direction as the traffic – in other words don't cross oncoming traffic to park on the right.

Vehicle rental

To **rent** a car you need a full, clean driving licence; usually, a minimum age of 21 is stipulated by the major car-rental companies, rising to 25 for 4WDs. Check on any mileage limits or other restrictions, extras, and what you're covered for in an accident, before signing. The multinational operators Hertz, Budget, Avis and Thrifty have offices in Sydney. **Local firms** – of which there are many – are almost always better value, and the bottom-line "rent-a-bomb" agencies go as low as $29 a day; however, these places often have restrictions on how far away from Sydney you're allowed to go. A city-based non-multinational rental agency will supply new cars for around $60 a day with unlimited kilometres.

Four-wheel drives are best used for specific areas rather than long term, as rental and fuel costs are steep, starting at around $120 a day. Some 4WD agents actually don't allow their vehicles to be driven off sealed roads, so check the small print first.

You can reserve a vehicle before you arrive with the businesses below, or once you're in Sydney from any of the companies listed in the "Directory".

Rental Companies

Sydney-based companies are listed in the "Directory", p.265.

Autos Abroad ☏ 020 7287 6000, ⓦ www.autosabroad.co.uk.

Avis In the UK ☏ 0870/606 0100; in Ireland ☏ 01/874 5844; in the US ☏ 1-800/230-4898; in Canada ☏ 1-800/272-5871; in New Zealand ☏ 09/526 2847; ⓦ www.avis.com.

Budget In the UK ☏ 0800/181181; in Ireland ☏ 0800/973159; in the US ☏ 1-800/527-0700; in New Zealand ☏ 09/375 2222; ⓦ www.budget.com.

Hertz In the UK ☏ 0870/844 8844; in Ireland ☏ 01/676 7476; in the US ☏ 1-800/654-3001; in Canada ☏ 1-800/263-0600 or 416/620-9620 from Toronto; ⓦ www.hertz.com.

Holiday Autos In the UK ☏ 0870/400 0011; in Ireland ☏ 01/872 9366; ⓦ www.holidayautos.com.

Kemwel Holiday Autos In the US ☏ 1-800/678-0678, ⓦ www.kemwel.com.

National In the US ☏ 1-800/CAR-RENT, ⓦ www.nationalcar.com.

Post, phones and email

As you might expect, Sydney has an efficient postal service, a good telephone network and plenty of places to go online and check email.

Post

Australia's national **postal service** is called Australia Post. Post offices are generally open Monday to Friday 9am to 5pm but the General Post Office (GPO) in Martin Place has longer hours (Mon–Fri 8.15am–5.30pm, Sat 9am–1pm). There are red post boxes outside post offices and on streets throughout the city. Make sure you put letters in the red box outside post offices, and not the yellow, which is for express post parcels. This guaranteed overnight express delivery service from Sydney to other major cities is handy and relatively inexpensive but ordinary mail is much less reliable: even a letter from Sydney to Katoomba in the Blue Mountains can take two days or more. **International mail** is extremely efficient, taking five to ten days to reach Europe, Asia and the US. **Stamps** are sold at post offices and agencies; most newsagencies sell them for standard local letters only. A standard letter or postcard within Australia costs 45¢; printed aerogrammes for international letters anywhere in the world cost 70¢; postcards cost 95¢ to the US and Canada, $1 to Europe; regular letters start at $1.05 to the US and Canada, $1.20 to Europe. If you're sending anything bigger in or outside Australia, there are many different services: get some advice from the post office. Large parcels are reasonably cheap to send home by surface mail, but it will take up to three months for them to get there. Economy Air is a good compromise for packages that you want to see again soon – expect a fortnight to Europe.

You can receive mail at any post office in or around Sydney: address the letter to **Poste Restante** followed by the town or suburb, state of NSW and post code, but the best address to give friends before you leave is: Poste Restante, Sydney GPO, Sydney, NSW 2000, Australia. However, confusingly, the address to pick up this Poste Restante mail is not at the Martin Place GPO but at the post office in the Hunter Connection shopping mall at 310 George St (Mon–Fri 8.15am–6pm), opposite Wynyard Station. You need a passport or other ID to collect mail, which is kept for a month and then returned; it's possible to get mail redirected if you change your plans – ask for a form at any post office. Some smaller post offices will allow you to phone and check if you have any mail waiting.

Most **hostels** and **hotels** will also hold mail for you if it's clearly marked, preferably with a date of arrival, or holders of Amex cards or travellers' cheques can have it sent to American Express offices.

Addresses and floor levels

The way that **addresses** are written for apartments (also more commonly known as a flats, units or home units) or offices in Australia can cause some confusion when you're trying to visit someone. What might be written in full elsewhere as, for example, Apartment 4, 6 Smith St, is always given as 4/6 Smith St; some travellers confuse this as meaning flat 6, 4 Smith St. Just remember, the apartment or office number is first, then the street address number follows. Contrary to the US system, floor levels are given as ground, first, second, third or ground, level 1, level 2, level 3 etc. Basement levels are often called lower ground floor.

Phones, phonecards and mobile phones

The two major phone operators in Australia are the partially privatized Telstra, and Optus. As a mainly government-run organization, Telstra's coverage is wider but their rates, on a day-to-day basis, are pretty similar. All public phones are Telstra-operated. Post offices (but not agencies) always have a bank of **telephones** outside; otherwise head for the nearest bar or service station. Public telephones take coins or **Telstra phonecards**, which are sold through newsagents and other stores for $5, $10, $20 or $50. You can also buy Telstra PhoneAway cards which can be used with both private and public phones using a PIN number. You can make international calls from virtually any public Telstra phones as from a private phone (though rates are much higher). Many bars, shops and restaurants have orange or blue **payphones**, but these cost more than a regular call box, and inter-national dialling is not advised because

they'll start to gobble money the moment you're connected, even if the call goes unanswered. Whatever their type, pay-phones do not accept incoming calls. The unattended Telstra Pay Phone Centre, 231 Elizabeth St (Mon–Fri 7am–11pm, Sat & Sun 7am–5pm) has private booths for more pri-vacy and quiet, but bring change or a phone card with you.

Creditphones accept most major credit cards such as Amex, Visa and Diners International, and can be found at interna-tional and domestic airports, central loca-tions in major cities, and many hotels. You can make free **reverse charge** calls using the 1800 REVERSE.

Rates for calls within Australia are cheap-est in the evenings from Monday to Saturday, and all day Sunday. **Local calls** are untimed, allowing you to talk for as long as you like; this costs 15¢–25¢ on a domes-tic phone, though Telstra public phones charge 40¢. Many businesses and services operate **free-call numbers**, prefixed

---

Operators and international codes

Operator services
Local Directory Assistance ☎12 23
Operator ☎12 3
National Directory Assistance ☎12 45 5
International Operator ☎12 34
International Directory Assistance ☎12 45 5

International calls
To call Australia from overseas dial the international access code (☎00 from the UK or New Zealand, ☎011 from the US and Canada), followed by ☎61, the area code minus its initial zero, and the number. To dial out of Australia it's ☎0011, followed by the country code, then the area code (without the zero, if there is one), followed by the number:
UK ☎0011 44
Ireland ☎0011 353
US and Canada ☎0011 1
New Zealand ☎0011 64

Country direct
UK
BT operator ☎1800 881 440
BT automatic ☎1800 881 441
Ireland
Telecom ☎1800 881 353
US
AT&T ☎1-800/881-011
LDDS Worldcom ☎1-800/881-212

MCI ☎1-800/881-100
Sprint ☎1-800/881-877
Canada
Teleglobe ☎1-800/881-490
New Zealand
Clear ☎1800 124 333
Telecom ☎1800 881 640

① 1800, while others have six-digit numbers beginning with ① 13 or 1300 that incur a one-off fee of 25¢ (or 40¢ from a public phone) no matter where you are calling from within Australia. However, you cannot call 1800 numbers from outside Australia. Numbers starting ① 0055 are private information services (often recorded), costing between 35¢ and 70¢ a minute, but with a minimum charge of 40¢ from public phones.

International calls are charged at a flat per-minute rate depending on the country called, whatever the hour or day of the week that the call is made. All incur a connection fee of 22¢, then it costs 37.4¢ per minute to the UK; 31¢ to the US; 44¢ for Canada; and 31¢ for New Zealand. If you plan to speak for a while, you can save money by buying half-hour blocks to all the above countries for $6.60 by dialling ① 0018 (instead of ① 0011), then the country code and number. Hang up within the first minute and you only pay a $2 connection fee, otherwise you'll be charged for the full half-hour; speak for over thirty minutes and you'll pay double.

Phonecards can be a far cheaper way to call cross-country or abroad. Various brands are available such as Say G'day or Go Talk, but all require a minimum of 40¢ to call the local centre, after which you key in your scratch number and telephone number. Rates are incredibly low: as little as 5¢ a minute with Go Talk. Global Gossip (see "Email", opposite) offers discount-rate international calls from private phone booths and Backpackers' Travel Centres (see "Travel agents", p.267) sell their own rechargeable discount phone card.

It's also possible to pop into K-Mart and buy a **prepaid mobile phone** for as little as $99 including a rechargeable SIM card with $25 credit that lasts three months. Or you can just buy the prepaid SIM card alone in various denominations, which slips into your own phone to give you an instant personal number once you've registered – very handy if you need to keep in touch when trying to get a job, for example. Telstra's communic8 network (ⓦ www.communic8.com.au) is the main provider. You'll need to check whether your own mobile is a GSM 900 or dual-band GSM 900/1800 and be warned that the rates are not so special: about 20¢ to connect and 77¢/minute thereafter. Texting is cheap at around 22¢ but by communic8's own admission, texting overseas was "hit and miss" at the time of writing.

Email

Public Internet access is widespread across Australia and keeping in touch via the Web is easy, fast and cheap in Sydney. **Internet cafés** are everywhere, typically charging $3–6 an hour with concessions as well as happy hours early in the morning. Many accommodation places – especially **hostels** – also provide terminals for their guests at similar rates (hotels will charge more) although some places still opt for the user-reviled coin-op booths; at some YHAs you buy a card that works like a phone card. The best machines and setups are what you'd want at home: modern, clean and fast with conventional controls and large screens. Otherwise, **local libraries** almost always provide free access, though time is generally limited to one hour and you'll have to sign up in advance on a waiting list. Some, like the State Library on Macquarie Street (see p.65), let you surf the Net for free but don't allow email access.

Darlinghurst Road in Kings Cross (see p.98) is crammed with cut-rate Internet places, with rates as low as $3 per hour. The chain Global Gossip has seven offices (all daily 9am–11pm; $3.95 for 30min–1hr; ① 02/9212 1466, ⓦ www.globalgossip.com), in the city at 770 & 790 George St, 415 Pitt St and 14 Wentworth Ave; at 111 Darlinghurst Rd, Kings Cross; 37 Hall St, Bondi; and 92 Oxford St, Darlinghurst. *Well Connected*, 35 Glebe Point Rd, Glebe (daily 7am–midnight; $5 per hour; see p.100), and the *Phone.Net Cafe*, 73–75 Hall St, Bondi Beach (daily 8am–10pm; $3.30 per hour) are both lively cybercafés with good food and coffee. You can surf the Net as part of your admission to the Australian Museum (p.75).

The media

There is a wide range of print media in Sydney, a rather American-influenced variety of TV channels, and a number of radio stations worth tuning into.

The press

The Murdoch-owned *Australian* is Australia's only national daily (that is, Mon–Sat) newspaper; aimed mainly at the business community, it has good overseas coverage but local news is often built around statistics. However, its bumper weekend (Sat) edition is much more lively and interesting. The *Australian Financial Review* is the in-depth business and finance paper to buy. Each state (or more properly, each state capital) has its own daily broadsheet, the best of which are two Fairfax-owned papers, the *Sydney Morning Herald* and Melbourne's venerable *The Age*. *The Age* is also widely available in Sydney but be warned that the two papers share similar content in their Saturday-edition weekend magazines. Sydney also has a tabloid, the Murdoch-owned *Daily Telegraph*. Both Sydney dailies have a more low-brow, advertisement-packed, multi-section Sunday version, the *Sun Herald* and the *Sunday Telegraph*. But the *Sydney Morning Herald* (*SMH*; Ⓦ www.smh.com.au) is *the* paper to buy to find out what's on in Sydney and there's usually a speciality supplement each day: the most useful are Monday's "The Guide", a programme and review of the week's TV; Tuesday's "Good Living", which focuses on the restaurant, foodie and bar scene; and Friday's "Metro", the entertainment supplement which includes listings and film, art and music reviews. Friday's *SMH* also has "The Form", a weekly racing guide. There are employment and rental sections daily, but the big Saturday edition is the best for these.

The *Guardian Weekly* and the *International Herald Tribune* are two easy-to-buy **international papers**. The City of Sydney Public Library, behind the Town Hall (Mon–Thurs 9am–7pm, Fri 9am–6pm, Sat 9am–noon), keeps a large selection of overseas newspapers, though nowadays it's probably easier to search for your favourite home newspaper's website and browse headlines and selected articles in a cybercafé (see "Email", p.34).

The weekly *Time Australia* and *The Bulletin* are Australia's current-affairs **magazines**. The monthly *HQ* focuses on literature, the arts and current affairs from a younger but sophisticated international and Australian perspective, while *Juice* is an intelligent and amusing music/popular culture mag. If you're interested in wildlife, pick up a copy of the quarterly *Australian Geographic* (related only in name to the US magazine) for some excellent photography and in-depth coverage of Australia's remoter corners. Overseas magazines are air-freighted in at exorbitant cost, but you'll find Australian versions of all the fashion mags, from *Vogue* to *Marie Claire*, plus enduring publications like the *Australian Women's Weekly* (now monthly) which is well-known for its excellent recipes, while the excellent *Australian Gourmet Traveller* celebrates both fine food and travel. Gossipy magazines like *Who Weekly* feature the lowdown on the antics of international and Australian celebs. On a different note, the Australian version of *The Big Issue*, produced out of Melbourne, is called *The Big Issue Australia* and has been operating since 1996. Vendors are homeless, ex-homeless or long-term unemployed and make half of the cover price.

TV

Australia's first **television station** opened in 1956 and the country didn't get colour television until 1974 – both much later than other Westernized countries. Australian television isn't particularly exciting unless you're into sport, of which there's plenty, and commercial stations put on frequent commercial breaks – with often annoyingly unsophisticated advertisements – throughout films.

There are Australian content rulings that ensure a good amount of Australian dramas, series and soap operas, many of which go on to make it big overseas, from the Melbourne-set *Neighbours* and *The Secret Life of Us* to *Home and Away*, filmed at Sydney's Palm Beach (see p.139). However, there's a predominance of American programmes and lots of repeats. Australian TV is also fairly permissive in terms of sexual content compared to the programming of Britain or North America. There are three predictable commercial stations: Channel Seven; Channel Nine, which aims for an older market with more conservative programming; and Channel Ten, which tries to grab the younger market with reality TV programmes like the Australian version of *Big Brother* and some good comedy programmes including the irreverent talk show *The Panel*. There is also the more serious ABC (Australian Broadcasting Corporation; ⊛www.abc.net.au) – a government-funded, national, advertisement-free station still with a British bias, showing all the best British sitcoms and mini-series, and excellent current affairs programmes such as Monday night's *Four Corners*. The livelier SBS, a mostly government-sponsored, multicultural station, has the best coverage of world news, as well as interesting current affairs programmes and plenty of foreign-language films, with high-quality advertisements (in between programmes only). There are two **pay TV** stations, Optus and the Murdoch-owned Foxtel, though the pay-TV culture is not as firmly established yet as in other countries, and even expensive hotels often still only have terrestrial TV. You can look at both free-to-air and pay-TV channel guides on ⊛www.ebroadcast.com.au, with links to all the TV stations and even your favourite Aussie TV shows.

Radio

The best **radio** is on the various ABC stations, both local and national: Radio National (576 AM) offers a popular mix of arty intellectual topics; 2BL (702 AM), intelligent talkback radio; News Radio (630 AM), 24-hour local and international news, current affairs, sports, science and finance, also utilizing a diverse range of foreign radio networks including the BBC World Service, the US's National Public Radio (NPR) and Germany's Radio Deutsche Welle; ABC Classic FM (92.9 FM), for classical music; and 2JJJ ("Triple J"; 105.7 FM), which supports local bands and alternative rock – aimed squarely at the nation's youth. You can listen to various ABC radio stations on the Web with live or on-demand audio (⊛www.abc.net.au/ streaming). Koori Radio (94.5FM; ⊛www .gadigal.org.au) gives voice to Aboriginal and Torres Strait Island communities in Sydney; the city's only "black" radio station, it plays a great mix of indigenous Australian, indigenous World music, and other black musicians. Sydney's "underground" radio station is the university-run – though largely self-supporting – 2SER (107.3FM; ⊛www .2ser.com).

Opening hours and public holidays

Business and post office hours are generally Monday to Friday 9am to 5pm. Shops and services usually open Monday to Saturday 9am to 5pm and until 9pm on Thursday night. The major retailers and several shopping malls in the city and in tourist areas also open on Sunday between 11am and 5pm, and big supermarkets generally open seven days from 8am until 8 or 9pm, though some close around 4pm on Sundays. There are several 24-hour 7/11 convenience stores/supermarkets in the inner city and suburbs.

Tourist attractions – museums, galleries and historic monuments – are open daily, usually between 10am and 5pm. All close on Christmas Day and Good Friday but otherwise specific opening hours are given throughout the Guide.

Public holidays

When an official holiday falls at the weekend, there may be an extra day off immediately before or after. The school holiday dates, when accommodation gets booked up and prices rise, are given on p.229.

New Year's Day (Jan 1)
Australia Day (Jan 26)
Good Friday
Easter Monday
Anzac Day (April 25)
Queen's Birthday (1st Mon in June)
Bank Holiday (1st Mon in Aug)
Labour Day (1st Mon in Oct)
Christmas Day (Dec 25)
Boxing Day (Dec 26)

Travellers with disabilities

Disability needn't interfere with your sightseeing: the attitude of the management at Sydney's major tourist attractions is excellent, and they will provide assistance where they can, and even most national parks have wheelchair accessible walks (including the Royal National Park, see p.309, and the Blue Mountains National Park, see p.289; also check ⓦwww.npws.nsw.gov.au). After cheerfully hosting the Paralympics in 2000, Sydney is now one of the most experienced cities at welcoming disabled travellers.

The Australian federal government provides information and various nationwide services for people with disabilities through the **National Information Communication Awareness Network** (NICAN) and the **Australian Council for the Rehabilitation of the Disabled** (ACROD) – see p.39 for contact details. The **Australian Tourist Commission** offices provide a helpline service and publish a factsheet, *Travelling in Australia for People with Disabilities*, available from its offices worldwide (see p.18 for addresses and phone numbers).

Planning a holiday

There are **organized tours and holidays** specifically for people with disabilities (including mobility, hearing, vision and intellectual restrictions). Some arrange travel only, some travel and accommodation, and others provide a complete package – travel, accommodation, meals and carer support. This last type, as well as catering fully for special needs, provides company for the trip. The contacts opposite will be able to put you in touch with any specialists for trips to Sydney; several are listed in the Australian Tourist Commission factsheet. If you want to be more independent, it's important to become an authority on where you must be self-reliant and where you may expect help, especially regarding transport and accommodation. It is also vital to be honest – with travel agencies, insurance companies and travel companions. Know your limitations and make sure others know them. If you do not use a **wheelchair** all the time but your walking capabilities are limited, remember that you are likely to need to cover greater distances while travelling (often over rougher terrain and in hotter temperatures) than you are used to. If you use a wheelchair, have it serviced before you go and carry a repair kit.

Read your **travel insurance** small print carefully to make sure that people with a pre-existing medical condition are not excluded. And use your travel agent to make your journey simpler: airline or bus companies can cope better if they are expecting you, with a wheelchair provided at airports and staff primed to help. A **medical certificate** of your fitness to travel (provided by your doctor) is also extremely useful; some airlines or insurance companies may insist on it. Make sure that you have extra supplies of medication – carried with you if you fly – and a prescription including the generic name in case of emergency.

Several **books** give a good overview of accessible travel in Australia, and include: *Smooth Ride Guides: Australia and New Zealand, Freewheeling Made Easy* (FT Publishing), which lists support organizations, airports and transport, specialist tour operators and places to visit and stay; *Easy Access Australia – A Travel Guide to Australia*, a comprehensive guide written by a wheelchair-user for anyone with a mobility difficulty, which is available over the Internet via ⓦwww.easyaccessaustralia.com.au (AU$45; includes postage and handling);

and *A Wheelie's Handbook of Australia* (Program Print).

Useful contacts

ⓦ**www.wheelabout.com**, ⓦ**e-bility .com/travel** Both have lists of accommodation and transport in Australia for people with disabilities as well as access maps of major Australian cities.

In the UK and Ireland

Irish Wheelchair Association Blackheath Drive, Clontarf, Dublin 3 ☎01/833 8241, ℻833 3873, ℮iwa@iol.ie. Useful information provided about travelling abroad with a wheelchair.
Tripscope Alexandra House, Albany Rd, Brentford, Middlesex TW8 0NE ☎0845/7585 641, ⓦwww.justmobility.co.uk/tripscope, ℮tripscope@cableinet.co.uk. This registered charity provides a national telephone information service offering free advice on UK and international transport for those with a mobility problem.

In the US and Canada

Access-Able ⓦwww.access-able.com. Online resource for travellers with disabilities.
Directions Unlimited 123 Green Lane, Bedford Hills, NY 10507 ☎1-800/533-5343 or 914/241-1700. Tour operator specializing in custom tours for people with disabilities.
Mobility International USA 451 Broadway, Eugene, OR 97401, voice and TDD ☎541/343-1284, ⓦwww.miusa.org. Information and referral services, access guides, tours and exchange programmes. Annual membership $35 (includes quarterly newsletter).
Society for the Advancement of Travelers with Handicaps (SATH) 347 5th Ave, New York, NY 10016 ☎212/447-7284, ⓦwww.sath.org. Non-profit educational organization that has actively represented travellers with disabilities since 1976.
Travel Information Service ☎215/456-9600. Telephone-only information and referral service.
Twin Peaks Press Box 129, Vancouver, WA 98661 ☎360/694-2462 or 1-800/637-2256. Publisher of the *Directory of Travel Agencies for the Disabled* ($19.95), listing more than 370 agencies worldwide; *Travel for the Disabled* ($19.95); the *Directory of Accessible Van Rentals* ($12.95); and *Wheelchair Vagabond* ($19.95), loaded with personal tips.
Wheels Up! ☎1-888/389-4335, ⓦwww.wheelsup.com. Provides discounted air fare, tour and cruise prices for disabled travellers, also

publishes a free monthly newsletter and has a comprehensive website.

In Australia

ACROD (Australian Council for Rehabilitation of the Disabled) NSW branch, Suite 103, 1st Floor, 1–5 Commercial Rd, Kingsgrove, NSW 2208 ☎02/9554 3666, ℱ9554 3188, ⓦwww.acrod.org.au. Provides lists of help organizations, accommodation, travel agencies and tour operators.
NICAN (National Information Communication Awareness Network) PO Box 407, Curtin, ACT 2605 ☎02/6285 3713 or 1800 806 769, ℱ6285 3714, ⓦwww.nican.com.au. A national, non-profit, free information service on recreation, sport, tourism, the arts, and much more, for people with disabilities. Has a database of 4500 organizations – such as wheelchair-accessible tourist accommodation venues, sports and recreation organizations, and rental companies who have accessible buses and vans.
Paraplegic and Quadriplegic Association New South Wales, 33–35 Burlington Rd, Homebush, NSW 2140 ☎02/9764 4166, ⓦwww.paraquad-nsw.asn.au. Organization serving the interests of the spinally injured.
People with Disabilities NSW 52 Pitt St, Redfern, NSW 2016 ☎02/9319 6622.

Accommodation

Much of Australia's tourist accommodation is well set up for people with disabilities, because buildings tend to be built outwards rather than upwards. New buildings in Australia must comply with a legal minimum **accessibility standard**, requiring that bathrooms contain toilets at the appropriate height, proper circulation and transfer space, wheel-in showers (sometimes with fold-down seat, but if this is lacking, proprietors will provide a plastic chair), grab rails, adequate doorways, and space next to toilets and beds for transfer. There are, of course, many older hotels which may have no wheelchair access at all or perhaps just one or two rooms with full wheelchair access. Most hotels also have refrigerators for medication which needs to be kept cool.

The best place to start looking for accommodation is the *A–Z Australian Accommodation Guide* published by the Australian Automobile Association (AAA) – the umbrella organization for state- and territory-based motoring associations that rate accommodation. They also offer some specialized services, a centralized **booking service** and a repair service for motorized wheelchairs, with reciprocal rights if you are a member of an affiliated overseas motoring organization. The guide is available from any of the state organizations; NICAN also has access to its database via computer, so you can choose your accommodation over the phone. Many travel shops and bookshops have accommodation guides which detail places that have wheelchair access.

In Sydney, accessible accommodation is most likely found in the big chain hotels which often have rooms with wheelchair access. Some of the smaller hotels do provide accessible accommodation, and a large proportion of suburban motels will have one or two suitable rooms. In the **country** around Sydney, there are fewer specially equipped hotels, but many motels have accessible units; this is particularly true of those that belong to a chain such as Flag – get hold of one of their directories for locations or check their website (ⓦwww.flag-choice.com.au). The newest YHA **hostels** are all accessible, and there has been an effort to improve facilities throughout; accessible hostels are detailed in the YHA *Handbook*, or check their website (ⓦwww.yha.com.au). **Caravan parks** are also worth considering, since some have accessible cabins. Others may have accessible toilets and washing facilities.

Transport

Post-Olympic improvements in Sydney include many wheelchair-accessible trains stations. However, as not all stations have lifts, check Station Facilities on the ⓦwww.cityrail.info before setting out, or call the Transport Infoline (☎13 15 00). For **taxis**, an organization called Wheelchair Accessible Taxis takes bookings on behalf of all taxi companies: call ☎02/8322 0200. To arrange a taxi from the airport call ☎1800 043 187. Of the major car-rental agencies, Hertz and Avis offer **vehicles with hand controls** at no extra cost, but advance notice is required. Reserved **parking** is available for vehicles displaying the wheelchair symbol (available from local council offices). There is no formal acceptance of overseas parking permits, but states will generally accept most home-country permits as sufficient evidence to obtain a temporary permit (call NICAN for further information).

The City of Sydney Council has a Disabled Access section on their website which includes access maps (ⓦwww.cityofsydney.nsw.gov.au/cs_disabled_services.asp). **Mobility maps**, showing accessible paths, car parking, toilets and so on, can be obtained from local councils such as Randwick Council, who will post them out (Customer Services, 30 Francis St, Randwick, NSW 2031; ☎02/9399 0999). Randwick Council has installed wheelchair accessible ramps at Clovelly and Malabar beaches. In 2002 the Australian Quadriplegic Association published the very useful *Access Sydney* which can be ordered on-line ($24.95; ⓦwww.aqa.com/accesssydneyguidebook .htm). The disability information resource website has a very useful city guide to Sydney (ⓦwww.accessibility.com.au/sydney/sydney .htm).

Crime and personal safety

You should take the same precautions in Sydney as you would in any other major city in the Western world, though the city's "heavy" areas would seem tame compared to similar areas in Europe or North America.

Drunk males may pose the usual problems on Friday and Saturday nights, though there is no sudden spill out onto the streets as closing times are variable, and you might find **restless teenagers** getting themselves into trouble in the city. CCTV cameras have been installed in city areas where there are often problems: in The Rocks, which gets very rowdy on Friday and Saturday nights, and on the George Street cinema strip, which is a popular suburban teenage hangout and, though crowded, a prime area for personal theft. Kings Cross is the red-light district and has a major drug problem. The main strips are crowded but there are assaults and muggings – you should be careful with your belongings here at any time and try not to walk down backstreets at night. Nearby Woolloomooloo, though going upmarket, has some troubled public housing, so it's wise to be careful at night, but Sydney's only no-go zone is Everleigh Street in Redfern (see p.91).

You're more likely to fall victim to a fellow traveller or an opportunist crime: **theft** is not unusual in hostels and so many provide lockable boxes; if you leave valuables lying around, or on view in cars, you can expect them to be stolen. Be careful with valuables at the beach; either leave them at your accommodation if you are alone, or take turns swimming. There are lockers at Bondi Beach (see p.133) and at Manly (p.125).

Exercise caution, don't forget common-sense streetwise precautions, and you should be fine; at night stay in areas that are well lit and full of people, look like you know where you are going and don't carry excess cash or anything else you can't afford to lose.

Rape and serious trouble

If the worst happens, it's best to contact the **Rape Crisis Line** (24hr; ☎02/9819 6565; outside the Metropolitan area ☎1800 424 017) before going straight to the police. Women police officers form a large part of the force, and in general the police deal sensitively with sexual assault cases.

To **avoid** physical attack, don't get too relaxed about Australia's friendly, easy-going

Police stations in popular and tourist areas

NSW Police Headquarters are at 14–24 College St, Darlinghurst (℡02/9339 0277). If you have any problems, or need to report a theft for insurance purposes or any other crime, you can call or drop in here or a local police station. For **emergencies** ℡000 is a free number which summons the police, ambulance or fire service. The following stations are open 24 hours:

Balmain 368 Darling St (℡02/9556 0699).

Bondi Beach 30 Hastings Parade (℡02/9365 9699).

Broadway 3-9 Regent St, Chippendale (℡02/9219 2199).

Darling Harbour 192 Day St (℡02/9265 6499).

Glebe 1–3 Talford St, cnr St Johns Rd (℡02/9552 8099)

Kings Cross 1–15 Elizabeth Bay Rd (℡02/8356 0099).

Manly 3 Belgrave St (℡02/9977 9499).

Mosman 96 Bradleys Head Rd (℡02/9969 1933).

Newtown 222 Australia St (℡02/9550 8199).

North Sydney 273 Pacific Highway (℡02/9956 3199).

Paddington 16 Jersey Rd (℡02/8356 8299).

Randwick 196 Alison Rd (℡02/9697 1099).

Redfern 30 Turner St (℡02/9690 4600).

Surry Hills 151 Goulburn St (℡02/9265 4144).

The Rocks 91 George St, cnr Argyle St (℡02/9265 6333).

Town Hall Sydney Electricity Bulding, 570 George St (℡02/9265 6595).

Woolloomooloo 164 Cathedral St (℡02/9265 6280).

attitude. The usual defensive tactics apply. Buses are generally safer than trains – on the train, always sit next to the guard in the carriage. Pick somewhere to stay that's close to public transport so you don't have to walk far at night – an area with busy nightlife may well be safer than a dead suburban backstreet. If you're going to have to walk for long stretches at night, take a cab unless the streets are busy with traffic and people.

Police and the law

The NSW **Police** Service – all armed – were formerly notoriously corrupt and have a poor public image. Perhaps as a result they tend to keep a low profile; you should have no trouble in your dealings with them. Indeed you'll hardly see them, unless you're out on a Friday or Saturday night when they cruise in search of drink-related brawls.

Things to watch out for, most of all, are drugs. A lot of marijuana is grown and its use is widespread, but you'd be foolish to carry it when you travel, and crazy to carry any other illicit narcotic, especially as sniffer dogs now do random searches at Sydney train stations. Driving in general makes you more likely to have a confrontation of some kind, if only for a minor traffic infringement: **drunk driving** is regarded extremely seriously, so don't risk it – random breath tests are common around all cities and larger towns.

Lesser potential problems are **alcohol** – there are all sorts of controls on where and when you can drink in public; **smoking**, which is increasingly being banned in public places; and nude or **topless** sunbathing, which is quite acceptable in many places, but absolutely not in others – follow the locals' lead.

If for any reason you are **arrested** or need help (and you can be arrested merely on suspicion of committing an offence), you are entitled to contact a friend or lawyer before answering any questions. You could call your consulate, but don't expect much sympathy. If necessary, the police will provide a lawyer, and you can usually get legal aid to settle the bill.

The City

The City

Sydney Harbour Bridge and The Rocks

he Rocks, immediately beneath the **Sydney Harbour Bridge**, is the heart of historic Sydney. On this rocky outcrop between Sydney Cove and Walsh Bay, Captain Arthur Phillip proclaimed the establishment of Sydney Town in 1788, the first permanent European settlement in Australia. Within decades, however, the area had become little more than a **slum** of dingy dwellings, narrow alleys and dubious taverns and brothels. In the 1830s and 1840s, merchants began building fine stone warehouses here, but as the focus for Sydney's shipping moved to Woolloomooloo, the area again fell into decline. By the 1870s and 1880s, the notorious Rocks "pushes", gangs of "larrikins" (louts), mugged passers-by when they weren't beating each other up. The narrow street named Suez Canal was a favourite place to jump out from. Some say the name is a shortening of Sewers' Canal, and indeed the area was so filthy and rat-ridden that whole street fronts had to be torn down in 1900 to contain an outbreak of bubonic plague. In 1924, the construction of the approaches to the Sydney Harbour Bridge began, again seeing mass **demolition** in The Rocks area, as hundreds of families were displaced, uncompensated.

The Rocks remained a run-down, depressed and depressing quarter until the 1970s, when there were plans to raze the remaining cottages, terraces and warehouses to make way for office blocks. However, due to the foresight of the Builders' Labourers Federation (BLF), a radical building workers' union (headed by its secretary, and now hero Jack Mundey), which opposed the demolition, the restored and renovated **historic quarter** is now one of Sydney's major tourist attractions. Despite a passing resemblance to a historic theme park, it's worth exploring. It's also the best place, apart from the airport, for tax-free shopping.

There are times when the old atmosphere still seems to prevail: Friday and Saturday nights can be thoroughly drunken – so much so that there's a prominent police station and officers patrolling on horseback; CCTV has also been installed. New Year's Eve is riotously celebrated here, as fireworks explode over the harbour. The best time to come for a more relaxed drink is Sunday afternoon, when many of the pubs offer live jazz or folk music.

The Sydney Harbour Bridge

The awe-inspiring **Sydney Harbour Bridge** has spanned the water dividing north and south Sydney since the early 1930s. It's hard to imagine the view of the harbour without the castle-like sandstone pylons anchoring the bridge to the shore and the crisscross of steel arch against the sky. At 503m, it was the longest single span arch bridge in the world when it was built; construction began in 1924 and continued to provide employment through the height of the Great Depression – sixteen workers also lost their lives to it.

As the New South Wales premier, J.T. Lang, of the Labor party, prepared to cut the ribbon to open the bridge in 1932, further excitement was provided by the dashing horseman and royalist fanatic, Francis de Groot, who galloped up like a cavalryman and cut the opening ribbon with a sabre declaring "I open this bridge in the name of the Majesty of the King and all the decent citizens of New South Wales" in protest at Lang's socialist leanings.

Residents of the north of England might find the bridge familiar: the much tinier Tyne Bridge in Newcastle-upon-Tyne, built in 1929, was the model for Sydney's. Construction costs for the altogether huger Sydney project weren't paid off until 1988, but there's still a $3 toll to drive across, payable when heading south; this is now used for maintenance costs and to pay off the newer Sydney Harbour Tunnel which runs below, starting south of the Opera House – the ever-increasing volume of traffic in recent years proved too much for the bridge to bear. However, you can walk or cycle the bridge for free: pedestrians should head up the steps to the bridge from Cumberland Street, reached from The Rocks via the Argyle Steps off Argyle Street, and walk on the eastern side (the western side is the preserve of cyclists).

The bridge demands full-time maintenance, protected from rust by continuous painting in trademark steel-grey. One of Australia's best-known comedians, Paul Hogan of *Crocodile Dundee* fame, worked as a rigger on "the coathanger" before being rescued by a New Faces talent quest in the 1970s. To check out Hoge's vista, you can follow a rigger's route and climb the bridge (see below) – once the favoured illegal pastime of drunken uni students. If you can't stomach (or afford) the climb, there's a **lookout point** (daily 10am–5pm; $5; Ⓦ www.pylonlookout.com.au; 5min walk from Cumberland St then 200 steps) actually inside the bridge's southern pylon where, as well as gazing out across the harbour, you can study a photo exhibition on the bridge's history.

Climbing the bridge

Bridge Climb take small, specially equipped groups (maximum twelve people) to the top of the bridge from sunrise through to the city lights of night-time daily, roughly every ten to twenty minutes (Mon–Fri daytime climbs and Mon–Thurs & Sun night-time climbs $145; dawn, twilight, Sat & Sun daytime climbs and Fri & Sat night-time climbs $175; minimum age 12; ℡ 02/8274 7777, Ⓦ www.bridgeclimb.com). Booking ahead is advised, particularly if you want to climb at weekends. Though the experience takes three-and-a-half hours, only two hours is spent on the bridge, gradually ascending and pausing while the guide points out landmarks and offers interesting background snippets. The hour spent checking in and getting kitted up at the "Base" at 5 Cumberland St, The Rocks, makes you feel as if you're preparing to go into outer space, as do the grey *Star Trek*-style suits specially designed so that you blend in with the bridge – no colourful crawling ants to spoil ground-level views. It's really not as scary as it looks – there's no way you can fall off, fully harnessed as you are into a cable system, and this can calm a normal fear of heights, though phobics beware.

To avoid the dangers of things accidentally being dropped on cars and passers-by, the only thing you're allowed to take up are your glasses, attached to the suit by special cords – everything from handkerchiefs to caps are provided and similarly attached. Annoyingly, as this has to be one of the world's greatest photo opportunities, this precaution also means you can't take your camera with you. You do get one group photo – taken by the guide – on top of the bridge free with the price of the climb, but the group – of jolly strangers, arms akimbo – crowds out the panoramic background. To get a good shot showing yourself with the splendours of the harbour behind, you'll need to fork out $15.95 for one extra individual photo, $24.95 for a large A4-size photo or $29.95 for four different small ones.

The Rocks

The best place to start your **tour** of The Rocks is the **Sailors' Home** at 106 George St (daily 9am–6pm; also see p.18) built in 1864 to provide decent lodgings for visiting sailors as an alternative to the area's brothels and inns. The building continued to house sailors until the early 1980s but is now the **Sydney Visitor Centre**, supplying tourist information about The Rocks along with a re-creation of the sailors' sleeping quarters. You can pick up a guided tour leaflet of The Rocks here ($2.20). Nearby, you can arrange to go on an excellent guided walking tour with the long-running **The Rocks Walking Tours**, whose office is at Shop 4, Kendall Lane, where the walks commence (Mon–Fri 10.30am, 12.30pm & 2.30pm, Jan 10.30am & 2.30pm only, Sat & Sun 11.30am & 2pm; $17.50; bookings ℡02/9247 6678; Ⓦwww.rockswalkingtours.com.au). For a cyber tour of the area, the website Ⓦwww.rocksvillage.com.au focuses on The Rocks precinct.

The small sandstone house next door to the information centre and beside tiny, grassy Barney & Bligh Reserve, at 110 George St, is **Cadman's Cottage**, the oldest private house still standing in Sydney, built in 1816 for John Cadman, ex-convict and Government coxswain. It's now the **National Parks and Wildlife Service** bookshop and information centre (Mon–Fri 9.30am–4.30pm, Sat & Sun 10am–4.30pm; ℡02/9247 5033, Ⓦwww.npws .nsw.gov.au), providing information about the Sydney Harbour National Park, and taking bookings for trips to Fort Denison (see p.112) and other harbour islands which are part of the park.

The corner of Argyle and Kent streets, Millers Point, is a terminus for several useful **bus routes**, so you could aim to walk through The Rocks from Circular Quay train station or ferry terminus and then catch a bus back: bus routes #431–434 go along George Street to Railway Square and from there to varying locations including Glebe and Balmain, while the #339 goes to the eastern beaches suburb of Clovelly via George Street in the city and Elizabeth and Albion streets in Surry Hills.

Campbells Cove to Argyle Street

Just exploring the narrow alleys and streets hewn out of the original rocky spur

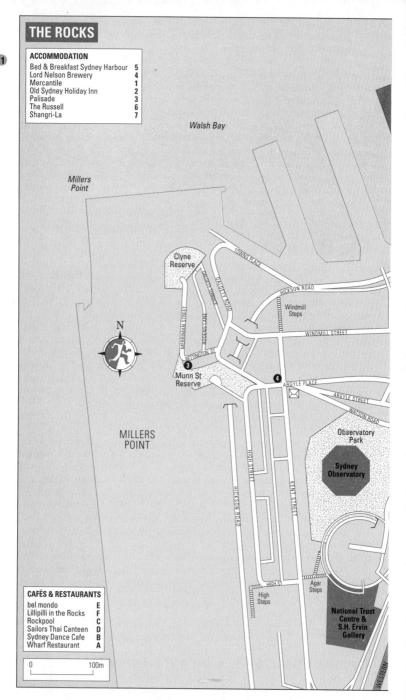

THE ROCKS

ACCOMMODATION

Bed & Breakfast Sydney Harbour	5
Lord Nelson Brewery	4
Mercantile	1
Old Sydney Holiday Inn	2
Palisade	3
The Russell	6
Shangri-La	7

Walsh Bay

Millers Point

Clyne Reserve

TOWNS PLACE

HICKSON ROAD

Windmill Steps

WINDMILL STREET

MERRIMAN STREET

DALGETY ROAD

POTTINGER ST.

N

3

Munn St Reserve

4 ARGYLE PLACE

ARGYLE STREET

WATSON ROAD

MILLERS POINT

Observatory Park

HIGH STREET

KENT STREET

Sydney Observatory

HICKSON ROAD

HIGH ST

Agar Steps

High Steps

High Steps

National Trust Centre & S.H. Ervin Gallery

WESTERN

CAFÉS & RESTAURANTS

bel mondo	E
Lillipilli in the Rocks	F
Rockpool	C
Sailors Thai Canteen	D
Sydney Dance Cafe	B
Wharf Restaurant	A

0   100m

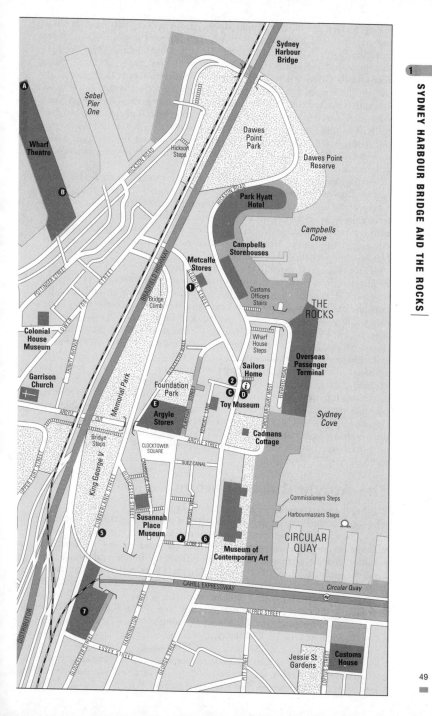

is the chief delight of **The Rocks**, a voyage of discovery that involves climbing and descending several stairs and cuts to different levels. Down the steps from the Sydney Visitor Centre, a stroll north along Circular Quay West past the revamped Overseas Passenger Terminal (see p.56), brings you to **Campbells Cove**, where the **Campbell's Storehouses** is fairly representative of The Rocks' focus on eating and shopping for souvenirs, clothing and arts and crafts in beautifully restored sandstone warehouses; these storehouses were once part of the private wharf of the merchant Robert Campbell, built in 1839 to hold everything from tea to liquor. A replica of Captain Bligh's ship, the *Bounty*, is normally moored here between cruises (see box on p.29), adding a Disneyish atmosphere, while a luxury hotel, the *Park Hyatt*, overlooks the whole area.

Going past the hotel to Dawes Point Park under the Harbour Bridge brings you to **Dawes Point**, a favourite spot for photographers, separating Sydney Cove, on the Circular Quay side, from Walsh Bay and its several old, now-renovated piers on Hickson Road, which is part of the still mostly residential and working-port area called Millers Point (see p.52). Looking out from Dawes Point, past the Opera House on a small harbour island, you can see Fort Denison, the fort-turned-prison (see p.112).

Heading back to Campbells Cove, you can climb the Customs Officer's Stairs to Hickson Road where you can browse in the **Metcalfe Stores**, another warehouse-turned-shopping complex, this time dating from around 1912. Exit from the old bond stores onto George Street, where at weekends you can further satisfy your shopping urge at the **Rocks Market** (see p.260), which takes over the entire Harbour-Bridge-end of the street with more than a hundred stores – shaded by big white umbrellas – selling souvenirs, bric-a-brac and arts and crafts with an Australiana slant.

There's more shopping at the **Argyle Stores**, on the corner of Argyle and Playfair streets, a complex of decidedly more tasteful and upmarket boutiques in a beautifully restored set of former bond stores; on the top floor you can take in great views from the bar of *bel mondo* (see p.181), also accessible from Gloucester Walk (see below). Also off Argyle Street, narrow **Kendall Lane** has a couple of great attractions for children, **The Rocks Toy Museum** and next door, free puppet shows at **The Puppet Cottage** (see "Kids Sydney", p.233).

The Argyle Cut and around

The Argyle Stores is just near the impressive **Argyle Cut**, which slices through solid stone to the more residential and working port area of **Millers Point** (see p.52). The Cut took eighteen years to complete, carved first with chisel and hammer by convict chain gangs who began the work in 1843; when transportation ended ten years later the tunnel was still unfinished, and it took hired hands to complete it in 1859. Up the **Argyle Steps** and along the narrow brick pedestrian walkway of peaceful **Gloucester Walk** you come to the tiny **Foundation Park**. It's quite a delight to stumble across – remains of cottage foundations discovered in architectural digs have formed the basis for an arrangement of sculptural installations representing Victorian furniture. You can follow Gloucester Walk back to the northern end of George Street for a drink at *The Mercantile*, one of Sydney's best Irish watering holes (see p.196). Gloucester Walk also leads to the pedestrian entrance of the Harbour Bridge on **Cumberland Street**, the location of a couple of classic old boozers, the *Glenmore* (see p.196) and the *Australian Hotel* (see p.196).

△ Sydney Harbour Bridge

From the *Australian*, head down **Gloucester Street** to the **Susannah Place Museum** at nos. 58–64 (Jan daily 10am–5pm; Feb–Dec Sat & Sun 10am–5pm; $7; Ⓦ www.hht.nsw.gov.au), a row of four brick terraces built in 1844 and continuously occupied by householders until 1990; the buildings are now a "house museum" (including a re-created corner store selling great old-fashioned sweets) that conserves the domestic history of Sydney's working class.

Millers Point

Looking west towards Darling Harbour, mostly residential **Millers Point** is a reminder of how The Rocks used to be – many of the homes are still government or housing association-owned and there's a surprisingly real community feel so close to the tourist hype. Of course, the area has its upmarket pockets, such as the very swish *Observatory Hotel* on Kent Street, and the renovated piers on **Walsh Bay**, but for the moment the traditional street-corner pubs and shabby terraced houses on the hill are reminiscent of the raffish atmosphere once typical of the whole area, and the peaceful leafy streets are a delight to wander in.

Lower Fort Street

You can reach the western side of the area through the Argyle Cut or from the end of George Street, heading onto **Lower Fort Street**. The **Colonial House Museum**, at no. 53 (daily 10am–5pm, but by arrangement only on ☏02/9247 6008; $1), takes up most of a residential 1883 terrace house where local character Shirley Ball has lived for over fifty years; her collection is crammed into six rooms, and includes period furnishings, hundreds of photographs of the area, etchings, artefacts and models. If you continue to wander up Lower Fort Street, don't pass up the opportunity to have a bevvy in the **Hero of Waterloo** at no. 81 (see p.196), built from sandstone excavated from the Argyle Cut in 1844, then peek in at the **Garrison Church** (or Holy Trinity, as it's officially called; daily 9am–5pm), on the corner of Argyle Street which was the place of worship for the military stationed at Dawes Point Fort from the 1840s. Next to the church, the volunteer-run **Garrison Gallery Museum** (Tues, Wed, Fri & Sat 11am–3pm, Sun noon–4pm; free) is housed in what was once the parish schoolhouse. Australia's first Prime Minister, Edmund Barton, was educated here and the collection of turn-of-the-twentieth century photographs, complete with images of ragged barefoot children and muddy dirt roads, gives a good indication of the conditions of his tutelage. Beside the church, **Argyle Place** has some of the area's prettiest terrace houses.

Walsh Bay

You can reach the northeastern side of Millers Point from Dawes Point (see p.50), where **Hickson Road** continues alongside **Walsh Bay.** Here, nearly all of the charmingly dilapidated old piers have been or are in the process of being transformed. At no. 11 Hickson Rd, the first pier has recently been taken over by a luxurious hotel, *Sebel Pier One*, while pier 4/5 has long been home to the **Wharf Theatre**, base of the prestigious Sydney Theatre Company (STC; also see p.216), established in 1978, and the internationally acclaimed Sydney Dance Company (see p.215) as well as about twenty other smaller arts organizations. From the **Wharf Restaurant** (see p.184) and its bar, you can revel in the sublime view across Walsh Bay to Balmain, Goat Island and the North

Shore, or get closer to the water (and the arts workers) at the cute little *Dance Cafe* (see p.173) on the ground floor that looks across to the brand-new luxury apartments on the opposite pier. If you're keen, you can even attend a drop-in dance class at the complex. The exhibition of posters of past STC productions, featuring such luminaries as Judy Davis and Cate Blanchett, lining the hallway to the restaurant might tempt you to come back for a performance (the STC also puts on productions at the Opera House – see p.60). **Guided tours** of the theatre, including the costume department and a look at set construction, are also available (last Thurs of month; 1hr–1hr 30min; $15; bookings on ☎02/9250 1777). Sydney's literati converge on the Wharf Theatre complex in May of each year, for the wonderfully sited and mostly free **Sydney Writers Festival** (see p.251).

Observatory Park

Opposite the Garrison Church, climb up the steps on Argyle Street to the well-chosen spot for **Sydney Observatory**, above **Observatory Park**. The park, with its shady Moreton Bay figs, park benches and lawns, has a marvellous hilltop view over the architecture below and the whole harbour in all its different aspects – glitzy Darling Harbour, the spectacularly cabled Anzac Bridge in one direction and the older Sydney Harbour Bridge in the other, gritty container terminals, ferries gliding by – and on a rainy day enjoy it from the bandstand which dominates the park. It's also easy to reach the park from the Bridge Stairs off Cumberland Street by the Argyle Cut.

Sydney Observatory

The Italianate-style **Sydney Observatory** from which the park takes its name marked the beginning of an accurate time standard for the city when it opened in 1858, calculating the correct time from the stars and signalling it to ships in the harbour and Martin Place's GPO by the dropping of a time ball in its tower at 1pm every day – a custom which still continues. Set amongst some very pretty gardens, the Observatory has had a **museum of astronomy** since 1982 and the excellent, modern museum is well worth a visit (museum and gardens daily 10am–5pm; free; ⓦwww.phm.gov.au).

A large section of the museum is devoted to the **Transit of Venus**, the rare astronomical event which takes place about twice every century – Venus is due to transit over the disk of the sun on June 8, 2004, visible from Europe, Africa, Asia and eastern parts of North America (for more infomation and exact locations, check out ⓦwww.transitofvenus.org); it was this occurrence which prompted Captain Cook's 1769 voyage of exploration, during which time he charted Australia's east coast. The extensive collection of astronomical equipment, both archaic and high-tech, includes the still-working telescope installed under the copper dome to observe the 1874 Transit of Venus (the last until 2004's). Another highlight, in the "Stars of the Southern Sky" section, are three animated videos of Aboriginal creation stories, retellings of how the stars came to be, from the Milky Way to Orion.

Every evening you can view the southern sky through telescopes and learn about the Southern Cross and other southern constellations; the two-hour tours include a lecture, film, the exhibitions, a guided view of the telescopes and a look at the sky, weather permitting. Otherwise, the small planetarium is used when the sky is not clear enough for observation (tour times vary seasonally; booking essential, usually up to a week in advance, on ☎02/9217 0485; $10).

National Trust Centre and S.H. Ervin Gallery

Also in the park, south of Sydney Observatory, is the **National Trust Centre**, located in a former military hospital dating from 1815, with a café (Tues–Fri 11am–3pm, Sat & Sun 1–5pm), and a specialist bookshop (Tues–Fri 11am–5pm, Sat & Sun noon–5pm) where you can pick up leaflets about other historic buildings and settlements in New South Wales.

The rear of the building, purpose-built as a school in 1850 in neo-Regency style, houses the **S.H. Ervin Gallery** (hours as bookshop; free; entry to special exhibitions $6; ⓦ www.nsw.nationaltrust.org.au), the result of a 1978 million-dollar bequest by Ervin to devote to Australian art; changing thematic exhibitions are of scholarly non-mainstream art, focusing on subjects such as Aboriginal or women artists.

2

Circular Quay and the Sydney Opera House

A t the southern end of Sydney Cove, sandwiched between Sydney's first settlement, The Rocks, and its modern emblem, the Opera House, **Circular Quay** is the launching pad for harbour and river ferries and sightseeing cruises. Less attractively, it's also the terminal for buses from the eastern and southern suburbs, and a major suburban train station to boot, with the ugly 1960s Cahill Expressway also spoiling the views. However, one of the most fantastic views of the harbour can now be seen from the above-ground platforms of Circular Quay train station, which has been opened up by the partial removal of a wall.

It's a popular stroll from the Quay to the **Opera House** and the Royal Botanic Gardens (see p.62) just beyond, enjoying an ice cream or stopping for some oysters and a beer at a waterfront bar; all the necessities for a picnic in the Gardens, including bubbly and fresh prawns, can be purchased at the Quay.

Circular Quay and around

Always bustling with commuters during the week, "The Quay", as the locals call it, is crammed with people simply out to enjoy themselves at the weekend. Restaurants, cafés and fast-food outlets stay open until late and buskers entertain the crowds, while vendors of newspapers and trinkets add to the general hubbub. For intellectual stimulation, you need only look beneath your feet as you stroll along: the inscribed bronze pavement plaques of **Writers' Walk** provide an introduction to the Australian literary canon. There are short biographies of writers ranging from Miles Franklin, author of *My Brilliant Career*, Booker Prize-winner Peter Carey and Nobel Prize-awardee Patrick White, to the feminist Germaine Greer, as well as quotations on what it means to be Australian. Notable literati who've visited Australia – including Joseph Conrad, Charles Darwin and Mark Twain – also feature.

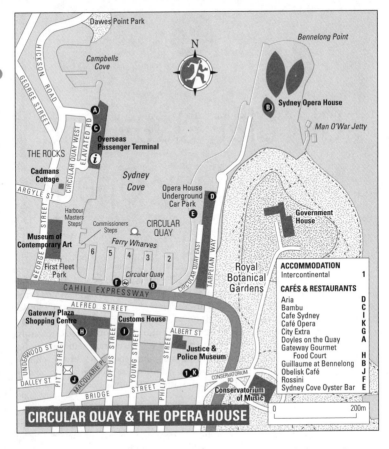

CIRCULAR QUAY & THE OPERA HOUSE

Leading up to the Opera House is the once-controversial **Opera Quays** development which runs the length of **East Circular Quay**. Locals and tourists flock to promenade along the pleasant colonnaded lower level with its outdoor cafés, bars and bistros, upmarket shops and Dendy Quays Cinema (see p.219), all looking out to sublime harbour views. The ugly apartment building above, dubbed "The Toaster" by locals and described by Robert Hughes, the famous expat Australian art critic and historian, as "that dull brash, intrusive apartment block which now obscures the Opera House from three directions", caused massive protests, but went up anyway, opening in 1999.

Besides ferries (for a comprehensive review of the huge range of cruises starting from Circular Quay, see pp.27–30), the Quay still acts as a passenger terminal for ocean liners, though it's been a long time since the crowds waved their hankies regularly from the **Sydney Cove Passenger Terminal**, looking for all the world like the deck of a ship itself, but you may still see an ocean liner docked here. To reach it, head in the opposite direction past the **Museum of Contemporary Art** to **Circular Quay West**; even if there's no ship, take the escalator and the flight of stairs up for excellent views of the harbour. The rest of the recently redeveloped terminal is now given over to super-trendy and expensive restaurants and bars such as *Aria* (see p.184) and *Cruise Bar* (see p.197).

Behind the Quay on **Alfred Street**, you can check out contemporary craft and a scale model of modern Sydney at the recently renovated **Customs House**, or peruse the exhibits at the nearby **Justice and Police Museum**.

Museum of Contemporary Art

The **Museum of Contemporary Art** (MCA) on Circular Quay West, with another entrance on 140 George Street (daily 10am–5pm; free; free tours Mon–Fri 11am & 2pm, Sat & Sun noon & 1.30pm; Ⓦ www.mca.com.au), was developed out of a bequest to Sydney University by the art collector John Power in the 1940s to purchase international contemporary art. The growing collection finally found a permanent home in 1991 in the former Maritime Services Building, provided for peppercorn rent by the state government. Since John Power left no recurrent funding, the museum now has to raise ninety percent of its own funding and has been financially troubled since opening; the free entry is courtesy of corporate sponsorship and means the MCA is now chock-a-block with locals at weekends. In 1999 Sydney City Council considered funding the redevelopment of the MCA, but when the Lord Mayor abandoned the plans, Bob Carr's state government stepped in to the rescue with $3 million.

The striking Art Deco-style 1950s building is dedicated to international twentieth- and twenty-first-century art, with an eclectic approach encompassing lithographs, sculpture, installations, film, video, photography, drawings, paintings and Aboriginal art, mostly shown in themed exhibitions. Some past exhibitions have featured the work of Robert Mapplethorpe and Jeff Koons, looked at contemporary Japanese art, and examined popular culture in the 1950s.

The museum's permanent collection of 1600 works, including pieces by Keith Haring, Bridget Riley, Jasper Johns, David Hockney and Jean Tinguely, is mostly kept in storage, though a selection is shown in special exhibitions twice a year. The museum's superbly sited, if expensive and rather snooty **café** (Mon–Fri 11am–4.30pm, Sat & Sun 9am–4.30pm) has outdoor tables overlooking the waterfront.

Customs House

Immediately opposite Circular Quay on Alfred Street is an architectural gem, the sandstone and granite **Customs House**. First constructed in 1845 and redesigned in 1885 by the colonial architect James Barnet to give its current Classical Revival-style facade, the building was then neglected for many years. However, with over $20 million spent on refurbishing the exterior and completely transforming the interior, it reopened as a cultural centre in 1999. Entering the building, the first impression is of space and light: the six floors are galleried and crowned by a glass-roofed central atrium. Escalators slant up three levels against a back glass wall providing a feeling of movement and high-tech modernity, while lifts continue up to the other floors.

The **Australian Centre for Craft and Design** has its exhibition gallery, **Object**, on level 3 (Tues–Sun 10am–5pm; free), displaying themed groupings and single shows of Australia's best artisans. On the ground floor, the centre's retail outlet, **Object Galleries** (Mon–Fri 10am–5.30pm, Sat & Sun noon–5pm), sells beautifully designed glass, ceramics, woodwork and jewellery, all labelled with the artisan and state of origin.

On level 4, the **City Exhibition Space** (daily 9am–5pm; free) keeps pace with the sometimes bewildering development of Sydney with an up-to-the-minute 500:1 scale model of the city accompanied by history boards and video screens. If you're really interested in the city's modern architecture, **Sydney Architecture Walks** have various on-foot tours led by young architects leaving from here every Wednesday and Saturday at 10am and on the first and last Sunday of the month (first Sun 2pm, last Sun 10am; all tours 2hr 30min; $22; bookings on ☎02/9242 8555 or ✉info@sydneyarchitecture.org).

The Customs House is blessed with some great **places to eat**: on the top floor a pricey contemporary-style brasserie, *Cafe Sydney* (see p.185), comes with some of the best Harbour Bridge views, while on the ground floor, you can take a coffee at *Caffe Bianchi*, or eat oysters and have a beer at *Quay Bar*, both with alfresco seating on Customs House Square out front.

Justice and Police Museum

A block east of the Customs House, on the corner of Phillip Street, the **Justice and Police Museum** (Jan daily except Fri 10am–5pm; Feb–Dec Sat & Sun 10am–5pm; $7; ⓦwww.hht.nsw.gov.au) is housed in the former Water Police station, an 1858 sandstone building whose verandah is decorated with some particularly fine ironwork.

The social history museum focuses on law, policing and crime in New South Wales with several temporary themed exhibitions throughout the year, often giving a contemporary viewpoint on crime and its milieu – past ones have delved into the art of tattooing and scrutinized the relationship between the police and environmental protestors. The permanent crime displays, including some truly macabre death masks, gruesome confiscated weapons (some of them murder implements) and other souvenirs of Sydney's murky past, are all shown within the context of a late-nineteenth-century police station and court mock-up. There's also an interesting display on bushrangers.

The Sydney Opera House

The **Sydney Opera House**, such an icon of Australiana that it almost seems kitsch, is just a short stroll from Circular Quay, by the water's edge on **Bennelong Point**. It's best seen in profile, when its high white roofs, at the same time evocative of full sails and white shells, give the building an almost ethereal quality. Some say the inspiration for the distinctive design came from the simple peeling of an orange into segments, though perhaps Danish architect **Jørn Utzon**'s childhood as the son of a yacht designer had something to do with their sail-like shape – he certainly envisaged a building which would appear to "float" on water. Close-up, you can see that the shimmering effect is created by thousands of chevron-shaped white tiles.

The feat of structural engineering required to bring to life Utzon's "sculpture", which he compared to a Gothic church and a Mayan temple, made the final price tag $102 million, fourteen times original estimates. Now almost universally loved and admired, it's hard to believe quite how controversial a project this was during its long haul from plan (as a result of an international competition in the late 1950s) to completion in 1973. It's a wonder Utzon even won the competition: Eero Saarinen, architect of New

York's JFK airport terminal, who was on the selection committee, vetoed the shortlist and flicked through the reject pile, pronouncing Utzon's way-out design the work of a genius. For sixteen years, construction was plagued by quarrels and scandal (the winner of the Opera House fund lottery even had his young son kidnapped for ransom and murdered, Australia's first such crime), so much so that Utzon, who won the competition in 1957, was forced to resign in 1966, calling the whole sorry situation "Malice in Blunderland". Many believe that he was hounded out of the country by politicians – the newly elected Askin New South Wales' state government disagreeing over his plans for the completion of the interior – and jealous, xenophobic local architects. Seven years and three Australian architects later, the interior, which never matched Utzon's vision, was finished: the focal Concert Hall, for instance, was completely designed by **Peter Hall** and his team.

The building's twenty-fifth birthday was celebrated with free concerts in October 1998 and the announcement of a $70 million ten-year plan to renew and modify the interior, which refocused media attention on past mistakes. However, Utzon, in his mid-eighties, now has a chance to have the final say: in 1999 he was invited by New South Wales' Premier Bob Carr to be the principal design consultant in the preparation of a Statement of Design Principles for the building, which will become the permanent reference for its conservation and development. The invitation was both a gesture of goodwill to make up for past slights and a real attempt to finally realize his full design. Some of these ideas might be used in decades to come, but as part of the current renovation, Utzon has made plans for a remodelled western exterior, and designed a huge wall tapestry, a "homage to Bach", for the Reception Hall; the sound-absorbing tapestry will allow the installation of a parquet floor with a pattern echoing the ribbed ceiling. Jørn Utzon is continuing his consultancy with the help of his architect and business-partner son Jan, who spent several childhood years in Sydney (Jørn's granddaughter Anna is a permanent Sydney resident). Although Jan Utzon has returned for a visit in his father's place – the pair are working from Jørn's homes in Copenhagen and Majorca – Utzon senior has still never seen the finished building he designed. The statement is intended to be publicly available by the end of 2003; check the Opera House website (see p.216) for the latest information.

Around the house

"Opera House" is actually a misnomer: it's really a performing arts centre, one of the busiest in the world, with five performance venues inside its shells, plus two restaurants, several popular cafés and bars, an Aboriginal artists' gallery, and a stash of upmarket souvenir shops.

The building's initial impetus, in fact, was as a home for the **Sydney Symphony Orchestra** (SSO), the cherished dream of Sir **Eugene Goossens**, the British conductor invited in 1947 to transform the SSO into a world-class orchestra and head the Conservatorium of Sydney. By 1955, the SSO was considered to be on the world's top ten list, Goossens had been knighted by the governor-general for his sterling effort, and the Australian Broadcasting Corporation (ABC) had the whole of Australia swooning with its radio broadcasts. Before the Opera House, however, their only venue was the too-small, draughty and acoustically challenged, though splendid Town Hall (see p.88). Like Utzon, Goosens never got to see the Opera House, which was designed with the huge **Concert Hall** (seating 2690) for the SSO as the focal point. Soon after he was knighted, he left for a holiday to Europe and on his return was found to be carrying a huge haul of pornography. Australia's censorship laws were notoriously tight, its climate parochial and puritanical, and the £100 fine came with a judgement from the QC that it was "difficult to imagine a worse case ... the exhibits speak for themselves ...". Hundreds of prominent international and local supporters were appalled at the witchhunt and subsequent career ruination of Goossens, who resigned in disgrace and left for Europe; he died alone on a plane flight in 1962.

The smaller **Opera Theatre** (1547 seats) is used as the Sydney performance base for Opera Australia (seasons Feb–March & June–Nov), the Australian Ballet (mid-March to May & Nov–Dec) and the Sydney Dance Company (see p.215). There are three theatrical venues: the **Drama Theatre** and **The Playhouse**, both used primarily by the Sydney Theatre Company (see p.52 and p.216), and the more intimate **The Studio**. The last was added in 1999 as part of the ten-year redevelopment plan; The Studio aims to draw in a younger audience, offering cheaper tickets for innovative Australian drama, comedy, cabaret and contemporary dance, performed in an adaptable theatre-in-the-round format.

There's plenty of action outside the Opera House too, with the use of the Mayan-temple-inspired **Forecourt** and Monumental Steps as an amphitheatre for free and ticketed concerts – rock, jazz and classical – with a capacity for around 5000 people. But on a more regular basis, Sunday is the liveliest day outside, when the **Tarpeian Markets** (10am–4pm), with an emphasis on Australian crafts, are held.

There are also a number of great **places to eat and drink** at the Opera House; you could choose to dine at what is considered to be one of Sydney's best restaurants, *Guillame at Bennelong*, overlooking the city skyline (see p.185), or take a drink at the *Opera Bar* on the lower concourse, with wonderful views from the outside tables and an affordable all-day menu. In addition there is also a sidewalk café, a bistro and several theatre bars.

Seeing the Opera House – tours and packages

If you're not content with gazing at the outside – much the building's best feature – and can't attend a performance, there are **guided tours** available: the Front-of-House tour gives an overview of the site, looking at the public areas and discussing the unique architecture (daily 8.30am–5pm, every 30–40min; 45min; $17). Backstage tours run about once or twice a week and include access to the scenery docks, rehearsal rooms and technical areas (1hr 30min; $28; bookings on ☏02/9250 7250 or via ⓦ www.soh.nsw.gov.au). It's only on these tours that you can see the small exhibition area in the foyer of The Playhouse where two original Utzon models of the Opera House are displayed, alongside a series of small oil paintings depicting the life of **Bennelong**, the Iora tribesman who was initially kidnapped as little more than an Aboriginal "specimen" but later became a much-loved addition to Governor Arthur Phillip's household; Phillip later built a hut for him on what is now the site of the Opera House, hence the name Bennelong Point. History buffs who would like to learn more can go on a history tour, offered by arrangement on the booking number above.

The best way to appreciate the Opera House, of course, is to attend an evening **performance** (see p.216): the building is particularly stunning when floodlit and, once you're inside, the huge windows come into their own as the dark harbour waters reflect a shimmering image of the night-time city – interval drinks certainly aren't like this anywhere else in the world. **Packages** which include tours, meals, drinks and performances can be purchased on-site or over the phone or Internet (see p.216) and can be good value.

3

Royal Botanic Gardens to Macquarie Street

t was Governor Arthur Phillip, at the helm of the new city from 1788 to 1792, who decreed that the picturesquely sited land around the harbour, east of his newly built Government House (now the site of the Museum of Sydney, see p.85) should always be in the public domain, a great park for the people to enjoy. Over two decades later Governor Lachlan Macquarie formalized his generous idea. The area remains public, but in two distinct parts: the open expanse of **The Domain**, long used for public celebrations and protests, which stretches from the stately strip of civic buildings envisaged by Governor Macquarie on the southern end of **Macquarie Street** to either side of the **Art Gallery of New South Wales** and down to the water alongside Mrs Macquaries Road; and spreading west of here, the much larger, varied expanse of the **Royal Botanic Gardens**, around 75 acres from the northern end of Macquarie Street to the Opera House (see p.58) and around Farm Cove.

The Royal Botanic Gardens

The **Royal Botanic Gardens** (daily 7am–sunset; free; Ⓦ www.rbgsyd.gov.au), established in 1816 by Governor Macquarie, occupy a huge waterfront area between The Domain and the Opera House, around the headland on Farm Cove where the first white settlers struggled to grow vegetables for the hungry colony. Today's gardeners are much more successful, judging by the well-tended flower beds. While duck ponds, a romantic rose garden and fragrant herb garden strike a very English air, look out for native birds and, at dusk, the fruit bats which fly overhead as the nocturnal possums begin to stir (you can also see hundreds of the giant bats hanging by day in the Palm Grove area near the restaurant). There are examples of trees and plants from all over the world, although it's the huge, gnarled native Moreton Bay figs that stand out. The gar-

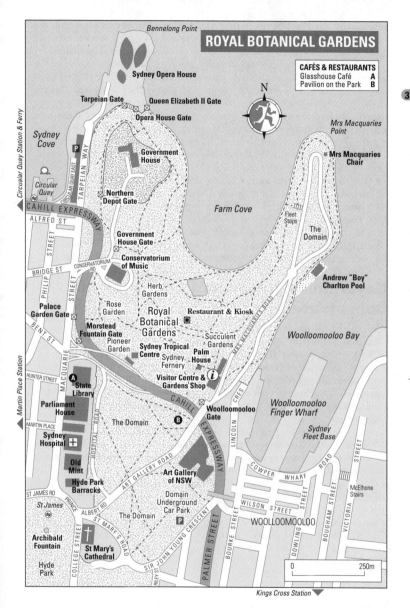

ROYAL BOTANICAL GARDENS

Bennelong Point

Sydney Opera House

Tarpeian Gate
Queen Elizabeth II Gate
Opera House Gate

CAFÉS & RESTAURANTS
Glasshouse Café   A
Pavilion on the Park   B

N

Circualar Quay Station & Ferry

Sydney
Cove

Circular
Quay

CAHILL EXPRESSWAY

ALFRED ST

BRIDGE ST

PHILIP STREET

Government
House

Northern
Depot Gate

Government
House Gate

Conservatorium
of Music

CONSERVATORIUM RD

Mrs Macquaries
Point

Mrs Macquaries
Chair

Farm Cove

Fleet
Steps

The
Domain

Herb
Gardens

Rose
Garden

Palace
Garden Gate

BENT ST

Morstead
Fountain Gate

Pioneer
Garden

Royal
Botanical
Gardens

Restaurant & Kiosk

Andrew "Boy"
Charlton Pool

Succulent
Gardens

Woolloomooloo Bay

MACQUARIE STREET

Martin Place Station

HUNTER STREET

Sydney Tropical
Centre

Sydney
Fernery

Palm
House

Visitor Centre &
Gardens Shop

Sydney Tropical
Centre

MRS MACQUARIES ROAD

A
State
Library

Parliament
House

MARTIN PLACE

Sydney
Hospital

Old
Mint

Hyde Park
Barracks

HOSPITAL ROAD

CAHILL

The Domain

B

Woolloomooloo
Gate

CAHILL EXPRESSWAY

LINCOLN CRES

Woolloomooloo
Finger Wharf

Sydney
Fleet Base

ST JAMES RD

St James

Archibald
Fountain

Hyde
Park

COLLEGE STREET

PRINCE ALBERT RD

St Mary's
Cathedral

ST MARY'S ROAD

ART GALLERY ROAD

Art Gallery
of NSW

The Domain

Domain
Underground
Car Park

SIR JOHN YOUNG CRESCENT

RILEY ST

PALMER STREET

COWPER   WHARF   ROAD

WILSON   STREET

BOURKE STREET

DOWLING STREET

BOUGHAM STREET

VICTORIA STREET

McElhone
Stairs

WOOLLOOMOOLOO

0   250m

Kings Cross Station ▼

dens provide some of the most stunning **views** of Sydney Harbour and are always crowded with workers at lunch time, picnickers on fine weekends, and lovers entwined beneath the trees.

Many **paths** run through the gardens. A popular and speedy route (roughly 15min) is to start at the northern gates near the Opera House and stroll along the waterfront path to the gates which separate it from The Domain, through here and up the **Fleet Steps** to Mrs Macquaries Chair (see p.68). Within the northern boundaries of the park, you can visit the original residence of the governor of New South Wales, and listen to lunch-time recitals at the nearby Conservatorium. Below the music school, the remaining southern area of the gardens has a herb garden, a cooling palm grove established in the 1860s, a popular café/restaurant by the duck ponds, and the **Sydney Tropical Centre** (daily 10am–4pm; $2.20) – a striking glass pyramid and adjacent glass arc respectively housing native tropical plants and exotics. Nearby, **the Rare and Threatened Plants** garden has the first example of a cultivated Wollemi Pine, planted in 1998. The "dinosaur" tree, thought long-extinct, was discovered by a national park ranger in 1994; there are only 38 of these trees in the world, growing in the Blue Mountains (see p.301).

At the southeast-corner entrance, near the Art Gallery of New South Wales, off Mrs Macquaries Road, free **guided tours** of the gardens commence from the **visitors centre** (daily 9.30am–5pm; tours daily 10.30am; 1hr–1hr 30min). The **Trackless Train**, which runs through the gardens about every twenty minutes, picks up from here; the main pick-up point is the entrance near the Opera House and there are also stops along the way (Mon–Fri 9.30am–5pm, Sat & Sun 9.30am–6pm; all-day hop-on-hop-off service $10, child $5).

Government House and the Conservatorium of Music

Within the northern boundaries of the Royal Botanic Gardens on Conservatorium Road, the sandstone mansion glimpsed through a garden and enclosure is the Gothic Revival-style **Government House** (built 1837–45), seat of the governor of New South Wales, and still used for official engagements by the governor, who now lives in a private residence. The stately interior has limited opening hours by free guided tour only (Fri–Sun 10am–3pm; tour 45min; Ⓦ www.hht.net.au) but you are at liberty to roam the grounds (daily 10am–4pm).

Further south of Government House, just inside the gardens at the end of Bridge Street, the **Conservatorium of Music** is housed in what was intended to be the servants' quarters and stables of Government House. Public opinion in 1821, however, deemed the imposing castellated building far too grand for such a purpose and a complete conversion, including the addition of a concert hall, gave it the loftier aim of training the colony's future musicians. A two-year renovation project, finished in 2000, uncovered an earlier convict-era site which led to an archeological dig being incorporated into the final redesign. Conservatorium students have traditionally given free lunch-time recitals every Tuesday and Friday at 1.10pm during term time (see p.215 for details of other classical music venues).

Macquarie Street

Lachlan Macquarie, reformist governor of New South Wales between 1809 and 1821, gave the early settlement its first imposing public buildings, clustered on the southern half of his namesake **Macquarie Street**. He had a vision of an elegant, prosperous city, but the Imperial Office in London didn't share his enthusiasm for expensive civic projects. Refused both money and expertise, Macquarie was forced to be resourceful: many of the city's finest buildings were designed by the ex-convict **Francis Greenway** – the convicted forger who went on to be appointed civil architect and design forty buildings, eleven of which survive – and paid for with "rum-money", the proceeds of a monopoly on liquor sales.

Modern Sydney – wealthy and international – shows itself on the corner of Bent and Macquarie streets in the curved glass sails of the 41-storey **Aurora Place Tower**, designed by Italian architect Renzo Piano, co-creator of the extraordinary Georges Pompidou Centre in Paris.

The closest **train** station to Macquarie Street is Martin Place CityRail.

State Library of New South Wales

The **State Library of New South Wales** (Mon–Fri 9am–9pm, Sat & Sun 11am–5pm, Mitchell Library closed Sun; free guided tours Tues 11am & Thurs 2pm; Ⓦwww.sl.nsw.gov.au) heads the row of public architecture on the eastern side of Macquarie Street. The complex of old and new buildings includes the 1906 sandstone **Mitchell Library**, its imposing Neoclassical facade gazing across to the Botanic Gardens. Inside, an archive of old maps, illustrations and records relating to the early days of white settlement and exploration in Australia includes the **Tasman Map**, drawn by the Dutch explorer Abel Tasman in the 1640s. The floor mosaic in the foyer replicates his curious map of the continent, still without an east coast, and its northern extremity joined to Papua New Guinea.

A glass walkway links the Mitchell Library with the modern building housing the **General Reference Library**. Free exhibitions relating to Australian history, art, photography and literature are a regular feature of the Reference Library vestibules while lectures, films and video shows take place regularly in the **Metcalfe Auditorium** (free and ticketed events; ☎02/9273 1414 for details and bookings). You can refresh yourself at the glass-roofed plant-filled **Glasshouse Cafe** on level 7 (see p.174). The library's **bookshop** on the ground floor has the best collection of Australia-related books in Sydney.

Sydney Hospital, NSW Parliament House and the Royal Mint

Sandstone **Sydney Hospital**, the so-called "Rum Hospital", funded by liquor-trade profits, was Macquarie's first enterprise, commissioned in 1814; the two remaining convict-built original wings therefore form one of the oldest buildings in Australia. The central section was pulled down in 1879 when it began collapsing; rebuilt by 1894, the Classical Revival buildings, still functioning as a small general and eye hospital, are also impressive – peep inside at the entrance hall's flower-themed stained glass and the decorative staircase, or you can take an interesting short cut through the grounds to The Domain and across to the Art Gallery of New South Wales (see p.67). Outside on Macquarie Street, the bronze statue of a boar, *Il Porcellino*, is a copy of one from Florence; his nose has long been rubbed shiny for luck by patients and their families.

One of the original wings of the hospital is now the **NSW Parliament House** (Mon–Fri 9.30am–4pm; free guided tours Mon & Fri 10am, 11am & 2pm; question time Tues–Thurs 2.15pm, call ☎02/9230 2111 or check

Ⓦ www.parliament.nsw.gov.au for parliamentary recesses), where as early as 1829 local councils called by the governor started to meet, making it by some way the oldest parliament building in Australia. However, it wasn't until the May 2003 state elections that an Aboriginal Australian was elected to the NSW Parliament – Linda Burney, former head of the NSW Department of Aboriginal Affairs and now Labor member for multicultural Canterbury; Labor was returned to office for the third time under the premiership of former journalist Bob Carr. You can listen in on Carr, Burney and other politicians during question time when the Parliament is sitting. Look out for the varied exhibitions in the foyer which change every fortnight or so – all represent community or public-sector interests and range from painting, craft and sculpture to particularly excellent photographic displays that often have an overt political content.

The other hospital wing was converted into a branch of the **Royal Mint** in response to the first Australian goldrush. It closed in 1927, and for some time served as a museum of gold mining; since the museum shut in 1997, the building has been taken over by NSW Historic Houses Trust offices. The organization has added a **café** (Mon–Fri 9am–5pm) that extends onto the verandah looking over Macquarie Street; interpretive boards detail the mint's history. Plans are afoot, however, for a $14 million redevelopment, finished by mid-2004, which will include a public auditorium created by combining the stone walls of the 1854 coining factory with a glass pavilion. Most daring though, is the plan to get rid of the ramshackle additions where the mint site borders the Hyde Park Barracks (see below) and link Macquarie Street with The Domain via this corridor.

The Hyde Park Barracks

Next door to the old Royal Mint, the **Hyde Park Barracks** (daily 9.30am–5pm; $7; Ⓦ www.hht.nsw.gov.au), designed by convict-architect Francis Greenway, was built in 1819, again without permission from London, to house six hundred male convicts. Now a **museum** of the social and architectural history of Sydney, it's a great place to visit for a taste of convict life during the early years of the colony. Start at the top floor, where you can swing in re-creations of the prisoners' rough hammocks. Computer terminals allow you to search for information on a selection of convicts' histories and backgrounds – several of those logged were American sailors nabbed for misdeeds while in Dublin or English ports (look up poor William Pink). Later the Barracks took in single immigrant women, many of them Irish, escaping the potato famine; an exhibition looks at their lives, and there's a moving monument in the grounds erected by the local Irish community. Look out too for the excellent temporary historical exhibitions and there's also a great **café** with an outdoor courtyard.

The Domain

The Domain is a large, quite plain, open space that stretches from behind the historic precinct on Macquarie Street to the waterfront, divided from the Botanic Gardens by the Cahill Expressway and Mrs Macquaries Road. Often filled with workers eating lunch under the shady Moreton Bay fig trees and people playing volleyball, or even swimming in its outdoor pool, the **Andrew "Boy" Charlton**, it's a popular place for a stroll from the city across to the **Art Gallery of New South Wales** or down to the harbour for wonderful views from **Mrs Macquaries Chair**. For many more years it has been a truly public site, as Sydney's focus for anti-establishment protests. Since the 1890s, assorted cranks and soapbox revolutionaries have assembled on Sundays for the city's version of **Speakers' Corner**, and huge crowds have registered their disquiet, notably during anti-conscription rallies in 1916 and after the Whitlam Labor government's dismissal in 1975. Every January thousands of people gather on the lawns to enjoy the wonderful free open-air concerts of the Sydney Festival (see p.249); in February the Tropfest short film festival (see p.219) takes over the grass, while December sees a night of Christmas carols (see p.253) and the all-Australian band line-up of the outdoor rock festival, Homebake (see p.210). The closest **train** stations to the Domain are Martin Place or St James CityRail, or you can take bus #441 from Market Street outside the QVB (see p.73).

Art Gallery of New South Wales

Art Gallery Road runs through The Domain to the **Art Gallery of New South Wales** (daily 10am–5pm; free general tours Mon & Sat 1pm & 2pm, Tues–Fri 11am, noon, 1pm & 2pm; free except for special exhibitions; Ⓦ www.artgallery.nsw.gov.au), whose collection was established in 1874. The original part of the building (1897), an imposing Neoclassical structure with a facade inscribed with the names of Renaissance artists, principally contains the large collection of European art dating from the eleventh century to the twenty-first – extensions were added in 1988 which doubled the gallery space and provided a home for mainly Australian art.

On level 1, the **Yiribana Gallery** is devoted to the art and cultural artefacts of Aboriginal and Torres Strait Islanders; the most striking exhibit is the **Pukumani Grave Posts**, carved by the Tiwi people of Melville Island. There is a highly recommended half-hour talk and performance of dance and didgeridoo by an indigenous Australian in this gallery (Tues–Sat noon), best combined with the free one-hour tour of the indigenous collection (Tues–Sun 11am).

Other highlights include some classic **Australian paintings** on level 4: Tom Roberts' romanticized shearing-shed scene *The Golden Fleece* (1894) and an altogether less idyllic look at rural Australia in Russell Drysdale's *Sofala* (1947), a depressing vision of a drought-stricken town. On level 5, the **photographic collection** includes Max Dupain's iconic *Sunbaker* (1937), an early study of Australian hedonism that looks as if it could have been taken yesterday.

A $16.4 million **extension** to the Art Gallery was due to open in October 2003; on the Woolloomooloo facade, the gigantic cube of white glass, dubbed the "lightbox", will be home to a Southeast Asian collection.

In addition to the galleries, there is also an auditorium used for art lectures, an excellent bookshop, a coffee shop (level 2), and a well-regarded restaurant (level 5). Opposite the gallery, within the Domain, is the scenically sited *Pavilion in the Park* (see p.174), with a pricey restaurant, a café and kiosk. A pedestrian walkway behind the Art Gallery leads quickly down to Woolloomooloo and its finger wharf on Cowper Wharf Road; as well as restaurants, bars and cafés on the wharf itself (see p.179, p.190 and p.203), you could eat cheaply at the pie cart, *Harry's Café de Wheels* (see p.179), or have some food or refreshment at the lively *Woolloomooloo Bay Hotel* (see p.190).

Mrs Macquaries Chair and "the Boy"

Beyond the Art Gallery, an overpass used to give a good view of the speeding traffic of the ugly 1960s Cahill Expressway, but, largely as a result of lobbying by the Art Gallery itself, a large section has been covered over and grassed. The landscaping greatly reduces the problem of noise and fumes, and no longer disgraces the beginning of one of Sydney's most scenic routes: Mrs Macquaries Road, built in 1816 at the urging of the governor's wife, Elizabeth. The road curves down from Art Gallery Road to Mrs Macquaries Point, which separates idyllic Farm Cove from the grittier Woolloomooloo Bay and its naval base. At the end is the celebrated lookout point known as **Mrs Macquaries Chair**, a seat fashioned out of the rock, from which Elizabeth could admire her favourite view of the harbour on her daily walk from the original Government House.

On the route down to Mrs Macquaries Point, the **Andrew "Boy" Charlton Pool** (see "Sports and activities", p.260) is an open-air, saltwater swimming pool safely isolated from the harbour waters on the Woolloomooloo side of the promontory, with excellent views across to the engrossingly functional Garden Island Naval Depot. "The Boy", as the locals fondly call it, was named after the champion swimmer, a Manly local, who turned 17 during the 1924 Paris Olympics, where he won a gold medal in the 1500-metre freestyle. He was beaten at the 400-metre event by Johnny Weissmuller, later the famous Hollywood Tarzan. The pool is a popular hangout for groovy Darlinghurst types (it's quick to get to from Kings Cross via Woolloomooloo by descending the McElhone Stairs from Victoria Street) and sun-worshipping gays. Revamped in 2002, the much-glamorized pool has its own café, yoga classes, and even a weekly biathlon.

City Centre

From Circular Quay to as far south as King Street is Sydney's **Central Business District**, often referred to as the CBD, with Martin Place as its commercial nerve centre (with its own underground train station), and the **Museum of Sydney** as its most compelling attraction. Stretching south of here to the Town Hall – with George and Pitt streets being the main thoroughfares – is a shopaholics' oasis, where you'll find all the department stores and several shopping malls, including the celebrated **Queen Victoria Building**; you can walk right from the underground Town Hall train station through into the basement levels of the building. The lavish **State Theatre** and the decorative **Town Hall** are also worth a peek, and overlooking it all, with supreme views of the city, is **Sydney Tower**. Several nearby monorail stops can get you here from Darling Harbour (see p.77).

The city centre's rest and recreation zone is **Hyde Park**, three blocks east of Town Hall across Elizabeth Street. It was fenced off by Governor Macquarie in 1810 to mark the outskirts of his township, and is still very much a formal city park with its war memorials and church. There are two very London Underground-like train stations at either end, opened in 1926 and well preserved (Museum Station to the south and St James Station to the north), and a peripheral natural history museum, cathedral and synagogue.

The short stretch between the Town Hall and Liverpool Street is for the most part teenage territory, a frenetic zone of multiscreen cinemas, pinball halls and fast-food joints. This stretch is trouble-prone on Friday and Saturday nights when there are pleasanter places to choose to catch a film. Things change pace at Liverpool Street, where Sydney's "**Spanish corner**" consists basically of a clutch of Spanish restaurants and a Spanish club. George Street becomes increasingly downmarket as it heads to Central Station – but along the way you'll pass Chinatown and Paddy's Market in the area known as Haymarket (see p.85).

The CBD

As you stroll from Circular Quay to the open space of Martin Place, the cramped streets of the CBD, overshadowed by high-rise office buildings, have little to offer. However, for some impression of the commerce going on here, check out the **Australian Stock Exchange**, opposite Australia Square at 20 Bond St, and join the throng gazing intently at the computerized display of stocks and shares through the glass of the ground floor. For a glimpse at how all this wealth might be spent, head over to Sydney's most upmarket shopping

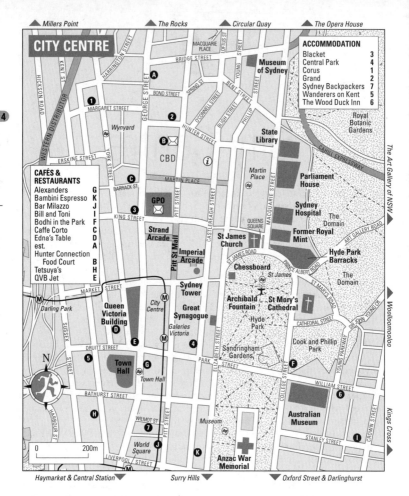

centre, **Chifley Plaza**, on the corner of Hunter and Phillip streets, where you'll find Leona Edmiston, Max Mara and other exclusive labels; a huge stencil-like **sculpture** of former Australian Labor Prime Minister Ben Chifley (1945–49), by artist Simeon Nelson, stands on the pleasant palm-filled square outside.

Martin Place

Martin Place, a pedestrian mall stretching five blocks between George and Macquarie streets, with its own underground rail station, is lined with imposing banks and investment companies, many with splendid interiors. The mall has its less serious moments at summer lunch times, when street performances are held at the little amphitheatre, and all year round stalls of flower- and fruit-sellers add some colour. The vast Renaissance-style **General Post Office**, designed by colonial architect James Barnet (see also Customs House, p.57 and Callan Park, p.109) and built between 1865 and 1887, with its landmark clock tower added in 1900, broods over the George Street end of Martin Place in all its Victorian-era pomp. The upper floors have been incorporated into part of a five-star luxury hotel, the *Westin Sydney*, which opened in late 1999; the rest of the hotel resides in the 31-storey tower behind (there is still a small post office on the ground floor of the building). The old building and the new tower meet in the grand **Atrium Courtyard**, in the lower ground floor, with its restaurants, bars (see p.199 for details on *Senate Bar*), classy designer stores and the **GPO Store**, a gastronome's delight featuring a butcher, fish shop, deli, cheese room, wine merchant and greengrocer.

At the other end of Martin Place, the fine mist which emerges from ground-level grilles marks the outlines of an early colonial home that once stood there, creating a ghostly house on still days; the artwork, called *Passage*, is by Anne Graham and is part of the **Sydney Sculpture Walk** (see box below). Opposite this eastern end of Martin Place is Parliament House (see p.65), one of the Colonial-era civic buildings on lower Macquarie Street.

Museum of Sydney

North of Martin Place, on the corner of Bridge and Phillip streets, is the **Museum of Sydney** (daily 9.30am–5pm; $7; ⓦ www.hht.net.au). From 1983 a ten-year archeological dig unearthed the foundations of the first Government House here, built by Governor Phillip in 1788 and home to eight subsequent governors of New South Wales before it was demolished in 1846. The museum, built next to the site, is totally original in its approach, presenting history in an interactive manner, through exhibitions, film, photography and multimedia; you may, however, come away feeling less informed than you expected. A key feature of the museum is the special exhibitions, about four each year, which make for a fuller experience; these range in subject from Sydney's Art Deco architecture to exhibitions of Aboriginal art, so it's worth finding out what's on before you go.

First Government Place, a public square in front of the museum, preserves the site of the original Government House: its foundations are marked out in different coloured sandstone on the pavement. The museum itself is built of honey-coloured sandstone blocks, using the different types of tooling available from the earliest days of the colony right up to modern times; you can trace this stylistic development from the bottom to the top of the facade.

Near the entrance, **Edge of the Trees**, an emotive sculptural installation that was a collaboration between a European and an Aboriginal artist, conveys the complexity of a shared history that began in 1788. Entering the museum, you hear a dramatized dialogue between the Eora woman Patyegarang and the First Fleeter Lieutenant Dawes, giving a strong impression of the meeting and misunderstanding between the two cultures.

Sydney Sculpture Walk

The specially commissioned artworks of the **Sydney Sculpture Walk** – a City of Sydney Council initiative for the 2000 Olympics and the 2001 Centenary of Federation – form a circuit from the Royal Botanic Gardens, through the Domain, Cook and Phillip Park, the streets of the CBD, Hyde Park and East Circular Quay. One of the most striking of the ten site-specific pieces is Anne Graham's *Passage*, at the eastern end of Martin Place (see opposite). A map showing the sculpture sites is available from Sydney Town Hall (p.74) or there are details on ⓦ www .cityofsydney.nsw.gov.au.

If you decide to pay to get into the rest of the museum, it's best to first go upstairs to the **auditorium** on level 2 and watch the fifteen-minute video explaining the background and aims of the museum. Back on level 1 a video screen extends up through all three levels, showing images of the bush, sea and sandstone Sydney as it was before the arrival of Europeans. On level 2, recordings of Sydney Kooris (Aboriginal people) are combined with video images to help the viewer reflect on contemporary experience. At the dark and creepy **Bond Store** on level 3, holographic "ghosts" relate tales of old Sydney as an ocean port. On the same level, a whole area is devoted to some rather wonderful **panoramas** of Sydney Harbour with views of the harbour itself from the windows.

There is also an excellent **gift shop** with a wide range of photos, artworks and books on Sydney. Quite separate from the museum is the expensive, licensed *MOS* **café**, on First Government Place; usually filled with lawyers at lunch time, it's agreeably peaceful for a (reasonably priced) coffee at other times.

King Street to Park Street

Further south from Martin Place, the rectangle between Elizabeth, King, George and Park streets is Sydney's prime shopping area, with a number of beautifully restored **Victorian arcades** (the Imperial Arcade, Strand Arcade on p.242 and Queen Victoria Building opposite and p.242 are all worth a look) and Sydney's two **department stores**, the very upmarket David Jones (see p.241), on the corner of Market and Elizabeth streets, established over 160 years ago, and the more populist but still quality-focused Grace Bros (see p.241), on Pitt Street Mall. All are overlooked by Sydney skyline's landmark, **Sydney Tower**.

Sydney Tower and Skytour

The **Sydney Tower** (daily 9am–10.30pm, Sat until 11.30pm; viewing gallery and Skytour $19.80, child $13.20; ⓦ www.sydneyskytour.com.au), long known to the locals as Centrepoint Tower, on the corner of Market and Pitt streets is the tallest poppy in the Sydney skyline. Its observation level is the highest in the entire southern hemisphere, and although the giant golden gearstick reaches to 305m, the management ruefully have to admit that the height of the tower is just beaten by the spire of the Sky Tower in Auckland, New Zealand, which is 23m taller. The 360-degree view from the observation level is especially fine at sunset, and on clear days you can even see the Blue Mountains,

---

Sydney Tower's revolving restaurants

To see the same view, without the crowds, and help put the saved $20 towards a meal, there are a couple of **revolving restaurants** at the top of the tower; the revolution takes about one hour ten minutes and nearly all the tables are by the windows (bookings on ☏02/8223 3800, ⓦwww.sydney-tower-restaurant.com). You can choose from a $75 3-course dinner in the level 1 restaurant (Tues–Sat from 5pm) or a daily buffet lunch or dinner on level 2 (Mon–Sat lunch $40, dinner and Sun lunch $50).

100km away. It can get crowded and to see the view in more peace, head down the stairs to the **café**, where you can enjoy floor-to-ceiling views along with a cup of tea.

The observation level is now packaged with the **Skytour** on entry-lift level, a tacky "virtual ride" introduction to a clichéd Australia that lasts forty long minutes. Unfortunately, the addition of Skytour has doubled the entry price to Sydney Tower and tower-only tickets are not available; the best advice is to steer clear of this assault on the intellect and the senses and go straight up to the top.

The State Theatre

Near the Sydney Tower the restored **State Theatre**, just across from the Pitt Street Mall at 49 Market St, provides a pointed architectural contrast. Step inside and take a look at the ornate and glorious interior of this picture palace which opened in 1929 – a lavishly painted, gilded and sculpted corridor leads to the lush, red and wood-panelled foyer. To see more – decorations include crystal chandeliers in the dress circle – you'll need to attend a concert or play, or catch the Sydney Film Festival (see p.218), held here annually in June. You can also go on a **self-guided tour** (Mon–Fri 11.30am–3pm; 1hr; $12; Ⓦwww.statetheatre.com.au) or pop into the beautiful little *Retro Café*, attached, for a coffee.

The Queen Victoria Building

The stately **Queen Victoria Building** (abbreviated by the locals to QVB), taking up the block bounded by Market, Druitt, George and York streets, is another of Sydney's finest. Built as a market hall in 1898, two years before Queen Victoria's death, the long-neglected building was beautifully restored and reborn in 1986 as an upmarket shopping mall with the focus on fashion: from the basement up, the four levels become progressively posh (shopping hours Mon–Sat 9am–6pm, Thurs until 9pm, Sun 11am–5pm, cafés and restaurants open longer, building open 24hr; Ⓦwww.qvb.com.au; for more on the shops here see p.242). From Town Hall Station you can walk right through the basement level (mainly bustling food stalls) and continue via the Sydney Central Plaza to Grace Bros (see p.241), emerging on Pitt Street without having to go outside – very cooling on a hot day.

Stern and matronly, a huge **statue of Queen Victoria** herself sits outside the Town Hall end of the magnificent domed, Romanesque-style building. She was sourced as part of the $75 million restoration from the Irish Republic, having been wrenched in 1947 from outside the Irish Houses of Parliament in Dublin. A small bronze statue of her favourite dog, Islay, fronts the nearby wishing well; money dropped in goes to a charity for deaf and blind children.

The **interior** is magnificent, with its beautiful woodwork, mosaic-tiled floors, stained-glass windows, gallery levels, exhibits and antique lifts. A brochure listing all the shops and main features is available from the information desks on the ground level and level two; a one-hour **guided tour** leaves from the ground-floor desk twice daily (Mon–Sat 11.30am & 2.30pm, Sun noon & 2.30pm; $8).

On **Level Two**, there are several exhibits including the Imperial Bridal Carriage, made from 300 tonnes of jade; a tableau of Queen Victoria's 1838 coronation, complete with copies of the Crown Jewels (the originals are in the Tower of London); a couple of pianolas constantly playing, and two huge clocks hanging from the ceiling. At the south end, the five-metre-high, one-tonne mechanical **Royal Automata Clock** shows a pageant of British royal history, every hour on the hour, including scenes of Charles I being beheaded. But in complete contrast, and outdoing it in size and weight, is the ten-metre-high, four-tonne, animated **Great Australian Clock** at the northern end, which details Australian history from the point of view of indigenous people and European settlers (animated display every half-hour).

The Town Hall

In the realm of architectural excess, however, the **Town Hall** is king – you'll find it across from the QVB on the corner of George and Druitt streets. It was built during the boom years of the 1870s and 1880s as a homage to Victorian England, and has a huge organ inside its Centennial Hall, giving it the air of a secular cathedral. Until the Opera House opened in 1973, this was Sydney's concert hall, where the Sydney Symphony Orchestra performed. Throughout the interior different styles of ornamentation compete for attention in a riot of colour and detail; the splendidly dignified toilets are a must-see.

The occasional concerts and theatre **performances** still held here set off the splendiferous interior perfectly, though it's more often used nowadays for public lectures (details on the City Infoline Mon–Fri 9am–6pm, ☏02/9265 9007 or ⓦwww.cityofsydney.nsw.gov.au).

Around Hyde Park

From the Town Hall, it's a short three-block walk east to **Hyde Park** along Park Street, which divides the park into two sections. The **Anzac War Memorial** and Museum Station are in the southern half, with the **Australian Museum** just across College Street. In the northern section, the **Sandringham Memorial Gardens** are near Park Street, and just across Elizabeth Street at no. 187 is the finely wrought **Great Synagogue** (also with an entrance on parallel Castlereagh Street at no. 166; free tours Tues & Thurs noon), consecrated in 1878 and inspired by English synagogues of the time in London and Liverpool. At the far northern end, near St James Station, the **Archibald Fountain** is overlooked by **St James's Church** across the northern boundary and **Cook and Philip Park** and **St Mary's Cathedral** across College Street.

Hyde Park

From Queens Square at the very south end of Macquarie Street, **St James's Church** (daily 9am–5pm; free tours 2.30pm) marks the northern entry to the park. The Anglican church, completed in 1824, is Sydney's oldest existing place of worship. It was one of Macquarie's schemes, built to ex-convict Greenway's design; the architect originally planned it as a courthouse – you can see how the simple design has been converted into a graceful church. It's worth popping into the crypt to see the richly coloured **Children's Chapel** mural painted in the 1930s.

Behind St James Station, the **Archibald Fountain** commemorates the association of Australia and France during World War I and nearby is a **giant chess**

The Anzacs

In Australia almost every town, large or small, has a war memorial dedicated to the memory of the Anzacs, the **Australia and New Zealand Army Corps**. When war erupted in Europe in 1914, Australia was overwhelmed by a wave of pro-British sentiment. On August 5, one day after Great Britain had declared war against the German empire, the Australian prime minister summed up the feelings of his compatriots: "When the Empire is at war so Australia is at war." On November 1, a contingent of twenty thousand enthusiastic volunteers – the **Anzacs** – left from the port of Albany in Western Australia to assist the mother country in her struggle.

In Europe, Turkey had entered the war on the German side in October 1914. At the beginning of 1915, military planners in London (Winston Churchill prominent among them) came up with a plan to capture the strategically important Turkish peninsula of the Dardanelles, with a surprise attack near **Gallipoli**, thus opening the way to the Black Sea. On April 25, 1915, sixteen thousand Australian soldiers landed at dawn in a small bay flanked by steep cliffs; by nightfall, two thousand men had died in a hail of Turkish bullets from above. The plan, whose one chance of success was the element of surprise, had been signalled by troop and ship movements long in advance, thus rendering it useless. Nonetheless, Allied soldiers continued to lose their lives for another eight months without ever gaining more than a feeble foothold.

In December, London finally issued the order to **withdraw**. Eleven thousand Australians and New Zealanders had been killed, along with as many French and three times as many British troops. The Turks lost eighty-six thousand men.

Official Australian historiography continues to mythologize the battle for Gallipoli, elevating it to the level of a national legend on which Australian identity is founded. The Anzac soldiers proved themselves heroes of the new nation, their loyalty and bravery evidence of how far Australia had developed. This "birth of a nation" was at the same time a loss of innocence and a national rite of passage: never again would Australians so unquestioningly involve themselves in foreign ventures.

Today, the legend is as fiercely defended as ever and April 25, **Anzac Day**, is commemorated annually, the focal point of Australian national pride. Although it may seem like a one-battle flag-waving ceremony to outsiders, it is akin to Britain's Remembrance Day and the USA's Veterans' Day, solemn occasions when one is asked to reflect on the sacrifices made by those who fought in all wars.

set where you can challenge the locals to a match. Further south near Park Street, the **Sandringham Memorial Gardens** also commemorate Australia's military dead, but the most potent of these monuments is the famous **Anzac War Memorial** at the southern end of the park (museum daily 9am–5pm; tours 11.30am & 1.30pm; free). Fronted by the tree-lined Pool of Remembrance, the thirty-metre-high cenotaph, unveiled in 1934, is classic Art Deco right down to the detail of Raynor Hoff's stylized soldier figures solemnly decorating the exterior. Downstairs, a free, mainly photographic, exhibition looks at Australian wartime experiences. The war memorial is the Sydney focus for the solemn annual Anzac Day march and wreath-laying on April 25 (see box above).

The Australian Museum

Facing Hyde Park across College Street, at the junction of William Street as it heads up to Kings Cross, the **Australian Museum** (daily 9.30am–5pm; $8, extra for special exhibitions; tours 10am–3pm on the hour; 30min; Ⓦ www.austmus.gov.au) is primarily a museum of natural history, with an interest in human evolution and Aboriginal culture and history. The collection

4

CITY CENTRE | Around Hyde Park

was founded in 1827, but the actual building, a grand sandstone affair with a facade of Corinthian pillars, wasn't fully finished until the 1860s and was extended in the 1980s. As well as the permanent exhibitions below, there are also special exhibitions throughout the year.

The core of the old museum is the three levels of the **Long Gallery**, Australia's first exhibition gallery, opened in 1855 to a Victorian public keen to gawk at the colony's curiosities. Many of the classic displays of the following hundred years remain here, Heritage-listed, contrasting with a very modern approach in the rest of the museum.

On the **ground floor**, the impressive **Indigenous Australian** exhibition looks at the history of Australia's Aboriginal people from the Dreamtime to more contemporary issues of the Stolen Generation and the freedom rides. The ground-floor level of the Long Gallery houses the **Skeletons** exhibit, where you can see a skeletal human going through the motions of riding a bicycle, for example.

Level 1 is devoted to **minerals**, but far more exciting are the disparate collections on **level 2** – especially the Long Gallery's **Birds and Insects** exhibit, which includes chilling contextual displays of dangerous spiders such as redbacks and funnelwebs. Past this section is the **Biodiversity: Life Supporting Life** exhibition that looks at the impact of environmental change on the ecosystems of Australian animals, plants, and micro-organisms, around eighty percent of which do not naturally occur elsewhere. Beyond is **Kids' Island**, a fun play-space for under-5s (also see p.230 for more on kids at the museum), while the **Tracks Through Time: Human Evolution** gallery traces the development of fossil evidence worldwide and ends with an exploration of archeological evidence of Aboriginal occupation of Australia. In the following gallery, **More Than Dinosaurs** deals with fossil skeletons of dinosaurs and giant marsupials: best of all is the model of the largest of Australia's megafauna, the wombat-like Diprotodon, which may have roamed the mainland as recently as ten thousand years ago. Finally on Level 2, **Search and Discover** is aimed at both adults and children, a flora and fauna identification centre with Internet access and books to consult.

St Mary's Cathedral and Cook and Phillip Park

North up College Street is the Catholic **St Mary's Cathedral** (Mon–Fri & Sun 6.30am–6.30pm, Sat 8am–6.30pm), overlooking the northeast corner of Hyde Park. The huge Gothic-style church opened in 1882, though the foundation stone was laid in 1821. In 1999 the cathedral at last gained the twin stone spires originally planned for the two southern towers by architect William Wardell in 1865, with $8 million of the project funded by state and federal governments. The cathedral also gained an impressive new forecourt – a pedestrianized terrace with fountains and pools – with the consolidation of two traffic-isolated parks into the large **Cook and Phillip Park**. The park includes a **recreation centre** with a fifty-metre swimming pool and gym (see "Sports and activities", p.260) and an excellent vegetarian restaurant, *Bodhi in the Park* (see p.174). The remodelling also created a green link to The Domain (see p.66).

Darling Harbour and around

W est of the city centre the 1980s redevelopment of the old wharf area around Cockle Bay saw the birth of the **Darling Harbour** entertainment and retail precinct, with several of the city's major tourist attractions located here and in the surrounding areas of Haymarket, Ultimo and Pyrmont. In Darling Harbour itself, you'll find the **Sydney Aquarium**, the **National Maritime Museum**, an **IMAX cinema**, and the **Chinese Garden**. Adjacent **Pyrmont** has the **Star City Casino** and the **Fish Market**, and the **Powerhouse Museum** is located in **Ultimo**. Darling Harbour's neighbouring area of **Haymarket**, heading towards Central Station, contains Sydney's **Chinatown**, as well as its oldest market.

Getting to and around Darling Harbour

To **get to Darling Harbour** you could **walk** – it's only ten minutes on foot from the Town Hall; from the Queen Victoria Building, walk down Market Street and along the overhead walkway. Further south there's a pedestrian bridge from Bathurst Street or you can cut through on Liverpool Street to Tumbalong Park, both bringing you out near the Chinese Garden.

Alternatively, the **monorail** (see p.30) runs from the city centre to one of five stops around Darling Harbour, and has the views to recommend it. Getting there by **ferry** from Circular Quay, to the wharf outside the Sydney Aquarium, gives you a chance to see a bit of the harbour. State Transit ferries leave from Wharf 5, and stop at McMahons Point and Balmain en route. The *Matilda Ferry* runs from the Commissioners Steps, outside the Museum of Contemporary Art, and goes via the casino at Pyrmont.

Many **buses** go from Circular Quay or Central up and down George Street, where you can alight outside the QVB, or the #443 goes from Circular Quay via the QVB, Pyrmont and the casino and the #449 does a road trip between the casino, the Powerhouse Museum, the Broadway shopping centre and Glebe.

There's actually quite a bit of walking involved in getting around the large site and if you're exhausted, or just for fun, you might consider hopping on board the dinky **People Mover train** (daily: summer 10am–6pm, winter 10am–5pm; full circuit 20min; $3.50) leaving every fifteen minutes from various points around Darling Harbour.

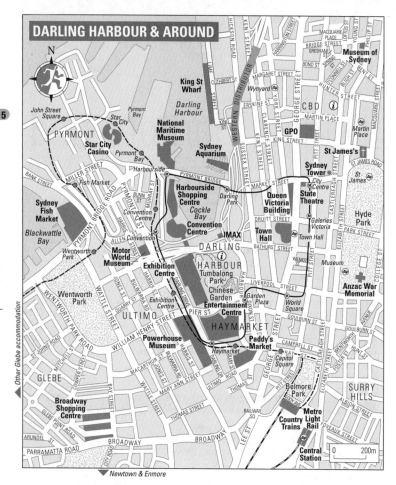

▼ Newtown & Enmore

Darling Harbour

Darling Harbour, once a grimy industrial docks area, lay moribund until the 1980s, when the state government chose to pump millions of dollars into the regeneration of this prime city real estate as part of the Bicentenary Project. The huge redevelopment scheme around Cockle Bay included the building of the much-protested above-ground monorail, which particularly irked environmentalists; the new shopping and entertainment precinct opened in 1988.

In many ways it's a thoroughly stylish redevelopment of the old wharves – the glistening water channels that run alongside Tumbalong Park and the Exhibition Centre are a great piece of modern design – and Darling Harbour has plenty to offer: a museum, an aquarium, entertainment areas, a shopping mall, an IMAX cinema, a Chinese Garden, a children's playground and a convention and exhibition centre.

Tourists have long flocked to Darling Harbour but it's only recently that Sydneysiders themselves have embraced it. Sneered at for years by locals as tacky and touristy, it took the recent Cockle Bay and King Street Wharf development – an upmarket café and restaurant precinct on the eastern side of the waterfront, with several lively bars and a huge two-thousand-capacity nightclub (*Home*, see p.212) – to finally lure locals in to the much-maligned area.

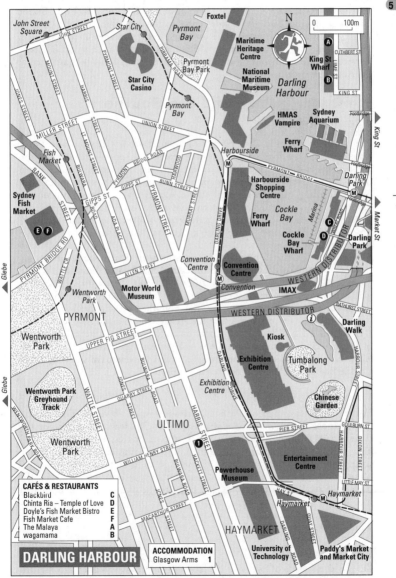

CAFÉS & RESTAURANTS
Blackbird	C
Chinta Ria – Temple of Love	D
Doyle's Fish Market Bistro	E
Fish Market Cafe	F
The Malaya	A
wagamama	B

DARLING HARBOUR

ACCOMMODATION
Glasgow Arms 1

Behind the development, and accessible from it, is **Darling Park**, with paths laid out in the shape of a waratah flower. The western side of Darling Harbour is dominated by rather ugly modern chain hotels – the *Novotel*, *Hotel Ibis* and *Grand Mercure* – providing the view for the stylish Cockle Bay Wharf diners.

There are always festivals and events, particularly during school holidays; to find out what's on, visit the **Darling Harbour Visitor Information Centre** (daily 9.30am–5.30pm; ☎02/9281 0788, ⓦwww.darlingharbour.com.au), next door to the IMAX cinema. The convenient **Darling Harbour Super Ticket** ($48, child $32.60) includes entry to the Aquarium and the Chinese Garden, a ride on the monorail, a one-hour cruise on the *Matilda Rocket*, a meal at the Aquarium's café and discounts at the IMAX cinema, the Powerhouse Museum and on the People Mover train; it can be purchased at the Aquarium (see below).

Tumbalong Park and the Southern Promenade

The southern half of Darling Harbour is focused around **Tumbalong Park**, reached from the city via Liverpool Street. Backed by the Exhibition Centre, this is the "village green" of the harbour and serves as a venue for open-air concerts and free public entertainment. The area surrounding it is perhaps Darling Harbour's most frenetic – at least at weekends and during school holidays – as most of the attractions, including a free playground and a stage for holiday concerts, are aimed at **children** (see "Kids' Sydney" pp.228–233). For some peace and quiet you can head for the adjacent **Chinese Garden**.

Beyond the children's playground, the **Southern Promenade** of Darling Harbour is dominated by the **Panasonic IMAX Theatre** (films hourly from 10am; 2-D films $16.20, 3-D $17.30; ☎02/9281 3300, ⓦwww.imax.com.au). Its giant cinema screen – which at eight storeys high is said to be the world's largest – shows a constantly changing programme from their one-hundred-film library, with an emphasis on scenic wonders, the animal kingdom and adventure sports.

The Cockle Bay Wharf development extends along the Eastern Promenade of Darling Harbour from the IMAX to **Pyrmont Bridge**, the world's first electrically operated swing span bridge, and now a pedestrian walkway across Cockle Bay, linking the two sides of the harbour.

The Chinese Garden

In the southeast corner of Darling Harbour, just northwest of Chinatown, the **Chinese Garden** (daily 9.30am–5pm; $4.50) was completed for the Bicentenary Festival in 1988 as a gift from Sydney's sister city Guangdong. The "Garden of Friendship" is designed in the traditional southern Chinese style. Although not large, it feels remarkably calm and spacious – a great place to retreat to from the commercial hubbub to read a book, smell the fragrant flowers that attract birds, and listen to the lilting Chinese music that fills the air. The balcony of the traditional tearoom offers a bird's-eye view of the dragon wall, waterfalls, a pagoda on a hill and carp swimming in winding lakes.

Sydney Aquarium

On the eastern side of Pyrmont Bridge is the impressive **Sydney Aquarium** (daily 9.30am–10pm; $23, child $11, also an Aquarium Pass including STA ferry from Circular Quay $27.40, child $13.20; also see Darling Harbour Super Ticket, above; Ⓦ www.sydneyaquarium.com.au), which has its own wharf. You can also visit the aquarium with Captain Cook Cruises from Circular Quay (see pp.27–28). If you're not going to get the chance to explore the Barrier Reef, the aquarium makes a surprisingly passable substitute.

The entry level exhibits freshwater fish from the Murray–Darling basin, Australia's biggest river system, but speed past these to get to the two **underwater walkways**, where you can wander in complete safety among sharks and gigantic stingrays. The Great Barrier Reef Oceanarium features exotic species, including a mass of glowing, undulating Moon Jellyfish. The Oceanarium finishes with a huge floor-to-ceiling tank where you can sit and be mesmerized by the movement and colour of the underwater world while classical music plays.

Alongside all the fish, there are also platypus, seals and fairy penguins on display. Removed here after becoming lost or injured, the seals at least seem to be enjoying themselves in their glass-walled outdoor pool, but the sad-looking fairy penguins appear most out of place.

The National Maritime Museum and around

On the western side of Pyrmont Bridge the **National Maritime Museum** (daily 9.30am–5pm, Jan until 6pm; $10, or with guided tours: of destroyers HMAS *Vampire* and HMAS *Onslow* $14, of barque *James Craig* $14, of destroyers and *James Craig* $20; Ⓦ www.anmm.gov.au), with its distinctive modern architecture topped by a wave-shaped roof, highlights the history of Australia as a seafaring nation. It also looks at how the sea has shaped Australian life, covering everything from immigration to beach culture and Aboriginal fishing methods in seven core themed exhibitions. Highlights include the "Merana Eora Nora – First People" exhibition which delves into indigenous culture, and "Navigators – Defining Australia" which focuses on the seventeenth-century Dutch explorers.

Outside are its own wharves, with several vessels moored: the navy destroyer the *Vampire* and a submarine the *Onslow* are permanently on display, while a collection of historic vessels, including a 1970s Vietnamese refugee boat, is on show on a rotational basis. There is a pleasant alfresco **café** here, which you don't have to enter the museum to use, with views of the boats. The bronze **Welcome Wall**, also outside the museum, unveiled in mid-2000, pays homage to Australia's six million immigrants; over 30,000 names will eventually be added to the wall – members of the public pay $100 to have the name of their immigrant forebear inscribed.

Included in the museum entry charge is a behind-the-scenes tour of the **Maritime Heritage Centre**, just beyond the museum off Pirrama Road and beside Pyrmont Bay Park at Wharf 7 (same hours as museum), where conservation and model-making work takes place and part of the museum's collection is stored. At the wharf, the Sydney Heritage Fleet's restored boats and ships are moored, including the beautifully restored 1874 square-rigger the *James Craig* (cruises available on Saturdays; see p.29) and the replica of James Cook's *Endeavour*.

Just south of the Maritime Museum, the two-level **Harbourside Shopping Centre** provides opportunities for souvenir shopping. Don't miss the first-floor **Gavala: Aboriginal Art & Cultural Education Centre** (daily 10am–7pm; Ⓦ www.gavala.com.au), a very spacious and relaxed store selling Aboriginal art, clothing, accessories and music; it is the only fully Aboriginal-owned and -run store in Sydney, with all profits going back to the artists.

Ultimo: the Powerhouse Museum and around

From Tumbalong Park, a signposted walkway leads to **Ultimo** and its **Powerhouse Museum** on Harris Street. It's a lively area, with the University of Technology campus on either side of Harris Street and the headquarters of both television and radio of national broadcaster, the ABC. Harris Street and the Powerhouse Museum can also be easily reached from Central Station via the Devonshire Street pedestrian tunnel, emerging at the northwestern end, from where it's signposted.

The Powerhouse Museum

The **Powerhouse Museum** (daily 10am–5pm; $10, child $3; free first Sat in month; free tours daily 11.30am & 1.30pm; 45min; monorail to Haymarket; Ⓦ www.phm.gov.au) is located, as the name suggests, in a former power station and is arguably the best museum in Sydney, combining arts and sciences, design, sociology and technology under the same roof; there's also fashion, with the much-anticipated "Fashion of the Year" display every November. Each year sees several big temporary exhibitions, with themes as varied as "Star Wars: The Magic of Myth", "Tokyo Street Style" and "Bush Tucker Connections".

The permanent displays are varied and presented with an interactive approach that means you'll need hours, or several trips, to investigate the five-level museum properly. The entrance level is dominated by the huge **Boulton and Watt Steam Engine**, first put to use in 1875 in a British brewery; still operational, the engine is often loudly demonstrated. The **Kings Cinema** on level 3, with its original Art Deco fittings, suitably shows the sorts of newsreels and films a Sydneysider would have watched in the 1930s. Judging by the tears at closing time, the special **children's areas** have proved a great success (see "Kids' Sydney" p.230). On level 5, there's a licensed **restaurant**, and also a less expensive courtyard cafeteria on the ground floor. The souvenir shop is also worth a browse for some unusual gifts.

The Motor World Museum

Three blocks north of the Powerhouse Museum, at 320 Harris St, Ultimo, the **Motor World Museum** (Fri–Sun, public holidays & daily during school holidays 10am–5pm; $11; monorail to Convention) houses just under two hundred vehicles on three levels. There's the usual mix of vintage cars and 1950s American-style cruisers, a comprehensive collection of Australian automobilia, plus the latest model cars, rally cars and motorcycles.

Pyrmont: Star City Casino and the Sydney Fish Market

Frantic redevelopment is taking place at **Pyrmont**, which juts out into the water between Darling Harbour and Blackwattle Bay. The once dilapidated suburb was Sydney's answer to Ellis Island in the 1950s when thousands of immigrants disembarked at the city's main overseas passenger terminal, Pier 13. Today, the former industrial suburb, which had a population of only nine hundred in 1988, is in the process of being transformed into a residential suburb of twenty thousand with $2 billion worth of investment. With the New South Wales government selling $97 million worth of property, this is one of the biggest concentrated sell-offs of land in Australia. The area has certainly become glitzier, with Sydney's casino, **Star City**, and two TV companies – Channel Ten and Foxtel – now based here. Harris Street has filled up with new shops and cafés, and the area's old pubs have been given a new lease of life. The approach to the spectacularly cabled **Anzac Bridge** – Sydney's newest – complete with statue of an Anzac soldier (see box, p.75), cuts through Pyrmont and saves between fifteen and twenty minutes' travelling time to Sydney's inner west. The main reason to visit this area, though, is the **Sydney Fish Market**.

Star City Casino

Beyond the Maritime Museum, on Pyrmont Bay is the palm-fronted **Star City**, the spectacularly tasteless Sydney casino (☎1300/300 711 for more information; ⓦwww.starcity.com.au); the only one in New South Wales, it opens 24 hours a day. As well as the two hundred gaming tables (from Blackjack to Pai Gow – there are heaps of Asian games, and gamblers), a big TAB lounge and sports bar, for putting bets on the horses and dogs and watching the results, and 1500 noisy poker machines, the building houses fourteen restaurants, cafés and theme bars, two theatres (see p.216), souvenir shops, a convenience store and a nightclub (see p.211). It's certainly somewhere to come for late-night eats, with some quite good-value places such as *Trophies Food Court* – with everything from stir-fries to sandwiches – staying open until 6am. The casino interior itself is a riot of giant palm sculptures, prize cars spinning on rotating bases, Aboriginal painting motifs on the ceiling, Australian critters scurrying across a red desert-coloured carpet and an endless array of flashing poker machines. Dress smart casual to get in.

Nearby, **Pyrmont Bay Park** is a shady spot in which to rest, and on the first Saturday of the month it hosts an early morning **Growers Market** (7–11am).

To **get to the casino** by bus, you can take the #888, which runs in a loop to and from Gresham Street in the city via the QVB to the casino and the Exhibition Centre in Darling Harbour, or take the #443 from Circular Quay via Phillip and Market streets and the QVB on York Street. The Light Rail (see p.30) pulls in right underneath the casino building.

Sydney Fish Market

On the corner of Pyrmont Bridge Road and Bank Street, the **Sydney Fish Market** (daily 7am–4pm; ⓦwww.sydneyfishmarket.com.au) is only a ten-minute walk via Pyrmont Bridge Road from Darling Harbour. Now a popular tourist attraction, it's a frenetic, early-morning spectacle. The market has the

△ Monorail, Darling Harbour

Sydney Seafood School

The **Sydney Seafood School** (☎02/9004 1111) offers seafood cookery lessons starting from $70 for a two-hour course, from Thai-style to French provincial, under the expert tuition of resident home economists as well as guest chefs drawn from the city's top restaurants. The most popular course, for which you need to book three or more months in advance, is the **Seafood Barbecue** run at weekends (4hr; $115). The school also does a two-hour early morning tour of the Fish Market's selling floor (first Thurs of month; $20 includes a coffee).

second-largest variety of fish on offer in the world, after the massive Tsukiji market in Tokyo. You need to visit early to see the **auctions** (Mon–Fri), with the biggest auction floor on Friday; the buyers begin viewing the fish at 4.30am and auctions begin 5.30am, but the public viewing platform opens at 7am. Buyers log into computer terminals to register their bids.

You can take away oysters, prawns and cooked seafood and eat picnic-style on waterfront tables. Everything is set up for throwing together an impromptu meal – there's a nearby bakery, deli, bottle shop and grocer. Alternatively, you can eat in at the fish restaurant, *Doyles* (see p.186), an excellent sushi bar, or have dirt-cheap fish and chips at the *Fish Market Cafe* (see p.175); retail shops open at 7am. For more on the Fish Market, see "Shopping" p.243.

To **get to** the Fish Market by public transport, take the Light Rail service from Central to Fish Market Station on Miller Street, near the entrance to the market. Bus #501 runs from outside the Sydney Electricity Building, on the corner of George and Bathurst streets opposite the Town Hall, to right outside the market on Bank Street; otherwise take bus #443 from Circular Quay or the QVB, and it's a five-minute walk from the corner of Harris Street and Pyrmont Bridge Road.

Haymarket

Immediately west of Central Station on either side of the downmarket end of George Street is the area known as **Haymarket**. The Light Rail (see p.30) heads through here from Central Station, past Capitol Square and the **Capitol Theatre**. Built as a deluxe picture palace in the 1920s, the theatre now hosts big-budget musicals and ballet under a star-studded ceiling representing the southern skies (also see p.216). The surrounding area is renowned for its pop culture pleasures, with the ugly concrete bunker of the **Sydney Entertainment Centre**, the city's mainstream concert venue (see p.209), on the other side of **Chinatown**.

Chinatown

Sydney's **Chinatown** is a much more full-blooded affair than "Spanish corner" on nearby Liverpool Street (see p.69). No mere tourist attraction, but a gutsy Chinese quarter, Chinatown has its share of social problems. Winter 2002 saw unprecedented incidents when several restaurants were wrecked, in front of terrified diners, by rival triad gangs conducting turf wars. Chinese people first began arriving in "New Gold Mountain", as they called Australia, in the 1850s

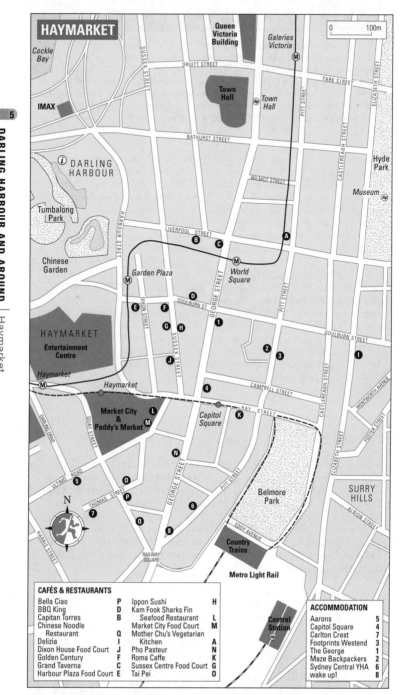

HAYMARKET

Cockle Bay

IMAX

DARLING HARBOUR

Tumbalong Park

Chinese Garden

Garden Plaza

HAYMARKET

Entertainment Centre

Haymarket

Haymarket

Market City & Paddy's Market

N

Queen Victoria Building

Galleries Victoria

DRUITT STREET

Town Hall

Town Hall

BATHURST STREET

Hyde Park

Museum

PARK STREET

WILMOT STREET

LIVERPOOL STREET

World Square

GOULBURN ST

GOULBURN STREET

CAMPBELL STREET

HAY STREET

Capitol Square

Belmore Park

SURRY HILLS

ALBION STREET

WENTWORTH AVENUE

FOSTER STREET

ELIZABETH STREET

CASTLEREAGH STREET

PITT STREET

GEORGE STREET

SUSSEX STREET

DIXON STREET

HARBOUR STREET

QUAY STREET

ULTIMO ROAD

THOMAS STREET

HARRIS STREET

DARLING DRIVE

RAILWAY SQUARE

EDDY AVENUE

Country Trains

Metro Light Rail

Central Station

0   100m

CAFÉS & RESTAURANTS

Bella Ciao	P	Ippon Sushi	H
BBQ King	D	Kam Fook Sharks Fin	
Capitan Torres	B	Seafood Restaurant	L
Chinese Noodle		Market City Food Court	M
Restaurant	Q	Mother Chu's Vegetarian	
Delizia	I	Kitchen	A
Dixon House Food Court	J	Pho Pasteur	N
Golden Century	F	Roma Caffe	K
Grand Taverna	C	Sussex Centre Food Court	G
Harbour Plaza Food Court	E	Tai Pei	O

ACCOMMODATION

Aarons	5
Capitol Square	4
Carlton Crest	7
Footprints Westend	3
The George	1
Maze Backpackers	2
Sydney Central YHA	6
wake up!	8

during the time of the goldrushes; after the 1880s most went back, but many stayed on and set up businesses – wholesaling and running market gardens were popular occupations and Chinatown grew up around what has been the traditional wholesale market area for over 150 years. It was only in 1980, however, that Dixon Street became Sydney's official Chinatown.

Through the Chinese gates, **Dixon Street Mall** is the main drag, buzzing day and night as people crowd into numerous restaurants, pubs, cafés, cinemas, food stalls and Asian grocery stores. Towards the end of January or in the first weeks of February, Chinese New Year is celebrated here with gusto: dragon and lion dances, food festivals and musical entertainment compete with the noise and smoke from strings of Chinese crackers. Friday nights are also a good time to visit, when a **night market** takes over Dixon and Little Hay streets (6pm–11pm).

Every Thursday, Friday, Saturday and Sunday, **Paddy's Market**, Sydney's oldest (1869), is conducted in its undercover home at the corner of Thomas and Hay streets, across from the Entertainment Centre (Thurs 10am–6pm, Fri, Sat & Sun 9am–4.30pm; Ⓦwww.paddymarket.com.au). It has around one thousand stalls and is a good place to buy cheap vegetables, seafood, plants, clothes and bric-a-brac. Above the old market, the multilevel **Market City Shopping Centre**, has a very Asian feel – you could easily imagine yourself in one of the air-conditioned centres of Bangkok or Kuala Lumpur; there's an excellent Asian food court (see p.177) on the top floor next to the Reading multiscreen cinema (see p.219).

Inner east

To the east of the city centre **Surry Hills**, **Darlinghurst** and **Paddington** were once rather scruffy working-class suburbs, but since the 1970s they have gradually been taken over and revamped by the young, arty and upwardly mobile. **Oxford Street**, from Hyde Park to Paddington and beyond, is a major amusement strip and waiting to be discovered, here and in the side streets, is an array of nightclubs, restaurants, cafés and pubs. **Kings Cross** is home to Sydney's red-light district as well as many of its tourists, and can be reached by a series of steps from **Woolloomooloo** and the

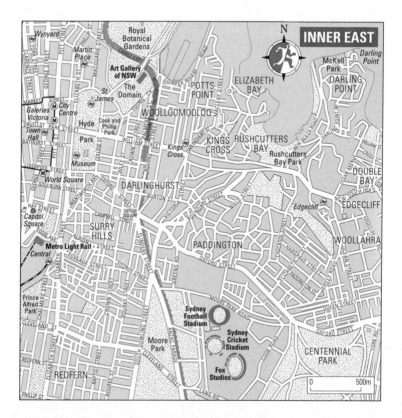

busy naval dockyards, or by walking straight up William Street from Hyde Park past East Sydney. Further east, "the Cross" (as locals call it) fades into the more elegant neighbourhoods of **Potts Point** and **Elizabeth Bay**, which trade on their harbour views.

Surry Hills

Surry Hills, directly east of Central Station from Elizabeth Street, was traditionally the centre of the rag trade, which still finds its focus on Devonshire Street. Rows of tiny terraces once housed its original poor, working–class population, many of them of Irish origin. Considered a slum by the rest of Sydney, the dire and overcrowded conditions were given fictional life in Ruth Park's *The Harp in the South* trilogy (see "Books", p.330), set in the Surry Hills of the 1940s. The area became something of a cultural melting pot with European postwar immigration, and doubled as a grungy, studenty, muso heartland in the 1980s.

By the mid-1990s, however, the slickly fashionable scene of neighbouring Darlinghurst and Paddington had finally taken over Surry Hills' twin focal points of parallel **Crown Street**, filled with cafés, swanky restaurants (such as *MG Garage*, where you dine alongside classic cars – see p.187), funky clothes shops and designer galleries, and leafy **Bourke Street**, where a couple of Sydney's best cafés lurk among the trees. As rents have gone up, only **Cleveland Street**, running west to Redfern (see box, p.91) and east towards Moore Park and the Sydney Cricket Ground (see p.95), traffic-snarled and lined with cheap Indian, Lebanese and Turkish restaurants (see pp.187–189), retains its ethnically varied population.

A good time to visit Surry Hills is the first Saturday of the month when a lively **flea market**, complete with tempting food stalls, takes over the small Shannon Reserve, on the corner of Crown and Fouveaux streets, overlooked by the **Clock Hotel** (see p.200). The hotel, which has expanded out of all recognition from its 1840s roots, is emblematic of the new Surry Hills, and its swish restaurant and cocktail bar attract a very different crowd from the rough and ready pool-playing crew of former years.

The Brett Whiteley Studio

The artistic side of Surry Hills can be experienced nearby at the **Brett Whiteley Studio** at 2 Raper St, off Davies St (Sat & Sun 10am–4pm, by appointment Thurs & Fri ☎02/9225 1881; $7). Whitely was one of Australia's best-known contemporary painters with an international reputation by the time he died of a heroin overdose at the age of 53 in 1992; wild self-portraits

---

Getting to Surry Hills

Surry Hills is a short **walk** uphill from Central Station (Devonshire Street or Elizabeth Street exit): take Fouveax or Devonshire streets and you'll soon hit Crown Street, or it's an even quicker stroll from Oxford Street, Darlinghurst, heading south along Crown or Bourke streets. Several **buses** also run here from Circular Quay, including the #301 and #303, both to Crown Street.

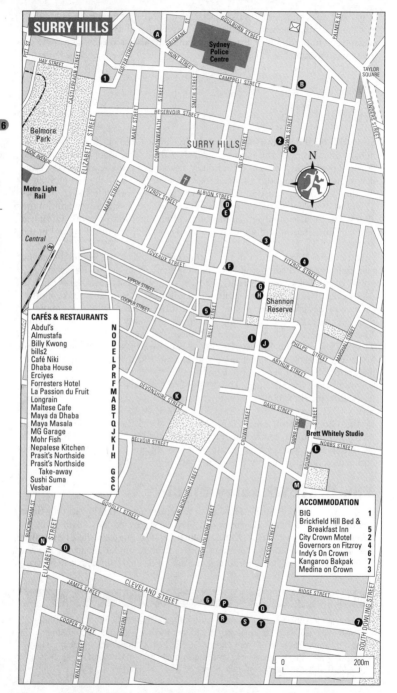

SURRY HILLS

Sydney Police Centre

TAYLOR SQUARE

SURRY HILLS

Belmore Park

Metro Light Rail

Central

Shannon Reserve

Brett Whitely Studio

CAFÉS & RESTAURANTS

Abdul's	N
Almustafa	O
Billy Kwong	D
bills2	E
Café Niki	L
Dhaba House	P
Erciyes	R
Forresters Hotel	F
La Passion du Fruit	M
Longrain	A
Maltese Cafe	B
Maya da Dhaba	T
Maya Masala	Q
MG Garage	J
Mohr Fish	K
Nepalese Kitchen	I
Prasit's Northside	H
Prasit's Northside	
Take-away	G
Sushi Suma	S
Vesbar	C

ACCOMMODATION

BIG	1
Brickfield Hill Bed &	
Breakfast Inn	5
City Crown Motel	2
Governors on Fitzroy	4
Indy's On Crown	6
Kangaroo Bakpak	7
Medina on Crown	3

0   200m

Just beyond Surry Hills, and only 2km from the glitter and sparkle of Darling Harbour, **Redfern** is Sydney's underbelly. Around the **Eveleigh Street** area, Australia's biggest urban Aboriginal community lives in "**the Block**", a squalid streetscape of derelict terraced houses and rubbish-strewn streets not far from Redfern train station; this is the closest Sydney has to a no-go zone. The Aboriginal Housing Company, set up as a cooperative in 1973, has been unable to pay for repairs and renovation work, and Eveleigh Street appears in shocking contrast to Paddington's cutesy restored terraces and the harbour-view mansions of Sydney's rich and beautiful. Recently the Company began knocking down derelict houses and relocating residents, which has upset many who want to keep the community together.

and expressive female nudes were some of his subjects, but it is his sensual views of Sydney Harbour painted from his home in Lavender Bay for which he is best known. In 1986 Whitely converted this one-time factory into a studio and living space, and since his death it has become a museum and gallery showing his paintings and memorabilia.

Darlinghurst

Oxford Street, stretching from Hyde Park through **Darlinghurst** to Paddington and beyond, is lined with nightclubs, restaurants, cafés, pubs, bookshops, cinemas and fashion stores. The Darlinghurst end is the focus of Sydney's very active **gay and lesbian** movement (see "Gay Sydney" pp.221–227), and the art college on Forbes Street, near the Darlinghurst Courthouse, means there's a new crop of self-conscious young stylemongers every year. Hip and bohemian, Darlinghurst mingles seediness with a certain hedonistic style: some art students and pale, wasted clubbers never leave the district – save for a *caffe-latte* at the Cross or a swim at "the Boy" in The Domain (see pp.96 & 260).

There's a concentration of cafés north of Oxford Street (and heading towards Kings Cross) on **Victoria Street**, a classic posing strip radiating around the legendary street-smart *Bar Coluzzi* (see p.177); this area also harbours some popular restaurants and bars. More cafés, restaurants and fashion are found on **Liverpool Street,** heading east and downhill from Oxford towards **East Sydney** near the Australian Museum. Here **Stanley Street** has a cluster of cheap Italian cafés and restaurants including the long-running *Bill and Toni* (see p.174).

Sydney Jewish Museum

The impressive **Sydney Jewish Museum**, at 148 Darlinghurst Rd (Mon–Thurs & Sun 10am–4pm, Fri 10am–2pm; $10; Ⓦ www.sydneyjewishmuseum.com.au), is housed in the old Maccabean Hall, which has been a Jewish meeting point for over seventy years.

Sixteen Jews were among the convicts who arrived with the First Fleet, and the high-tech, interactive museum explores over two hundred years of Australian Jewish experience. An introductory fifteen-minute film discusses

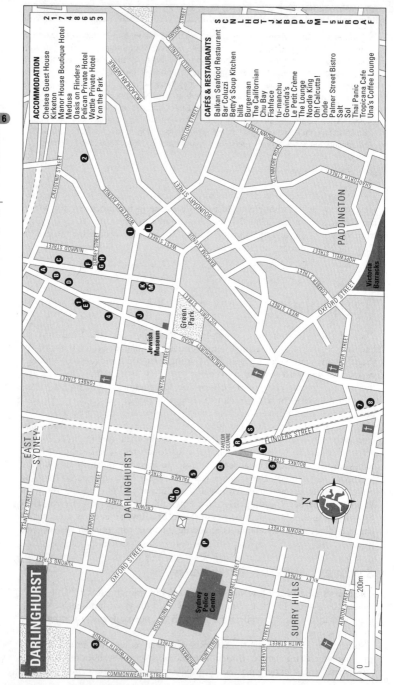

DARLINGHURST

ACCOMMODATION

Chelsea Guest House	2
Kirketon	1
Manor House Boutique Hotel	7
Medusa	4
Oasis on Flinders	8
Pelican Private Hotel	6
Wattle Private Hotel	5
Y on the Park	3

CAFÉS & RESTAURANTS

Balkan Seafood Restaurant	S
Bar Coluzzi	C
Betty's Soup Kitchen	N
bills	L
Burgerman	H
The Californian	Q
Chu Bay	T
Fishface	J
fu-manchu	K
Govinda's	B
Le Petit Crème	D
The Lounge	P
Noodle King	G
Oh! Calcutta!	M
Onde	I
Palmer Street Bistro	E
Salt	R
Sol	O
Thai Panic	A
Tropicana Cafe	A
Una's Coffee Lounge	F

EAST
SYDNEY

DARLINGHURST

Jewish
Museum

Green
Park

PADDINGTON

Victoria
Barracks

TAYLOR
SQUARE

SURRY HILLS

Sydney
Police
Centre

N

0   200m

anti-Semitism through the ages, and the Holocaust is covered in harrowing detail with Australian survivors' videotaped testimonies.

You can pick up the pamphlet *Guide to Jewish Sydney* from the museum and there's a **kosher café** on site. You might also like to visit the **Great Synagogue** in the city opposite Hyde Park (see p.74), and there is a concentration of **kosher** Jewish cafés, butchers and supermarkets on Hall Street in Bondi (see p.126). The great modern Israeli **restaurant** *Yulla* has glorious beach views of Bondi Beach (see p.193).

Paddington and Woollahra

From the intersection with South Dowling Street in Darlinghurst, Oxford Street strikes southeast through trendy, upmarket **Paddington** and wealthy, staid **Woollahra** to the verdant expanse of Centennial Park (see p.94).

Transport heading in this direction includes **buses** #380 and #382 from Circular Quay, which both run up Elizabeth Street and along Oxford Street. The #378, from Central Station, also heads along Oxford Street. Bus #389 from Circular Quay runs via Elizabeth and William streets in the city and along Glenmore Road and Hargrave Street, Paddington, to emerge on Oxford Street.

Paddington was a slum at the turn of the century but became a popular hangout for hipsters during the late 1960s and 1970s. Since then, yuppies have taken over and turned Paddington into the smart and fashionable suburb it is today: the Victorian-era terraced houses, with their iron-lace verandahs reminiscent of New Orleans, have been beautifully restored. Many of the terraces were originally built in the 1840s to house the artisans who worked on the graceful, sandstone **Victoria Barracks** on the southern side of Oxford Street, its walls stretching seven blocks, from Greens Road to just before Paddington Town Hall on Oatley Road. **Shadforth Street**, opposite the entrance gates, has many examples of the original artisans' homes. Though the barracks are still used by the army, there are free guided tours (Thurs 10am) – complete with army band – while a small **museum** is open to visitors (Sun 10am–3pm).

On the other side of Oxford Street, the small, winding, tree-lined streets are a pleasant place for a stroll, and offer a chance to wander into the many small art galleries (see pp.243–245) or to take some liquid refreshment. Head via Underwood and Heeley streets to **Five Ways**, where you'll find cafés, speciality shops and a typically gracious old boozer, the *Royal Hotel* (see p.190). There are more shops on Elizabeth Street running off Oxford Street, but the main action is, of course, on Oxford Street itself, with the emphasis on fashion; every major fashion chain store is represented here, as well as exclusive boutiques and Australian designer label shops (see "Shopping", pp.237–239). Oxford Street is most lively on Saturday from 10am to around 4pm, when the crowds descend on the fashion-conscious **Paddington Market** in the church grounds at no. 395 (see p.246).

Woollahra, along Oxford Street from Paddington, is even more moneyed but contrastingly staid, with its expensive **antique shops** and **art galleries** on **Queen Street**. Leafy Moncur Street hides *jones the grocer*, at no. 68, where Woollahra locals gather for coffee at the long central table; it sells stylishly packaged, outlandishly priced and utterly delicious groceries and gourmet treats to eat in or take away (see p.243).

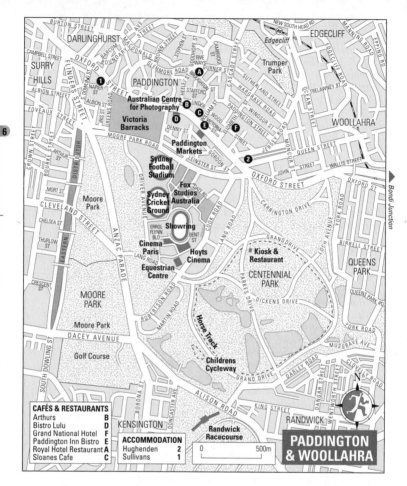

Map labels (within image):

BURTON STREET
DARLINGHURST
Edgecliff
EDGECLIFF
CAMPBELL STREET
SURRY
HILLS
OXFORD STREET
PADDINGTON
Trumper Park
ALBION STREET
ALBION STREET
FOVEAUX STREET
Australian Centre for Photography
WOOLLAHRA
Victoria Barracks
Paddington Markets
MOORE PARK ROAD
QUEEN STREET
WALLIS STREET
Sydney Football Stadium
Fox Studios Australia
OXFORD STREET
Moore Park
Sydney Cricket Ground
CLEVELAND STREET
CARRINGTON DRIVE
ERROL FLYNN BLD
Showring
BENT ST
GRAND DRIVE
BIRRELL STREET
Cinema Paris
Hoyts Cinema
Kiosk & Restaurant
QUEENS PARK
Equestrian Centre
CENTENNIAL PARK
ANZAC PARADE
QUEENS PARK RD
MOORE PARK
DICKENS DRIVE
YORK ROAD
Moore Park
DACEY AVENUE
Horse Track
MUSGRAVE AVE
Golf Course
Childrens Cycleway
GRAND DRIVE
SOUTH DOWLING ST
ALISON ROAD
KING STREET
RANDWICK
N

CAFÉS & RESTAURANTS
Arthurs — B
Bistro Lulu — D
Grand National Hotel — F
Paddington Inn Bistro — E
Royal Hotel Restaurant — A
Sloanes Cafe — C

KENSINGTON

ACCOMMODATION
Hughenden — 2
Sullivans — 1

Randwick Racecourse

0 — 500m

PADDINGTON & WOOLLAHRA

6

Centennial Parklands and Fox Studios

South of Paddington and Woollahra lies the green expanse of **Centennial Park** (daily sunrise to sunset; ⓦwww.cp.nsw.gov.au), opened to the citizens of Sydney at the Centennial Festival in 1888 (the bicentennial version was opened at Homebush in 1988, see p.147). With its vast lawns, rose gardens and extensive network of ponds, complete with ducks, it resembles an English country park, but is reclaimed at dawn and dusk by distinctly antipodean residents, including possums and flying foxes. The park is criss-crossed by walking paths and tracks for cycling, rollerblading, jogging and horse riding; you can rent a bike or rollerblades nearby (see p.262) or hire a horse from the adjacent equestrian centre (see p.262) and then recover from your exertions in the café with its popular outside tables (though packed and hideously slow at weekends, even for takeaways). In the finer months you can stay on until dark and catch an outdoor film with the Moonlight Cinema (see p.220).

Adjoining **Moore Park** is incorporated under the banner of **Centennial Parklands** and has facilities for tennis, golf, grass-skiing, bowling, cricket and hockey; it's also home to the Sydney Cricket Ground (SCG; see "Sports and activities", p.256) and Fox Studios (see below). You can get a free map of the Centennial Parklands from the Park Office (Mon–Fri 8.30am–5.30pm; ☎02/9339 6699) which is near Centennial Park's café and easily reached from the Paddington gates off Oxford Street (opposite Queen Street).

Fox Studios

Also within Moore Park, immediately southeast of the SCG, are the Murdoch-owned **Fox Studios** (Ⓦwww.foxstudios.com.au), constructed at a cost of $300 million within the old Showgrounds site, where the Royal Agricultural Society held its annual Royal Easter Show (see p.251) from 1882 until 1997; in 1998 the huge show took place for the first time at the Sydney Showground at the Olympic site at Homebush Bay (see p.145). The **Professional Studio** (Ⓦwww.foxmovies.com.au), opened in May 1998, takes up over half the site and has facilities for both film and television production, with six high-tech stages and industry tenants on site providing everything from casting services to stunt professionals. Films made here so far include *The Matrix*, *Mission Impossible II*, *The Quiet American*, Baz Luhrmann's *Moulin Rouge*, and Episodes I and II of the *Star Wars* saga.

The **public areas** of the site opened in late 1999, focused around a mega state-of-the-art twelve-screen **cinema complex**, complete with digital surround sound and VIP lounges (see p.219), and a smaller four-screen arthouse Cinema Paris (see p.218); international film premieres are often held here. For information on keeping children amused at Fox Studios, see p.233.

The Show Ring

The old **Show Ring**, once the preserve of wood-chopping competitions and rodeo events for the Easter Show, is now used for everything from open-air cinema and circuses to the **weekend market** (Sat & Sun 10am–6pm) and the midweek **Farmers' Market** (Wed noon–7pm; see p.243). The **Bungy Trampoline** (Wed–Sun 10am–6pm; $10) here is a permanent fixture: an ordinary trampoline but with several bungy cords, designed to give you the thrill of a bungy jump but without the danger. During the colder months, from the end of April, an ice-skating rink operates on the Show Ring (see p.262).

Bent Street

The Show Ring is surrounded by the gleaming shops, cafés, restaurants, bars and children's playgrounds of pedestrianized **Bent Street**; this is a bit like a Darling Harbour for locals (it's car-friendly) rather than tourists (who find it too hard to get to). The upmarket **shops**, over twenty of them, stay open late (daily 10am–10pm) and include lots of casual clothing, beach, sports and fashion chains, a bookshop, record store and a bush outfitters. The two major **bars** are close to each other – the contemporary-styled but casual *Dog Gone Bar* and the more traditional *Fox and Lion* – by the big outdoor screen which shows the music-video channel **Channel [V]**. The screen is outside the channel's live studio and there are often shows being taped both inside and outside which are free to attend; check the What's On page of their website ⓦwww.channelv.com.au for show times. Other bars include the action-focused **Sports Central** which has everything from ten-pin bowling to American pool (see p.203) and Fox Sports broadcasts, of course. There's also a music venue, *City Live* (see p.209).

Including the bars, there are fifteen **places to eat** on Bent Street, which include an eat-in gourmet deli, wood-fired pizza, Chinese seafood, noodles and classy contemporary Australian. There's also a **stand-up comedy** venue, the *Comedy Store*, on Driver Avenue (see p.217).

Kings Cross, Potts Point and Elizabeth Bay

The preserve of Sydney's bohemians in the 1950s, **Kings Cross** became an R&R spot for American soldiers during the Vietnam war, and is now the city's red-light district, its streets prowled by prostitutes, drug abusers, drunks, strippers and homeless teenagers. It is also a bustling centre for backpackers and other travellers, especially around leafy and quieter Victoria Street; the two sides of the Cross coexist with little trouble, though some tourists seem a little surprised at where they've ended up, and it can be rather intimidating for lone women. It's always lively, however, with places to eat and drink that stay open all hours, and the constant flow of people makes it relatively safe.

South Sydney Council has produced a free **Kings Cross Walking Tour** map available from the library off Fitzroy Gardens that points out some of the Art Deco architecture the area is known for, and provides some background history.

William Street

Heading up the rise of **William Street** from Hyde Park and past Cook and Phillip Park and the Australian Museum, **Kings Cross** beckons with its giant neon Coca-Cola sign. By day, William Street is hardly attractive with its car-

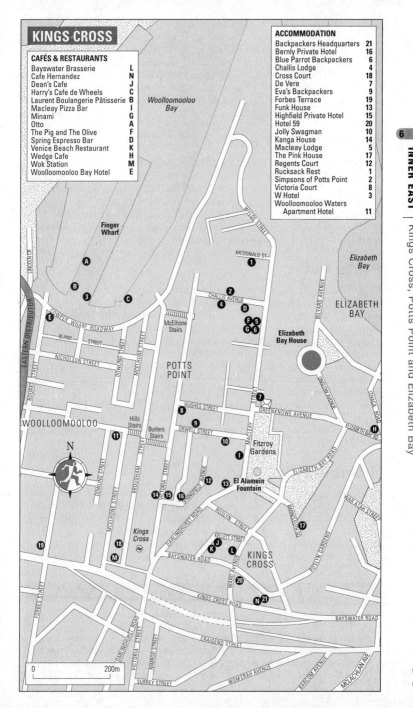

KINGS CROSS

CAFÉS & RESTAURANTS

Bayswater Brasserie	L
Cafe Hernandez	N
Dean's Cafe	J
Harry's Cafe de Wheels	C
Laurent Boulangerie Pâtisserie	B
Macleay Pizza Bar	I
Minami	G
Otto	A
The Pig and The Olive	F
Spring Espresso Bar	D
Venice Beach Restaurant	K
Wedge Cafe	H
Wok Station	M
Woolloomooloo Bay Hotel	E

ACCOMMODATION

Backpackers Headquarters	21
Bernly Private Hotel	16
Blue Parrot Backpackers	6
Challis Lodge	4
Cross Court	18
De Vere	7
Eva's Backpackers	9
Forbes Terrace	19
Funk House	13
Highfield Private Hotel	15
Hotel 59	20
Jolly Swagman	10
Kanga House	14
Macleay Lodge	5
The Pink House	17
Regents Court	12
Rucksack Rest	1
Simpsons of Potts Point	2
Victoria Court	8
W Hotel	3
Woolloomooloo Waters Apartment Hotel	11

Woolloomooloo Bay

Elizabeth Bay

Finger Wharf

MCDONALD ST.

CHALLIS AVENUE

McElhone Stairs

ELIZABETH BAY

Elizabeth Bay House

POTTS POINT

WOOLLOOMOOLOO

Hills Stairs

Butlers Stairs

HUGHES STREET

ORWELL STREET

Fitzroy Gardens

El Alamein Fountain

Kings Cross

BAYSWATER ROAD

KINGS CROSS

KINGS CROSS ROAD

BAYSWATER ROAD

CRAIGEND STREET

SURREY STREET

WOMERAH AVENUE

0   200m

rental firms and streams of fast and fumy traffic heading to the Eastern and Western distributors; at night, there are even fewer pedestrians as hard-core streetwalkers and kerbcrawling patrons go about their business. However, with the development of the Cross City Tunnel, planned to be open to traffic by the end of 2004, there's a grand vision for William Street to become a European-style boulevard – tree-lined, traffic-calmed, and with wide pavements for café tables and strolling pedestrians (check ⓦ www.rta.nsw.gov.au for the latest on the developments).

Darlinghurst Road

At the top of the hill, **Darlinghurst Road** is the Cross's action zone. At weekends, an endless stream of ice-cream-licking suburban voyeurs trawl along the street to the El Alamein fountain in Fitzroy Gardens, as touts try their best to haul them into tacky strip-joints and sleazy nightclubs. It's much more subdued during the day, with a slightly hung-over feel; local residents emerge and it's a good time to hang out in the cafés. Every Sunday there's a small **art and crafts market** in Fitzroy Gardens by the fountain.

Potts Point

From Fitzroy Gardens, the sin strip ends and tree-lined Macleay Street runs through quieter, upmarket **Potts Point** with its tree-lined streets, apartment blocks, classy boutique hotels, stylish restaurants and buzzy cafés, and also occasional harbour glimpses over wealthier Elizabeth Bay, just east. This is as close to European living as Sydney gets. This area was the city's first suburb, from land grants to John Wylde in 1822 and Alexander Macleay in 1826. The grand villas of colonial bureaucrats gave way in the 1920s and 1930s to **Art Deco** residential apartments and in the 1950s splendid hotels were added to the scene. The area is set to go more upmarket and residential as all but one of its large hotels have been, or is in the process of being, made over into luxury apartments. Beyond Macleay Street, Wylde Street heads downhill to Woolloomooloo; you may spot white-clad sailors and officers here, strolling up through the streets from the naval base.

Elizabeth Bay

Barely five minutes' walk northwest of Kings Cross, **Elizabeth Bay** is a well-heeled residential area, centred on **Elizabeth Bay House**, at 7 Onslow Ave (Tues–Sun 10am–4.30pm; $7; ⓦ www.hht.com.au). The grand Greek Revival villa was built between 1835 and 1839 for Alexander Macleay, colonial secretary of New South Wales. The large Macleay family, who arrived from Britain in 1826, were obsessed with botany and entomology and the original

---

Getting to the Kings Cross area

You can get to Kings Cross by **train** (Eastern Suburbs line) or **bus** (#311, #324 or #325 from Circular Quay; #327 from Gresham Street in the city; many others from the city to Darlinghurst Road), or it's not too far to **walk**: straight up William Street from Hyde Park. For a quieter route, you could head up from the Domain via Cowper Wharf Road in Woolloomooloo, and then up the McElhone Stairs to Victoria Street. To get to Elizabeth Bay House, take bus #311 or walk from Kings Cross Station.

54-acre waterfront grounds were said to be a botanist's paradise – the Macleay Museum at Sydney University (see p.116) was formed from the Macleays' natural history collection. The views from the windows of the yachts and water of Elizabeth Bay are stunning.

Woolloomooloo

North of William Street, just below Kings Cross, **Woolloomooloo** occupies the old harbourside quarter between The Domain and the grey-painted fleet of the **Garden Island Naval Depot**. Once a slum of narrow streets, Woolloomooloo is quickly being transformed, although its upmarket apartment developments sit uneasily side by side with problematic community housing, and you should still be careful at night in the backstreets. There are some lively pubs and some old-fashioned quiet locals, such as the *Woolloomooloo Hotel* which serves good meals, as well as the legendary **Harry's Café de Wheels** on Cowper Road, a 24-hour pie-cart operating since 1945 and popular nowadays with Sydney cabbies and hungry clubbers in the small hours. Across Cowper Wharf Road at nos. 43–51, an old stone warehouse is home to **The Gunnery Arts Centre**; its gallery (Tues–Sat 11am–6pm) shows provocative young artists with a focus on installations and new media and is worth a look.

Woolloomooloo Finger Wharf

Next door to the naval base, the once picturesquely dilapidated **Woolloomooloo Finger Wharf**, dating from 1917, has been redeveloped into an upmarket complex comprising a marina, luxury residential apartments, the cool *W Hotel* (see p.155) and its funky *Water Bar* (see p.203), and some slick restaurants with alfresco dining – *Otto* (see p.190), *Manta Ray* and *Shimbashi Soba* are the swankiest. The general public are free to wander along the wharf and even go inside: there's a free exhibition space with a changing theme in the centre. Anyone can afford a cake and pastry at the Parisian-feel *Laurent Pâtisserie* (see p.179), or you can grab a pie from *Harry's* and sit for free on the other side of the wharf.

Getting to Woolloomooloo

Woolloomooloo is best reached **on foot** from Kings Cross by taking the McElhone Stairs or the Butlers Stairs from Victoria Street; alternatively take **bus** #311 from Kings Cross, Circular Quay or Central Station. It's also easily reached from a walkway behind the Art Gallery of New South Wales (see p.67).

Inner west

West of the centre, immediately beyond Darling Harbour, the inner-city areas of **Glebe** and **Newtown** surround Sydney University, their vibrant cultural mix enlivened by large student populations. On a peninsula north of Glebe and west of The Rocks, **Balmain** is a gentrified working-class dock area popular for its village atmosphere and big old pubs; up-and-coming **Rozelle** next door has both an art college and a writers' centre in the grounds of waterfront Callan Park, while en route, **Leichhardt** and its neighbour **Haberfield** are the focus of Sydney's Italian community.

Glebe

Glebe, right by Australia's oldest university, has gradually been evolving from a café-oriented student quarter to a more upmarket thirtysomething territory, with a New Age slant. Indeed, it's very much the centre of alternative culture in Sydney, with places selling organic food (such as Russells Natural Food Markets, see p.243), yoga schools and healing centres offering every kind of therapy from Chinese massage to homeopathy and floatation tanks. **Glebe Point Road**, the focal point of the area, is filled with an eclectic mix of cafés with trademark leafy courtyards, restaurants, bookshops and secondhand and speciality shops as it runs uphill from **Broadway**, becoming quietly residential as it slopes down towards the water of Rozelle Bay. The side streets are fringed with renovated two-storey terraced houses

---

Getting to Glebe

Buses #431, #433 and #434 run to Glebe from Millers Point, George Street and Central Station; #431 and #434 run right down the length of Glebe Point Road to Jubilee Park, with the #434 continuing on to Balmain, while the #433 runs half-way, turning at Wigram Road, and heads on to Balmain. You can also reach Glebe via the Metro Monorail (see p.30), which runs between Central Station, Pyrmont and Rozelle: the "Glebe" stop is just off Pyrmont Bridge Road (follow Allum Place and Marlborough Street to emerge on Glebe Point Road near the Valhalla Cinema), while the "Jubilee" stop is at Jubilee Park (follow Victoria Road and Cotter Lane to emerge at Glebe Point Road by the YHA). Otherwise it's a fifteen-minute **walk** from Central Station up Broadway to the beginning of Glebe Point Road.

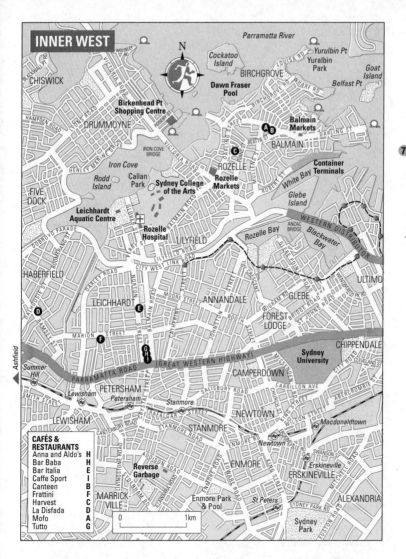

INNER WEST

CHISWICK

Parramatta River

Cockatoo Island

BIRCHGROVE

Yurulbin Pt
Yuralbin Park

Goat Island

Belfast Pt

Dawn Fraser Pool

Birkenhead Pt Shopping Centre

DRUMMOYNE

Balmain Markets

BALMAIN

Iron Cove

Rodd Island

Callan Park

Sydney College of the Arts

ROZELLE

Rozelle Markets

Container Terminals

White Bay

Glebe Island

FIVE DOCK

Leichhardt Aquatic Centre

Rozelle Hospital

LILYFIELD

Rozelle Bay

Blackwater Bay

WESTERN DISTRIBUTOR

ANZAC BRIDGE

ULTIMO

HABERFIELD

ANNANDALE

GLEBE

FOREST LODGE

CHIPPENDALE

LEICHHARDT

MARION STREET

(GREAT WESTERN HIGHWAY)

Sydney University

Ashfield

Summer Hill

PARRAMATTA ROAD

CAMPERDOWN

PETERSHAM

Lewisham

Petersham

Stanmore

NEWTOWN

Macdonaldtown

LEWISHAM

STANMORE

Newtown

ERSKINEVILLE

CAFÉS & RESTAURANTS	
Anna and Aldo's	H
Bar Baba	E
Bar Italia	I
Caffe Sport	B
Canteen	C
Frattini	F
Harvest	D
La Disfada	A
Mofo	G
Tutto	

Reverse Garbage

MARRICK-VILLE

Enmore Park & Pool

St Peters

ALEXANDRIA

Sydney Park

0   1km

ENMORE

with white-iron lacework verandahs. The laid-back, villagey feel makes Glebe a popular **place to stay**, with some of Sydney's best hostels, as well as motels and B&Bs (see "Accommodation", pp.154–168); for **longer stays**, check the many café notice boards for flat shares. There's also an Internet café, and the handy **Broadway Shopping Centre** on nearby Broadway, with its supermarkets, speciality food shops, huge food court, record, book and clothes shops and twelve-screen cinema. It's linked to Glebe by an overhead walkway from Glebe Point Road opposite one of the street's best cafés *Badde Manors* (see p.179).

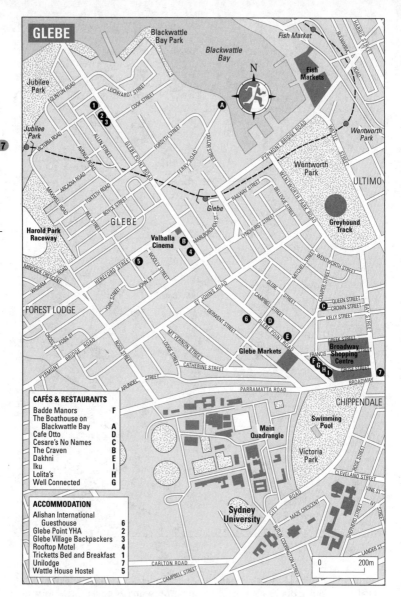

GLEBE

Blackwattle
Bay Park

Fish Market

Blackwattle
Bay

N

Fish
Markets

Jubilee
Park

LEICHHARDT STREET

COOK STREET

①
②③

Jubilee
Park

VICTORIA ROAD

AVENUE ROAD

ALLEN STREET

EGLINTON ROAD

GLEBE POINT ROAD

FORSYTH STREET

FERRY ROAD

TAYLOR STREET

Ⓐ

PYRMONT BRIDGE ROAD

Wentworth
Park

RAILWAY STREET

WATTLE STREET

Wentworth
Park

ULTIMO

ARCADIA ROAD

MAXWELL ROAD

TOXTETH ROAD

BOYCE STREET

BELL STREET

GLEBE

Glebe

MARLBOROUGH ST.

BELLEVUE STREET

WENTWORTH PARK ROAD

LYNDHURST STREET

Greyhound
Track

**Harold Park
Raceway**

MINOGUE CRESCENT

WIGRAM ROAD

HEREFORD STREET

WOOLLY STREET

JOHN ST.

⑤

**Valhalla
Cinema**

Ⓑ
④

MITCHELL STREET

WENTWORTH STREET

COWPER STREET

BAY STREET

FOREST LODGE

CROSS ST.

FOSS ST.

YORK STREET

JOHN ST.

ST JOHN'S ROAD

DERWENT STREET

CAMPBELL STREET

GLEBE STREET

QUEEN STREET

CROWN STREET

KELLY STREET

Ⓒ

PYRMONT

ROSS STREET

MT VERNON STREET

LODGE STREET

⑥

GLEBE POINT ROAD

Ⓓ

Ⓔ

GREEK STREET

**Broadway
Shopping
Centre**

BRIDGE ROAD

ARUNDEL STREET

CATHERINE STREET

Glebe Markets

FRANCIS

**ⒻⒼ
ⒽⒾ**

ROSE STREET

⑦

BROADWAY

PARRAMATTA ROAD

CHIPPENDALE

CAFÉS & RESTAURANTS

Badde Manors	**F**
The Boathouse on Blackwattle Bay	**A**
Cafe Otto	**D**
Cesare's No Names	**C**
The Craven	**B**
Dakhni	**E**
Iku	**I**
Lolita's	**H**
Well Connected	**G**

**Main
Quadrangle**

Swimming
Pool

Victoria
Park

ROSE STREET

CLEVELAND STREET

VINE ST.

IVY ST.

ACCOMMODATION

Alishan International Guesthouse	**6**
Glebe Point YHA	**2**
Glebe Village Backpackers	**3**
Rooftop Motel	**4**
Tricketts Bed and Breakfast	**1**
Unilodge	**7**
Wattle House Hostel	**5**

**Sydney
University**

CITY ROAD

BUTLIN COCKINGTON STREET

MAZE CRESCENT

SHEPHERD STREET

LANDER ST.

CARLTON ROAD

CAMPBELL STREET

0   200m

Sydney University and Victoria Park

Just before the beginning of Glebe Point Road, on Broadway, **Victoria Park**
with its duck pond, huge expanse of lawn and shady trees, has a very pleasant,
heated outdoor swimming pool (see p.261), with an attached gym and

sophisticated café. Leading up from the park is a path and steps into **Sydney University** (ⓦwww.usyd.edu.au), Australia's oldest tertiary educational institution, inaugurated in 1850 and today catering to 42,300 students. Your gaze is led from the walkway up to the Main Quadrangle and the stone clock tower, reminiscent of England's Oxford University and complete with gargoyles. The university's cedar-ceilinged, stained-glass-windowed **Great Hall** makes a glorious concert venue. You are free to walk through the gates and wander around the pleasant grounds, which take up a suburb-sized area between Parramatta Road and City Road, running up to King Street, Newtown (see p.105). Famous alumni include Germaine Greer, Clive James, Jane Campion and the current prime minister, John Howard; there's a small exhibit relating to well-known former students in Fisher Library, near the Victoria Park entrance.

Museum collections

There are several **free museums** and galleries you can visit on weekdays. The **War Memorial Art Gallery** (Main Quadrangle; Tues–Thurs noon–4pm) holds regular temporary exhibitions, including works from the Sydney University Art Collection, gathered since 1850. The **Nicholson Museum** specializes in antiquities (Main Quadrangle; Mon–Fri 10am–4.30pm; closed Jan), while the natural history collection of the **Macleay Museum**, on Science Road (Mon–Fri 9am–4pm), was formed from that of the botany-obsessed Macleay family who built Elizabeth Bay House (see p.98).

Glebe Point Road to Jubilee Park

Glebe itself is at its best on Saturday, when **Glebe Market**, which takes place on the shady primary school playground, a couple of blocks up from Broadway, is in full swing (see p.246). Just across the road at 49 Glebe Point Rd, you'll find the excellent **Gleebooks** – one of Sydney's best-loved bookshops (see "Shopping", p.237 and "Books", p.326). The original Gleebooks, now selling secondhand and children's books only, is worth the trek further up at 191 Glebe Point Rd, past St Johns Road and Glebe's pretty park. Across the street from the secondhand bookshop, and a couple of blocks further on, is one of Sydney's best independent cinemas, the Valhalla (see p.220), established in 1976; stop for a coffee next door in the relaxed and very popular *Craven Cafe* (p.179).

A few blocks on from here, the action stops and Glebe Point Road trails off into a more residential area, petering out at **Jubilee Park**, with characterful views across the water to Rozelle Bay's container terminal. The pleasantly landscaped waterfront park, complete with huge, shady Moreton Bay fig trees and a children's playground, offers an unusual view of far-off Sydney Harbour Bridge framed within Sydney's newest, the spectacularly cabled Anzac Bridge (see p.83).

Newtown and around

Newtown, separated from Glebe by Sydney University and easily reached by train (to Newtown Station), is another up-and-coming inner-city neighbourhood. What was once a working-class district – a hotchpotch of derelict factories,

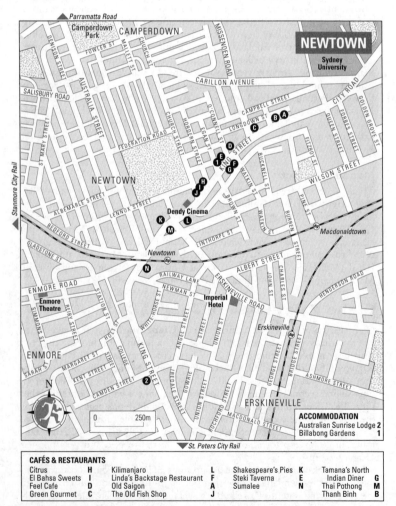

CAFÉS & RESTAURANTS

Citrus	**H**	Kilimanjaro	**L**	Shakespeare's Pies	**K**	Tamana's North
El Bahsa Sweets	**I**	Linda's Backstage Restaurant	**F**	Steki Taverna	**E**	Indian Diner	**G**
Feel Cafe	**D**	Old Saigon	**A**	Sumalee	**N**	Thai Pothong	**M**
Green Gourmet	**C**	The Old Fish Shop	**J**			Thanh Binh	**B**

ACCOMMODATION
Australian Sunrise Lodge 2
Billabong Gardens 1

Getting to the Newtown area

Buses #422, #423, #426 and #428 run to Newtown from Circular Quay via Castlereagh Street, Railway Square and City Road. They all go down King Street as far as Newtown Station, where the #422 continues to St Peters and the others turn off to Enmore and Marrickville. You can also get to the area by **train** to Newtown, St Peters or Erskineville train stations.

junkyards and cheap accommodation – has been transformed into a trendy but still offbeat area where body piercing, shaved heads and weird fashions rule. The neighbourhood is characterized by a large gay and lesbian population, a rich cultural mix and a healthy dose of students and lecturers from the nearby university. It also has an enviable number of great cafés and diverse restaurants, especially Thai.

King Street

Newtown's main drag, gritty, traffic-fumed and invariably pedestrian-laden **King Street**, is filled with unusual secondhand, funky fashion and speciality and homeware shops. The Dendy Cinema complex at no. 261 (see p.219), is a central focus, more like a cultural centre than just a film theatre; it has an attached bookshop, excellent record store, and street-front café, all open daily and into the night. During the **Newtown Festival** (early Oct to early Nov; Ⓦwww.newtowncentre.org) various shop windows display irreverent and in-your-face art, and the festival ends with a huge party in Camperdown Memorial Park, with hundreds of stalls and live music. On the book front, check out Gould's Book Arcade, way back near the Sydney Univeristy end of King Street at no. 32, a vast and chaotic secondhand book warehouse that is a Sydney institution, browsable until midnight.

King Street becomes less crowded south of Newtown train station as it heads for a kilometre towards **St Peters** train station. It's well worth strolling down to look at the more unusual speciality shops (buttons, ribbons, cacti, Chinese medicine amongst them), as well as several small art galleries and yet more retro clothes shops. The street is also stacked with culturally diverse restaurants which range from Turkish to African, and closer to St Peters Station are several colourful businesses aimed at the local Indian community. You'll also find a couple of theatres and a High School for the Performing Arts, reputed to be one of the top-five performing-arts schools in the world.

Enmore Road

Enmore Road, stretching west from King Street, opposite Newtown Station, is a similar mix of speciality shops and evidence of a migrant population. Look out for the long-established Mocha Coffee, at no. 16, which sells a large range of blends; Amera's Palace, at no. 83, stocking everything a belly dancer might need; Lemon Spread at no. 101, full of new and secondhand quirky collectable items; The Bead Company at no. 116; and Artwise Amazing Paper at no. 186. There's a range of restaurants, too, from Swedish to Thai. Enmore is generally much quieter than Newtown, except when a big-name band or comedian is playing at the Art Deco **Enmore Theatre**, at no. 130 (see p.209). When it's closed, you can play board games at the cosy booths of the *Box Office Cafe*. At the end of Enmore Road, Enmore Park hides the **Annette Kellerman**

△ Balmain Market

Aquatic Centre and its tiny heated 33-metre pool (see p.260). Combine a swim with a home-made ice cream from *Serendipity Icecream*, just across the road at no. 333.

Marrickville

Beyond Enmore, the very multicultural, lively but down-at-heel suburb of **Marrickville** stretches out. It has some great places to eat, particularly Greek and Vietnamese: two standouts are the *Corinthian Rotisserie Restaurant* at 283 Marrickville Rd and *Bay Tinh* at 318 Victoria Rd. Marrickville's other notable feature, and of great interest if you're committed to recycling, is the very commendable **Reverse Garbage**, in the grounds of the Addison Road Community Centre, 8/142 Addison Rd (Mon–Sat 9am–5pm, Sun 11am–3pm; ☎02/9569 3132, ⓦwww.reversegarbage.org.au), which was formed as a cooperative in 1976 by a group of schoolteachers who wanted to save useful industrial discards and offcuts from landfill to use in school arts and crafts projects instead. The sustainable, not-for-profit business now employs twenty, not just on the shop floor but teaching people how to use the resources in art and craft and DIY classes; the warehouses are always being scoured by creative-looking types, from set-builders to artists, and parents with toddlers in tow. To reach Reverse Garbage, catch the #428 **bus** from Circular Quay, Railway Square or Newtown Station.

Erskineville

Erskineville Road, stretching from the eastern side of King Street, marks the beginning of the adjoining suburb of **Erskineville**, a favourite gay address. The *Imperial Hotel* here at 35 Erskineville Rd (see also p.225) has long hosted popular drag shows, and is famous as the starting point of the gang in the hit film *The Adventures of Priscilla, Queen of the Desert*, directed by Stephan Elliot in 1994 and with an all-star cast including Terence Stamp, Hugo Weaving and Guy Pearce. The drag shows no longer include Priscilla tributes but the cocktail bar, the *Priscilla Lounge*, is lined with photos, and if you must re-create the movie, the *Venus Room* at Kings Cross (see p.227) now does the Priscilla thing. Another good pub, *The Rose of Australia*, at 1 Swanson St (see p.210), focuses on live music. Just near Swanson Street, Erskineville has its own **train** station on Bridge Street.

Leichhardt and Haberfield

It's almost an hour from The Rocks to Balmain by the #440 bus, via **Leichhardt**, Sydney's "Little Italy", where the famous **Norton Street** strip of cafés and restaurants runs off ugly **Parramatta Road**. Leichhardt is full of Italian businesses and cafés but the real heart of Italian Sydney is a little further west on Ramsay Street in **Haberfield**, also one of the best places to gaze at a whole suburb of charming, turn-of-the-twentieth-century federation-style houses.

Leichhardt

Leichhardt is very much up and coming – shiny, trendy, Italian cafés keep popping up all along the Norton Street strip, though its focus is the upmarket cinema complex, The Palace, at no. 99 (which hosts an Italian film festival in early December), with its attached record store, bookshop and Internet café (see p.218). Just opposite, at no. 70, the huge Beurkelow's new and secondhand bookstore is run by a family who've been in the antiquarian book trade since 1812; there are also CDs to browse, and two cafés (see also "Shopping" p.236). Back on the other side of Norton Street, closer to Parramatta Road at no. 39, is an upmarket shopping and dining centre and showcase for all things Italian, the **Italian Forum**. The Forum is arranged around a central square, with two colonnaded levels surrounding it. The top level is filled with upmarket fashion shops, several featuring Italian fashion of course, while downstairs are a host of mostly Italian eateries with alfresco tables on the square; they are hugely popular for lunch on a Sunday when the whole Forum is full of Italian families. An Italian Cultural Centre and a local library branch have been planned to open down here for years now but the spaces still stand empty. It's also worth heading on to the lively, much-loved and enduring *Bar Italia* (see p.180), a fifteen-minute walk further down Norton at the extent of the tempting array of eateries; it's still the best Italian café in Leichhardt, and it was one of the first.

To get to Leichhardt you can take **bus** #436, #437, #438 or #440 from Circular Quay, George Street in the city or Railway Square.

Haberfield

The real heart of Italian Sydney is a little further west on Ramsay Street in **Haberfield**; catch **bus** #436 from Leichhardt (or from Circular Quay or George Street in the city centre, or it's a twenty-minute walk from Summer Hill CityRail – take the northern exit and follow Sloane Street across Parramatta Road from where it's quite far along Ramsay Street to the shops).

Between Parramatta Road and Iron Cove on the Parramatta River, Haberfield was an entirely planned suburb. "Slum-less, Lane-less, and Pub-less" was the vision of the post-federation developers; the new nation was to have the ultimate urban environment. The style of the 1500 homes, all designed by the architect J. Spencer-Stanfield, is a classic Australian confection called **Federation Style**, which spread around the country from 1901. Eminently suited to the climate, the houses are a pleasing combination of the functional – wide verandahs that allow cooling breezes to circulate – with the fanciful, such as turrets. Stained glass is an important decorative element, often with very Australian motifs such as kookaburras and native flowers or flowing Art Nouveau designs. Elaborate chimneys, fretted woodwork, and gables and eaves are other key features. Every Spencer-Stanfield house in Haberfield is different, so you can easily spend a fascinating afternoon wandering its tranquil, leafy streets.

You still won't find a pub in Haberfield, but the many Italians who have moved to the area have opened up cafés, restaurants and delis, concentrated on Ramsay Road and Dalhousie Street. One of Sydney's best pizzerias, *La Disfida* is here at no. 109 Ramsay Rd (see p.191) and some great pasticcerias, including *A and P Sulfaro* at no.119, where you can also sit outside and have a coffee. There are also lots of speciality shops in Haberfield – model toy cars and antiques among them.

Rozelle

From Leichhardt, the #440 bus continues to Darling Street, which runs from **Rozelle** right down to Balmain's waterfront. Rozelle, once very much the

To **get to Rozelle**, the #440 **bus** continues from Norton Street, Leichhardt to Rozelle (or catch it from Circular Quay, George Street in the city or Railway Square), or you can catch the #445 from Norton Street, Leichhardt. You can also take the Metro Light Rail (see p.30) to Rozelle from Central, Pyrmont or Glebe; the "Lilyfield" stop is about 500m from Balmain Road: follow Catherine Street and Grove Street to emerge opposite the Sydney College of the Arts campus.

down-at-heel, poorer sister to Balmain is now emergently trendy with the Sydney College of the Arts and the NSW Writers' Centre based here in the grounds of the 61-hectare waterfront **Callan Park** on Balmain Road. There are lots of cafés, bookshops, speciality shops, gourmet grocers, restaurants, made-over pubs, and designer home-goods stores on Darling Street. A weekend **flea market** takes place in the grounds of Rozelle Primary School on Darling Street, Rozelle, near Victoria Road (Sat & Sun 9am–4pm). There's also the new, very ritzy **Rozelle Bay Super Yacht Marina** on James Craig Road; enjoy the views with a glass of wine at the bar-restaurant *Liquidity*, with its huge glass front overlooking the water.

Callan Park

The **Callan Park** site was bought by the government for a new lunatic asylum in the 1870s, but an enlightened one for the time, under the guiding hand of the American doctor, Thomas Kirkbride, who believed that the beauty of nature could calm troubled minds. The set of Neoclassical buildings, built from sandstone quarried from the site and linked by courtyards, was designed by colonial architect James Barnet (also responsible for Customs House, see p.57), and finished in 1885. They formed the core of the mental hospital, and were named after Kirkbride. The picturesque parklands sloping down to over a kilometre of waterfront were designed by the then Royal Botanic Gardens director.

In 1996 the Kirkbride Block was taken over by Sydney College of the Arts, while the still-functioning mental institution, now called Rozelle Hospital, moved to a more ramshackle collection of buildings; the **NSW Writers' Centre** (information and bookings ☏02/9555 9757; ⓦ www.nswwriterscentre.org.au) has for many years occupied the Greek Revival-style Gary Owen House, an information centre and venue for readings and literary events open to the public.

Indeed, for as long as there has been a hospital at Callan Park, the public have freely been allowed to use the grounds as their recreation area. Several attempts to sell off some of the land for private housing have been stopped in their tracks by local opposition, most vocally from the Friends of Callan Park (ⓦ www.callanpark.com) who were behind the 2002 opposition which resulted in the state government finally declaring it would forever remain in public ownership.

Balmain and Birchgrove

Balmain, directly north of Glebe, is less than 2km from the Opera House by ferry from Circular Quay to Darling Street Wharf. But, stuck out on a spur in the harbour and kept apart from the centre by Darling Harbour and Johnston's

Getting to and around Balmain and Birchgrove

For a **self-guided tour** of Balmain and Birchgrove, you can buy a *Balmain Walks* leaflet ($2.20) from Balmain Library, 370 Darling St. To **get to Balmain**, you can catch a ferry from Circular Quay to Darling Street Wharf in Balmain East, where the #442 bus waits to take you up Darling Street to Balmain proper. Buses #433 and #434 run out to Balmain via George Street, Railway Square and Glebe Point Road and down Darling Street; faster is the #442 from the QVB, which crosses Anzac Bridge and heads to Balmain Wharf. **Birchgrove** can be reached via ferry from Circular Quay or on the #441 from the QVB. You can also catch the #445 from Norton Street in Leichhardt.

Bay, it has a degree of separation that has helped retain its slow, villagey atmosphere and made it the favoured abode of many writers, film-makers and actors. Like better-known Paddington, Balmain was once a working-class quarter of terraced houses that has gradually been gentrified. The docks at White Bay are still important, though, and Balmain hasn't completely forsaken its roots. Darling Street rewards a leisurely stroll, with a bit of browsing in its speciality shops (focused on clothes and gifts), and grazing in its restaurants and cafés. It, and the surrounding backstreets, are also blessed with enough watering holes to warrant a pub crawl – two classics are the *London Hotel* on Darling Street (see p.204) and the *Exchange Hotel* on Beattie Street (see p.204).

The best time to come is on Saturday, when the lively **Balmain Market** occupies the shady grounds of St Andrews Church (7.30am–4pm; see p.246), on the corner opposite the *London Hotel*.

On the Parramatta River side of Balmain, looking across to Cockatoo Island, Elkington Park contains the quaint **Dawn Fraser Swimming Pool** (Oct–April daily 6.30am–7.30pm; $3), an old-fashioned harbour pool named after the famous Australian Olympic swimmer, a Balmain local. For long, stunning sunsets and wow-worthy real estate, meander from here down the backstreets towards water-surrounded **Birchgrove** on its finger of land, where Louisa Road leads to Birchgrove Wharf; from here you can catch a ferry back to Circular Quay, or stay and relax in the small park on Yurulbin Point.

The harbour

The harbour

Loftily flanking the mouth of Port Jackson – **Sydney Harbour**'s main body of water – are the rugged sandstone cliffs of North Head and South Head, providing spectacular viewing points across the calm water to the city, where the Harbour Bridge spans the sunken valley at its deepest point, 11km away. The many coves, bays, points and headlands of the harbour, and their parks, bushland and swimmable beaches are rewarding to explore. However, harbour beaches are not as clean as ocean ones, and after storms are often closed to swimmers (see p.127). Finding your way by ferry is the most pleasurable method of exploring: services run to much of the **North Shore** and to harbourfront areas of the **eastern suburbs**. The eastern shores are characterized by a certain glitziness and are the haunt of the nouveaux riches, while the leafy North Shore is very much old money.

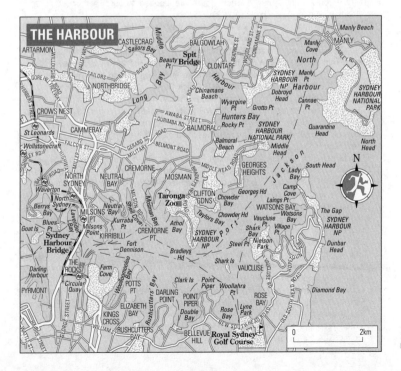

Sydney Harbour National Park

Both sides of the harbour have pockets of bushland which have been incorporated into **Sydney Harbour National Park**, along with five islands, two of which – Goat Island and Fort Denison – can be visited on tours (see box); the other three – Shark Island, Clark Island and Rodd Island – are bookable for picnics but you must provide your own transport. The NPWS publish an excellent free map detailing the areas of the national park and its many walking tracks (☎02/9337 5511 or ⊛www.npws.nsw.gov.au for general information, or visit Cadman's Cottage in The Rocks or NPWS office in Nielson Park – see p.47 and p.114 respectively).

Rushcutters Bay to South Head

The suburbs on the hilly southeast shores of the harbour are rich and exclusive. The area around **Darling Point**, the enviable postcode 2027, is the wealthiest in Australia, the waterfront mansions and yacht club memberships

Harbour islands tours

Two **harbour islands**, Fort Denison and Goat Island, can be regularly visited on NPWS tours with Sydney Ferries. Tours are booked through and meet up at Cadman's Cottage (see p.47; ☎02/9247 5033).

Fort Denison, a small island east of the Opera House and visible from Bennelong Point, was originally used as a special prison for the tough nuts the penal colony couldn't crack: locals still call it "Pinchgut". During the Crimean Wars in the mid-nineteenth century, however, old fears of a Russian invasion were rekindled and the fort was built as part of a defence ring around the harbour. If it's around lunchtime you'll hear the One O'Clock Gun, originally fired so sailors could accurately set their ship chronometers. For those interested in Australian history, there are tours organized by the NPWS from Circular Quay, either daytime tours (Mon–Sat 11.30am & 3pm, Sun 11.30am & 2.30pm; 2hr 30min; $22) or more leisurely Saturday brunch tours with a cooked meal in the fort's café included (Sat 9am, Sun 9.15am; 3hr; $47).

Just across the water from Balmain East, **Goat Island** is the site of a well-preserved gunpowder magazine complex. The sandstone buildings, including a barracks, were built by two hundred convicts between 1833 and 1839. Treatment of the convicts was harsh: 18-year-old Charles Anderson, a mentally impaired convict with a wild, seemingly untameable temper who made several attempts to escape, received over twelve hundred lashes in 1835 – and if that wasn't enough, he was sentenced to be chained to a rock for two years in an attempt to control him, a cruel punishment even by the standards of the day. Tethered to the rock, which you can still see, his unhealed back crawling with maggots, he slept in a cavity hewn into the sandstone "couch". Sydneysiders would row up and tease him for entertainment. Eventually Anderson ended up on Norfolk Island, where under the humane prisoner reform experiments of Alexander Maconochie, the once feral, abused 24-year-old was transformed. The NPWS make the most of the island's gruesome history: tours range from a Heritage Tour (Mon & Fri–Sun 1pm; 2hr15min; $19.80), and a night-time Gruesome Tales Tour for over-12s only (Sat 6pm depending on sunset; 3hr 20min; $24.20; supper included).

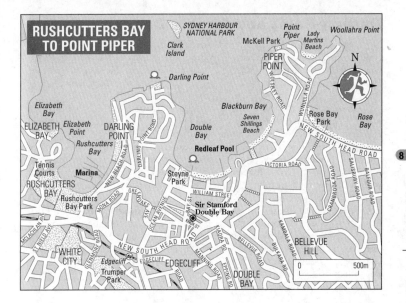

enjoyed by residents such as Nicole Kidman and Lachlan Murdoch. A couple of early nineteenth-century mansions, Elizabeth Bay House (see p.98) and **Vaucluse House**, are open to visitors, giving an insight into the lifestyle of the pioneering upper crust, while the ferry to Rose Bay gives a good view of the pricey contemporary real estate, and is close to beautiful Nielson Park and the surrounding chunk of Sydney Harbour National Park. At **South Head**, Watsons Bay was once a fishing village, and there are spectacular views from The Gap in another section of the national park.

Buses #324 and #325 from Circular Quay via Pitt Street, Kings Cross and Edgecliff cover the places listed below, heading to Watsons Bay via New South Head Road; #325 detours at Vaucluse for Nielson Park. Bus #327 runs between Bondi Junction station and Martin Place in the city via Edgecliff station and Darling Point.

Rushcutters Bay

Only ten minutes' walk northwest from Kings Cross train station, **Rushcutters Bay Park** is set against a wonderful backdrop of the yacht- and cruiser-packed marina in the bay; the marina was revamped for the 2000 Olympics sailing competition. You can take it all in from the tables outside the very popular *Rushcutters Bay Kiosk* (good coffee and café fare). Gangs of friends book out the **tennis courts** at the Rushcutters Bay Tennis Centre (see "Sports and activities" p.257), but if you don't have anyone to play, the friendly managers will try to provide a hitting partner for you; there's a nice little coffee bar too, with outdoor tables under vines and a resident squawking galah.

Woollahra Council has developed the 5.5-kilometre (3hr) Rushcutters Bay to Rose Bay harbour **walk** (see p.115), which takes in exclusive streets, pretty parks and harbour views.

Darling Point and Double Bay

Northeast from Rushcutters Bay is **Darling Point**, Australia's wealthiest post-code zone, according to the tax office. From the point's McKell Park are wonderful views across to Clarke Island and Bradleys Head, both part of Sydney Harbour National Park (see p.112); to get to the park, follow Darling Point Road (or take bus #327 from Edgecliff Station).

The next port of call is **Double Bay**, dubbed "Double Pay" for obvious reasons. The noise and traffic of New South Head Road are redeemed by several excellent antiquarian and secondhand bookshops (see p.237), while in the quieter "village" are some of the most exclusive shops in Sydney, full of imported designer labels and expensive jewellery. The eastern suburbs' socialites meet on **Cross Street**, where the swanky pavement cafés are filled with well-groomed women in Armani outfits sipping coffee, their Mercedes parked illegally outside.

If all this sounds like a turn-off, Double Bay's real delight is **Redleaf Pool** (daily Sept–May dawn–dusk; free), a peaceful, shady harbour beach – one of the cleanest – enclosed by a wooden pier you can wander around, dive off or just laze on; there's also an excellent café famed for its fruit salad and coffee. A ferry from Circular Quay (Wharf 2) stops at both Darling Point and Double Bay; otherwise, catch bus #324 or #325, also from Circular Quay, or the #327 from Bondi Junction, Martin Place or Edgecliff stations.

Rose Bay

The ferry to **Rose Bay** from Circular Quay gives you a chance to check out the waterfront mansions of **Point Piper** (where Opera singer Joan Sutherland was born) as you skim past. You can also catch buses #324 or #325 to get here (see p.113).

Rose Bay itself is quite a haven of exclusivity, with the verdant expanse of the members-only Royal Sydney Golf Course. Directly across New South Head Road from the course, waterfront **Lyne Park** provides welcome distraction in the form of a **seaplane** service, based here since the 1930s; planes can be chartered to go to Palm Beach or Berowra Waters, and there are also scenic flights (☏020/9388 1978). Rose Bay is also a popular **windsurfing** spot, and you can rent equipment to join in from Rose Bay Aquatic Hire (see p.259).

Woollahra Council has developed an eight-kilometre (4.5hr) harbour walk from Rose Bay to Watsons Bay via the cliffs, coves and bushland of the Sydney Harbour National Park (they will post a walk-map out, or it is downloadable from their website; see "Coastal walks" opposite).

Nielson Park

Sydney Harbour National Park (see p.112) emerges onto the waterfront at Bay View Hill, where the 1.5-kilometre **Hermitage walking track** to Nielson Park begins; the starting point, Bay View Hill Road, is off South Head Road between two exclusive educational establishments, the Kambala School and the Rose Bay Convent (on bus routes #324 and #325). The walk takes about an hour, with great views of the Opera House and Harbour Bridge, some lovely little coves to swim in and a picnic ground and sandy beach at yacht-filled **Hermit Point**.

Extensive, tree-filled **Nielson Park**, on Shark Bay, is one of Sydney's delights (don't worry about Shark Bay's ominous name – it's netted), a great place for a daytime swim, a night-time skinny-dip, a picnic, or refreshment at the popular café. Within the park, the decorative Victorian-era mansion, **Greycliffe House**, built for William Wentworth's daughter in 1852 (see below), is now the headquarters of Sydney Harbour National Park (see p.112); if the ranger is around (there are no regular hours) pop in for information on other waterfront walks. With views across to the city skyline, the park is a popular spot to watch the New Years' Eve fireworks display (see p.249), and its position also makes it a prime spot to view the yachts racing out for the heads on Boxing Day (see p.252).

Vaucluse House and Parsley Bay

Beyond Shark Bay, Vaucluse Bay shelters the magnificent Gothic-style 1803 **Vaucluse House** and its large park-like estate on Wentworth Road (Tues–Sun 10am–4.30pm & public holiday Mondays, grounds open daily 10am–5pm; $7), with tearooms in the grounds for refreshment. The house dates from 1803, but its most famous owner was the influential Australian-born explorer and reformer **William Wentworth**, whose mother was a former convict and father a doctor with a dubious past; a major figure in the colony, William was a member of the first party to cross the Blue Mountains (see p.288). The house is restored to the middle period of the Wentworths' occupation (1829–1853), and has some of the original furniture.

In 1831 Wentworth invited four thousand guests to Vaucluse House to celebrate the departure of the hated Governor Darling (1824–31). In his struggle for popular rights in the colony, Wentworth detested Darling's upholding of the king's authority and his favouring of the large landholders. The climax of the evening was a fireworks display which burned "Down with the Tyrant" into the night sky.

Coastal walks

Woollahra Council (☎02/9391 7000, ⊛www.woollahra.nsw.gov.au/your_area) publishes brochures detailing three waterside walks: the 5.5-kilometre (3hr) Rushcutters Bay to Rose Bay harbour walk (see p.113), the eight-kilometre (4.5hr) harbour walk from Rose Bay to Watsons Bay (see opposite), and the five-kilometre (3hr) cliffside walk from Vaucluse to Watsons Bay and South Head – this is detailed below. The maps are downloadable or can be posted out.

On the southern, ocean side of the South Head peninsula, **Christison Park** (bus #382), off Old South Head Road in Vaucluse, is the start of a magnificent coastal cliff walk heading north to the sheer drop of The Gap near Watsons Bay (2.3km) and on to South Head and the beach at Camp Cove. At the north end of Christison Park, the serenely white-painted **Macquarie Lighthouse** was the site of Australia's first, erected in 1818, and designed by convict-architect Francis Greenway who was then pardoned for his efforts. The present 1883 tower was built to the same plan.

The walk continues through **Lighthouse Reserve**; at its north end, facing out over Dunbar Head, is a **signal station** built in 1848. A watchpost was set up here from the very beginnings of the colony to alert the Sydney Town community, by use of flags, of ships arriving in the harbour. Continuing north, the rocks below the cliffs of **Signal Hill Reserve** wrecked the *Dunbar*, in 1857; the sole survivor, of 122 on board, was dragged up **Jacob's Ladder**, the jagged cleft in the cliffs here. The path heads upwards to **Gap Park**, where the *Dunbar*'s anchor is on display. Continue north along the path through the Sydney Harbour National Park to South Head (5km from Vaucluse) or cross Military Road for the settlement of Watsons Bay (see p.116).

To get to Vaucluse House, walk from Nielson Park (see p.114) along Coolong Road, or take bus #325 right to the door. From Christison Park off Old South Head in Vaucluse, a one-hour coastal walk heads to Watsons Bay, detailed in the box on p.115.

Beyond Vaucluse Bay, narrow **Parsley Bay**'s shady finger of a park is a popular picnic and (shark-netted) swimming spot, crossed by a picturesque pedestrian suspension bridge.

Watsons Bay

On the finger of land culminating in South Head, with an expansive sheltered harbour bay on its west side, and the treacherous cliffs of The Gap on its ocean side, **Watsons Bay** was one of the earliest settlements outside of Sydney Cove. In 1790 Robert Watson was one of the first signalmen to man the clifftop flagstaffs nearby, and by 1792 the bay was the focus of a successful fishing village. The suburb has retained a villagey feel with quaint old wooden fishermen's cottages still found on the tight streets around Camp Cove. It's an appropriate location for one of Sydney's longest-running fish restaurants, *Doyles*, right out on the bay by the old Fishermans Wharf (see p.192), now the ferry terminal: it's accessible by ferry from Circular Quay, or by Matilda Rocket Express from Darling Harbour. In fact *Doyle's* has virtually taken over the waterfront here, with two restaurants, a takeaway fish and chip shop, and a seafood bistro in the bayfront beergarden of the adjacent *Doyle's Watsons Bay Hotel* (see p.205).

The Gap and Camp Cove

Spectacular ocean views are just a two-minute walk away from *Doyle's* through grassy Robertson Park, across Gap Road to **The Gap** (buses terminate just opposite – the #324, #325 and faster #L24 from Circular Quay, and the #L82 from Circular Quay via Bondi Beach), whose high cliffs are notorious as a place to commit suicide. You can follow a walking **track** north from here to South Head through another chunk of **Sydney Harbour National Park**, past the HMAS *Watson* Military Reserve where you can detour up the road to look at the Memorial Chapel (daily 9am–4pm) and beautifully framed water views from its picture window. The track heads back to the bay side, and onto Cliff Street which leads to **Camp Cove**, a tiny palm-fronted harbour beach (not netted) popular with families; a small kiosk provides refreshments. Camp Cove can also be reached by walking along the beach of Watsons Bay then along Pacific Street and through Green Point Reserve.

South Head

Alternatively, reach Camp Cove by walking along the beach of Watsons Bay then along Pacific Street and through Green Point Reserve. From the northern end of Camp Cove, steps lead up to a boardwalk which will take you to **South Head** (470-metre circuit), the lower jaw of the harbour mouth affording fantastic views of Port Jackson and the city, via Sydney's best-known **nude beach**, Lady Jane (officially "Lady Bay" on maps), a favourite gay beat. It's not very private, however: a lookout point on the track provides full views and ogling tour boats cruise past all weekend. From Lady Bay, it's a further fifteen minutes' walk to South Head itself, along a boardwalked path past nineteenth-century fortifications, lighthouse cottages, and the picturesquely red-and-white-striped Hornby Lighthouse.

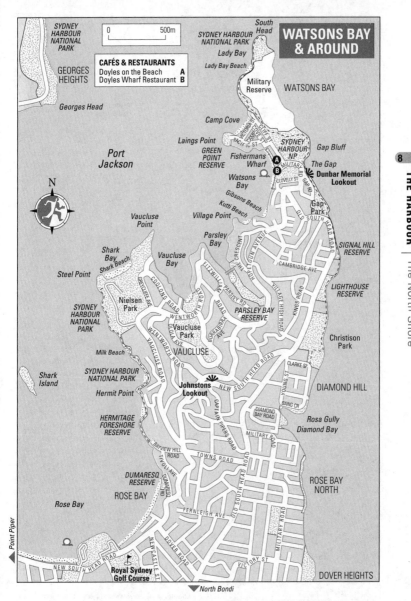

WATSONS BAY & AROUND

SYDNEY HARBOUR NATIONAL PARK

GEORGES HEIGHTS

Georges Head

CAFÉS & RESTAURANTS
Doyles on the Beach   A
Doyles Wharf Restaurant   B

SYDNEY HARBOUR NATIONAL PARK

South Head

Lady Bay
Lady Bay Beach

Military Reserve

WATSONS BAY

Camp Cove

Laings Point

Port Jackson

GREEN POINT RESERVE

Fishermans Wharf

Watsons Bay

Gibsons Beach

Kutti Beach

Village Point

SYDNEY HARBOUR NP

Gap Bluff

The Gap

Dunbar Memorial Lookout

Gap Park

Parsley Bay

Shark Bay
Shark Beach

Vaucluse Point

Vaucluse Bay

Steel Point

SIGNAL HILL RESERVE

CAMBRIDGE AVE

LIGHTHOUSE RESERVE

Nielsen Park

SYDNEY HARBOUR NATIONAL PARK

PARSLEY BAY RESERVE

Vaucluse Park

Milk Beach

VAUCLUSE

Christison Park

NEW SOUTH HEAD ROAD

Shark Island

SYDNEY HARBOUR NATIONAL PARK

Hermit Point

Johnstons Lookout

DIAMOND HILL

DIAMOND BAY ROAD

HERMITAGE FORESHORE RESERVE

Rosa Gully
Diamond Bay

MILITARY ROAD

BAYVIEW HILL ROAD

TOWNS ROAD

DUMARESQ RESERVE

ROSE BAY

Rose Bay

ROSE BAY NORTH

FERNLEIGH AVE

DOVER ROAD

Point Piper

NEW SOUTH HEAD ROAD

VICTORY ST

Royal Sydney Golf Course

North Bondi

DOVER HEIGHTS

0   500m

N

The North Shore

The **North Shore**, where Sydney's "old money" is mainly found, is generally more affluent than the rest of Sydney. **Mosman** and **Neutral Bay** in particular have some stunning waterfront real estate, priced to match. Upmarket

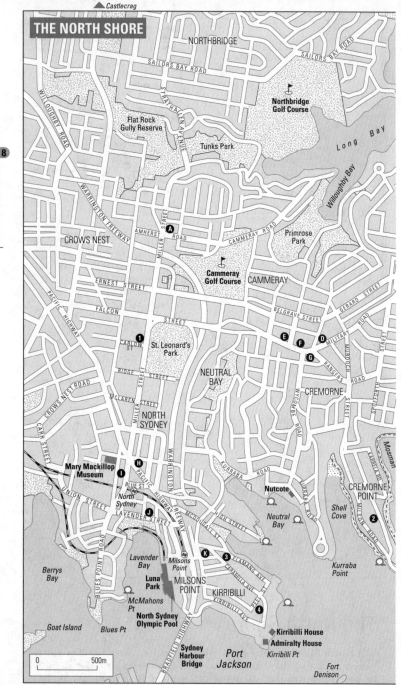

THE NORTH SHORE

▲ Castlecrag

NORTHBRIDGE

SAILORS BAY ROAD

SAILORS BAY ROAD

WILLOUGHBY ROAD

STRATHALLEN AVENUE

Northbridge
Golf Course

Flat Rock
Gully Reserve

Long Bay

Tunks Park

Willoughby Bay

WARRINGTON FREEWAY

AMHERST

MILLER STREET

A

ROAD

CAMMERAY ROAD

Primrose
Park

CROWS NEST

ERNEST STREET

Cammeray
Golf Course

CAMMERAY

GERARD STREET

FALCON

STREET

BELGRAVE STREET

MILITARY ROAD

PACIFIC HIGHWAY

1

CARLOW ST

St. Leonard's
Park

E **F** **D**

MURDOCH STREET

G

RANGERS ROAD

CROWS NEST ROAD

RIDGE STREET

STREET

NEUTRAL
BAY

WYCOMBE ROAD

CREMORNE

McLAREN STREET

MILLER STREET

NORTH
SYDNEY

CARR STREET

KURRABA ROAD

Mosman

CREMORNE
POINT

Mary Mackillop
Museum

H

I

BLUE ST

North
Sydney

Nutcote

CABRELLA RD

UNION STREET

PACIFIC HIGHWAY

WARRINGTON FREEWAY

HIGH STREET

Neutral
Bay

Shell
Cove

MILSON ROAD

J

LAVENDER STREET

McDOUGALL ST

Berrys
Bay

BLUES POINT ROAD

Lavender
Bay

Milsons
Point

K

3

ELAMANG AVE

Kurraba
Point

2

Luna
Park

MILSONS
POINT

CARABELLA AVE

KIRRIBILLI

KIRRIBILLI AVE

4

Goat Island

McMahons
Pt

North Sydney
Olympic Pool

Blues Pt

BRADFIELD HIGHWAY

Sydney
Harbour
Bridge

Port
Jackson

Kirribilli Pt

◆ **Kirribilli House**
■ **Admiralty House**

Fort
Denison

0   500m

▼ Circular Quay & Opera House

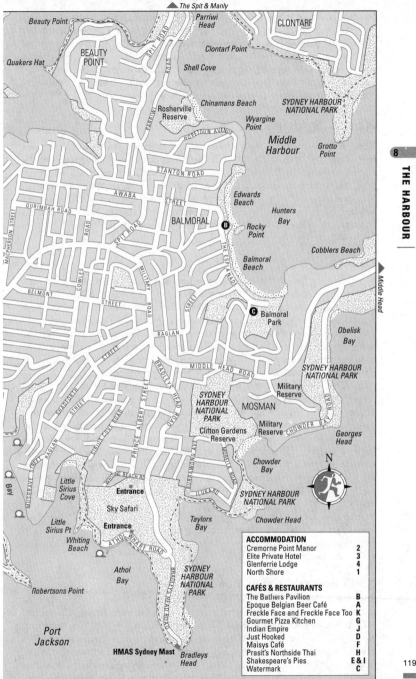

The Spit & Manly

Beauty Point
Parriwi Head
CLONTARF

Quakers Hat
BEAUTY POINT
Clontarf Point

Shell Cove

Rosherville Reserve
Chinamans Beach
SYDNEY HARBOUR NATIONAL PARK

Wyargine Point

HOPETOUN AVENUE
Middle Harbour
Grotto Point

STANTON ROAD

AWABA STREET
Edwards Beach
Hunters Bay

OURIMBAH ROAD
BALMORAL
B
Rocky Point

BELMONT STREET
Cobblers Beach

Balmoral Beach

THE ESPLANADE
RAGLAN
C Balmoral Park
Obelisk Bay

MIDDLE HEAD ROAD
SYDNEY HARBOUR NATIONAL PARK

Military Reserve
SYDNEY HARBOUR NATIONAL PARK
MOSMAN
Military Reserve
CHOWDER BAY
Georges Head

Clifton Gardens Reserve
Chowder Bay

N

Entrance
Sky Safari
SYDNEY HARBOUR NATIONAL PARK
Chowder Head

Little Sirius Cove
Taylors Bay

Little Sirius Pt
Entrance

Whiting Beach
ATHOL WHARF ROAD

Athol Bay
SYDNEY HARBOUR NATIONAL PARK

Robertsons Point

Port Jackson

HMAS Sydney Mast
Bradleys Head

ACCOMMODATION

Cremorne Point Manor	2
Elite Private Hotel	3
Glenferrie Lodge	4
North Shore	1

CAFÉS & RESTAURANTS

The Bathers Pavilion	B
Epoque Belgian Beer Café	A
Freckle Face and Freckle Face Too	K
Gourmet Pizza Kitchen	G
Indian Empire	J
Just Hooked	D
Maisys Café	F
Prasit's Northside Thai	H
Shakespeare's Pies	E & I
Watermark	C

Middle Head

Military Road, running from Neutral Bay to Mosman, is something of a gourmet strip with a string of excellent, albeit expensive, restaurants, and a number of tempting patisseries and well-stocked delis. Around the water, it's surprising just how much harbourside bushland remains intact here – "leafy" just doesn't do it justice – and superbly sited amongst it all is **Taronga Zoo**.

A ride on any ferry lets you gaze at beaches, bush, yachts and swish harbourfront houses and is one of the chief joys of this area.

North Sydney

Though it's easy for the area's white-collar workers to get into the city, there's also a busy high-rise office district in **North Sydney**, on the north side of the Harbour Bridge. You'll also find a famous fun park, a gloriously sited swimming pool, and a museum devoted to Mary MacKillop, Australia's saint-in-waiting. You can get here in a couple of minutes by train from Circular Quay to Milsons Point or North Sydney train stations, or take the ferry to Milsons Point wharf, or even walk straight across the Harbour Bridge from The Rocks (see p.47).

Luna Park

North Sydney has been associated with pure fun since the 1930s – beside the Bridge on Lavender Bay at **Milsons Point**, you can't miss the huge laughing clown's face that belongs to **Luna Park**. Generations of Sydneysiders have walked through the grinning mouth, and the park's old rides and conserved 1930s fun hall, complete with period wall murals, slot machines, silly mirrors and giant slippery dips, have great nostalgia value for locals. The water views from the park's rides, particularly the Ferris wheel, with the Harbour Bridge as a backdrop, are sensational – it's worth coming for these alone.

Luna Park was closed down for several years from the late 1980s until a grand reopening in January 1995 with a new clown's face – the eighth since the park began – closely resembling the 1950s model. Unfortunately, the amusement park noise upset nearby residents who'd grown used to peace and quiet, and the park promptly closed again, losing developers millions of dollars. Back in business in 2000, it shut down again in early 2001 for yet another bout of redevelopment, which will include the dismantling of its classic old roller-coaster, the Big Dipper; redevelopment has been stalled and the park should reopen in the first half of 2004 (check ⓦwww.lunaparksydney.com for the latest information).

Getting to Luna Park can be pleasant too: the ferry to Milsons Point wharf from Circular Quay or Darling Harbour pulls up right outside (or catch a train from Circular Quay to Milsons Point Station). Beyond the park there's a boardwalk right around Lavender Bay.

North Sydney Olympic Pool

Right next door to the amusement park is Sydney's most picturesquely sited public swimming pool, with terrific views of the Harbour Bridge. The heated **North Sydney Olympic Pool**, Alfred South Street (see p.261), is open year round and was revamped in 2001, with a new indoor 25-metre pool as well as the old 50-metre outdoor pool, a gym, sauna, spa, café and a restaurant, *Aqua*, overlooking the pool (expensive contemporary Australian; bookings ⓣ02/9955 2309) – be prepared to be ogled by diners as you swim your laps.

Mary MacKillop Place Museum

Beyond Luna Park and the pool, worth visiting in amongst North Sydney's impersonal corporate zone, is the Catholic Church-run **Mary MacKillop Place Museum**, 7 Mount St (daily 10am–4pm; $8.25; ⓦ www.marymackillopplace .org.au). Housed in a former convent, it provides a surprisingly broadminded look at the life and times of Australia's first would-be saint – MacKillop was beatified in 1995 and is entombed here – and sainthood itself. The late nun's charitable educational work began in Penola in the Coonawarra region of South Australia in the 1860s. The best way to get here directly is to take the train to North Sydney station and head north along Miller Street for about five minutes.

Kirribilli, Neutral Bay and Cremorne Point

Just east of the Harbour Bridge and immediately opposite the Opera House, **Kirribilli** on Kirribilli Bay is a mainly residential area, although Kirribilli hosts a great **market** on the last Saturday of the month in Bradfield Park (7am–3.30pm), the best and biggest of several rotating markets on the North Shore (see "Markets" p.246). On Kirribilli Point, the current prime minister, native Sydneysider John Howard, lives in an official residence, **Kirribilli House**, snubbing Canberra, the usual PM's residence – a sore point with ACT locals. Admiralty House, next door, is the Sydney home of the governor general, and is where the British family stay when they're in town.

Following the harbour around from Kirribilli is upmarket **Neutral Bay**. A five-minute walk from Neutral Bay ferry wharf via Hayes Street and Lower Wycombe Road is **Nutcote**, 5 Wallaringa Ave (Wed–Sun 11am–3pm; $7). This was the home for 45 years of May Gibbs (1867–1969), the author and illustrator of the famous Australian children's book about two little gum nuts who come to life, *Snugglepot and Cuddlepie*, published in 1918 and an enduring classic. The highlight of North Shore **drinking** is the shady **beer garden** at Neutral Bay's *Oaks Hotel* on Military Road (see p.205); for more listings in Neutral Bay, see p.183 for the 24-hour *Maisy's Café*, and p.192 for restaurants.

Bush-covered **Cremorne Point**, which juts into the harbour here, is also worth a jaunt. Catch the ferry from Circular Quay and you'll find a quaint open-access sea pool to swim in by the wharf; from here, you can walk right around the point to Mosman Bay (just under 2km; see below), or in the other direction, past the pool, there's a very pretty walk along **Shell Cove** (1km).

Mosman Bay

Mosman Bay's seclusion was first recognized as a virtue during its early days as a whaling station, since it kept the stench of rotting whale flesh from the Sydney Cove settlement. Now the seclusion is a corollary of wealth. The ferry ride into the narrow, yacht-filled bay is a choice one – get off at Mosman Wharf, not South Mosman (Musgrave St) – and fittingly finished off with a beer at the unpretentious *Mosman Rowers' Club* (visitors welcome).

Taronga Zoo

What Mosman is most famous for is **Taronga Zoological Park** on Bradleys Head Road, with its superb hilltop position overlooking the city (daily: Jan 9am–9pm; Feb–Dec 9am–5pm; $23, child $12.50, family $57, Zoo Pass from Circular Quay including return ferry and entry $28.40, child pass $14.30;

The wonderful views and the natural bush surrounds are as much an attraction as the chance to get up close to some animals. The zoo houses bounding Australian marsupials, native birds (including kookaburras, galahs and cockatoos), reptiles, and sea lions and seals from the sub-Antarctic region. You'll also find exotic beasts from around the world, including the frequently photographed giraffes, who stick their necks out across a sublime harbour view.

Established in 1916, the zoo has come a long way from its Victorian roots, and the animals now live in more natural habitats. You can get close to kangaroos and wallabies in the **Australian Walkabout** area, and the **koala house** gives you eye-level views; you can get closer by arranging to have your photo taken patting a koala, but for a guaranteed **hands-on experience** with a native animal, a VIP Gold Tour (daily 9.15am & 1.15pm; 1hr 30min–2hr; $55 includes zoo entry; book 24hr in advance on ℡02/9969 2777) will give you and a small group a session with a zookeeper, guiding you through the Australian animals. There are keeper talks and feeding sessions – including a free-flight bird show and a seal show – throughout the day, detailed on the free souvenir map handed out when you arrive; if you want to coordinate timing in advance, check the website for show times or call for details. The zoo also hosts concerts on summer evenings; again, check the website for details.

Though there has been a lot of criticism lately that the enclosures are very shabby, the zoo has masterplanned a **redevelopment** which started in 2001 and will continue until 2007. The latest part of this redevelopment is the fun and creative **Backyard to Bush**, which opened in April 2003. A typical urban house, full of the usual Sydney creepy crawlies and pests, is yours to explore, giving way to a farm setting and then some bush (complete with a gigantic wombat burrow). Another recent feature is the **Wollemi Pine area**, where six small and very rare pines (see p.301) are growing amongst warm-temperate rainforest species.

The zoo is best reached by taking the **ferry** from Circular Quay to the Taronga Zoo wharf (also known as Athol wharf; every 30min). Though there's a lower entrance near the wharf on Athol Road, it's best to start your zoo visit from the upper entrance so you can spend several leisurely hours winding your way downhill and exit for the ferry: State Transit buses still meet the ferries for the trip uphill, or take the **Sky Safari** cable car (the cable car is included in the entry price and can be taken as often as you want). You can also get to the zoo on bus #247 from Wynyard or the QVB.

Bradleys Head To Chowder Bay

Beyond the zoo, at the termination of Bradleys Head Road, **Bradleys Head** itself is marked by an enormous mast that towers over the rocky point. The mast once belonged to HMS *Sydney*, a victorious World War II battleship, long since gone to the wrecker's yard. It's a peaceful spot with a dinky lighthouse and, of course, a fabulous view back over the south shore. A colony of ring-tailed possums nests here, and boisterous flocks of rainbow lorikeets visit.

The headland comprises another large chunk of **Sydney Harbour National Park** and you can walk to Bradleys Head via the six-kilometre Ashton Park **walking track**, which starts near the ferry wharf, opposite the zoo entrance, and continues beyond the headland to Taylors Bay and Chowder Head, finishing at **Clifton Gardens**, where there's a jetty and sea baths on **Chowder Bay**. The defunct military reserve which separates Chowder Bay from another chunk of Sydney Harbour National Park on Middle Head is now open to the public (see below) and reached by a boardwalk from the northern end of Clifton Gardens.

The NPWS offer a two-hour **Bush Food tour** of Bradleys Head on the first and third Sunday of the month (1.30pm; $13.20; bookings essential ☎02/9247 5033), departing from the rear entrance of the zoo, giving you a chance to see and taste some of the bush tucker the local Aboriginal people once survived on.

Middle Harbour

Middle Harbour is the largest inlet of Port Jackson, its two sides joined across the narrowest point at **The Spit**. The Spit Bridge opens regularly to let tall-masted yachts through – much the best way to explore its pretty, quiet coves and bays; several cruises pass by (see pp.27–30). Crossing the Spit Bridge, you can walk all the way to Manly Beach along the ten-kilometre Manly Scenic Walkway (see p.137), while bus #144 runs from Spit Road to Manly Wharf, taking in a scenic route uphill overlooking the Spit marina.

Middle Head

Between Clifton Gardens and Balmoral Beach, a military reserve and naval depot at **Chowder Bay** blocked coastal access to both **Georges Head** and the more spectacular **Middle Head** by foot for over a century, although they could always be reached by road. However, since the military's recent withdrawal from the site, walkers can now trek all the way between Bradleys Head and Middle Head. The 1890s military settlement itself is open to visitors as a reserve, and NPWS offer tours exploring its underground fortifications (second & fourth Sun of each month; 10.30am; 2hr; $13.20). You can reach the military reserve entrance from the northern end of Clifton Gardens (see opposite) or walk from Balmoral Beach, below.

Balmoral Beach and around

The bush setting provided by Middle Head helps lend **Balmoral**, on Hunters Bay, the peaceful secluded air that makes it so popular with families (it's netted, too, which helps). There's something very Edwardian and genteel about palm-filled, grassy Hunters Park and its bandstand, which is still used for Sunday jazz concerts or even Shakespeare recitals in summer. The civilized air is added to by the pretty white-painted **Bathers Pavilion** at the northern end, now converted into a restaurant and café (see p.191). There are really two beaches at Balmoral, separated by the island-like **Rocky Point**, a noted picnicking spot. The low-key esplanade has some takeaways including an excellent fish-and-chip place, a quiet café, and a fine bottle shop – all you need for a day at the beach. South of Rocky Point, the "baths" – actually a netted bit of beach with a boardwalk and lanes for swimming laps – have been here in one form or another since 1899; you can rent sailboards and catamarans and take lessons from the neighbouring boat shed (see p.259). This end of the beach is great for kids – the big trees actually shade the sand and there's a popular playground and a kiosk selling ice creams.

To get to Balmoral, catch a **ferry** from Circular Quay to Athol Wharf (Taronga Zoo) and then bus #238 via Bradleys Head Road, or the ferry to

Musgrave Street wharf, at nearby Mosman, then bus #233 or #257 via Military Road (#257 originates from Wynyard in the city).

Cobblers and Chinamans beaches

On the Hunters Bay side of Middle Head, tiny **Cobblers Beach** is officially **nude**, and is a much more peaceful, secluded option than the more famous Lady Jane at South Head (see p.116). The hillside houses overlooking Balmoral have some of the highest price tags in Sydney: for a stroll through some prime real estate, head for **Chinamans Beach**, via Hopetoun Avenue and Rosherville Road.

Northbridge and Castlecrag

There are some architectural gems lurking around Middle Harbour: the 1889 bridge leading to **Northbridge**, which Jan Morris describes rather fancifully in *Sydney* as "an enormously castellated mock-Gothic bridge, with hefty towers, arches, crests and arrow-slits, such as might have been thrown across a river in Saxe-Coburg by some quixotic nineteenth-century princeling"; and the idyllic enclave of **Castlecrag**, which was designed in 1924 by **Walter Burley Griffin**, the Chicago landscape architect who had won the international competition in 1912 to design the nation's new capital, Canberra, which he worked on until 1920. Burley Griffin's plan for Canberra envisaged a garden city, taking into account the natural features of the landscape. His plans for Castlecrag were similar: he was intent on building an environmentally friendly suburb – free of the fences and the red-tiled roofs he hated – that would be "for ever part of the bush".

To get to Castlecrag, take **bus** #207 from Wynyard or North Sydney train station or #275 from Chatswood train station; to get to Northbridge, take bus #202 from Wynyard or North Sydney train stations.

9

Ocean beaches

Sydney's **beaches** are among its great natural joys, key elements in the equation that makes the city special. The water and sand are remarkably clean – people actually fish in the harbour, and don't just catch old condoms and plimsolls – and at Long Reef, just north of Manly, you can find rock pools teeming with starfish, anemones, sea-snails and crabs, and even a few shy moray eels. There's good snorkelling and diving at various spots (see "Diving" on p.259), especially at the underwater nature trail at Gordons Bay (see p.131). In recent years, **humpback whales** have begun to be regularly sighted from the Sydney headlands in June and July on their migratory path from the Antarctic to the tropical waters of Queensland, and southern right whales even occasionally make an exciting appearance in the harbour itself – the three whales cavorting in July 2002 caused a sensation (for more information consult the Australian Museum website – Ⓦ www.livingharbour.net).

With the ocean splitting the harbour in half, the two stretches of ocean beaches on either side are deemed the **northern beaches** – which continue beyond Manly for 30km up to Barrenjoey Heads and Palm Beach and the **eastern beaches**, which stretch south from Bondi to Maroubra.

Bondi Beach

Bondi Beach is synonymous with Australian beach culture, and indeed the mile-long curve of golden sand (now free of the controversial Olympic beach-volleyball stadium) must be one of the best-known beaches in the world. It's the closest ocean beach to the city centre; you can take a train to Bondi Junction and then a ten-minute bus ride, or drive there in twenty minutes (parking is another story). Big, brash and action-packed, it's probably not the best place for a quiet sunbathe and swim, but the sprawling sandy crescent really is spectacular. Red-tiled houses and apartment buildings crowd in to catch the view, many of them erected in the 1920s when Bondi was a working-class suburb.

Although still residential, Bondi is now one of Sydney's trendiest suburbs, with escalating real estate and rental prices, and a thriving café and restaurant scene packed out with the young and fashionable. There's also the Saturday night "hoon" culture when suburban youngsters drive their souped-up cars up and down Campbell Parade (though police regularly crack down), and it's an alternative to the city centre for weekend drinking and dining. Backpackers create another large part of the culture, drinking and otherwise, especially in summer when they turn Christmas Day into a big beach event

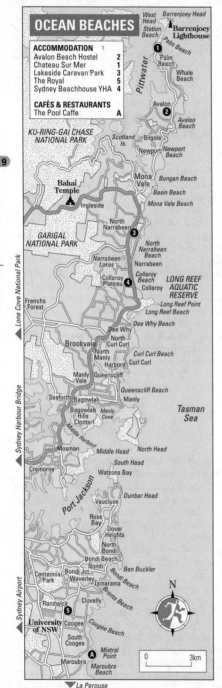

OCEAN BEACHES

ACCOMMODATION	
Avalon Beach Hostel	2
Chateau Sur Mer	1
Lakeside Caravan Park	3
The Royal	5
Sydney Beachhouse YHA	4

CAFÉS & RESTAURANTS	
The Pool Caffe	A

KU-RING-GAI CHASE NATIONAL PARK

West Head
Station Beach
Barrenjoey Head
Barrenjoey Lighthouse

Palm Beach

Whale Beach

Avalon
Avalon Beach

Scotland Is.
Bilgola
Newport
Newport Beach

Bahai Temple

Ingleside

Mona Vale
Bungan Beach
Basin Beach
Mona Vale Beach

GARIGAL NATIONAL PARK

North Narrabeen

North Narrabeen Beach

Narrabeen Lakes
Narrabeen

Collaroy Plateau
Collaroy Beach
Collaroy

LONG REEF AQUATIC RESERVE
Long Reef Point
Long Reef Beach

Frenchs Forest

Dee Why
Dee Why Beach

Brookvale
North Curl Curl
North Manly
Harbord
Curl Curl Beach
Curl Curl

Manly Vale
Bagowlah
Queenscliff
Queenscliff Beach

Seaforth
Bagowlah Hills
Clontarf
Manly Cove
Manly

Tasman Sea

Mosman
Middle Head
North Head

Cremorne
South Head
Watsons Bay

Dunbar Head

Vaucluse

Rose Bay
Dover Heights

North Bondi
Bondi Beach
Bondi
Ben Buckler
Bondi Jct.
Waverley
Tamarama Beach
Bronte Beach

Centennial Park

Randwick
Clovelly

University of NSW
Coogee
Coogee Beach

South Coogee

Mistral Point

Maroubra
Maroubra Beach

La Perouse

Pittwater

Port Jackson

Lone Cove National Park

Sydney Harbour Bridge

Middle Harbour

Sydney Airport

N

0 ——— 3km

126

(see "Festivals and Events" p.253, and for a list of Bondi accommodation see pp.158–169).

You can reach Bondi on **bus** #380, #L82 or #389 from Circular Quay via Oxford Street and Bondi Junction, or take the train directly to Bondi Junction, then transfer to these buses or to the #361, #381 and #382.

Campbell Parade and Hall Street

Beachfront **Campbell Parade** is both cosmopolitan and highly commercialized, lined with alfresco cafés, bars, restaurants, record, fashion and surfwear shops. On Sunday the **Bondi Beach markets** (10am–5pm) – in the grounds of the primary school on the corner of Campbell Parade and Warners Avenue, facing the northern end of the beach – place great emphasis on fashion and jewellery.

You'll find the locals' favourite cafés and more day-to-day shops and facilities on the calmer side streets. **Hall Street**, heading gently uphill from Campbell Parade, is Bondi Beach's real nerve centre, with a post office (and public phones), banks, bakeries, supermarkets, an assortment of kosher delis and butchers and other shops that serve the area's Jewish community, cybercafés, laundries, a health-food store with a great notice board for share accommodation, bookshops (try *Martin Smith's* at no. 3 for new books and *Gertrude & Alice Cafe Bookstore* at no. 40 for secondhand, also see p.181), and some of Bondi's best cafés.

Bondi Park and the Bondi Pavilion

Between Campbell Parade and the beach, grassy (though mostly shadeless except for the few picnic

Beach and sun safety

Don't be lulled into a false sense of security: the beaches do have **perils** as well as pleasures. Some beaches are protected by special shark nets, but they don't keep out stingers such as bluebottles, which can suddenly swamp an entire beach; listen for loudspeaker announcements that will summon you from the water in the event of shark sightings or other dangers.

Pacific **currents** can be very strong indeed – inexperienced swimmers and those with small children would do better sticking to the sheltered **harbour beaches** (see "The Harbour" p.111–124 and "Kids' Sydney" p.232) or **sea pools** at the ocean beaches. Ocean beaches are generally patrolled by **surf lifesavers** during the day between October and April (all year at Bondi): red and yellow flags (generally up from 6am until 6pm or 7pm) indicate the safe areas to swim, avoiding dangerous rips and undertows. It can't be stressed strongly enough that you must try to swim between the flags – people have drowned in strong surf. If you do get into difficulty, stay calm and raise one arm above your head as a signal to be rescued. It's hard not to be impressed as **surfers** paddle out on a seething ocean that you wouldn't dip your big toe in, but don't follow them unless you're confident you know what you're doing. Surf schools can teach you the basic skills and enlighten you on surfing etiquette and lingo: see "Surfing" on p.258 for recommended schools. You can check daily **surf reports** on ⓦwww .realsurf.com.

Don't underestimate the strength of the southern **sun**: follow the local slogan and Slip (on a shirt), Slop (on the sun block), Slap (on a hat). The final hazard, despite the apparent cleanliness, is **pollution**. Monitoring shows that it is nearly always safe to swim at all of Sydney's beaches – except after storms, when storm water, currents and onshore breezes wash up sewage and other rubbish onto certain beaches (though usually harbour beaches – see p.111) making them – as signs will indicate – unsuitable for swimming and surfing. To check pollution levels, call the Beachwatch Bulletin on ☎1800/036 677 (ⓦwww.epa.nsw.gov.au).

A final note: topless bathing for women is accepted on many beaches but frowned on on others, so if in doubt, do as the locals do. There are two official **nude** beaches around the harbour (see pp.116 and 124).

---

groups shelters) **Bondi Park** slopes down to the promenade, and is always full of sprawling feasting on fish and chips with seagulls mobbing them. Along the promenade there are two board ramps for **rollerblading** and **skateboarding**. For places to hire rollerblades, see p.262.

The focus of the promenade is the arcaded, Spanish-style **Bondi Pavilion**, built in 1928 as a deluxe changing-room complex and now converted to a community centre hosting an array of workshops, classes and events, from drama and comedy in the theatre and the Seagull Room (the former ballroom) to daytime dance parties and outdoor film festivals in the courtyard (programme details on ☎02/9130 3325 Mon–Fri, ☎02/9368 1253 Sat & Sun; ⓦwww.waverley.nsw.gov.au). The pavilion is now also the base for the Sydney Fringe Festival in January (see p.250). Downstairs in the foyer, photos of Bondi's past are worth checking out, with some classic beach images of men in 1930s bathing suits, and there's an excellent **souvenir shop** (daily 9.30am–5.30am) which utilizes lots of old-fashioned Bondi imagery. There's even a community-access **art gallery** (daily 10am–5pm) featuring changing exhibitions by local artists, and some alfresco cafés and restaurants. In September, the Festival of the Winds, Australia's largest **kite festival**, takes over the beach (see p.251).

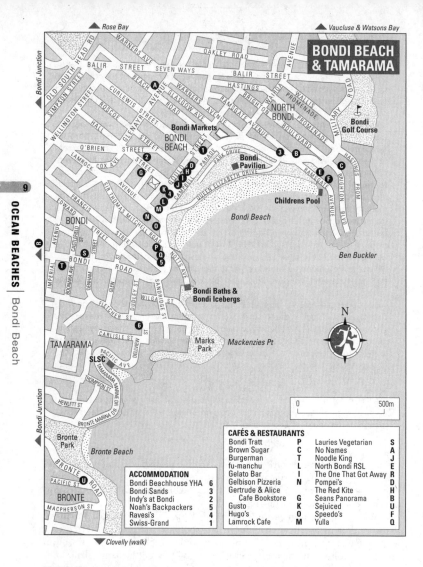

BONDI BEACH & TAMARAMA

ACCOMMODATION

Bondi Beachhouse YHA	6
Bondi Sands	3
Indy's at Bondi	2
Noah's Backpackers	5
Ravesi's	4
Swiss-Grand	1

CAFÉS & RESTAURANTS

Bondi Tratt	P	Lauries Vegetarian	S
Brown Sugar	C	No Names	A
Burgerman	T	Noodle King	J
fu-manchu	L	North Bondi RSL	E
Gelato Bar	I	The One That Got Away	R
Gelbison Pizzeria	N	Pompei's	D
Gertrude & Alice		The Red Kite	H
Cafe Bookstore	G	Seans Panorama	B
Gusto	K	Sejuiced	U
Hugo's	O	Speedo's	F
Lamrock Cafe	M	Yulla	Q

The beach

Surfing is part of the Bondi legend, the big waves ensuring that there's always a pack of damp young things hanging around, bristling with surfboards. However, the beach is carefully delineated, with surfers using its southern end, so you shouldn't have to fear catapulting surfboards. There are two sets of flags for swimmers and boogie-boarders. Families congregate at the northern end near the shallow sheltered saltwater pool (free) that's popular with kids, with a park with BBQs and a playground above, and everybody else uses the middle flags. The beach is netted and there hasn't been a shark attack for over forty years.

Bondi's surf lifesavers

Surf lifesavers are what made Bondi famous; there's a bronze sculpture of one outside the Bondi Pavilion. The surf lifesaving movement began in 1906 with the founding of the Bondi Surf Life Bathers' Lifesaving Club in response to the drownings that accompanied the increasing popularity of swimming. From the beginning of the colony, swimming was harshly discouraged as an unsuitable bare-fleshed activity. However, by the 1890s swimming in the ocean had become the latest fad, and a Pacific Islander introduced the concept of catching waves or **bodysurfing** that was to become an enduring national craze. Although "wowsers" (teetotal puritanical types) attempted to put a stop to it, by 1903 all-day swimming was every Sydneysider's right.

The bronzed and muscled surf lifesavers in their distinctive red and yellow caps are a highly photographed, world-famous Australian image. Surf lifesavers (members of what are now called Surf Life Saving Clubs, abbreviated to SLSC) are volunteers who work the beach at weekends, so come then to watch their exploits – or look out for a surf carnival; lifeguards, on the other hand, are employed by the council and work all week during swimming season (year-round at Bondi).

If the sea is too rough, or if you want to swim laps, head for the seawater swimming pool at the southern end of the beach under the **Bondi Icebergs Club** building entrance on Notts Avenue, with a 50-metre lap pool, kids' pool, gym, sauna, massage service and poolside café (pool Mon–Wed & Fri 6am–8pm, Sat & Sun 6am–6.30pm; $3.30). The Icebergs Club has been part of the Bondi legend since 1929; members must swim throughout the winter, and media coverage of their plunge, made truly wintry with the addition of huge chunks of ice, heralds the first day of winter. The very dilapidated club building was knocked down and rebuilt to the tune of $10 million, reopening in 2002; one floor has been appropriately leased to Surf Lifesaving Australia, who have an information room with a small collection of memorabilia (Mon–Fri 10am–3pm; free). On the top floor is a posh new restaurant, but the club floor itself is as unpretentious as ever, with the addition of wonderful open balconies and a decent café (see p.206).

Topless bathing is condoned at Bondi – a long way from conditions right up to the late 1960s when stern beach inspectors were constantly on the lookout for indecent exposure. If you want to join in the sun and splash but don't have the gear, Beached at Bondi, below the lifeguard lookout tower, rents out everything from umbrellas, wetsuits, cozzies and towels to surfboards and body-boards. They also sell hats and sun block and have lockers for valuables.

The eastern beaches

Sydney's eastern beaches stretch from **Bondi** down to **Maroubra**. Many people find the smaller, quieter beaches to the south of Bondi more enticing, and it's a popular walk or jog right around the oceanfront and clifftop **walking track** to Bondi's smaller, less brazen but very lively cousin **Coogee** (about 2hr 30min). The track also includes a fitness circuit, so you'll see plenty of joggers. En route you'll pass through gay favourite **Tamarama**; family-focused, café-cultured **Bronte**; narrow **Clovelly**; and a popular diving and snorkelling spot Gordons Bay (see "Diving" p.259). Randwick Council have designed the

"Eastern Beaches Coast Walk" from Clovelly to Coogee and beyond to more downmarket Maroubra, with stretches of boardwalk and interpretive boards detailing environmental features. A free guide-map detailing the walk can be picked up from the council's Customer Service Office, 30 Francis St, Randwick (☎02/9399 0999, ⓦwww.randwickcitytourism.com.au), or from Coogee at the beachfront Coogee Bay Kiosk, Goldstein Reserve, Arden Street, opposite *McDonald's*.

Tamarama

From Bondi Beach, walk past the Bondi Icebergs Club on Notts Avenue (see p.129) round Mackenzies Point, through Marks Park, until you reach the modest and secluded **Mackenzies Bay**. Next is **Tamarama**, a deep, narrow beach favoured by the smart set and a hedonistic gay crowd ("Glamarama" to the locals), as well as surfers. The surf here is very rough and the flags are often taken down and swimmers advised not to go into the water, hence the sun-worshipping rather than swimming crowd. Topless sunbathing is the norm for women here. Apart from the small Surf Life Saving Club (SLSC), which offers drop-in yoga classes, the intimate beach has a popular café, and a small grassy park (not very shady) with picnic shelters, barbecues and a basic children's playground.

The **Sculpture by the Sea festival** turns the walk between Bondi and Tamarama into a temporary art gallery for ten days in October (see "Festivals and events", p.252).

Tamarama Bay is a fifteen-minute walk from Bondi, or if you want to come here directly, it's a 300-metre walk from the #380 bus stop on Fletcher Street (from Circular Quay or Oxford St), or hop on bus #360 or #361 from Bondi Junction.

Bronte

Walk through Tamarama's small park and follow the oceanfront road for five minutes to the next beach along, **Bronte Beach** on Nelson Bay, where the 2000 Olympic road-cycling races picturesquely terminated. More of a family affair with a large green park, a popular café strip and sea baths, it's also easily reached on bus #378 from Central Station via Oxford Street and Bondi Junction. The **northern end** as you arrive from Tamarama has inviting flat-rock platforms, popular as fishing and relaxation spots, and the beach here is cliff-backed, providing some shade. The valley-like **park** beyond is extensive and shady; a **mini-train ride** for small children ($3 or 4 rides for $10) has been operating here since 1947, while further back there's an imaginative children's playground.

At the **southern end** of the beach, palm trees give a suitably holiday feel as you relax at one of the outside tables of Bronte Road's wonderful café strip, with a clutch of eight to choose from, plus a fish-and-chip shop. Back on the water at this end, a natural rock enclosure makes a calm area for kids to swim in, and there are rock ledges to lie on around the enclosed sea swimming pool known as **Bronte Baths** (open access; free), often a better option than the surf here, which can be very rough.

It's a pleasant five-minute walk past the Bronte Baths to **Waverly Cemetery**, a fantastic spot to spend eternity. Established in 1877, it contains the graves of many famous Australians, with the bush poet contingent well represented. **Henry Lawson**, described on his headstone as poet, journalist and patriot, languishes in section 3G 516, while **Dorothea Mackellar**, who penned the famous poem "I love a sunburnt country", is in section 6 832–833.

Clovelly and Gordons Bay

Beyond Waverly Cemetery – another five-minute walk – on the other side of the ominously named Shark Point, is channel-like **Clovelly Bay**, with concrete platforms on either side and several sets of steps leading into the very deep water. Rocks at the far end keep out the waves and the sheltered bay is popular with lap-swimmers – there's a free swimming pool too – and snorkellers, while a grassy park with several terraces extends far back and is a good spot for a picnic. You can hire snorkels up the road at the set of shops (see p.260). There's a divinely sited café next to the surf club that gets packed at weekends (see p.182), while on Sunday afternoons and evenings, the nearby *Clovelly Hotel* is a popular hangout for locals and travellers, with free live music and a great bistro. Otherwise, go for the rock-bottom-priced drinks and fab views at the Clovelly Bowling Club, also on the walk route. To get to Clovelly directly, take bus #339 from Millers Point via Central Station and Albion Street, Surry Hills; #360 from Bondi Junction; or the weekday peak-hour X39 from Wynyard.

Gordons Bay

From Clovelly you can rock-hop around to equally narrow **Gordon's Bay**, though this can be a little tricky – backed by high sandstone cliffs with some rocky tunnels to pass through – and without local knowledge you're probably better off sticking to the road route along Cliffbrook Parade. The secluded rocks are popular with locals for peaceful fishing or sunbathing, and rescuing stranded tourists tends to shatter the equilibrium. Unsupervised, undeveloped Gordons Bay itself is not a pretty beach, but another world exists beneath the sheltered water: the protected **underwater nature trail** makes it diving and snorkelling heaven (see p.259 for diving operators). From here, a walkway leads around the waterfront to Major Street and then on to **Dunningham Reserve** overlooking the northern end of Coogee Beach; the walk to Coogee proper takes about fifteen minutes in all.

Coogee

Coogee is another long-popular seaside resort, almost on a par with Manly and Bondi. Dominated by the extensive *Coogee Bay Hotel* on beachfront Arden Street, one of Sydney's best-known music venues, Coogee has had a reputation for entertaining Sydneysiders since Victorian times. At the northern end of the beach, the dome you can see over the *Beach Palace Hotel* is an 1980s restoration of the 1887 Coogee Palace Aquarium – in its heyday a gigantic dance floor that could accommodate three thousand pleasure-seekers. Today the hotel is a popular drinking spot for backpackers, who crowd out its oceanfront balcony (see p.193).

With its hilly streets of California-style houses looking onto a compact pretty beach enclosed by headlands, Coogee has a snugness and a friendly local feel that its cousin Bondi just can't match – there's just something more laid-back and community-oriented about it, and you can happily wear your old shorts to the beach. Everything is close to hand: **Arden Street** has a down-to-earth strip of cafés that compete with each other to sell the cheapest cooked breakfast, while the main shopping street, **Coogee Bay Road**, running uphill from the beach, has a choice selection of coffee spots and eateries plus a big supermarket. The imaginatively modernized promenade is a great place to stroll and hang out; between it and the beach a grassy park has free electric barbecues, picnic tables and shelters. The beach is popular with families (there's an excellent children's playground above the southern end; see p.233) and young

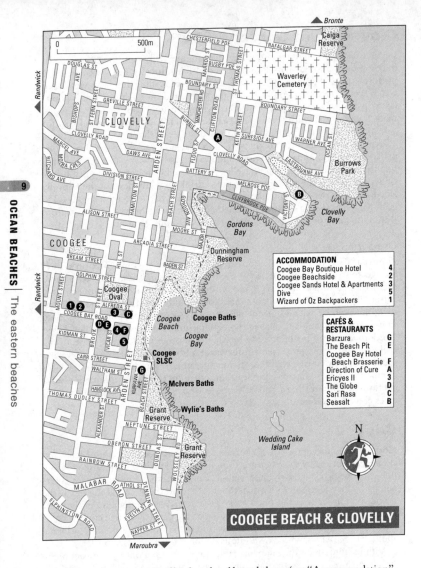

ACCOMMODATION

Coogee Bay Boutique Hotel	4
Coogee Beachside	2
Coogee Sands Hotel & Apartments	3
Dive	5
Wizard of Oz Backpackers	1

CAFÉS & RESTAURANTS

Barzura	G
The Beach Pit	E
Coogee Bay Hotel Beach Brasserie	F
Direction of Cure	A
Ericyes II	3
The Globe	D
Sari Rasa	C
Seasalt	B

COOGEE BEACH & CLOVELLY

travellers, as there's a stack of backpackers' hostels here (see "Accommodation", pp.159–169).

You can reach Coogee on **bus** #373 or #374 from Circular Quay via Randwick, or #372 from Eddy Avenue, outside Central Station; the journey time from Central is about 25min. There are also buses from Bondi Junction via Randwick: #313 and #314.

Coogee's baths

One of Coogee's chief pleasures is its baths, beyond the southern end of the beach. The first, the secluded McIvers Baths, traditionally for women and children only, is known by locals as **Coogee Women's Pool** (noon–5pm; volunteer-run, entry by donation). Opposite the entrance to the women's pool, Grant Reserve has a full-on adventure playground. Just south of the women's pool, the unisex **Wylies Baths**, a saltwater pool on the edge of the sea, is at the end of Neptune Street (Oct–April 7am–7pm, May–Sept 7am–5pm; $2.50), with big decks to lie on and solar-heated showers; its kiosk serves excellent coffee. Immediately south of Wylie's, **Trenerry Reserve** is a huge green park jutting out into the ocean; its spread of big, flat rocks offers tremendous views and makes a great place to chill out.

South to Maroubra Beach

Probably the most impressive section of Randwick Council's **Eastern Beaches Coast Walk** (see p.130) commences from Trenerry Reserve (above). The council is attempting to regenerate the native flora, and the walk, sometimes on boards, is accompanied by interpretive panels detailing the surrounding plant- and birdlife. Steps lead down to a rock platform full of small pools – you can wander down and look at the creatures there, and there's a large tearshaped pool you can swim in. It's quite thrilling with the waves crashing over – but be careful of both the waves and the blue-ringed octopus found here. At low tide you can continue walking along the rocks around Lurline Bay – otherwise you must follow the streets inland for a bit, rejoining the waterfront from Mermaid Avenue. Jack Vanny Memorial Park is fronted by the large rocks of Mistral Point, a great spot to sit and look at the water, and down by the sea there's the **Mahon Pool** (free; open access), a small, pleasant pool surrounded by great boulders, with an unspoilt secluded feel. The isolated *Pool Caffe* across the road makes a wonderful lunch or coffee spot (see p.182).

At the southern end of the Memorial Park, the kilometre-long stretch of **Maroubra Beach** begins. With the Anzac Rifle Range at the southern end and the far-off sound of gunfire, this traditionally working-class suburb with a down-at-heel set of shops has never been a popular beach resort. However, things are changing fast, most noticeably with the opening of the phenomenally popular *Pavilion Cafe* right on the sand on Marine Parade in the former kiosk; the views are fantastic but the atmosphere and food is casual.

To get to Maroubra by public transport, take **bus** #376 or #377 from Circular Quay, Eddy Avenue at Central Station, Randwick or Coogee or the #317 from Bondi Junction station.

Manly

Manly, just above North Head at the northern mouth of the harbour, is blessed with both ocean and harbour beaches, plus bushwalking in the nearby stretch of Sydney Harbour National Park (also see p.112) – a cycling track heads in the other direction.

When Captain Arthur Phillip, the commander of the First Fleet, was exploring Sydney Harbour in 1788, he saw a group of well-built Aboriginal men onshore, proclaimed them to be "manly" and named the cove in the process. During the Edwardian era it became fashionable as a recreational retreat from the city, and the cheesy promotional slogan of the time "Manly – seven miles from Sydney, but a thousand miles from care" still holds true today. The area

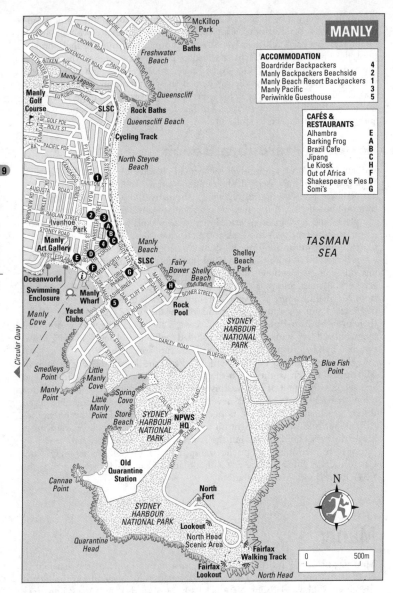

MANLY

ACCOMMODATION
Boardrider Backpackers 4
Manly Backpackers Beachside 2
Manly Beach Resort Backpackers ... 1
Manly Pacific 3
Periwinkle Guesthouse 5

CAFÉS &
RESTAURANTS
Alhambra .... E
Barking Frog .... A
Brazil Cafe .... B
Jipang C
Le Kiosk .... H
Out of Africa .... F
Shakespeare's Pies .... D
Somi's .... G

TASMAN SEA

0 ———— 500m

has become quite a travellers' centre in recent years with some of Sydney's best backpackers' hostels plus some good B&Bs and hotels. An excellent time to visit is over the Labour Day long weekend in early October, when there's an international **Jazz Festival** with free outdoor concerts (see p.251).

Ferries leave wharves 2 and 3 at Circular Quay for Manly approximately twice an hour (30min; $5.40). The last ferry service from Circular Quay is at 7pm after which time the faster JetCat catamarans operate until midnight, 11pm on Saturdays. The JetCat ($6.70) goes twice as fast as the regular ferries but is about half as much fun. After it finishes, night bus #E50 runs from Wynyard Terminal.

Around Manly Wharf

A day-trip to Manly, rounded off with a dinner of fish and chips, offers a classic taste of Sydney life. The ferry trip out here is an essential part of the experience: the legendary Manly Ferry service has been running from Circular Quay since 1854, and the huge old boats come complete with snack bars selling the ubiquitous meat pies. Ferries terminate at **Manly Wharf** in Manly Cove, near a small section of harbour beach with a netted-off swimming area popular with families. **Manly Wharf** until recently always had a funfair; now it's all very grown up, with a **David Jones food hall**, *Food Chain*, a swathe of cafés and multicultural food stalls and a swish new pub, the *Manly Wharf Hotel*. You'll also find the **Manly Visitor Information Centre** (Mon–Fri 9am–5pm, Sat & Sun 10am–4pm; ☏02/9977 1088, ⓦwww.manlyweb .com.au; lockers $2) handily located here.

The streets between Manly Cove and the surf beach are lively and interesting and there are plenty of great places to eat or find the makings of a beachside picnic – for cafés and restaurants in Manly see p.183 and p.193. There's the food hall and outlets at the wharf but the nearby streets are also very quality-food oriented: opposite the wharf, on the corner of Wentworth Street, there's an organic food store, and if you head past this a block to the intersection with **Darley Road**, you'll find a corner awash with upmarket food shops, delis and gleaming European-style cafés as well as an above-average Coles supermarket. And **Belgrave Street**, running north from Manly Wharf, is Manly's alternative strip, where you'll find some good cafés tucked away, interesting shops to browse, yoga schools and the Manly Environment Centre at no. 41.

Oceanworld

From the wharf, walk west, either along the beach with the pool or along West Esplanade to **Oceanworld** (daily 10am–5.30pm; $15.90, child $8, family ticket $39.90; ⓦwww.oceanworldmanly.com), where clear acrylic walls hold back the water so you can saunter along the harbour floor, gazing at huge sharks and stingrays. Divers hand-feed sharks every Monday, Wednesday and Friday at 11am and there's also a thirty-minute Shark Tunnel Tour (daily 2.30pm & Tues, Thurs, Sat & Sun 11am). You can even arrange to dive amongst the sharks for half an hour (qualified diver $150; unqualified diver $195; bookings ☏02/9949 2644).

Water activities and cruises

Manly Wharf is now also a hub for adventure activity, with three **watersports** companies based here. Manly Parasailing (☏02/9977 6781, ⓦwww.parasail.net; Oct to April only) offer the only parasailing experience in Sydney: a ten-minute "lift" costs $59 if you're on your own, but the $99 tandem is more fun; expect to be on the boat for an hour. Manly Boat & Kayak Hire (☏0412 622 662) are here daily Oct to April and weekends the rest of the year; single kayaks cost from $15 per hour and the five-seater motorboats start from $35 for 30min. Epic Surftours (☏02/8900 1018, ⓦwww.epicsurf.com.au; $60) operate all year – their small-group one-hour tours through crashing surf to the cliffs of North Head are not for the faint-hearted.

△ Bondi Beach

Manly Waterworks and the art gallery

The original vividly painted aquarium now houses a restaurant and the **Manly Waterworks** (Oct to Easter: Sat, Sun, school & pub hols 10am–5pm; 1hr $13.50, all day $19) – three giant **waterslides** which kids adore (they must be aged over 6). Between the waterslides and Ocean World is the **Manly Art Gallery and Museum** (Tues–Sun 10am–5pm; $3.50), with a collection of unremarkable Australian paintings, drawings, prints and etchings which was started in the 1920s, and a fun stash of beach memorabilia including huge old wooden surfboards and old-fashioned swimming costumes.

The beaches

Many visitors mistake Manly Cove for the ocean beach, which in fact lies on the other side of the isthmus, 500m down **The Corso**, Manly's busy pedestrianized main drag which is lined with shops, cafés, restaurants and pubs. The ocean beach, **South Steyne**, is characterized by stands of Norfolk pine which line the shore. Every summer, there's a beach-hire concession which hires out just about anything to make the beach more fun, from surfboards to snorkel sets; they also have a bag-minding service. A six-kilometre-long **cycle path** (shared with pedestrians) begins at South Steyne and runs north to Seaforth, past North Steyne Beach and Queenscliff. You can rent bikes from Manly Cycles, a block back from the beach at 36 Pittwater Rd (☎02/9977 1189; mountain bikes 1hr $12, $25 day), and Manly Blades & Skates, 49 North Steyne (☎02/9976 3833) have inline skates and skateboards from $12 per hour ($20 all day) as well as nifty electric scooters (1hr $20) and power-assisted bikes (2hr $44) for the truly lazy.

For a more idyllic beach, follow the footpath from the southern end of South Steyne around the headland to Cabbage Tree Bay, with two very pretty, green-backed beaches at either end – **Fairy Bower** to the west and **Shelley Beach** to the east.

Manly Scenic Walkway

The wonderful **Manly Scenic Walkway** starts at Manly Cove, following the harbour shore inland all the way to Spit Bridge on Middle Harbour, where you can catch bus #180 back to Wynyard Station in the city centre (20min). The 9.5-kilometre walk takes you through a section of **Sydney Harbour National Park**, past a number of small beaches and coves, Aboriginal middens and some subtropical rainforest. The entire walk takes three to four hours but is broken up into six sections with obvious exit/entry points if you're not up to doing the whole thing; pick up a map from the Manly Visitor Information Centre (see p.135) or NPWS offices (see "Parks and wildlife information" in Basics on p.19).

North Head

You can take in more of the Sydney Harbour National Park at **North Head**, the harbour mouth's upper jaw, where the short but circuitous Fairfax Walking Track leads to three dramatic lookout points, including the **Fairfax Lookout**. There's a regular #135 **bus** from Manly Wharf (10–14 daily; last bus returns Mon–Fri 3.55pm, Sat & Sun 4.25pm), or if you have your own car (parking $3 per hour, $5 per day) you can drop in en route to the NPWS office (daily 9am–4.30pm), a kilometre or so before the lookouts, to pick up free information leaflets.

Smack bang in the middle of the national park is a military reserve with its own **National Artillery Museum** (Wed, Sat, Sun & public holidays noon–4pm; $6) sited in the historic **North Fort**, a curious system of tunnels built into the headland here during the Crimean Wars in the nineteenth century, as a reaction against fears of a Russian invasion. It takes up to two hours to wander through the tunnels.

The Quarantine Station

The old **Quarantine Station**, on the harbour side of North Head, was used from 1828 until 1984: arriving passengers or crew who had a contagious disease were set down at Spring Cove to serve a spell of isolation at the station, all at the shipping companies' expense. Sydney residents, too, were forced here, most memorably during the plague which broke out in The Rocks in 1900, when 1832 people were quarantined (104 plague victims are buried in the grounds).

The site, its buildings still intact, is now looked after by the NPWS, which offers **guided history tours** (Mon, Wed & Fri–Sun 1.15pm; 1hr 30min–2hr; $11; booking essential on ☏02/9247 5033; ⓦwww.manlyquarantine.com), giving an insight not only into Sydney's immigration history but also the evolution of medical science in the past century and a half, often in gory detail. The night-time **ghost tours** (Wed & Fri–Sun 7.15pm; 3hr 15min; $22 Wed, $27.50 Fri–Sun, including a light supper) are very popular; children under 12 have a less hair-raising, once-weekly Kids Ghost Tour (Fri 5.45pm; 2hr 15min; $13.20, no supper). Unfortunately, no public transport is available for the night-time visits, so without your own vehicle you'll have to catch a taxi.

The tours, which coordinate with the #135 bus from Manly Wharf (bus fare extra), provide the only opportunity to get out to this beautiful isolated harbour spot with its views across to Balmoral Beach. It's so beautiful that a hotel group has proposed to lease and run the site for 45 years and build a three-star hotel there, to local protest; at the same time the station has suffered two recent fires and consequent claims of NPWS mismanagement.

The northern beaches

Beyond Manly, the **northern beaches** continue for 30km up to Barrenjoey Heads and **Palm Beach**. It's a good idea to pick up the excellent free *Sydney's Northern Beaches Map* from the Manly Visitor Centre (see p.135) or check out the associated website, ⓦwww.sydneybeaches.com.au.

The northern beaches can be reached by regular **bus** from Wynyard in the city or from Manly. Bus #190 and #L90 run up the peninsula from Railway Square at Central via Wynyard to Avalon, continuing to Palm Beach via the Pittwater side; change at Avalon for bus #193 to Whale Beach. Bus #L88 goes from Central and Wynyard to Avalon, and the #187 from Milsons Point in The Rocks to Newport.

Freshwater to Bilgola Beach

Immediately north of the long stretch of Manly's North Steyne Beach, **Freshwater**, sitting snugly between two rocky headlands on Queenscliff Bay, is one of the most picturesque of the northern beaches. There's plenty of surf culture around the headland at **Curl Curl**, and a walking track at its northern end, commencing from Huston Parade, will take you above the rocky coastline to the curve of **Dee Why Beach**. Dee Why provides consistently good surf, while its sheltered lagoon makes it popular with families. Beyond the lagoon, windsurfers gather around **Long Reef**, where the point is surrounded by a wide rock shelf pitted with pools and protected as an aquatic reserve – it's well worth a wander to peek at the creatures within.

The long, beautiful sweep of **Collaroy Beach**, with its popular YHA (see p.170), shades into **Narrabeen Beach**, an idyllic spot backed by the extensive, swimmable and fishable **Narrabeen Lakes**, popular with anglers and families; there's also a good campsite here (see p.165). Beyond Narrabeen, **Mona Vale** is a long, straight stretch of beach with a large park behind and a sea pool dividing it from sheltered **Bongin Bongin Bay**, whose headland reserve, and rocks to clamber on, make it ideal for children.

Inland from Mona Vale at Ingleside, the domed **Bahá'í Temple** in extensive gardens on Mona Vale Road (daily 9am–5pm; ⓦ www.bahai.org; bus #195, #196, #285) is one of only seven in the world; the Bahá'í faith teaches the unity of religion, and at Sunday services (11am) there are readings from the texts of the world's main religions.

After Bongin Bongin Bay the Barrenjoey Peninsula begins, with calm Pittwater (see p.140) on its western side and ocean beaches running up its eastern side until it spears into Broken Bay. **Newport** boasts a fine stretch of ocean beach between two rocky headlands; on Sunday crowds gather to listen to live jazz in the beer garden of the *Newport Arms* on Kalinya Street (see p.205), overlooking Heron Cove on Pittwater. Unassuming **Bilgola Beach**, next door to Newport, is one of the prettiest of the northern beaches.

Avalon and Whale beaches

From Bilgola Beach, a trio of Sydney's best beaches, for both surf and scenery, run up the eastern fringe of the mushroom-shaped peninsula: Avalon and Whale Beach are less fashionable than Palm Beach, and are popular surfie territory.

Backed by bush-covered hills, and reached by three kilometres of winding road, small **Avalon Beach** has a secluded feel and is like a slice of paradise on a summer's day. An attractive set of shops and eateries runs perpendicular from the beach on Avalon Parade; *Avalon Beach Cafe* at no. 23 is a good licensed café with a very contemporary feel – it's popular with the travellers who stay nearby at the marvellous hostel (see p.169). The people of Avalon memorably rejected the proposed filming of a series of *Baywatch* in early 1999, though the beach did feature in a tacky *Baywatch* special.

Whale Beach, 8km further north via Barrenjoey Road and Whale Beach Road, is much less of a settlement, with the beach fronted by the inevitable Surf Life Saving Club and the classy *Whale Beach Restaurant* (☎02/9974 4009; closed Mon), which dishes up six-course $85 menus alongside stunning views – it also has a much cheaper, very pleasant garden café.

Palm Beach

You can continue following Whale Beach Road north to reach **Palm Beach** which, living up to its name, is a hangout for the rich and famous: you can even get here by Hollywood-style seaplane from Rose Bay (see p.114). The ocean beach, on the western side of the peninsula, leads a double life as "Summer Bay" in the famous, long-running Aussie soap *Home and Away*, with the picturesque **Barrenjoey Lighthouse** and bushcovered headland – part of Ku-Ring-Gai Chase National Park – regularly in shot.

There's a steep path to the summit of **Barrenjoey Headland** from the car park at the base on the Pittwater side of Palm Beach which the NWPS advises takes 40 minutes, but fit walkers can do in half the time. There is no drinking water or toilets when you reach the top, but you'll be rewarded by a stunning panorama of Palm Beach, Pittwater and the Hawkesbury River. If you want to see inside the lighthouse – built from local sandstone in 1881 and recently renovated – and get an even better view from the top, the NPWS offer weekend and holiday tours (bookings only ℡02/9247 5033; 11.30am, 12.45pm & 2pm; 1hr; $10), which include the lighthouse keeper's cottage.

The bulk of Ku-Ring-Gai Chase National Park is across **Pittwater**, and can be visited by ferry from a wharf on the eastern, Pittwater side of the peninsula beside calm Snapperman Beach. The beach and wharf are surrounded by yachts and a shady park, while across Barrenjoey Road you can **eat** at *Barrenjoey House*, an upmarket guesthouse and restaurant. You can also dine well at *Ancora*, or try the excellent milk bar serving cheap fish and chips, hamburgers and good sandwiches. There are a few interesting **shops** to browse in on Barrenjoey Road, offering Indian clothes and accessories, funky secondhand furniture and women's clothing.

Palm Beach and Hawkesbury River Cruises (℡02/9997 4815, ⓦwww.sydneysceniccruises.com) depart from the wharf at 11am, back at 3.30pm, with a one-hour lunch break at Bobbin Head in Ku-Ring-Gai Chase National Park (cruise $32); they also offer ordinary transport to Patonga one to three times daily – see p.278). Alternatively, the Palm Beach Ferry Service runs from Palm Beach wharf via The Basin to Mackeral Beach, reaching picnicking and camping spots on Pittwater (hourly 9–11am & 1–5pm, plus noon Oct–May; Sat & Sun until 6pm; Fri also 6pm, 7pm & 8pm; $4 one-way, $8 return; ℡02/9918 2747 or 9973 2704, ⓦwww.palmbeachferry.com.au). They also go to Ettalong on the Central Coast (see p.276 for details).

Besides the regular bus services detailed on p.138, you can get to Palm Beach via **minibus** on the Palm Beach Express with Barrenjoey Adventures (℡1800/23 23 30, ⓦwww.sydneytrips.com; $18), who pick up from the city, Kings Cross and eastern beaches accommodation in the morning and steer you in the direction of the *Home and Away* film set, providing a map plus a drink at the *Newport Arms* on the way home in the late afternoon. They can also arrange two-hour kayaking tours on Pittwater ($40) or straight kayak hire ($16.50 per hour), as well as surfing lessons (2hr; $40) and board hire ($20).

The southern and western outskirts

S ydney's mostly unattractive **western suburbs** cover the flat plains heading to the Blue Mountains, the ultimate destination of most travellers heading westward (see p.288). The city's first successful farming area, **Parramatta**, on the Parramatta River, has a cluster of historic colonial buildings not swallowed up by development and there are several **wildlife parks** out this way and in the northwestern suburbs, where the conjunction of the Lane Cove River and the Parramatta River create gorgeous scenery at well-heeled **Woolwich** and **Hunters Hill**, and there's the nearby **Lane Cove National Park**. The **southern suburbs** of Sydney have pockets of beauty and interest at **La Perouse**, and **Botany Bay National Park** and a superb surf beach at **Cronulla**.

South

The southern suburbs of Sydney, arranged around huge **Botany Bay**, are seen as the heartland of red-roofed suburbia – a terracotta sea spied from above as the planes land at **Mascot**. Clive James, the area's most famous son, hails from Kogarah, described as a 1950s suburban wasteland in his tongue-in-cheek *Unreliable Memoirs*. The popular perception of Botany Bay is coloured by its proximity to an airport, a high-security prison (Long Bay), an oil refinery, a container terminal and a sewerage outlet which causes high pollution levels. Yet the surprisingly clean-looking water is fringed by quiet, sandy beaches and the marshlands shelter a profusion of birdlife. Whole areas of the waterfront, at **La Perouse**, with its associations with eighteenth-century French exploration, and on the **Kurnell Peninsula** where Captain Cook first dropped anchor, are designated as part of **Botany Bay National Park**, and large stretches on either side of the Georges River form a State Recreation Area. Beyond Botany Bay lies the beach surburb of **Cronulla** on **Port Hacking**, and the Royal National Park (see p.309) is just across the water, reached by ferry to Bundeena (see p.311).

La Perouse

La Perouse, tucked into the northern shore of Botany Bay where it meets the

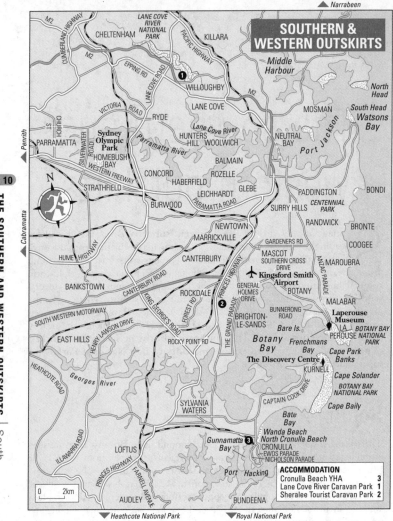

ACCOMMODATION

Cronulla Beach YHA	**3**
Lane Cove River Caravan Park	**1**
Sheralee Tourist Caravan Park	**2**

Pacific Ocean, contains Sydney's oldest Aboriginal settlement, the legacy of a Christian mission. The suburb took its name from the eighteenth-century French explorer, **Laperouse**, who set up camp here for six weeks, briefly and cordially meeting Captain Arthur Phillip, who was making his historic decision to forgo swampy Botany Bay and move on to Port Jackson; after leaving Botany Bay, the Laperouse expedition was never seen again.

The surrounding headlands and foreshore have been incorporated into the northern half of **Botany Bay National Park** (no entry fee; the other half is across Botany Bay on the Kurnell Peninsula, see p.144). A **visitor centre** (℡02/9311 3379), in the same building as the Laperouse Museum, can give details of walks including a fine one past **Congwong Bay Beach** to Henry

Head and its lighthouse (5km round trip). The idyllic verandah of the *Boatshed Cafe*, on the small headland between Congwong and Frenchmans bays, sits right over the water with pelicans floating about below. La Perouse is at its most lively on Sundays (and public holidays) when, following a tradition established at the turn of the twentieth century, Aboriginal people come down to sell boomerangs and other crafts, and demonstrate snake-handling skills and boomerang throwing (from 1.30pm).

Across from the **Frenchmans Bay** beach and park there are a few places **to eat** on Endeavour Avenue, including the popular, casual and affordable *Paris Seafood Cafe* at no. 51; you can eat in, or get fish and chips to take away and devour in the park.

To **get to** La Perouse, catch bus #394 or #399 from Circular Quay via Darlinghurst and Moore Park, or #393 from Railway Square via Surry Hills and Moore Park, or the #L94 express from Circular Quay.

The Laperouse Museum

At least, is there any news of Monsieur de Laperouse?

Louis XVI, about to be guillotined, 1793

A monument erected in 1825 and the excellent NPWS-run **Laperouse Museum** (Wed–Sun 10am–4pm; $5.50), which sits on a grassy headland between the pretty beaches of Congwong Bay and Frenchmans Bay, tell the whole fascinating story. Tracing Laperouse's voyage in great detail, the museum displays are enlivened by relics from the wrecks, exhibits of antique French maps and copies of etchings by the naturalists on board.

The voyage was commissioned by the French king Louis XVI in 1785 as a purely scientific exploration of the Pacific to rival Cook's voyages, and strict instructions were given for Laperouse to "act with great gentleness and humanity towards the different people whom he will visit". After an astonishing three-and-a-half-year journey through South America, the Easter Islands, Hawaii, the northwest coast of America, and past China and Japan to Russia, the *Astrolobe* and the *Boussole* struck disaster – first encountering hostility in the Solomon Islands and then in their doomed sailing from Botany Bay, on March 10, 1788. Their disappearance remained a mystery until 1828, when relics were discovered on Vanikoro in the Solomon Islands; the wrecks themselves were found only in 1958 and 1964.

An additional exhibition here looks at the Aboriginal history and culture of the area.

Bare Island

There are also tours of the nineteenth-century fortifications on **Bare Island** (Sat, Sun & public holidays 12.30pm, 1.30pm, 2.30pm & 3.30pm; $7.70; no booking required, wait at the gate to the island), joined to La Perouse by a walkway; the island featured in *Mission Impossible II*, starring Tom Cruise. Lantern-led twilight tours happen once a month, and include coffee and cake served up in the old barracks (7pm last Sat of month; $13.20; 2hr 30min).

Botany Bay National Park

From La Perouse you can see across Botany Bay to Kurnell and the red buoy marking the spot where Captain James Cook and the crew of the *Endeavour* anchored on April 29, 1770 for an eight-day exploration. Back in England, many refused to believe that the uniquely Australian plants and animals they had recorded actually existed – the kangaroo in particular was thought to be a hoax. **Captain Cook's Landing Place** is now the south head of **Botany Bay National Park**, where the informative **Discovery Centre** (Mon–Fri 10am–4pm, Sat & Sun 9.30am–4.30pm; $7.50 fee per car, otherwise free; ☎02/9668 9111) looks at the wetlands ecology of the park and tells the story of Cook's visit and its implications for Aboriginal people. Indeed the political sensitivity of the spot, which effectively marks the beginning of the decline of an ancient culture, has led to a search for an Aboriginal name for the park: one suggestion was "Gillingarie", from the language of the original Dharawal people of the area, which means "land that belongs to us all", but the name which has been settled on (though the park has not yet been officially renamed) is Kamay-Botany Bay National Park – "Kamay" being the Dharawal name for the bay.

Set aside as a public recreation area in 1899, the heath and woodland is unspoilt and there are some secluded beaches for **swimming**; you may even spot parrots and honeyeaters if you keep your eyes peeled. Cape Solander provides a great vantage point to spot humpback or southern right whales on their migratory path in June or July (call the ranger to find out if there have been any sightings; also see p.125). To get here by **public transport**, take the train to Cronulla and then Kurnell Bus Services route #987 (call ☎02/9524 8977 for times).

Cronulla

On the ocean side of the **Kurnell Peninsula** is Sydney's longest beach: the ten-kilometre stretch begins at **CRONULLA** and continues as deserted, dune-backed **Wanda Beach**. This is prime surfing territory – and the only Sydney beach accessible by train (Sutherland line from Bondi Junction; surfboards carried free). Like Manly (see p.133), Cronulla has both sheltered bay beaches and ocean frontage, situated as it is on a finger of land jutting into **Port Hacking**. Its modern residential and commercial developments can give it the feel of a Gold Coast resort, but at heart it's just a down-to-earth outer suburb, though with the opening of a purpose-built YHA hostel (see p.170) a couple of years ago, travellers have been added into the mix. Life revolves around the beaches and the shopping strip on **Cronulla Street**, which becomes a pedestrianized mall between Kingsway and Purley Place. The train station is at the southern end of this street, along with Cronulla's more interesting shops and a hip young café-bar *Nulla Nulla*, at no. 75, which also has Internet access.

Serious surfing is done at the main beach, **North Cronulla**, straight down Kingsway. It's fronted by a commercial-looking eating precinct and the very modern *Northies* pub across the road, which has outdoor tables. Follow the concreted walkway, **The Esplanade**, south along the rock platform and past a couple of delightful sea pools to reach the smaller, more sheltered and less developed **South Cronulla** beach. Above, shady Cronulla Park, popular with families, slopes down to the water while the Cronulla Sports Complex on The Esplanade has indoor heated pools and a gym (see p.260); next door, the *Cronulla Kiosk* is a magic spot for breakfast or lunch. Behind the Sports Centre, the unpretentious *Cronulla RSL Memorial Club* has stunning ocean views from its wall-to-ceiling windows, which can be enjoyed with a cheap drink or meal. Keep following The Esplanade right around to Darook Park on sheltered **Gunnamatta Bay**, where you can catch a ferry to Bundeena in the Royal National Park (see p.309) from the Tonkin Street Wharf (Tonkin St is just behind the train station if you want to get to it quickly).

West

For over fifty years, Sydney has been sliding ever westwards in a monotonous sprawl of shopping centres, brick-veneer homes and fast-food chains, along the way swallowing up towns and villages, some of which date back to colonial times. The first settlers to explore inland found well-watered, fertile river flats, and quickly established agricultural outposts to support the fledgling colony. **Parramatta**, **Liverpool**, **Penrith** and **Campbelltown**, once separate communities, have now become satellite towns inside Sydney's commuter belt. Yet, despite Sydney's advance, bushwalkers will find there's still plenty of wild west to explore. Three wildlife parks keep suburbia at bay, and the beauty of the **Blue Mountains** (see p.288) is a far cry from the modernity of Sydney. Heading west, however, now starts for many travellers with a visit to the Olympic site at **Homebush Bay**.

Sydney Olympic Park at Homebush Bay

The main focus of the 2000 Olympic events was **Sydney Olympic Park** at **Homebush Bay**, a down-at-heel working-class area in the city's west, far removed from the glamour of Sydney's harbour. Virtually the geographical heart of a city that sprawls westwards, Homebush Bay already had some heavy-duty sporting facilities – the State Sports Centre and the Aquatic Centre – in place. The Sydney Olympic Park Authority is turning Sydney Olympic Park into an entertainment and sporting complex with family-oriented recreation in mind, with events such as outdoor movies and a free, two-day Aboriginal arts festival, Sydney Dreaming, which was inaugurated in mid-November 2002 and will hopefully become an annual event. For details call ☎02/9714 7888 or check ⓦ www.sydneyolympicpark.nsw.gov.au.

To get an overview of the site, there is an **observation centre** on the 17th floor of the *Novotel Hotel* (daily 10am–4pm; $4; ⓦ www.sydneyolympicparkhotels .com.au), on Olympic Boulevard between Telstra Stadium and the Aquatic Centre. The *Novotel* is the social focus of the Olympic Park, with several places to eat and drink including a *McDonald's* and the popular *Homebush Bay Brewery*.

Visiting the sporting venues

The A$470 million Olympic site was centred around the 110,000-seat **Telstra Stadium** (previously called Stadium Australia), the venue for the opening and closing ceremonies, track and field events, and marathon and soccer finals. A recent A$68 million overhaul has reduced the number of seats to 80,000 – a more realistic number for its use as an Australian Rules football, cricket, rugby league, rugby union, soccer and concert venue. Tours of the stadium, with commentary, are available daily in one hour or half-hour versions (hourly 10.30am–3.30pm; 30min tour $15, 1hr $26; turn up at Gate C but check it's a non-event day first by calling ☎02/8765 2360 or finding ⓦ www.telstrastadium.com.au).

Just south of the stadium is the **State Sports Centre** (daily 9am–5pm; ☎02/9763 0111, ⓦ www.sscbay.nsw.gov.au), where you can visit the **NSW Hall of Champions**, devoted to the state's sporting heroes (same hours as centre; free; the Hall of Champions is closed when events are being held at the the State Sports Centre, so call the latter before setting out); and the **Sydney International Aquatic Centre** (April–Oct Mon–Fri 5am–8.45pm, Sat &

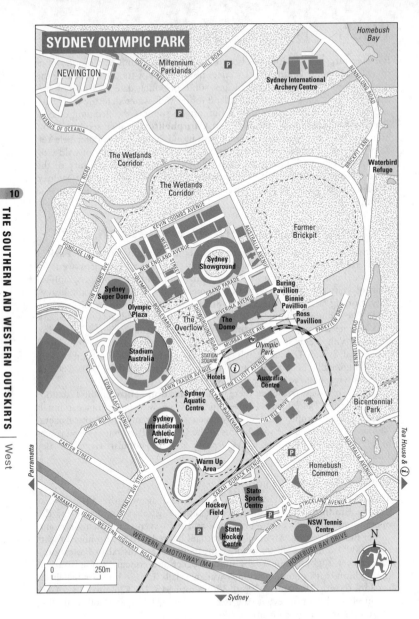

Sun 6am–6.45pm; Nov–March Mon–Fri 5am–8.45pm, Sat & Sun 6am–7.45pm; swim & spa $5.80; guided behind-the-scenes 1hr tours – which also include a swim and spa afterwards in the price – daily noon, 1pm & 2pm, $16; ☎02/9752 3666, ⓦwww.sydneyaquaticcentre.com.au; also see p.261).

On the south side of the site, you can watch tennis tournaments or hire a court at the **Sydney International Tennis Centre** (☎02/8746 0777,

ⓦ www.sydneytennis.com.au), while on the north side, the **Sydney Superdome** (tours Mon–Fri 11am & 3pm; 45min; $15.40; ⓣ02/8765 4321, ⓦ www.superdome.com.au), which hosted the basketball, rhythmic gymnastics and paralympic basketball, is Sydney's basketball stadium. The Royal Agricultural Society Showground, taking up an extensive area at the very north of the site, hosts the annual Easter Show (see p.251).

Bicentennial Park and around

Opposite the Olympic site, is the huge **Bicentennial Park**, opened in 1988; more than half of the expanse is conservation wetlands. The park's own visitor centre (Mon–Fri 10am–4pm, Sat & Sun 9.30am–4.30pm; ⓣ02/9714 7545) at the Australia Avenue entrance can give details of around 8km of cycling and walking tracks, and of the "Explorer Train" that tours the wetlands on Sundays (12.30pm; 1hr 30min; $4.40).

Further north, the site of the green-friendly Athletes' Village consisted mostly of modular dwellings, which have been moved and reused elsewhere; it is now incorporated into a new solar-powered suburb, **Newington**.

The nicest way to **reach** Olympic Park is to take a ferry up the Parramatta River: the **RiverCat** from Circular Quay ($5.40 one-way to Homebush Bay) stops off frequently en route to Parramatta. The second best option is the direct **train** from Central to Olympic Park station (at the centre of Sydney Olympic Park on Dawn Fraser Avenue, a few minutes' walk to the Telstra Stadium on Olympic Boulevard), which runs four times daily on weekdays (otherwise and at weekends change at Lidcombe station from where trains depart every 10min). You can also take a more direct route to some of the venues from

Cuddly Koalas: wildlife parks around Sydney

It is no longer legal to pick up and hold a koala in New South Wales' wildlife parks but photo-opportunity "patting" sessions are still on offer. Several hands-on wildlife experiences on the outskirts of Sydney are listed on p.230. Also see Taronga Zoo (p.121) and the Australian Reptile Park (p.277).

About 10km northwest of Parramatta at **Featherdale Wildlife Park** (217 Kildare Rd, Doonside; daily 9am–5pm; $16; ⓦ www.featherdale.com.au), patting koalas is the special all-day attraction. It's located 30km west of Sydney's city centre off the M4 Motorway between Parramatta and Penrith (see p.230). To get there by public transport, take the train from Central to Blacktown station then bus #725. You can also visit on a WonderBus day tour to the Blue Mountains on its Discovery Tour ($95 including lunch; ⓣ02/9555 9800 or 1800 669 800, ⓦ www.wonderbus.com.au).

The **Koala Park Sanctuary** (daily 9am–5pm; $17; ⓦ www.koalaparksanctuary .com.au) was established as a safe haven for koalas in 1935 and has since opened its gates to wombats, possums, kangaroos and native birds of all kinds. Koala-feeding sessions (daily 10.20am, 11.45am, 2pm & 3pm) are the patting and photo-opportunity times. The Sanctuary is situated 25km north of Sydney, not far from the Pacific Highway on Castle Hill Road, West Pennant Hills; or take the train from Central Station to Pennant Hills then bus #651 or #655 towards Glenorie (Mon–Sat).

At the **Australian Wildlife Park** (daily 9am–5pm; $17.60; ⓦ www.wonderland .com.au), the "meet the animals" experience includes koalas, kangaroos and echidnas. It's next door to the fun park Wonderland Sydney (see p.234) on Wallgrove Road, Rooty Hill, just off the M4 approaching Penrith. Take the train to Rooty Hill station then the Busways service (ⓣ02/9625 8900 for times) from outside the Commonwealth Bank. AAT Kings (ⓣ02/9518 6095; ⓦ www.aatkings.com.au) offer a bus, transfer and admission package for a hefty $64.

△ Telstra Stadium, Sydney Olympic Park at Homebush Bay

Strathfield train station: **buses** #401–#404 run regularly from Strathfield to the Homebush Bay Olympic Centre, the State Sports Centre and the Athletic Centre. Parking is available at several parking stations for $2 per hour ($10 per day); to find out how to pre-book on event days or to check availability, call ☎1900 95 7275 ($0.55 per min).

Tours of the ex-Olympic venues leave from the **Olympic Park Visitor Centre**, set within a pleasant garden at 1 Herb Elliot Avenue, near the train station (daily 9am–5pm; ☎02/9714 7958). The hop-on-hop-off STA-run **Explorer Bus**, with tour commentary, does a circuit of the venues, picking up from the visitor centre (daily 9.17am–3.47pm; every 30min; $10). Another bus, without commentary, the **People Mover** operates continuously between Olympic Park station and the venues (daily 10am–5pm; all-day ticket $11, one-way $2.20, return $5.50). Entry fees to the venues are not included in the price of either bus.

Parramatta

Situated on the Parramatta River, a little over 20km upstream from the harbour mouth, **PARRAMATTA** was the first of Sydney's rural satellites – the first farm settlement in Australia, in fact. The fertile soil of "Rosehill", as it was originally called, saved the fledgling colony from starvation with its first wheat crop of 1789. It's hard to believe today but dotted here and there among the malls and busy roads are a few eighteenth-century public buildings and original settlers' dwellings that warrant a visit if you're interested in Australian history. Today Parramatta is the headquarters of many government agencies and has a multicultural community and a lively restaurant scene on its main drag, Church Street.

You can **stop off** in Parramatta on your way out of Sydney – a rather depressing drive along the ugly and congested Parramatta Road – or endure the dreary thirty-minute suburban train ride from Central Station. But much the most enjoyable way to get here is on the sleek RiverCat **ferry** from Circular Quay up the Parramatta River (1hr; $6.40 one-way). The wharf at Parramatta is on Phillip Street, a couple of blocks away from the helpful visitor centre within the **Parramatta Heritage Centre**, on the corner of Church and Market streets (Mon–Fri 10am–4pm, Sat 9am–1pm, Sun 10.30am–3.30pm; ☎02/9630 3703, ⓦwww.parracity.nsw.gov.au), which hands out free walking route maps which guide you to the places of interest listed below. From the ferry wharf, you can walk to the centre in around ten minutes along the colourful paved Riverside Walk, decorated with Aboriginal motifs and interpretative plaques, which tell the story of the Burramatagal people. Alternatively, STA run a hop-on-hop-off weekend-only **Parramatta Explorer bus**, with commentary, leaving from Parramatta Wharf (Sat & Sun 10am–4.30pm; every 20min; $10), visiting the places mentioned below.

One block south of the visitor centre, the area around the corner of Church and Phillip streets has become something of an "**eat street**" with around twenty cafés and restaurants, from Filipino through Chinese and Malaysian to Japanese, reflecting Parramatta's multicultural mix.

Historic buildings

Parramatta's most important historic feature is the National Trust-owned **Old Government House** (Mon–Fri 10am–4pm, Sat & Sun 10.30am–4pm; last admission 3.30pm; $7) in **Parramatta Park** by the river. To get there turn left onto Marsden Street from the visitors centre, cross the river, then go right onto

Lane Cove River

Some of Sydney's prettiest suburbs lie on the **Lane Cove River**, which runs into the Parramatta River a few kilometres west of the city centre. Exclusive Hunters Hill and Woolwich are found on a peninsula, with the Parramatta River on its southern side and the Lane Cove River on its northern side. As Lane Cove River meanders north from Hunters Hill, a valley of bushland between North Ryde and Chatswood forms the Lane Cove National Park.

Hunters Hill and Woolwich
The impressive houses in **Hunters Hill** and **Woolwich** with beautiful gardens and views over both rivers, provide the setting for an elegant stroll. A great way to explore the area is to take a ferry from Circular Quay to Woolwich's Valentia Street Wharf, then bus #538 up the hill from the wharf to Hunters Hill, and then wander back down Woolwich Road, Gale Street and The Point Road to the wharf. Turn right off Woolwich Road at Elgin Street and follow it down into Clarke Road for Clarke Point Reserve with its lookout. On a Sunday afternoon, you might also like to drop in to look at an example of early Sydney domestic architecture – the tiny, National Trust-owned four-room Vienna Cottage (38 Alexandra St, Hunters Hill; Sun 2pm–4pm, other times by appointment; $4; ☎02/9817 2240, ⊕www.nationaltrust.org.au), built in 1871 with an adjoining park and orchard. At the end of Gale Street, the big old *Woolwich Pier Hotel* is a terrific place to stop for a drink or a simple pub meal (lots of seafood and steaks), with fantastic water views. A walking track runs opposite the hotel through parkland to Woolwich Dock, carved into the sandstone cliff, taking you beyond to Clarkes Point Reserve.

Lane Cove National Park
Lane Cove National Park (☎02/9412 1811; Chatswood CityRail, then bus #550 or #551) offers riverside walking tracks, a wildlife shelter and boat rental. You can camp or stay in en-suite cabins at an adjoining caravan park (see p.165). If you're driving, the park is accessed by Delhi Road, Lane Cove Road or Lady Game Drive.

George Street. Entered through the 1885 gatehouse on O'Connell Street, the park – filled with native trees – rises up to the gracious old Georgian-style building, the oldest remaining public edifice in Australia. It was built between 1799 and 1816 and used as the Viceregal residence until 1855; one wing has been converted into a pleasant teahouse.

The three other main historic attractions are close together: from Parramatta Park, follow Macquarie Street and turn right at its end onto Harris Street. Running off here is Ruse Street, where the aptly named **Experiment Farm Cottage** at 9 Ruse St (Tues–Fri 10.30am–3.30pm, Sat & Sun 11am–3.30pm; $5.50), another National Trust property, was built on the site of the first land grant, given in 1790 to reformed convict James Ruse. On parallel Alice Street, at no. 70, **Elizabeth Farm** (daily 10am–5pm; $7) dates from 1793 and claims to be the oldest surviving home in the country. The farm was built and run by the Macarthurs, who bred the first of the merino sheep that made Australian wealth "ride on a sheep's back"; a small café here serves refreshments. Nearby **Hambledon Cottage**, 63 Hassel St (Wed, Thurs, Sat & Sun 11am–4pm; $3), built in 1824, was part of the Macarthur estate.

Listings

Listings

Accommodation

T here are a tremendous number of places to stay in Sydney, and fierce competition helps keep prices down. Finding somewhere to stay is only a problem during peak holiday periods from Christmas to the end of January, during Mardi Gras in late February/early March and over Easter: at these times you'll definitely need to **book ahead**.

Many places offer a discount for **weekly bookings**, and may also reduce prices considerably during the **low season** (roughly May–Oct, school holidays excepted; see box on p.229 for school vacation times). We've divided our accommodation listings into the following categories: hotels (p.154); B&Bs and guesthouses (p.160); pubs (p.163); and hostels (p.164).

All accommodation is marked on the relevant chapter maps throughout the Guide.

Where to stay

The listings below are arranged by area. For short visits, you'll want to stay in the **city centre** or the immediate vicinity: The Rocks, the CBD and Darling Harbour have the greatest concentration of expensive hotels and now also several backpackers' hostels, while the area around Central Station and Chinatown, known as Haymarket, has some cheaper, more downmarket places and an ever greater concentration of hostels led by the huge YHA. **Kings Cross** is still hanging on as a travellers' centre, with more backpackers' accommodation and cheaper hotels than elsewhere, but it's falling out of favour as travellers head for the new establishments in town to avoid the sleaze and all-night partying. In its favour, lively Kings Cross can make a convenient base as it's only a ten-minute walk from the city and has its own train station. The adjacent suburbs of **Woolloomooloo** and **Potts Point** are moving gradually

---

Accommodation price codes

Rates are highest in December and January and during school holidays. Our listings for hotels, motels and B&Bs feature a code (eg ❶) for the least expensive double room available outside these peak holiday periods. Dorm rates are given in dollars.

❶ Under $50		❺ $95–120	
❷ $50–65		❻ $120–150	
❸ $65–80		❼ $150–200	
❹ $80–95		❽ $200 and over	

upmarket, and what little you lose in terms of accessibility, you gain in peace and quiet. To the west, leafy and more peaceful **Glebe** is another slice of prime backpackers' territory, featuring a large YHA hostel, as well as several other backpackers' places and a number of small guesthouses.

If you're staying longer, consider somewhere further out, on the **North Shore**, for example, where you'll get more for your money and more of a resident's feel for Sydney as a city. **Kirribilli**, **Neutral Bay** or **Cremorne Point** offer some serenity and maybe an affordable water view as well: they're only a short ferry ride from Circular Quay. Large old private hotels out this way are increasingly being converted into guesthouses. **Manly**, tucked away in the northeast corner of the harbour, is a seaside suburb with ocean and harbour beaches and a concentration of hostels as well as more upmarket accommodation, just thirty minutes from Circular Quay by ferry. The **eastern suburbs** also have a couple of great beachside locations close to the city – **Bondi** and **Coogee** – both with hostels and budget accommodation.

Hotels

The term "**hotel**" does not necessarily mean the same in Australia as it does elsewhere in the world – traditionally, an Australian hotel was a pub, a place to drink which also always had rooms above. Today, plenty of **pubs** have cleaned up their act and offer more pleasant accommodation (see listings on p.163). Some budget places use the name **private hotel**, to distinguish themselves from licensed establishments. The city's larger **international hotels** are concentrated in The Rocks and the CBD, and charge around $150 to $250 for a double room, and from $250 to $400 for the best five-star establishments. Rates in Kings Cross and nearby Potts Point and Woolloomooloo are much less expensive, with budget hotels charging around $55 to $90 (cheaper rooms share bathrooms), and three- or four-star hotels from $90 to $160. **Motels**, such as ones we've listed in Glebe and Surry Hills, charge around $100. **Holiday apartments** (see box on pp.158–159) can be very good value for a group, but are generally heavily booked.

The Rocks

Old Sydney Holiday Inn 55 George St ℡02/9252 0524, ⊛www.sydney.holiday -inn.com. Circular Quay CityRail/ferry. In a great location right in the heart of The Rocks, this four-and-a-half-star hotel has eight impressively designed levels of rooms around a central atrium, which creates a remarkable feeling of space. The best rooms have harbour views but the rooftop swimming pool (plus spa and sauna) also gives fantastic vistas. 24hr room service. ❽
Shangri-La 176 Cumberland St ℡02/9250 6000, ⊛www.shangri-la.com. Circular Quay CityRail/ferry. Luxurious five-star hotel on 36 floors with over five hundred rooms – all with fantastic harbour views from huge windows. The best panorama, however, is from the top floor *Horizons Bar* (see p.196).

Facilities include a gym, indoor pool, spa, sauna and several restaurants and bars. Hefty prices start at $450 per night (but cheaper packages are often available). ❽

Circular Quay

Intercontinental 117 Macquarie St ℡02/9230 0200, ⊛www.intercontinental.com. Circular Quay CityRail/ferry. The old sandstone Treasury building forms the lower floors of this 31-storey five-star property, with stunning views of the Botanic Gardens, Opera House and harbour. The café/bar is the perfect place for everything from champagne to afternoon tea, and there are three other eateries, a cigar divan, and a pool and gym on the top floor. Rooms cost from $275 for city view and $345 harbour view. Parking is $25 per night. ❽

City centre

Blacket 70 King St ☎02/9279 3030, ⓦwww.blackethotel.com.au. Town Hall or Wynyard CityRail. Totally stylish four-and-a-half-star small hotel (42 rooms) in a converted nineteenth-century bank, with original features such as the 1850s staircase contrasting with the minimalist modern interiors in muted charcoals, blues and off-whites. Many of the rooms are studios, with designer kitchenettes complete with washing machines and there are also loft suites, two-bedroom apartments and a suite with its own terrace. Rates start from $210 and go up to $410 for the terrace suite. The basement bar, *Minc Lounge*, is very trendy, and there's a smart on-site restaurant where breakfast (included) is served. ❻

Central Park 185 Castlereagh St ☎02/9283 5000, ⓦwww.centralpark.com.au. Town Hall CityRail. A small chic hotel in a great position amid the city bustle (right near the Town Hall and Hyde Park) though rooms remain quiet. Larger rooms have king-size beds and smart and spacious bathrooms with big bathtub and shower. Standard rooms, while smaller, are still spacious but minus the tub; all come with sofa, desk, air-con, kitchenette with sink, toaster, kettle, coffee plunger, crockery, fridge and iron. The small lobby café runs daytime only, but there's a 24hr reception. Light breakfast included. ❼–❽

Corus 7–9 York St ☎02/9274 1222, ⓦwww.corushotels.com.au. Wynyard CityRail. Central position for both the CBD and The Rocks. This 22-storey four-star hotel has the usual motel-style rooms but excels with its spacious studios, which come with kitchen area, CD player, voicemail and a safe. Small gym; 24hr room service; pleasant café-brasserie. Cheaper weekend packages available. Rooms ❼, studios ❽

Grand 30 Hunter St ☎02/9232 3755, ☏9232 1073. Wynyard CityRail. Very well-located budget accommodation occupying several floors above one of Sydney's oldest, but not necessarily nicest, pubs (open until 3am Thurs–Sat). Pub and hotel have quite separate entrances and rooms (all sharing bathrooms), are brightly painted, with colourful bed covers, fridge, kettle, TV, heating and ceiling fans. ❻

Darling Harbour and around

See map p.86 for locations.

Aarons 37 Ultimo Rd, Haymarket ☎02/9281 5555, ⓦwww.aaronshotel.com.au. Central CityRail. Large, three-star hotel right in the heart of Chinatown, with its own modern café downstairs where a light breakfast is available. Comfortable en suites, all with TV and air-con. The least expensive are internal, small and box-like, with skylight only, while the pricier courtyard rooms have their own balconies. Rates are cheaper midweek. Parking $15 per day. ❻

Capitol Square Capitol Square, cnr Campbell and George streets, Haymarket ☎02/9211 8633, ⓦwww.goldspear.com.au. Central CityRail. One of the centre's most affordable four-stars (rooms from $165 but often specials at $110), this place is small enough not to feel impersonal, but the service could be improved. Decor in the rooms is modern if a little chintzy. In an excellent location right next to the Capitol Theatre and cafés, and across from Chinatown; it also has its own restaurant serving Asian and European food. Price includes buffet breakfast. Parking $18. ❼

Carlton Crest 169–179 Thomas St, Haymarket ☎02/9281 6888, ⓦwww.carltonhotels.com.au. Central CityRail. Architecturally interesting, this modern eighteen-storey tower is fronted by the charming nineteenth-century facade of the site's former hospital. In a quiet street but right near Chinatown and the fringes of Darling Harbour. Modern decor plain enough to suit all tastes. Heated outdoor swimming pool and spa; terrace garden with BBQ area; 24hr room service. ❼

The George 700A George St, Haymarket ☎02/9211 1800, ⓦwww.georgehotel.com.au. Central CityRail. Budget private hotel on three floors opposite Chinatown. Though the key deposit and payment-in-advance are off-putting, the bargain-priced rooms – all but two sharing bathrooms – are clean and acceptable. Facilities include a small combined kitchen and TV room and a laundry. ❷–❸

Woolloomooloo

See map p.97 for locations.

W Hotel 6 Cowper Wharf Rd ☎02/9331 9000, ⓦwww.whotels.com. Bus #311 from Circular

Quay CityRail. This luxury boutique hotel, with bags of colourful contemporary style and fantastic service and facilities, is Sydney's hippest. On the redeveloped finger wharf, it couldn't be any closer to the water and is a dream choice for a splurge. One end of the wharf is an apartment complex and a marina, and along its length are restaurants and cafés, including some of Sydney's best. *W Hotel's lobby* is spacious and striking in design, often host to art exhibitions, and its lush *Water Bar* is one of Sydney's trendiest watering holes (see p.203). The rooms have everything including a CD player (with a CD library to choose from), big-screen TV with Internet, cordless phone, writing desk and coffee-maker; loft rooms have a lounge or work area downstairs and bedroom and bath-room upstairs. 24hr room service; day spa, indoor heated pool and gym. Prices from $288 to $363 for a loft room. ❽

Woolloomooloo Waters Apartment Hotel 88 Dowling St ☎02/9358 3100, ⓦwoolloomooloo -waldorf-apartments.com.au. Kings Cross CityRail. Serviced studio, one- two- and three-bedroom apartments with balcony views over Woolloomooloo Bay or the city. Pool, spa and sauna. Light breakfast in the ground-floor *Waldorf Lounge* included. Cheaper weekly rates available. ❼

Surry Hills

BIG 212 Elizabeth St ☎02/9281 6030, ⓦwww.bigonelizabeth.com. Central CityRail. Stylish new 140-bed part-hotel, part-hostel. Lousy location opposite the railway line but just a five- or ten-minute walk to Central Station, Chinatown and Oxford Street. Sunny rooms have extra-thick glass and good curtains to block out noise and light, and contemporary decor in natural colours; all have air-con and TV and video, but no lamps or telephones. The ground-floor lobby, which has a colourful feature wall, designer sofas and Internet terminals, doubles as the common area with a high-tech guest kitchen to the side. An organic café serves breakfast through to dinner (with $5 specials). Four-, six- and eight-bed dorms; rates include linen, towels and breakfast (pancakes, fresh scones and juice). Roof terrace BBQ area. Guest laundry. Dorms $32.50, rooms ❺

City Crown Motel 289 Crown St, cnr Reservoir

Street ☎02/9331 2433, wwww.citycrown motel.com.au. Bus #301– 303 from Circular Quay CityRail or Castlereagh Street, City. A fairly typical motel but in a great location. The en-suite units are air-con with free in-house movies. One self-catering unit, sleeping six, is available. Some parking space (enter on Reservoir Street) at an extra $15 per night. Rooms ❺, apartment ❽

Medina on Crown 359 Crown St ☎02/9360 6666, ⓦwww.medinaapartments.com.au. Bus #301– 303 from Circular Quay CityRail or Castlereagh St, City. Tastefully decorated one- or two-bedroom serviced apartments, with well-equipped kitchen, laundry and balcony, air-con, lounge suite, dining area, TV, video and telephone – all from $287 nightly. There's also an on-site café, gym, sauna, swimming pool and rooftop tennis court. 24hr reception and free covered parking. *Medina* also have a range of apartments around Sydney – see box p.159. ❽

Darlinghurst

Kirketon 229–231 Darlinghurst Rd ☎02/9332 2011, ⓦwww.kirketon.com.au. Kings Cross CityRail. This hotel comes top in the fashion stakes, thanks to the big-name Australian designers who created the swish interiors. Swish bars – including *Fix*– and a top con-temporary restaurant, *Salt* (see p.201 and p.189), beckon on the ground level, while the forty rooms (costing from $220 to $365) boast toiletries by Aveda, mohair throw rugs and CD players. You may feel less beautiful than the staff, but service is slick. Free pass to gym and pool at nearby facilities; free parking; room service. ❽

Paddington

Sullivans 21 Oxford St ☎02/9361 0211, ⓦwww.sullivans.com.au. Bus #378 from Central CityRail; #380 & #382 from Circular Quay CityRail. Medium-sized (64-bed) con-temporary-style private hotel in a trendy location, run by staff tuned into the local scene (they'll even give you a walking tour of Paddington). Comfortable, modern en-suite rooms with TV and telephones. Free (but limited) parking, garden courtyard and swimming pool, in-house movies, free Internet access, free guest bicycles, laundry, 24hr reception, tour-booking service, and a café open for breakfast. **6**

Kings Cross and Potts Point

Bernly Private Hotel 15 Springfield Ave, Kings Cross ☎02/9358 3122, ⊛www.bernlyprivate hotel.com.au. **Kings Cross CityRail.** This clean budget hotel, which also has a few dorms, is just removed from the seedy heart of the Cross but has good security including 24hr reception, and staff are courteous. All private rooms come with TV, sink and fridge, and are available en suite and with air-con or share bathroom. Facilities include a tidy kitchen and TV lounge and a big sunroof with deck chairs and a view of the Harbour Bridge. Good single rates. Dorms $22–25, rooms **2**, en suite **4**

Cross Court 201–203 Brougham St, Kings Cross ☎02/9368 1822, ⊛www .crosscourthotel.com.au. **Kings Cross CityRail.** In a terraced house in a leafy side street, this small, well-run budget hotel offers smartly decorated spacious doubles, some en suite, plus a couple of self-catering apartments and some good-value small singles; all come with fridge, TV, ceiling fans and lamps. Rooms at the rear have fantastic views over the city to the Opera House and the self-catering rooms have big balconies at the front. The drawback is it's near a noisy, late-closing pub. Rooms **3**–**4**, apartments **5**

De Vere 44–46 Macleay St, Potts Point ☎9358 1211, ⊛www.devere.com.au. **Kings Cross CityRail.** Comfortable three-star hotel in a great position, close to cafés and restaurants. Third- and fourth-floor rooms have stunning views of Elizabeth Bay; studios with kitchenette are also available. Some rooms have balconies and all are air-con. There is also a breakfast room (buffet-style), guest laundry and 24hr reception. Rooms **5**, studios **6**

Highfield Private Hotel 166 Victoria St, Kings Cross ☎02/9326 9539, ⊛www.highfield hotel.com. **Kings Cross CityRail.** Swedish-run, very clean, modern and secure budget hotel well located on leafy Victoria Street. Rooms are well equipped with fans, heating and sinks. Three-bed dorms also available. Tiny kitchen/common room with TV, microwave, kettle and toaster; no laundry but there's one a few doors down. Dorms $23, rooms **2**

Hotel 59 59 Bayswater Rd, Kings Cross ☎02/9360 5900, ⊛www.hotel59.com.au. **Kings Cross CityRail.** Small, pleasant hotel (just eight rooms), reminiscent of a European *pensione*, with a friendly owner and small but tastefully decorated air-con rooms. Situated in a quiet leafy location, but close to the action, and with a downstairs café where delicious cooked breakfasts are served (included in the room rate). Very popular, so book in advance. One family room (sleeps four) has a small kitchenette. Outdoor courtyard. Rooms **5**, family room **6**

Macleay Lodge 71 Macleay St, Potts Point ☎02/9368 0660, ⊛www.budgethotels sydney.com. **Kings Cross CityRail.** Don't expect anything fancy from this budget option, but it's perfectly fine and in a fab spot in the midst of Potts Point's café and restaurant scene. All rooms (bar one) share bathrooms and come with sink, plates, cutlery, kettle, fridge and wonky colour TV. Best ones have access to the balcony. **2**

Glebe

Rooftop Motel 146 Glebe Point Rd ☎02/9660 7777, ©reservations@rooftopmotel.com.au. **Bus #431, #433 & #434 from Central CityRail.** Reasonably priced motel right in the heart of Glebe. On three floors (no lift), it has light and spacious, very clean air-con rooms with plain, acceptable decor. Most have a double and a single bed. There's a rooftop courtyard with city views, BBQ and an L-shaped pool. 24hr reception. Parking included. **5**

Unilodge Cnr Bay St and Broadway, near Glebe ☎02/9338 5000, ⊛www.unilodge.com.au. **Bus #431, #433, #434, #438 & #440 from Central CityRail.** Converted from a former department store and retaining some striking original fixtures, this hotel close to Sydney and the University of Technology has a luxury feel, but rates are very reasonable for the facilities. Rooms are all studios, with kitchenettes. There's a small gym, lap-pool, spa and sauna, rooftop running track and BBQ. 24hr reception, and 24hr convenience store and food court in the foyer. Children under 12 free. Parking $6 per day. **6**

The North Shore

Elite Private Hotel 133 Carabella St, Kirribilli ☎02/9929 6365, ⊛www.elitehotel.com.au.

Holiday apartments

The following places rent out **apartments**, generally for a minimum of a week. Expect to pay between $350 and $600 per week, depending on the size and the season; all are completely furnished and equipped – though occasionally you're expected to provide linen and towels: check first. Those listed below are only serviced if stated. Many hotels (some called apartment hotels) have serviced apartments or self-catering studios available at a nightly rate, which we have listed under "Hotels" – see *Coogee Sands Hotel & Apartments* (p.159), *Corus* (p.155), *Cross Court* (p.157), *City Crown Motel* (p.156), *De Vere* (p.157), *Hotel 59* (p.157), *Unilodge* (p.157), *Regents Court* (p.160) and *Y on the Park* (p.166). All hostels also have communal self-catering facilities – see pp.164–170 for details – and on-site vans and cabins at caravan parks are another affordable option (see box, p.165).

Bondi Serviced Apartments 212 Bondi Rd, Bondi ☎02/9387 1122, ⊛www .bondi-serviced-apartments.com.au. Bus #380 & #382 from Bondi Junction CityRail. Good-value serviced motel studio apartments halfway between Bondi Junction and Bondi Beach – a ten-minute walk to either but in the thick of the local shops and on bus routes. Air-conditioned units all have clean modern furniture, TV, telephone, kitchen and a balcony with sea view. There are more stylish recently decorated rooms, and some older-style apartments without views which are cheaper. The rooftop pool has far-off ocean views. Nightly rates $89–129; cheaper rates if you stay a week or more. Parking included.

Enochs Holiday Flats ☎02/9388 1477, ℗9388 1353. Bus #380, #382 & #389 from Bondi Junction CityRail. One-, two- or three-bedroom apartments, all close to Bondi Beach, sleeping four to six people. $500–2000 weekly, depending on the size and season.

Manly National 22 Central Ave, Manly ☎02/9977 6469, ℗9977 3760. Ferry to Manly Wharf. One- and two-bedroom apartments accommodate up to four people; swimming pool; linen not supplied. One-bedroom $575–700 weekly, two-bedroom $745–1045.

Milsons Point CityRail or ferry to Kirribilli Wharf. Bright place surrounded by plants offering good rooms with sink, TV, fridge and kettle; some dearer ones have a harbour view and most share bathrooms. Small communal cooking facility but no laundry; garden courtyard. Cheaper weekly rates. ❸–❹

North Shore 310 Miller St, North Sydney ☎02/9955 1012, ⊛www.smallandunique hotels.com. Bus #207 & #208 from Clarence Street, City and North Sydney CityRail. Two-storey mansion with balconies in a quiet location opposite St Leonards Park but within walking distance (10–15min) of the cafés and restaurants of North Sydney and Crows Nest, or a bus runs from outside. En-suite rooms or family studios sleeping four, all with air-con, TV, fridge, hot drinks and telephone. Shared kitchen and laundry facilities; breakfast available. ❹–❺

Sir Stamford Double Bay 22 Knox St, Double Bay ☎02/9363 0100, ⊛www.stamford.com.au. Ferry to Double Bay Wharf. See map p.113. Mid-sized (73-room) hotel in a great spot amongst the wealthy village atmosphere of Double Bay, surrounded by posh fashion shops, sidewalk cafés and restaurants. Rooms are either romantic with four poster beds or urbane New York-loft style. Pool, spa and sauna. Breakfast included. ❼

Bondi

Bondi Sands 252 Campbell Parade, Bondi Beach ☎02/9365 3703 or 1800 026 634, ⊛www.bondisands.com. Bus #380, #382 & #389 from Bondi Junction CityRail. This budget hotel, straight across from the northern end of the beach, has fantastic views from its oceanfront rooms, and also from its best feature, the rooftop common area, which has a BBQ, and a handy kitchen and laundry. Rooms all share bath-rooms but come with sinks; the pricier oceanfront ones have more furniture and

Medina Executive Apartments Head office, Level 1, 155 Crown St, Surry Hills, ☎02/9360 1699, ⓦwww.medinaapartments.com.au. Upmarket studio or one-, two- and three-bedroom serviced apartments in salubrious locales with resident managers and reception. Various locations in the city include Lee Street near Central Station, Kent Street and Martin Place in the CBD, King Street Wharf at Darling Habour; inner-city and eastern suburbs include Chippendale, Surry Hills (see Medina on Crown, p.156), Paddington, Double Bay, Randwick and Coogee; on the lower North Shore at Crows Nest, and at North Ryde handy for Macquarie University. All include covered parking. From $1085 weekly.

The Park Agency 190 Arden St, Coogee ☎02/9315 7777, ⓦwww.parkagency .com.au. Bus #372 from Central CityRail & #373, #374 & #376 from Circular Quay CityRail. Very friendly staff who offer several spacious well-set-up studio-, one-, two- and three-bedroom apartments near the beach from $700 per week for the smaller units, and $800 and $1000 per week respectively for the two- and three-bedroom options. Much cheaper quarterly leases are also available. All fully furnished including linen, blankets and washing machine.

Raine and Horne 255 Miller St, North Sydney ☎02/9959 5906, ⓦwww .accommodationinsydney.com. Modern executive/upmarket fully furnished apartments fitted out by interior designers, on the leafy North Shore: North Sydney, Kirribilli, Milsons Point and McMahons Point. Studios from $550, one-bed from $650, two-bed from $850, three-bed from $1200 per week. All have TV, video, CD player, telephone; several have spas, pools or gyms. One-off cleaning fee of $120 for studios and one-bedders and $220 for larger apartments.

Sydney City Centre Serviced Apartments 7 Elizabeth St, Martin Place ☎02/9233 6677, ℻9235 3432. Martin Place CityRail. Fully equipped open-plan studio apartments that can sleep up to three people with kitchenette, laundry, TV, video and fans; basic, but in an excellent location. This is a good one for long-stayers, as they rent out for a minimum of nine weeks. $300–390 weekly.

queen-size beds, while the cheaper rooms have tri-bunks (single over a double). Often booked up in advance. ❸

Swiss-Grand Cnr Campbell Parade and Bondi Road, Bondi Beach ☎02/9365 5666, ⓦwww.swissgrand.com.au. Bus #380 & #382 from Bondi Junction CityRail. Four-and-half-star hotel on five floors opposite the beach, which suffers from tacky-looking architec-tural design from the outside (it looks like a big wedding cake) but which is suitably luxurious within. It would want to be, with rates from $300 per night (though cheaper packages are available from $165). All rooms have fab ocean views. Health club, gym, rooftop and indoor pools, two bars and restaurants, free parking. ❻

Coogee

Coogee Bay Boutique Hotel 9 Vicar St, Coogee ☎02/9665 0000, ⓦwww .c-inc.com.au. Bus #372 from Central CityRail

& #373, #374 & #376 from Circular Quay CityRail. New hotel attached to the rear of a pub, the older, sprawling *Coogee Bay Hotel*. Rooms – all with balconies, half with ocean views – look like something from *Vogue Interior*; luxurious touches include marble floors in the bathrooms, minibars, in-room safes and data ports. Cheaper rooms in the old hotel are noisy at weekends but are just as stylish; sev-eral offer splendid water views. Parking included. 24hr reception. The pub has an excellent brasserie, several bars and a nightclub. ❺–❼

Coogee Sands Hotel & Apartments 161 Dolphin St, Coogee ☎02/9665 8588, ⓦwww.coogeesands.com.au. Bus #372 from Central CityRail & #373, #374 & #376 from Circular Quay CityRail. Very pleasant one-, two- and three-bedroom beachside apart-ments (from $270) with all mod cons plus spacious, well-set-up self-catering studios, some with beach views. Studios ❼–❽

Manly Pacific 55 North Steyne, Manly ☎02/9977 7666, ⓦwww.accorhotels.com. Ferry to Manly Wharf. Beachfront, multistoreyed four-star hotel with 24hr reception, room service, spa, sauna, gym and heated rooftop pool. Rooms with an ocean view are pricier. ❽

B&Bs and guesthouses

We have included places that label themselves **boutique hotels** in this section. Generally small and upmarket, they offer more personal service; you'll pay around $100 to $160 for a double en-suite room. **Guesthouses** and **B&Bs**, which are generally cheaper, are often pleasant, renovated old houses; some have shared bathrooms (and possibly kitchen facilities), with prices from around $60 per room up to about $120.

The Rocks

Bed & Breakfast Sydney Harbour 140–142 Cumberland St, The Rocks ☎02/9247 1130, ⓦwww.bedandbreakfastsydney.com. Circular Quay CityRail. This charming brick building close to the start of the Harbour Bridge began life as a boarding house in 1901 and original features include its cedar doors and staircase. The friendly, local-family-run, nine-bedroom B&B has been furnished in period style from Australian hardwood timber recycled from a colonial courthouse. Every room is different; one has a kitchenette and all have top-of-the-range mattresses. The gorgeous garden courtyard is a peaceful haven and although the cooked breakfast can be eaten in the guest sitting room, most people prefer to hang out here – braziers keep it warm in winter. Thick walls and double insulated windows keep out bridge-traffic noise. ❼–❽

The Russell 143A George St ☎02/9241 3543, ⓦwww.therussell.com.au. Circular Quay CityRail/ferry. Charming, small National Trust-listed hotel. Rooms have Colonial-style decor; some are en suite but the small shared bathroom options are very popular – and at $140 are a great price for the area. Other rooms range from $195 to $290, the best with views of the Quay. Sunny central courtyard and a rooftop garden, sitting room and bar, and downstairs restaurant for continental breakfast. ❼–❽

Woollahra

Hughenden 14 Queen St ☎02/9363 4863, ⓦwww.hughendenhotel.com.au. Bus #327 & #389 from Circular Quay CityRail. See map p.94. Old-fashioned Victorian-era guesthouse, built in 1876, situated opposite Centennial Park. Expensive en-suite singles and doubles with rates ranging from $128 to $268, depending on size of room. Hot breakfast included. ❻–❽

Kings Cross and Potts Point

Challis Lodge 21–23 Challis Ave, Potts Point ☎02/9358 5422, ⓦwww.budgethotels sydney.com. Kings Cross CityRail. Budget accommodation in a wonderful old mansion with polished timber floors throughout. Great location on a quiet, tree-filled street that has three good cafés. Best rooms open off the extensive balcony frontage (these are all en suite). All rooms have TV, fridge and sink; there's a laundry but no kitchen. ❷–❹

Regents Court 18 Springfield Ave, Kings Cross ☎02/9358 1533, ⓦwww.regentscourt.com.au. Kings Cross CityRail. Small hotel raved about by international style mags – yet despite lots of arty guests, the place is very friendly and homy. Classic designer furniture, and each studio-style room has a sleek kitchen area. Instead of a bar downstairs, you'll find a well-chosen wine list (at bottle-shop prices), and you can help yourself to coffee and *biscotti*. A small kitchen and BBQ area is located on the rooftop, amongst citrus trees growing in pots. A breakfast of fresh, baked goodies and just-squeezed juice costs extra. Expect to pay between $220 and $255. ❽

Simpsons of Potts Point 8 Challis Ave, Potts Point ☎02/9356 2199, ⓦwww.simpsonspotts

point.com.au. **Kings Cross CityRail**. Small personal hotel, designed in 1892 for a parliamentarian, and beautifully restored. Carpeted and quiet, the three floors of comfortable rooms, all en suite, are furnished with antiques (the guest sitting-room even has a piano); breakfast (included in price) is served in a sunny conservatory. ⑥–⑧

Victoria Court 122 Victoria St, Kings Cross ☎02/9357 3200, ⊚www.victoriacourt.com.au. **Kings Cross CityRail**. Boutique hotel in two interlinked Victorian terraced houses; very tasteful and quiet. En-suite rooms with all mod cons, some with balconies; buffet breakfast included and served in the conservatory. Secure parking a bonus. ⑥

Glebe

Alishan International Guesthouse 100 Glebe Point Rd ☎02/9566 4048, ⊚www.alishan .com.au. Bus #431, #433 & #434 from Central CityRail. Beautifully restored old villa in a handy spot at the bottom of Glebe Point Road, close to Victoria Park pool, Sydney Uni and the shopping centre. En-suite doubles and rather bland but very clean motel-style rooms are available, plus one furnished contrastingly in Japanese fashion (minus an actual futon), as well as some four- and six-bed dorms that are getting a little shabby. Facilities include a kitchen, spa, an airy common room, garden patio and BBQ area. Internet access. Children are most welcome: there's a very spacious family room sleeping six and cots are available. Dorms $27–33, rooms ⑤

Tricketts Bed and Breakfast 270 Glebe Point Rd ☎02/9552 1141, ⊚www.tricketts.com.au. Bus #431, #433 & #434 from Central CityRail. Luxury B&B in an 1880 mansion. En-suite rooms are furnished with antiques and Persian rugs, and the lounge, complete with a billiard table and leather armchairs, was originally a small ballroom. There's also a fully self-contained one-bedroom garden apartment with its own verandah. Delicious, generous and sociable breakfast. ⑦

Newtown

Australian Sunrise Lodge 485 King St ☎02/9550 4999, ⑥9550 4457. **Newtown CityRail**. Inexpensive, tastefully furnished and well-managed small, private hotel with guest kitchen. Sunny single and double rooms, all with TV, fridge and toaster, and en-suite bathroom; most have balconies. Family rooms available. ④–⑥

The North Shore

Cremorne Point Manor 6 Cremorne Rd, Cremorne Point ☎02/9953 7899, ⊚www .cremornepointmanor.com.au. Ferry to **Cremorne Point Wharf**. Huge restored federation-style villa run by a friendly couple, offering very cheap singles (from $52) and good-value doubles. Nearly all rooms are en suite – except for a few singles which do, however, have their own toilet and sink – with TV, fridge, kettle and a fan. Pricier rooms have harbour views as does the guest balcony. One family room has its own kitchen, but there's also a communal kitchen and a laundry. Rate includes continental breakfast. Reception sells bus and ferry passes and books tours. ⑤–⑥

Glenferrie Lodge 12A Carabella St, Kirribilli ☎02/9955 1685, ⊚www.glenferrielodge.com. **Milsons Point CityRail or ferry to Kirribilli Wharf**. A made-over Kirribilli mansion, clean, light and secure with 24hr reception. Rates include a continental breakfast whether you're in a three-share dorm, single, double or family room (all share bathrooms). Some pricier rooms have their own balcony and harbour glimpses but guests can also hang out in the garden and on the guest verandahs. Facilities include a TV lounge, laundry and dining room with free tea and coffee and buffet-style $7 dinner. Dorms $32, rooms ③

Bondi

Ravesi's Cnr Campbell Parade and Hall St ☎02/9365 4422, ⊚www.ravesis.com.au. Bus #380, #382 & #389 from Bondi Junction CityRail. The first-floor restaurant and most rooms at this boutique hotel have glorious ocean views. The facade is pure 1914, but interiors are totally modern: well-thought-out rooms (sixteen in all) have minimalist Asian-style decor and ceiling fans (in addition to air-con). Most of the second-floor rooms have French windows opening onto small balconies; split-level and penthouse suites have spacious ones. Smaller standard rooms don't have views, but offer great value. Large, popular bar at ground level. ⑥–⑧

Gay and lesbian accommodation

Gay men and lesbians won't encounter any problems booking into a regular hotel, but here are several places that are particularly gay-friendly or close to Oxford Street in Darlinghurst. Some other particularly welcoming places in our general listings include *BIG* (p.156), *Coogee Sands Hotel and Apartments* (p.159) *Cross Court* (p.157), *De Vere* (p.157), *Kirketon* (p.156), *Sullivans* (p.156) and *Victoria Court* (p.161). For **flat shares** check the community press and café notice boards.

Brickfield Hill Bed & Breakfast Inn 403 Riley St, Surry Hills ☎02/9211 4886, ⊛www.zipworld.com.au/~fields. Central CityRail or bus #301 from Circular Quay CityRail. See map p.90. In a terraced house, five minutes' walk from Oxford Street and convenient for Surry Hills' diverse cafés, restaurants and bars, this gay-owned and -operated place is definitely for old-fashioned romantics, with antique-style furnished rooms, window drapes, chandelier lights and four poster beds. Mostly male guests. Cheaper rooms share bathrooms. Full cooked breakfast included. Rooms ❺, en suite ❼

Chelsea Guest House 49 Womerah Ave, Darlinghurst ☎02/9380 5994, ⊛www.chelsea.citysearch.com.au. Kings Cross CityRail. See map p.91. In a tastefully decorated terraced house in the leafy residential backstreets of Darlinghurst, this gay-owned guesthouse is in a quiet location but not far from the action. The double rooms are en suite; singles ($94) share bathrooms but have sinks. All rooms have fridge, kettle and TV and the price includes a light breakfast which is served in the courtyard. ❻–❼

Governors on Fitzroy 64 Fitzroy St, Surry Hills ☎02/9331 4652, ⊛www.governors.com.au. Bus #378 from Central CityRail; #380 & #382 from Circular Quay CityRail. See map p.90. Long-established gay B&B in a restored Victorian terrace just a few blocks from Oxford Street. The six guest rooms share two bathrooms but have their own sinks. The rooms are big, well appointed and each has its own style. A full cooked breakfast is served in the dining room or the garden courtyard. Guests – mostly men – can also meet and mingle in the spa. ❻

Manor House Boutique Hotel 86 Flinders St, Darlinghurst ☎02/9380 6633, ⊛www.manorhouse.com.au. Bus #397–#399 from Circular Quay CityRail. See map p.91. This grand mansion was the residence of Sydney's first lord mayor, and is now gay-owned and run mostly for men. Rooms (all en suite) have decks overlooking the courtyard, where there's a heated pool and a spa. Licensed

Coogee

Dive 234 Arden St, Coogee Beach ☎02/9665 5538, ⊛www.divehotel.com.au. Bus #372 from Central CityRail & #373, #374 & #376 from Circular Quay CityRail. Far from living up to its name, this is a wonderful small hotel in a renovated former boarding house opposite the beach. The hall features Art Deco tiling and high, decorative-plaster ceilings and there's a pleasant, bamboo-fringed courtyard (with BBQ and discreet guest laundry) that opens out from a spacious breakfast room for prepare-yourself breakfasts. Two larger rooms at the front have splendid ocean views; one at the back has its own balcony. All have funky little bathrooms, CD players, cable TV, queen-size beds and a handy kitchenette with microwave and crockery. Free Internet access. ❼–❽

Manly

Periwinkle Guesthouse 18–19 East Esplanade ☎02/9977 4668, ⊛www.periwinkle manlycove.com.au. Ferry to Manly Wharf. Pleasant B&B in a turn-of-the-twentieth-century homestead near Manly Cove. Rooms, furnished in Colonial style, have fridge and fans. Several en suites, with big bathtubs to soak in; larger rooms suitable for families. Guest kitchen, BBQ and parking. ❻–❼

Northern beaches

Chateau Sur Mer 124 Pacific Palm Rd, Palm

restaurant and bar. Continental breakfast included. **⑦–⑧**

Medusa 267 Darlinghurst Rd, Darlinghurst ☎02/9331 1000, ⊛www.medusa
.com.au. Kings Cross CityRail. See map p.91. This Victorian-era terrace houses one
of Sydney's swankiest boutique hotels, close to Oxford Street and very popular
with gay guests. Interiors were designed by architect Scott Western, known for his
innovative use of colour, and the furnishings are funky. Luxurious marble
bathrooms, sleek kitchenettes, and stereos and VCRs in the rooms (with plenty of
CDs and videos to choose from). From $270. **⑧**

Oasis on Flinders 106 Flinders St, Darlinghurst ☎02/9331 8791,
⊛www.oasisonflinders.com.au. Bus #397–#399 from Circular Quay CityRail. See
map p.91. Small men-only nudist B&B retreat in a three-storey terraced house. Two
of the guest rooms share a bathroom, the other is en suite; all have ceiling fans and
TV and video. Spa and sundeck in the courtyard. **⑥**

Pelican Private Hotel 411 Bourke St, Darlinghurst ☎02/9331 5344, ⊛www.pelican
privatehotel.iwarp.com. Bus #378 from Central CityRail; #380 & #382 from Circular
Quay CityRail. See map p.91.Recently renovated and redecorated comfortable budget
accommodation in one of Sydney's oldest gay guesthouses, a short walk from Oxford
Street. The mid-nineteenth-century sandstone building's wonderful tree-filled garden is
like an inner-city oasis and the communal kitchen and laundry out here make it even
more of a sociable hangout. Appealing, good-sized, well-furnished rooms have fans,
TV and fridge, but share bathroom facilities. Back rooms overlook the garden; front
rooms are much bigger. Rate includes help-yourself continental breakfast from the
kitchen. At the time of writing, a streetside cafe was being added. **③**

Wattle Private Hotel 108 Oxford St, cnr Palmer Street, Darlinghurst ☎02/9332
4118, ⊛www.sydneywattle.com. Bus #378 from Central CityRail; #380 & #382 from
Circular Quay CityRail. See map p.91. You can't get any closer to the action at this
long-established gay-friendly hotel, with it's stylish café/bistro-cum-reception area,
opening onto the street. There's a cushion room to relax in, and an intimate
basement bar for guests only. The air-con en-suite rooms are very spacious, clean
and well maintained, appointed with everything from telephones to ceiling fans and
desks; decor – dark green carpets, yellow walls and floral bedspreads – is so dated
it actually looks cutely retro. Ask for the room on the roof, which opens out to the
rooftop garden with spectacular city and harbour views. **⑤**

Beach ☎02/9974 4220, ⊛www.palmbeach
chateau.com.au. Bus #L90 from Central CityRail
or Wynyard CityRail. See map p.126. "Chateau"
is not too grand a description for this
Mediterranean-style mansion perched on a
hilltop with ocean views in one of Sydney's
most sought-after streets. The three guest
rooms – the Riveria Suite, St Tropez Suite

and Parisienne Room – are within the family
home, much like a British B&B, but the
friendly English couple who run it don't
intrude on their guests' privacy, and rooms
have their own bathroom and balcony. A
fridge comes stocked with breakfast things
and more goodies arrive on a tray in the
morning. **⑦–⑧**

Pubs

Plenty of **pubs** have cleaned up their act and offer pleasant old-fashioned
rooms, usually sharing bathrooms. The main drawback can be the noise from
the bar; ask for a room well away from the action.

The Rocks

Lord Nelson Brewery Cnr Argyle and Kent

streets ☎02/9251 4044, ⊛www.lordnelson
.com.au. Circular Quay CityRail/ferry. B&B in a
historic pub (see p.196). The ten very

smart Colonial-style rooms are mostly en suite and come with all mod cons. Price varies according to size and position ($120–180): best is the corner room with views of Argyle Street. Meals served in the upmarket brasserie. Breakfast included. **⑤–⑦**

Mercantile 25 George St, The Rocks ☎02/9247 3570, ⓔmerc@tpg.com.au. **Circular Quay CityRail/ferry.** Sydney's best-known Irish pub (see p.196), right on the edge of The Rocks near the Harbour Bridge, has a stash of fab rooms upstairs which are always booked out – get in early. Original features include huge fireplaces in several rooms, all furnished in Colonial style. Several have bathrooms complete with spa baths. Cooked breakfast included. **⑤–⑥**

Palisade 35 Bettington St, Millers Point ☎02/9247 2272, ⓦwww.palisadehotel.com. **Circular Quay CityRail/ferry.** Magnificent tiled pub standing like an observatory over Millers Point; plenty of old-world charm about its bar (no pokies) and its simple, clean and bright shared-bath rooms, some of which have fantastic views over the inner harbour and Harbour Bridge. Also has a stylish, contemporary restaurant (see p.184). **⑤**

Darling Harbour

Glasgow Arms 527 Harris St, Ultimo ☎9211 2354, ⓕ9281 9439. **Central CityRail.** Handy for Darling Harbour, and opposite the Powerhouse Museum, this pleasant pub with courtyard dining (see p.186) has accommodation upstairs. The high-ceilinged rooms are nicely decorated, all air-con and en suite with TV and radio. Bar shuts around 10pm so noise levels aren't a worry. Light breakfast included. **⑥**

Randwick

For pub location see map p.126.

The Royal 2 Perouse Rd, cnr Cuthill St, Randwick ☎02/9399 3006 or 9399 5659, ⓦwww.royalhotel-sydney.com. Bus #372, #374 & #376 from Central CityRail; bus #373 & #377 from Circular Quay CityRail or Oxford Street. Big, historic pub (listed by the National Trust), with fairly upmarket rooms – TV, fridge, fan, telephone, kettle – but all sharing bathrooms. The stylish pub is a very popular drinking hole (open until very late nightly, but there are no live bands to disturb sleepers) and has a traditional Italian restaurant. Good transport to the city and beaches. **③–④**

Hostels

All **hostels** have a laundry, kitchen, and common room with TV unless stated otherwise. Most include linen but sometimes not blankets, which makes it a good idea to travel with a sleeping bag. Office hours are generally restricted, typically 8am–noon and 4.30–6pm, so it's best to call and arrange an arrival time. The **Kings Cross** area, which includes Potts Point and Woolloomooloo, has a heavy concentration of hostels. It's best to avoid the dodgy places that spring up overnight on Darlinghurst Road; nearby leafy Victoria Street and the backstreets of Potts Point offer a more pleasant atmosphere. **Glebe** is a laid-back, inner-city locale, and the beachside hostels at **Bondi**, **Coogee** and **Manly** are popular. Private rooms cost around $50–65 ($70–90 for an en suite), while dorm beds range from $22 to $30. *Alishan Guesthouse* (p.161), *Bernly Private Hotel* (p.157), *BIG* (p.156), *Glenferrie Lodge* and *Highfield Private Hotel* (p.157) also offer dorm beds.

City centre

Sydney Backpackers Victoria House, 7 Wilmot St ☎02/9267 7772 or 1800 88 77 66, ⓦwww.sydneybackpackers.com. **Town Hall CityRail.** Very central choice off the George Street cinema strip (though you could find the alley-like street a bit scary at night).

Clean and spacious, although lacking a little in atmosphere, staff encourage sociability and there's a comfortable, colourful common room with cable TV, books and Internet access. Small but clean kitchen. Four-, eight-, ten- and twelve-bed dorms – one en-suite dorm on every floor – and spacious doubles and twins; all have air-con, cable TV,

Campsites around Sydney

It's possible to camp or stay in a self-catering on-site van or cabin in one of several well-equipped **caravan parks** around Sydney, though your own bed linen is usually required for the latter two options. The three listed below are the closest sites to the centre. Camping will cost around $20–22 for two people in an unpowered site to $24–29 for a powered site.

Lakeside Caravan Park Lake Park Road, Narrabeen, 26km north of the city ☏02/9913 7845, ⊛www.sydneylakeside.com.au. Bus #L90 from Wynyard CityRail and then a 10min walk. See map p.126. Great spot by Narrabeen Lakes on Sydney's northern beaches. Free gas BBQs, camp kitchen and a nearby shop. Minimum two-night stay in cabins (all are en suite). Cabins ❻

Lane Cove River Caravan Park Plassey Road, North Ryde, 14km northwest of the city ☏02/9888 9133, ⊛www.lanecoveriver.com. Bus #550 & #551 from Chatswood CityRail. See map p.141. Wonderful bush location beside Lane Cove National Park, right on the river, in Sydney's northern suburbs. Great facilities include a bush kitchen (with fridge), TV room and swimming pool. En-suite cabins ❹

Sheralee Tourist Caravan Park 88 Bryant St, Rockdale, 13km south of the city ☏02/9567 7161. Rockdale CityRail, then a 10min walk. See map p.141. Small park with camp kitchen. On-site vans ❶

fridges and lockers. Modern but cramped bathrooms. Dorms $21–29, rooms ❹
Wanderers on Kent 477 Kent St ☏02/9267 7718, ⊛www.wanderersonkent.com.au. Town Hall CityRail. This huge modern 360-bed hostel is in a good location near the Town Hall. Though popular, facilities and atmosphere are somewhat lacking and bathrooms and kitchens are inadequate. The bustling reception has a help and job-search desk, Internet lounge, travel agency and attached café and bar. Well-furnished rooms and dorms (four- to ten-bed), are all air-con with shared bathrooms; doubles are fairly small. Rooms over the bar can be noisy. Dorms $24–32, rooms ❹
The Wood Duck Inn 49 William St, East Sydney ☏02/9358 5856 or 1800 110 025, ⊛www.woodduckinn.com.au. Hostel in a great spot right near the Australian Museum and Hyde Park and at the safer city end of William Street. The dingy and seemingly endless flights of concrete steps are off-putting, but you emerge onto a sunny rooftop, the nerve centre of the hostel, with fantastic park and city views. Here you'll find the all-day reception-cum-bar, BBQ, a small but functional kitchen (plenty of fridge space), laundry and a TV/dining room with quirky surfboard table-tops. Accommodation is on the floors below; polished wood floors, citrus-coloured walls, high ceilings, fresh flowers

in the hall. Spacious, clean dorms (mostly four- and six-bed; one en-suite for women) have fans, good mattresses (complete with Aboriginal-motif bed linen) and cage lockers under the bunks; the two doubles have TV. The two young brothers who run the place are friendly and organize lots of activities, including free lifts to the beach. Good security. Dorms $20–24, rooms ❷

Haymarket

See map p.86 for locations.
Footprints Westend 412 Pitt St, Haymarket ☏02/9211 4588 or 1800 013 186, ⊛www.footprintswestend.com.au. Central CityRail. Bright and contemporary hostel in a large renovated hotel close to Chinatown. Common areas are spick-and-span with funky furniture and there's a big modern kitchen and dining area, and a pool table. The young staff are local, clued-up and organize nights out and tours. All rooms have TV and/or mini-fridge while dorms (four- and six-bed) come with lockers; all are en suite and with nice bedding. Many rooms have air-con: request these in summer, as there are no fans. In-house yoga classes ($5), travel centre and small café downstairs. 24hr reception. Dorms $28–30, rooms ❸–❹
Maze Backpackers 417 Pitt St, Haymarket ☏02/9211 5115 or 1800 813 522, ⊛www.nomadsworld.com. Central CityRail.

With charming original 1908 features, this huge hostel is a good choice if you're after a single room ($49); there's sixty of them although they're tiny, cubicle-like and dim. The atmosphere is sociable and all rooms and dorms (four- to six-bed) have ceiling fans, but stark fluoro lighting and shared bathrooms. Doubles have a wardrobe, chair and bedside table. The kitchens are small and lacking in facilities. Daily yoga classes. 24hr reception. Dorms $22–24, rooms ❷

Sydney Central YHA Cnr Pitt St and Rawson Place ☎02/9281 9111, ✉sydcentral@yhansw.org.au. **Central CityRail.** Very successful YHA in a centrally located listed building transformed into a huge and snazzy hostel (over 550 beds); it's still the best choice in the area. Hotel-like facilities but still very sociable. Spacious four- and six-bed dorms and twins sharing bathrooms or en-suite twins and doubles. Wide range of amenities, including employment desk, travel agency, rooftop pool, sauna, and BBQ area. 24hr reception. Licensed bistro plus a cute, very popular basement bar, Scu Bar (see p.200). Some parking available. Maximum stay fourteen days. For longer stays, the YHA also have a "working holidaymaker hostel" at Dulwich Hill (☎02/9550 0054). Dorms $25–31, rooms ❸–❹

wake up! 509 Pitt St, opposite Railway Square ☎02/9264 4121, ⊛www.wakeup.com.au. **Central CityRail.** The latest mega-backpackers' – over five hundred beds – is almost too trendy. The vibrant interior sits inside a characterful turn-of-the-twentieth-century corner building. Very styled, right down to the black-clad staff in the huge intimidating foyer with its banks of Internet terminals. Rooms, which aren't as stylish as you'd expect, are light-filled and well-furnished but only nine doubles are en suite. Dorms (four-, six-, eight- and ten-bed) have lockers. Facilities include a streetside café and an underground late-opening bar and eatery. The best feature is the huge modern kitchen, on a corner with gigantic windows overlooking busy Railway Square. Lockers that you have to pay for are the only storage possibility on checkout day. Dorms $25–30, rooms ❸–❹

Surry Hills

Indy's On Crown 589 Crown St, cnr Cleveland Street, above the *Crown Hotel* ☎02/8300 8804 or 1800 889 449, ⊛www.indysbackpackers.com.au. **Bus #372, #393 & #395 from Central CityRail.** Above a pub but completely separate from it, this hostel is in a very lively locale but has a surprisingly relaxed and homy atmosphere. Cute and sunny kitchen has huge windows overlooking Crown Street; sociable lounge with comfy couches, cable TV and a big table. Indy's attracts working travellers, and most people end up as long-termers here hence the share-house atmosphere. The dorms (four- and six-bed) are better furnished than most and beds are very comfortable; also a couple of sought-after doubles. There's a handy supermarket just across the road, though tea, coffee and muesli (and Internet access) are thrown in for free. Dorms $23, rooms ❸

Kangaroo Bakpak 665 South Dowling St, Surry Hills ☎02/9319 5915, ⊛www.kangaroobakpak.com.au. **Bus #372, #393 & #395 from Central CityRail.** Small, clean and very friendly family-run backpackers' hostel in a terraced house on a major traffic artery – though it's surprisingly calm inside. Spacious dorms (three-, four- or six-bed) are well furnished and most have lockers. There's a BBQ in a green area out back. The owners also run *Gracelands Budget Accommodation* on nearby Cleveland Street, which is aimed more at long-stayers (weekly rates only), with more twins and doubles; rooms are brightly painted and there's a great common room downstairs. Dorms $20–22, rooms ❷

Darlinghurst

Y on the Park 5–11 Wentworth Ave ☎9264 2451, ⊛www.ywca-sydney.com.au. **Museum CityRail.** This YWCA (both sexes welcome) is in a great location just off Oxford Street and near Hyde Park; recently renovated, it's surprisingly stylish and very comfortable. Rooms have all you'd expect in a good hotel, and come in en-suite, share-bathroom or self-catering studio varieties; there are good-value singles ($70) and four-bed dorms (made-up beds with towel, no bunks). There's no common kitchen, but facilities include a café (open 7am–8pm) and a laundry. Rates include a light breakfast. Dorms $29, rooms ❺–❻

Kings Cross and Potts Point

Backpackers Headquarters 79 Bayswater Rd, Kings Cross ☏02/9331 6180, ⊛www.back packershqhostel.com.au. Kings Cross CityRail. Closer to Rushcutters Bay than Kings Cross, this modern, light and clean hostel is well run by very courteous management and benefits from its quieter position. Large, bright, partitioned dorms with firm mattresses, fans, heaters and mirrors; only two doubles. Usual amenities plus big-screen TV in the lounge area, sun deck and BBQ area on the roof. Excellent security. Dorms $22, rooms ❷

Blue Parrot Backpackers 87 Macleay St, Potts Point ☏02/9356 4888, ⊛www.blueparrot .com.au. Kings Cross CityRail. In a great position in the trendy (and quieter) part of Potts Point and with helpful management, this converted mansion is sunny, airy, brightly painted and tastefully furnished. One of its best features is the huge courtyard garden out back with wooden furniture and big shady trees, looking onto a heritage building. Mostly six- and eight-bed dorms but no doubles or twins. Common room has cable TV and gas fire. Dorms $22.

Eva's Backpackers 6–8 Orwell St, Potts Point ☏02/9358 2185, ⊕9358 3259. Kings Cross CityRail. Family-run, safe and friendly hostel away from the clamour of Darlinghurst Road. Colourfully painted, clean rooms, well set up with fans, mirrors and lamps. Dorms are four-, six-, eight- and ten-bed; four-bed dorms are en suite. A bonus is the peaceful rooftop garden with table umbrellas, greenery, BBQ area and fantastic views over The Domain. The guest kitchen/dining room, positioned at street level, feels like a café and is conducive to socializing, though this isn't a "party" hostel. Dorms $22, rooms ❷–❸

Forbes Terrace 153 Forbes St, Woolloomooloo ☏02/9319 4031, ⊕9318 1306, ⊛www .alfredpark.com.au/forbes. Kings Cross CityRail. Small, well-run and clean hostel in a restored terraced house; well positioned just off William Street. Dorms are four- to ten-bed and rooms (all share bathroom) come with TV and fridge. Leafy courtyard with BBQ. Dorms $22, rooms ❹

Funk House 23 Darlinghurst Rd, Kings Cross ☏02/9358 6455 or 1800 247 600, ⊛www.funkhouse.com.au. Kings Cross CityRail. This hostel is plonked in the seedy heart of Kings Cross – though its more sheltered entrance is off the main drag – and with colourful murals on every door and upbeat music playing in the corridors and showers, it attracts travellers who want a place with a pulse. The fairly basic dorms, all with fans, benefit from being only three- or four-bed. Doubles and twins also come with fridge and TV. There are plenty of cheap places to eat nearby, which is just as well as the kitchen is very small and inadequate; a rooftop garden with BBQ extends the cooking possibilites. Also licensed travel agents. 24hr reception. Dorms $20, rooms ❷

Jolly Swagman 27 Orwell St, Kings Cross ☏02/9358 6400, ⊛www.jollyswagman.com.au. Kings Cross CityRail. Big, long-established hostel that's colourful, clean and lively, with good notice boards and work connections. They run their own events with anything from sports teams to pub crawls, and sell tours from the in-house travel centre. Along with the usual communal facilities, every room has its own fridge and lockers; four- to six-bed dorms. A cheap licensed café with Internet access out front. 24hr reception. Dorms $21, rooms ❷

Kanga House 141 Victoria St, Kings Cross ☏02/9357 7897, ⊛www.kangahouse.com.au. Kings Cross CityRail. On leafy Victoria Street, this terraced-house hostel may have fairly ordinary-to-rundown facilities – though it's recently been repainted and carpeted – but the city views are tremendous from the back rooms, taking in the bridge and Opera House. It's still one of the cheapest hostels in the Cross. Dorms are four-, six- and eight-bed and doubles have sink, TV, microwave and fridge. Single rooms and rates available. Dorms $20–22, rooms ❷

The Pink House 6–8 Barncleuth Square, Kings Cross ☏02/9358 1689 or ☏1800 806 385, ⊛www.pinkhouse.com.au. Kings Cross CityRail. Attractive Art Deco mansion with big dorms – four-, six- and eight-bed – and a few doubles (some en suite), with fans and sinks. All the expected amenities plus cable TV in the common room and garden courtyards with BBQ. Friendly, very peaceful place but close to the action. Dorms $22–24, rooms ❷

Rucksack Rest 9 McDonald St, Potts Point ☏02/9358 2348. Kings Cross CityRail. Small (thirty-bed) and well-run private hostel in a lovely old terraced house, exuding a shabby charm, which benefits from a friendly atmosphere, quiet leafy location and on-site local owner-manager. Facilities include a BBQ area and an outdoor kitchen perfect for summer. Dorms are maximum three-bed. Not a party hostel. Dorms $20, rooms ❷

Glebe

Glebe Point YHA 262 Glebe Point Rd ☎02/9692 8418, ⓔglebe@yhansw.org.au. Bus #431, #433 & #434 from Central CityRail. Reliable YHA standard with helpful staff who organize lots of activities. The hostel sleeps just over 150 in a mix of private rooms – no en suites – as well as three-, four- and five-bed dorms. Facilities include the usual plus a TV and video lounge, pool table, Internet access, luggage storage and roof terrace with city views. Dorms $22–24, rooms ❸

Glebe Village Backpackers 256 Glebe Point Rd ☎02/9660 8133 or 1800 801 983, ⓦwww.bakpak.com/glebevillage. Bus #431, #433 & #434 from Central CityRail. Three large old houses with a mellow, sociable atmosphere, feeling more like a guesthouse than a hostel – the generally laid-back guests hang out and socialize in the leafy fairy-lit garden overlooking the street. It's staffed by young locals who know what's going on around town. However, despite attempts at renovation, the place is very shabby, so come here for the scene, not the clean factor. Double and twin rooms as well as four-, six- and ten- or twelve-bed dorms $22–24, rooms ❸

Wattle House Hostel 44 Hereford St ☎02/9552 4997, ⓦwww.wattlehouse.com.au. Bus #431, #433 & #434 from Central CityRail. Top-class small, cosy and clean privately owned hostel in a restored terraced house on a quiet street. Four-bed dorms and well-furnished doubles. Pretty gardens and an outdoor eating area make staying here very pleasant, and there's even a library room. Rates include linen and towels. Very popular, so book in advance. Dorms $25, rooms ❸

Newtown

Billabong Gardens 5–11 Egan St ☎02/9550 3236, ⓦwww.billabonggardens.com.au.

Newtown CityRail. In a quiet street but close to the action, and run by a friendly team, this purpose-built hostel is arranged around a peaceful inner courtyard with swimming pool. It offers clean dorms (up to six-bed; some en suite), and rooms and motel-style en suites. Communal facilities include Internet access. Covered car park $5 per night. Dorms $20–23, rooms ❸–❹

Bondi

Bondi Beachhouse YHA 63 Fletcher St, cnr Dellview Street ☎02/9365 2088, ⓔbondi@intercoast.com.au. Bus #380 & #382 from Bondi Junction CityRail. The YHA's latest beach hostel, a former student boarding house, is actually closer to Tamarama Beach than its namesake Bondi but benefits from being slightly removed from the latter's often overly frenetic atmosphere, and the cafés, restaurants and shops of Bondi Road are close by. International students still form a large slice of its guests, hence the availability of buffet-style breakfasts and dinners at cut-rate prices in the big dining room; there's also a small but very well-equipped guest kitchen. Brightly painted with a sunny internal courtyard with BBQ, and a rooftop deck with fabulous ocean views. Spacious high-ceilinged dorms (four-, six- and eight-bed, with lockers) and rooms – some en suite, with fridges and kettles – all have ceiling fans. Bag a beach-view room which go for the same price. Lots of local info; free surf talks. Dorms $26, rooms ❸–❹

Indy's at Bondi 35A Hall Street, Bondi ☎02/9365 4900, ⓦwww.indysbackpackers .com.au. Bus #380, #382 & #389 from Bondi Junction CityRail. Justifiably popular, this spacious hostel feels like a friendly student house-share – except it's well organized and there's every amenity, including a pool table, outdoor area with seating, excellent security, Internet access, and free use of sporting equipment: surf and snorkelling gear (except surfboards themselves which are for rent), mountain bikes, rollerblades, and various ball games. Social events and trips organized; also travel bookings. The laid-back *Indy's at Coogee* is now only for longer-term stayers of a month or more; enquire here for details. Dorms $26, rooms ❸

Noah's Backpackers 2 Campbell Parade, Bondi Beach ☎02/9365 7100, ⓦwww

.noahsbondibeach.com. **Bus #380 & #382 from Bondi Junction CityRail.** Huge hostel right opposite the beach. Fantastic ocean views from the rooftop deck with a BBQ area and kitchen conveniently on hand. Beach-view rooms with sink, TV, fridge, fan, chair and lockable cupboard. Four-, six- and eight-bed dorms have sinks, lockers, table and chairs. Clean and well run but with cramped bathrooms. On-site bar, TV room (wide-screen TV) and pool table; greasy-spoon food available. Excellent security. Dorms $19–25, rooms ❷

Coogee

Coogee Beachside 178 Coogee Bay Rd, Coogee ☎02/9315 8511, ⊛www.sydneybeach side.com.au. **Bus #372 from Central CityRail & #373, #374 & #376 from Circular Quay CityRail.** Airy old two-storey house, pleasantly renovated, with wooden floors. All rooms and dorms (four- and six-bed) come with TV, in-house videos and fans but share bathrooms. Doubles and family rooms also have fridge. Small well-equipped kitchen but no common room – everyone hangs out in the big sunny back garden. Up the hill from the beach but handy for shops and the supermarket. Dorms $22, rooms ❷

Wizard of Oz Backpackers 172 Coogee Bay Rd, Coogee ☎02/9315 7876, ⊛www.wizard ofoz.com.au. **Bus #372 from Central CityRail & #373, #374 & #376 from Circular Quay CityRail.** Top-class hostel run by a friendly local couple in a big and beautiful Californian-style house with a huge verandah and polished wooden floors. Spacious, vibrantly painted dorms with ceiling fans, and some well-set-up doubles. TV/video room, dining area, modern kitchen, good showers and big pleasant backyard with BBQ. The owners also rent out furnished one-bedroom apartments nearby from $420 per week. Dorms $22–25, rooms ❷–❸

Manly

Boardrider Backpackers 63 The Corso, Manly ☎02/9977 6077, ⊛www.boardrider.com.au. **Ferry to Manly Wharf.** Brand-new hostel in a great spot right on the lively pedestrianized Corso, en route to the surf beach, with a balcony overlooking the action and views to the beach. It can be noisy at night, however, with nearby pubs and clubs creating a racket. Up-to-date facilities including a large, well-equipped modern kitchen and dining area and big common room, lockers in the bedrooms and good security. Several rooms and dorms have balconies, some of which have ocean views, and some private rooms have en suites. There's a rooftop terrace with a BBQ. Dorms $25, rooms ❷

Manly Backpackers Beachside 28 Raglan St, Manly ☎02/9977 3411, ⊛www.manlyback packers.com.au. **Ferry to Manly Wharf.** Well-run modern purpose-built two-storey hostel one block from the surf. Though it's pricier than others in the area, its super-cleanliness, spacious well-equipped kitchen and outside terrace with BBQ make it worth it, and it attracts many long-stayers as one of the few hostels that manages to be both clean and fun. Accommodation is in twin and double rooms – some en suite – plus small three-bed dorms (six-bed is largest). The best dorm is at the front with a balcony. Free use of boogie-boards. Dorms $21, rooms ❷

Manly Beach Resort Backpackers 6 Carlton St, Manly ☎02/9977 4188, ⓔmanlybeachre sort@ozemail.com.au. **Ferry to Manly Wharf.** Located one block from the beach. Clean, four- to eight-bed en-suite dorms and a few very reasonable doubles. There is also a more upmarket motel section. The attached café is good for breakfast. 24hr reception. Dorms $24, hostel rooms ❷, motel rooms B&B ❻

Northern beaches

See map p.126 for locations.

Avalon Beach Hostel 59 Avalon Parade, Avalon ☎02/918 9709, ⓔgunilla@avalonbeach .com.au. **Bus #L88 & #L90 from Central CityRail or Wynyard CityRail.** This hostel has seen better days, but its location and atmosphere still make a stay worthwhile. Located at one of Sydney's best – and most beautiful – surf beaches, this owner-managed hostel is certainly conducive to year-round relaxation, with warming fireplaces, breezy balconies and plenty of greenery and rainbow lorikeets to gaze at. Built mainly of timber, it has a real airy beach-house feel – but the level of cleanliness is not great, and bathroom facilities are severely stretched at

Staying longer

If you're staying for any length of time, you might want to consider a **flat-share** as an alternative to hotels or hostels. The best place to look is in Saturday's real-estate section of the *Sydney Morning Herald* or on café notice boards, especially in King Street in Newtown, Glebe Point Road in Glebe and Hall Street in Bondi Beach (the window of the health-food store at 29 Hall St is crammed with house-share notices aimed at travellers). The average room price in a shared house in these areas is $150 a week (rent is usually two weeks in advance, plus a deposit of four weeks' rent, and you'll normally need to provide at least your own bedroom furniture and linen). Sleeping With The Enemy, 373 Bulwara Rd, Ultimo (☎02/9211 8878, ⍟www.sleepingwiththeenemy.com) organizes travellers' house-shares in inner-city terraced houses; homes are fully equipped, but expect to share a room with up to five others (from $135 per week for a one-month stay, cheaper for longer stays).

peak times. Dorms (four- and six-bed) and rooms have storage area and fans. Boat trips on Pittwater and surfboard rental available. Excellent local work contacts. Dorms $20–22, rooms ❷

Sydney Beachhouse YHA 4 Collaroy St, Collaroy Beach ☎02/9981 1177, ⍟www .sydneybeachouse.com.au. Bus from Manly Ferry Wharf: #151, #155 & #156; bus from Central CityRail and Wynyard CityRail: #L88 & #L90. Purpose-built beachside YHA hostel just across (traffic-laden) Pittwater Road from Collaroy Beach. The hostel has everything, from a heated outdoor swimming pool, sun deck, BBQs, open fireplaces, video lounge to games and pool rooms. There are four- to six-bed dorms plus several doubles (some en suite) and family rooms. You wouldn't base yourself here for your entire Sydney stay as it's too far out – a 45-minute bus ride from the city – and the immediate area isn't very lively, but it's a good base for exploring the northern

beaches – bikes are free for guests – or just relaxing by the beach for a few days. There's free use of surfboards, boogie-boards, and surfing lessons for weekly guests (or try the mechanical surfboard in the common room). Free car parking. Dorms $20–24, rooms ❷

Cronulla

See map p.141 for location.

Cronulla Beach YHA 40 Kingsway, Cronulla ☎9527 7772, ⍟www.cronullabeachyha .com.au. Cronulla CityRail. Newish hostel in this unpretentious, surf-oriented suburb that's well situated for trips to the Royal National Park; the friendly live-in manager offers surf trips to Garie Beach and drop-offs to Wattamolla. Surfboards, kayaks and bicycles for rent. Private rooms are en suite and there are four- and six-bed dorms, all with fans and lockers. Dorms $24, rooms ❷

Eating

S ydney has blossomed into one of the great **restaurant** capitals of the world, and offers a fantastic range of cosmopolitan eateries, covering every imaginable cuisine. Quality is uniformly high, with the freshest produce, meat and seafood always on hand, and a culinary culture of discerning, well-informed diners. The places we've listed below barely scratch the surface of what's available and, as the restaurant scene is highly fashionable, businesses rise in favour, fall in popularity and close down or change names and style at an astonishing rate. For a comprehensive guide, consider investing in the latest edition of *Cheap Eats in Sydney* or the *Sydney Morning Herald Good Food Guide*, both of which try to keep track of the best places in town.

Sydney has several great eat streets, each with a glut of cafés and restaurants: **Victoria Street** and **Oxford Street** in Darlinghurst; **Macleay Street** in Potts Point; **Crown Street** in Surry Hills; **King Street** in Newtown; **Glebe Point Road** in Glebe; the **Darling Street strip** running from Rozelle to Balmain; and on the North Shore, **Military Road**, running from Neutral Bay to Mosman and **Miller Street**, from North Sydney to Cammeray. By the sea, **Bondi Beach**, **Coogee** and **Manly** all have countless café and dining options. All New South Wales's restaurants are nonsmoking, except for at reception areas and outside tables.

Cafés, snacks and light meals

The city boasts a thriving café scene, and a selection of the best can be found along **Victoria Street** in Darlinghurst; **Challis Avenue** in Potts Point; **Glebe Point Road** in Glebe; **King Street** in Newtown; and in the beachside neighbourhoods of **Bondi**, **Bronte** and **Coogee**. Sydney can thank its sizeable Italian population for having elevated **coffee-drinking** to the status of a serious pastime: in the local coffee lingo, a flat white is a cappuccino without the froth; a cafe latte is a milkier version served in a glass; a long black is a regular black coffee; and a short black is an espresso (transformed by a splash of milk into a *macchiato*). Any of these will cost $2.50–3. Most cafés are open for breakfast, particularly those in the beach areas, and some stay open until the small hours. All those listed are inexpensive, many serving main courses for $12 or less.

The Rocks

There isn't really a café culture in **The Rocks** and it's hard to find a decent cup of coffee or a reasonably priced light meal or snack. Pubs rule supreme, and many of those in The Rocks serve great light meals and bar snacks at lunchtime; see p.196 of the "Drinking" chapter, where we've

African *Le Kilimanjaro* (p.191).

Belgian *Epoque Belgian Beer Café* (p.192)

Chinese *BBQ King* (p.186), *Billy Kwong* (p.187), *fu-manchu* (p.177), *Golden Century* (p.186), *Kam Fook* (p.186), *Mother Chu's Vegetarian Kitchen* (p.187), *Tai Pei* (p.176).

Contemporary Australian *Barzura* (p.182), *Bayswater Brasserie* (p.190), *Blackbird* (p.186), *Beach Pit* (p.193), *Brazil Café* (p.183), *Bathers Pavilion* (p.191), *Cafe Otto* (p.180), *Café Sydney* (p.185), *Hugo's* (p.192), *Le Kiosk* (p.194), *MG Garage* (p.187), *Rockpool* (p.184), *Sean's Panroma* (p.193), *Tetsuya's* (p.186), *Watermark* (p.192), *Wharf Restaurant* (p.184).

Bistros & pubs *Coogee Bay Hotel* (p.193), *Grand National* (p.190), *Venice Beach* (p.190), *Paddington Inn* (p.190), *Palisade* (p.184), *Royal Hotel Restaurant* (p.190).

French/French fusion *Bistro Lulu* (p.189), *Le Petit Crème* (p.178), *Guillaume at Bennelong* (p.185), *Onde* (p.189), *Tetsuya's* (p.186).

Fish and seafood *Balkan Seafood* (p.189), *Fishface* (p.189), *Fish Market Cafe* (p.175), *Just Hooked* (p.192), *Doyles* (p.192, p.185 & p.187), *Mohr Fish* (p.176), *Rockpool* (p.184), *Sydney Cove Oyster Bar* (p.174).

German *Una's* (p.178), *Lowenbrau Keller* (p.196).

Greek *Steki Taverna* (p.191), *Gertrude & Alice Cafe Bookstore* (p.181).

Indian *Indian Empire* (p.192), *Dakhni* (p.190), *Dabha House* (p.187), *Govinda's* (p.189), *Maya Masala* (p.176)

Indonesian *Sari Rasa* (p.193)

Israeli *Yulla* (p.193)

Italian *Anna & Aldo's* (p.191), *Bar Baba* (p.180), *Bar Coluzzi* (p.177), *Bar Italia* (p.180), *Bar Milazzo* ("City coffee hits" box p.175), *Bambini Espresso* ("City coffee hits" box on p.175), *Caffe Corto* ("City coffee hits" box p.175), *bel mondo* (p.184), *Bondi Tratt* (p.192), *Bill and Toni* (p.174), *Cesare's No Names* (p.190), *Delizia* (p.175), *Frattini* (p.191), *No Names* (p.193), *Otto* (p.204), *QVB Jet* (p.175), *Roma Caffe* (p.176), *Rossini* (p.173), *Tutto* (p.191).

Japanese *Ippon Sushi* (p.176), *Jipang* (p.193), *Minami* (p.179), *Sushi Suma* (p.189), *Tetsuya's* (186), *wagamama* (p.175).

Juice/heath *Direction of Cure* (p.182), *Sejuiced* (p.182). Also see vegetarian box p.185.

Middle Eastern *Abdul's* (p.176), *Almustafa* (p.187), *El Bahsa* (p.180), *Erciyes* (p.187)

Malaysian/Singaporean *The Malaya* (p.186), *McLuksa* (see "Food courts" box on p.177).

North African *Alhambra* (p.193), *Out of Africa* (p.194).

Native Australian *Edna's Table* (p.185), *Lillipilli at The Rocks* (p.184).

Nepalese *Nepalese Kitchen* (p.187).

Noodles See box p.175

Pies See box p.174

Pizza *Arthurs* (p.178), *Blackbird* (p.186), *La Disfada* (p.191), *Gelbison* (p.192), *Gourmet Pizza Kitchen* (p.192), *Macleays* (p.179), *The Pig and the Olive* (p.190).

Spanish/Latin American *Alhambra Café* (p.193), *Cafe Hernandez* (p.178), *Capitan Torres* (p.186), *La Grand Taverna* (p.186).

Thai *Longgrain* (p.187), *Prasit's* (p.189), *Sailors Thai* (p.184), *Somi's* (p.194), *Sumalee* (p.191), *Thai Potong* (p.191), *Wok Station* (p.179), *Thai Panic* (p.224).

Steak *Brooklyn Hotel* (p.198), *Forresters* (p.187).

Vegetarian See box p.185

Vietnamese *Chu Bay* (p.189), *Old Saigon* (p.191), *Pho Pasteur* (p.176), *Than Binh* (p.191 & box p.175).

mentioned the kind of meals served. It's also only a hop, skip and jump from Circular Quay, where there's a much wider choice.

Sydney Dance Cafe Pier 4, Hickson Rd, Millers Point. Circular Quay CityRail/ferry. On the ground level of the Wharf Theatre complex, home to the Sydney Dance Company and several other dance, theatre and arts organizations, this is a relaxing spot for a coffee or a light meal with water views and an interesting, arty crew of fellow customers. Mon–Sat 8am–8pm.

Circular Quay and the Opera House

In addition to these listings, there's a wide choice of snacks and light meals at the Gateway Gourmet Food Court (see "Food courts", box, p.171).

City Extra East Podium, Circular Quay. Circular Quay CityRail/ferry. Licensed 24hr coffee shop with a stop-the-press theme – and of course, newspapers for customers to read. Breakfast is served round the clock plus burgers, pasta, steaks and desserts. Quayside seating too.

Obelisk Café Shop 1, 7 Macquarie Place. Circular Quay CityRail/ferry. Stylish outdoor café close to Circular Quay. Fab spot on a historic square with big shady trees, or you can sit inside on stools and listen to jazzy music on a wet day. Attracts a working crowd who plunge in for great coffee, *pizzetta*, focaccia, pasta, steak sandwiches and healthy filled wraps. Mon–Fri 6am–5pm.

Rossini Between wharves 5 and 6, Circular Quay. Circular Quay CityRail/ferry. Eat quality Italian fast food alfresco while you're

12

EATING | Cafés, snacks and light meals

Ethnic eats

Sydney features many diverse enclaves, many of them in far-flung suburbs, where you can sample authentic cuisines from around the world and buy imported goods from local shops and delis. Where the areas are detailed in the text, we've given page references; where they are not, we have provided transport details to point you in the right direction.

African On King Street, Newtown (see p.105).

Chinese In the Chinatown section of Haymarket (see p.85) and in Ashfield (Ashfield CityRail).

Eastern European Around Hall Street, Bondi (p.126).

Indian On Elizabeth Street and Cleveland Street in Surry Hills (p.89) and on King Street, St Peters (p.105).

Indonesian On Anzac Parade, Kingsford and Kensington (bus #393 or #395 from Central CityRail);

Italian On Stanley Street in East Sydney (p.91), Norton Street in Leichhardt (p.107), Ramsay Street in Haberfield (p.108) and Great North Road, Five Dock (bus #438 from Central CityRail).

Japanese There's a concentration at Bondi Junction (Bondi Junction CityRail), Neutral Bay (see p.121) and Crows Nest (bus #273 from WynyardCityRail).

Jewish On and around Hall Street, Bondi (p.126).

Korean In Campsie (Campsie CityRail).

Lebanese On Elizabeth Street and Cleveland Street in Surry Hills; in Punchbowl (Punchbowl CityRail) and Lakemba (Lakemba CityRail).

Portuguese At New Canterbury Rd, Petersham (Petersham CityRail); Greek at Marrickville (see p.107), Earlwood (bus #409 from Ashfield CityRail), and Brighton Le Sands (bus #302 or #303 from Circular Quay CityRail).

Spanish On Liverpool Street in the city (p.69);

Turkish On Elizabeth Street and Cleveland Street in Surry Hills (p.89).

Vietnamese Concentrated in Cabramatta, far to the west of the CBD (fourteen stops from Central CityRail); there are some superb restaurants clustered along Park Road and John Street, just west of Cabramatta Station.

waiting for a ferry. *Panzerotto* – big, cinnamon-flavoured and ricotta-filled doughnuts – are a speciality. Pricey but excellent coffee. Licensed. Daily 7am–11pm.

Sydney Cove Oyster Bar Circular Quay East. Circular Quay CityRail/ferry. It's hard not to be lured into this place on a stroll to the Opera House. The quaint little building housing the bar and kitchen was once a public toilet, but don't let that put you off. Outdoor tables provide a magical location to sample Sydney Rock Pacific oysters (around $15.50 for half a dozen). There's other seafood as well, or just come for coffee, cake and the view. Daily 11am–11pm.

Royal Botanical Gardens to Macquarie Street

There are also great cafés in this area at the Hyde Park Barracks (see p.66), the old Mint building (see p.66), and within the Botanical Gardens (see p.62) and the Art Gallery of NSW (see p.67).

Glasshouse Café Level 7, State Library, Macquarie St. Martin Place CityRail. Airy and with masses of plants, this glass-roofed space at the State Library is a relaxing spot for lunch or just coffee and cake. Mon–Fri 10am–4.30pm, Sat & Sun 11am–3.30pm.

Pavilion on the Park 1 Art Gallery Rd. Martin Place or St James CityRail. Right opposite the Art Gallery of New South Wales and just by the Botanical Gardens entrance, this is a great place to take a break from sightseeing – there's an outdoor kiosk, a café section and an upmarket restaurant (bookings ☎02/9232 1322) and great views of the city too. Licensed. Restaurant moderate to expensive. Café daily 9am–5pm; restaurant lunch daily except Sun.

City Centre

Nearly all of the **city centre** pubs and bars serve great light meals and bar snacks at lunchtime; see the listings on pp.197–199. There are also several cosmopolitan food courts which are a great source of cheap and tasty snacks and light meals (see "Food courts" box, p.177), and loads of great little Italian espresso bars (see box "City coffee hits" opposite). You can also get scrummy snacks and light meals from the wonderful David Jones Food Hall (see "Shopping", p.241).

Alexanders 550 George St, City. Town Hall CityRail. A 24hr licensed café close to the cinemas, which only closes its doors Mon 2am–8am. The continental food – cakes, coffee, steaks and pasta – is pricey, but it's handy for night owls.

Bill and Toni 74 Stanley St, East Sydney. Museum CityRail. Atmospheric, cheap Italian restaurant with balcony tables. There's generally a queue to get in. The café downstairs is a popular Stanley St local (daily 7am–midnight) and serves tasty Italian sandwiches. BYO.

Bodhi in the Park Cook and Phillip Park, College St, East Sydney. Museum CityRail. (another branch at Capitol Square, 730–742 George St, Haymarket). Top-notch Chinese vegetarian and vegan food, with the focus on delicious *yum cha* which is served daily until 5pm. Organic and biodynamic produce is used. Licensed. Daily 11am–11pm.

The great Australian pie

Before all the sophisticated "modern Australian cuisine" hit the scene, the humble Aussie **meat pie** ruled, preferably "with sauce" (tomato ketchup). Many old-fashioned pubs have a hot oven warming up the pies all day, and they are a staple at milk bars and bakeries. The classic location to have a "pie with sauce" is on the Manly ferry or at the all-night *Harry's Café de Wheels* (p.179) where pea and pie floater versions are available. And of course, the pie chain *Shakespeare's* reckon they serve up "the best pies on the planet". With a pie of the week for around $3.50, this place is a cheap eat par excellence for a whole range of savoury and sweet pies plus muffins and coffee. *Shakespeare's* locations include 283 King St, Newtown (Newtown CityRail; Mon–Wed 8am–9pm, Thurs to midnight, Fri & Sat 8am–2am, Sun 10am–9pm), Neutral Bay and Manly (see maps on pp.104, 118–119 and 134).

QVB Jet Cnr York and Druitt streets. Town Hall CityRail. On the corner of the QVB building looking across to the Town Hall, with big windows and outdoor seating providing people-watching opportunities, this is a very lively Italian café/bar. The coffee is predictably excellent, and the menu is big on breakfast. The rest of the day choose from pasta, risotto and soups, salads and sandwiches. Licensed. Mon–Fri 8am–10pm, Sat 9am–10pm.

Darling Harbour and around

Also check out the "Food courts" box for several great Asian-style food courts around Chinatown.

Fish Market Cafe Sydney Fish Markets, Pyrmont. Fish Market Light Rail. Come and watch the early morning fish-market action (or just head here after a very late night out) and grab breakfast and an excellent coffee at this Italian-run café. You can eat inexpensive fresh fish and chips later in the day. Mon–Fri 4am–4pm, Sat & Sun 5am–5pm. See map on p.79.

wagamama 10/45 Lime St, King St Wharf. Town Hall CityRail. Huge high-tech Japanese noodle bar based on the London model: young trendy staff equipped with a computerized ordering system, communal

tables and no bookings (which can mean long queues), though service and turnover is fast. No desserts. Licensed but a basic drinks list, which includes sake. Mon–Thurs & Sun noon to 11pm, Fri & Sat noon to midnight. See map on p.79.

Haymarket

Bella Ciao Shop 5, 187 Thomas St, cnr Quay St, Haymarket. Central CityRail. A café culture spot in Chinatown is a find: colourful 1950s fish-shop feel, huge windows and funky music. Breakfast until 2pm – blueberry bagels with fresh ricotta and Hank's legendary jam go well with the excellent Italian coffee. Lunch on woodfired bread sandwiches, soups and salads; very reasonable prices. Mon–Fri 7am–6pm, Sat 8.30am–2pm.

Chinese Noodle Restaurant 8 Quay St, Haymarket. Central CityRail. Scrumptious and very fresh dumplings and noodles, northwest China style. Very cheap. BYO. Daily 11am–9pm.

Delizia 148 Elizabeth St, City. Museum CityRail. A high-ceilinged Italian deli-café bustling with black-clad staff: the gleaming glass counters groan with pasta and the shelves are stacked with gourmet goods. It looks pricey, but there's nothing over $10 on the menu. With a secondhand

City coffee hits

Italian **espresso bars** are all over the CBD, many with outside seating for sunny days (and smokers ...), and braziers for the winter. We've listed three of the best below. See map of City Centre for locations.

Bar Milazzo 379 Pitt St. Museum or Town Hall CityRail. Mon–Fri 7am–6pm.

Bambini Espresso 299 Elizabeth St. Museum or Town Hall CityRail. Mon–Fri 7am–6pm.

Caffe Corto 10 Barrack St. Martin Place CityRail. Mon–Fri 7am–4.30pm.

literary bookshop tucked out the back (an offshoot of Bondi's popular *Gertrude and Alice* – see p.181), there's nothing else like it the city; the tables and lounge chairs amongst the bookshelves create a private haven. Popular with lawyers and judges from the courts opposite, and everyone else. Weekend breakfasts here are very popular – most other city cafés are closed then. Mon–Fri 7am–6pm, Sat & Sun 8am–4pm.

Ippon Sushi 404 Sussex St, Haymarket. Central CityRail. Fun, inexpensive Japanese sushi train downstairs, with a revolving choice of delectables ($2–5.50. Licensed and BYO. Daily 11am–11pm.

Pho Pasteur 709 George St, Haymarket. Central CityRail. The speciality at this very popular Vietnamese cheap eat is *pho* – rice noodle soup, served with fresh herbs, lemon wedges and bean sprouts. Nearly all the people crowding out the formica tables are Asian, a testament to the food and the prices – most noodles (mainly pork, chicken and beef) are $7, and there's nothing over $10. A refreshing pot of jasmine tea is included. BYO. Daily 10am–9pm.

Roma Caffe 191 Hay St, Haymarket. Central CityRail. The *Roma* has been in the area for over 35 years offering fabulous coffee, great breakfasts and a huge gleaming display of wicked Italian desserts, plus delicious focaccia and fresh pasta – try the home-made pumpkin tortellini. Mon–Sat 8am–6pm.

Tai Pei Shop 2, Prince Centre, 8 Quay St, Haymarket. Central CityRail. Tiny, congenial and cheap Taiwanese eatery offering generous servings; great dumplings, and very tasty Mama Pho's tofu (with pork – like most things on the menu). Popular with students from the nearby University of Technology. Daily 11am–9pm.

Inner east

The **inner east** has probably the greatest concentration of cafés and also several late-night and all-night options (see box "Eating around the clock", p.178). Its equally vast range of pubs and bars also serve up great light meals : see p.200 of "Drinking".

Surry Hills

Abdul's 563 Elizabeth St, cnr Cleveland St. Bus #393, #395 from Central CityRail. This cheap Lebanese place is a late-night, post-pub institution. Eat-in or takeaway; belly-dancing Fri & Sat nights. BYO. Daily 10am–midnight (Thurs–Sat until 2am).

Café Niki 544 Bourke St, Surry Hills. Bus #301–#303 from Circular Quay CityRail. Corner café with a relaxed ambience, which manages to feel groovy but not pretentious. Cheap and delicious food – best are their soups and focaccia – plus excellent coffee. Mon–Fri 7am–10pm, Sat 8am–10pm, Sun 8am–4pm.

La Passion du Fruit 633 Bourke St, cnr Devonshire St, Surry Hills. Bus #301–#303 from Circular Quay CityRail. One of the best brunches in town is served at this bright and friendly place. Also interesting salads, sandwiches and light meals, and some of the freshest fruit drinks and frappés in town. Mon–Sat 8am–5pm.

Maltese Cafe 310 Crown St, Surry Hills. Bus #378 from Central CityRail; bus #380 & #382 from Circular Quay CityRail. Café just off Oxford Street known for its delicious Maltese *pastizzi* – flaky pastry pockets of ricotta cheese, plain or with meat, spinach or peas – to eat in or take away. They're ridiculously cheap (70c each) and satisfying. Mon 10am–6pm, Tues–Sun 8am–6pm.

Maya Masala 470 Cleveland St, Surry Hills. Bus #393, #395 from Central CityRail. Fantastic and very cheap authentic South Indian vegetarian food served all day in a bustling cafeteria-style interior. Popular with local Indian families, especially at weekends for the chaat menu. BYO. Daily 10am–10.30pm.

Mohr Fish 202 Devonshire St, Surry Hills. Central CityRail. This tiny but stylish fish-and-chip bar, with stools and tiled walls, packs in the customers. Inexpensive. BYO. Daily 10am–10pm.

Vesbar 368 Crown St, Surry Hills. Cool, fun and friendly Italian café and pizzeria that doubles as a vespa showroom with a repair garage attached. Daily 10am–10pm.

Darlinghurst

Darlinghurst also boasts a branch of the gourmet burger joint, *Burgerman*

Food courts

Some of the best cheap eats in Sydney, with hot dishes from $6–9, are to be had in the multitude of cosmopolitan **food courts** in city shopping malls. Those around Chinatown are particularly good, serving everything from Japanese to Vietnamese, and of course Chinese food.

Dixon House Food Court Off Dixon St, basement level, corner of Little Hay and Dixon streets. Central CityRail. Chinese noodles, Vietnamese, Thai, Indonesian, Malaysian, Japanese and Korean plus a bar. Daily 10.30am–8.30pm. See map, p.86.

Gateway Gourmet Quayside Shopping Centre, ground floor, bounded by Alfred St, Reiby Pl and Loftus St, Circular Quay. Circular Quay Cityrail/ferry. Pizza, pasta, seafood, patisserie, healthy sandwiches and Asian food. Business hours See map, p.56.

Harbour Plaza Corner Factory and Dixon streets, Haymarket. Central CityRail. Food court in basement. More lacklustre than other Chinatown food courts. Malaysian, Japanese, Korean, Indonesian, and Vietnamese. Licensed bar. Daily 10am–1pm. See map, p.86.

Hunter Connection 310 George St, City. Wynyard CityRail. Fantastic and frenetically busy food court on the first floor with a small supermarket, sushi bar, fresh juice shop, sandwiches, noodles, seafood, pasta, Asian buffet, plus Mexican, Filipino, Malaysian and Chinese food. Business hours. See map, p.70.

Market City Food Court Level 3, Market City Shopping Centre, corner Quay and Thomas streets, Haymarket. Central CityRail. Apart from one Italian place they are all Asian – Vietnamese, Chinese, Japanese, Thai and Singaporean. The best stall is *McLuksa* – the spicy coconut noodle soups which give it its name are delicious. Daily 8am–10pm. See map, p.86.

Sydney Central 450 George St, City. Town Hall CityRail. Buzzing basement food court beneath Grace Bros department store. Enter from Pitt St Mall or via the QVB. Mon–Wed 7am–7pm, Thurs 7am–10pm, Sat 8am–7pm, Sun 10am–6pm. See map, p.70.

Sussex Centre 401 Sussex St, Haymarket. Central CityRail. Food court on first floor. Vietnamese, Japanese, several Chinese. Delicious natural ice cream. Daily 10am–9pm. See map, p.86.

(see p.181), and you can get cheap but fresh noodles nearby at *Noodle King* (see "Noodles" on p.175).

Bar Coluzzi 322 Victoria St, Darlinghurst. Kings Cross CityRail. Famous Italian café: tiny and always packed with a characterful crew of regulars spilling out onto stools on the pavement. The trendier, though equally tiny and very popular *Latteria* is next door. Daily 5am–7.30pm.

Betty's Soup Kitchen 84 Oxford St, Darlinghurst. Bus #378 from Central CityRail; bus #380 & #382 from Circular Quay CityRail. Soup is the speciality ($6.50), and makes for a cheap meal, served with damper, but there are also all the simple things your fantasy granny might serve: stews, sausages or fish fingers with mash, pasta, salads and desserts too. Yummy home-made ginger beer or lemonade. Nothing over $11. BYO. Daily noon to 10.30pm (11.30pm Fri & Sat).

bills 433 Liverpool St, Darlinghurst. Kings Cross CityRail. This sunny corner café in the quieter backstreets of Darlinghurst is one of Sydney's favourite breakfast spots. Top three on the breakfast list are the ricotta hotcakes, the huge muffins and the deliciously creamy scrambled eggs. Breakfast isn't cheap, at $14.50 for the hotcakes, but definitely worth it; the mod Oz lunch costs $17.50–23. It feels like a stylish restaurant with a café at its heart – the heart being the huge communal table with its stash of glossy mags. Mon–Sat 7.30am–3pm; breakfast until noon and all day on Saturday; BYO. Bistro-style *bills 2* is at 359 Crown St, Surry Hills (no bookings; licensed; see map, p.91).

fu-manchu 249 Victoria St, Darlinghurst. Kings Cross CityRail. Perch yourself on red stools at stainless-steel counters and enjoy stylish but inexpensive Chinese and Malaysian noodles. BYO. Daily lunch and dinner.

(Also a branch at Level 1, 80 Campbell Parade, Bondi Beach with fabulous ocean views; see map, p.128). **The Lounge 277 Goulburn St, Darlinghurst. Bus #378 from Central CityRail; bus #380 & #382 from Circular Quay CityRail.** Somewhere between a vegetarian café, a bar, an art gallery and a music venue, this place yells "alternative" and is popular with students from the nearby art college. By day, it feels like a regular café – the menu is virtually all vegetarian and vegan with big servings and delicious recipes – and you eat outside at basement level, or inside where changing exhibitions cover the walls. By night, it seems more like a bar and music venue with DJs, open-mic nights, spoken-word performances, bands and projected images. Entertainment might be any night at this unconventional café, but there's usually something happening on Fridays. Licensed. Tues–Thurs & Sun 9am–11pm, Fri & Sat 9am–midnight.

Le Petit Crème 116 Darlinghurst Rd, Darlinghurst. Kings Cross CityRail. Friendly and thriving French café whose speciality is huge, good-value filled baguettes. Also steak and *frites*, omelettes, home-made pâté, *pain au chocolat* and big bowls of café au lait. Bread and pastries are baked on the premises. Mon–Sat 7am–3pm, Sun 8am–3pm.

Tropicana Café 227B Victoria St, Darlinghurst. Kings Cross CityRail. The birthplace of the Tropfest film festival (see box on pp.218–219) and still a hugely popular place to hang out and pose, at the weekend especially. The huge but cheap Trop salad could fuel you all day. Daily 5am–11pm, Fri & Sat until midnight.

Una's Coffee Lounge 340 Victoria St, Darlinghurst. Kings Cross CityRail. Cosy café that's been here for years, dishing up schnitzel and other cheap and tasty German dishes. The big breakfasts are very popular. BYO. Mon–Sat 6.30am–11pm, Sun 8am–11pm.

Paddington and Woollahra

See p.243 of "Shopping" for details of Woollahra's foodie focus, *jones the grocer*, which has a small eat-in café section.

Arthurs 260 Oxford Street, Paddington. Bus #378 from Central CityRail; bus #380 & #382 from Circular Quay CityRail. Paddington pizza institution where queuing to get in is mandatory (no bookings). Pizzas here are the thin kind, with a huge range of top-pings, and start from around $14 for a small one; the fresh pasta is also excellent. BYO. Mon–Fri 5pm–midnight, Sat & Sun noon–midnight.

Sloanes Cafe 312 Oxford St, Paddington. Bus #378 from Central CityRail; bus #380 & #382 from Circular Quay CityRail. The emphasis in this veteran café is on unusual and moder-ately priced vegetarian food, but some meatier dishes have slipped into the menu. The fresh juice bar has always been phe-nomenal. A stone-floored dining room opens onto the street, or for more peace eat out back under vines in the delightful courtyard. Breakfast served all day. BYO. Mon–Sat 6.15am–5pm, Sun 7am–5pm.

Kings Cross and around

Cafe Hernandez 60 Kings Cross Rd, Kings Cross. Kings Cross CityRail. This veteran

---

Eating around the clock

Loads of places in Sydney cater to hungry night owls, or those in need of a late-night caffeine fix, and some are open **24 hours**. At Circular Quay, *City Extra* is a 24-hour licensed coffee shop; *Alexanders* (see p.174), virtually opposite the Town Hall, is another. There's a **late-night food court** at the *Star City Casino* in Pyrmont (see p.216); nearby at the **Sydney Fish Market**, you can stay the day at 4am at the Italian-run *Fish Market Café* (see p.175). Several late-night options can be found in **Chinatown**, such as *BBQ King* (p.186) and *Golden Century* (p.186). In **Kings Cross**, there's the 24-hour *Café Hernandez* (see above), late-opening *Deans* (see opposite) and *Macleay's Pizza Bar* (see opposite). At nearby **Woolloomooloo**, *Harry's Café de Wheels* (see opposite) has dished up pies through the night for nearly sixty years. On the **North Shore** you'll find *Maisys Cafe* (p.183), open 24hr.

Argentinian-run 24hr coffee shop, open daily, is relaxed and friendly: you can dawdle here for ages and no one will make you feel unwelcome. Popular with taxi drivers and a mixed clientele of locals. Spanish food is served – *churros*, tortilla, *empanadas* and good pastries – but the coffee is really the focus.

Dean's Cafe 5 Kellett St, Kings Cross. Kings Cross CityRail. A haven after a night out in the Cross: toasted sandwiches plus other favourites like pumpkin soup, nachos and cakes. Licensed and BYO. Mon–Thurs 7pm–3am, Sat & Sun 7pm–6am.

Harry's Café de Wheels Cnr Cowper Wharf Rd and Brougham St, Woolloomooloo. Kings Cross CityRail. Colourful 24hr pie cart stationed outside the naval fleet base since 1945, covered with photographs of the sailors and the famous who've eaten here, from Brooke Shields to Kevin Costner and Elton John – and could that really be Colonel Sanders of *Kentucky Fried Chicken* trying out the competition?

Laurent Boulangerie Pâtisserie The Wharf, 6 Cowper Wharf Rd, Woolloomooloo. Kings Cross CityRail. Paris meets Sydney at this bakery café: the gleaming glass counters hold a tempting array of pastries plus filled baguettes and *croque monsieurs*. The most affordable of the eight eateries in the upmarket Woolloomooloo restaurant precinct, with nothing much over $10. Order at the counter. Daily 7.30am–8pm.

Macleay Pizza Bar 101 Macleay St, Potts Point. Kings Cross CityRail. Unassuming pizza bar: great prices and great pizzas. Daily noon–2.30am except Fri & Sat until 4.30am.

Minami 87C Macleay St, Potts Point. Kings Cross CityRail. Tiny, authentic Japanese noodle bar, where you'll find both Japanese residents and visitors squeezed around one large counter; popular choices include *ramen*, *yakisoba* and *kushikatsu*. BYO. Cheap. Mon–Sat noon–1am, Sun noon–midnight.

Spring Espresso Bar Challis Ave, near cnr Macleay St, Potts Point. Kings Cross CityRail. Once nominated by *wallpaper* magazine as serving the best breakfast in the world, this crowded bolt hole with street seating also serves some of the best coffee in Sydney and some great pastries and *panini*. BYO. Mon–Sat 7am–7pm, Sun 8am–7pm.

Wedge Cafe 70 Elizabeth Bay Road, Elizabeth Bay. Kings Cross CityRail. Trendy little local café with counter seats along the front window or pavement tables. You can have your breakfast coffee in a bowl, accompanied by the delicious cakes, muffins and biscuits made here. Also tasty filled rolls and bruschetta. Daily 7am–6pm.

Wok Station 230 William St, Kings Cross. Kings Cross CityRail. Tiny frenetic Thai café with friendly young staff cooking in the open kitchen to the sugary strains of Thai pop. Food is inexpensive and delicious; there's an inventive line in daily specials.

Inner west

The **inner west**, stretching from Newtown and Glebe west to the very Italian Leichhardt and Haberfield, and harbourside Balmain, has a well-established café culture and plenty of casual eateries. The area's pubs also usually serve up bar snacks and light meals; for more options, see p.203 of "Drinking".

Glebe

Badde Manors 37 Glebe Point Rd. Bus #431, #433 & #434 from Central CityRail. Veteran vegetarian corner café with a wonderful light-and-airy ambience, eclectic decor and laid-back staff; always packed, especially for weekend brunch. One of the best cafés on this strip, with yummy cakes and ice cream, and inexpensive and generous servings – nothing over $12. Mon–Fri 8am until midnight, Sat 8am–1am, Sun 9am–midnight.

The Craven 166 Glebe Point Rd, next door to the Valhalla Cinema. Bus #431, #433 & #434 from Central CityRail. At the other end of the street to *Badde Manors* and just as popular, this café is a great place to devour tasty titbits before or after the pictures, or plough into more substantial North African and Mediterranean-style fare from the daily blackboard specials. The atmosphere is friendly and relaxed, and there's plenty of space, light and air in the split-level shop-front building with big ceiling fans. You can sit outside too, though it's a bit bus-fumy. Mon–Fri 8am–10.30pm, Sat & Sun 9am–10.30pm.

Iku 25A Glebe Point Rd. Bus #431, #433 & #434 from Central CityRail. (Also at 612a Darling St, Rozelle; 168 Military Rd, Neutral Bay; 279 Bronte Rd, Waverly; and 62 Oxford St, Darlinghurst). The original *Iku* at Glebe proved so popular it keeps branching out. Healthy but delicious macrobiotic meals and snacks, all vegetarian or vegan, plus organic, pesticide-free coffee. Meditative interior and outdoor dining area. Mon–Fri 11am–9pm, Sat 11am–7pm, Sun 12.30–7.30pm.

Lolita's 29 Glebe Point Rd, Glebe. Bus #431, #433 & #434 from Central CityRail. The place for a big weekend breakfast (Sat & Sun 9am–1pm), with a great deck to soak up the sun and an upstairs balcony to relax on. Mon–Fri 10am–10pm, Sat & Sun 9am–10pm.

Cafe Otto 79 Glebe Point Rd, Glebe. Bus #431, #433 & #434 from Central CityRail. Varied, eclectic menu, ranging from Thai fishcakes to pasta, pizza, open baguettes and veal dishes, and a small Australian wine list. Has a glorious street-front garden. Licensed and BYO. Daily 9am–11pm, to midnight Fri & Sat.

Well Connected 35 Glebe Point Rd. Bus #431, #433 & #434 from Central CityRail. This colourful, funky café is a popular Glebe hangout, and there are lots of different areas to do just that, from tables on the street to lounges upstairs and the balcony overlooking the street, and in front of the computers peppered about the place. Yes, this is a cyber café, but that's just part of the scene – with breakfast served until 6pm, when dinner starts, people blow in and out all day. The simple menu is good value – Turkish bread sandwiches, lasagne, soup and salad – with loads for vegetarians, and servings are generous. The Moroccan vegetable curry with couscous is a dinner favourite. Internet access $1 per ten minutes to $5 per hour. Daily 7am–midnight.

Newtown

Citrus 227 King St. Newtown CityRail. The zingy-coloured walls of this café are just what you'd expect from the name. Big fold-back windows give good views of Newtown's unconventional innercity dwellers and there's a stash of papers and mags if people-watching's not your thing. This is a Newtown favourite: service

is friendly, and the servings of food are huge and delicious – the Mediterranean-inspired chicken breast burger and the steak sandwich are stand-outs – with nothing much over $12. BYO. Mon–Thurs & Sun 8am–10pm, Fri & Sat 8am–midnight.

El Bahsa Sweets 233 King St. Newtown CityRail. Lebanese coffee lounge with a huge range of traditional sweets, all home-made. Daily until 11pm, later at weekends.

Feel Cafe 165 King St, Newtown Newtown CityRail. This popular, bright, noisy café, its multi-coloured walls covered with art for sale, feels more like a busy bar. As well as coffee and cake, you can eat tasty meals, from scallop risotto through to sirloin steak. Garden courtyard outside. BYO. Daily 8am–midnight.

The Old Fish Shop 239 King St. Newtown CityRail. This little corner place, decorated with strands of dried garlic and chilli, is pure Newtown: lots of shaven heads, body piercings, tattoos and bizarre fashions. Food is simple – mainly focaccia and mini-pizzas – and the excellent raisin loaf goes well with a coffee. Daily 6am–11pm.

Tamana's North Indian Diner 196 and 236 King St. Newtown CityRail. Very cheap, absolutely delicious fast meals to eat in or take away. Licensed and BYO.

Leichhardt

Bar Baba 31 Norton St, Leichhardt ☏02/9564 2044. Bus #438 & #440 from Central CityRail. This gleaming but relaxed veteran family-run Italian place is open all day. Great desserts include baked ricotta cheesecake and tiramisu. On two levels; there's a courtyard and balcony too. Mon–Sat 8.30am–11.30pm, Sun 9am–11.30pm.

Bar Italia 169 Norton St, Leichhardt. Bus #438 or #440 from Central CityRail. Like a community centre with the day-long comings and goings of Leichhardt locals, and positively packed at night. The focaccia, served during the day, comes big and tasty, and coffee is spot-on. Some of the best *gelato* in Sydney; pasta costs from $9, and the extra night-time menu includes more substantial meat dishes. Don't overlook the shady courtyard out the back when you hunt for a table. BYO. Sun &

EATING | Cafés, snacks and light meals

Mon 10am–midnight, Tues–Thurs 9am–midnight, Fri 9am–1am, Sat 10am–1am.

Caffe Sport 2A Norton St, Leichhardt. Bus #438 & #440 from Central CityRail. One of the original Norton Street cafés, decorated with Italian sporting paraphernalia. Very casual, very Italian and very friendly. Cheap prices and generous helpings of focaccia. Daily 7am (Sun 8am) to 6pm.

Balmain

See map on p.101 for locations.

Canteen 332 Darling St, Balmain. Bus #432, #433 & #434 from Central CityRail. Airy, high-ceilinged café with whitewashed walls, inside the old Working Men's Institute. Simple fare: generous baguettes, burgers and salads, and big cooked breakfasts particularly popular at weekends when customers spill onto the sunny outside tables. Order and pay at the counter. Mon–Fri & Sun 7am–5pm, Sat 6am–5pm.

Mofo 354 Darling St, Balmain Bus #432, #433 & #434 from Central CityRail. Funky, slightly crazy but laidback vegetarian café. The background sounds are groovy, and even the menus are on antiquated vinyls. Mon–Fri 8am–7.30pm, Sat 8am–4.30pm; closed Sun.

Ocean beaches

From Bondi south to Maroubra, and from Manly north to Palm Beach, the **ocean beaches** have a stash of great cafés and relaxed eating places: early breakfasts are a beachside speciality. The beaches' pubs also usually offer bar snacks and light meals: p.206 of "Drinking" for more options. There's a branch of the noodle eatery, *fu-manchu* (see p.177) at Bondi, with great ocean views from its balcony.

Bondi

Brown Sugar 100 Brighton Boulevarde, North Bondi. Bus #389 from Bondi Junction CityRail. A stroll from the northern end of the beach, this little café is tucked in a quiet residential street around the corner from the North Bondi shops. The decor is funky distressed and the staff – cooking at the open kitchen – are suitably sweet and the atmosphere comfortable and relaxed. Locals straggle in for the very good breakfast menu; they have an interesting way with eggs, from green eggs (with pesto) to dill salmon eggs. Lunch on toasted Turkish sandwiches, salad and pasta. Great coffee. Daily 7.30am–4.30pm.

Burgerman 249 Bondi Rd, Bondi. Bus #380 & #382 from Bondi Junction CityRail. Gourmet burgers to slaver over, at bargain prices and vegetarian options too. Busy takeaway service and small eat-in area. Daily noon–10pm. There's another branch at 116 Surrey St, off Victoria St, Darlinghurst. See map, p.91.

Gelato Bar 140 Campbell Parade, Bondi Beach. Bus #380 & #382 from Bondi Junction CityRail. A gleaming window display of indulgent creamy continental cakes and strudels lure beachgoers to this Hungarian-run place. For over thirty years it has been serving up Eastern European dishes, huge portions of cake and gelato (though the best is at *Pompei's*, round the corner on Roscoe St). The coffee is among the best in Bondi. Old-fashioned coffee-lounge decor. Daily 8am–midnight.

Gertrude & Alice Cafe Bookstore 40 Hall St, cnr Consett Ave, Bondi Beach. Bus #380, #382 & #389 from Bondi Junction CityRail. It's hard to decide if *Gertrude & Alice*'s, open daily from 7.30am until late night, is a café or a secondhand bookshop. With small tables crammed into every available space, a big communal table and a comfy couch to lounge on, it can be hard for browsers to get to the books at busy café times. Tables outside and stools and a counter at the window – inside, it's a homy hang with generous, affordable serves of Greek and Mediterranean food, great cakes and coffee and lots of conversation. There's another *branch* tucked within a city café (*see Delizia*, p.175).

Gusto 16 Hall St, Bondi Beach. Bus #380, #382 & #389 from Bondi Junction CityRail. Deli-café which creates quite a Bondi scene, with its cosmopolitan crew of regulars and travellers blocking the pavement outside. Excellent coffee, delicious edibles piled high on platters and a separate deli counter too. There's just enough room for a few more people to perch on stools inside and along the front. Good notice board. Daily 6.15am–7.30pm.

Lamrock Cafe 72 Campbell Parade, cnr Lamrock Ave, Bondi Beach. Bus #380 & #382 from Bondi Junction CityRail. Stalwart Bondi café, always lively. The unpretentious local crowd come for magnificent ocean views, uncomplicated food – *panini*, salads, pasta, burgers and fish and chips – and the breakfasts. You can even have a cocktail with your brunch. Umbrella-covered tables outside, cushions inside. Licensed. Daily 7am–midnight.

Lauries Vegetarian 286 Bondi Rd, Bondi. Bus #380 & #382 from Bondi Junction CityRail. Excellent veggie takeaway with a couple of eat-in tables. Daily 11am–10pm.

The One That Got Away 163 Bondi Rd, Bondi. Bus #380 & #382 from Bondi Junction CityRail. Award-winning fish shop which even sells kosher fish plus sushi; also BBQ grills and fish and chips. There's a small eat-in section where salads and unusual yam chips are served. Daily 10am–9pm.

The Red Kite 95 Roscoe St, Bondi Beach. Bus #380 & #382 from Bondi Junction CityRail. Funky vegetarian café just back from Campbell Parade, with outside tables to catch the breeze. Fresh, imaginative food and freshly squeezed juices; yummy spiced Indian tea. Nothing over $12. Daily 8am–6pm.

Sejuiced 487 Bronte Rd, Bronte. Bus #378 from Central CityRail. Delicious fresh juices, smoothies and frappés, combined with ocean and palm-tree views, make this tiny place a beauty to kick-start a summer's day. Salads, soups and pasta are terrific too. If it's full, choose from several other great options on this wonderful café strip. Daily 6.30am–6pm.

Speedo's 126 Ramsgate Ave, North Bondi. Bus #380, #382 & #389 from Bondi Junction CityRail. Totally casual café bang opposite the north end of the beach, where the locals and their kids and dogs hang out, with no busy road between you and the view. The inexpensive breakfast specials are very popular; expect long waits for your order. Daily 6am–6pm.

Eastern beaches: Clovelly, Coogee and Maroubra

Barzura 62 Carr St, Coogee. Bus #372 from Central CityRail & #373, #374 & #376 from Circular Quay CityRail. Fantastic spot with ocean views. Both café and restaurant, with wholesome breakfast until 1pm, snacks until 7pm, and restaurant meals – seafood spaghetti or grilled kangaroo rump

– served at lunch and dinner. Unpretentious though stylish service encourages a local crowd and it's always packed. Moderate; licensed and BYO. Daily 7am–11pm. See map, p.132

Direction of Cure 23 Burnie St, Clovelly. Bus #339 from Circular Quay and Central CityRail. Homeopathic store that's also a licensed café (also BYO), serving up really healthy, fresh, delicious and inexpensive food from an eclectic seasonal menu. Lots of wholesome fresh juices too. Outside tables. Thurs–Sun 8am–6pm. See map, p.132.

Ericyes II 240 Coogee Bay Rd, Coogee. Bus #372 from Central CityRail & #373, #374, #376 from Circular Quay CityRail. This casual eat-in or takeaway place has delicious pide – Turkish-style pizzas – and just-baked bread and tasty dips that are perfect for a beach picnic. BYO. Daily 10am–midnight. See map, on p.132.

The Globe 203 Coogee Bay Rd, Coogee. Bus #372 from Central CityRail & #373, #374 & #376 from Circular Quay CityRail. This relaxed local daytime hangout good coffee. Interesting, healthy food, from gourmet sandwiches to Mediterranean-slanted mains. Mon–Sat 8am–6pm, Sun 9am–6pm. See map, p.132

The Pool Caffe 94 Marine Parade, Maroubra ☎02/9314 0364. Bus #376 & #377 from Circular Quay CityRail. In a quiet residential spot opposite the Mahon sea pool on the Coogee–Maroubra coastal walk, this café has a relaxed holiday feel. Breakfast on organic porridge and fresh-fruit plates, have a coffee with fresh muffins, biscuits and cakes, or tuck into more expensive restaurant-style meaty modern food, often with an Indian flavour (bookings recommended weekends). Inexpensive to moderate. Breakfast Sat & Sun, lunch & dinner Wed–Sun. See map, p.126

Seasalt 1 Donnellan Circuit Clovelly. Bus #339 from Circular Quay and Central CityRail. The old kiosk has been made over into a contemporary café-restaurant. Open-fronted, with fantastic views over the beach to cliffs, greenery and houses, it looks really smart, but it's the sort of place you can come into covered in sand and in your cossie and have just a casual coffee or a full meal with wine. The cuisine is fresh and modern with a seafood basis; lunch mains range from $13 to $17, and summer-only dinner (when fully clothed and groomed is the idea) starts from $16. The sophisticated, extensive

EATING | Cafés, snacks and light meals

breakfast – dishes like goats ricotta and fresh herb omelette – packs the punters in at the weekends. Get in early to be sure of a seat – or get a takeaway from the small kiosk section. Licensed. Mon–Fri 9am–5pm, Sat & Sun 8.30pm–5.30pm. See map, p.132

Manly and the northern beaches

Barking Frog 48 North Steyne Manly. Ferry to Manly Wharf. Two of Manly's most popular surf-front breakfast spots – *Barking Frog and Brazil* – are side by side: if one's full, try the other. The fave breakfast is their version of eggs hollandaise ("Barking Frog's eggs") and the huge pancakes are delicious and inexpensive. Lunch fare includes packed-full baguettes. Like *Brazil, Barking Frog* has a restaurant menu and feel in the evenings, but it's also a great late-night spot for coffee and cake. Mon & Tues noon to midnight, Wed–Sun 8am to midnight.

Brazil Cafe 46 North Steyne, Manly. Ferry to Manly Wharf. A classy surf-front café that's more Italian/eclectic than Brazilian, and transforms into a pricey restaurant in the evenings (bookings ☎02/9977 3825). A popular local hangout, particularly for the breakfasts and famed Sunday brunch. Licensed. Daily 8am–10pm.

The harbour

Several pubs around the **harbour** – in Neutral Bay, Watsons Bay and North Sydney – all with great beer gardens, serve good snacks and light meals. See the box "Legendary Beer Gardens" on p.205 and the *Greenwood Hotel* (p.205). To locate these places, see the map on pp.118–119.

Freckle Face and Freckle Face Too 32 & 32C Burton St, Kirribilli. Milsons Point CityRail or ferry to Kirribilli Wharf. These two almost adjacent cafés run by sisters are a good place to recharge after walking over the Harbour Bridge;: they're near the north side of the bridge at Milsons Point. Coffee is good and comes with a Freckle chocolate. Healthy fare – fresh juices, smoothies, salads and sandwiches.

Maisys Cafe 164 Military Rd, Neutral Bay. Bus #247 from Clarence St, City. Cool hangout on a hot day or night (open 24hr), with funky interior and music. Good for breakfast – from croissants to bacon and eggs – or delicious Maltese *pastizzi* plus soups, burgers, pasta and cakes. Not cheap, but servings are generous. BYO.

Restaurants

You're likely to come across the term **"contemporary Australian"**, "modern Australian" or "Pacific Rim" in various restaurant descriptions. This refers to an adventurous blend of influences from around the world – mostly Asian and Mediterranean – combined with fresh local produce (including kangaroo, emu and crocodile); the result is a dynamic, eclectic and very healthy cuisine.

An average Sydney restaurant main is about $18; top dollar at the city's finest is around $40. Many places allow you to **BYO** (Bring Your Own) wine or beer, but will probably add a corkage charge ($1–2 per person). Several **pubs** have well-regarded restaurants; pub meals rarely cost more than $16 in their bistro sections, with huge steaks likely to be at the top of the menu.

Restaurant prices

All the restaurant section listings are **price-coded** into five categories, going on the price of a typical main course:

Cheap	under $14
Inexpensive	$14–18
Moderate	$18–25
Expensive	$25–35
Very expensive	$35 plus

All restaurants listed below are open daily for lunch and dinner, unless otherwise stated (hours vary, so it's advisable to phone and check).

The Rocks

bel mondo Level 3, the Argyle Stores, 12–24 Argyle St, The Rocks ☎02/9241 3700. Circular Quay CityRail/ferry. The North Italian food served here is probably the best of its kind in Sydney and comes with fabulous views over The Rocks and the harbour. Attracts a sophisticated crowd, but for less cash you can get views and similar food at the fashionable *Antibar* at the front. Very expensive; licensed. Restaurant closed Mon, Sat & Sun lunch.

Lillipilli in the Rocks 1 Globe St, cnr Nurses Walk, The Rocks ☎02/9251 6988. Circular Quay CityRail/ferry. A chance to sample some authentic but upmarket bushtucker among Aboriginal artwork. Run by a Koori from the south coast, this has the best pedigree of any restaurant serving contemporary native Australian cuisine in Sydney. Expect vegetarian dishes like fettucine with wild spinach, bush mushrooms and bunya bunya nuts, or meatier dishes such as wallaby with local honey. The best time to come is Fri or Sat night, when there's an Aboriginal dance performance at 8pm. BYO. Expensive.

Palisade Hotel Restaurant 35–37 Bettington St, Millers Point ☎02/9251 7225. Circular Quay CityRail/ferry; bus #431–#434. On the first floor of a classic tiled pub which stands sentinel-like over Millers Point, the intimate dining room provides absorbing water and city views. Cuisine is expensive modern Australian and service is friendly. Have a drink downstairs first in the wonderfully unspoilt pub. Licensed. Closed Sat lunch and all Sun.

Rockpool 107 George St, The Rocks ☎02/9252 1888. Circular Quay CityRail/ferry. Owned by top chef Neil Perry, the raved-about seafood – blue swimmer crab omelette, mud crab ravioli – and other contemporary creations make this one of Sydney's best dining spots. With mains around $45, however, it's definitely splurge material. Licensed. Closed Sat lunch & Sun. Very expensive. A less expensive Perry restaurant, inspired by Asian cuisines, is *XO*, 155 Victoria St, Kings Cross (☎02/9331 8881).

Sailors Thai Canteen 106 George St, The Rocks. Circular Quay CityRail/ferry. The cheaper version of the much-praised, pricey downstairs restaurant (☎02/9251 2466 for bookings), housed in the restored Sailors' Home. Its ground-level canteen with a long stainless-steel communal table looks onto an open kitchen, where the chefs chop away to produce simple one-bowl meals. Come early for dinner in the canteen. Licensed. Daily noon–8pm. Inexpensive to moderate.

Wharf Restaurant Pier 4, Hickson Rd, Millers Point ☎02/9250 1761, next to the Wharf Theatre. Circular Quay CityRail/ferry. Enterprising modern food (lots of seafood), served up in an old dock building with heaps of raw charm and a harbour vista; bag the outside tables for the best views. Cocktail bar open from noon until end of evening performance. Moderate to expensive. Closed Sun.

Circular Quay and the Opera House

Aria 1 Macquarie St, East Circular Quay ☎02/9252 2555 Circular Quay CityRail/ferry.

Veggies are well catered for on just about every café menu, and most contemporary restaurant menus too. The following are specifically or virtually **vegetarian**: *Badde Manors* (p.179), *Bodhi in the Park* (p.174), *Green Gourmet* (p.191), *Harvest* (p.191), *Iku* (p.180), *The Lounge* (p.178), *Maya Masala* (p.176), *Mofo* (p.181), *Mother Chu's Vegetarian Kitchen* (p.187), *Red Kite* (p.182) and *Sloanes* (p.178).

On the first floor of the Opera Quays building (aka the much-maligned "Toaster" – see p.56), the 200-seater Aria has knock-out harbour views, one of Sydney's best chefs, Matthew Moran (dishing up modern Australian fare), and wonderful service to recommend it. The interiors are also pretty slick. All this comes at a price, but there are more affordable set lunch menus and pre-theatre dinners (5.30–7.30pm). Licensed. Closed lunch Sat & Sun.

Bambu Bay 4, Overseas Passenger Terminal, Circular Quay West ☎02/9247 6044. **Circular Quay CityRail/ferry.** The breathtaking views vie with the sensational interiors of this brand-new 200 seater harbourside restaurant. The food from chef Anthony Flowers encompasses Oriental and European, from about $30 a main. If you can't afford the food, the bar is a great place to enjoy the views and ambience. Expensive. Licensed. Dinner Mon–Sat.

Cafe Sydney Level 5, Customs House, 31 Alfred St, Circular Quay ☎02/9251 8683. **Closed Sun dinner. Licensed. Seats 275. Circular Quay CityRail/ferry.** Though the food here has never been that highly rated (wide-ranging, from a tandoor oven to French- and Greek-inspired dishes), the views of the Harbour Bridge and Opera House from the balcony are jaw-dropping – *Café Sydney* is firmly on the tourist agenda. Service is great and the atmosphere is fun, especially with the live jazz accompaniment on Fri nights. A drink at the bar is the affordable option. Lunch daily, dinner Mon–Sat.

Café Opera Intercontinental 117 Macquarie St ☎02/9240 1260. **Circular Quay CityRail/ferry.** The five-star *Intercontinental* (see p.154) has long been a hit with the locals, not just tourists, and the buffet offered by its Café Opera, groaning under the display of seafood, is legendary. You can stuff yourself silly for $42 at lunchtime ($59 Sun, with live jazz), $48 at dinner ($54 Fri & Sat,

$52 Sun) or $28.50 at supper from 10pm on Friday and Saturday. Licensed. Expensive to very expensive.

Doyles on the Quay Overseas Passenger Terminal, Circular Quay West ☎02/9252 3400. **Circular Quay CityRail/ferry.** Downtown branch of the Watsons Bay seafood institution (see p.192; branch at Sydney Fish Market p.186); pricey but excellent, with great harbour views from the outdoor waterfront tables. You'll probably need to book. Licensed. Expensive.

Guillaume at Bennelong Sydney Opera House, Bennelong Point ☎02/9241 1999. **Circular Quay CityRail/ferry.** French chef Guillaime Brahimi has fused his name with the enduring *Bennelong*, the Opera House's top-notch restaurant. If you want to have one splash-out romantic meal in Sydney, come here. The restaurant fills one of the iconic building's smaller shells, with dramatic rib-vaulted ceilings, huge windows providing stunning harbour views, and sensuous lighting. With mains at around $35, this is not the priciest in town, but if you can't afford it, you could opt for a drink at the bar. Expensive to very expensive. Lunch Fri only, dinner Mon–Sat.

City Centre

Edna's Table 204 Clarence St ☎02/9267 3933. **Wynyard CityRail.** A chance to sample some *haute cuisine* bushtucker among upmarket kitsch Australian decor. The chargrilled kangaroo fillet served with a warm salad of wild yams and curried dressing is ever popular. Closed Sat lunch and all Sun. Licensed. Expensive.

est. Level 1, Establishment Hotel, 252 George St, City 02/9240 3010 **Seats 85. Wynyard CityRail.** Above one of Sydney's most deluxe bars (see p.198), this top-notch restaurant has a dramatic classical but contemporary interior, complete with columns. The food is contemporary

Australian but with quite a French slant. Expensive to very expensive. Licensed. Closed Sat lunch and all Sun.

Tetsuya's 529 Kent St ☎02/9267 2900, ☏9799 7099. **Town Hall CityRail.** Stylish premises – a Japanese timber interior and a beautiful Japanese garden outside – and the internationally renowned chef Tetsuya Wakuda creates exquisite Japanese/French-style fare. The waiting list is a month ahead – worth it to sample his twelve-course *dégustation* menu ($170); wine teamed with each course starts from $60. Licensed and BYO. Lunch Fri & Sat, dinner Tues–Sat.

Darling Harbour and around

BBQ King 18 Goulburn St, Haymarket ☎02/9267 2433. **Central CityRail.** Unprepossessing but perpetually crowded Chinese restaurant specializing in barbecued meat. There is also, surprisingly, a big vegetarian section in the menu. Licensed. Cheap to inexpensive. Daily 11.30am–2am (last orders 1.30am). See map, p.86.

Blackbird Cockle Bay Wharf, Darling Harbour ☎02/9283 7835. **Town Hall CityRail.** This place has the feel of a funky American diner; sit on stools at the bar or couches out the back, or enjoy the water views from the terrace. Generous, good-value meals – from dhal to spaghetti, noodles, salads, pizzas from a hot-stone oven, and breakfast until 4pm. Licensed. Inexpensive. Daily 7am–1am. See map, p.79.

Capitan Torres 73 Liverpool St ☎02/9264 5574. **Town Hall CityRail.** An atmospheric and enduring Spanish place, specializing in seafood – a fresh display helps you choose – and paella. Licensed. Moderate. Sit downstairs at the bar or upstairs in the restaurant. See map, Haymarket.

Chinta Ria – Temple of Love Roof Terrace, 201 Sussex St, Cockle Bay Wharf development, Darling Harbour ☎02/9264 3211. **Town Hall CityRail.** People queue to get in here (bookings lunch only) as much for the fun atmosphere – a blues and jazz soundtrack and decor which mixes a giant Buddha, a lotus pond and 50s-style furniture – as for the yummy Malaysian food from the frenzied open kitchen; popular dishes include *lohbak*, a starter of bean-curd skin wrapped around minced chicken and deep fried, and the coconut milk-based noodle soup, curry laksa. Licensed. Inexpensive to

moderate. See map, p.79.

Doyles Fish Market Bistro Sydney Fish Market, Pyrmont ☎02/9552 4339. **Metro Light Rail to Fish Market stop.** A very casual and more affordable version of the famous Doyles fish restaurant in Watsons Bay (p.192); you sit at plastic tables and order at the counter. Daily specials from the best fish market offers served all day. Inexpensive to moderate. BYO. Mon–Thurs 11am–3pm, Fri & Sat 11am–9pm, Sun 11am–5pm. See map, p.79.

Golden Century 393 Sussex St, City ☎02/9281 1598. **Central CityRail.** Seafood is the thing here, and it's very fresh – you can watch your potential dinner swimming around in the tanks. Be adventurous – try the oysters sitting on black moss, or the raved-about Pipis in XO sauce. And you can eat as dawn approaches – this one's open very late. Mains range from inexpensive to expensive. Licensed and BYO. Daily noon–4am. See map, p.86.

Grand Taverna Sir John Young Hotel, 557 George St, cnr Liverpool St, Haymarket ☎02/9267 3608. **Town Hall CityRail.** Spanish food, including tapas, at the heart of the Spanish quarter. Authentically lively atmosphere and no-frills setting for some of the best paella and sangria in town. Licensed. Inexpensive. See map, p.86.

Glasgow Arms Hotel 527 Harris St, Ultimo, opposite the Powerhouse Museum. **Haymarket Monorail.** Very pleasant pub with leafy courtyard dining. Sat dinner only and Sun restaurant is closed. Inexpensive to moderate. See map, p.79.

Kam Fook Sharks Fin Seafood Restaurant Level 3, Market City complex, cnr Quay and Haymarket streets, Haymarket ☎02/9211 8988. **Central CityRail.** This Cantonese establishment is officially Australia's largest restaurant, seating 800, though you'll still have to queue if you haven't booked. Some of the best *yum cha* in Sydney is served here. Moderate; licensed. *Yum cha* Mon–Fri 10am–5.30pm, Sat & Sun 9am–5.30pm, dinner nightly. See map, p.86.

The Malaya 39 Lime St, King Street Wharf, Darling Harbour ☎02/9211 0946. **Town Hall CityRail.** Popular, veteran Chinese-Malaysian place now in swish waterside surrounds, serving some of the best, most authentic and spicy laksa in town. Inexpensive to moderate; licensed. Closed Sun. See map, p.79.

Mother Chu's Vegetarian Kitchen 367 Pitt St, Haymarket ☎02/9283 2828. **Central CityRail.** Taiwanese Buddhist cuisine in a suitably plain setting, and true to its name, it's family-run. Though onion and garlic aren't used, the eats here certainly aren't bland, such as the vegetarian Peking Duck which you have to order a day in advance (serves two). Don't try to BYO – there's a no-alcohol policy. Closed Sun. Cheap. See map, p.86.

See map, p.86.

Inner east

The **inner east** has the biggest concentration of places to eat in Sydney, and some of its best restaurants.

Surry Hills

Almustafa 276 Cleveland St, Surry Hills ☎02/9319 5632. **Bus #393, #395 from Central CityRail.** Very homy Lebanese place where you relax on low couches in the traditional manner while eating. Tasty home-style food too – you can sample a wide range with a shareable meze platter. Cheap. BYO. Closed lunch Mon–Wed; open until 12.30am Fri & Sat.

Billy Kwong 355 Crown St, Surry Hills ☎02/9332 3300. **Bus #301–#303 from Circular Quay CityRail or Castlereagh St, City.** Raved-about chef Kylie Kwong gives traditional Chinese cooking a stylish new slant. The space itself provides a similar contrast, with Chinese antiques but contemporary fittings: bright light, stools and bare tables. Licensed & BYO. Inexpensive to moderate. Dinner nightly.

Dhaba House 466 Cleveland Surry Hills ☎02/9319 6260. **Bus #393, #395 from Central CityRail.** Downmarket decor matches the cheap prices at this invariably crowded Indian restaurant, but the dishes are well above average in quality. BYO. Lunch Wed–Sun, dinner nightly.

Erciyes 409 Cleveland St, Surry Hills ☎02/9319 1309. **Bus #393, #395 from Central CityRail.** Among the offerings of this busy Turkish restaurant is delicious *pide* – a bit like pizza – available with a range of toppings, many vegetarian. There's a take-out section too. Belly dancing Fri & Sat nights. BYO. Cheap. Daily 10am–midnight.

Forresters Hotel 336 Riley St, Surry Hills ☎02/9211 2095. **Central CityRail.** The Sunday to Wednesday steak and chicken specials (and until 6pm on Saturday) have become a legend and attract punters in the hundreds: try a 300g scotch fillet, T-bone steak or chargrilled chicken breast with mash and Asian greens and a different sauce depending on the day, all for $5. The catch, and it's not much of one, is that you must buy a drink. The three-levelled pub itself is very pleasant and there are some streetside tables.

Longrain 85 Commonwealth St, Surry Hills ☎02/280 2888. **Central CityRail.** This popular bar-restaurant is all warm, sensuous woods – big communal tables made of jarrah, black Japanese-style floorboards and pine walls. Superb Thai food, among the best in Sydney, and a hip clientele. Moderate to expensive. Lunch Tues–Fri, dinner Tues–Sun.

Maya da Dhaba 431 Cleveland St, Surry Hills ☎02/8399 3785. **Bus #393, #395 from Central CityRail.** The more upmarket, non-veg version of the phenomenally popular vegetarian *Maya Masala* (see p.176) across the road. This one is also noisy and crowded, but it's much comfier and decor extends to craft-covered walls. The tender lamb curries in particular are superb, and prices are low. Lunch Fri–Sun, dinner nightly.

MG Garage 490 Crown St, Surry Hills ☎02/9383 9383. **Bus #301–#303 from Circular Quay CityRail or Castlereagh St, City.** Flash restaurant which doubles as a car showroom, with MGs sharing the dining room. The modern Australian fare on offer is superb (by top chef Janni Kyritsis), and if you can afford the very expensive prices, this makes a fun night out. Next door, *Fuel* is the moderate café/bistro version – phenomenally popular for weekend brunch – or you can have a cocktail and some bar nibbles at *Tow Bar*. MG Garage is closed Sun & lunch Sat and licensed; *Fuel* is open Mon–Fri lunch, dinner nightly, plus breakfast from 8am Sat & Sun; and *Tow Bar* is open daily 5.30pm–11pm.

Nepalese Kitchen 481 Crown St, Surry Hills ☎02/9319 4264. **Bus #301– #303 from Circular Quay CityRail or Castlereagh St, City.** The speciality here is goat curry, served with *achars*, freshly cooked relishes which traditionally accompany the mild Nepalese dishes. There's also a whole range of vegetarian options. Cosy, calming atmosphere, with traditional music; you can sit outside

△ *Harry's Café de Wheels*, Woolloomooloo

in the courtyard on a fine night. Dinner nightly. BYO. Cheap to inexpensive.

Prasit's Northside Take-away 395 Crown St, and Prasit's Northside on Crown, 415 Crown St, Surry Hills ☎02/9319 0748. Also 77 Mount St, North Sydney ☎02/9957 2271, see map on pp.118–119. Bus #301–#303 from Circular Quay CityRail or Castlereagh St, City. Be prepared for some great Thai taste sensations amongst the bold purple colour scheme. Since entrees are available, you can attempt to work your way through their delicious repertoire; plenty of vegetarian options too. The takeaway branch can squeeze diners out front on stools, with a few more places upstairs. BYO. Inexpensive to moderate. Takeaway closed Mon; restaurant open dinner Mon–Sat. See map on p.90.

Sushi Suma 421 Cleveland St, Surry Hills ☎02/9698 8873. Bus #393, #395 from Central CityRail. That this small, noisy Japanese restaurant is extremely popular with Japanese locals and visitors says it all. You'll need to book a table to avoid disappointment. Inexpensive. BYO. Closed Mon & lunch Sat & Sun.

Darlinghurst

Balkan Seafood Restaurant 217 Oxford St, Darlinghurst ☎02/9331 7670. Bus #378 from Central CityRail, bus #380 & #382 from Circular Quay CityRail. This long-running Croatian/Italian place is a bustling Darlinghurst institution: fish and seafood is the best choice, but you can also get huge schnitzels and other continental meat dishes and Balkan specialities like *cevapci* and *razjnici*. Licensed and BYO. Moderate. Dinner Tues–Sun. There's another *Balkan Seafood* at Bent St, Fox Studios, Moore Park (☎02/9360 0097).

Chu Bay 312A Bourke St, Darlinghurst ☎02/9331 3386. Bus #378 from Central CityRail, bus #380 & #382 from Circular Quay CityRail. Tiny, cheap Vietnamese restaurant, just off Oxford Street, that's authentic and very popular. BYO. Dinner nightly.

Fishface 132 Darlinghurst Rd, Darlinghurst ☎02/9332 4803. Kings Cross CityRail. Best market buys of fish, and a chance to taste some unusual varieties (imaginatively cooked), served at stools and benches. Delicious corn bread. Moderate. BYO. Dinner Mon–Sat.

Govinda's 112 Darlinghurst Rd, Darlinghurst ☎02/9380 5155. Kings Cross CityRail. Excellent, cheap Indian vegetarian restaurant, in the Hare Krishna centre. All-you-can-eat specials cost $15.90 with a film thrown in at their own cinema (or an extra ten percent of the cost of the meal; see p.220). It's worth booking for the meal-and-movie deal. Dinner nightly from 6pm.

Oh! Calcutta! 252 Victoria St, Darlinghurst ☎02/9360 3650. Kings Cross CityRail. This place was fitted out by Australia's star interior decorator Iain Halliday. It gets suitably exclamatory reviews for its authentic – and occasionally inventive – food, and despite the decor, prices remain inexpensive to moderate. Licensed. Lunch Fri only, dinner Mon–Sat.

Onde 346 Liverpool St, Darlinghurst ☎02/9331 8749. Kings Cross CityRail. The French owner is onto a winner with this popular restaurant in Darlinghurst's quieter backstreets, that offers very good-value authentic bistro food: soups and pâtés to start, mains like steak and *frites* or confit of duck, and decadent desserts. Serves are generous, service excellent, and it's invariably squeezed full of happy diners. Licensed, and all wine is available by the glass. Inexpensive. Dinner nightly. No bookings, so be prepared to queue.

Salt Kirketon Hotel, 229 Darlinghurst Rd, Darlinghurst 02/9332 2556. Kings Cross CityRail. The restaurant of one of Sydney's coolest hotels (see p.156), highly fashionable *Salt* boasts one of Sydney's best chefs, Luke Mangan. The food is inventive, using the best, freshest ingredients around. Vegetarians do very well too. Licensed. Very expensive. Closed lunch Sat & Sun.

Paddington

Bistro Lulu 257 Oxford Street, Paddington ☎02/9380 6888. Bus #378 from Central CityRail, bus #380 & #382 from Circular Quay CityRail. Attached to the Australian Centre for Photography (see p.245), this French-style bistro is sleekly modern with huge fold-back windows and views of street action. With a chef trained by some of the city's finest, the food here is heavenly but it's not all fancy – even the old French favourite, *steak frites*, is on the menu. Moderate; licensed. Lunch Thurs–Sat, dinner nightly.

Grand National Hotel 161 Underwood St, cnr of Elizabeth St, Paddington ☎02/9963 4557. Bus #378 from Central CityRail, bus #380 & #382 from Circular Quay CityRail. One of the best pub-restaurants in Sydney, dishing up imaginative fare but with old-fashioned attentive service. Booking essential at weekends. Expensive. Lunch Tues–Sun, dinner Tues–Sat.

Paddington Inn Bistro 338 Oxford St, Paddington. Bus #378 from Central CityRail, bus #380 & #382 from Circular Quay CityRail. Busy upmarket pub-bistro with an extensive and eclectic menu. Interior decor of textured glass, cushioned booths, polished concrete floors and fabric-lined walls. Packed on Saturdays, as it's opposite the market. Cheap to inexpensive.

Royal Hotel Restaurant Royal Hotel, 237 Glenmore Rd, off Five Ways, Paddington ☎02/9331 5055. Bus #389 from Circular Quay CityRail. Pub-restaurant serving some of the best steaks in Sydney, nonstop from noon to 11pm (9pm Sun). Smart interior and staff but moderate prices. Eating on the verandah is a real treat, with views over the art gallery and Five Ways action below, but places fill fast – and they don't take bookings. Wait to be called in the charming top floor *Elephant Bar* (from 4.30pm daily; see p.202).

Kings Cross and Woolloomooloo

Bayswater Brasserie 32 Bayswater Rd, Kings Cross ☎02/9357 2177. Kings Cross CityRail. Busy, lively, upmarket brasserie consistently rated for its interesting modern food (constantly changing seasonal menu) – it's a long-time hangout for Sydney's media types. Moderate to expensive; licensed. Lunch Fri only, dinner Mon–Sat.

Otto The Wharf, 6 Cowper Wharf Rd, Woolloomooloo. Kings Cross CityRail. The sort of restaurant where agents take actors and models out to lunch, and where a well-known politician could be dining at the next table – every Sydneysider secretly wants to be taken to lunch at Otto. Trendy and glamorous, it serves top-of-the-range, very expensive Italian cuisine. Service is friendly, and the atmosphere is lively, so don't feel intimidated if you're not a celeb. Expensive to very expensive.

The Pig and The Olive 71A Macleay St, Potts Point ☎02/9357 3745. Kings Cross CityRail. Gourmet pizza bar with wild toppings like marinated lamb with feta. Also check out

the small menu of contemporary dishes, which includes grilled polenta and spicy rack of lamb. Licensed & BYO. Moderate. Mon–Sat 6–11pm, Sun 6–10pm.

Venice Beach Restaurant 3 Kellet St, Kings Cross ☎02/9326 9928. Kings Cross CityRail. In a big Victorian terrace house with a courtyard and a cushion room, this is a seriously stylish cheap eat. All entrees are $6.90 (except for a half-dozen oysters; $7.90), and mains range from pasta ($12.90) to steak ($15.90). A giant chargrilled seafood platter feeding two costs $49. Licensed. Dinner nightly from 6pm. Cheap.

Woolloomooloo Bay Hotel 2 Bourke St, Woolloomooloo ☎02/9357 1177. Kings Cross CityRail. This big old pub has long been a popular place to eat and drink but with the upmarket wharf development opposite it has come into its own. It's a fabulous space, with outside tables at the front and on the big upstairs balcony and lots of little nooks to discover. Well-known for its $35 seafood platters, the bistro food includes the usual pub steaks and pasta, with mains under $20.

Inner west

Though the **inner west** is heavy on café culture, it also has some great, often multicultural, restaurants and pub bistros.

Glebe

The Boathouse on Blackwattle Bay End of Ferry Rd, Glebe ☎02/9518 9011. Bus #431, #433 & #434 from Central CityRail. Atmospheric restaurant located in a former boatshed, with fantastic views across the bay to Anzac Bridge and the fishmarkets opposite. Fittingly, seafood is the thing here, from the six different kinds of oysters to the raved-about fish pie with smoked tomatoes. One of the best fish restaurants in Sydney; very expensive but worth it. Licensed. Closed Mon.

Cesare's No Names Friend in Hand Hotel, 58 Cowper St, Glebe ☎02/9660 2326. Bus #431, #433 & #434 from Central CityRail. Excellent, cheap Italian restaurant in the gazebo and beer garden of the characterful backstreet pub (see p.203). Generous pasta meals from $9 and pricier meaty main courses like schnitzels. Restaurant closed Sun lunch.

Dakhni 65 Glebe Point Rd ☎02/9660 4887. Bus #431, #433 & #434 from Central CityRail. A range of Indian dishes from tandoori through to delicious South Indian vegetarian *masala dosai* (filled pancakes). A meat or vegetarian *thali* costs around $18.90, plus it's BYO. Inexpensive to moderate. A popular spot, so book. Closed Mon lunch.

Newtown

Green Gourmet 115–117 King St ☎02/9519 5330. Newtown CityRail. This loud and busy Chinese vegetarian eatery always has plenty of Asian customers, including the odd Buddhist monk. Buffet meals are sold per 100g weight at dinner, or by the plate (around $8) at lunch; you can also order off the menu. Closed Sun. Cheap to inexpensive.

Kilimanjaro 280 King St ☎02/9557 4565. Newtown CityRail. Newtown is the focus of a small African community, with the African International Market providing supplies at 2a Enmore Rd, just around the corner. This long-running Senegalese-owned place serves authentic and simple dishes that span Africa – from West African marinated chicken to North African couscous. Casual and friendly atmosphere, with African art and craft adorning the walls. Cheap to inexpensive. BYO.

Old Saigon 107 King St ☎02/9519 5931. Newtown CityRail. Vietnamese food with French, Thai and Japanese influences. Saigon memorabilia covers the walls of this cosy restaurant run by a former war correspondent and his Vietnamese wife. Inexpensive to moderate. Licensed and BYO. Lunch Wed–Fri, dinner Tues–Sun.

Steki Taverna 2 O'Connell St, off King St ☎02/9516 2191. Newtown CityRail. Atmospheric and moderately priced Greek taverna, with live music and dancing at weekends – when you'll need to book. Licensed. Inexpensive. Dinner Wed–Sun.

Sumalee Courtyard of the Bank Hotel, 324 King St ☎02/9565 1730. Newtown CityRail. Great Thai restaurant in a pub; you can eat in the leafy beer garden. Inexpensive to moderate. Closed Mon.

Thai Pothong 294 King St ☎02/9550 6277. Newtown CityRail. King Street's best Thai; excellent service and inexpensive to moderate prices. Essential to book at the weekend. Licensed and BYO. Closed Mon lunch.

Thanh Binh 111 King St ☎02/9557 1175. Newtown CityRail. With a celebrated original in Cabramatta (see box, p.173), the Vietnamese food at this Newtown offspring is just as fresh, delicious and inexpensive. The roll-your-own rice-paper rolls are sensational (and fun) and there are a huge range of noodles to choose from. Licensed and BYO. Inexpensive. Closed lunch Mon–Wed.

Leichhardt, Haberfield and Rozelle

See map, p.101 for locations.

Anna and Aldo's 9 Norton St, Leichhardt ☎02/9550 9760. Bus #438 & #440 from Central CityRail. Enduringly popular and very traditional Italian trattoria. Cheap to inexpensive. Licensed & BYO. Closed Sun dinner.

Frattini 122 Marion St, Leichhardt ☎02/9569 2997. Bus #438 & #440 from Central CityRail. One of the best Italian restaurants in Little Italy, run by a genial family. Modern, airy space but old-fashioned service. The fish is recommended, especially the whitebait fritters. BYO. Moderate. Closed Sat lunch and all Sun.

Harvest 71 Evans St, Rozelle ☎02/9818 4201. Bus #440 from Central CityRail. Established for over thirty years, this vegan and vegetarian restaurant has kept up with the times, dipping into Vietnamese, Japanese, Italian and a whole range of cuisines. The moderately priced food is delicious, desserts decadent and the coffee gets the thumbs up. Licensed & BYO. Dinner only; closed Sun.

La Disfada 109 Ramsay St, Haberfied ☎02/9798 8299. A little off the beaten track in Sydney's true Italian heartland, but reckoned to serve the best pizza in town; no bookings so you might have to queue as it's so popular. The pasta is also delicious. BYO. Dinner Wed–Sun.

Tutto Shop 20, The Italian Forum, 39 Norton St, Leichhardt ☎02/9568 4242. Bus #438 & #440 from Central CityRail. One of a stash of popular Italian restaurants set around the central square of the Italian Forum (see p.108). Book a table for Sunday lunch, when the whole Forum is abuzz with Italian families enjoying alfresco dining. Licensed. Moderate.

The harbour

The Bathers Pavilion 4 The Esplanade,

Balmoral Beach ☎02/9969 5050. Bus #257 from North Sydney CityRail. Indulgent beachhouse-style dining in the former (1930s) changing rooms on Balmoral Beach, now a very pricey restaurant and café double-act, presided over by one of Sydney's top chefs, Serge Dansereau. The fixed-price dinner menu in the restaurant starts from $87 for two courses (from $60 lunch-time). Weekend breakfast in the café is a North Shore ritual – expect to queue to get in (the resto has Sun breakfast only, for which you can book) – while the wood-fired pizzas are popular later in the day. Café daily 7am–midnight, restaurant lunch and dinner daily. Licensed. Expensive to very expensive. See map, pp.118–119.

Doyles on the Beach 11 Marine Parade, Watsons Bay ☎02/9337 1350; also *Doyles Wharf Restaurant* ☎02/9337 1572 next door. Ferry to Watsons Bay Wharf. The original of the long-running Sydney fish-restaurant institution is the first of these, but both serve great if overpriced seafood and have views of the city across the water. They have also taken over the adjacent pub, which serves pub versions in its beer garden. A water taxi can transport you from Circular Quay to Watsons Bay. Licensed. Expensive. Daily lunch and dinner. See map, p.116.

Epoque Belgian Beer Café 429 Miller St, Cammeray ☎02/9954 3811. Bus #202, #207 & #208 from Wynyard CityRail. With a Belgian owner and original wood panelling and fittings, this is a slice of Belgium in Sydney. Draught beer taps dispense Hoegaarden, Leffe Blonde and Brune and Stella Artois, and there are 24 other beers by the bottle. There's only room for eighteen people at the bar, so best to book a table and come to eat. Mussels, of course, are the thing, served with *frites* and mayo, or try the satisfying *andouillettes* (sausage) and mashed potato. Very popular; bookings recommended. Closed Sun. Licensed. Moderate. See map, pp.118–119.

Gourmet Pizza Kitchen 199 Military Rd, Neutral Bay ☎02/9953 9000. Bus #257 from North Sydney CityRail. Spacious, busy place that's especially popular with families – how many other pizza joints provide dough for the kids to play with? Inexpensive. Licensed. See map, pp.118–119.

Indian Empire 5 Walker St, North Sydney ☎02/9923 2909. North Sydney CityRail.

Spectacular view of the city across Lavender Bay, plus everything you'd expect from a good Indian restaurant. Inexpensive to moderate. Closed Sat & Sun lunch. BYO. See map, pp.118–119.

Just Hooked 236 Military Rd, Neutral Bay ☎02/9904 0428. Bus #257 from North Sydney CityRail. A small range of delicious fresh fish in a classy version of a classic fish shop, with white-tiled walls and high but comfortable stools. They do all sorts of inspired, often spicy things with seafood, from Thai curries to pasta dishes, but the simple fish and chips is just as popular. BYO. Inexpensive to moderate. Dinner Mon–Sat. See map, pp.118–119.

Watermark 2A The Esplanade, Balmoral Beach ☎02/9968 3433. Bus #257 from North Sydney CityRail. For a memorable Sydney meal, both for location and food, you can't go wrong here. Chef Kenneth Leung is well-known for his fusion of Eastern and Western cooking styles and ingredients, plus there are views right across the water, a terrace to dine on under the sun or stars (or sit by the fireplace in winter), a stylish interior and fabulous service. Very expensive; licensed. See map, pp.118–119.

Bondi

Bondi Tratt 34B Campbell Parade, Bondi Beach ☎02/9365 4303. Bus #380 & #382 from Bondi Junction CityRail. Considering the setting, with outdoor seating overlooking the beach, *Bondi Tratt* is not at all expensive. Come here to take in the view and the invariably buzzing atmosphere over breakfast, lunch and dinner, or just a coffee. Serves contemporary Australian and Italian food. Daily from 7am–11pm. Moderate. Licensed and BYO.

Gelbison Pizzeria 10 Lamrock Ave, Bondi Beach ☎02/9130 4022. Bus #380 & #382 from Bondi Junction CityRail. Popular breezy pizza restaurant with sea views from a couple of pavement tables. The pizzas get the critical thumbs up and range from traditional to the inspired – their potato pizza (*patate all'aglio*) is surprisingly yummy. Big range of pasta too. Worth booking later in the week as fills up fast. BYO. Inexpensive to moderate.

Hugo's 70 Campbell Parade, Bondi Beach ☎02/9300 0900. Bus #380 & #382 from Bondi Junction CityRail. Set smack amongst the parade of posers, surfers and travellers, this is contemporary Bondi – part café, part fine dining – with a casual, young and friendly flair. At weekends it opens for all-day brunch (Sat & Sun 9am–4pm; no bookings), while every night white table-cloths and softly glowing lamps appear and everyone seems to be having noisy fun. Service is wonderful and honed for your comfort, including blankets for those chilly sea breezes if you sit outside. Generous portions of modern Asian and Mediterranean-slanted creations. Expensive; licensed.

No Names Beach Road Hotel, 71 Beach Rd, corner Glenayr Ave, Bondi ☎02/9130 7247. Bus #389 from Bondi Junction CityRail. This is the choice for a big, filling, cheap and tasty Italian feast after a day at the beach. Eat in the sunny beer garden. Licensed. Pasta $8, mains like schnitzel $12.

North Bondi RSL 120 Ramsgate Avenue, North Bondi. Bus #380, #382 & #389 from Bondi Junction CityRail. Luke Mangan of *Salt* restaurant fame (see p.189) has taken over the dining room of the once downmarket North Bondi RSL and has installed a pro-tégé as chef. Huge windows look right over the north end of the beach, and the modern Australian food is sensational. Moderate to expensive. Licensed.

Sean's Panaroma 270 Campbell Parade, Bondi Beach ☎02/9365 4924. Bus #380, #382 & #389 from Bondi Junction CityRail. A funky, relaxed little restaurant across from the north end of the beach. Sean Moran's food is considered to be some of the best and most inventive in Sydney – the blackboard menu reflects the latest inspirations, though the Mediterranean is the touch-stone. Moderate to expensive. BYO. Lunch Sat & Sun, dinner Wed–Sat.

Yulla 1st Floor, 38 Campbell Parade, Bondi Beach ☎02/9365 1788. Bus #380 & #382 from Bondi Junction CityRail. You could almost miss the discreet orange sign for *Yulla*, which will send you upstairs via a lift. But this is no exclusive restaurant, though the beach views from the balcony are certainly million-dollar. Instead, you'll find a relaxed café atmosphere – colourful glowing walls, shining wooden floors and a window of blue sea – and very affordable contempo-rary Israeli food, which means a mix of Middle Eastern and North African dishes. When Bondi's cafés get packed out for

weekend breakfast, this is a great choice, as so many people don't realize it's here – breakfast is served till noon. Licensed. Inexpensive to moderate. Mon–Thurs 5.30pm–10pm, Fri noon–10.30pm, Sat & Sun 7am–10.30pm.

Coogee

The Beach Pit 211 Coogee Bay Rd, Coogee ☎02/9665 0068. Bus #372 From Central CityRail & #373, #374 & #376 from Circular Quay CityRail. Really enjoyable café-restaurant with Coogee's trademark informality and friendliness. Small but succulent menu has European and Asian influences and plenty of fish and seafood on offer; dishes are generous, well-priced and presented. You can breakfast here at the weekend too. BYO. Inexpensive to moderate. Closed Tues & Wed.

Coogee Bay Hotel Beach Brasserie 212 Arden St, Coogee ☎02/9665 0000. Bus #372From Central CityRail & #373, #374 & #376 from Circular Quay CityRail. Very reasonably priced pub food, with an interesting menu, but traditionalists can cook their own steaks on the barbie. Licensed. Inexpensive.

Sari Rasa 186 Arden St, above McDonald's, Coogee Beach ☎02/9665 5649. Bus #372 From Central CityRail & #373, #374 & #376 from Circular Quay CityRail. A mostly Indonesian menu, plus delicious Malaysian and Indian specialities, accompanied by ocean views – some tables outside on the balcony. Generous servings and low prices; BYO. Inexpensive. Daily noon–3pm & 6pm–late.

Manly and the northern beaches

Alhambra 54 West Esplanade, Manly ☎02/9976 2975. Ferry to Manly Wharf. Opposite the wharf, you can't miss this place when you get off the ferry. The owner is from Spanish Morocco, and the food is both authentic North African and Spanish – tapas, paella, *merguez* sausage, lamb and fish *tagines*, seven vegetable couscous, and a chicken version of *b'stilla* all feature. There are even flamenco dancers some nights (Thurs–Sun) and a classical Spanish guitarist on Tues nights. Moderate. Licensed and BYO.

Jipang 37 The Corso, Manly ☎02/9977 4436. Ferry to Manly Wharf. Excellent Japanese noodle house; very inexpensive. BYO. Closed Mon.

Le Kiosk 1 Marine Parade, Shelly Beach ☎02/9977 4122. **Ferry to Manly Wharf.** The coastal walk from Manly Wharf to secluded Shelly Beach is a delight in itself, and *Le Kiosk* has just the right laid-back beach-house feel. If you can't afford the generous but expensive contemporary fare, fish and chips from the attached kiosk is an excellent alternative. Licensed.

Out of Africa 43–45 East Esplanade, Manly ☎02/9977 0055. **Ferry to Manly Wharf.** Another North African eatery in Manly: *Out of Africa's* friendly owners come from Casablanca and serve authentic, delicious Moroccan fare (except the disappointing desserts), in a brightly coloured restaurant displaying traditional art and craft. You can also eat outside facing the water. There's live African music with your meal Thurs, Fri & Sat nights. Inexpensive to moderate. Licensed & BYO. Lunch Thurs-Sun, dinner nightly.

Somi's 48 Victoria Parade, cnr South Steyne, Manly ☎02/9977 7511. **Ferry to Manly Wharf.** Inexpensive Thai restaurant across from the beach – fantastic views – with an appropriately fresh and delicious range of spicy seafood dishes on the menu, and quite a few vegetarian dishes too. Inexpensive to moderate. Licensed and BYO. Daily noon–11pm.

Drinking

ustralians have a reputation for enjoying a drink, and hotels – more commonly known as **pubs** – are where this mostly takes place. Typically, a pub will have at least a public bar (traditionally rowdier) and a lounge bar (more sedate), a pool table, and in some cases a beer garden. Many offer meals, either in a restaurant or bistro setting, or served up informally at the bar. Ten percent of the world's **poker machines** are found in New South Wales, and the noisy, money-eating things have taken over many Sydney pubs. We have chosen places where these monsters are absent, or at the least, few and unobtrusive. More relaxed licensing laws – including allowing restaurants to serve drinks to non-diners in their bars – has finally seen the burgeoning growth of a sophisticated **bar scene** in Sydney as punters escape pubs and their poker machines.

Some pubs and bars have 24-hour licences, though few actually stay open continuously (we have indicated those that have them, and their normal hours of operation). Standard **opening hours** are Monday to Saturday 11am–11pm/midnight and Sunday 11am–10pm, but many places stay open until at least 2am or later, particularly on Friday and Saturday nights. In July 2003, **smoking** at bar or service counters was banned in New South Wales; a designated non smoking area must also be provided within at least one bar area. By July 2004 a full non smoking bar must be provided in venues with more than one bar.

Draught **beer** is served in a ten-ounce (half-pint) glass known as a **middy** (around $2.80) or the fifteen-ounce **schooner** (around $3.80). Imports such as Guinness and Stella cost a bit more. Three local beers readily available on tap are: Toohey's New, a pretty standard lager; Toohey's Old, a darker, more bitter brew; and Reschs, a tastier, Pilsner-style beer. Upmarket places may only serve beer in bottles, costing from $5. Wine by the glass is available at many places, usually from $5, but expect to pay at least $7 for something choicer. Cocktail bars are very popular, and happy hour (times given in reviews) at one of these can be a great chance to catch the sunset over cheap drinks; outside these times a cocktail will set you back $8.50–14.50.

We have divided our drinking account into areas, starting from The Rocks and ending with Bondi. A few **CBD** bars are closed on Saturday and most also close Sunday (the big nights out downtown are Thursday and Friday). **The Rocks**, with its huge range of lively watering holes, is a fair option on any night, though it does attract a pretty boisterous, beery crowd. A better choice for a cool, gay, or arty scene is **Darlinghurst,** or nearby **Paddington** and **Surry Hills**. You can get a drink any time, day or night, in **Kings Cross**; there's a burgeoning gay and lesbian pub scene in inner-city **Newtown**, and the old neighbourhood pubs of **Balmain** make for a great pub crawl. The best seaside drinking spots are **Bondi**, **Coogee**, **Watsons Bay**, **Manly** and **Newport**. Some pubs serve such good food that we have listed them separately in the "Eating" chapter. Likewise, some pubs listed in the "Live music and clubs" chapter are among the city's best watering holes.

Sydney has many **Art Deco pubs**, a classic 1930s style notably seen in the tilework; see *Burdekin Hotel* (p.201), *Civic Hotel* (p.199), *Palace Hotel* (p.202), *Palisade Hotel* (p.184) and *Piccadilly Hotel* (see *Soho Bar* p.203).

The Rocks

Australian Hotel 100 Cumberland St, The Rocks. Circular Quay CityRail/ferry. Convivial corner hotel with crowded outside tables facing across to the lively basketball courts tucked beneath the Harbour Bridge. Inside, original fittings give a lovely old-pub feel. Known for its Bavarian-style draught beer brewed in Picton, south of Sydney, plus gourmet pizzas with toppings which extend to native creatures – emu, kangaroo and crocodile. Mon–Sat 11am–midnight, Sun 11am–10pm.

Glenmore Hotel 96 Cumberland St, The Rocks. Circular Quay CityRail/ferry. Unpretentious, inexpensive breezy pub perched over The Rocks, with great views from large windows in the public bar, and spectacular ones from the rooftop beer garden (not always open, but Fridays are a good bet). A handy refresher before or after the Harbour Bridge walk, it's opposite the pedestrian walkway entrance and serves up reasonably priced pub grub. Mon–Sat 11am–11pm/midnight, Sun noon–10pm.

Hero of Waterloo 81 Lower Fort St, Millers Point. Circular Quay CityRail/ferry. One of Sydney's oldest pubs, built in 1843 from sandstone dug out from the Argyle Cut (see p.50), this place has plenty of atmosphere. Open fireplaces make it a good choice for a winter drink, and it serves simple meals. Mon–Sat 10am–11pm, Sun 10am–10pm.

Horizons Bar 36th floor, *Shangri-La Hotel*, 176 Cumberland St, The Rocks. Circular Quay CityRail/ferry. *Horizons* is the top-floor bar of the towering five-star *Shangri-La* and has a stunning 270-degree view which takes in

the Opera House, Darling Harbour, Middle Harbour, and Homebush Bay to the Blue Mountains. Smart dress is essential to get in – tables are allocated – and even then it can be too crowded, so prepare for disappointment. It's mega-expensive but worth it for the view (and free nuts at the table); pricey bar snacks include smoked salmon and oysters. Mon–Sat noon–1am, Sun noon–midnight.

Lord Nelson Brewery Hotel Cnr Argyle and Kent streets, Millers Point. Circular Quay CityRail/ferry. Licensed in 1841, this pub serves beer brewed on the premises, plus bar food daily and upmarket meals from its first-floor brasserie (lunch Mon–Fri, dinner Mon–Sat). Ask for a tour of the brewery. Mon–Sat 11am–11pm, Sun noon–10pm.

Lowenbrau Keller Argyle St (corner of Playfair St), The Rocks. Circular Quay CityRail/ferry. It's Oktoberfest all year round in this Bavarian beer hall in a historic Rocks courtyard. This is the only place in Australia that serves Löwenbräu Original and Franziskaner Weissbier on tap, and you can also eat Bavarian food for breakfast, lunch and dinner. If you like it rowdy, this is for you. Mon–Thurs 10am–11pm/midnight, Fri 10am–1/2am, Sat 8.30am–1/2am, Sun 8.30am–11pm.

Mercantile Hotel 25 George St, The Rocks. Circular Quay CityRail/ferry. High-spirited Irish pub with Sydney's best-poured Guinness on offer; bistro meals. Outdoor tables are a fine spot to watch the weekend market crowds. Mon–Wed & Sun 10am–midnight, Thurs–Sat 10am–1am.

Circular Quay and the Sydney Opera House

As well as those listed below, another pleasant place for a drink on **Circular Quay** is the *Sydney Cove Oyster Bar* (see p.174). *Bambu Restaurant* (see p.185) also has a great bar with wonderful views, as does *bel mondo* (see p.184). The

Sydney Opera House has several bars, including the very swish one at its top-notch restaurant, *Guillaume at Bennelong* (see p.185).

Aqua Luna Bar Building 2, Shop 18, Opera Quays, Circular Quay East. Circular Quay CityRail/ferry. Be lured by the blue light into this slick ground-floor bar near the Opera House. Fantastic views of the harbour from the terrace. A speciality is infused vodka, with over 60 flavours to choose from. Restaurant upstairs. Mon–Wed & Sun 11am–11pm, Thurs 11am–midnight, Fri & Sat 11am–2am.

Bridge Bar Level 10, Building 2, Opera Quays, Circular Quay East. Circular Quay CityRail/ferry. Located on top of the infamous "Toaster" building, there's no better place to watch the sun go down: a see-through curtain drops down to minimize glare and ensure an unspoiled view of the harbour. Despite the plush surrounds, the crowd is not as exclusive as you would expect. Meze platters to snack on. Daily noon till late.

Cruise Bar Level 2, Overseas Passenger Terminal, Circular Quay West. Circular Quay CityRail/ferry. With glass walls providing an uninterrupted view of the harbour, the location of this fun and bright addition to the Sydney scene has ensured it's a popular destination for the young and urbane. You'll need to dress well, but drink prices aren't exorbitant. Mon, Tues & Sun 11am–midnight, Wed & Thurs 11am–1am, Fri & Sat 11am–2am.

Customs House Bar 19 Macquarie Place, off Bridge St. Circular Quay CityRail/ferry. Attractive building (circa 1826) fronting onto a city square near Circular Quay (but not at Customs House itself). A suited crowd spills out the doors and schmoozes amongst the palm trees and statues. Cheap bar lunches. Mon–Fri 11am–10pm; closed Sat & Sun.

Opera Bar Lower forecourt, Sydney Opera House, Bennelong Point. Circular Quay CityRail/ferry. *Opera Bar* is part of the Opera House's plan to attract a younger audience and is a fabulous spot for a drink, with outdoor tables right on the harbour and braziers to keep you out here on cool nights. The long, narrow interior is oriented to make the most of the views and has cosy booths or tables to dine at: pre-theatre meals start at 6pm (nothing over $25), and there are very reasonable bar snacks. There's great free live music too – mellow jazz, blues, soul and funk (Tues–Sat at 8.30pm, Sat 2–5pm & Sun 2–8pm). Mon–Sat 10am–1am, Sun 11am–midnight.

Posh Level 3, Overseas Passenger Terminal, Circular Quay West. Circular Quay CityRail/ferry. On the top floor above *Cruise Bar* (see above), *Posh* is also a level up in class: views are even better, and decor is seriously sultry – expect steep drink prices. Mon–Fri 2pm till late, Sat 6pm till late. Closed Sun.

City centre

Art House Hotel 275 Pitt St. Town Hall CityRail. The grand nineteenth-century School of Arts building has been converted into a popular new drinking venue with four bars. High sky-lit ceilings, polished wooden floorboards and beautiful Victorian-era design, plus some modern touches make for a dramatic setting in the main downstairs bar, *The Verge* (a converted chapel), which contrasts with the cosy, quirky *Attic Bar*. True to its name, the *Arthouse* is a great place to learn about art or music, with life-drawing classes in the library, art exhibitions, short-film screenings and guest DJs. The restaurant prices are reasonable and lunch-time bar specials – such as the Mon–Wed $5 steaks – are fantastic value. Mon–Wed 11am–midnight, Thurs 11am–1am, Fri 11am–4am, Sat 5pm–4am. Closed Sun.

Bar Luca 52 Phillip St. Circular Quay CityRail. Trendy European-style licensed bar doubles as an Italian café, with breakfast from 7am and main meals, coffee and cake available throughout the day. The interior is all natural woods, mellow-coloured walls, and fresh flowers, and there's a street-side patio for some fresh air; busy as a drinking spot most nights. Mon–Wed 7am–midnight, Thurs & Fri 7am till late.

Brooklyn Hotel 225 George St, cnr Grosvenor St. Wynyard or Circular Quay CityRail. Rather posh, the *Brooklyn* has a well-regarded, pricey restaurant (specializing in prime beef from the char-grill), magenta walls and gleaming wood floors. Stools run along the length of the big glass windows from where you can watch the city crowds. Popular with cashed-up traders from the nearby Sydney Futures Exchange but also now attracting a younger crowd for the Fri and Sat night DJs. Upmarket eclectic bar food includes $5 steaks. Mon–Thurs 11am–midnight, Fri & Sat to 1/2am, closed Sun.

CBD 75 York St, cnr King St. Wynyard CityRail. Clamorous and swanky ground-floor bar in a renovated Art Deco bank, popular with an after-work crowd. The hotel covers four floors, which include an award-winning modern Australian restaurant (mains $26, extra for salads and side dishes) and two other bars. Mon–Thurs 11.30am–1am, Fri & Sat 11.30am–2am.

Dendy Bar Dendy Cinema, 19 Martin Place. Martin Place CityRail. This basement bar, separate from the Dendy cinema, makes a cool downtown meeting spot, especially as neither the dreaded poker machines nor city suits are found here. There's cushioned seating along the wall and a popular pool room. Happy hour Mon–Fri 4.30–6.30pm. DJs Fri & Sat nights (10pm–6am; $15). Mon–Fri noon–11pm, Sat & Sun noon–6am.

Establishment 252 George St. Wynyard CityRail. One of the new breed of deluxe bars in Sydney aimed at twenty-somethings with a yearning for some old-school glamour. The huge main room boasts an extraordinarily long marble bar, white pillars, high decorative ceilings, and an atrium and

fountain at the back. Despite the size, it gets jam-packed, particularly on Fri nights, and the door policy is very strict, so pre-pare for humiliation. On site there's a ball-room, restaurants (see p.185), the *Tank* nightclub (see p.213), and thirty-odd luxu-rious hotel rooms. Mon & Tues 11am–1am, Wed 11am–2am, Thurs & Fri 11am–3am, Sat noon–3am.

Forbes Hotel Cnr King and York streets. Wynyard CityRail. Atmospheric, turn-of-the-twentieth-century corner hotel with a lively downstairs bar; resolutely untrendy. Upstairs is more sedate, with a pool table and plenty of window seating – the best spot is the tiny cast-iron balcony, with just enough room for two. Very popular Thurs & Fri nights. Mon–Thurs 11am–midnight, Fri & Sat to 3am, Sun to 8pm.

Industrie Bar 107 Pitt St. Martin Place CityRail. The theme is "south of France" yet the biggest point of difference from the prolifer-ation of cocktail bars springing up in the city is *Industrie*'s intimacy. Located in the Pitt Street corporate precinct, it's an ideal spot to shift down a gear from the hustle and bustle of the world outside. Cocktails are $14 and baguettes and omelettes make up the all-day brasserie-style menu. Mon–Wed 7.30am–midnight, Thurs & Fri 7.30am–2am, Sat 6pm–2am. Closed Sun.

Innc basement 244 Pitt St. Town Hall CityRail. A comfortable cocktail environment, with moody lighting and plenty of sofas and inti-mate mesh-curtained booths to relax in. It's popular with young twenty-somethings unwinding after work to funky lounge music. It's not cooler than thou, though: there are free pool tables and pokies to play. A more style-conscious crowd on Saturday nights. Mon–Wed 11am–11pm, Thurs to midnight, Fri to 3am, Sat to 4am.

The Marble Bar *Hilton Hotel*, 259 Pitt St. Town Hall CityRail. As much a sightseeing stopoff as a good spot for a drink. This was the original 1893 basement bar of the *Tattersalls Hotel*, replaced by the *Hilton* in 1973. The *Hilton* is itself undergoing a mas-sive multimillion dollar refurbishment, but the iconic bar will remain the same (but shinier) and will reopen in mid-2004. Mon & Tues 11am–1am, Wed 11am–2am, Thurs & Fri 11am–3am, Sat noon–3am.

Martin Place Bar (MPB) 51 Martin Place. Martin Place CityRail. A new bar that's pop-ular with professionals for breakfast, lunch or after-work drinks. The terrace onto Martin Place is great in the evenings, if you don't mind rubbing shoulders with bankers and lawyers. There are DJs most nights providing a groovy soundtrack. Good-value $9.50 cocktails, and pizza to snack on outside of meal times. Mon–Thurs 7am–midnight, Fri 7am–3am, Sat 9pm–6am.

Orbit Lounge Level 47, Australia Square, 264 George St. Wynyard CityRail. Australia's first Manhattan-style skyscraper, designed by perhaps Sydney's best-known architect Harry Seidler, was built in 1968, and the fifty-storey building was Sydney's tallest for many years. The views from the revolving bar on level 47, attached to the *Summit Restaurant*, are best when darkness falls and the city is dramatically lit up. It's much easier to get in here than the crowded *Horizons Bar* (see p.196); dress code is smart casual. Delicious cocktails from $13.50, snacks from $8. Daily 5pm–midnight.

Senate Bar Lower ground floor, 1 Martin Place. Martin Place CityRail. Elegant, stylish bar below the old GPO, where lawyers and bankers come to sip on imported beers. Sandstone walls and funky ottomans provide a sophisticated feel. Good-value $10

curry-of-the-day lunch includes a drink, and draws them in during the day. Mon–Fri noon–11pm, Sat 5pm till late. Closed Sun.

Slip Inn 111 Sussex St, cnr King St. Town Hall CityRail. On three levels overlooking Darling Harbour, this huge place has several bars, a bistro and a nightclub, the *Chinese Laundry*. A young style-conscious crowd still comes here, but it's dropped some of its past pretension (you can now get a Thai meal for just $7.50 Mon–Thurs). Front bars have a pool room, while downstairs a boisterous beer garden fills up on sultry nights, with the quieter, more sophisticated *Sand Bar* beside it. Excellent wine list, with lots available by the glass. Mon–Thurs noon–midnight, Fri noon–4am, Sat 5.30pm–4am. Closed Sun.

Verandah Bar 60 Castlereagh St. Town Hall CityRail. Lively after-work crowd packs out the *Verandah* on Fridays, when it's impossible to appreciate the wonderful spacious, white and shiny glass interior. You'll need to get in early for a prime position on the verandah overlooking Pitt Street or one of the great booths. If you're after a quiet chat, this isn't for you. Mon noon–10pm, Tues & Wed noon–11pm, Thurs noon–midnight, Fri noon to 1am. Closed Sat & Sun.

Darling Harbour and around

As well as those places that we cover below you can also drink 24 hours in **Darling Harbour** at the Star City Casino (see p.216); *Home* nightclub (p.212) has its own waterfront bar and the area also has a sports bar (see box p.203). The *Glasgow Arms Hotel* (see "Eating" p.186), opposite the Powerhouse Museum, is a pleasant spot for a drink, too.

Cargo Bar 52 The Promenade, King Street Wharf, Darling Harbour. Town Hall CityRail. Popular, stylish waterfront bar attracts a young, good-looking crowd. So great is the buzz, you have to queue to get in on Fri and Sat nights when the music is pumping and it stays open until the small hours. There's a bar upstairs with a balcony and a promenade-level bar with outside tables. Delicious gourmet pizzas. Mon–Wed 11.30am–1am, Thurs–Sun 11.30 to late (to 5am Sat).

Civic Hotel 388 Pitt St, cnr Goulburn St, Haymarket. Town Hall or Central CityRail. Beautiful rejuvenated 1940s Deco-style pub, with original features. Upstairs, there's

a glamorous dining room and cocktail bar where live jazz is often performed. Handy meeting point for Chinatown and George Street cinemas. Mon–Wed 11am–midnight, Thurs 11am–1am, Fri 11am–3/4am, Sat 5pm–3/4am. Closed Sun.

Pontoon Cockle Bay Wharf, Darling Harbour. Town Hall CityRail. This open-fronted bar with outside tables feels like one big lively beer garden, right on the water opposite the new marina. Pool tables inside. Attracts a young casual crowd, despite the upmarket restaurants surrounding it. Daily noon till late.

Scruffy Murphy's 43 Goulburn St, Haymarket. Central CityRail. Rowdy, late-opening Irish pub with Guinness on tap; phenomenally popular, particularly with travellers. Just around the corner from Central Station. 24hr licence: daily 11am–3.30/4.30am.

Scu Bar Basement, 4 Rawson Place, off Pitt St. Central CityRail. This is the bar of the adjacent YHA but it's open to all-comers. Not surprisingly, it's most popular with the many backpackers staying in the area. There's crab racing on Mon nights, and a summer-party theme Thurs. Affordable pub prices and a casual atmosphere. Mon–Fri noon–late, Sat & Sun 5pm–late.

Inner East

The **inner east** of Sydney has the biggest concentration of places to drink, from fun pubs where you can play pool to some of the city's hippest bars, with a huge concentration in Darlinghurst. Many gay bars (see p.224) are also worth checking out: the legendary *Taxi Club* (p.226) is a weird and wonderful place to end a big night out.

Surry Hills

Surry Hills is packed with great pubs, and a couple listed in the "Live music and clubs" and "Eating" chapters are also fun drinking spots: check out the lively *Hopetoun Hotel* (p.210) and the sprawling cheap-eats venue the *Forresters Hotel* (p.187).

Bar Cleveland Cnr Cleveland and Bourke streets. Bus #372, #393 & #395 from Central CityRail. Huge plate-glass windows have opened this pub up onto the busy, gritty street, and punters have packed it ever since for an authentic urban brew. There's a pool table in the main bar, or head for the cosier rear bar. 24hr licence: Mon–Wed 11am–2am, Thurs–Sat 11am–4am, Sun noon–midnight.

Clock Hotel 470 Crown St. Central CityRail. This huge hotel has expanded out of all touch with its 1840s roots (the landmark clock tower was only added in the 1960s). Upstairs, a swish restaurant and cocktail bar runs off the huge balcony – a great place to hang out. There's a popular pool hall and basement gaming room. Mon–Sat 11am–midnight, Sun noon–10pm.

Cricketers Arms 106 Fitzroy St. Central CityRail. Just down the road from the live music scene at the *Hopetoun* (p.210), the *Cricketers* has an equally dedicated clientele. A young, offbeat crowd – plenty of piercings and shaved heads – cram in and fall about the bar, pool room, and tiny beer garden, and yell at each other over a funky soundtrack. Hearty bar snacks and a bistro (Tues–Sun 3–10pm). Mon–Sat noon–midnight, Sun noon–10pm.

Dolphin Hotel 412 Crown St. Central CityRail or bus #301–#303 from Circular Quay CityRail or Castlereagh St, City. Fashionably renovated pub; the lounge bar doubles as a café, while the public bar is as down-to-earth as ever. The tiny upstairs bar, overlooking the stunning architecture of the *Dolphin*'s restaurant, is a good spot for a chat and a glass of wine. Mon–Sat 10am–midnight, Sun noon–10pm.

Mars Lounge 16 Wentworth Ave. Central CityRail. With its high ceilings, red and black decor, subdued lighting and heaps of seating, *Mars* is both comfortable and stylish. Though it's a bar not a club, the emphasis is on music, with an eclectic approach and a different flavour each night: retro jazz, world grooves, Latin, Seventies funk, uplifting house, electronica and more. There's Mediterranean food on the menu, including lots of shareable platters. Tues, Wed & Sun 5pm–1am, Thurs 5pm–1am, Fri & Sat 5pm–3am.

O Bar *Clarendon Hotel*, 156 Devonshire St, cnr of Waterloo St. Central CityRail. The name comes from the perfectly round bar of this upmarket pub near Central Station, popular with youngish professionals. A complete absence of poker machines makes this a good place for a chat over a glass of wine from the well-considered list. It's a particularly attractive stop before dinner on nearby Crown Street – or you could try their own highly regarded bar food. There's also a smaller area with sofas, and a tiny courtyard. Cheap cocktails 5pm–7pm. Mon–Wed noon–midnight, Thurs–Sat noon to 3am. closed Sun.

Darlinghurst

Burdekin 2 Oxford St, Darlinghurst. Museum CityRail. This well-preserved Art Deco pub near Hyde Park has several trendy bars on four levels. The basement *Dug Out Bar* (from 5pm) is tiny and beautifully tiled, and has table service and generous cocktails, while the spacious, ground-level *Main Bar* sports dramatic columns and a huge round bar. *Main Bar* Mon–Thurs noon–1am, Fri noon–4/5am, Sat 3.30pm–4/5am; *Dug Out Bar* Tues–Thurs 5pm–midnight, Fri 5pm–2am, Sat 6pm–3am. Closed Sun.

Chicane 1A Burton St, Darlinghurst, just off Oxford St. Museum CityRail. Located at the "Paris end" of Burton Street, *Chicane* is self-consciously trying to create a *Sex and the City*-style bar atmosphere. The intimate space – it was once a barber's – is seriously ambient, with a warm colour scheme, candles and a fireplace, luxurious armchair and lounge seating, and DJs playing mellow sounds. Dress smartly and you'll fit in. The bar separates the drinking space from the restaurant dining area (quality formal dining, mains from $30). Tues–Thurs & Sat 6pm–3am, Fri noon–3am, Sun 6pm–1am.

Darlo Bar *Royal Sovereign Hotel*, cnr Darlinghurst Rd and Liverpool St, Darlinghurst. Kings Cross CityRail. Popular Darlinghurst meeting place, with a lounge-room atmosphere. Comfy colourful chairs, sofas and lamps have a 1950s feel, the crowd is mixed and unpretentious and drinks, including the house wines, aren't expensive. At night you can order from the menu of nearby *Fishface* (see p.189) and also a local Thai restaurant, and from neighbouring *Eca Bar* during the day; staff fetch the food for you. Mon–Sat 10am–midnight, Sun noon–10pm.

East Village Hotel 234 Palmer St, cnr Liverpool St, Darlinghurst. Kings Cross CityRail. Downhill from the main Darlinghurst bar and café action, this beautifully tiled corner pub, built in 1917, sits alone in a grittier backstreet area with lots of roaming prostitutes – tables on the street provide a glimpse of the street life. The bar is self-consciously stylish, with wooden floors and Sixties-style white swivel chairs – and they won't serve anything as downmarket as a schooner; fellow drinkers resemble young arts

professionals. Mon–Fri 11am–midnight, Sat 2pm–midnight, Sun 3–10.30pm.

Fix *Kirketon Hotel*, 229 Darlinghurst Rd, Darlinghurst. Kings Cross CityRail. This intimate little bar, with its walls lacquered red and its moody lighting, is very sexy and upmarket. The long communal table with its leather bar stools heightens the intimacy, putting the almost-too-cool customers in close proximity. Drinkers here are quite often celebs, who come here for a pre-dinner drink before dining at the adjacent restaurant *Salt* (see p.189). Very expensive. Mon–Thurs & Sun 7pm to midnight, Fri & Sat 6pm–1am.

Green Park Hotel 360 Victoria St, Darlinghurst. Kings Cross CityRail. A Darlinghurst stalwart. Always lively, packed and cruisy at night with a crowd of young regulars. The stash of pool tables out back are a big part of the attraction. Mon–Sat 10am–1am, Sun noon–midnight.

Judgement Bar *Courthouse Hotel*, 189 Oxford St, Darlinghurst. Bus #378 from Central CityRail, #380 & #382 from Circular Quay CityRail. Overlooking Taylor Square, the upstairs bar of this pub is often open 24hr. Totally undiscriminating – you may find yourself here in the wee hours among an assortment of young clubbers and old drunks – and drinks aren't pricey. Wakes up around 1am. 24hr licence: Mon–Thurs 11am–3am, Fri & Sat 24hr, Sun 11am–midnight.

Lizard Lounge *Exchange Hotel*, 34 Oxford St, Darlinghurst. Museum CityRail. Stylish, (mostly) straight bar in a gay strip – Tues night from 11pm is girls only and the *Phoenix Bar* downstairs is gay on Sat & Sun nights – this place has a spacious interior, wooden floorboards, changing art exhibitions and comfy leather couches in the corner (bag one of these early). Happy hour (Mon–Fri 5–8pm) gets them in, and as the crowd gathers, posing becomes the main game. At weekends after 11pm the bar becomes a club called *Stereo* (Fri $15, Sat $20), which leads through an entrance into *Q Bar* (see p.212). Otherwise the bar runs Mon–Sat 5pm to around 3am.

Middle Bar 1st floor, *Kinsela's*, 383 Bourke St, Darlinghurst. Bus #378 from Central CityRail #380 & #382 from Circular Quay CityRail. Once a deluxe Art Deco funeral parlour, *Kinsela's* has long been transformed into a drinking and dancing spot. The *Middle Bar* is seriously sexy, from its lush decor and sunken seating area to the young good-looking crowd who drink here. You can gaze at the action in Taylor Square from the open-air balcony. In contrast, the unglamorous ground-floor bar is full of noisy poker machines. *Middle Bar* Tues, Wed & Sun 5pm–1am, Thurs 5pm–3am, Fri & Sat 5pm–4am; ground-floor bar 24hr.

Palace Hotel 122 Flinders St, cnr South Dowling St, Darlinghurst. Bus #397–#399 from Circular Quay CityRail. Classic Art Deco tiled corner pub, fashionably done-up. Noisy boho and student hangout downstairs, and a tiny eating area services the recommended Thai kitchen (students get discounts on Tues nights); eat meals where you can find a spot. Star attraction is the several rooms of pool tables upstairs. Mon–Wed 4pm–midnight, Thurs–Sat 4pm–1am, Sun 4–11pm.

Savage 182 Campbell St, Darlinghurst, just off Taylor Square. Bus #378 from Central CityRail, Bus #380 & #382 from Circular Quay CityRail. Upstairs, above the restaurant of the same name (the usual modern Australian fare), this new bar has a vinyl record store attached, and a cool soundtrack to go with your drinks. Tues–Sun noon–midnight.

Will and Toby's Level 1, 294 Victoria St, Darlinghurst. Kings Cross CityRail. Fashionable new bistro and bar run by two young brothers. The interior design is summery white and Sixties retro, right down to the cube seats; the small space and a legendary friendly service gives the relaxed atmosphere of a private party. Mon–Sat 6pm–1am.

Paddington and Woollahra

Two lively drinking spots reviewed in the "Eating" chapter, the *Paddington Inn* (see p.190) and the *Grand National Hotel* (see p.190) shouldn't be overlooked. Likewise, the *Fringe Bar* (see p.217) is known for its comedy nights but is also good for a drink anytime.

Elephant Bar *Royal Hotel*, 237 Glenmore Rd, Paddington. Bus #389 from Circular Quay CityRail. The top-floor bar of this beautifully renovated, Victorian-era hotel has knockout views of the city, best appreciated at sunset (happy hour 6–7pm). The small interior is great too, with fireplaces, paintings and elephant prints. As it gets crowded later on, people cram onto the

stairwell and it feels like a party. Mon–Fri 5pm–midnight, Sat 4.30pm–midnight, Sun 4.30–10pm.

Grand Pacific Blue Room Cnr Oxford and South Dowling streets, Paddington. Bus #378 from Central CityRail, #380 & #382 from Circular Quay CityRail. Housed in an Art Deco building, this cross between a bar, restaurant and club is as grand as its name suggests. But the bar is surprisingly cosy and diners eat below (Chinese/modern Australian menu). This is where the chill-out lounge culture in Sydney began, and young and now not-so-young trendy locals come to drink and dance – the DJs get going at 11pm. Mon–Wed 6pm–1am, Thurs–Sat 6pm–3am.

Lord Dudley 236 Jersey Rd, Woollahra. Bus #389 from Circular Quay CityRail. Sydney's most British pub, complete with fireplaces, fox-hunting pictures, dark wood furniture – and a dartboard. Thirty-six beers on tap, many imported, including Newcastle Brown Ale. The bistro serves up hearty British fare. Mon–Sat 10am–midnight, Sun 10am–10pm.

Kings Cross and Woolloomooloo

There are several pubs and bars in **Kings Cross**, many of them back-packers' hangouts, which we've listed in the "Live music and clubs" chapter, as the emphasis is on DJs and dancing – see *Kings Cross Hotel* (p.212) and *The World* (p.213); the bars reviewed here are more sophisticated options. There are several boisterous pubs in **Woolloomooloo** opposite the naval base including the *Woolloomooloo Bay Hotel* (see "Eating", p.190).

Hugo's Lounge 33 Bayswater Rd, Kings Cross. Kings Cross CityRail. The same people who run the very successful *Hugo's* restaurant opposite Bondi Beach (see p.192) have opened this very cool bar and restaurant. The beautiful bar, complete with ottomans to loll on, has a very decadent Oriental feel and attracts a beautiful crowd – it can be hard to get into. Expensive drinks. Tues–Sat 6pm–1am.

Peppermint Lounge 281 Victoria St, Kings Cross. Kings Cross CityRail. Decor is sexy and plush in this European-style bar, with plenty of couches and private booths to relax in.

Young crowd. Wed & Thurs 6pm–4am, Fri & Sat 6pm–5am, Sun 6pm–3am.

Soho Bar & Lounge Piccadilly Hotel, 171 Victoria St, Kings Cross. Kings Cross CityRail. This trendy Art Deco pub on leafy Victoria Street has recently been refurbished and is looking better than ever. The downstairs *Soho Bar* is the most Deco, but locals head for the upstairs *Lounge Bar* (Tues–Sun nights only) to hang out on the back balcony and play pool. The attached nightclub, *Yu*, operates on Fri and Sat nights. Daily 5pm–5am.

Water Bar *W Hotel*, Cowper Wharf Rd, Woolloomooloo. Kings Cross CityRail. The bar of Sydney's hippest hotel (see p.155), this place is fabulously located in a dramatically renovated old iron and timber finger wharf. The sense of space is sensational, the lighting lush, and the sofas gorgeously designed and comfortable. A favourite with local celebrities, you may even spot an Australian actor you recognize. The pricey drinks (cocktails from $15.50) and the extortionate cost of the snacks (nuts from $8) are worth it for the architecture and ambience. Mon & Sun 4pm–1am, Tues–Sat 4pm–midnight.

Inner West

The areas around the Sydney University – **Glebe**, **Chippendale** and **Newtown** – have always had plenty of lively pubs. Further west, **Leichhardt** and **Balmain** also have some great boozers and the latter is a good place for a crawl.

Glebe

Ancient Briton 225 Glebe Point Road, cnr Bridge Rd, Glebe. Bus #431, #433 & #434 from Central CityRail. This lively pub is popular with the area's travellers, helped by claims of the coldest beer in Sydney, plus free Internet access (15min) for every drink bought, and cheap drink deals (happy hour daily 4.30pm–7.30pm). There's inexpensive Asian noodles on offer, and a stash of cheap pool tables upstairs, as well as a cosier cocktail bar. Mon–Sat 8am–midnight, Sun 1am–10pm.

Friend in Hand 58 Cowper St, cnr Queen St. Bus #431, #433 & #434 from Central CityRail. This characterful pub in the leafy back-streets of Glebe, with all manner of curious objects dangling from the walls and ceilings of the public bar, is a popular haunt for backpackers. Diverse entertainment in the upstairs bar (where you can also play

Sports bars

As well as the two places listed below, you can catch live big-screen **sport** at many other drinking spots, including Star City Casino (see p.216) and the *Ivanhoe Hotel* at Manly (p.206). You can also imbibe happily at Sydney's several race tracks (see "Sports and activities", p.257).

One World Sports Bar 25 Harbour St, Darling Harbour. Town Hall CityRail. ⓦ www.oneworldsport.com.au. Seventy-three TVs plus three megascreens here show everything from Fox Sports to SBS football coverage. There are even TVs in the toilets, and some booths at the back where you can control your viewing. Sporting paraphernalia covers the walls, and bar snacks are suitably unfancy. 24hr licence: Mon–Thurs & Sun 10am–10.30pm, Fri & Sat 10am–3/4am, but opens earlier/later for specific sporting events (check website for details).

Sports Central Bent St, Fox Studios ⓦ www.sportscentralatfox.com. Bus #339, #392, #394 & #396 from Central CityRail. A sports-themed place with three bars, ten-pin bowling lanes ($6 before 5pm, $12.50 after), American pool tables ($3 per game), electronic games ($2 per game), 45 television screens and one huge screen, and Fox Sports broadcasts. Bar snacks served. Mon–Thurs & Sun noon–midnight, Fri & Sat noon–2am.

pool) includes script-reading (Mon), poetry nights (Tues), and quizzes (Thurs). In the public bar, crab racing takes over Wed nights, and there's a piano player on Sat nights. There's also a cheap Italian restaurant, *Cesare's No Names* (see p.190). Mon–Sat 10am–midnight, Sun noon–10pm.

Nag's Head 162 St Johns Rd, off Glebe Point Rd. Bus #470 from Central CityRail. Calling itself a "posh pub", this is a good place for a quiet drink. With several imported beers on tap (Guinness, Boddingtons, Stella and Becks), and pints and half-pints available, decor and atmosphere is British. The bistro dishes up excellent steaks and other grills, and there's an extensive bar menu. For more action, there's a loft area upstairs with pool tables. Mon–Sat 11am–midnight, Sun noon–midnight.

Chippendale and Newtown

In addition to the watering holes included here the *Lansdowne Hotel* in **Chippendale** opposite Victoria Park (see p.102) has a great little cocktail bar upstairs and popular pool tables downstairs, while the *Sandringham Hotel* ("Sando") in **Newtown** (see p.104) has long been one of the area's favourite places to drink.

Bank Hotel 324 King St, next to Newtown Station. Newtown CityRail. Smart-looking pub that's always packed and open late. Pool table out front, cocktail bar out back and a big beer garden downstairs (with Thai restaurant). 24hr licence: Mon & Tues noon–12.30am, Wed & Thurs noon–1.30/2am, Fri & Sat noon–4am, Sun noon–midnight.

Kellys on King 285 King St, Newtown. Newtown CityRail. Celtic mysticism meets outback charm in this quaint Irish pub in the middle of Newtown. Colourful locals drink with students and backpackers in a relaxed setting. A good selection of Irish beers on tap. Mon–Thurs 10am–2am, Fri to 10am–3am, Sat to 10am–4am, Sun to 11am to midnight.

Kuleto's 157 King St, Newtown. Newtown CityRail. Small but lively and unpretentious cocktail bar, packed with inner-city types for the two-for-one cocktails during happy hour (Mon–Sat 6–7.30pm & bonus happy hour Thurs 9.30–10.30pm). Ideal meeting point

before a King Street dinner. Daily 4pm till late.

Marlborough Hotel 145 King St, Newtown. Newtown CityRail. A local favourite for a pre-dinner drink and a hangout for students from nearby Sydney University, the "Marly" is benefiting from almost a decade of major structural work. The spacious pub with several bars and a great beer garden also has a popular, good-value restaurant, *Bar Prego*, serving a diverse assortment of meals with an Italian slant. Cover bands Tues & Sat and a funk band on Sun, trivia nights Wed and DJs Thurs. 24hr licence: Mon–Wed 10am–2am, Thurs–Sat 10am–3am, Sun noon–midnight.

The Rose 54 Cleveland St, Chippendale. Bus #423, #424, #426 & #428 from Central CityRail. This funkily decorated pub near Victoria Park is a real treasure, despite the unpromising location at the traffic-laden end of Cleveland Street. A mock-Renaissance ceiling mural overlooks a popular pool table, while a bizarrely decorated rocking horse is suspended over the partly covered beer garden out back (doubling as a modern Australian eatery with a huge blackboard menu). Good wine list, available by the glass. Mon–Sat 11.30am–midnight, Sun 11.30am–10pm.

Balmain and Leichhardt

Exchange Hotel Cnr Beattie and Mullens streets, Balmain. Bus #442 from Darling Street Wharf or the QVB. This classic Balmain back-street corner pub, built in 1885, has a large iron-lace balcony, which is the perfect place to sample the weekend early-morning Bloody Mary specials. Daily 10am–midnight.

Leichhardt Hotel 95 Norton St, Leichhardt. Bus #438 & #440 from Central CityRail. With a courtyard opening onto the busy Italian restaurant strip and a first-floor balcony also providing a vantage point, the newly incarnated *Leichhardt Hotel* is a very slick designer pub. The dramatic contemporary interior includes a huge Caravaggio-style mural, a modern Italian restaurant (bar snacks also available) and a good selection of Italian bottled beers. Mon–Wed noon–midnight, Thurs–Sat noon–3am.

London Hotel 234 Darling St, Balmain. Bus

#442 from Darling Street Wharf or the QVB.
Convivial British-style pub, with a high
verandah overlooking the Saturday market.
Attracts a typically mixed Balmain crowd.
Mon–Sat 11am–midnight, Sun
noon–10pm.
**Monkey Bar 255 Darling St, Balmain. Bus #442
from Darling Street wharf or the QVB.** Stylish

bar overlooking an atrium restaurant.
Twenty- and thirty-something professionals
drink in this loud and crowded space.
There's a small stage for the free live music
– blues, soul, jazz or acoustic rock – Tues
8–11pm and Sun 6–9pm. Inexpenisve bar
menu and a variety of wine by the glass.
Mon–Sat noon–midnight, Sun noon–10pm.

The harbour

Three of the best places to drink around the harbour, **Watsons Bay**,
Newport and **Neutral Bay**, are listed in the "Legendary beer gardens" box
below.

**Greenwood Hotel 36 Blue St, North Sydney.
North Sydney CityRail.** A former school, this
gorgeous old sandstone building has been
turned into a very pleasant, extensive pub,
with the big courtyard serving as a haven
from the corporate bustle of the North
Shore's high-rise business district. There
are four bars, one of which includes a
restaurant area serving lunch Mon–Fri
(modern Australian with mains at around
$16–19); you can also eat outside and bar
snacks are available in the evenings. From

Thurs to Sun there is much more of a party
atmosphere here; the best time to come is
on Sun, when around a thousand trendy
young people flock to the day club which
takes over the whole pub; between twelve
and fifteen DJs in three different areas,
including the courtyard, play everything
from funky house to hip hop ($15). There's
a free student night, also with DJs, on
Thurs (7pm–3am). Mon–Wed 11am–11pm,
Thurs–Fri 11am–3am, Sat 4pm–3am, Sun
noon–10pm.

Legendary beer gardens

Many Sydney pubs have an outdoor drinking area, perfect for enjoying the sunny
weather – the four listed below, however, are outright legends.

Doyle's Watsons Bay Hotel 10 Marine Parade, Watsons Bay. Ferry to Watsons
Bay Wharf or bus #324 & #325 from Edgecliff CityRail. Relaxing garden with views
over Watsons Bay and good-value bistro meals, crowded at weekends with people
enjoying a beer with their fish and chips. Mon–Thurs & Sun 10am–10pm, Fri & Sat
till midnight.

The Mean Fiddler Lot 3, Windsor Rd, Rouse Hill ⓦwww.meanfiddler.com.au. No
public transport. About an hour's drive from Sydney's CBD, the *Fiddler* is well
worth the effort, as evidenced by the huge crowds it consistently attracts. An Irish
pub with something for everyone – small intimate rooms, a big courtyard with live
entertainment or live sport on the TVs in the sports bar. One of the best beer
gardens in Sydney. Mon–Thurs 11am–11pm, Fri & Sat 11am–2am, Sun
11am–10pm.

Newport Arms Hotel 2 Kalinya St, Newport. Bus #190 from Wynyard CityRail.
Overlooking Pittwater. Sunday is the big day, with free jazz outside (1–5pm), and
the bistro serving food from noon right through until closing time. Mon–Sat
10am–midnight, Sun 10am–9.30pm.

The Oaks Hotel 118 Military Rd, Neutral Bay. Bus #247 & #263 from Wynyard
CityRail. The North Shore's most popular pub takes its name from the huge oak
that shades the entire beer garden. Make use of the BBQ and cook your own
(expensive) steak, or if you're feeling lazy, there's a gourmet pizza restaurant inside.
Mon–Thurs & Sun 10am–midnight, Fri & Sat till 1am.

Ocean beaches

The relaxed pubs and bars at Sydney's **ocean beaches** are great places to come for a daytime or early-evening drink; come back later in the evening, dressed up for a night of fun, as entertainment and seaside pubs are a traditional Sydney combo.

Bondi and the eastern beaches

There's great food and views at the *North Bondi RSL*, and it's also a lively drinking hole (see p.193). Also check out the legendary *Coogee Bay Hotel* (see p.159 and p.193).

Beach Palace Hotel 169 Dolphin St, Coogee. Bus #372 & #373 from Central CityRail. Home to a young and drunken crowd, made up of locals, beach babes and backpackers. Features seven bars, two restaurants and a great view of the beach from the balcony under the distinctive dome. There are DJs on the middle level Wed–Sat (Wed & Thurs 8pm–1am, Fri & Sat 10pm–3am) and on the top floor Thur & Fri (8pm to midnight); entrance for which is free except on Sat after 10pm when it's $5. Mon–Thurs 11am–1am, Fri & Sat 11am–3am, Sun 11am–midnight.

Beach Road Hotel 71 Beach Rd, Bondi Beach. Bus #389 from Bondi Junction CityRail. Huge, stylishly decorated pub with a bewildering range of bars on two levels and a beer garden. Popular with both travellers and locals for its good vibe. Entertainment, mostly free, comes from rock bands, DJs and a jazz supper club. The hotel also has a cheap Italian bistro, *No Names* (see p.193), and an upmarket contemporary Australian restaurant.

Bondi Hotel 178 Campbell Parade, Bondi Beach. Bus #380 & #382 from Bondi Junction CityRail. Huge pub dating from the 1920s, with many of its original features intact. Sedate during the day but at night an over-the-top, late-night backpackers' hangout. Mon–Sat till 4am.

Bondi Icebergs Club 1 Notts Ave, Bondi Beach. Bus #380 & #382 from Bondi Junction CityRail. Famous for its winter swimming club (see p.129), the *Icebergs* is a fantastic place to soak up the atmosphere of Bondi Beach. You'll find a crowd of backpackers and other tourists enjoying the cheap drinks, live entertainment and fabulous view of the southern end of the beach, complete with surfers catching the waves. Cover bands play Wed and Fri–Sun and there's trivia on Mon. Meals at the *Sundeck Café* with its open-air balconies range from $5–20 or there's a pricey restaurant upstairs. To guarantee entry, bring your passport or other ID to show you're an out-of-towner. Daily 11am–11pm.

Clovelly Hotel 381 Clovelly Rd, Clovelly. Bus #360 from Bondi Junction CityRail. Known to the locals as the "Cloey", this huge hotel perched above the beach has four bars and a fantastic, very popular bistro complete with a great terrace eating area with beach views. Come on Sunday, when there's a DJ in the bar upstairs (from 7pm; free). Pool tables. Mon–Sat 10am–midnight, Sun 10am–10pm.

Ravesi's Campbell Parade, cnr Hall St, Bondi Beach. Bus #380 & #382 from Bondi CityRail. A former shoe store was wasted in this corner spot looking across to the beach and it's now a very popular and stylish bar attached to the boutique hotel above (see p.161). Huge windows ensure full people- and ocean-watching opportunities. There's a dress policy in the evening but you can get away with beach gear by day. There's beer on tap, but it's pricier than elsewhere. Wine by the glass starts from $6. There is also a basement bar open Thurs–Sun and a bistro-style restaurant upstairs, with more great views from its balcony tables. Mon–Sat 10am–midnight, Sun 10am–10pm.

Manly and the northern beaches

Ivanhoe Hotel 27 The Corso, Manly. Ferry to Manly Wharf. This huge Corso pub combines several bars with a nightclub and brasserie over four floors and includes a terrace and balcony where you can take in some sun. Locals and backpackers crowd the place out, from the oldtimers in the public bar, to the smartly dressed twenty-somethings in the lounge bar. The weekend two-for-one cocktail deals (before 11pm Fri & Sat, before 9pm Sun) ensure a merry atmosphere, and there's various live music and also DJs Wed–Sat nights (free or $5–$10). 24hr licence but generally: Mon–Wed 9am–midnight, Thurs 9am–1am, Fri & Sat 9am–5am, Sun 9am–midnight.

Old Manly Boatshed 40 The Corso, Manly. **Ferry to Manly Wharf** ☏02/9977 4443; ⓦwww.manlyboatshed.com.au. Characterful and relaxed basement bar filled with Manly Surf Club paraphernalia is popular with both the area's backpackers and a crew of local regulars. There's Mon night stand-up comedy (8.30pm; $7) and free live music every night (Tues–Thurs & Sun 8.30pm; Fri & Sat 9.30pm); Thurs is the night for emerging songwriters. Food is served until midnight – the café-style menu includes good-value steaks ($15) and the *Boatshed*'s legendary steak sandwich ($10.50). Mon–Sat 6pm–3am, Sun 6pm to midnight.

U-Turn Bar 36–38 South Steyne Rd. **Ferry to Manly Wharf.** This is the sophisticated but trendy bar choice in Manly, and is in a great spot opposite the beach. Half of the area is a restaurant, for early breakfasts at the weekend right through to expensive dinners with an emphasis on seafood; bar food served into the small hours. Sun night DJ (8.30pm–midnight; free). Mon–Fri noon–3am, Sat 7am–3am, Sun 7am to midnight.

DRINKING | Ocean beaches

Live music and clubs

t's easy enough to find out exactly what's going on in the Sydney music and club scene. You'll find **listings** of music events in the "Metro" supplement in Friday's *Sydney Morning Herald* and "Time Out", a weekly entertainment lift-out in Sunday's *Sun-Herald*, but the best listings are in the excellent new "Sydney Live Magazine" in the *Daily Telegraph* every Wednesday, aimed squarely at the 18–30 market; there's also a more general what's on pull-out, "Seven Days", in Thursday's *Daily Telegraph*. A plethora of **free magazines** give information on more alternative goings-on – clubbing, fashion, and the like – and band interviews and reviews, and can be found in the cafés, record shops and boutiques of Surry Hills, Darlinghurst, Glebe and Newtown: *On the Street, Drum Media* (with an online gig guide at ⓦ www.drummedia.com.au) and *Revolver* have weekly listings and reviews; *3D World* and *Beat* cover the clubbing scene. Best of all is *Revolver*, which offers informed and well-written critiques (as opposed to the more illiterate diary entries printed elsewhere). **Radio** station 2 MMM (FM 104.9MHz) details music gigs around town daily on the hour between 2 and 6pm. There's also a handy web-based gig guide prepared by ABC Radio's youth station Triple J (ⓦ www.abc.net.au /triplej/gigs). Also check the useful **website** ⓦ www.sydney.citysearch.com.au, a kind of listings mag on the net, with plenty about the music and club scene.

Live music

Australia in general, and Sydney in particular, has a well-deserved reputation for producing quality **live bands**: the thriving pub scene of the late 1970s and early 1980s produced a spectrum of great acts, from indie stars Nick Cave, The Church and the Triffids, to globe-straddling stadium-shakers like INXS.

Sadly, the live music scene in Sydney has passed its boom time, and pub venues keep closing down to make way for the dreaded poker machines.

Buying tickets

Ticketek is the main **booking agency**, with branches located throughout Sydney, including 195 Elizabeth St; inside Grace Bros department store at the corner of George and Market streets; and within the Entertainment Centre by Darling Harbour (☏ 02/9266 4800, ⓦ www.ticketek.com.au). There's also Ticketmaster7, at the Capitol Theatre, 13 Campbell St, Haymarket or 480 Elizabeth St, Surry Hills (bookings ☏ 02/9310 5020, ⓦ www.ticketmaster7.com). Fish Records sell tickets to selected gigs in-store (see "Shopping" p.247 for locations or ⓦ www.fishrecords .com.au) or over the phone on Fish Tix (☏ 02/9410 1444).

However, there are still enough venues to nourish a steady stream of local, interstate and overseas acts passing through every month, peaking in summer with several huge open-air festivals (see box on p.210).

Besides the big concert halls, Sydney's live music action still centres around **pub venues** (see below). Pub bands are often free, especially if you arrive early (bands generally go on stage around 9.30–10.30pm, earlier on Sundays); otherwise, $5–8 is a standard entry fee for local bands, $12–15 for the latest interstate sensation and upwards of $20 for smaller international acts. Late Sunday afternoon and early evenings are notably laid-back – an excellent time to catch some, funk or mellow jazz bands, which are usually free.

Concert venues

Capitol Theatre 13 Campbell St, Haymarket ☎02/9266 4800. Central CityRail. Refurbished, older theatre with balcony seating and room for around 2000 people. The Capitol hosts musicals and even ballet, but crooners and mellow pop groups occasionally appear here (see also p.216).

City Live Bent St, cnr Errol Flynn Boulevard, Fox Studios, Moore Park ☎02/9358 8000, ⓦwww.citylive.com.au. Bus #339 from Central CityRail. This massive three-floor, six-bar venue has a capacity of 1800. From all-ages gigs to CD launches, it plays host to a wide range of special events and concerts. A versatile venue with great acoustics but drink prices are ridiculous.

Enmore Theatre 118–132 Enmore Rd, Enmore ☎02/9550 3666, ⓦwww.enmoretheatre.com.au. Newtown CityRail. A pleasingly intimate, old-world theatre venue for 1500 people – dingier than the Capitol, a fact which sits comfortably with its location, near to inner-city Newtown. Elvis Costello, the Pogues, Kraftwerk and the Cranberries are among notables to have played here.

Metro Theatre 624 George St ☎02/9264 2666, ⓦwww.metrotheatre.com.au. Town Hall CityRail. Purpose-designed to handle everything from musicals to bands and dance parties, the Metro is exceptionally well laid out and has an excellent sound system; holds up to 1200 people.

Selina's *Coogee Bay Hotel*, 212 Arden St, Coogee Bay ☎02/9665 0000, ⓦwww.c-inc.com.au. Bus #372 from Central CityRail, #373 & 374 from Circular Quay CityRail. Woeful interior design has the audience peeping around pillars, and the acoustics are terrible, but a dearth of competition sees *Selina's* survive as Sydney's largest genuine pub venue. Room for 1100 punters.

State Theatre 49 Market St ☎02/9373 6655,

ⓦwww.statetheatre.com.au. Town Hall CityRail. This 2000-seat theatre is decked out perhaps a bit too opulently in marble and statuary, but performers who insist on a bit of grandeur play here.

Sydney Entertainment Centre Haymarket, beside Darling Harbour ☎02/9266 4800, ⓦwww.sydentcent.com.au. Central CityRail. Soulless, 12,000-seat arena with video screens and a good sound system – Sydney's largest indoor venue, for big international acts.

Pub venues

As well as the places listed below which are well known as live music venues, many of the **pubs and bars** reviewed in the "Drinking" chapter also have regular music nights: see the *Opera Bar* at the Opera House (p.197), the *Civic Hotel* in the city (p.199), the *Marlborough Hotel* in Newtown (p.204), the *Monkey Bar* in Balmain (p.205), in Bondi the *Beach Road Hotel* (p.206) and the *Bondi Icebergs Club* (p.206), in Manly the *Ivanhoe Hotel* (p.206)and the *Old Manly Boatshed* (p.207), and the *Newport Arms Hotel* (p.205) in Newport.

Annandale Hotel Cnr Nelson St and Parramatta Rd, Annandale ☎02/9550 1078, ⓦwww.annandalehotel.com. Bus #438 & #440 from Central CityRail. One of Sydney's best showcases for local and interstate indie bands, from up-and-comers to headline international acts, through rock, funk, metal and groove, with a capacity of 450. Music Tues–Sat nights. Entry $5–12.

The Basement 29 Reiby Place, Circular Quay ☎02/9251 2797, ⓦwww.thebasement.com.au. Circular Quay CityRail/ferry. A great place to see jazz, acoustic and world music, as well as a roster of renowned blues performers. The best option is to book a table and dine in front of the low stage; if you don't and it's a largish crowd, you'll might find yourself in a cramped spot with an obstructed view.

Bridge Hotel 135 Victoria Rd, Rozelle ☎02/9810 1260. Bus #501 from Central CityRail. A legendary inner-west venue, specializing in blues and pub rock, with mostly local acts and occasional international artists. Also pub theatre and comedy nights.

Excelsior Hotel 64 Foveaux St, Surry Hills ☎02/9211 4945. Central CityRail. Something of a muso's pub, this place is now back in action with jazz four nights a week: residencies cover every style, from swing to avant garde (Mon–Wed & Sun 8pm). Sun evening from 6pm is usually a jamming session. Bistro. Bar till 3am Fri & Sat. Entry $5.

Hopetoun Hotel 416 Bourke St, cnr Fitzroy St, Surry Hills ☎02/9361 5257. Central CityRail. The "Hoey" is one of Sydney's best venues for the indie band scene, focusing on new, young bands: local, interstate and inter-

national all play in the small and inevitably packed front bar Mon–Sat (from 7.30pm; cover charge depends on the act, though sometimes free), and on Sun there are DJs (5–10pm; $5). There's also a popular pool room, a drinking pit in the basement, and an inexpensive little restaurant upstairs (meals from $5–8.50). Closes midnight.

Rose of Australia Hotel 1 Swanson St, Erskineville ☎02/9565 1441. Erskineville CityRail. Trendy inner-city types mix with, goths, locals and gays to sample some of the favourites of the pub circuit. Tues nights is Jazz and Soul Residency, Wed is popular local performer Bernie Hayes and a special guest appearance (laid-back Australian sounds). Bands play Fri and Sun on a rotational basis, so you can catch anything from an original rock act, to a country-and-western cover band. Music starts from 8.30pm (from 6.30pm Sun) and is always free. The bistro is cheap (from $5) and popular.

Sandringham Hotel 387 King St, Newtown ☎02/9557 1254. Newtown CityRail. The only

Outdoor music festivals

There are now several big outdoor rock concerts in Sydney, throughout spring and summer, but the **Big Day Out** in late January is the original and the best (around $90 plus booking fee; ⊛www.bigdayout.com). Held at the showground at the Sydney Olympic Park at Homebush Bay (see p.145), it features big international names such as the Foo Fighters and PJ Harvey, as well as local talent, and attracts crowds of over 50,000. One of the latest additions to the rock circuit is **Livid**, the one-day Brisbane music festival which was held in Moore Park (see p.95) for the first time in late October 2002. It attracted audiences of 20,000, with 43 acts from internationals such as Oasis, to locals Machine Gun Fellatio (around $90 plus booking fee; ⊛www.livid.com.au). **Homebake** (around $60 plus booking fee; ⊛www.homebake.com.au) is a huge annual open-air festival in The Domain (see p.66) in early December with food and market stalls, rides and a line-up of over fifty famous and underground Australian bands from Killing Heidi to Grinspoon.

The big outdoor dance music festival is **Vibes on a Summers Day**, a sweltering day of sultry beats, trip-hop, reggae flavours and excruciatingly beautiful bodies at the end of January, either in and around the Bondi Pavilion at Bondi or at the Arthur Byrne Reserve at Maroubra Beach (around $88; ⊛www.vibes.net.au); past guests have included the Afro Celt Sound System and Jazzanova.

Tickets for all of the above festivals are available from Fish Records (see p.247).

The **Manly International Jazz Festival** runs over the Labour Day long weekend in early October. Free outdoor stages include one on the scenic harbourfront and one on the oceanfront; there are also a number of indoor concert venues charging admission. The wide-ranging guests of previous years have included a Slovenian band playing Gypsy swing, a Japanese jazz orchestra and an Italian trio, plus well known local, US and UK acts. You can get advance details from Manly Council (⊛www.manly.nsw.gov.au). For other musical events through the year, see the "Festivals and events" chapter pp.249–253.

remaining music venue in Newtown, which once had a thriving music scene; even the veteran "Sando" stopped playing music for a while but once again features local and interstate indie bands. Bands are no longer squeezed beside the bar but play on a stage upstairs. Music Thurs–Sat 8.30pm–midnight, Sun 7–10pm; usually $5–8, more well-known bands $12–15.

Side On Cafe 83 Parramatta Rd, Annandale ℡02/9519 0055, 🌐www.side-on.com.au. Bus #438, #440 from Central CityRail. Sydney's most interesting venue calls itself a "multi-arts complex", and on Fri and Sat nights you can hear jazz here in an intimate café atmosphere – everything from popular trios to the latest experimental fusions. Wed night is artist's residency, Thurs is world music/Latin. Book if you want to dine (℡02/9516 3077); mains such as steak with roasted vegetables cost around $20. The venue also offers Sun night cabaret plus there's an art gallery and sometimes film screenings and script readings. Entry $10–15.

Soup Plus 383 George St, City ℡02/9299 7728. Wynyard CityRail. This simple restaurant, in a basement near the Strand Arcade, has been serving up live jazz with its bowls of soup ($5) for over 25 years; other simple meals, from fish through to pasta, are also served. Music Mon–Sat 7–11.30pm (Fri & Sat $25 cover charge includes a two-course meal). Closed Sun.

Wine Banc 53 Martin Place ℡02/9233 5399. Martin Place CityRail. Very good cutting-edge jazz, playing to an upmarket well-heeled wine-bar crowd. Located downstairs off the main street, the soft lighting and funky music creates a chill-out atmosphere. You can get a delicious French-style meal at a reasonable price (mains around $16) while you're waiting for a band to begin. Live music Fri (entry $10) and Sat nights ($15) from 9pm. After midnight there's a "jam session", with jazz on Fri and Latino music Sat. The wine list is both extensive and expensive. Mon–Fri noon–11pm/midnight, Sat 6pm–2am. Closed Sun.

Clubs

Many of Sydney's best clubs are at **gay** or **lesbian** venues, and although we've listed these separately on p.226, the divisions are not always clear – many places have specific gay, lesbian and straight nights scheduled each week. A long strip of thriving clubs stretches from Kings Cross to Oxford Street and down towards Hyde Park, with *D.C.M.* (see p.226) perhaps the most popular. There are also clubs attached to several of the pubs we've listed – see *Slip Inn* for the *Chinese Laundry* (p.199) – and some pubs actually transform into clubs, such as the hugely popular Sunday day club which takes over the entire *Greenwood Hotel* in North Sydney (see p.205), even the beer garden. Most other pubs and bars don't push things quite so far, but DJs are fast taking over from the live music scene and you'll find people dancing at least one night a week in the city at the *Art House Hotel* (p.197), *Brooklyn Hotel* (p.198), *Dendy Bar* (p.198), *Martin Place Bar* (p.198), in Paddington at the *Grand Pacific Blue Room* (p.202), in Newtown at the *Marlborough Hotel* (p.204) and by the beaches at the *Clovelly Hotel* (p.206), the *Beach Palace Hotel* in Coogee (p.206), *Beach Road Hotel* in Bondi (p.206), and the *U-Turn Bar* in Manly (p.207).

The **club scene** can be pretty snobby, with door gorillas frequently vetting your style. **Admission** ranges from $5 to $30, depending on the club; many stay open until 5am Saturday morning and until 6am Sunday morning.

BJ's 195 Oxford St Mall, Bondi Junction ℡02/9388 9100. Bondi Junction CityRail. Lively club for lovers of South American sounds and salsa. A Latino band plays three sets through the night, while DJs offer up merengue plus house and techno in two different club rooms. Sat 9.30pm–3am only. Entry $15.

Cave Nightclub Star City Casino, Pirrama Rd, Pyrmont ℡02/9566 4755, 🌐www.cavenight club.com.au. Star City Light Rail. Located at the northern end of the casino complex,

Cave draws a well-dressed crowd that's keen to be seen. DJs play funk, soul and R&B on Fri ($15), and uplifting house and dance on Sat ($20). Fri & Sat 9pm–6am, Sun 9pm till late.

Club 77 77 William St, East Sydney ☎02/9361 4981. Kings Cross CityRail. Rock venue which has post-band indie and alternative dance parties on Fri & Sat nights until 5am. Popular with students. Drink prices aren't as high as at other clubs. Entry $6.

Gas 467 Pitt St, Haymarket, entered through the foyer of an office building ☎02/9211 3088, ⊕www.gasnightclub.com. Central CityRail. There's one huge cutting-edge room downstairs where international DJs appear about once a month and a mezzanine level which acts as a viewing area over the dance floor, with chill-out lounges attached. Three bar areas. Thurs–Sun 10pm–6am. Entry Thurs $15, Fri & Sat $20.

Globe 60 Park St, cnr Elizabeth St ☎02/9264 4844, ⊕www.sydneyglobe.net. Town Hall CityRail. *Globe*'s cocktail bar lounge is open 24 hours. On Thurs to Sat nights from 10pm (till 4am Thurs, till 6am Fri & Sat) it's linked to a downstairs club section – you'll have to dress very cool to get past the door. With a long legacy of quality nights and talented DJs, this is a great place for soul, energetic house and hip-hop sounds. Wed nights are Get Down (funk and soul; $10), Thurs is Funk Trust ($15), resident and international DJs on Fri ($15) and Fly on Sat (from deep sexy house to break beat $15).

Home Cockle Bay Wharf, Darling Harbour ☎02/9266 0600, ⊕www.homesydney.com.au. Town Hall CityRail. The first really big club venture in Sydney, the lavish *Home* can cram 2000 punters into its cool, cavernous interior; there's also a mezzanine, a chill-out room, and outdoor balconies. The decks are often manned by big-name DJs, drinks are expensive and staff beautiful. Attracts a younger crowd on Fri for its packed, flagship night Sublime, with four musical styles across four levels. On Sat, Together at Home plays progressive and funky house. Sat & Sun 11pm till late (waterfront public bar open regular pub hours). Entry $25.

Kings Cross Hotel Cnr William St and Darlinghurst Rd, Kings Cross ☎02/9358 3377. Kings Cross CityRail. Popular with backpackers, a brash in-your-face pub section at ground level has activity nights

Mon–Wed & Sun from 8pm: homesick Brits can watch *Eastenders* on Mon nights, Tues is trivia, there's a pool comp on Wed and on Sun nights you can watch a big-screen movie. Thurs is "Loaded" (from 10pm), an indie night, very big with the British crowd and on Fri and Sat there's live drag shows (11pm, midnight & 1am) and DJs playing club classics. Daily 12pm–2am. Free entry.

Powercuts Reggae Club *Castles Hotel*, 114 Castlereagh St ☎02/9261 2238. TownHall CityRail. DJs play the "smoothest reggae known to man" every Saturday night from 10pm till late; $10. The venue for Powercuts can change, so check the website or call the pub before setting out.

Q Bar 44 Oxford St, Darlinghurst ☎02/9360 1375. Museum CityRail. As the name suggests, this is a huge pool hall, but the main game is looking good in an elite crowd: it is exclusive and difficult to penetrate, particularly if you're male and don't have a stunning babe on your arm. Inside it's another world altogether – entry is via a lift (although you can also get in through the *Lizard Lounge*; see p.201) and the club is decked out with rich kid's toys, such as arcade machines and a photo booth to capture your insobriety. Daily 7pm till late (except Fri from 5pm).

Rogues Cnr Oxford and Riley streets, Darlinghurst ☎02/9380 9244. Museum CityRail. Popular with the younger straight Oxford Street clubbing crowd who can afford the hefty cover charge (Wed & Fri $16.50, Sat $25) and the $15 cocktails, proceeds of which go towards employing the good-looking, skimpily dressed bar staff. The sandstone basement with its stone arches makes a very architecturally attractive main dance floor. Predominantly commercial dance and R&B at the weekends, although Eighties funk on Wed nights pulls an older crowd. Wed, Fri & Sat 9.30pm–6am.

Sugareef 20 Bayswater Rd, Kings Cross ☎02/9368 4256. Kings Cross CityRail. After the sweaty writhing of neighbouring *The World* (see p.opposite), *Sugareef* presents a more chilled, sophisticated atmosphere; deep house and breakbeat attract a regular crowd. Two rooms, two DJs and a popular pool table too. Well-attended on Tues nights when there's not much happening elsewhere. Free on Wed ("DJ Discovery" night), otherwise entry $5–15. Tues–Sun 9pm–6am.

Tank 3 Bridge Lane, off George St, City ☎ 02/9240 3094, ✆ www.tankclub.com.au. **Wynyard CityRail.** This is for the glamorous industry crowd – fashion, music and film aficionados. If you don't belong, the style police can spot you a mile away. All very "funky" – from the house music played by regular or guest DJs to the mirrors and wash basins in the toilets. There are three amazing bars and a VIP section. Attire is smart casual to funky street wear, but attitude and good looks override the dress code. Fri & Sat 10pm–6am. Entry Fri $15, Sat $20.

Tantra 169 Oxford St, Darlinghurst ☎ 02/9331 7729, ✆ www.tantrabar.com.au. Bus #378 from Central CityRail or #380 & #382 from Circular Quay CityRail. Rotating resident DJs and live musicians/percussionists ensure that there's always something new happening here. The younger crowd comes on Fri for the high-octane beats, while Sat sees predominantly 25–30 year olds. Entry $10–30.

The World 24 Bayswater Rd, Kings Cross ☎ 02/9357 7700. **Kings Cross CityRail.** With cheap drinks on Fri and Sat nights and a relatively relaxed door policy, *The World* is popular with a fun party-loving crowd of travellers who jive to a pleasing mix of funk and house grooves in a pleasant Victorian-era building with a big front balcony. The atmosphere throughout is lively, if a little beery in the front bar. Fri & Sat noon–6am, Mon–Thurs & Sun noon–4am.

Performing arts
and film

From Shakespeare to gay film festivals, Sydney's arts scene takes itself seriously while managing never to lose its sense of fun. Free summertime outdoor performances, such as the Sydney Festival's **Opera in The Domain** (see p.249), are among the year's highlights, as Sydneysiders turn out in their thousands to picnic and share in the atmosphere.

For **listings** of **what's on** at the venues below, check the *Sydney Morning Herald*'s Friday supplement "Metro", or the *Daily Telegraph*'s Thursday pull-out "Seven Days". The Sydney Citysearch **website** ⓦwww.sydney.citysearch .com.au also has listings and reviews, while Sydney City Council produce *City Life*, a free weekly list of theatrical productions, classical concerts and other events which comes out on Wednesdays; you can pick it up at the Town Hall or at tourist offices, or download it from their website, ⓦwww.cityofsydney .nsw.gov.au.

Classical music, opera and ballet

The **Sydney Opera House** is the centre of high culture in Sydney, and while it's not necessary to don tie-and-tails or an evening dress when attending a performance, it's still about the only place you're likely to see locals in formal attire.

Sydney's five most prestigious performing arts companies, the Australian Ballet, Opera Australia, the Sydney Symphony Orchestra, the Sydney Theatre Company (see p.216) and the Sydney Dance Company (see box opposite) all have Opera House seasons. The **Australian Ballet**, which features contemporary as well as classical dance (tickets from $55; information ⓦwww.australian

---

Buying tickets

You can book through Ticketek, the main **booking agency** or Ticketmaster7; details of both can be found in the box on p.208.

For theatre, concerts, opera and ballet you can always try for cheap, same-day tickets at the **Halftix** office at 91 York St (Mon–Fri 9.30am–5pm, Sat 10am-3pm; enquiries ☎02/9279 0855, bookings ⓦwww.halftix.com.au); they also sell regular tickets.

ballet.com.au), shifts between Sydney and Melbourne – it's based in the latter, but performs at the Opera House from mid-March to early May, and November through December, and sometimes at the Capitol Theatre. **Opera Australia** (tickets from $90; information ⓦ www.opera-australia.org.au) also alternates between the two cities, with Opera House seasons in either the Concert Hall or the Opera Theatre from June to November and during February and March; it also performs at the Capitol Theatre. The **Sydney Symphony Orchestra** (tickets from $40; information and bookings ⓦ www.sso.com.au) performs at the Sydney Opera House Concert Hall and the City Recital Hall.

City Recital Hall Angel Place, between George and Pitt streets. Martin Place CityRail. On-site box office ☎ 02/8256 2222, ⓦ www.cityrecital-hall.com. Opened in 1999, this classical music venue right next to Martin Place was specifically designed for chamber music. Seats 1238, but on three levels giving it an intimate atmosphere.

Conservatorium of Music Off Macquarie St, in the Botanic Gardens ☎ 02/9351 1263, ⓦ www.usyd.edu.au/su/conmusic. Circular Quay CityRail/ferry. Students at the "Con", a prestigious branch of Sydney University, have traditionally given free lunch-time recitals every Wednesday and Friday at 1.10pm during term time in Recital Hall West. Other concerts involving staff and students (some free, otherwise up to $30) are held here and at various venues around town; a programme is available from the concert department or check the website. Also see p.64.

Eugene Goosens Hall ABC Centre, Harris St, Ultimo ☎ 02/9333 1500, ⓦ www.abc.net.au/classic. Central CityRail. Auditorium (320-seater) with state-of-the-art

acoustics within the radio headquarters of the ABC, used for very reasonably priced ABC Classic FM Recital Series and some-times free lunch-time concerts; check the website for event details. Named after the British conductor who brought the Sydney Symphony Orchestra to world-class stan-dards in the 1940s and 1950s (see p.59). The four-week Sydney Spring International Festival of New Music is held here from the end of August/beginning of September.

St James' Church King St, beside Hyde Park ☎ 02/9232 3022, ⓦ www.stjameschurch sydney.org.au. St James or Town Hall CityRail. This beautiful little Anglican church (see p.74) has long been associated with fine music. It has its own director of music and a highly acclaimed semi-professional ten-member chamber choir, whose repertoire extends from Gregorian chants to more contemporary pieces. The choir can be heard every Sun morning at 11am and on the last Sun of the month at 3.30pm. Evening events – concerts and choirs – are held once a month, usually on a Thurs at 6.30pm ($22; check website for dates).

Contemporary dance companies

NAISDA Dance College 3 Cumberland St, The Rocks ☎ 02/9252 0199, ⓦ www.naisda .com.au. Established in 1976, this famous training company for young Aboriginal and Islander dancers, based in The Rocks, puts on mid-year and end of year performances at the NAISDA Studios at the college; call or check the website for times.

Bangarra Dance Theatre Pier 4, Hickson Rd, Millers Point ☎ 02/9251 5333, ⓦ www.bangarra .com.au. Formed in 1989, Bangarra's innovative style fuses contemporary movement with the traditional dances and culture of the Yirrkala Community in Arnhemland. They are based at the same pier as the Wharf Theatre but perform at other venues in Sydney and tour nationally and internationally – check their website for the latest details.

Sydney Dance Company ☎ 02/9221 4811, ⓦ www.sydneydance.com.au. Graeme Murphy, Australia's doyen of dance, has been at the helm of the Sydney Dance Company since 1976, and continues to set the standard with ambitious sets and beautifully designed costumes. The company is based at the Wharf Theatre (see p.216 and p.52), with Opera House seasons April–May and Sept–Oct.

Sydney Opera House Bennelong Point
☎02/9250 7777, ⓦwww.sydneyopera
house.com. Circular Quay CityRail/ferry. The
Opera House is Sydney's prestige venue for
opera, classical music and ballet. Forget
quibbles about acoustics or ticket prices –
it's worth going just to say you've been.
The huge Concert Hall, seating 2690, is
home to the Sydney Symphony Orchestra
and also hosts opera; the smaller Opera
Theatre (1547 seats) hosts opera, ballet
and contemporary dance. See below for
details of performances at the Opera
House's three theatrical venues. See also
p.58.

Town Hall Cnr Druitt and George streets
☎02/9265 9007, ⓦwww.cityofsydney.nsw
.gov.au. Town Hall CityRail. Centrally located
concert hall (seats 2000) with a splendid
high-Victorian interior – hosts everything
from chamber orchestras to bush dances
and public lectures. See also p.74.

Theatre

Prices for mainstream theatre performances are fairly high, from $25 to $70
for the best seat at a Sydney Theatre Company performance; tickets in smaller,
fringe venues cost from around $22.

Major venues

Capitol Theatre 13 Campbell St, Haymarket
☎02/9320 5000. Central CityRail. Built as a
deluxe picture theatre in the 1920s, the
Capitol was saved from demolition and beautifully restored in the mid-1990s. The 2000-
seater now hosts big-budget musicals, ballet
and opera, which you watch from beneath its
best feature, the deep blue ceiling spangled
with the stars of the southern skies.

Footbridge Theatre Sydney University,
Parramatta Rd ☎02/9692 9955. Bus #436–#440
from Central CityRail. Rich and varied repertoire, from *Cabaret* to Shakespeare.

Star City Casino 20–80 Pyrmont St, Pyrmont
☎02/9657 9657, ⓦwww.starcity.com.au. Star
City Light Rail. Sydney's Vegas-style casino
has two theatres catering to popular tastes.
The technically advanced Lyric Theatre,
seating 2000, stages hit musicals such as
Showboat, while the smaller Star City
Showroom puts on more off-beat musicals
– such as the *Rocky Horror Picture Show* –
and comedy.

Theatre Royal MLC Centre, King St, City
☎02/9266 4800. Martin Place CityRail.
Imported musicals and blockbuster plays in
a Harry Seidler-designed building opened in
1976; seats 1180.

Drama and performance

Belvoir St Theatre 25 Belvoir St, Surry Hills
☎02/9699 3444, ⓦwww.belvoir.com.au.
Central CityRail. Highly regarded two-stage
venue for a wide range of contemporary

Australian and international theatre.

Ensemble Theatre 78 McDougall St, Milsons
Point ☎02/9929 0644, ⓦwww.ensemble
.com.au. Milsons Point CityRail. Australian
contemporary and classical theatre.

Sydney Opera House Bennelong Point
☎02/9250 7777, ⓦwww.sydneyopera
house.com. Circular Quay CityRail/ferry. The
Opera House has three theatrical venues.
The Playhouse and the Drama Theatre
show modern and traditional Australian and
international plays mostly put on by the
Sydney Theatre Company (also see p.52
and below) while The Studio, the Opera
House's smallest venue (and with the most
affordable ticket prices) is flexible in design
with a theatre-in-the-round format, and
offers an innovative and wide-ranging programme of contemporary performance:
theatre, cabaret, dance, comedy, and
hybrid works.

Wharf Theatre Pier 4, Hickson Rd, Millers Point
☎02/9250 1777, ⓦwww.sydneytheatre
.com.au. Circular Quay CityRail/ferry. Home to
the highly regarded Sydney Theatre
Company (STC) – which produces
Shakespeare and modern pieces and has
two theatres here – and to the Sydney
Dance Company (see p.215). Atmospheric
waterfront location, and a well-regarded
restaurant, bar and café. See also p.184.

Fringe and repertory

New Theatre 542 King St, Newtown ☎02/9519
3403, ⓦwww.ramin.com.au/online/newtheatre.
Newtown or St Peters CityRail. Professional and

amateur actors (all unpaid) perform contemporary dramas with socially relevant themes.
NIDA Studio 215 Anzac Parade, Kensington ☎02/9697 7613, ⓦ www.nida.unsw.edu.au. Bus #390–#394 from Central CityRail. Australia's premier dramatic training ground – the National Institute of Dramatic Art – where the likes of Mel Gibson and Judy Davis started out. The three seasons of student productions (March–April, July–Aug &

Sept–Oct), in a brand-new auditorium, are open to the public as well as talent-spotters.
The Performance Space 199 Cleveland St, Redfern ☎02/9319 5091, ⓦ www.performance space.com.au. Central CityRail. Stages experimental performances.
Stables Theatre 10 Nimrod St, Darlinghurst ☎02/9361 3817, ⓦ www.griffintheatre.com.au. Kings Cross CityRail. Develops and fosters new Australian playwrights.

Comedy and cabaret

As well as the listings below, the **drag shows** at the *Imperial Hotel* in Erskineville (see p.225) are also great fun. And there's occasional comedy at the *Bridge Hotel* in Rozelle (see p.210) and the *Exchange Hotel* in Balmain (see p.204).

Comedy Store Fox Studios, Driver Ave, Moore Park ☎02/9357 1419, ⓦ www.comedystore .com.au. Bus #339 from Central CityRail. International (often American) and established Australian stand-up comics Thurs–Sat nights; new comics and open mic nights Tues & Wed. Bar open from 4pm, shows 8.30pm. Meals aren't available inside, but the sleek *Arena Bar & Bistro* offers meal discounts for Comedy Store ticket holders. Entry Tues & Wed $15, Thurs–Sat $27.50. Bookings recommended for Thurs–Sat.
The Fringe Bar *Unicorn Hotel*, 106 Oxford St, Paddington ☎02/9360 3554. Bus #378 from Central CityRail or #380 & #382 from Circular Quay CityRail. The popular Mon night Comedy Circuit features local stand-up comics from 8.30pm. Dinner and show $25, show only $9.
The Laugh Garage Comedy Club *Agincourt*

Hotel, Cnr George and Harris streets, Broadway ☎02/8883 1111, ⓦ www.thelaughgarage.com. Central CityRail. Comedy line-ups of local, interstate and international comedians from 9pm Thurs–Sat. Dinner and show $40, show only $20.
Old Manly Boatshed 40 The Corso, Manly ☎02/9977 4443 ⓦ www.manlyboatshed .com.au. Ferry to Manly Wharf. Characterful and relaxed basement bar with Mon night stand-up comedy (8.30pm; $7) and a café-style menu (also see p.207).
Theatresports Belvoir Street Theatre, 25 Belvoir St, Surry Hills ☎02/9699 3444. Central CityRail. Theatresports is the intellectual's answer to footy – pure performance improvisation on-the-run. The teams square off most Sun evenings at Belvoir Street, and occasionally at other venues around town such as the Enmore Theatre. Tickets around $24.

Cinema

Sydneysiders love going to **the pictures**, and in recent years Hollywood itself has come to town in the shape of the Fox Studios site (see also p.95), which offers superb facilities and filming locations in the heart of the city, plus sixteen cinema screens to choose from. During the summer you can watch films **outdoors**, either at one of Sydney's open-air cinemas (see box on p.220), or at one of the city's lively film festivals (see box on pp.218–219).

Main venues

The commercial movie centre of Sydney is two blocks south of the

Town Hall at 505–525 George Street, where you'll find the three big **chains** – Hoyts (☎02/9273 7431, ⓦ www.hoyts.com.au), Greater

Film Festivals

The great variety of **film festivals** in Sydney provides opportunities to catch a movie in one of a number of attractive outdoor settings.

Sydney Film Festival

The **Sydney Film Festival** (☎ 02/9660 3844, ⓦ www.sydneyfilmfestival.org), held annually over two weeks in early June, is an exciting programme of features, shorts, documentaries and retrospective screenings from Australia and around the world. Founded at Sydney University in 1954, the festival struggled with prudish censors until freedom from censorship for festival films was introduced in 1971. From the early, relaxed atmosphere of picnics on the lawns between screenings, it has gradually moved off-campus, to find a home from 1974 in the magnificent State Theatre (see p.73). Films are also shown at the wonderfully located three-screen Dendy Quays on Circular Quay East (see p.219).

The festival was once mainly sold on a subscription basis, but subscriptions now only apply to screenings at the State Theatre; the more provocative line-up of films at the Dendy Quays aims to attract a new, under-35 audience to the festival on a single or packaged ticket basis. Single **tickets** cost around $14, packages of five to ten tickets $12.50 or eleven or more $11. **Subscriptions** for the entire State Theatre programme start from $155 for day-time only unreserved stalls seating, and go up to $260 for two weeks' reserved dress circle night-time screenings. You can also get a one-week unreserved evening subscription for $120.

Flickerfest and Tropfest

There are now also two short-film festivals in Sydney, both of which echo the young and irreverent attitude that once fuelled the Sydney Film Festival. Stars above and the sound of waves accompany the week-long **Flickerfest International Short Film Festival** (☎ 02/9365 6888, ⓦ www.flickerfest.com.au; single ticket $13.50, season pass $110), held in early January in the amphitheatre of the Bondi Pavilion; foreign and Australian productions are screened, including documentaries.

Union (☎ 02/9267 8666, ⓦ www.greaterunion.com.au) and Village (☎ 02/9273 7409, ⓦ www.villagecinemas.com.au) – under one roof. This is mainstream, fast-food, teenager territory and there are much nicer places to watch a film. Other more pleasantly located Hoyts can be found at the Broadway Shopping Centre, on Broadway near Glebe (☎ 02/9211 1911), and at Fox Studios (see below). Standard tickets cost around $14, but Tuesdays are reduced-price (around $9.50) at all Hoyts, Greater Union and Village cinemas and their suburban outlets, and Monday or Tuesday at the arthouse and local cinemas listed below.

Cinema Paris Driver Ave, off Lang Rd, Moore Park ☎ 02/9332 1633, ⓦ www.hoyts.com.au. Bus #339 from Central CityRail. Hoyts' "art-house" option; the teenagers drop away and the atmosphere is suddenly very adult in this pleasant four-screen cinema which also offers Sun double features.

Palace Academy 3A Oxford St, cnr South Dowling St, Paddington ☎ 02/9361 4453, ⓦ www.biziworks.com.au. Bus #378 from Central CityRail, #380, #382 from Circular Quay CityRail. One of a chain of three inner-city cinemas showing foreign-language, art-house and new releases, with discounts on Mon. If you are going to be in Sydney for a while, and will be staying or working near one of these cinemas, it's worth buying a Palace Card ($16.50 for 12 months), which gives you discount-price ($9.50) tickets anytime for yourself and a friend; it doesn't take long to recoup the membership price.

Palace Verona 17 Oxford St, cnr Verona St, Paddington ☎ 02/9360 6099; bus #378 from Central CityRail, #380, #382 from Circular Quay CityRail. Arthouse and foreign-language fare, plus new releases. Also has a trendy

The **Tropfest** (☎9368 0434, ⓦwww.tropfest.com.au) is a competition festival for short films held annually on the last Sunday of February. Its name comes from the *Tropicana Café* (see p.178) on Victoria Street, Darlinghurst, where the festival began almost by chance in 1993 when young actor John Polsen persuaded his local coffee spot to show the short film he had made. He pushed other filmmakers to follow suit, and the following year a huge crowd packed themselves into the café to watch around twenty films. These days the entire street is closed to traffic to enable an outdoor screening, while cafés along the strip screen films on TVs inside. The festival has grown enormously over the years and the focus of the event has now moved to The Domain, with live entertainment from 3pm and huge crowds turning up to watch the free 8pm screening and picnic on the grass. Films must be specifically produced for the festival and be up-to-the-minute, and to this end an item which must feature in the shorts is announced a few months in advance of the entry date; in 2003 it was a "rock" – however you wanted to interpret it. The judges, who turn up for the screenings, are often famous international actors, which adds a bit of excitement, and Polsen himself, the festival's director, has made it as a Hollywood director with his recent film *Swimfan* (and you can also see him in *Mission Impossible II* alongside Tom Cruise).

Other film festivals

Other film festivals include the **Women on Women Film Festival** (ⓦwww.wift.org/wow), held over three days in late September at the Chauvel Cinema, Paddington. There is also a **Gay and Lesbian Film Festival** in late February as part of the Sydney Gay Lesbian Mardi Gras (see p.221), and French, Italian, Spanish and Greek film festivals – look out for ads. The latest, and quirkiest addition to the scene, is the outdoor **Goat Island Film Festival** (late Nov or early Dec; ⓦwww.cityofsydney.nsw.gov.au), an outdoor event with a different theme each year, which takes over the island (special ferries are put on to get you there).

first-floor bar. Another branch, the Palace Norton, at 99 Norton St, Leichhardt (☎02/9550 0122; bus #438 & #440 from Central CityRail), has a bookshop and cybercafé and hosts an Italian film festival in early Dec.

The Dendy MLC Centre, Martin Place ☎02/9233 8166, ⓦwww.dendy.com.au. Martin Place CityRail. Trendy single-screen cinema showing prestige, arthouse and foreign new-release films; also has a café, bar and pool-room (see p.198). Other branches of the Dendy chain can be found at the four-screen Dendy Newtown, 261 King St, Newtown (☎02/9550 5699; Newtown CityRail), with attached café, bar and book-shop, and the superbly sited three-screen Dendy Quays, 2 East Circular Quay (☎02/9247 3800; Circular Quay CityRail/ferry). Discount day Mon but if you're staying in Sydney longer and will be living or working near one of these cin-emas, it's worth investing in a Club Dendy card ($15 for twelve months) which gives discount tickets ($9.50) for yourself and a friend anytime.

Hoyts at Fox Studios Driver Ave, off Lang Rd, Moore Park ☎02/9332 1300, ⓦwww.hoyts.com.au. Bus #339 from Central CityRail. Twelve-screen multiplex showing mainstream new releases. La Premiere, the special deluxe section aimed at couples (bookings ☎02/9266 4887), provides custom-made sofa seats for two with wine holders and tables for food – cheese plates are provided when you purchase a bottle of wine, though tea, coffee and popcorn are all included in the ticket price; prices start at $22, rising to $27.50 on Saturday night.

Reading Cinema Level 3, Market City Shopping Centre, Haymarket ☎02/9280 1202, ⓦwww.readingcinemas.com.au. Central CityRail. Mainstream five-screen multiplex with longer runs of new films. Adjacent Asian food court and bar handy for quick

Outdoor cinema

In the summer, two open-air cinemas set up shop. From November to mid-February the **Moonlight Cinema**, in the Centennial Park Amphitheatre on Oxford Street (Woollahra entrance; Tues–Sun, films start 8.45pm, tickets from 7.30pm or via Ticketek on ☎02/9266 4800; $14; ⓦwww.moonlight.com.au; bus #378 from Central CityRail or #380 & #382 from Bondi Junction CityRail), shows classic, arthouse and cult films. Throughout January as part of the Sydney Festival, the **Open Air Cinema** is erected at Mrs Macquaries Point in the Royal Botanic Gardens (tickets from 6.30pm or bookings on ☎13 06 100; $17.50), screening mainly mainstream recent releases and some classics. Other opportunities to watch films under the stars are detailed in the "Film festivals" box on pp.218–219.

pre- or post-movie meals. Cheap day Tues plus discounted tickets before 6pm, though generally cheaper than Hoyts.

Panasonic IMAX Theatre Southern Promenade, Darling Harbour ☎02/9281 3300, ⓦwww.imax.com.au. Town Hall CityRail. State-of-the-art giant cinema screen showing a choice of four films designed to thrill your senses, for $15 for 2-D version, $17 for 3-D.

Locals and independents

Chauvel Twin Cinema Paddington Town Hall, cnr Oatley Rd and Oxford St, Paddington ☎02/9361 5398, ⓦwww.chauvelcinema .com.au. Bus #378 from Central CityRail or #380 & #382 from Circular Quay or Bondi Junction CityRail. This grandiose Town Hall is a beautiful setting to taste the varied programme of Australian and foreign films plus classics. An Australian Film Institue (AFI) cinema, and a definite cineaste haunt. Discount days Mon & Tues. The $38 four-film pass can also be used at the Valhalla (see below).

Cremorne Orpheum 380 Military Rd, Cremorne ☎02/9908 4344, ⓦwww.orpheum.com.au. Bus #243 from Wynyard CityRail or #246 & 247 from Clarence St. Charming Heritage-listed four-screen cinema built in 1935 with a splendid Art Deco interior. The main cinema keeps up a tradition of Wurlitzer organ recitals preceding the Sat and Sun night films (also sometimes Tues & Fri nights). Mainstream and foreign new releases. Discount day Tues.

Govinda's Movie Room 112 Darlinghurst Rd, Darlinghurst ☎02/9380 5162, ⓦwww .govindas.com.au. Kings Cross CityRail. Run by the Hare Krishnas (but definitely no indoctrination), Govinda's shows two films every night from a range of classics and recent releases in a pleasantly unorthodox cushion-room atmosphere (you have to take off your shoes if you lie on the cushions so choose unsmelly footwear). The movie and dinner deal (all-you-can-eat vegetarian buffet) is popular – $15.90 for the meal and then an extra 10 percent to see the movie – and you may need to book.

Randwick Ritz 45 St Paul St, Randwick ☎02/9611 4811. Bus #339 from Central CityRail or #372, #373, #374 & #377 from Circular Quay CityRail. Characterful old cinema handy if you're staying in Coogee, with five screens showing mainstream new releases and always at discount prices. "Bubs Clubs" child-friendly sessions for parents every fortnight (first & third Mon of month 10.30am). The area around the cinema known to the locals as "the Spot", has a big concentration of cafés and culturally diverse restaurants to eat at before or afterwards.

Valhalla 166 Glebe Point Rd, Glebe ☎02/9660 8050, ⓦwww.valhallacinemas.com.au. Bus #431, #433, #434 from Central CityRail. The beloved Valhalla, Sydney's first alternative cinema (established in 1976), shows documentaries, foreign films, new-release independents and Australian films. Also hosts specialist evenings – including short-film nights – which draw in local filmmakers for screenings and discussions. The $38 four-film pass can also be used at the Chauvel (see above).

Gay Sydney

S ydney is indisputably one of the world's great **gay** cities – indeed, many people think it capable of snatching San Francisco's crown as the queen of them all. There's something for everyone – whether you want to lie on a beach during the warmer months (April–Oct) or party hard all year round. The weather is at its steamiest in February – just in time for the **Sydney Gay + Lesbian Mardi Gras**. As things start to warm up again, the beginning of spring is celebrated with the **Sleaze Ball**, an annual Mardi Gras fundraiser in late September/early October.

But don't despair if you can't be here for Mardi Gras or Sleaze. The city has much more to offer. **Oxford Street** is Sydney's official "pink strip" of gay restaurants, coffee shops, bookshops and bars, and here you'll find countless tight-T-shirted guys strolling hand-in-hand, or checking out the passing talent from a hip streetside café. However, the gay-straight divide in Sydney has less relevance for a new generation, perhaps ironically a result of Mardi Gras' mainstream success. Many of the long-running gay venues on and around Oxford Street have closed down and many of the remaining ones attract older customers, as younger gays and lesbians embrace inclusiveness and party with their straight friends and peers. **King Street**, Newtown, and nearby **Erskineville**, is another centre of gay culture, while lesbian communities have carved out territory of their own in **Leichhardt** (known affectionately as "Dykehart"). The bar and club listings on pp.224–227 have not been split into separate gay and lesbian listings, as the scene thankfully doesn't split so neatly into "them and us".

A good starting point for **information** is The Bookshop, 207 Oxford St, Darlinghurst ☎02/9331 1103, ⓦwww.thebookshop.com.au, which has a complete stock of gay- and lesbian-related books, cards and magazines, including the free gay and lesbian weeklies, *Sydney Star Observer* (ⓦwww.sssonet.com.au) and *SX* (ⓦwww.sxnews.com.au), which both come out on Thursdays; the free lesbian-specific monthly *LOTL* (*Lesbians on the Loose;* ⓦwww.lotl.com); and the monthly nationally distributed *DNA* (ⓦwww.dnamagazine.com.au), an upmarket lifestyle glossy for gay men ($7.60). The websites of all these magazines are also worth checking out before you leave home. For **accommodation**, see pp.162–163.

The Mardi Gras and Sleaze

The first **Sydney Gay + Lesbian Mardi Gras** was held in 1978 as a gay-rights protest. Things have come a long way since then, when 53 people were arrested following a violent struggle with the police, and today it's the biggest celebration of gay and lesbian culture in the world. Hysteria about AIDS saw the Mardi Gras parade nearly cancelled in 1985. By 1992, however, an unprecedented crowd of 400,000, including a broad spectrum of straight society, meant the event was firmly on the summer festival calendar – two years later it began to be broadcast nationally on television. The festival goes for four weeks, starting the first week of **February**. There are hundreds of arts and community events, beginning with a community fair day in Victoria Park (see p.102) and culminating in the parade and party on the last weekend of February or the first weekend of March. In 1982, the first **Sleaze Ball**, an annual Mardi Gras fundraiser in late **September/early October**, was added to the calendar, and has been a much anticipated event ever since.

Mardi Gras turned 25 in 2003, but for a while it looked like it wouldn't make it. By 1999, the combined festival, parade and party was making the local economy $100 million dollars richer, with the increasing **commercialization** drawing criticisms from the gay and lesbian community. The bubble burst in 2002, after financial mismanagement saw the Mardi Gras organization in the red to the tune of $500,000. Instead of throwing in the towel, the fundraising organization was rebuilt as the "New Mardi Gras" – less cash-rich but drawing on the resources and creativity of its talented community. There may have been fewer floats in 2003, but the desire to keep the festival going has revived the old Mardi Gras spirit.

The festival and parade

Four weeks of exhibitions, performances and other events – including the ten-day **Mardi Gras Film Festival** in mid-February at the Palace Academy cinema (see p.218) showcasing the latest in Queer cinema – represent the largest lesbian and gay arts festival in the world, paving the way for the main event, an exuberant night-time **parade** down Oxford Street, when up to half-a-million gays and straights jostle for the best viewing positions, before the Dykes on Bikes, traditional leaders of the parade since 1988 (though the boys on bikes, The Roadrunners, made their debut in 2003), roar into view. Participants devote months to the preparation of outlandish floats and outrageous costumes at Mardi Gras workshops, and even more time is devoted to the preparation of beautiful bodies in Sydney's packed gyms (see p.227). The parade begins at 7.30pm (finishing around 10.30pm), but people line the barricades along Oxford Street from mid-morning (brandishing stolen milk crates to get a better view). If you can't get to

Oxford Street until late afternoon, your best chance of finding a spot is along Flinders Street near Moore Park Road, where the parade ends. Otherwise, AIDS charity The Bobby Goldsmith Foundation (☎02/9283 8666, ⓦ www.bgf.org.au) has around 7000 grandstand seats on Moore Park Road, at $75 each.

The post-parade, wild-and-sexy **dance party** is one of the hottest tickets in Sydney. Twenty-thousand people sashay and strut through several differently themed dance spaces at Fox Studios, Moore Park (including a women's space, *G-Spot*). The two biggest are the Hordern Pavilion and the Royal Hall of Industries, where past performers have included Kylie Minogue, Boy George and Grace Jones. You have to plan ahead if you want to get a **ticket** ($95); they often sell out by the end of January. The purchase of tickets used to be restricted to "Mardi Gras members" to keep the event Queer, with special provisions for visitors from interstate and overseas, but as the New Mardi Gras is rebuilding the old memberships and procedures no longer exist, it's best to contact the

First stop is **Pinkboard** (ⓦ www.pinkboard.com.au), a popular long-running Australian website featuring personal ads and classifieds sections with everything from houseshares, party tickets for sale, employment and a help and advice section. It's free to run your own personal or classified.

Press and multimedia

For Sydney-specific listings mags and the lesbian monthly *LOTL*, see p.221. Below are some useful national publications and Web-based guides; printed publications are available at The Bookshop (see p.221)

ALSO Foundation ⓦ www.also.org.au. Based in Victoria, they have a good website with an excellent nationwide business and community directory.

Gay Australia Guide ⓦ www.gayaustraliaguide.bigstep.com. Handy general guide. Information on where to stay, what to do, nightlife and community groups – covers Sydney and the state capitals.

Pink + Blue ⓦ www.pinkandblue.com.au. A useful online gay and lesbian lifestyle magazine.

The Pink Directory ⓦ www.thepinkdirectory.com.au. Launched in 2001, this is an online and print directory of gay and lesbian business and community information.

Support networks

Gay & Lesbian Counselling Service ☎ 02/9207 2800, ⓦ www.glcsnsw.org.au. Daily 4pm–midnight.

AIDS Council of NSW (ACON) 9 Commonwealth St, Surry Hills ☎ 02/9206 2000, ⓦ www.acon.org.au.

Albion Street Centre 150–154 Albion St, Surry Hills ☎ 02/9332 1090; counselling, testing clinic, information and library.

Anti-Discrimination Board ☎ 02/9318 5444

Tour operators and travel agents

Friends of Dorothy Travel 96 Crystal St, Petersham ☎ 02/9569 5331, ⓦ www.fod.com.au. Offers special tours designed for gay men and lesbians, and can advise about travel during Mardi Gras.

redOyster.com ATS Pacific Pty, Level 10, 130 Elizabeth St, Sydney ☎ 02/9268 2188, ⓦ www. redOyster.com. A gay- and lesbian-branded tour operator that can arrange packages for Mardi Gras, and other festivals and destinations.

Silke's Travel PO Box 1099, Darlinghurst, NSW 1300 ☎ 02/8347 2000, ⓦ www.silkes.com.au. Offers advice and bookings for domestic and international travel and accommodation from a gay and lesbian perspective. Lots of experience with backpacker tours.

Tourist services

GALTA (Gay and Lesbian Tourism Australia ☎ 02/8379 7498, ⓦ www.galta.com.au. A non-profit organization set up to promote the gay and lesbian tourism industry. Its website has links to accommodation, travel agents and tour operators, and gay and lesbian printed and online guides.

Q Beds ⓦ www.qbeds.com. An online accommodation directory and booking service for gay and lesbian-owned, -operated or -friendly businesses.

New Mardi Gras office (☎ 02/9557 4332, ⓕ 9557 8259, ⓦ www.mardigras.org.au) for details. For credit-card bookings for festival events visit ⓦ www.ticketek.com.au. Your local gay-friendly travel agent can also organize tickets as can the Sydney travel agents listed in box above.

For details of festival events, the free *Sydney Gay + Lesbian Mardi Gras*

Guide, available from mid-December, can be picked up from bookshops, cafés and restaurants around Oxford Street or at the New Mardi Gras office.

The Sleaze Ball and PRIDE

Sydney just can't wait all year for Mardi Gras, so the **Sleaze Ball** is a very welcome stopgap in early October. It was set up in 1982 as a fundraiser for the first Mardi Gras Party, and has since become an annual fixture. There's not quite the same

frenzied build-up as for Mardi Gras, but it's just as wild and can be every bit as much fun. It's held the first Saturday night in October, also at the old showground site at Moore Park, and is attended by up to 15,000 people. Tickets cost $82 and are organized by New Mardi Gras (see p.223).

The community centre **PRIDE** (℡02/9331 1333; ⊛www.pridecentre .com.au), arranges a similarly priced and over-the-top **New Year's Eve party**, usually at Fox Studios; contact them for details.

Cafés and restaurants

For a full listing of places to eat, see pp.171–194. Below we've listed a few gay favourites on Oxford Street and in Newtown. See maps of Darlinghurst and Newtown for locations.

The Californian 177 Oxford St, Darlinghurst ℡02/9331 5587. Bus #378 from Central CityRail, bus #380, #382 from Circular Quay CityRail. Marilyn gazes down at you from the front counter in provocative pose, while Fifties rock blasts from the jukebox. The all-day Californian breakfast ($14) is fuel for the boys streaming in from the clubs at 5am. Mon–Wed 8am–midnight/1am, Thurs–Sun 24hr.

Linda's Backstage Restaurant Newtown Hotel 174 King St, corner Watkin St, Newtown ℡02/9557 1329. Newtown CityRail. At the rear of Newtown's popular gay hangout, well-regarded *Linda's* serves up delicious, very reasonably priced modern Australian fare. Dinner Mon–Sat.

Palmer Street Bistro *Wattle Private Hotel*, 108 Oxford St, cnr Palmer St, Darlinghurst ℡02/9332 4118, ⊛www.sydneywattle.com.au. Bus #378 from Central CityRail; #380, #382 from Circular Quay CityRail. This long-running gay-friendly hotel has a stylish café/bistro

cum reception area open to the street antics. Big cooked breakfasts, toasted Turkish sandwiches, pasta and salads by day, and a simple pub-style menu at night (mains $16.50–22.50). Licensed. Inexpensive to moderate.

Sol Restaurant and Bar Level 2, 191 Oxford St ℡02/9380 4400. Bus #378 from Central CityRail, bus #380, #382 from Circular Quay CityRail. *Sol*'s huge windows look out over Taylor Square and it makes the perfect celebrity and media base for Mardi Gras: there's a sexy New York-style bar, and fine dining in the warmly coloured restaurant. Wed–Sun: restaurant 7–10.30pm, bar 6pm–3am. Licensed.

Thai Panic 80 Oxford St, Darlinghurst ℡02/9361 6406. Museum CityRail. This noisy corner eatery, serving spicy meals continuously from noon, is very popular day and night with young gays and lesbians. Good-value lunch specials (noon–4pm). BYO. Cheap. Daily noon–11pm.

Pubs and bars

Several of the **bars** listed here have dance floors and regular DJs, and could just as well be included in the club listings on p.226.

Bank Hotel 324 King St, Newtown ℡02/9557 1692. Newtown CityRail. This stylish bar is a

dyke favourite on Wednesday nights, when the long-running women's pool competition

(8pm) draws large crowds to socialize and maybe even compete. 24hr licence: Mon & Tues noon–12.30am, Wed & Thurs noon–1.30/2am, Fri & Sat noon–4am, Sun noon–midnight.

The Colombian 117–123 Oxford St, corner Crown St, Darlinghurst ☎02/9360 2151, ⊛www.colombian.com.au. Bus #378 from Central CityRail or #380 & #382 from Circular Quay CityRail. Gay bars have been closing in rapid numbers around Oxford Street, but this lavish bar, in a commanding corner position in a renovated bank, opened in late 2002. The fun and funky *faux* South American-style interior – which includes a giant red tribal mask in the ground-floor public bar – was designed by Andrew Parr, who was responsible for *Middle Bar* (p.201) and *Establishment* (p.198). Upstairs, there's a more intimate cocktail bar. There are different DJs and musical styles every night, from R&B to funky house and drag-cum-variety nights Wed & Thurs. Hip but not pretentious. Mon & Tues 10am–3pm, Wed–Sun 9am–5am.

Imperial Hotel 35 Erskineville Rd, Erskineville ☎02/9519 9899, ⊛www.theimperial.com.au. Erskineville CityRail. A notorious late-night gay and lesbian venue, with four bars including a popular hot and sweaty dance floor in the basement (progressive, commercial, high energy; Fri & Sat 11pm–6am; $5), and a riotous drag-show line-up in the Cabaret Room. This is where *Priscilla, Queen of the Desert* both started and ended. It was the *Imperial*'s finest hour, and the memories are kept alive in the cocktail bar, the *Priscilla Lounge*, with photos from the movie lining its walls. The drag shows here are hilarious, inventive and constantly changing: expect anything from the gay-version of *Survivor* ("Ten queens, ten weeks, one winner") to the *Rocky Horror Drag Show* (Wed 9.30pm, 10.30pm & 11.30pm; Thurs–Sat 10pm, 11pm, midnight & 1am; free). There's also cabaret in the cocktail bar on Fri and Sat nights from 10.30pm; to escape the live entertainment you can play pool (free all day Mon), watch music videos and talk in the public bar. "Go Girl" on Thursday nights in the cellar bar is a girls' only club night from 10pm (free). Mon–Thurs 3pm–2/3am, Fri & Sat 3pm–7am, Sun 3pm to midnight.

Newtown Hotel 174 King St, corner Watkin St, Newtown ☎02/9557 1329, ⊛www.newtown hotel.com.au. Newtown CityRail. A stalwart of the Sydney scene. Laid-back mix of Newtown lesbians and gays (though predominantly male), drag shows (Tues–Sat 10pm & 11pm, Sun 8.30pm & 9.15pm) and pool tables (free on Mon nights). There's a tiny dance floor and nightly DJs. At the rear, the well-regarded *Linda's Backstage Restaurant* (Mon–Sat from 6pm) serves up delicious, very reasonably priced modern Australian fare. Upstairs, but with a separate entrance, *Bar 2* is a quiet intimate space – no entertainment, but a couple of pool tables to amuse. Mon–Sat 11am–midnight, Sun 11am–10pm; *Bar 2* Wed–Sun 6pm–midnight.

Oxford Hotel 134 Oxford St, Darlinghurst ☎02/9331 3467. Bus #378 from Central CityRail, bus #380, #382 from Circular Quay CityRail. With bars on three levels, there's something for everyone here. The ground-floor bar, open 24 hours, is the macho pillar of the Sydney gay community, with dim lights, hard music and a packed crowd after 11pm – it's particularly busy on Fri and Sat nights. On the first floor, *Gilligans* is a very different scene, a very popular cocktail bar which attracts a mixed crowd of gay boys, lesbians and the straight party set (daily 5pm–3am; happy hour 5–7pm). On the second floor, *Gingers* is a quieter, more women-friendly bar – decor is plush, and several small cosy rooms provide intimacy; open Thurs–Sat from 6pm.

Stonewall Hotel 175 Oxford St, Darlinghurst ☎02/9360 1963, ⊛www.stonewallhotel.com.au. Bus #378 from Central CityRail, bus #380, #382 from Circular Quay CityRail. Extending over three action-packed levels, this pub is a big hit with young gays and lesbians and their straight friends. You can expect theme nights like karaoke, celebrity drag, or Mailbox (a dating game), and there are DJs in the various different bars Wed–Sat. The downstairs bar plays commercial dance music, the cocktail bar on the next level accelerates on uplifting house, while the top-floor, weekend-only *VIP Bar* gets off on campy, "handbag" sounds (Fri & Sat 11pm–6am; free). There's natural light and outside tables downstairs, where you can also order in a meal from the neighbouring café, *The Californian* (see opposite). Tues–Sun noon–5am.

Clubs

The scene is rapidly changing, and bars and **clubs** have recently been closing down at an alarming rate: check before going out of your way for a big night. Entry is free unless otherwise indicated.

Arq 16 Flinders St, cnr Taylor Square, Darlinghurst ☎02/9380 8700, ⊛www.arqsydney.com.au. Bus #378 from Central CityRail, bus #380, #382 from Circular Quay CityRail. A huge 900-person capacity, state-of-the-art club with everything from DJs and drag shows to pool competitions. There are two levels each with a very different scene: the *Arena*, on the top floor, is strictly gay; while the ground-floor *Vortex* is a quieter, less crowded mix of gay and straight, with pool tables. Chilling out booths, laser lighting on the dance floors, viewing decks and fishtanks add to the fun and friendly atmosphere. The attached gaming lounge is open 24hr. Sunday is the big night. Thurs–Sun from 9pm. Fri & Sat $15–20, Sun $5.

BumpHer Bar Burdekin Hotel, 2 Oxford St, Darlinghurst ☎02/9331 3066. Museum CityRail. On Friday nights on the top floors of this stylish hotel, lush *Lava Lounge* and the *Bat Bar* are taken over by *BumpHer Bar* (9pm–3am; $5; see p.201), a girl's cocktail and club night – gay friends are also welcome.

DCM 31–33 Oxford St, Darlinghurst ☎02/9267 7036. Bus #378 from Central CityRail, bus #380, #382 from Circular Quay CityRail. Young, fast, mixed gay, lesbian and straight venue. A long-running but still-renowned nightclub which, like most Sydney clubs, doesn't really liven up till after midnight, when you can be assured of a wild night of dancing. Entry $15–25.Thurs, Fri & Sun 10pm–6am, Sat 10pm–noon.

Exchange Hotel 34 Oxford St, Darlinghurst ☎02/9331 1936. Museum CityRail. In the downstairs *Phoenix* bar, Sat night's *Crash* underground "alternative" dance club is mostly gay men, but on Sun nights there's a happy mix of gays and dykes who go wild to some groovy music (Sat & Sun from 10pm; $5 Sat, free Sun). In the upstairs *Lizard Lounge* (also see p.201) on Tues nights from 11pm, *Furbar* is strictly for girls (free entry).

Icebox 2 Kellet St, Kings Cross ☎02/9331 0058, ⊛www.icebox.com.au. Kings Cross CityRail. Friday nights at this small club are usually gay and lesbian; no two nights are ever the same, but the music is a mix of techno, house and hard house and the light show is lavish. The new decor is bright and funky, but it's still kept cosily dark with candlelight, and there are more intimate lounges to chill out on around the walls. Drinks aren't too pricey and dress is casual. Tues & Wed 10pm–3am, Thurs–Sun 10pm–6am. Door charge $5–15, $10 Fri.

Midnight Shift 85 Oxford St, Darlinghurst ☎02/9360 4319, ⊛www.midnightshift.com.au. Bus #378 from Central CityRail, bus #380, #382 from Circular Quay CityRail. Commonly known as "The Shift", this veteran of the Oxford Street scene has now been running for over twenty years. On the ground floor, the *Shift Video Bar* is a large drinking and cruising space to a music-video backdrop, with pool tables out the back. Upstairs, the weekend-only club has been hugely revamped; the massive place is now rather splendid, with everything from a waterfall to a cutting-edge laser light show. The club hosts drag shows (usually Fri nights), DJs and events, with a cover charge of $5 and upwards, depending on the event. Mainly men. Bar daily noon–6am, club Fri & Sat 11pm–7am.

The Red Room Lansdowne Hotel, 2–6 City Rd, Chippendale, just off Broadway ☎02/9211 2325. Central CityRail; bus #422, #423, #426, #428 from Central CityRail. Upstairs at the *Lansdowne* on Saturday nights (8pm–3am), this classy funk and soul night is strictly for girls, including the female DJs and special guests. The motto is "dress to impress" but really anything goes, from cargo pants to sequinned splendour. Entry $5.

Taxi Club 40 Flinders St, Darlinghurst ☎02/9331 4256, ⊛www.thetaxiclub.com. Bus #378 from Central CityRail, #380, #382 from Circular Quay CityRail. If you made it here, congratulations, you're a true bar hopper. It's a Sydney legend, but don't bother before 2 or 3am, and you'll need to be suitably intoxicated to appreciate it fully. There's a strange blend of drag queens, taxi drivers, lesbians and boys (straight and gay) to observe, and the cheapest drinks in gay

Sydney. An upstairs dance club (free) operates Fri & Sat from 1am, and the ground-floor café stays open until 5am on Fri & Sat nights (until midnight Tues–Thurs & Sun; closed Mon). Overseas and interstate visitors with some home id don't have to become members, but locals need to join at the door. Free entry. Basically 24hr except for a daily closure from 6am–9am.

Venus Room 2 Roslyn St, Kings Cross. Kings Cross CityRail. ☏ 02/8354 0888. The *Priscilla* tribute shows have finished at Erskinville's the *Imperial* after a decade (see p.225), but you can now catch them at Sydney's resuscitated drag venue – the old Les Girls venue is once again putting on drag shows (Mon & Thurs–Sat after 10pm). Happy hour 8pm–10pm and all night Wed.

Gyms

The prices below are for a casual pass, which can last all day if you want it to, and includes any fitness classes on offer. Many **gyms** have a one-week free introductory offer, which is a cheeky way for travellers to do the rounds and get a buff bod for nothing.

Bayswater Fitness 33 Bayswater Rd, Kings Cross ☏ 02/9356 2555, ⓦ www.bayswaterfitness.com.au. Kings Cross CityRail. Clientele of mostly gay men, although lesbians are also welcome. Weights, circuit-fitness and aerobics classes. Mon–Thurs 6am–midnight, Fri 6am–11pm, Sat 7am–10pm, Sun 7am–9pm. $15.
City Gym 107–113 Crown St, East Sydney ☏ 02/9360 6247, ⓦ www.citygym.com.au. Museum CityRail. Unbelievably popular (at all hours) among gay men, lesbians and straights. There are plenty of weights, aerobics, body combat and yoga classes and a sauna – which can be cruisey. $13.50. 24hr Mon 7am–Sat 10pm, Sun 8am–10pm.
Newtown Gym Level 1, 294 King St, Newtown ☏ 020/9519 6969. Newtown CityRail. Large lesbian membership. Step, stretch and yoga classes, weight training, solarium and sauna. Free childcare facilities (Mon–Sat 9am–noon). Mon–Fri 6am–10pm, Sat & Sun 8am–8pm. $13.

Beaches and swimming pools

During Sydney's hot summer, a popular choice among the gay set is **Tamarama** (known locally as Glamarama, see p.130), a fifteen-minute walk from the southern end of Bondi Beach. But if showing off is not your thing, **Bondi** (p.125) or nearby **Bronte** (p.130) may suit you better. The calm harbour waters of **Red Leaf** at Double Bay (p.114) also lure a big gay crowd and, if you want to get your gear off, try **Lady Jane Beach** at Watsons Bay (p.116).

Pools of choice are Red Leaf harbour pool at Double Bay and the appropriately named Andrew "Boy" Charlton pool in The Domain (pp.67 & 260). The Coogee Women's Baths, at the southern end of Coogee Beach (p.132), are popular with lesbians.

Kids' Sydney

W
ith its sunny climate, fabulous beaches and wide open spaces, Sydney is a great place to holiday with kids. There are lots of parks, playgrounds, sheltered bays and public pools for safe swimming, and a range of indoor options for rainy days. Museums are mostly child-friendly, in particular the **Powerhouse Museum** and the **Australian Museum**, both of which have exhibits and activities designed to entertain as well as educate, and most offer a range of special school-holiday programmes. Three areas, **The Rocks**, **Darling Harbour** and **Fox Studios** have much to keep children amused and all offer lots of free activities during the school holidays; check these websites for the latest goings on: ⓦwww.rocksvillage .com.au; ⓦwww.darlingharbour.com.au; and ⓦwww.foxstudios.com.au.

Also see the "Sports and activities" chapter for details on the many options for children, from renting bikes or rollerblades to the free pony rides and jumping castle at Canterbury Racetrack (p.257). And check out the "Festivals" chapter where everything from Sydney's kite festival at Bondi to the balmy evening Christmas carols in The Domain will keep the kids happy.

Costs and access

Children under 5 get **entry into museums** for free, while those aged from 5 to 15 have a half-price or reduced rate (teenagers 16 or older should bring a student card or better still get hold of an ISIC card to get concession rates – see p.21); discounted family tickets, usually based on two adults and two children, are also offered in most places (over-16s will count as adults in this case). We give the child and family entry prices in this chapter and while we don't list these rates in the rest of the Guide, assume they are available.

Children under 5 also travel on **public transport** for free, while children from 5 to 15 travel at half rates. There are also "family fares" – when one fare-paying adult travels with their children, the first child travels at half-price and the rest are free. Special family discounts are also available on the Sydney Pass, Airport Express buses, Sydney Explorer and Bondi Explorer services, ferry cruises and the Aquarium Pass. Local full-time students 16 and over are eligible for concession rates on transport but they are provided with a special concession card, so your older teenager will have to travel at full-price rates and also count as an adult regarding transport discounts.

If you're travelling with a pram, refer to the "Travellers with disabilities" section in Basics on p.37, which gives information about accessible transport and even bushwalks, all relevant to pram-pushers as well.

Public toilets and parents' rooms

Sydney is well serviced with **public toilets** (see p.267), and those in shopping malls and department stores invariably have a quite separate unisex **parents' room** attached, where you can change nappies. There's often even a microwave to heat bottles or baby food, and curtained booths with vaguely comfy chairs for breastfeeding. However, it's your legal right to breastfeed in public and on the whole most people are pretty unfazed, given the amount of flesh routinely bared on Sydney's beaches.

Information and childminding

Sydney's Child is an excellent free monthly magazine with intelligent articles, detailed listings of **what's on**, and adverts for a range of services including **babysitting**; pick up a copy at libraries, major museums and many kid-oriented shops and services, or check out Ⓦ www.sydneyschild.com.au.

Some hotels, usually the most expensive variety, offer in-house babysitting; enquire when you're booking. There are casual **childminding services** at many gyms (see Newtown Gym, p.227) and swimming pools (see Leichhardt Park Aquatic Centre, p.260), usually with a limit of up to two hours, but if you are going to be in Sydney for a while and need some time to yourself during the day, you could try **occasional care** at a childcare centre; the City of Sydney website's list of childcare centres (Ⓦ www.cityofsydney.nsw.gov.au/cs_childcare_centres.asp) details where this kind of service is offered in different areas and the fees applicable.

Museums and galleries

The **Historic Houses Trust of New South Wales**, consisting of the Justice and Police Museum (p.58), the Museum of Sydney (p.71), Hyde Park Barracks (p.66), Elizabeth Bay House (p.98), Vaucluse House (p.115), Government House (p.64) and Elizabeth Farm in Parramatta (p.150), offer a huge range of school-holiday programmes for children aged 6 to 12, from music performances and workshops in the Government House ballroom to pretending to be a servant at Vaucluse House (2hr; $7–10; ☏02/9518 6866, Ⓦ www.hht .nsw.gov.au).

Art Gallery of New South Wales The Domain Ⓦ www.artgallery.nsw.gov.au. **Martin Place or St James CityRail.** The gallery's free "Fundays at the Gallery" Sunday performances (11.30pm & 1.45pm) for families – art appreciation, drama, storytelling, dance and mime – run most of the year and also daily except Sat during school holidays. Also during the vacation periods there are kids' practical art workshops (2hr–2hr 30min; $15–20; 5–9 years and 9–13 years; booking essential on ☏02/9225 1740).

New South Wales' school holidays

Summer, six weeks, beginning roughly ten days before Christmas, to last week in January; **autumn**, two weeks coinciding with Easter (normally early to mid-April); **winter**, two weeks, beginning the second week of July; **spring**, two weeks, beginning the last week of September. Check the public schools section of the New South Wales Department of Education website for exact dates: Ⓦ www.schools.nsw.edu.au/calendar.

Daily 10am–5pm. Entry free, except for special exhibitions. Also see p.67.

Australian Museum Cnr College and William streets, East Sydney ⊛www.austmus.gov.au. Museum or Town Hall CityRail. The people here clearly know a thing or two about the special relationship kids have with dinosaurs – their dino exhibition is aimed squarely at the 5–12-year-olds. The museum's biodiversity section has a Search and Discover room, complete with microscopes, specimens (and books to help with identifying them), and a child-size kitchen where kids can learn about being environmentally friendly. Kids Island is for under-5s; it has a shipwreck boat and all sorts of crawling pits and cubby houses to explore, plus a baby change area. Daily 9.30am–5pm. Entry $8, child $4 (under-5 free), family $19. Also see p.75.

Powerhouse Museum 500 Harris St, Ultimo ⊛www.phm.gov.au. **Central CityRail.** Each level of this science and technology museum has a noisy and colourful corner aimed at small children, with hands-on exhibits exploring machines and movement, domestic activities, music, and film and television. The general exhibits, from the huge steam engine to the chiming Strasbourg clock, will interest older kids. During school holidays there are activities, from crafts to storytelling sessions ($6 adult, $4 child). The Powerhouse Shop in the foyer is crammed with quirky and educational toys. Daily 10am–5pm. $10, child $3, family $23.

The Rocks Toy Museum Kendall Lane, off Argyle St, The Rocks ⊛www.rocksvillage .com.au. Circular Quay CityRail. Two floors of collectable toys from the nineteenth and twentieth centuries, housed in a sandstone 1850s coach house. Daily 10am–6pm. Entry free.

Parks and wildlife

Sydney and the surrounding area provide plenty of opportunities to see – and in some cases touch – native wildlife. The kids can pat koalas at Taronga Zoo (see opposite), and at **Featherdale Wildlife Park** (p.147) and the **Koala Park Sanctuary** (p.147), and get close to the animals at the **Australian Wildlife Park** (p.147). They can also meet Eric the giant crocodile and watch snakes and spiders being milked at the **Australian Reptile Park** on the Central Coast (p.277). Children also love observing the sea creatures, seals, and fairy penguins at **Sydney Aquarium** (see p.80) and the scary sharks at Manly's **Oceanworld** (see p.135).

Centennial Park Cnr Oxford St and Lang Rd, Paddington ⊛www.cp.nsw.gov.au. Bus #378 from Central CityRail or #380 & #382 from Circular Quay CityRail. Offering typical park pleasures such as feeding ducks and climbing trees, you'll also find bike paths (and a learners' cycleway) and bridleways here. You can rent kids' bikes and rollerblades nearby (see p.262) and the Equestrian Centre offers horse and pony rides. If children are over 5, they can go on an escorted horse ride around the park, while younger ones (upwards of 3) can go on an escorted pony ride in the grounds of the centre; Centennial Stables, in Pavilion B (☎02/9360 5650), allow several children to share one pony over 30min for $55 but don't offer shorter individual and cheaper rides. Also see p.262 for more on horse riding. If you can't afford a ride, it's great fun and perfectly fine for kids to wander through the Equestrian Centre and see the different horses in their stables. Back in the park, there are regular ranger-led "Spotlight Prowls" searching for wildlife on the first Fri of the month and during school holidays ($8.50 per adult or child; bookings essential on ☎02/9339 6699), and there's school-holiday activities, aimed at varying age groups from 2 years up, which might be anything from a bushtucker tour to a basics of gardening course ($8–12). The child-friendly café even serves up "babyccinos" (hot frothy milk). Daily 8am–6pm, to 8pm during Daylight Saving.

Cumberland State Forest 95 Castle Hill Rd, West Pennant Hills ☎02/9871 3377, ⊛www.forest.nsw.gov.au/cumberland. Pennant Hills CityRail, then bus #631–#635. Australia's only metropolitan state forest covers 40 hectares in Sydney's northwestern suburbs. There's over half a century of native forest growth here – the land was cleared in 1908 and bought by the government for a forestry project in 1938. The Information Centre (Mon–Fri 9am–4.30pm, Sat & Sun 10am–4.30pm) has displays and videos on the park and a great range of wooden toys among its Forest Shop stock, and an attached café. There are bushwalking trails, a Native Plant Nursery and free barbecues and picnic areas. Free ranger-guided tours operate at weekends (call for times) and there's a school-holiday programme which includes craft activities such as making an animal mask, an introduction to bushtucker, and dusk wildlife-spotting walks. Walks are free; crafts and other activities (most for kids 5 and over but some 'mini-ranger' activities for kids aged 3–6) last an hour and cost $4.40–5.50 (bookings necessary). On the last Sun in October, the free Family Forest Fair takes over – great fun for kids, with theatre and craft activities, pony rides, visiting fire-engines, wood choppers, wood craftspeople, food and environmental stalls, and live music. **Sydney Harbour National Park** National Parks and Wildlife Service, Cadman's Cottage, 110 George St, The Rocks ☎ 02/9247 5033, ⓦ www.npws.nsw.gov.au. The NPWS offers special ranger-led walks for families in the school holidays (from $7.70 per child or adult) and special activities for kids, detailed on their website; they also lead a Kids Ghost Tour of the Quarantine Station near Manly on Fri nights (2hr; $13.20 child or adult; see p.138).

Taronga Zoo Bradleys Head, Mosman Bay ⓦ www.zoo.nsw.gov.au. Ferry to Taronga Zoo (Athol) Wharf. Taronga Zoo occupies an enviable position high over the harbour, and the ferry ride there plus the cable car up the hill are half the fun. Favourites with the kids are the lumbering kodiak bears, playful gorillas, poised meerkats, the native animal walka-bout enclosure and aviaries where you wander among native birds. There's also a petting zoo with domestic animals (milking show 11am, farm feed 2pm), a seal training show, a free-flight bird show, plus keeper talks and feedings throughout the day. Children's concerts are featured during school holidays. Daily: Jan 9am–9pm; Feb–Dec 9am–5pm. Entry $23, child $12.50, family $57, Zoo Pass including return ferry $28.40, child pass $14.30.

Shops

Suburban K-Mart, Target, Best and Less and Pumpkin Patch stores sell affordable kidswear, and the department stores in the city centre stock a full range of quality clothes and toys. The huge Toys "R" Us stores are found at various suburban locations. More interesting shops are detailed below. Also see p.237 for Lesley McKay's Childrens Bookshop in Double Bay.

ABC Shop Level 1, Albert Walk, QVB ⓦ shop.abc.net.au. Town Hall CityRail. ABC (and BBC) television's merchandising outlet – books, audio, video, toys, clothing and accessories – sells all the Australian favourites, from *Bananas in Pyjamas* to *The Wiggles*. Mon–Fri 9am–5.30pm (Thurs to 8pm), Sat 9am–5pm, Sun 11am–5pm.

Gleebooks Children's Books 191 Glebe Point Rd, Glebe ⓦ www.gleebooks.com.au. Bus #431–#434 from Central CityRail. Children's bookshop, attached to the well-respected Gleebooks secondhand store (see p.237). Mon–Wed & Sun 10am–8pm, Thurs & Fri 10am–9pm, Sat 9am–9pm.

Hobbyco Gallery Level, Mid-City Centre, Pitt St Mall ⓦ www.hobbyco.com.au. Town Hall CityRail. Established as a business in 1935, this huge hobby shop has everything from dolls' houses to kites, Meccano sets, trains and slot cars. The working model railway is a major attraction. Mon–Sat 9am–6pm (Thurs to 9pm), Sun 11am–5pm.

The Kids' Room 83 Paddington St, Paddington ☎ 02/9328 6864. Bus #378 from Central CityRail or #380 & #382 from Circular Quay or Bondi Junction CityRail. Quality clothes and shoes, for babies through to early teens. Stocks Australian brands like Fred Bare, Scooter and Gumboots. Mon–Fri 10.30am–5.30pm, Sat 10am–4.30pm.

Play House Toy Shop 152 Clarence St ☎ 02/9299 5498. Town Hall CityRail. Catering for younger children, from babies up to about 9 years. Playhouses, lots of hand-made wooden toys, and attentive service and advice. Mon–Fri 9am–5.30pm, Sat 9am–4pm.

Swimming and water sports

Beware Sydney's **strong surf** – young children are safer swimming at sheltered harbour beaches or ocean pools. Public swimming pools (typically outdoor and unheated), generally have a toddlers' **paddling pool**. For year-round swimming there's a heated pool at North Sydney (p.261), right beside Luna Park, or at the indoor Sydney International Aquatic Centre (p.261), which has a rapid water ride and slides. The Cook and Phillip Park Aquatic and Leisure Centre (p.260) is another good place to take kids, while the Leichhardt Park Aquatic Centre (p.260) has creche facilities. If you're going to be in Sydney for a while and your children can't swim, or are weak swimmers (or you're envisaging a future Olympic career for them), the NSW Department of Sport and Recreation conduct excellent inexpensive small-group **Swimsafe courses** at local swimming pools, held over nine consecutive days (information and bookings ☎13 13 02, ⓦ www.dsr.nsw.gov.au; pre-schoolers from 18 months, 30min per day, $35; school-age, 40min per day, $46; shorter courses available). Manly Surf School (☎02/9970 6300, ⓦ www.manlysurfschool.com) and Bondi's Lets Go Surfing (☎02/9365 1800, ⓦ www.letsgosurfing.com.au) both offer group lessons in **board-riding** and **surf safety** for kids aged 7–11 and 12–16 (2hr; younger kids $30, older kids $45), including longer surf camps in school holidays (4 days; 2hr per day; $180), and individual and family lessons. Balmoral Windsurf, Sail and Kayak School at Balmoral Beach has a **learn to sail** camp during summer and Easter holidays (ages 6–13; 5 days; 9.30am–3pm; $325; ☎02/9960 5344, ⓦ www.sailboard.net.au). Northside Sailing School, Spit Bridge, Mosman (☎02/9969 3972, ⓦ www.northsidesailing.com.au) specializes in weekend dinghy sailing courses on Middle Harbour during the sailing season (Sept–April) and they also have lessons for kids (8–15 years; 2hr lesson for 2 children $80) and holiday camp programmes (3-, 4- or 5-day programmes; $240/$305/$365) during all school holidays except the winter break.

Beaches

Balmoral Beach On the north side of the harbour, around the corner from Taronga Zoo, this is the pick of the family beaches for its wide sandy bays, sheltered from the wind and waves. Much of the sand is shaded by big trees, and there's a great children's playground right next to the beach kiosk where you can buy ice creams and takeaway coffee (there's fish and chips across the road). See p.123.

Bronte Beach The most popular of the eastern beaches for families, fronted by an extensive and shady park with picnic shelters and barbecues (plus a stash of good alfresco cafés across the road), a mini-train ride ($3 per ride; $10 for 4 rides) and an imaginative children's playground. A natural

---

Sun protection

A broad-spectrum, water-resistant **sunscreen** (with a minimum SPF of 20) is a must, and colourful zinc cream on nose and cheeks is a good extra protectant when swimming. Most local kids wear UV-resistant lycra **swim tops** or wetsuit-style all-in-ones to the beach, and schoolchildren wear **hats** in the playground – the legionnaire-style ones are especially popular, as they shade the face and the back of the neck. All these items can be purchased at surfwear shops, department stores, or at the NSW Cancer Council Shop in the Glasshouse shopping centre, Pitt St Mall (ⓦ www.nswcc.org.au; Town Hall CityRail).

rock enclosure provides a calm area for swimming. See p.130.

Coogee Bay Coogee Bay is popular with families, with a grassy park with picnic shelters and barbecues. Past the southern end of the beach, Coogee Women's Pool (see p.133) is for women and children only (boys are welcome up to age 12). There's a big adventure playground in Grant Reserve opposite the pool. See p.133.

Manly On the north side of the harbour, tucked in beside Manly Wharf, Manly Cove has a small harbour beach with a netted-off swimming area and, on the ocean side of Manly, there are sheltered beaches on Cabbage Tree Bay – Fower Bower (with a rock pool) and Shelly Beach (fronted by a big park). The ferry ride over is lots of fun, and there are plenty of attractions for kids in the area, including an aquarium and a water slide. The family can rent bikes or rollerblades and get onto the Manly bike path, which is shared with pedestrians. See p.133.

Northern beaches Stretching from Manly, the northern beaches also have some good family choices – Dee Why Beach is backed by a sheltered lagoon, Long Reef's creature-filled rockpools provide wonderful exploration opportunities, while Narrabeen Beach fronts extensive, swimmable lakes. Beyond Narrabeen, sheltered Bongin Bongin Bay, with a headland reserve and rocks to clamber on, is ideal for children.

Theatre

Marian Street Theatre for Young People 2 Marian St, Killara ✆02/9498 3166. Killara CityRail. Bookings are essential for the popular matinees for kids aged 3–10, often involving audience participation (Sat 1pm; school holidays: Mon–Fri 10.30am & 1pm; $9.50, child $7.50).

The Rocks Puppet Cottage Kendall Lane, off Argyle St, The Rocks ✆02/9255 1788. Circular Quay CityRail/ferry. Free weekend and school-holiday puppet shows (11am, 12.30pm & 2pm).

Sydney Opera House Bennelong Point, Circular Quay ✆02/9250 7777, ✆www.sydney operahouse.com. Circular Quay CityRail/ferry. The popular Kids @ the House programme includes "Babies' Proms" for 2–5 year olds to learn about orchestral music (1hr; $13 child or adult), "Family Proms" for children aged 5–9 and their families ($14), and for older children (suitable for aged 10 and upwards) an "Introduction to the Ballet" with dancers from the Australian National Ballet (1hr 30min; $14).

Theme parks and playgrounds

Sydney's first theme park, harbourfront **Luna Park**, opened in the 1930s but has been shutting down and reopening since the 1980s and is currently closed (see p.120). You can head out west to **Wonderland Sydney** or, if you're in town around April, to Homebush Bay for the biggest annual funfair at the **Royal Easter Show** (see p.251).

Darling Harbour (see p.77) is never short of kids' amusements and is big on family festivals. The area along Darling Walk is particularly child-focused – there's a watery playground with fountains to race amongst and colourful stationary bikes spouting water, plus naughty sweetshops and a rainforest-theme café. During school holidays, events are held on the floating stage on Darling Walk's small lake. West of the lake, a colourful children's playground area (albeit commercially sponsored by an ice-cream company and covered in advertising) has a host of vivid climbing frames, slides, swings, and a sandpit with bright tubing and there's a merry-go-round right next door.

At **Fox Studios** (see p.95) there's plenty on tap for little kids to teenagers: a big choice of movies at its cinemas, an outdoor music screen, lots of shops to browse in including a huge bookshop and a kids' dress-up store, a mini-golf course (Mon–Thurs & Sun 10am–8.30pm, Fri & Sat 10am–10pm; $9, child

$6.50), a winter ice-skating rink (p.262), a bungee-jumping trampoline (p.263), two outdoor adventure playgrounds, one for small children and another for bigger, more adventurous kids, and beside them, a carousel ($2.50 per ride) and a (pricey) indoor playground, Lollipops (see below), that's perfect for rainy days.

Lollipops Playground Fox Studios, Driver Ave, Moore Park ⓦ www.lollipopsplayland.com.au. Bus #339 from Central CityRail. This indoor playground is aimed at children aged 1–10, and is guaranteed to physically exhaust them, with a jungle gym, giant mazes, tunnels, and everything from a ball pool to a tea-cup merry-go-round ride, books, toys, dress-ups and games. Socks are obligatory. There are also two free playgrounds, and a merry-go-round outside. Mon–Thurs 9.30am–7pm, Fri 9.30am–8pm, Sat 9am–8pm, Sun 9am–7pm. Entry: 1–2 year olds $7.90, 2–9 year olds $10.90; adults $4 includes a coffee from the well-stocked café.

Wonderland Sydney Wallgrove Rd, Rooty Hill. Rooty Hill CityRail, then Busways service. ⓦ www.wonderland.com.au. Huge family entertainment complex with shows, water slides, roller coasters, and the Australian Wildlife Park, where you can "meet the animals" – koalas, kangaroos, echidnas, wombats, emus, saltwater crocodiles and forest birds in simulated natural habitats. Entry ticket includes all rides and events. Daily 10am–5pm, wildlife park from 9am. Entry $42.90, child $29.70; wildlife park only $16.50, child $9.90.

Shopping and galleries

The rectangle bounded by Elizabeth, King, York and Park streets is Sydney's prime shopping area, with a number of beautifully restored **Victorian arcades** and the main **department stores**. The city also has plenty of sparkling shopping complexes where you can hunt for fashion and accessories without raising a sweat. Still in the centre, The Rocks is packed with Australiana and **souvenir shops**, where you can satisfy the urge to buy boomerangs, didgeridoos and stuffed toy koalas, and it's also the best place for duty- and GST-free shopping.

Paddington is best for stylish one-stop shopping, with its enticing array of designer shops, funky fashion, some of the city's most appealing book-shops – and the best weekend market in town. The more avant-garde **Darlinghurst** and **Surry Hills** (notably the stretch of Crown Street between Devonshire and Oxford streets) have become a focus for retro-influenced interior design and clothes shops. In the inner west, **Balmain** has chic shops and gourmet delis to supplement its Saturday market, while cheerfully offbeat **Newtown** and neighbouring St Peters are great for sec-ondhand fashions and quirky speciality stores. Down at the beach, **Bondi Pavilion** has an excellent souvenir shop, and the Campbell Parade strip offers lots of beachwear and surf shops.

The main **sales** take place immediately after Christmas and into January, and in June and into July; there are also stock clearances throughout the year, often around public holidays.

Finally, if you've run out of time to buy presents and souvenirs, the revamped **Sydney Airport** has one of the biggest shopping malls in Sydney, with out-lets for everything from surfwear to R. M. Williams bushoutfitters, at the same prices as downtown stores; see box p.248.

Opening hours

Most stores are open Monday to Saturday from 9am or 10am until 5.30pm or 6pm, with late-night shopping on Thursdays until 9pm. Many of the larger shops and department stores are also open on Sunday from 10am or noon until 4 or 5pm, as are most malls and shopping centres at tourist hotspots such as Darling Harbour and The Rocks.

Books

In addition to the small selection of places listed below, there is a concentration of **secondhand bookshops** on King Street in Newtown, Glebe Point Road in Glebe and good secondhand stalls at Glebe, Balmain, Paddington and Bondi markets (see "Markets", p.246). *Gertrude & Alice Cafe Bookstore* at Bondi (see p.126) and *Delizia* in the city (see p.175) also sell secondhand books. The Bookshop, a specialist gay and lesbian bookshop in Darlinghurst, is detailed on p.221. The worldwide book **superstores** now have a presence in Sydney – there's Borders at the Skygarden shopping centre (see p.242) and Kinokuniya at The Galeries Victoria (see opposite), but the Australia-owned Collins, near Glebe, was the first and is still the best in terms of high-comfort level browsing – and this has prompted many bookshops to offer added value, in terms of instore coffee shops, Internet terminals, discounted bestsellers and author talks. For extended opening hours and knowledgeable staff, though, you'll still do better with the independents. The bookshop at the State Library (see p.65) has one of the best collections of Australian-related books in Sydney while if you're interested in Australian art, the Art Gallery of New South Wales (p.67) has an extensive bookshop. The shop at the Museum of Sydney (see p.71) has plenty on the city and there's a National Trust bookshop at the S.H. Ervin Gallery (p.54).

Abbey's 131 York St ⓦwww.abbeys.com.au. Town Hall CityRail. Big academic and general bookstore, established in 1968 and still mostly family-run, is one of Sydney's best-known independent booksellers – great at ordering in books – and in a prime spot opposite the QVB. The Language Book Centre on the first floor is the place to buy foreign-language books in Sydney. Abbey's also has Sydney's science fiction, fantasy and horror bookshop, Galaxy, which is two doors up at no. 143. Mon–Fri 8.30am–7pm (Thurs to 9pm), Sat 9am–6pm, Sun 10am–5pm.

Ariel 42 Oxford St, Paddington ☎02/9332 4581, ⓦwww.arielbooks.com.au. Bus #378 from Central CityRail or #380 & #382 from Circular Quay CityRail. Not too large, lively and very hip, Ariel is especially good for design books and cutting-edge fiction. It's a great place to browse in the evening after a movie (the Palace cinemas Verona and Academy are just across the road; see p.218) and often has author readings and book launches. The branch at 103 George St (Circular Quay CityRail) also offers respite from the stuffed-koala overdose that frequently afflicts shoppers in The Rocks. Both daily 9am–midnight.

Berkelouws 19 Oxford St, Paddington ⓦwww.berkelouw.com.au. Bus #378 from Central CityRail or #380 & #382 from Circular Quay CityRail. Catering to collectors as well as casual browsers, Berkelouws has been dealing in antiquarian books since 1812. New books are downstairs, and their upstairs coffee shop, with huge windows overlooking the busy Oxford Street strip, is a popular pre- and post-movie meeting place (the Palace Verona – see p.218 – is just next door); daily 9.30am–midnight. Also Berkelouw's Books and Music at 70 Norton St, Leichhardt for new and secondhand books and CDs (including a big range of World Music), an Aboriginal art gallery (Walkabout; see p.244) and two in-store cafés, one of which hosts fortnightly Philo Cafe philosophy discussions (first & third Tues; 8pm; $5 includes coffee) and even a performance space; Mon–Thurs & Sun 10am–11pm, Fri & Sat 10am–midnight

Duty-free shopping

If you have an air ticket out of Australia, you may be able to save around thirty percent on goods such as perfume, jewellery, imported clothing, cameras and electronic equipment. One of the main outlets is DFS (Duty Free Shoppers), with a major store at 155 George Street in The Rocks.

(bus #438 & #440 from Central CityRail). Berkelouw Discovery Bookstore in Gowings' Market Street store (see p.240) stocks travel-related books and maps.

Books Kinokuniya The Galeries Victoria, 500 George St, cnr Park St, City. Town Hall CityRail. Now Sydney's biggest book superstore, the Japanese-owned Kinokuniya has seventy percent of its estimated 300,000 titles in English. A range of books in Japanese and Chinese make up the rest, and the city's best stash of magazines, both local and imported. As you'd expect, there's a good range of comics, including Manga. The art and design section is also impressive and there's an antiquarian books section, an art gallery, a selection of world globes for sale, a fossil collection and the now-obligatory bookstore café. Mon–Sat 10am–7pm (Thurs to 9pm), Sun 10am–6pm.

Collins Superstore Level 2, Broadway Shopping Centre @www.collinsbooks.com.au. Buses #431–#434, #438 & #440 from Central CityRail. Vast bookstore – Sydney's first book superstore and Australian-owned – with curving bookshelves, soft lighting and comfy sofas and window seats in the arched windows where you can easily lose yourself for an afternoon. When it's time to face the real world again, make for the in-store coffee shop to ease the transition. Mon–Fri 9am–6pm (Thurs to 9pm) Sat 9am–7pm, Sun 10am–6pm.

Dymocks 428 George St @www.dymocks.com.au. Town Hall CityRail. Sprawled across several floors, Dymocks has a particularly impressive Australian selection, and an upstairs café where you can slurp generous smoothies; Mon–Fri 9am–6.30pm (Thurs to 9pm), Sat 9am–6pm, Sun 10am–5pm. Two other branches with longer hours and in-store espresso bars are: Level 2, Harbourside Shopping Centre, Darling Harbour (Mon–Sat 10am–9pm, Sun 10am–7pm; Harbourside Monorail) and Bent St, Fox Studios (daily 10am–10pm), with a big range of performing arts and design books.

Gleebooks 49 Glebe Point Rd, Glebe, @www.gleebooks.com.au. Bus #431–#434 from Central CityRail. Specializes in academic and alternative books, philosophy and cultural studies, contemporary Australian and international literature, plus author appearances and book-signings upstairs; daily 10am–9pm except Sat 9am–9pm. Further up the hill is Gleebooks Secondhand and Children's Books, at 191 Glebe Point Rd.

Gould's Book Arcade 32–38 King St, Newtown ☎02/9519 8947. Newtown CityRail. Chaotic piles of books greet you in this near legendary secondhand bookstore run by Bob Gould. The incredible range of non-fiction includes a whole host of leftie political tomes; you'd never find anything specific here unless you were incredibly lucky but it's great for browsing. Daily 7am–midnight.

Lesley McKay's Bookshop 346 New South Head Rd, Double Bay ☎02/9327 1354. Bus #324, #325 from Edgecliff CityRail. Excellent range and knowledgeable staff at this late-opening store (daily 10am–10pm); during the day you can wander upstairs to the secondhand Nicholas Pounder's (see below) and next door at 344 is the equally good Lesley McKay's Children's Bookshop (daily 10am–6pm).

Macleay Bookshop 103 Macleay St, Potts Point ☎02/9358 2908. Kings Cross CityRail. When you're sick of all the bigger stores, this tiny, independent and very literary bookstore is a peaceful choice for browsing, with a well-chosen selection. It also stocks books by local Kings Cross writers. Daily until 9pm.

Nicholas Pounder Level 1, 346 New South Head Rd, Double Bay ☎02/9328 7410. Bus #324 & #325 from Edgecliff CityRail. Well-known antiquarian and secondhand bookseller specializing in Australian first editions, above Lesley McKay's (see above). Mon–Sat 10am–6pm, Sun noon–6pm.

The Travel Bookshop Shop 3, 175 Liverpool St ☎02/9261 8200. Museum CityRail. The place for maps, guides, phrasebooks and travelogues, plus a good selection of Australiana and specialist walking and cycling books, as well as travel accessories. Also an American Express branch in store. Mon–Fri 9am–6pm, Sat 10am–5pm, Sun noon–5pm.

Clothes and accessories

For interesting **fashion** to suit a range of budgets, Oxford Street in Paddington is the place, along with the glitzy Sydney Central Mall in the city. With more time to explore, take a stroll down Crown Street, near the junction with Oxford Street, where there are great stores stuffed with Hawaiian shirts, frocks from the Fifties and cool clubbing gear. Or check out the **secondhand** stores on Newtown's King Street – though you'll probably find that prices are higher than for similar stuff in the UK or US. If you want to peek at expensive Australian **designer fashion**, head for David Jones Department Store (see p.241) or the shops of the designers themselves, mostly on Oxford Street in Paddington or the Strand Arcade in the city – see p.242.

Fashion

Country Road 142–144 Pitt St Ⓦwww.country road.com.au. Town Hall CityRail. Classic but stylish (if a little preppy) Australian-designed clothes for men and women, plus a high-quality range of shoes and accessories. Several other stores include one on the ground level of the QVB (see p.242) and a clearance outlet at Birkenhead Point, Drummoyne (see box, opposite). Mon–Fri 9am–5.30pm (Thurs to 9pm), Sat 9am–5pm, Sun 11am–5pm.

Hot Tuna 180 Oxford St, Paddington Ⓣ02/9361 5049. Bus #378 from Central CityRail or #380 & #382 from Circular Quay. Flagship store of this cool Australian surfwear label. As well as the casual clothes and swimming gear, there are great accessories – sunglasses, jewellery, hats, beach towels, and bags to stash it all in. Mon–Sat 10am–6pm, Sun noon–5pm.

Mambo 17 Oxford St, Paddington Ⓦwww.mambo.com.au. Bus #378 from Central CityRail or #380 & #382 from Circular Quay. Influenced by comic-strip and graffiti art, Reg Mombassa's designs are now emblazoned on T-shirts, surf gear, beach towels, watches and wallets around the world, promoting his tongue-in-cheek philosophy of "salvation through shopping". Mon–Fri 9am–6pm (Thurs to 9pm), Sat 9am–5pm, Sun 11am–5pm. Also at 80 Campbell Parade, Bondi Beach.

Marcs Pitt St Mall Ⓦwww.marcs.com.au. Town Hall CityRail. *The* place to buy great shirts for men and women. Also stocks a selection of hip European and US lines such as Diesel. Mon–Fri 9.30am–6pm (Thurs to 9pm), Sat 9am–5pm, Sun noon–4pm.

Mooks Clothing Co Shop 2, The Galeries Victoria Ⓦwww.mooks.com. Town Hall CityRail. Now known internationally, Mooks' trendy streetwear originated in Melbourne; clothing and footwear. Mon–Sat 10am–6pm, Sun 11am–5pm.

Sarah Jane 94 Oxford St, Paddington Ⓣ02/9380 7700. Bus #378 from Central CityRail or #380 & #382 from Circular Quay CityRail. Gorgeous, highly feminine frocks, from silky slip dresses to ethereal, floaty chiffon numbers, embroidered velvet coats and appliquéd tops, all with a vintage feel. Prices are mid-range, somewhere between chain store and designer levels, with substantial reductions during summer and winter clearances. Mon–Sat 9am–6pm (Thurs to 9pm), Sun noon–5pm. Also at 134 King St, Newtown and 340 Darling St, Balmain.

Zomp Shoez Shop 303, Mid-City Centre, Pitt St Mall, City Ⓣ02/9221 4027. Town Hall CityRail. A shoe fetishist's heaven, with styles (and prices) that run the gamut from sensible to extravagant; women's shoes only. Also at 468 Oxford St, Paddington. Mon–Fri 9am–5.30pm (Thurs to 9pm), Sat 9am–5pm, Sun 11am–5pm.

Designer fashion

Australian Fashion Week (Ⓦwww .afw.com.au) is held annually in May, with around sixty designers from Australia and the Asia–Pacific region showing their collections. Since Fashion Week's inception in the mid-1990s, there's been a stronger focus both at home and abroad on Australian designers, many of whom, such as **Collette Dinnigan**, are making a name for themselves internationally. We have listed designers with their own outlets below, all on (or just off) Oxford Street in Paddington and Woollahra and in the Strand Arcade ("Department stores and shopping malls", p.242). Some designers don't have their own shops, but look out for the signature low-cut jeans of **Sass & Bide** (ⓦ www.sassandbide.com.au for stockists) and **Michelle Janks'** rejigged vintage pieces. You can combine a visit to Paddington's boutiques with a visit to Saturday's Paddington Market (see p.246), where you'll find original fashion, but expect big crowds. The "Fashion of the Year" display in November at the Powerhouse Museum (see p.82) is also worth a look. All the stores below are open daily. To get to Oxford Street, Paddington, take bus #378 from Central CityRail or #380 or #382 from Circular Quay or Bondi Junction CityRail; the nearest train station to the Strand Arcade in the city is Town Hall CityRail.

The Akira Boutique 12A Queen St, Woollahra ☎02/9361 5221. Japanese-born designer Akira Isogawa has been living in Sydney since the mid-1980s. His ethereal, Japanese-influenced designs now also include clothes for men.

Alannah Hill 118–120 Oxford St, Paddington ☎02/9380 9147; Level 1, The Strand Arcade. Over-the-top, vintage-look, feminine clothing in rich fabrics; boudoir-like store.

Brave 302 Oxford St, Paddington ☎02/9332 2940. Wayne Cooper makes these hip but practical clothes for men and women in the latest high-tech fabrics; even the store feels futuristic. There's also a Wayne Cooper store at Level 1, The Strand Arcade.

Bettina Liano 440 Oxford St, Paddington; Shop 74–78, Level 1, The Strand Arcade ⓦ www.bettinaliano.com. Well-cut designer jeans for women.

Colette Dinnigan 33 William St, Paddington ☎02/9360 6691; also stocked in David Jones Department Store ⓦ www.collettedinnigan.com. Australia's most internationally recognized designer with her own shop in London and her designs stocked in Harrods and Harvey Nichols in the UK and Barneys in the US. Dinnigan is known for her very feminine, finely made clothes for women – lots of beading and embroidery.

Lisa Ho Shop 2A–6A Queen St Woollahra; Level 1, The Strand Arcade; ⓦ www.lisaho.com. Girly frocks; lots of evening wear.

Morrissey 372 Oxford St Paddington ☎02/9380 7422. Peter Morrissey designs sexy clothes with an edge, for men and women; also accessories. Other locations include 76A Oxford St, Darlinghurst; Sydney Central Plaza (see "Department stores and malls" p.242) and Direct Factory Outlets, Homebush (see "Factory outlets" box, below).

Saba 270 Oxford St, Paddington ⓦ www.saba.com.au. Understated, urbane range of clothing for men and women by veteran designer Joe Saba.

Scanlon & Theodore 443 Oxford St, Paddington ☎02/9361 6722. Original, stylish clothes for women; great cuts and fabrics.

Zimmermann Wear 387 Oxford St, Paddington and 24 Oxford St, Woollahra; Level 1, The Strand Arcade ⓦ www.zimmermannwear.com.

Factory outlets

If you like **designer labels** but not the price tags, there are several **factory outlets** in Sydney you can check out. In the city, designer outlets at the Market City shopping centre (see p.242) include Armani, Versace, Replay, Moschino, D&G, OshKosh B'Gosh, Esprit and Australian designer Marcs, but really determined bargain hunters head west for **Direct Factory Outlets** (DFO) on the corner of Homebush Bay Drive and Underwood Rd, Homebush (daily 10am–6pm; ⓦ www.dfo.com.au; North Strathfield CityRail) where there are clearance outlets of big fashion brands including Esprit, Jigsaw, Polo Ralph Lauren, Rivers and Australian designers Charlie Brown, Morrissey (see above) and Lisa Ho (see above). A much more pleasant spot for samples and seconds hunting is the **Birkenhead Point Outlet Centre** (ⓦ www.birkenheadsc.com.au), Roseby Street, Drummoyne, fronting the Parramatta River on Iron Cove. It can be reached on a very pleasant ferry trip from Circular Quay to Birkenhead Ferry Wharf, and you can enjoy more waterviews from the alfresco cafés; fashion outlets include Oroton, Country Road and David Jones bargain warehouse.

Simone Zimmermann is known for her trendy women's swimwear.

Secondhand

The Look 230 King St, Newtown ☏02/9550 2455. Newtown CityRail. A stylish variant on the charity shop, run by the Wesley Mission and worth a look for bargain buys. Mon–Thurs 10am–6pm, Fri–Sat 10am–10pm.

Pretty Dog 1 Brown St, Newtown, just off King St ☏02/9519 7839. Newtown CityRail. A good range of retro secondhand gear and over-the-top club and streetwear. Mon noon–6pm, Tues & Wed 11am–6pm, Thurs 11am–8pm, Fri 11am–5pm, Sat 10am–6pm, Sun noon–5pm.

Route 66 257 Crown St, Darlinghurst ☏02/9331 6686. Bus #378 from Central CityRail or #380 & #382 from Circular Quay CityRail. Taking its inspiration from America's legendary highway (Route 66) to the Wild West, this is where you'll find US vintage gear, and cowgirl-chic leather boots just made for line-dancing. Mon–Fri 10.30am–6pm, Sat 10am–6pm, Sun 11.30am–4.30pm.

The Vintage Clothing Shop 147 Castlereagh St, City ☏02/9267 7135. Town Hall CityRail. This is Sydney's (and probably Australia's) premier vintage clothing store, established in 1976. It has a fabulous range from the 1890s to the 1970s, including an incredible collection of beaded and sequinned tops and dresses from the 1960s. Mon–Fri 9.30am–6pm (Thurs to 7pm), Sat 10.30am–4pm.

Zoo Emporium 332 Crown St, Surry Hills ☏02/9380 5990. Bus #378 from Central CityRail or bus #380 & #382 from Circular Quay CityRail. The very best in Seventies disco gear, from a world where day-glo never died. Mon–Sat 11am–6pm (Thurs to 8pm), Sun noon–5pm.

Outdoor and workwear

Gowings 45 Market St, cnr George St ☏www.gowings.com. Town Hall CityRail. The place to go for Australian workwear is this delightfully old-fashioned men's department store, which has become a beloved Sydney institution since it was established in 1868. It has everything a bloke could want (or in some cases sheilas too), from Bonds T-shirts and Speedo swimwear, to Blundstone boots and a range of Akubra

hats – all at the best prices in town. With a floor devoted to outdoor pursuits, it's also a useful pitstop for basic camping equipment and there's also a travel bookstore courtesy of Berkelouw's (see p.237). Their very amusing catalogue is worth keeping as a souvenir. Mon–Fri 8.30am–6pm (Thurs to 9pm), Sat 9am–6pm, Sun 10am–5pm. Other central branches are located at 319 George St, Wynyard and 82 Oxford St, Darlinghurst.

R. M. Williams 389 George St ☏www.rmwilliams.com.au. Central CityRail. This quality bush outfitters is great for mole-skin pants and shirts, Drizabone coats and superb leather riding and dress boots. Mon–Fri 9am–5.30pm (Thurs to 9pm), Sat 9am–4.30pm, Sun 11am–4pm. Also at the airport.

Strand Hatters The Strand Arcade, 412 George St (through to Pitt St) ☏www.strand hatters.com.au. Town Hall CityRail. For the widest range of Akubra hats and other Australian classics, this old-fashioned store is the place. Mon–Fri 9am–5.30pm (Thurs to 7pm), Sat 9am–4.30pm, Sun 10am–4pm.

Accessories and jewellery

In addition to the following shops, it's worth checking out the **markets** (see p.246), **museum shops** (especially the MCA, see p.57, the Powerhouse Museum, see p.82 and the Art Gallery of New South Wales, see p.67) for unusual treasures and trinkets, as well as the smaller, **private galleries** (see p.243).

Dinosaur Designs Shop 77, The Strand Arcade, 412 George St (through to Pitt St) ☏www.dinosaurdesigns.com.au. Town Hall CityRail. Dinosaur's trademark chunky resin and silver jewellery, and beautifully tactile tableware in muted shades of amber and earth, are terribly hard to resist. Mon–Fri 9.30am–5.30pm (Thurs to 8.30pm), Sat 10am–4pm. Also at 339 Oxford St, Paddington.

Love and Hatred The Strand Arcade, 412 George St (through to Pitt St) ☏02/9233 3441. Town Hall CityRail. Funky Australian jewellery incorporating Gothic and medieval imagery. They will also make commissioned pieces here. Mon–Fri 9am–5.30pm (Thurs to 9pm), Sat 9am–5pm, Sun 10.30am–4.30pm.

SHOPPING AND GALLERIES | Clothes and accessories

Department stores and shopping malls

Australia has followed the American trend in shopping and you're bound to find yourself in mall-land at some stage. Although lacking in neighbourhood character, big city and suburban malls and department stores are handy for familiarizing yourself with prices and variety, especially if time is short. Mall air-conditioning, too, can be a big plus on hot, sticky days.

Department stores

Also see Gowings, a menswear department store, opposite.

David Jones Cnr Elizabeth and Castlereagh streets ⊛ www.davidjones.com.au. **St James or Town Hall CityRail.** Straddling Market Street, David Jones' twin buildings are linked by a walkway above street level. An utterly civilized shopping experience, the ground floor of this flagship store is graced with seasonal floral displays and a coiffured pianist playing tasteful tunes. There's a fantastic gourmet food hall in the Market Street store. Mon–Sat 9am–6pm (Thurs to 9pm), Sun 11am–5pm. A less salubrious version is located at 229 Oxford St, Bondi Junction (Bondi Junction CityRail) and there's a warehouse outlet at Birkenhead Point (see box on p.239).

Grace Bros 436 George St ⊛ www.gracebros
.com.au. **Town Hall CityRail.** Traditionally seen as the more workaday of Sydney's two main department stores, the reborn Grace Bros store, at the heart of the Sydney Central Plaza mall (see p.242), has sharpened up its act, with several gleaming floors of designer fashion and a tranquil Wellness Spa flanked by elegant minimalist homewares. Mon–Sat 9am–6pm (Thurs to 9pm), Sun 11am–5pm.

Shopping malls

Broadway Shopping Centre Cnr Broadway and Bay streets, Broadway. **Bus #431–#434, #438 & #440 from Central CityRail.** On Broadway, between Central Station and Glebe, this mall benefits from its proximity to Sydney University and the arty enclave of Glebe, with a less run-of-the-mill mix of street fashion and chain stores. A Hoyts

The face of Australia

In recent years, Aussie skincare companies have wowed the world with their minimalist approach to packaging, lavish use of essential oils and vibrant lippy colours – not to mention some savvy marketing.

All the following are available at David Jones and/or Grace Bros; Jurlique also has its own store in The Strand Arcade (see p.242), while Red Earth has its flagship store in the QVB (see p.242). Napoleon has its own stores, including one on the fashionista strip, Oxford Street, Paddington, at no. 74.

Aesop Divine skin balms and haircare products packed in pharmaceutical-grade brown glass, which rely on essential oils for their beneficial properties and fragrance, and eschew the usual exaggerated claims and hype.

Bliss Aromatherapy range of pure essential oils, massage oils and incense.

Bloom ⊛ www.bloomcosmetics.com. Whimsically packaged bath and body range, including fruity lip balms and body glitter.

Jurlique ⊛ www.jurlique.com.au. Pure, hypoallergenic skin and haircare based on essential oils produced organically in South Australia.

Napoleon ⊛ www.napoleoncosmetics.com. Individually colour-matched cosmetics to suit all types and shades of skin, as you might expect from a company that also runs a school for make-up artists.

Red Earth Skincare and cosmetics company that wears its environmental credentials on its sleeve, incorporating native herbs and plants in its products. They also boast a vast range of vividly coloured lipsticks and nail polish of every hue, all at bargain prices.

SHOPPING AND GALLERIES | Department stores

multiplex cinema shows art-house and mainstream movies, there's Collins Superstore (see p.237), and an extensive Asian section in the Coles supermarket.

The Galeries Victoria 500 George St, cnr Park St ⊛ www.tgv.com.au. Town Hall CityRail. Diagonally opposite the Town Hall, Sydney's latest upmarket shopping mall has a great sense of space provided by its central glass-roofed piazza with overhead pedestrian bridges running across the space, and a series of arcades throughout. All the fashion stores are mixed clothing or menswear – including the funky Mooks Clothing Co (see p.238), Polo Jeans and Nico Clothing and Footwear. Its main drawcard, however, is the city's biggest book superstore, Kinokuniya (see p.237). There are lots of cafés, patisseries, sandwich bars, a sushi shop and an ice-cream parlour on the lower ground floor, as well as a small IGA supermarket. You can enter the contrastingly Heritage *Art House Hotel* (see p.197) from one end of the ground floor, where there are also cheap eats by day.

Market City 9–13 Hay St, Haymarket ⊛ www.marketcity.com.au. Central CityRail. This cavernous mall above Paddy's Market houses two food courts, a multiplex cinema (see p.219) and a bar. The shopping centre has a distinctly Asian feel, with Chinese lanterns hanging from the ceiling and resident shiatsu masseurs. There are Asian supermarkets, factory outlets for big-name stores like Esprit and OshKosh and smaller boutiques selling cute street and club wear imported from Asia (think smaller sizes).

QVB (Queen Victoria Building) 455 George St, City ⊛ www.qvb.com.au. Town Hall CityRail. This splendid Victorian arcade is a sight in its own right, attracting more visitors than either the Harbour Bridge or the Opera House. The interior is magnificent, with beautiful woodwork, elevated walkways and antique lifts. Brave the weekend hordes for a wistful look at the designer shop fronts upstairs (the third level has several boutiques featuring the work of younger Australian designers) and a wander around the ubiquitous Esprit, Jigsaw or the Body Shop at ground level. Or come just for a coffee fix in *Bar Cupola* or *Jet* (see

p.175), both at street level. From Town Hall Station you can walk right through the basement level (mainly bustling food stalls) and continue via the Sydney Central Plaza to Grace Bros, emerging on the Pitt St Mall. Shopping hours Mon–Sat 9am–6pm (Thurs to 9pm), Sun 11am–5pm; ground level open 24hrs.

Skygarden 77 Castlereagh St and off Pitt St Mall ⊛ www.skygarden.com.au. Town Hall CityRail. Stylish shopping centre with lots of fashion for men and women, and the Borders book superstore (Mon–Wed & Fri 9.30am–5.30pm, Thurs 9.30am–8pm, Sat 9.30am–5pm, Sun 11am–4pm). If you're going to be in Sydney for a while, you might like to check out level 2, which is totally devoted to homewares. There's also a good food court on the top floor.

The Strand Arcade 412 George St (through to Pitt St) ⊛ www.strandarcade.com.au. Town Hall CityRail. Built in 1892, this elegant arcade with its wrought-iron balustrades houses tiny fashion boutiques including outlets of several of Australia's top designers on level 1 (see p.239), jewellers including Dinosaur Designs (see p.240) and Love and Hatred (see p.240), watchmakers, Sydney's best hat shop (see p.240), an outlet of Jurlique (see box, p.241), plus gourmet coffee shops and tea rooms.

Sydney Central Plaza 450 George St, City ☎02/9261 2266. Town Hall CityRail. Sprawling from George Street through to Pitt St Mall and linking with the Mid-City Centre, this maze of shops and fast-food outlets takes in Grace Bros and a whole host of mostly clothing and fashion stores, not to mention a stage where variable, but free, entertainers perform for the munching masses.

Westfield Centrepoint Cnr Pitt St Mall and Market St, City ⊛ www.westfield.com/centre point. Town Hall CityRail. At the base of the landmark Sydney Tower, Westfield Centrepoint has over 130 speciality stores, 60 of them focusing on fashion and accessories, though nothing terribly exciting. There's an excellent basement food court and the Australian Geographic Shop (p.248) and the Wilderness Society Shop (p.248) here are both good for quality souvenirs.

Food and drink

The handiest **supermarkets** for the city centre are Woolworths Metro, opposite the Town Hall (Mon–Wed 7am–8pm, Thurs & Fri 7am–9pm, Sat

9am–6.30pm, Sun 10am–5.30pm), and Coles Express, in the Wynyard Station complex (daily 6am–midnight); the Coles Express in Kings Cross, at 88 Darlinghurst Rd, is also handy for travellers (daily 6am–midnight). The Asian supermarkets on Sussex and Burlington streets in Chinatown and in the Market City complex offer more exotic alternatives, and for deli items and impromptu picnic supplies, head for the splendid food hall at David Jones (see "Department stores", p.241), its Food Chain outlet at Manly Wharf (see p.135) or one of the gourmet stores listed below. In the suburbs, the big supermarkets such as Coles stay open until about 10pm or midnight, and there are plenty of 24-hour, 7-Eleven convenience stores in the inner city and suburbs.

There are also several **food markets**: Paddy's Market in Chinatown (see p.87) has been selling fruit and vegetables since the nineteenth century, while rural growers and producers of gourmet goods distribute direct to Sydney's regular **produce markets**: at Pyrmont Bay Park in front of the Star City Casino on the first Saturday of the month (7–11am); at Fox Studio's Bent Street every Wednesday (noon–7pm) and on the third Saturday of the month (8am–noon); and at the Northside Produce Market at the Civic Centre, Miller Street, North Sydney, between Ridge and McClaren streets, on the third Saturday of the month (8am–noon).

Australian Wine Centre Shop 3, Goldfields House, 1 Alfred St, cnr George St, Circular Quay ⓦ www.australianwinecentre.com. Circular Quay CityRail/ferry. Basement store stocking more than a thousand wines from over 300 wineries around Australia, which holds regular tastings, or you can just buy a test-drive glass of wine at its in-house wine bar during the week (open till 7pm Fri, closed Sat & Sun). They also ship overseas. Mon–Sat 9.30am–6.30pm, Sun 11am–5pm.

Infinity Sourdough 225 Victoria St, Darlinghurst ☎ 02/9380 4320. Kings Cross CityRail. A great place for breakfasts on the hoof, and for the sheer pleasure of wonderful bread baked on the premises – from sourdough and wholemeal to the more exotic Guinness beer rye bread and oatmeal polenta loaves. Daily 6am–7pm or later.

jones the grocer 68 Moncur St, Woollahra ⓦ www.jonesthegrocer.com.au. Bus #389 from Circular Quay CityRail. Stylishly packaged, outlandishly priced and utterly delicious groceries and gourmet treats to eat in or take away; includes a cheese room. Mon–Sat 9am–5pm.

Russell's Natural Food Markets 53–55 Glebe Point Rd, Glebe ☎ 02/9660 8144. Bus #431–#433 from Central CityRail. Vast range

of wholefoods, organic fruit and vegetables, speciality honeys and tahini. Mon–Fri 9.30am–7pm (Thurs to 8pm), Sat 9am–6pm, Sun 10am–5pm.

Simon Johnson 181 Harris St, Pyrmont ⓦ www.simonjohnson.com.au. Pyrmont Light Rail. When only the best will do, try Simon Johnson's superb cheeses (in a dedicated conditioning room), teas and coffees, top-of-the-range pastas, oils and vinegars, as supplied to discriminating restaurateurs. Mon–Fri 10.30am–7pm, Sat 9am–5pm. Also at 55 Queen St, Woollahra (Mon–Fri 10.30am–7pm, Sat 9am–5pm, Sun 10am–4pm) and Quadrangle Shopping Village, 100 Edinburgh Rd, Castlecrag (Mon–Fri 9am–6pm, Sat 9am–5pm, Sun 10am–4pm).

Sydney Fish Markets Pyrmont Bay, Pyrmont ⓦ www.sydneyfishmarket.com.au. Fish Market Light Rail. Sydney's seafood comes straight off the fishing boats here, from where it's sold to retailers at the fish market auction and then goes on to the several fishmonger outlets. There's also excellent fruit and veg, flowers, a reliable deli, a bottle shop, plus takeaway (and eat-in) sushi and fish and chips for the picnic tables by the water's edge. Daily 7am–4pm. Also see p.83.

Galleries

Sydney's diverse arts scene is reflected in a myriad of **small art galleries**, which are concentrated in Paddington and Surry Hills, with a few smaller ones in King Street, Newtown. The useful *Artfind Guide* to selected Sydney art galleries and antique dealers is published by the Josef Lebovic Galleries (see p.246); its website has links to the galleries selected in their guide and includes maps (Ⓦ www.artfind .com.au). Alternatively, you can buy a copy of *Art and Australia Magazine* (Ⓦ www.artaustralia.com), Australia's authoritative national art journal which has major exhibition reviews and listings. It's published quarterly and available at bookshops and newsagents. The Citysearch Sydney website, Ⓦ www.sydney.citysearch .com.au, has comprehensive listings of art galleries and current exhibitions, while Friday's "Metro" section of the *Sydney Morning Herald* offers reviews of recently opened shows. For shops attached to Sydney's major galleries and museums see the individual reviews in the main Guide section.

If you're interested in buying **Aboriginal art and crafts**, try some of the galleries that direct profits back to Aboriginal communities, rather than settling for the standard tourist tat.

Aboriginal art and craft

For background on Aboriginal art styles and communities, visit the Art Gallery of New South Wales (see p.67) or check out the excellent Aboriginal Art Online website, Ⓦ www.aboriginalartonline.com. Also see Quadrivium (opposite), which exhibits work of Aboriginal artists.

Aboriginal and Tribal Art Centre 1st floor, 117 George St, The Rocks ☎ 02/9247 9625. Circular Quay CityRail. Has a huge collection of traditional Aboriginal art from around Australia including didgeridoos (live didj played Sat and the musician also offers advice to customers). Daily 10am–5pm.

Boomalli Aboriginal Artists Co-operative 119 Parramatta Rd, Annandale Ⓦ www.culture.com.au/boomalli.com.au. Bus #438 & #440 from Central CityRail. Boomalli, initiated by ten indigenous artists in the late

1980s is still wholly Aboriginal-operated. Unlike many other Aboriginal galleries, it prioritizes the work of New South Wales urban and rural Aboriginal artists: expect controversial, cutting-edge contemporary art including photography and mixed media. Mon–Fri 10am–4pm.

The Boomerang School 200 William St, Kings Cross ☎ 02/9358 2370. Kings Cross CityRail. Boomerangs sold here are mostly authentic, made by Aboriginal artisans from around Australia. The owner, Duncan MacLennon, has been giving free boomerang-throwing lessons every Sun in Yarranabbe Park near Rushcutters Bay (10am–noon) since 1958. Mon–Sat 9am–6.30pm, Sun 2–6pm.

Dreamtime Gallery Shop 35, The Rocks Centre, 10–26 Playfair St, The Rocks Ⓦ www.dt.citysearch.com.au. Circular Quay CityRail. Sells traditional Aboriginal art including didgeridoos. Daily 9.30am–5.30pm. Also a branch at the Opera House.

Gavala: Aboriginal Art & Cultural Centre Level 2, Harbourside Shopping Centre, Darling Harbour Ⓦ www.gavala.com.au. Town Hall CityRail. Highly credible Aboriginal-owned and -run arts and crafts store – all profits go to the artists and their communities, while the centre aims to raise awareness of indigenous cultures through education programmes. They also sell clothes and accessories from Balarinji, the Aboriginal-owned design studio based in The Rocks, most famous for the Aboriginal-art-covered Qantas planes. Daily 10am–7pm.

Hogarth Galleries Aboriginal Art Centre 7 Walker Lane (off Brown St), Paddington ☎ 02/9360 6839, Ⓦ www.hoggal.citysearch .com.au. Bus #378 from Central CityRail or #380 & #382 from Circular Quay CityRail. This long-established gallery has a sound reputation for its support of contemporary Aboriginal artists, and its broader commitment to reconciliation. Extensive collection of work by contemporary Aboriginal artists, both tribal and urban, and special exhibitions. Tues–Sat 10am–5pm.

Walkabout Art Berkelouw Books, 70 Norton St, Leichhardt, Ⓦ www.worldvision.com.au/walka boutart. Bus #438 & #440 from Central CityRail. This Aboriginal art gallery is a World Vision Australia project; as well as providing a source of income for individual artists, any profits fund education and health programmes in indigenous communities. Work is exhibited from communities all over Australia, with a focus on the Western Desert, and Utopia and Pintupi. Mon–Sat 10am–5pm, Sun 11am–4pm.

Contemporary painting and sculpture

Art House Gallery 66 McLachlan Ave, Rushcutters Bay ☎02/9332 1019. Kings Cross CityRail. This cavernous gallery showcases Australian artists and always has interesting exhibits, as well as pieces for sale. Tues–Fri 10am–5.30pm, Sat 10am–4pm.

Australian Galleries: Painting & Sculpture 15 Roylston St, Paddington ☎02/9360 5177. Edgecliff CityRail. Serene gallery exhibiting and selling contemporary Australian art, including works by Gary Shead, Jeffrey Smart and John Coburn. Tues–Sat 10am–6pm.

Australian Galleries: Works on Paper 24 Glenmore Rd, Paddington ☎02/9380 8744. Bus #378 from Central CityRail or #380 & #382 from Circular Quay CityRail. Works for sale here include drawings by William Robinson, Brett Whiteley and Arthur Boyd, as well as prints and sketches by young Australian artists. Tues–Sat 10am–6pm, Sun noon–5pm.

Quadrivium Level 2, QVB, 455 George St ⊛www.quadrivium.com.au. Town Hall CityRail. Upmarket gallery specializing in contemporary Australian craft and design objects, particularly glass, ceramics and jewellery; Aboriginal art from Utopia; and traditional Asian art. Representing over a 100 artists. Mon–Sat 10am–6pm (Thurs to 9pm), Sun 11am–5pm.

Ray Hughes Gallery 270 Devonshire St, Surry Hills. Central CityRail. ⊛www.rayhughes gallery.com. Influential dealer with a stable of high-profile contemporary Australian and New Zealand artists. Openings monthly, with two artists per show. Tues–Sat 10am–6pm.

Sherman Galleries 16–18 Goodhope St, Paddington ☎02/9331 1112, ⊛www.sherman galleries.com.au. Bus #389 from Circular Quay or Bondi Junction CityRail. There are two Sherman Galleries in Paddington, the other on Hargrave St (see p.246). The main focus of interest at the Goodhope Street gallery is the large outdoor sculpture garden presenting work by both international and Australian sculptors. Tues–Sat 11am–6pm.

Experimental, multimedia and installation

Artspace The Gunnery Arts Centre, 43–51 Cowper Wharf Rd, Woolloomooloo ⊛www .artspace.org.au. Kings Cross CityRail. In a wonderful location, showing provocative young artists with a focus on installations and new media. Tues–Sat 11am–6pm.

Ivan Dougherty Gallery Cnr Albion Ave and Selwyn St, Paddington ⊛www.cofa.unsw.edu. Bus #378 from Central CityRail or #382 from Circular Quay CityRail. This is the exhibition space for the College of Fine Arts, University of New South Wales. The ten shows per year focus on international contemporary art with accompanying forums, lectures and performances. Mon–Sat 10am–5pm.

The Performance Space 199 Cleveland St, Redfern, opposite Prince Alfred Park ⊛www.performancespace.com.au. Redfern or Central CityRail. Experimental multimedia and plastic arts: installations, sculpture, photography and painting. Wed–Fri noon–6pm.

Roslyn Oxley9 Gallery 8 Soudan Lane, off Hampden St, Paddington ☎02/9331 1919, ⊛www.roslynoxley9.com.au. Edgecliff CityRail. Avant-garde videos and installations among the Australian and international offerings. Tues–Fri 10am–6pm, Sat 11am–6pm.

Photography and prints

Australian Centre for Photography 257 Oxford St, Paddington ☎02/9332 1455, ⊛www.acp.au.com. Bus #378 from Central CityRail or #380 & #382 from Circular Quay CityRail. This non-profit organization is part-funded by various government agencies. Exhibitions of photo-based art from established and new international and Australian artists in two galleries. Emerging photographers are showcased on the Project Wall, and it's something of a developing (and visiting) photographers' Mecca, with basic and specialist courses and a darkroom available for use (daily noon–6pm). There's also a specialist bookshop plus the French-style *Bistro Lulu* (see p.189). Tues–Sun 11am–6pm.

Horden House 77 Victoria St, Potts Point ⊛www.horden.com. Kings Cross CityRail. Eminent antique dealer, trading in colonial art including antiquarian prints and maps, rare books and manuscripts. Tues–Fri 9am–5pm.

Josef Lebovic 34 Paddington St, Paddington Ⓦ www.joseflebovicgallery.com.au. Bus #378 from Central CityRail, #380, #382 from Circular Quay CityRail. Renowned print and graphic gallery specializing in Australian and international prints from the nineteenth and twentieth centuries, as well as vintage photography. Tues–Fri 1–6pm, Sat 11am–5pm.

Sherman Galleries 1 Hargrave St, Paddington Ⓦ www.shermangalleries.com.au. Bus #389 from Circular Quay or Bondi Junction CityRail. Specialists in contemporary prints and drawings. Tues–Sat 11am–6pm.

Stills Gallery 36 Gosbell St, Paddington Ⓦ www.stillsgallery.com.au. Kings Cross CityRail. One of the most high-profile Sydney photography galleries; exhibits contemporary Australian and international work. Wed–Sat 11am–6pm.

Markets

Weekend **markets** have become a feature of the leisurely lives of Sydneysiders, so be prepared for crowds. The best for general browsing are the trendy Paddington Bazaar, the more arty Balmain market and the relaxed market on Glebe Point Road. Apart from the markets listed below, there is a Sunday art and craft market in Kings Cross (see p.98); a Sunday craft market on the Opera House forecourt (see p.60); a monthly flea market in Shannon Reserve, on the corner of Crown and Foveaux streets, Surry Hills (see p.89); a weekend flea market in the grounds of Rozelle Primary School on Darling Street, Rozelle, near Victoria Rd (see p.109); and a Sunday Aboriginal craft market at La Perouse (see p.143).

In addition, a series of alternating Saturday markets takes place on the **North Shore**, the most well known being Kirribilli market (fourth Sat of month; see p.121; ☎02/9936 8197 for details of the others).

Balmain Markets St Andrews Church, cnr Darling St and Curtis Rd, Balmain. Bus #433 from Central CityRail or #442 from the QVB. An assortment of books, handmade jewellery, clothing and ceramics, antiques, homemade chocolates, cakes and gourmet foods and organic produce are sold. The highlight is an eclectic array of food stalls in the church hall where you can snack your way from the Himalayas to South India. Sat 7.30am–4pm.

Bondi Beach Markets Bondi Primary School, cnr of Campbell Parade and Warners Avenue. Bus #380, #382 & #389 from Bondi Junction CityRail. In the grounds of a lucky beach-facing primary school, these relaxed Sunday markets place great emphasis on groovy fashion – both new and secondhand – and jewellery. Sun 10am–4pm, to 6pm Dec–Feb.

Glebe Market Glebe Primary School, 38 Glebe Point Rd. Bus #431–#434 from Central CityRail. The market is shady, relaxed and quietly sociable, like Glebe itself. A mixture of funky new and secondhand clothes and accessories, including beach dresses, handbags, jewellery – plus plants, records and CDs, and the inevitable New Age knick-knacks and secondhand books. Chinese masseurs ply their trade, but the small range of food stalls are disappointing; there is, however, a strip of great cafés opposite, including *Badde Manors*, *Iku*, *Lolita's* and *Well Connected* (see pp.179–180). Sat 9am–4.30pm.

Paddington Markets 395 Oxford St, Paddington. Bus #378 from Central CityRail or #380 & #382 from Circular Quay or Bondi Junction CityRail. As well as being a great location for people-watching in the shady church grounds, these markets offer contemporary Australian crafts – particularly leather goods and jewellery – as well as original fashion, both old and new. Even if you're just here to browse, the atmosphere, music and buskers come free, and it's all conveniently located in the middle of an excellent shopping and grazing strip. Sat 10am–4pm.

The Rocks Market George St, The Rocks. Circular Quay CityRail/ferry. Completely taking over The Rocks end of George Street, this collection of more than a hundred stalls offers jewellery, antiques and art and crafts, mostly with an Australiana/souvenir slant and shaded from the sun by big white umbrellas. The excellent remain-

dered book stall is great for coffee-table books on Sydney. Sheltered from the sun and rain by huge canvas sails. Sat & Sun 10am–5pm.

Music

Tyranny of distance has traditionally kept many big-name bands from including Sydney on their world tours. As a result, perhaps, there is fierce loyalty here to home-grown music. In addition to specialist **Australian music** shops, you'll find a smattering of places catering for **jazz** and **folk** aficionados, as well as the usual megastores.

Australian Music Centre Shop Level 4, The Arts Exchange, 18 Hickson Rd, The Rocks ⓦwww.amcoz.com.au. Circular Quay CityRail/ferry. Specialist Australian music store of the Australian Music Centre, set up in 1974 to provide information, publications and scores relating to Australian music. The retail outlet covers genres from classical through jazz and folk to traditional Aboriginal music and experimental sounds. With its relaxed, listen-before-you-buy policy and knowledgeable staff, this is a great place to get a taste for antipodean music; you are also welcome to visit the centre's resource library, which has listening facilities (Mon–Thurs 10am–5pm). Mon–Fri 9am–5pm.

Birdland Records 3 Barrack St, City ⓦwww.birdland.com.au. Wynyard or Martin Place CityRail. This is arguably Sydney's premier jazz store, helped along by some blues and soul. Mon–Fri 9am–6pm (Thurs to 7pm), Sat 9am–4pm.

Central Station Records 46 Oxford St, Darlinghurst ⓦwww.centralstationrec.com. Museum CityRail. Sydney's dance music specialist, stocking the latest imported and local sounds on vinyl and CD. At the heart of the gay scene in Darlinghurst, they also put together and sell the official Mardi Gras compilations. Mon–Fri 10am–7pm (Thurs to 9pm), Sat 10am–6pm, Sun noon–6pm.

Fish Records 200, 285 & 350 George St, City ⓦwww.fishrecords.com.au. Circular Quay, Wynyard or Martin Place CityRail. Bus #378 from Central CityRail or #380 & #382 from Circular Quay CityRail. Australia's largest independent music chain but catering to

eclectic tastes – indie, drum and bass, acid jazz, top 40, soundtracks and some classical. Also in-store ticket sales for the best gigs. Mon–Sat 9am–11.30pm, Sun 10am–9.30pm. Also at Balmain, Bondi Junction, Broadway Shopping Centre, Leichhardt and Newtown and the international terminal at Sydney Airport.

Folkways 282 Oxford St, Paddington ☏02/9361 3980. Bus #378 from Central CityRail or #380 & #382 from Circular Quay CityRail. Long catering to Sydney's folk-music devotees; there's a comprehensive selection of folk recordings, plus some world music. Mon–Fri 9am–6pm (Thurs to 9pm), Sat 9.30am–6.30pm, Sun 11am–6pm.

HMV Mid-City Centre, Pitt St Mall ⓦwww.hmv.com.au. Martin Place or Town Hall CityRail. The most conspicuous of the city-centre music shops, this megastore stocks just about everything, including extensive classical and world music selections. Mon–Fri 9am–6pm (Thurs to 8pm), Sat 9am–5.30pm, Sun 11am–5pm.

Red Eye Records 66 King St, City ⓦwww.redeye.com.au. Martin Place CityRail. Sydney's biggest independent record store is the place to track down your favourite Australian bands on hard-to-find independent labels, plus rare, out-of-print and collectable items. The ground floor is all new, with everything from alternative to jazz; upstairs there's a huge range of secondhand vinyls, CDs and memorabilia. This is also where you can plug into the live music scene, with heaps of flyers available. They also ship overseas. Mon–Fri 9am–6pm (Thurs to 9pm), Sat 10am–5pm, Sun 11am–5pm.

Souvenirs

Also see the "Outdoor and workwear" section on p.240 and "Aboriginal art and craft" on p.244. For toys see "Kids' Sydney" p.231.

Aussie Koala Shop Shop 8, The Rocks Centre, 10–26 Playfair St, The Rocks ☏02/9247 6388. **Circular Quay CityRail.** The place for those kitsch souvenirs: lots of furry koalas, of course, snowdomes featuring the Harbour Bridge and the Opera House, and even mini-boomerangs. Daily 9am–6pm.

Australian Geographic Shop International Airport ☏02/8339 0027. **International CityRail.** Linked to the *Australian Geographic* magazine, similar to *National Geographic*, this is the place for quality souvenirs including portable indigenous art, coffee-table and travel books, and quirky novelty items. Perfect for last-minute shopping. Daily 6am–10pm. Also at Darling Harbour Harbourside Shopping Centre (see p.81) and Westfield Centrepoint in the city (see p.242).

Done Art and Design 123 George St, The Rocks ⓦ www.done.com.au. **Circular Quay CityRail/ferry.** Love the stuff or loathe it, there's no doubt that Ken Done's loud and colourful knitwear, T-shirts and other design oddments are as identifiably Sydney as the

Harbour Bridge. Appropriately, the bridge, Opera House and harbour scenery feature prominently in his artwork, which graces items from duvet covers to swimwear. Daily 10am–6pm. Also at 1 Hickson Rd, The Rocks (daily 10am–5.30pm) and at the international departure terminal at Sydney Airport (daily 6am–9pm).

Wilderness Society Shop Westfield Centrepoint, cnr Pitt St Mall and Market St, City ⓦ www.wildshop.com.au. **Town Hall CityRail.** The shop of Australia's national community environmental campaigning group, the Wilderness Society, is an oasis in a very commercial district, with friendly young staff and information about current campaigns. It's great for quality souvenirs, including a great range of cards, calendars and books, children's and adults' T-shirts (the one with the "Treehugger" caption is one of their bestsellers), children's picture books and games, native bush-scented candles and must-have chocolate bilby babies. Mon–Fri 9am–6pm (Thurs to 8pm), Sat 9am–5pm, Sun 11am–4pm.

Festivals and events

The Sydney year is interspersed with festivals, both sporting and cultural, with summer being the peak time for big events. The **Sydney to Hobart Yacht Race** starts on Boxing Day (December 26); then there's the **New Years Eve fireworks**, eclipsed by the big extravaganza of the **Australia Day** celebrations (January 26). Running throughout January is the **Sydney Festival** whose highlight is the free outdoor **Opera in The Domain** concert. The summer winds up in a whirl of feathers and sequins at the **Sydney Gay + Lesbian Mardi Gras**, held in late February/early March. An entirely different side of Sydney life is on view at the impressive summer **surf carnivals**, staged regularly by surf life-saving clubs; check the newspapers for details.

City of Sydney Council's website ⓦ www.cityofsydney.nsw.gov.au has details of festivals and events including the rundown of the Sydney Festival. Its free weekly list of what's on, *City Life*, comes out every Wednesday and can be picked up at the Town Hall (see p.74) and at tourist offices (see p.18).

January

New Year Sydney sees in the New Year with a spectacular multimillion-dollar fireworks display on Sydney Harbour. The more family-focused part of the proceedings begins at 9pm at Darling Harbour, with lots on for kids (for more information check ⓦ www.darlingharbour.com.au), followed by the main event at midnight, when themed fireworks are set off from the Harbour Bridge itself, synchronized to music. People crowd out vantage points including North Head, South Head, The Rocks, Cremorne Point, Blues Point and Neutral Bay – anywhere with the Bridge in sight is good – and many bag their spots from early morning; more information can be found at ⓦ www.cityofsydney.nsw.gov.au. Thousands of vessels also anchor on the water to take in the views; contact any of the ferry cruise companies listed under "Ferries and cruises" on p.26, as well as

Sydney Ferries (ⓦ www.sydneyferries .nsw.gov.au) and, if you can sail yourself, the boat and yacht charters on p.259 of "Sports and activities" to organise getting out on the water.

Sydney Festival After the New Year celebrations, there's a brief hiatus before the start of the Sydney Festival on January 2 (ⓣ 02/8248 6500, ⓦ www.sydneyfestival.org.au), an exhaustive (and exhausting) arts event that lasts until the Australia Day celebrations (Jan 26). Highlights include Opera in The Domain, Jazz in The Domain and Symphony in The Domain (all free); the outdoor cinema at Mrs Macquaries Chair; and a fantastic roster of international performers and exhibitions. Many events are free, and take place in public spaces such as Circular Quay, The Domain and Darling Harbour. International acts tend to be quite expensive. The general programme is usually printed in the *Sydney Morning Herald* in October or November, while a full eighty-plus-page (free) programme is available nearer the time from the Town Hall. A weekly listing of events appears in the *Sydney Morning Herald* during the festival. Darling Harbour also hosts its own festival (Dec 26–Jan 31); most attractions are aimed at children, but there's a free promenade jazz festival (more information on ⓦ www .darlingharbour.com.au).

Flickerfest International Short Film Festival Week-long film festival, held mostly outdoors in the amphitheatre of the Bondi Pavilion in early January; some films in the auditorium. More details on ⓦ www .flickerfest.com.au; see also p.218.

Sydney Fringe Festival Headquartered by the beach at the Bondi Pavilion (see p.127), the Sydney Fringe Festival (☎ 02/9130 3325, ⓦ www.waverly.nsw.gov.au) runs for two weeks from mid-January, and encompasses performance, music, visual art, workshops, kids' shows and some very unusual, irreverent sporting events, from the very camp Drag Race Meet to the Nude Night Surfing competition. The lively Festival Club, with DJs and performances, and ABC Triple J radio broadcasts, takes place nightly in the pavilion's balcony bar.

Big Day Out Sydney's biggest outdoor rock concert, held at the Showgrounds at Homebush Bay the weekend before or after Australia Day (Jan 26), features around sixty of the best local and international acts on several stages, with over 50,000 in the audience. More details on ⓦ www.big-dayout.com and on p.210.

Australia Day January 26 is the anniversary of the arrival of the First Fleet in Sydney Harbour in 1788 (see p.320), and Australia Day activities are focused on the harbour (Australia Day Council of NSW ⓦ www.adc.nsw.gov.au). Sydney's passenger ferries race from Fort Denison to the Harbour Bridge and there is a Tall Ships Race, from Bradley's Head to the Harbour Bridge, a 21-gun salute fired from the Man O'War steps at the Opera House and a military air show over the harbour. The Australia Day Regatta takes place in the afternoon, with hundreds of yachts racing at various harbour locations. There are also events and activities in The Rocks, Hyde Park and at Darling Harbour, where there's a 9pm fireworks display to rival the New Year's Eve extravaganza. The Survival concert, organized by the National Indigenous Arts Advocacy Association, is a celebration of indigenous culture and a tribute to, and acknowledgement of, the Stolen Generation, in pointed opposition to the mainstream Australia Day festivities. The concert features many of Australia's best Aboriginal bands and performers; around 10,000 attend (10am–7pm; $12; tickets at the gate; no alcohol; more details via ⓦ www.niaaa.com.au/survival or ⓦ www .waverley.nsw.gov.au). Coogee Beach hosts an outdoor jazz festival (information on ⓦ www.randwick.nsw.gov.au) and many Sydney museums have free entry all day.

Vibes on a Summers Day At the very end of January, either the Bondi Pavilion or the Arthur Byrne Reserve at Maroubra Beach host a weekend outdoor daytime dance party (noon–9pm) with the best of international DJs. More details at ⓦ www.vibes.net.au and on p.210.

February

Chinese New Year Towards the end of January or in the first weeks of February, Chinese New Year is celebrated in Chinatown – firecrackers, dragon and lion dances, food stalls and music. More details on ⓦ www.cityofsydney.nsw.gov.au.

Tropfest Hugely popular competition festival for short films, taking place at the end of February, with an outdoor screening in The Domain. More details on ⓦ www.tropfest .com.au; see also box on p.218.

Sydney Gay + Lesbian Mardi Gras The festival runs through February, and features films, theatre and exhibitions that range from cheeky to outrageous. It all culminates in one of the world's biggest street parades, when up to a million people line the streets on the last Saturday in February or the first Saturday in March. More details on ⓦ www.mardigras.com.au; see also pp.221–224.

March/April

Norton St Festival Sunday street festival in mid-March (10am–7pm), celebrating Sydney's most stridently Italian community. It's held along the Norton Street (see p.107) strip of cafés and restaurants. Lots of food stalls and entertainment, culminating in a fireworks display over Leichhardt Town Hall. More details on ⓦ www.lmc.nsw.gov.au.

Royal Easter Show The Royal Easter Show, an agricultural and garden show, moved in 1998 to the Sydney Showground at the Olympic site at Homebush Bay. For fourteen consecutive days in late March/early April (the Easter weekend is neatly sandwiched in between), the country comes to the city with parades of prized animals and various farm/agriculture related displays, plus a frantic array of amusement-park rides, and frenzied consumerism in the Showbag Pavilion. At night in the main arena, there's a celebration of Australian bush heritage, stunt shows, a rodeo and fireworks displays; by day, there are usually horse-related events, judging of show animals, and the traditional, and very popular, woodchopping competitions. Open 9.30am–10pm, last admission 8.30pm. Tickets $23, child $14.50, half-price tickets after 6pm; rides extra; Show Infoline ℡ 02/9704 1000; ⓦ www.greataustralian muster.com.au.

May–July

Biennale of Sydney Every alternate (even-numbered) year, this international contemporary art festival takes place over six weeks from mid-May until early July, featuring artists from every continent. Provocative contemporary exhibitions and events at various venues and outdoor spaces around town, including the Art Gallery of New South Wales, the Opera House, Customs House and the Museum of Contemporary Art. Usually free. More details on ⓦ www.biennaleofsydney.com.au.

Sydney Writers Festival Week-long high-profile mid-May event with readings, workshops and discussions, mostly free; Australian and international writers. Takes place in a very scenic location at the Wharf Theatre, Hickson Rd, Millers Point. More details on ⓦ www.swf.org.au.

Sydney Film Festival Takes over several of the city's screens for two weeks from early June. More details at ⓦ www .sydneyfilmfestival.org; see also box on p.218.

August

Sun Herald City-to-Surf Race A newspaper-sponsored 14-kilometre fun run from Park Street in the city to Bondi, held on the second Sunday of August. About 30,000 participants. Entry forms are in the *Sun* *Herald* from June 1 or entry is available online; entry costs $25, $18 for children up to 18. More details from the official website ⓦ city2surf.sunherald.com.au or ⓦ www.coolrunning.com.au/citytosurf.

September–October

Festival of the Winds In September, as the skies get bluer, Australia's largest kite festival takes over Bondi Beach. More details on ⓦ www.waverley.nsw.gov.au.

Carnivale Carnivale is a state-funded multicultural festival, celebrating the diverse talents of the ethnic peoples of Sydney through theatre, music and dance. Held each spring, September to early October. More details on ⓦ www.carnivale.com.au.

Manly International Jazz Festival Taking place over the Labour Day weekend in early October, this festival consists of mostly free outdoor, waterfront events with some indoor concerts charging entry for some of the bigger Australian and international acts. As Sydney gets into the swim of summer, and the beaches officially open for the year,

FESTIVALS AND EVENTS

this jazz-fest by the sea is a wonderful way to enjoy the warming weather. More details on ⓦwww.manly.nsw.gov.au; also see p.134.

Blessing of the Fleet Labour Day weekend (early October) sees revellers dressed in traditional fancy dress for the blessing of brightly decorated fishing boats for their life at sea. Most of Sydney's fishing industry workers come from the Italian community, hence this very Italian festival at Darling Harbour. More details on ⓦwww .darlinghabour.com.au.

Newtown Festival Organized by the Newtown Neighbourhood Centre, Town Hall, 1 Bedford St, Newtown (☎02/9516 4755, ⓦwww.newtowncentre.org), this is one of Sydney's biggest community festivals. Around Oct 8–Nov 8, various local venues host events, and shop windows lend themselves to the work of some young, irreverent, in-your-face artists. The highlight is the Fair Day (second Sun in

Nov) when Camperdown Park is overtaken by a bazaar with food, community and market stalls and live music. For more festival details drop into the Centre or check the website.

Taste of a Nation In mid-October, Fitzroy Gardens, Kings Cross, is host to a one-day food fair (the culmination of the week-long Cross Culture Festival), with Kings Cross restaurateurs showing their stuff; profits go to Community Aid Abroad. More details on ⓦwww.cityofsydney.nsw.gov.au and ⓦwww.caa.org.au.

Women on Women Film Festival Held over three days in mid-October at the Chauvel Cinema, Paddington. More details on ⓦwww.wift.org/wow and see box p.219.

City of Sydney Food and Wine Fair In late October, Hyde Park is overtaken for a day by around 80 stalls representing restaurants, wineries, cheese-makers and the like. More details on ⓦwww.cityofsydney.nsw.gov.au.

November

Sculpture By the Sea The coastal walk between Bondi and Tamarama becomes crowded during this fortnight-long installation (in the first two weeks of November) of around a hundred wonderfully playful and provocative sculptures by Australian and international artists, many designed to be site-specific. More details on ☎02/9357 1457, ⓦwww.sculpture bythesea.com.

Glebe Street Fair Second to last Sunday in November. Thousands flock to one of Sydney's great eat-streets, Glebe Point Road, for a vibrant street festival – notably fabulous food for sale, representing the

local restaurants and cafés, plus lots of arts and crafts. More details on ⓦwww.cityof sydney.nsw.gov.au.

Sydney Food and Wine Fair Last Saturday in November, Hyde Park. Sponsored by the *Sydney Morning Herald* and Heineken, restaurants and wineries set up food stalls selling cut-price samples of their wares. More details on ⓦwww.cityofsydney.nsw.gov.au and ⓦwww.smh.com.au.

Goat Island Film Festival Ten-day outdoor film festival from the last week of November. More details on ⓦwww.cityof sydney.nsw.gov.au; see also box on p.219.

December

Homebake Australian music is celebrated in The Domain with a line-up of bands from around the country. More details on ⓦwww.homebake.com.au; also see box on p.210.

Sydney to Hobart Yacht Race It seems like almost half of Sydney turns out at around 1pm on December 26 to cheer the start of this classic regatta, and watch the colourful spectacle of a hundred or so

yachts setting sail on their 630-nautical-mile slog. The toughest bit is the crossing of Bass Strait, which is swept by the "Roaring Forties". (Conditions were so rough in 1999 that many crews abandoned the race, and six sailors tragically died.) Good vantage points include South Head, Lady Bay and Nielson Park on the eastern shores, or Georges Head, Middle Head, Chowder Bay, North Head and

Christmas Day on Bondi

For years, backpackers and Bondi Beach on **Christmas Day** were synonymous. The beach was transformed into a drunken party scene, as those from colder climates lived out their fantasy of spending Christmas on the beach under a scorching sun. The behaviour and litter had been getting out of control over several years, and after riots in 1995, and a rubbish-strewn beach to clean up, the local council began strictly controlling the whole performance – but with the idea of trying to keep a spirit of goodwill towards the travellers, while also tempting local families back to the beach on what is regarded as a family day. Nowadays alcohol is banned from the beach on Christmas Day, and police enforce the rule with on-the-spot confiscations – even locals can't enjoy a bottle of beachfront bubbly.

However, a big **beach party** is organized for backpackers: a large area of sand is fenced off, with a bar, DJs, food and entertainment running from 11am to 8pm. Around three thousand revellers cram into "the cage", while thousands of others – including a greater proportion of the desired family groups – enjoy the alcohol-free beach outside. In 2002, tickets for what is now called A **Sunburnt Christmas** were $30 in advance from record stores or $33.20 from Ticketek (☎02/9266 4800).

Bradleys Head on the North Shore. For more background information, check out the Cruising Yacht Club of Australia's website ⊛www.cyca.com.au.

Carols in the Domain Mid-December; a balmy night of Christmas carols under the stars. More details on ⊛www.cityof sydney.nsw.gov.au.

FESTIVALS AND EVENTS

Sports and activities

Sydneysiders are sports mad, especially for the ostensibly passive spectator sports of Rugby League, Aussie Rules football, cricket, tennis and horse racing. No matter what it is, from surf life saving competitions to yacht races, it'll draw a crowd. They're keen participants too, whether it's a game of squash or the latest infatuation with yoga, but getting into (or onto) the water is their greatest joy. The *Sydney Morning Herald*'s Friday **listings** supplement, "Metro", has a Sport and Leisure section, with details of the best events around town. Most seats can be booked through Ticketek (☎02/9266 4800, ⓦwww.ticketek.com.au).

If you want to watch live televised sport, see the "Sports bars" box on p.203. See the "Festivals and events" chapter for details of the annual City-to-Surf race, a 14-kilometre fun run.

SPORTS AND ACTIVITIES | Rugby League

Rugby League

Rugby League is *the* football code in Sydney, and was for many years a bastion of working-class culture. Formerly run by the Australian Rugby

> ### Sydney Olympics 2000
>
> Sydney proudly beat Beijing and Manchester in the chase for the **Olympics** in the year 2000, but no one would have guessed that Juan Antonio Samaranch, Olympic Chairman, would pronounce it the "best games ever". Unseasonably fine spring weather, a public transport system that held up to the job, cheerful volunteers who gave it their all and a public who at the last minute pulled out the stops to buy tickets (91 percent of seats were sold) and party hard in the Live Sites dotted around town, all added up to a hitch-free three-week sporting fiesta. Cries of "Aussie Aussie Aussie Oi Oi Oi" filled the air as Australia won its biggest pile of gold medals ever, 16 in all (plus 25 silver and 17 bronze), putting it fourth on the list (behind the US, Russia and China), an amazing achievement for its population size. Cathy Freeman's lighting of the Olympic flame, and then her gold medal run in the women's 400m, became symbolic of the hopes for reconciliation between Aboriginal and white Australia. It was all over too soon as far as Sydney was concerned, though the 11th summer **Paralympics**, a few weeks later, extended the excitement somewhat as tickets sales far outran expectations, and tested the city's disabled access.
>
> Now a new body, the **Sydney Olympic Park Authority**, which came into existence on January 1, 2001, has the task of turning Sydney Olympic Park into an entertainment and sporting complex with family-oriented recreation in mind (see "The southern and western outskirts" chapter, p.000, for information on visiting the former Olympic site).

League (ARL), the game was split down the middle in 1996, when Rupert Murdoch launched Super League in an attempt to gain ratings for his Foxtel TV station. It quickly became obvious, however, that the game could not support two separate competitions, and in 1997 they united to form the **National Rugby League** (NRL; ☎02/9339 8500, ⓦwww.nrl.com.au). There are now fifteen clubs in the NRL, the majority of them Sydney-based. The Sydney teams are the Canterbury Bulldogs, Manly Sea Eagles, Parramatta Eels, Penrith Panthers, The Roosters, Sharks, South Sydney Rabbitohs, St George Illawarra Dragons and West Tigers, all with associated "leagues clubs" where you can drink, eat, be entertained and above all gamble on the pokies (see Penrith Panthers, p.295). The other NRL clubs are Brisbane Broncos, Canberra Raiders, New Zealand Warriors, Newcastle Knights, Melbourne Storm and North Queensland Cowboys. Brisbane Broncos is the glamour club, while Sydney's best teams are the Penrith Panthers, eastern-suburbs-based Roosters, the Canterbury Bulldogs and the Parramatta Eels. The western-suburbs clubs Canterbury Bulldogs, Parramatta Eels and Penrith Panthers have the most loyal and most boisterous supporters – expect any of their matches to be well attended. The NRL dropped the South Sydney Rabbitohs in 1999 but with a big, still strongly working-class supporter base, huge street rallies were organized, attended by up to 150,000 people, and the NRL bowed to pressure and allowed the Rabbitohs back into the premiership in 2001.

The season starts in early March, and the **Grand Final** is played at the end of September, when huge crowds pack out the Sydney Football Stadium next to the SCG at Moore Park (tours of the SCG also take in this stadium – see p.256) or the Telstra Stadium (formerly Stadium Australia) at Sydney Olympic Park.

The **State of Origin** series, where Queensland and New South Wales battle it out over three matches (at least one of which is held in Sydney), is incredibly hard-fought, and coverage of these matches consistently produces the highest ratings on Australian television.

Australian Rules

Victoria has traditionally been the home of **Australian Rules** ("Aussie Rules") football, and Victorian sides are still expected to win the AFL Flag – decided at the Grand Final in Melbourne in September – as a matter of course. However, the enormously popular **Sydney Swans** (ⓦwww.sydneyswans.com.au), New South Wales' contribution to the AFL, have ensured Aussie Rules a place in the city, helped along by legendary goal-kicker Tony "Plugger" Lockett. During the 1999 season, Plugger finally broke the game's all-time goal-scoring record, which had stood for 62 years. Born in 1966, he finished playing for the Swans in 2002. The game itself is a no-holds-barred, eighteen-a-side brawl, closely related to Gaelic football. Despite the violence on the pitch, crowds tend to be very well behaved; you'll be surrounded by boisterous fans, but perfectly safe, if you go to watch the Swans at their home base at the Sydney Cricket Ground (see p.256). See the website of the Australian Football League, ⓦwww.afl.com.au, for more details.

Rugby union

Rugby union, in spite of the huge success of the national team (the Wallabies, who play at Telstra Stadium), still lags behind Rugby League in popularity. However, the introduction of the **Super 12** competition, which runs from the end of February to the end of May, and involves regional teams from Australia, New Zealand and South Africa, has generated broader interest in what has traditionally been an elitist game. The state's contribution to the Super 12 is the **NSW Waratahs**, who play at the Sydney Football Stadium about six times per season. For more details and the latest rugby info check out the Australian Rugby Union (ARU) website at ⓌＷＷＷ .rugby.com.au.

Soccer

Soccer is still a minority sport in Australia. Around half the **National Soccer League** (NSL) clubs evolved from communities of postwar immigrants – mainly Italians, Greeks and Yugoslavs. (In the mid-1990s, a ban on clubs with these nation's flags in their team logos won considerable support, but also came in for accusations of "ethnic cleansing".) The four Sydney teams who compete in the NSL competition (Oct–May) for the Ericsson Cup are: Sydney United, Marconi-Fairfield, Sydney Olympic and Northern Spirit, but the best players invariably head off to play overseas, such as Harry Kewell, the former Leeds United striker who made a £5 million transfer to Liverpool in July 2003. Details of matches and grounds are through **Soccer Australia** on ☎02/9267 0799 or at Ⓦwww.socceraustralia.com.au. Australia's national team, the **Socceroos**, play in the Oceania group, against teams such as Fiji and Western Samoa. Their home matches at the Sydney Football Stadium still generate only limited interest.

Cricket

Sydney's cricket season runs from October to March, and offers some of the year's best sporting days out (locals go for the atmosphere, the sunshine and the beer as much as the game). The **Sydney Cricket Ground** (SCG) is the venue for four-day, interstate Sheffield Shield matches (not much interest for spectators, but a breeding ground for Australia's Test cricketers); five-day international **Test matches**; and the colourful, crowd-pleasing **one-day internationals**. The venerated institution of the SCG earned its place in cricketing history for Don Bradman's score of 452 not out in 1929, and for the controversy over England's bodyline bowling techniques in 1932. Ideally, you would watch today's proceedings from the Members Stand while sipping an icy gin and tonic – but unless you're invited by a member, you'll end up elsewhere, drinking beer from a plastic cup. Cricket spectators aren't a sedate lot in Sydney, and the noisiest barrackers come from "the Hill" – or the Doug Walters stand, as it's officially known. Still the cheapest spot to sit, the now concreted area was once a grassy hill, where rowdy supporters threw beer cans at players and each other. The Bill O'Reilly Stand gives comfortable viewing (until the afternoon, when you'll be blinded by the sun), whereas the Brewongle Stand provides a consistently good vantage. Best of all is the Bradman Stand, with a view from directly behind the bowler's arm. For information, scores, prices and times, call the Sydney Cricket Trust on ☎02/9360 6601 or check out Ⓦwww.scgt.nsw .gov.au. You can buy **tickets** in advance, or at the gates on the day (subject to availability), or purchase them in advance from Ticketek (☎02/9266 4800, Ⓦwww.ticketek.com.au). Cricket fans can take a **tour** of the SCG on non-match days (Mon–Fri 10am & 1pm; 1hr 30min; $19.50; bookings ☎02/9380 0383, Ⓦwww.scgt.nsw.gov.au).

Tennis and squash

Sydney's major tennis event is the **Adidas International**, held during the second week of January as a lead-up to the Australian Open in Melbourne; it's played at the 10,500-seat centre court of the **Sydney International Tennis Centre** (☎02/8746 0777; Ⓦwww.sydneytennis.com.au), at Sydney Olympic Park in Homebush Bay (see p.145). Tickets are available from September. You can play tennis on one of the fifteen outdoor courts (off-peak Mon–Fri 8am–6pm; $15 per hour; peak Mon–Fri 6pm–10pm, Sat & Sun 8am–6pm; $18 per hour; bookings ☎02/8746 0444). Another place to play nearby is **Rushcutters Bay Tennis Centre**, Rushcutters Bay Park, New South Head Road; the clay courts are in a picturesque park by the marina (daily 8am–9/10pm; $20 per hour, $24 after 4pm and on Sat & Sun; racquet hire $3; ☎02/9357 1675; Kings Cross CityRail).

A central place to play **squash** is Hiscoe's Fitness Centre, 525 Crown St, Surry Hills (Mon–Fri 6am–10pm, Sat 8am–8pm, Sun 9am–noon & 4–8pm; $22–24 per 45min; racquet $5; gym casual visit $15; squash bookings essential on ☎02/9699 3233).

Racetracks

Australians lose approximately $1000 a head each year succumbing to the temptation of a flutter. This eagerness to bet, coupled with relaxed **gambling** laws, has tax-collectors rubbing their hands as the revenue rolls in. Sydney offers plenty of opportunities for any punter heading for the fast lane to millionaires row – or the slippery slope to the poorhouse. Every Friday the *Sydney Morning Herald* publishes its racing guide, "The Form". Bets are placed at TAB (Totalisator Agency Board) shops; these are scattered throughout the city, and most pubs also have TAB access as does Star City Casino (see p.216).

There are **horse-racing** meetings on Wednesday, Saturday and most public holidays. This is due mainly to the accessibility of courses, the high quality of racing, the presence of bookmakers and cheap admission prices ($10, $15–20 for carnivals). The venues are well maintained and peopled with colourful racing characters and often massive crowds. Best times to hit the track are during the spring and autumn carnivals (respectively Aug–Sept and March–April), when prize money rockets, and the quality of racing rivals the best in the world. The principal racecourses are: **Royal Randwick** (Alison Rd, Randwick ☎02/9663 8400, Ⓦwww.ajc.org.au), which featured in *Mission Impossible II*; **Rosehill Gardens** (James Ruse Drive, Rosehill ☎02/9930 4070; Rosehill Gardens CityRail), which also has loads of free kids' entertainment including a bouncy castle and pony rides (entry for children is also free); and **Canterbury Park** (King St, Canterbury ☎02/9930 4000; Canterbury CityRail), which has midweek racing, plus floodlit night racing from September to March. For further information, contact the Sydney Turf Club (☎02/9930 4019, Ⓦwww.stc.com.au). There are also plenty of picturesque country venues to choose from; contact the Australian Jockey Club for more details on ☎02/9663 8400 or at Ⓦwww.ajc.org.au.

If the chariot scenes of *Ben Hur* are more to your taste, a trip to the trots might be the ticket. **Harness racing** occurs at **Harold Park Paceway**, Ross St, Glebe (℡02/9660 3688; $8), on Tuesday afternoons (1–6pm) and Friday evenings (7–11pm), though Tuesdays are best avoided unless you need to escape human contact for a few hours. There is more of a buzz on Friday nights, the excitement reaching its peak on the last Friday of November when the Miracle Mile is run. For some, watching horses lope around the fibres and course is too sedate, but, just around the corner, money is thrown away at greater speed as the **greyhounds** hurtle around **Wentworth Park** (℡02/9660 4308; $5.50) each Monday and Saturday night – gates open at 5.30pm and races run between 7.30pm and 10.30pm.

Surfing and surf carnivals

One peculiarly Australian institution is the **surf carnival**, where teams of volunteer life-savers demonstrate their skills in mostly inflatable life-saving boats, usually on summer weekends, which makes for a great day out on the beach. Community surf life-saving organizations began forming across Australia in 1905; the Surf Life Saving Association was established in 1907. Since 1980 women were allowed to join and now make up about forty percent of members (also see box on p.129). Contact Surf Life Saving NSW for details of the current season's carnivals (℡02/9984 7188, Ⓦwww.surflifesaving.com.au) or head for Surf Live Saving Australia's office at the Bondi Icebergs Club (see p.129), where they provide information on the organization and exhibit memorabilia. **Surfing** competitions are good opportunities to catch some hot wave-riding action. The NSW Surf Riders Association (℡02/9518 9410) can tell you where to find them.

Surf schools can teach you the basic skills, and enlighten you on surfing etiquette and lingo. The best two in Sydney, offering both individual and group lessons are Lets Go Surfing (℡02/9365 1800; Ⓦwww.letsgosurfing .com.au) which also has its own surf store renting and selling boards at 28 Ramsgate Ave, North Bondi (daily 9am–6pm); and Manly Surf School (℡02/9977 6977, Ⓦwww.manlysurfschool.com) which covers the northern beaches. Both charge $50–55 for a two-hour group lesson, including boards and wet suit, and private lessons for singles, pairs or families are available (1hr; $79 one person, $45 each extra person). You can **rent boards** from surfshops for $25 half-day to $40 full-day (wet suit often included but may cost extra): try Lets Go Surfing at Bondi 128 Ramsgate Ave North (℡02/9365 1800), or Aloha Surf, 44 Pittwater Rd, Manly (℡02/9977 3777, Ⓦwww.alohasurfboards .com.au). You can check daily **surf reports** on Ⓦwww.realsurf.com. Also see the box "Beach and sun safety" on p.127.

Canoeing, kayaking, sailboarding and sailing

The best time to sail in Sydney is from April to September, and some sail schools only offer lessons and rental during the sailing season. For other sailing courses and yacht rental check out the NSW Yachting Association's website Ⓦwww.nsw.yachting.org.au, or phone them on ℡02/9660 1266. If you want to try rafting, you can take a thrilling white-water rafting circuit at the Penrith Whitewater Stadium, a former Olympic venue at the foothills of the Blue Mountains (see p.296).

Balmoral Windsurfing, Kitesurfing, Sailing and Kayak School Balmoral Boatshed, southern end of the Esplanade, Balmoral Beach ☎02/9960 5344, ⊛www.sailboard.net.au. Bus #257 from Wynyard CityRail. Rents sailboards, kiteboards and Hobiecat dinghies as well as giving lessons. A full-day (5hr) kitesurfing course costs $165. Windsurfing courses start from $175 for beginners (5hr over 2 days) to $195 for improving technique (6hr over 2 days); there's also a Hobiecat sailing course (beginners' course 5hr over 2 days; $195). For classes for children, see p.232. Sailboard hire $27 per hour for beginners, $38 per hour for intermediate and advanced; Hobiecat hire $35 per hour. Open all year.

Natural Wanders Sea Kayak Adventures ☎02/9899 1001, ⊛www.naturalwanders .com.au. Guided sea-kayaking in the harbour: the most popular trip is the Bridge Paddle (4hr; $75; suitable for beginners), which starts from Lavender Bay near Luna Park, goes under the Harbour Bridge and explores the bush-clad, yacht-filled North Shore, with a picnic brunch included on a beach near Taronga Zoo.

Northside Sailing School Middle Harbour Skiff Club Spit Bridge, Mosman ☎02/9969 3972, ⊛www.northsidesailing.com.au. Bus #169, #175, #178, #L80 & #180 from Wynyard CityRail. Specializes in weekend dinghy sailing courses on Middle Harbour (Sept–April); tuition is one-on-one and costs $120 per 3hr lesson (4 lessons are equal to an Australian Yachting Federation

beginners' course). Also lessons for kids (see p.232).

Rose Bay Aquatic Hire 1 Vickery Ave, Rose Bay ☎02/9371 7036. Rose Bay Wharf; bus #323, #324 & #325 from Edgecliff CityRail. Rents out catamarans ($25 first hour, $15 thereafter), kayaks ($15 per hour) and motorboats (weekends $50 for the first 2 hours, $15 for each subsequent hour, plus charge for petrol). There are cheaper deals midweek and midwinter. No boat licence required, only a drivers' licence.

Sydney by Sail Based at the National Maritime Museum, Darling Harbour ☎02/9280 1110, ⊛www.sydneybysail.com. Town Hall CityRail. Learn To Sail programmes for yacht sailing throughout the year for all levels, from a Level 1 Introductory Course (12hr course over 2 days; $450) to a Level 4 Inshore Skipper Course (2-day 2-night live-aboard course; $660 includes all meals). Experienced sailors can also charter the yachts from $345 half-day to $995 for a weekend.

Teamsail Royal Prince Alfred Yacht Club, Mitala St, Newport ☎02/9999 3047, ⊛www.teamsail.com.au. Bus #L90 from Central CityRail and Wynyard CityRail. All-year yachting courses on Pittwater, from beginners to yacht master. The two-day course costs $405 (max 4 participants). A big feature is the follow-up social sailing, where you get a chance to develop your skills and meet others with the same interest, for a very reasonable $35: there are twilight sails (summer Mon & Thurs; 2hr) and Sunday sails (last Sun of month; 4hr).

Diving and snorkelling

Visibility in the waters around Sydney is good – and divers can expect to see to a distance of 10–15m. One of the best places to dive is at **Gordon's Bay** in Clovelly, where there is easy access to Sydney's only underwater nature trail – a sort of beneath-the-sea bushwalking track, marked by a series of chains connected to concrete drums. The trail includes typical Sydney shoreline life: sponges, sea jellies, anemones, shrimps and crabs, molluscs, cuttlefish, octopus, sea stars and sea squirts. The 700-metre trail takes around 35–40 minutes to cover, and has a maximum depth of 14m. It is one of Sydney's most dived locations; diving off North and South heads is also popular.

Aquatic Explorers 40 Kingsway, Cronulla ☎02/9523 7222, ⊛www.aquaticexplorers.com.au Cronulla CityRail. Local shore dives including Shiprock and the Botany Bay National Park

on the Kurnell Peninsula at weekends; dives are free but gear rental costs $50 per day. They also organize dives and weekends away up and down the coast of New South Wales.

Dive Centre Bondi 192 Bondi Rd ☏02/9369 3855, ⓦwww.divesydney.com. Bus #380 & #382 from Bondi Junction CityRail. Shore dives at Camp Cove (Watsons Bay) and Ben Buckler at North Bondi (double dive $95) and boat dives to South Head and Maroubra where there's a chance to see sharks.

Dive Centre Manly 10 Belgrave St, Manly ☏02/9977 4355, ⓦwww.divesydney.com. Ferry to Manly Wharf. Shore dives at Shelley Beach, Fairlight, Little Manly and Harbord, plus boat dives off North and South Head (single boat dive with full gear $85/double $130, shore dive with gear $75/double $130).

Deep 6 Diving 351–355 Clovelly Rd, cnr Beach St, Clovelly ☏02/9665 7427, ⓦwww.deep6diving.com.au. Bus #339 from Central CityRail. Closest dive shop to Gordons Bay, so naturally they run lots of trips there. Single boat dive $40, double $80; equipment $85 per 24hr. Snorkelling sets $10 per day.

Prodive Coogee 27 Alfreda St, Coogee ☏02/9665 6333, ⓦwww.prodive.com.au. Bus #373 & #374 from Circular Quay CityRail. Offer local boat and shore dives anywhere between Camp Cove (Watsons Bay) and La Perouse (double boat dive $135, shore $105; gear included), plus dives all over Sydney.

Swimming pools

Most public, council-run pool complexes are outdoors and have a fifty-metre pool, a smaller children's pool and a wading pool, all usually unheated. The **swimming season** is generally the warmer months, from the long weekend in October, until Easter. Many pools are closed to the public for several days in February when school swimming carnivals traditionally take place. There are over seventy public pools, plus 74 enclosed sea pools at beaches and on the harbour; several of the latter are detailed in the text, including the Women's Pool (p.133) and Wylie's Baths (p.133), both in Coogee; the pool at the Bondi Icebergs (p.129); and the Mahon Pool at Maroubra (p.133). The following are a selection of favourites in popular areas; check "Swiming pools" in the *Yellow Pages* for a full list.

Andrew "Boy" Charlton The Domain ☏02/9358 6686. Martin Place CityRail. Revamped in 2002, the much-glamorized pool, now has its own café-restaurant and yoga classes (Mon 6.45pm & Tues 6.30pm; $15), plus a regular Thurs night biathlon (running and swimming) open to all competitors. Sept–April daily 6.30am–8pm; $4.50.

Annette Kellerman Aquatic Centre Enmore Pool, Enmore Park off Enmore Rd, Enmore ☏02/9565 1906. Bus #423, #426 & #428 from Central CityRail. Not far from Newtown, and known to the locals simply as Enmore Pool, the heated 33m pool stays open all year. Mon–Sat 5.30am–8.30pm, Sun 8am–6pm; $3.50.

Cook and Phillip Park Aquatic and Leisure Centre Cnr William and College streets ☏02/9326 0444. Museum CityRail. State-of-the-art undercover complex with a 50m heated indoor pool for laps, a 25m leisure pool with a wave-making machine at weekends and during school holidays, a bubbling "river run" feature and toddlers area with its own beach, a hydrotherapy pool with disabled access and a gym. There's access to an outdoor courtyard and café, plus two external restaurants, one of which is vegetarian. Don't expect to linger long, though, with very annoying 2hr non-refundable lockers costing $3. Mon–Fri 6am–10pm, Sat & Sun 7am–8pm. Swim $5, swim and gym $13.

Cronulla Sports Complex The Esplanade, Cronulla ☏02/9523 5842. Cronulla CityRail. Beachfront complex with heated indoor pools and a gym. Mon–Fri 7am–3.45pm, Sat 7am–4.45pm, Sun 8am–4.45pm. Swim $3.50, gym and swim $8.60, gym, sauna & spa $11.

Leichhardt Park Aquatic Centre Mary St Leichhardt ☏02/9555 8344, ⓦwww.lmc.nsw.gov.au. Bus #440 from Central CityRail. A great spot for a swimming centre, on an extensive park on Iron Cove, an inlet of the Parramatta River. The pool grounds themselves are green and spacious. The heated outdoor 50m pool is a great place to swim in winter and there's also a diving pool or you can stay inside in the smaller 25m heated pool (with an indoor toddlers' pool and spa beside it). Just outside there's a popular, landscaped, gate-surrounded toddlers' pool. The gym has aerobics, aqua aerobics and yoga classes in its programme. There's a handy weekday child-minding service too (Mon–Fri 9am–1.30pm; $3.30 per hour, max 2hr; bookings essential), but the café is mediocre and the Norton Street ones are quite a long haul away. Daily 5.30am–8pm. Swim $5.20, gym & swim $14.

North Sydney Olympic Pool Alfred St South, Milsons Point. Milsons Point CityRail ℡02/9955 2309. The heated 50m outdoor pool here is open all year (covered in winter); situated by the water, in the shadow of the harbour bridge, it's one of Sydney's best. Revamped in 2001, it has a new indoor 25m pool, a gym, sauna, spa, café, and a slick restaurant *Aqua*, overlooking the swimmers. Mon–Fri 5.30am–9pm, Sat & Sun 7am–7pm; $4.20.

Sydney International Aquatic Centre Olympic Boulevard, Sydney Olympic Park, Homebush Bay ℡02/9752 3666, ⓦwww.sydneyaquaticcentre .com.au. Olympic Park CityRail. As well as being a great place to swim laps in the competition pools, there are landscaped leisure pools with amusements such as the rapid river-ride, as well as water slides. Also spas, steam rooms and saunas, a gym and fitness classes. Nov–March Mon–Fri 5am–8.45pm, Sat & Sun 6am–7.45pm; April–Oct Mon–Fri 5am–8.45pm, Sat & Sun 6am–6.45pm. Swim and spa $5.80, child $4.60 ($11.50 includes steam rooms and sauna; also including gym and fitness classes $14).

Victoria Park Pool Cnr City Rd and Broadway ℡02/9660 4181. Bus #431, #433, #434, #438 & #440 from Central CityRail. Heated outdoor pool next to Sydney University and close to Glebe Point Road, in a landscaped park. Great café. Mon–Fri 6am–7.15pm, Sat & Sun 7am–5.45pm; $3.50, swim & gym $7.

Cycling

The narrow maze of streets in Sydney's CBD, combined with traffic congestion, means that **cycling** has never been too popular. Bicycles can be carried free on trains (outside peak hours of Mon–Fri 6–9am & 3.30–7.30pm), and on ferries at all times if there is room in the bicycle racks. It is a legal requirement that you wear a helmet – police issue fines for non-compliance. The Roads and Traffic Authority (℡02/9218 6888, ⓦwww.rta.nsw.gov.au) produces a handy fold-out map, *Sydney Cycleways*, showing both off-road paths and suggested bicycle routes, which they will post out. The best source of information, however, is Bicycle NSW, Level 2, 209 Castlereagh St, cnr Bathurst St (Mon–Fri 9am–5.30pm; ℡02/9283 5200, ⓦwww.bicyclensw .org.au). Two useful publications available here are *Bike It Sydney* ($13), which has inner-city bike routes and is good for people new to Sydney, and *Discovering NSW and Canberra Bike and Walking Paths* ($18.50).

For leisure cycling, head for **Centennial Park** (p.94) or the **cycleway at Manly** (p.137). Critical Mass is an activist group "reclaiming the streets for cycling" which began in San Francisco and now has groups all over the world including Sydney. The Sydney movement organize a cycling event on the last Friday of the month; meet at the Archibald Fountain in Hyde Park between 4.30pm and 5.30pm for an hour-long ride through the city (or you can skate, jog, rollerblade and even runners turn up too).

Recommended central **bicycle shops** for sales and repairs include Clarence Street Cyclery, 104 Clarence St (℡02/9299 4962, ⓦwww.cyclery.com.au); Woolys Wheels, 82 Oxford St, Paddington (℡02/9331 2671, ⓦwww.woolyswheels.com.au); and Inner City Cycles, 31 Glebe Point Rd,

Glebe (☎02/9660 6605, ⓦwww.innercitycycles.com.au). The cheapest **bike rental** is at Cheeky Monkey Cycle Co, 456 Pitt St, Haymarket (open daily; ☎02/9212 4460, ⓦwww.cheekymonkey.com.au); mountain bikes cost $25 per day, and they also rent and sell cycle-touring equipment and sell bikes. Clarence Street Cyclery also rent mountain bikes ($65 per day, $100 per weekend; open daily), as do Inner City Cycles ($33 per 24hr, $55 per weekend; open daily). For a leisurely ride in the park, Centennial Park Cycles, 50 Clovelly Rd, Randwick, rent bikes (mountain bikes $9 per hour, $20 per 4hr; bikes for kids $7 per hour, $16 per 4hr; open daily; ☎02/9398 5027, ⓦwww.cyclehire .com.au), and to get onto Manly's bike path, you can rent bikes from Manly Cycles, a block back from the beach at 36 Pittwater Rd (mountain bikes $12 per hour, $25 per day; ☎02/9977 1189, ⓦwww.manlycycles.com.au).

Rollerblading, skateboarding and ice-skating

Rollerblading is banned in the CBD. The two most popular areas for bladers are along the bike track at Manly, and in Centennial Park. Teenagers also use the skateboarding ramp at Bondi Beach. **Rental places** charge $12 for the first hour for either inline skates or skateboards, inclusive of protective gear, then a decreasing rate per hour up to a maximum daily charge of $20–30: try Total Skate, corner of Oxford and Queen streets, Woollahra (☎02/9380 6356), handy for Centennial Park; Bondi Boards and Blades, 230 Oxford St, Bondi Junction (☎02/9369 2212, ⓦwww.bondiboardsandblades.com.au) handy for Bondi Beach; and Manly Blades & Skates, 49 North Steyne (☎02/9976 3833), close to Manly's bike track. The latter also have nifty electric scooters (1hr $20) and power-assisted bikes (2hr $44) for the truly lazy.

During the colder months, from the end of April to the middle of October, an outdoor ice-skating rink operates on the Showring at Fox Studios, Moore Park near Paddington (Mon–Thurs & Sun 10am–9pm, Fri & Sat 10am–10pm; adult $14, child $12 includes skate rental; lessons available Wed & Sat, enquiries on ☎02/9383 4175; bus #339 from Central CityRail).

Horse riding

The vast expanse of **Centennial Park** (see p.94) has extensive horse-riding tracks and people stable their horses at the Centennial Parklands Equestrian Centre at the southeast corner of the Fox Studios site, on the junction of Cook and Lang roads just through the Showground gate to Centennial Park. Several stables offer **horse riding**; you can just wander into the centre and enquire, or book in advance with one such as Centennial Stables, in Pavilion B (1hr escorted rides $55; 1hr lesson $80; ☎02/9360 5650, ⓦwww.centennial stables.com.au). There's more scenic horse riding in the Blue Mountains' Megalong Valley and in Wollombi en route to the Hunter Valley; for operators see p.295.

Abseiling, canyoning, climbing and bungee jumping

For **thrill sports**, from rap jumping to skydiving and aerobatic flights, contact the Adrenalin Club (☎02/9959 3934, ⓦwww.adrenalin.com.au). A popular spot for **hang-gliding** is Stanwell Park just south of the Royal National Park; the Sydney Hang Gliding Centre (℡02/4294 4294, Ⓦwww.hanggliding .com.au), offers tandem flights with an instructor ($180 during the week, $195 weekends; courses from $195 per day). The **Bungy Trampoline** at the Showring at Fox Studios (see p.95; Wed–Sun 10am–6pm; $10), is an ordinary trampoline but with several bungy cords, designed to give you the thrill of a bungy jump but without the danger.

See "The Blue Mountains" chapter, p.290, for information on operators offering abseiling and canyoning trips. There's also a great **indoor climbing centre** in the mountains at Blackheath (see p.294) and a brand-new one near Newtown: Sydney Indoor Climbing Gym, 4C Unwins Bridge Rd, St Peters (Mon & Fri 10am–9pm, Tues–Thurs 10am–9.30pm, Sat & Sun 10am–6pm; casual entry $10.50, harness, shoes and chalk bag rental $9; ℡02/9716 6949; Ⓦwww.indoorclimbing.com.au; St Peters CityRail).

Gyms

Most **gyms** charge between $13 and $15 for a casual visit, which applies all day, and includes access to aerobics and even yoga classes. In their quest for new members, many gyms have a no-obligation one-week free introductory offer, which is a cheeky way for travellers to do the rounds and get fit for free. Several gyms are reviewed in the "Gay Sydney" chapter, with the (nearly) 24-hour City Gym (see p.227) recommended. Many of the city's swimming pools also have gyms, and with a swim usually thrown in, the rates are much more reasonable (see p.260). Also see Hiscoe's Fitness Centre (p.257), where a casual gym visit costs $15.

Yoga

Yoga is very popular in Sydney, and and we've included three specific **yoga schools** allowing casual visits and offering different styles of yoga. Most gyms also organize yoga classes - see above and p.260, also p.295.

Bondi Beach Iyengar Yoga Institute Suite 10, 78 Campbell Parade, Bondi Beach ℡02/9130 1295, Ⓦwww.bondibeachyoga.com. Bus #380 & #382 from Central CityRail. All classes are Hatha yoga taught in the Iyengar method; 1hr 30min beginners and general classes $17.

Bikram's Yoga College of India Level 1, 256 Crown St, Darlinghurst ℡02/9356 4999, Ⓦwww.bikramyogaaustralia.com.au. Museum CityRail. The latest yoga craze, Bikram yoga consists of 26 set postures done in sequence in a very hot room (37°C), allowing your body to sweat out toxins. It's very exhausting but many people feel exhilarated afterwards. There's an introductory offer of $17 for the first ten days – they recommend coming three to five times – which is a bargain for a Sydney visitor wanting to try something different.

Yoga Synergy 115 Bronte Rd, Bondi Junction (Bondi Junction CityRail) and 196 Australia St, Newtown (Newtown CityRail) – bookings for both ℡02/9389 7399, Ⓦwww.yogasynergy .com.au. The directors here are also physiotherapists: the yoga taught is a synthesis between Hatha yoga and modern medical science. More strenuous Ashtanga yoga is also practised. Classes 1hr 30min, beginners to advanced; $16.

The Ginseng Bathhouse

After you've got all sweaty, try a traditional ginseng bath and skin-scrub treatment at the wonderful Korean-style **Ginseng Bathhouse**, *Crest Hotel*, 1st floor, 111 Darlinghurst Rd, Kings Cross (☎02/9358 2755; Kings Cross CityRail). There are separate bathhouses for men and women – everyone must take off all their clothes – but robes are provided for the unisex refreshment room where you can make yourself a herbal tea and read a magazine. The men's bathhouse can get a little cruisey. All-day bath access costs $25; extras include exfoliation scrub for $27 and Korean or shiatsu massage at $44 for 30min. Mon–Fri 10am–9.30pm, Sat & Sun 9am–9.30pm.

Dance classes

The prestigious Sydney Dance Company, Wharf 4–5, Hickson Rd, Millers Point (☎02/9221 4811, ⊛www.sydneydance.com.au; Circular Quay CityRail), holds day and evening open **dance** classes at their waterfront studios on an atmospheric converted wharf – ranging from funk and jazz, through contemporary to ballet. You can just turn up for a $15 casual class.

Directory

Airlines (domestic) Qantas ☏ 13 13 13, ⓦ www.qantas.com.au; Regional Express (REX) ☏ 13 17 13, ⓦ www.regionalexpress.com.au; Sydney Harbour Seaplanes ☏ 02/9388 1978, ⓦ www.sydneyseaplane.com.au; Virgin Blue ☏ 13 67 89, ⓦ www.virginblue.com.au.

Airlines (international) Aeroflot, 44 Market St ☏ 02/9262 2233; Aerolineas Argentinas, Level 4, 189 Kent St ☏ 02/9252 5150; Air Canada, Level 12, 92 Pitt St ☏ 02/9232 5222; Air New Zealand, Level 4, 10 Barrack St ☏ 13 24 76; Alitalia, 64 York St ☏ 02/9244 2400; British Airways, Level 19, 259 George St ☏ 02/9258 3200; Cathay Pacific ☏ 13 17 47; Continental, 64 York St ☏ 02/9244 2242; Delta, Level 9, 189 Kent St ☏ 02/9251 3211; Finnair, 64 York St ☏ 02/9244 2299; Garuda, 55 Hunter St ☏ 02/9334 9900; Gulf Air, 64 York St ☏ 02/9244 2199; Japan Airlines, Level 14, 201 Sussex St ☏ 02/9272 1111; KLM, 115 Pitt St ☏ 02/9231 6333; Korean Air ☏ 02/9262 6000; Lauda Air, Level 2, 1 York St ☏ 02/9251 6155; Malaysia Airlines, 16 Spring St ☏ 13 26 27; Olympic, 3rd floor, 37–49 Pitt St ☏ 02/9251 1048; Qantas, 70 Hunter St, cnr Phillip St, and 468 Oxford St, Bondi Junction ☏ 13 13 13; Scandinavian Airlines, Level 15, 31 Market St ☏ 1300 727 707; Singapore Airlines, 17–19 Bridge St ☏ 02/9350 0100; Swissair, Level 3, 117 York St ☏ 1300 724 666; Thai International, 75 Pitt St ☏ 02/9251 1922; United, Level 5, 10 Barrack St ☏ 13 17 77. For airline websites see "Getting there" p.9.

Bike rental See p.261 of "Sports and activities".

Campervans and 4WD rental All Seasons Campervans, 77 Planthurst Rd, South Hurstville (☏ 02/9547 0100, ⓦ www.allseasonscampervans.com.au) has a wide range of campervans, motor-homes, four-door sedans plus camping equipment; prices include free delivery to airport or accommodation, linen and sleeping bags. Australian Outback 4 Wheel Drive Hire Co., 184 Elizabeth St, City ☏ 02/9281 9676; Britz Australia, 263 Coward St, Mascot ☏ 02/9667 0402, ⓦ www.britz.com (campervans, 4WDs and camping gear); Travel Car Centre, 54 Orchard Rd, Brookvale ☏ 02/9905 6928, ⓦ www.travelcar.com.au (hatchbacks, station-wagons, campervans and 4WDs available for long- or short-term rental); Travellers Auto Barn ☏ 02/9360 1500; ⓦ www.travellers-autobarn.com.au (budget campervan rental).

Camping equipment and rental Kent Street in the city behind the Town Hall is nick-named "adventure alley" for its plethora of outdoor equipment stores; the best known is the high-quality Paddy Pallin at no. 507 (☏ 02/9264 2685, ⓦ www.paddypallin.com.au). Cheaper options include disposal stores at the downtown ends of George and Pitt streets near Central Station – try Boss Disposals, 708 George St (☏ 02/9211 1991) – and suburban K-Mart stores (closest stores to the city are at Spring St, Bondi Junction and at the Broadway shopping centre, Bay St) or hostel notice boards. Only a few places rent gear, mostly based in the suburbs: try Alpsport, 1045 Victoria Rd, West Ryde (☏ 02/9858 5844), with weekend rent of a backpack for around $32, sleeping bag from $29, and tent from $30.

Car rental and sales Most car-rental firms have a branch in William Street, Kings Cross; the big four, with new-model cars, are also at the airport. Average daily charge is $50–70 for a small manual. Avis, airport ☏ 02/9353 9000, 220 William St ☏ 02/9357 2000, ⓦ www.avis.com; Budget, 93 William St ☏ 13 27 27, ⓦ www.budget.com.au; Hertz, cnr William and Riley streets ☏ 13 30

39, ⓦwww.hertz.com; Thrifty, 75 William St
ⓣ1300 367 227, ⓦwww.thrifty.com.au.
Also at the airport, Network (ⓣ02/9317
3223, ⓦwww.networkrentals.com.au) offers
good-value longer-term deals. There are
cheaper deals with: Bayswater, 180 William
St, Kings Cross (ⓣ02/9360 3622,
ⓦwww.bayswatercarrental.com.au), which
has low rates but limited km; Kings Cross
Rent-A-Car, 169 William St (ⓣ02/9361
0637, ⓦwww.kxr.com.au), which is open
daily and also has low prices; Daytona
Rentals, 164 Parramatta Rd, Ashfield
(ⓣ02/9716 8777), which has slightly older
cars at very good rates for weekly rentals all
inclusive of insurance; and Apollo Car
Rental, 33 Pittwater Rd, Manly (ⓣ02/9977
5777, ⓦwww.apollo-car-rental.com), which
has new model cars and also incorporates
Rent-a-Ruffy, for cheap, older-model cars –
both have limited km. Travellers Auto Barn,
177 William St, Kings Cross (ⓣ02/9360
1500, ⓦwww.travellers-autobarn.com.au),
does cheap long-term rentals and sells station wagons and combivans with buy-back
deals; travellers can also easily buy a car at
the Backpackers Car Market, Kings Cross
Car Park, Level 2, Ward Ave, Kings Cross
(daily 9am–6pm; ⓣ02/9358 5000,
ⓦwww.carmarket.com.au).

Consulates Canada, Level 5, 111
Harrington St ⓣ02/9364 3000; New
Zealand, 55 Hunter St ⓣ02/8256 2000;
UK, Level 16, Gateway Building, 1
Macquarie Place ⓣ02/9247 7521; US,
Level 59, MLC Centre, 19–29 Martin Place
ⓣ02/9373 9200. For visas for onward
travel, consult "Consulates and Legations"
in the *Yellow Pages*.

Coach terminal Sydney Coach Terminal,
cnr Eddy Ave and Pitt St, next to Central
Station (daily 6am–10pm; ⓣ02/9281 9366).
You can make coach ticket bookings here
or at Backpackers Travel Centres (see
"Travel agents", opposite).

Electricity Australia's electrical current is
240/250v, 50Hz AC. British appliances will
work with an adaptor; American and
Canadian 110v appliances need a trans-
former.

Emergency ⓣ000 for fire, police or ambulance.

GST (Goods and Services Tax) A GST of ten
percent was introduced in 2000, and
caused a general across-the-board price
hike, though fresh foods are not included.

Visitors can claim GST refunds for goods
purchased in Australia as they clear customs, providing that individual receipts
exceed $300 and the claim is made within
thirty days of purchase. Many stores in The
Rocks and the airport have a "sealed bag"
system which lets you buy goods without
paying GST, and the minimum of $300 is
waived.

Hospitals Sydney Hospital, Macquarie St
ⓣ02/9382 7111; St Vincents Hospital, cnr
Victoria and Burton streets, Darlinghurst
ⓣ02/8382 1111.

Libraries City of Sydney Public Library,
just behind the Town Hall on Sydney
Square ⓣ02/9265 9470; Mon–Fri
8am–7pm, Sat 9am–noon. Also see the
State Library, p.65.

Medical centres and clinics See "Medical
Centres" in the *Yellow Pages* for the closest
clinic to where you're staying. Broadway
Medical Centre, 185–211 Broadway, near
Glebe ⓣ02/9212 2733: general practi-
tioners open Mon–Fri 9am–7pm, Sat & Sun
11am–5pm, no appointment necessary.
Skin Cancer Centre, ground floor, 403
George St ⓣ02/9262 4877; Sydney Sexual
Health Centre, Nightingale Wing, Sydney
Hospital, Macquarie St ⓣ02/9382 7440
(free tests, counselling and condoms);
Travellers Medical and Vaccination Centre,
7th floor, 428 George St ⓣ02/9221 7133,
ⓦwww.tmvc.com.au.

Motoring organizations The New South
Wales' motoring organization, the NRMA is
at 74–76 King St, City (ⓣ13 21 32,
ⓦwww.nrma.com.au), and is handy if you
belong to a motoring organization back
home, as the maps are free to associated
members. They provide road maps of New
South Wales and a useful map of Sydney;
lots more information is also available and
there's also an accommodation booking
service.

Immigration Department of Immigration, 26
Lee St, near Central Station, Haymarket
ⓣ13 18 81.

Laundries Virtually all accommodation will
have a coin-operated laundry and dryer and
possibly even a clothesline outside. If not,
there's always a few laundromats in busy
tourist and residential areas; a load of
washing costs about $3.50 at any of these.

Left luggage Cloakrooms at Town Hall
Station and Central Station (country trains)
are both open daily 6.30am–9.30pm

($8/$6/$4 per 24hr depending on size); also lockers at the airport and the Sydney Coach Terminal ($6/$9 per 24hr).

Motorbike rental and sales Wentworth Avenue in the city has a concentration of motorbike salerooms for new models; also see Vesbar (p.176). Bikescape, 191 William St, Kings Cross (☎1300 736 869, ⓦwww.bikescape.com.au), rents scooters from $65 per day and motorbikes from $95. Maverick Motorcycles, 133 Parramatta Rd, Homebush (☎02/9746 2005, ⓦwww.maverickmotorcycles.com.au), specializes in selling and exchanging travellers' motorbikes.

Pharmacy (late-night) Crest Hotel Pharmacy, 60A Darlinghurst Rd, Kings Cross (Tues–Sat 8.30am–2am, daily 8.30am–midnight; ☎02/9358 1822).

Police Headquarters at 14 College St, Darlinghurst (☎02/9339 0277; emergency ☎000). Also see box p.41.

Post office The General Post Office (GPO) is in Martin Place (Mon–Fri 8.15am–5.30pm, Sat 9am–1pm). Poste restante is located at the post office in the Hunter Connection shopping mall at 310 George St (Mon–Fri 8.15am–6pm), opposite Wynyard Station. The address to write to is: Poste Restante, Sydney GPO, Sydney NSW, 2000.

Public toilets Free public toilets are found at beaches, in parks, shopping arcades, train stations and department stores.

Time Sydney follows Australian Eastern Standard Time (AEST), half an hour ahead of South Australia and the Northern Territory, two hours ahead of Western Australia, ten hours ahead of Greenwich Mean Time (GMT) and fifteen ahead of US Eastern Standard Time. Clocks are put forward one hour in November and back again in March for daylight saving.

Tours Return tours from Sydney to the areas outside the city are covered in chapters 22–25. In addition, the coach tour company AAT Kings (☎02/9518 6095, ⓦwww.aatkings.com/aus), one of the largest operators, offer big-group, sedentary bus tours covering city sights, wildlife parks, the Blue Mountains, Jenolan Caves, the Hawkesbury River and the Hunter Valley; admissions and hotel pick-ups and drop-offs are included in their prices. CityRail (☎13 15 00, ⓦwww.131500.com.au) offer package day-trips by rail, which can be very good-value, generally covering all transport and entry fees – trips include the Blue Mountains, and the Hawkesbury River (which includes a cruise); details and tickets from CityRail at Circular Quay or Central Station. Also see "Tourist passes" in the box on pp.28–29 for information on the Sydney Explorer and Bondi Explorer hop-on-hop-off bus tours, and p.27 for cruises.

Trains All out-of-town trains depart from the country trains terminal of Central Station. Information and booking 6.30am–10pm ☎13 22 32.

Travel agents STA Travel does international and domestic flights, tours and accommodation. Branches include 855 George St ☎02/9212 1255; Shop 205, Broadway Shopping Centre, Bay St, Broadway ☎02/9211 2563; and Springfield Ave, Kings Cross ☎02/9368 1111, ⓦwww.statravelaus.com.au. The British travel agency Trailfinders have a branch in Sydney at 8 Spring St (☎02/9247 7666, ⓦwww.trailfinders.com). Flight Centre, 52 Martin Place (☎02/9235 0166, ⓦwww.flightcentre.com), also at several other locations, offer cheap domestic and international air tickets. YHA Travel, 422 Kent St, City (☎02/9261 1111, ⓦwww.yha.com.au), provides domestic and international travel services: transport, tours and accommodation as well as an excellent selection of day-trips around Sydney (branch at *Sydney Central YHA*, 11 Rawson Place off Eddy Ave ☎02/9281 9444). Backpackers Travel Centre, Shop 33, Imperial Arcade, off Pitt St Mall, Pitt St (☎02/9231 3699, ⓦwww.backpackerstravel.net.au), do everything from international flights to bus passes; offices also at 155 Oxford St, Bondi Junction ☎02/9369 1331; 37 Hall St, Bondi Beach ☎02/9300 0505; and 194 Coogee Bay Rd, Coogee ☎02/9315 7751. For details of day tours from Sydney, see p.112. and the day-trip sections themselves.

Women The big events are the Reclaim the Night march in late October and events around International Women's Day in March. Contact the Women's Information and Referral Service (Mon–Fri 9am–5pm; ☎1800 817 227) for information on this and women's organizations, services and referrals. The Women's Library, 8–10 Brown St, Newtown (Tues, Wed & Fri 11am–5pm,

Thurs 11am–8pm, Sat & Sun noon–4pm; ☎02/9557 7060), lends feminist and lesbian literature. Jesse Street National Women's Library, housed in the Town Hall, 456 Kent St (Mon–Fri 10am–2pm; ☎02/9265 9486), is an archive collecting literature detailing Australian women's history and writing. The Feminist Bookshop is in Orange Grove Plaza on Balmain Rd, Lilyfield ☎02/9810 2666.

Work If you have a working holiday visa, you shouldn't have too much trouble finding some sort of work, particularly in hospitality or retail. Offices of the government-run Centrelink (☎13 28 50) have a database of jobs. The most central of their offices are at 140 Redfern St, cnr of George St, Redfern; 151 Crown St, Darlinghurst; and 231 Oxford St, Bondi Junction. The private agency Troy's, Level 11, 89 York St (☎02/9290 2955, ⊛www.troys.com.au), specializes in the hospitality industry. If you have some office or professional skills, there are plenty of temp agencies that are more than keen to take on travellers: flick through "Employment Agencies" in the *Yellow Pages*. For a whole range of work, from unskilled to professional, the multinational Manpower (☎13 25 02, ⊛www .manpower.com.au), is a good bet. Otherwise, scour hostel notice boards and the *Sydney Morning Herald*'s employment pages – Saturday's bumper edition is best.

YHA NSW 422 Kent St, City ☎02/9261 1111. Youth Hostel Association membership and travel centre. Mon–Fri 9am–5pm (Thurs to 6pm), Sat 10am–2pm.

Beyond the City

Beyond the City

22

The Hawkesbury River and the Central Coast

N orth of Sydney the **Hawkesbury River** widens and slows as it approaches the South Pacific, joining Berowra Creek, Cowan Creek, Pittwater and Brisbane Water in the system of flooded valleys that form the jagged jaws of the aptly named **Broken Bay**. The bay and its surrounding inlets are a haven for anglers, sailors and windsurfers, while the entire area is surrounded by bush, with the huge spaces of the **Ku-Ring-Gai Chase National Park** in the south and the **Brisbane Waters National Park** in the north. Beyond Broken Bay, the **Central Coast** between Gosford and Newcastle is an ideal spot for fishing, sailing and lazing around.

The **Pacific Highway** up here, partly supplanted by the **Sydney–Newcastle Freeway**, is fast and efficient, though not particularly attractive until you approach Ku-Ring-Gai Chase; if you want to detour into the park or towards Brooklyn on the Hawkesbury River, don't take the freeway. The **rail** lines follow the road almost as far as Broken Bay, before they take a scenic diversion through Brooklyn and Brisbane Waters to Woy Woy and Gosford.

Ku-Ring-Gai Chase National Park

Ku-Ring-Gai Chase is much the best known of New South Wales' national parks and, with the Pacific Highway running all the way up one side, is also the easiest to get to. The bushland scenery is crisscrossed by walking tracks, which you can explore to seek out Aboriginal rock paintings, or just to get away from it all and see the forest and its wildlife. Only 24km from the city centre, the huge park's unspoilt beauty is enhanced by the presence of water on three sides: the Hawkesbury, its inlet Cowan Creek, and the expanse of **Pittwater**, an inlet of Broken Bay.

From Palm Beach you can take a **boat cruise** with the Palm Beach Ferry Service (see p.140) across Pittwater to the park's Bobbin Head. There are four

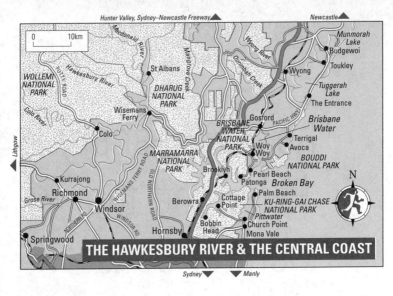

Hunter Valley, Sydney–Newcastle Freeway ▲   Newcastle ▲

THE HAWKESBURY RIVER & THE CENTRAL COAST

Sydney ▼   ▼ Manly

road entrances to the park and a $10 entrance fee for cars. Alternatively, take a **train** to Turramurra CityRail Station and then Hornsby Bus #577 (☎02/9457 8888 for times) to the Bobbin Head Road entrance; some buses continue down to Bobbin Head itself.

Bobbin Head

Ku-Ring-Gai Chase National Park's most popular picnic spot is at **Bobbin Head**, with its colourful marina on Cowan Creek. At the **Kalkari Visitor Centre** (daily 9am–5pm), on the Ku-Ring-Gai Chase Road, you can watch videos about the area's Aboriginal heritage and the wildlife you might encounter, pick up information about walks in the park or take a guided walk. The Birrawanna Walking Track leads from here for 1.5km to the park head-quarters in the *Bobbin Inn*, which can also be approached by car further along Ku-Ring-Gai Chase Road. The NPWS **Bobbin Head Information Centre** (daily 9am–4pm; ☎02/9472 8949) is located inside the Art Deco *Bobbin Inn*, which also has a very pleasant restaurant, popular for weekend breakfasts and Sunday afternoon jazz.

Pittwater and Scotland Island

From West Head at the northeastern corner of Ku-Ring-Gai Chase National Park, there are superb views across Pittwater to the Barrenjoey Lighthouse at Palm Beach (see p.140). The **Garigal Aboriginal Heritage Walk** (3.5km circuit) heads from West Head Road to the most accessible Aboriginal art site in the park, featuring Aboriginal rock engravings and hand art. The only place to **camp** is The Basin (☎02/9451 8124 for bookings) on Pittwater, reached via the Palm Beach Ferry Service (see p.140). Facilities at the site are minimal so bring everything with you.

If you want to stay in the park in rather more comfort, there's a very popu-lar **YHA hostel** (☎02/9999 5748, ✉pittwater@yhansw.org.au; rooms ❷, dorms $19–22; bookings essential and well in advance for weekends) at **Halls Wharf**. It's one of New South Wales' most scenically sited – a rambling old house surrounded by bush and with a verandah where you can feed rainbow lorikeets and look down onto the water; sailing lessons can also be arranged. You must bring everything with you – the last food (and bottle) shop is at Church Point where the **ferry** departs to Halls Wharf (last departure Mon–Fri 7pm, Sat & Sun 6.30pm; call ☎02/9999 3492 for times; $7.50 return).

Two direct **buses** run from Sydney to Church Point: #E86 from Central Station or #156 from Manly Wharf; it's then a ten-minute uphill walk. Alternatively a 24-hour **water-taxi** service operates from Newport (Pink Water Taxi ☎018 238 190); bus #190 from Wynyard runs up the coast to Newport.

The Church Point–Halls Wharf ferry service can also get you to and from **Scotland Island** at the southern end of Pittwater, which it stops at on the forty-minute round trip from Church Point. The bush-clad island is residential only, with no sealed roads or shops, just a school, a kindergarten and a bush-fire brigade, and makes for an interesting wander.

The Hawkesbury River

One of New South Wales' prettiest rivers, with bush covering its banks for much of its course, and some interesting old settlements alongside, the **Hawkesbury River** has its source in the Great Dividing Range and flows out to sea at Broken Bay. For information about the many national parks along the river, contact the NPWS in Sydney (see p.19) or at 370 Windsor Rd in Richmond (☎02/4588 5247). Short of chartering your own boat, the best way to explore the river system is to take a cruise (see box on p.274); the River Boat Mail Run is the most interesting.

Upstream: Wisemans Ferry and around

The first ferry across the Hawkesbury River was opened by ex-convict Solomon Wiseman in 1827, ten years after he was granted 200 acres of river frontage at the spot now known as **WISEMANS FERRY**. The crossing forged an inland connection between Sydney and the Hunter Valley via the convict-built Great North Road. Unfortunately, travellers on this isolated route were easy prey for marauding bushrangers and it was largely abandoned for the longer but safer coastal route. Today it's a popular recreational spot for day-trippers – just a little over an hour from Sydney by car, and with access to the **Dharug National Park** over the river by a free 24-hour car ferry. Dharug's rugged sandstone cliffs and gullies shelter Aboriginal rock engravings which can be visited only on ranger-led trips during school holidays; there's a camping area at Mill Creek (contact Gosford NPWS on ☎02/4324 4911 for details of walks and camping; bookings for both are essential at weekends and during holiday periods). Open to walkers, cyclists and horse-riders but not vehicles, the **Old Great North Road** was literally carved out of the rock by hundreds of convicts from 1829; you can camp en route at the Ten Mile Hollow camping area.

Taking the ferry across the river from Wisemans Ferry, it's a scenic nineteen-kilometre river drive north along Settlers Road, another convict-built route, to

Exploring the Hawkesbury River system

Brooklyn, just above the western mass of Ku-Ring-Gai Chase National Park, and reached directly by train from Central Station (Country Trains), is the base for Hawkesbury River Ferries (℡02/9985 7566), whose River Boat Mail Run still takes letters, as well as tourists, up and down the river. Departures are from Brooklyn Wharf on Dangar Road (Mon–Fri 9.30am excluding public holidays, connecting with trains from Sydney's Central Station and from Gosford; 4hr; $35 including morning tea; booking essential). They also run two-hour coffee cruises towards the mouth of the river (Mon–Thurs 11am & 1.30pm; $20), which can be used as transport to Patonga (see p.278; $10 one-way).

Gosford's Public Wharf is the starting point for the MV *Lady Kendall* (℡02/4323 1655, ⓦwww.starshipcruises.com.au), which cruises both Brisbane Water and Broken Bay (Mon–Wed, Sat & Sun, daily during school & public holidays, 10.15am & 1pm; 2hr 30min; $21; bookings essential; licensed kiosk on board).

Windsor is the base for the Hawkesbury Paddlewheeler (℡02/4575 1171; ⓦwww.paddlewheeler.com.au), which has a good-value Sunday afternoon Jazz Cruise: live jazz and a BBQ lunch for $28 (12.30pm–3pm; advance bookings essential).

Woy Woy is a port of call for the MV *Lady Kendall* (see above) at 10.35am and 12.10pm.

Boat and houseboat rentals

The Hawkesbury River Marina Boat Hire, on Dangar Road, opposite the railway station in Brooklyn (℡02/9985 7252), hires out **boats** which comfortably seat six people (from $70 half-day, $95 full day, more at weekends) and are perfect for fishing expeditions around the mouth of the Hawkesbury or Dangar Island. The centre has a fishing shop and sells bait supplies; you'll need to buy rather than hire rods here. **Houseboats** can be good value if you can get a group together, with prices starting from $560 a weekend and $1040 a week for four people. The Sydney Visitor Centre in Sydney (℡02/9667 6050) has details of operators, or try Able Hawkesbury River Houseboats, on River Road in Wisemans Ferry (℡02/4566 4308 or 1800 024 979, ⓦwww.hawkesburyhouseboats.com.au), or Ripples Houseboats, 87 Brooklyn Rd, Brooklyn (℡02/9985 7788, ⓦwww.ripples.com.au).

ST ALBANS, where you can partake of a cooling brew (or stay a while) at a pub built in 1836, the hewn sandstone *Settlers Arms Inn* (℡02/4568 2111, ⒻE4568 2046; en-suite rooms ❺). The pub is set on two-and-a-half acres and many of the vegetables and herbs for the delicious home-cooked food are organically grown on site (lunch daily, dinner Fri–Sun).

Wisemans Ferry accommodation and eating

The settlement of Wisemans Ferry was based around Wiseman's home, Cobham Hall, built in 1826. Much of the original building still exists in the blue-painted *Wisemans Ferry Inn* on the Old Great North Road (℡02/4566 4301, Ⓕ4566 4780; pub ❸–❹, motel ❷–❸), with characterful **rooms** upstairs sharing bathrooms, and en-suite motel-style rooms outside at the back. Bistro meals are served daily and there's entertainment on Sunday afternoons. Just across the road, with extensive grounds fronting onto the river, is the contrastingly modern *The Retreat at Wisemans* (℡02/4566 4422, ⓦwww.wisemans.com.au; B&B ❻), a 54-room resort. The upmarket motel rooms can't compete with the inn's colonial charm, but the location is superbly scenic and facilities include a restaurant, golf course, tennis courts, swimming pool, in-house masseuse and bike hire; cheaper rates are available during the week. Other accommodation in the surrounding area includes the *Del Rio Riverside Resort* (☎02/4566 4330, ⓦwww.delrioresort.com.au; en-suite cabins ❹–❺), a campsite in Webbs Creek across the Webbs Creek car ferry, 3km south of Wisemans Ferry; facilities include a Chinese restaurant, swimming pool, tennis court and golf course. *Rosevale Farm Resort*, 3km along Wisemans Ferry Road en route to Gosford (☎ & ⓕ 02/4566 4207; on–site vans ❶, en-suite cabins ❷), has more inexpensive camping and cabins – cheaper on weekdays – in extensive bushland close to Dharug National Park.

The Upper Hawkesbury: Windsor and beyond

About 50km inland from Sydney and just a few kilometres apart, Windsor and Richmond are two of five towns founded by Governor Macquarie in the early nineteenth century to capitalize on the fertile, well-watered soil of the Upper Hawkesbury River area. Both are reached easily by train from Central Station via Blacktown.

WINDSOR is probably the best preserved of all the historic Hawkesbury towns, with a lively centre of narrow streets, spacious old pubs and numerous historic colonial buildings. It's terrifically popular on Sundays, when a market takes over the shady, tree-lined mall end of the main drag, George Street, and the *Macquarie Arms Hotel*, which claims to be the oldest pub in Australia, puts on live music – raucous rock'n'roll to befit the crowd of bikies and assorted types crowding the front verandah – on Thompson Square, the grassy village green opposite. Next door to the pub, the **Hawkesbury River Museum and Tourist Information Centre** (daily 10am–4pm; museum $2.50; ☎02/4577 2310, ⓦwww.hawkesburyweb.com) doles out local info. There are picnic tables along the river and a Sunday cruise leaves from the jetty across the road from the tourist office (see box opposite).

Just 7km northwest of Windsor, **Richmond**'s attractions include its unspoilt riverside setting, an old graveyard and settlers' dwellings. Cinema buffs could take in a bargain-priced film at the beautifully preserved Regent Twin Cinema,

Scenic drives from Windsor and Richmond

Driving via the Hawkesbury River area from Sydney is a very scenic way to get to the Blue Mountains via the Bells Line of Road or Hawkesbury Road, and to the Hunter Valley via Putty Road.

From Windsor, **Putty Road** (Route 69) heads north through beautiful forest country, along the eastern edge of the Wollemi National Park, to Singleton in the Hunter Valley (see p.287).

From Richmond, the **Bells Line of Road** (Route 40), goes to Lithgow (see p.306) via Kurrajong, and is a great scenic drive; all along the way are fruit stalls stacked with produce from the valley. There's a wonderful view of the Upper Hawkesbury Valley from the lookout point at **Kurrajong Heights**, on the edge of the Blue Mountains.

Another scenic drive from Richmond to the Blue Mountains, emerging near Springwood (see p.296), is south along the **Hawkesbury Road**, with the **Hawkesbury Heights Lookout** halfway along providing panoramic views. Not far from the lookout is the modern solar-powered *Hawkesbury Heights YHA* (☎02/4754 5621; beds $18), with more views from its secluded bush setting, and no chance of overcrowding with only six twin rooms.

on the main road through town at 149 Windsor St (☎02/4578 1800, ⓦwww.richmondregent.com.au).

The Central Coast

The shoreline between Broken Bay and Newcastle, known as the **Central Coast**, is characterized by large **coastal lakes** – saltwater lagoons almost entirely enclosed, but connected to the ocean by small waterways. To travel anywhere on the Central Coast, you need to go through **Gosford**, perched on the north shore of Brisbane Water and just about within commuting distance of Sydney. Its proximity to the city has resulted in uncontrolled residential sprawl which has put a great strain on the once-unspoilt lakes. Around Gosford are two excellent **national parks** – Brisbane Water and Bouddi – and a couple of wildlife attractions: **Calga Springs Sanctuary** and the nearby **Australian Reptile Park**. Beyond the national parks, **Pearl Beach** and nearby **Patonga** are idyllic bay beach retreats, while on the ocean, **Terrigal**, **Avoca** and **The Entrance** are all enjoyable holiday resorts.

For tourist information on the whole region, and accommodation bookings, contact **Central Coast Tourism** (☎1800/806 258, ⓦwww.cctourism.com.au).

Gosford and around

Although there's plenty of accommodation in and around Gosford – details from **Central Coast Tourism**, near the train station at 200 Mann St

---

Transport on the coast

If you're **driving**, and want to enjoy the coastal scenery and lakes, follow the older Pacific Highway which heads to Newcastle via Gosford and Wyong, rather than the speedier Sydney–Newcastle Freeway which runs some way inland. The frequent **train** service from Central Station (Country Trains) to Gosford or Woy Woy also follows a very picturesque route. Bennetts Airport Shuttle (see "Airport Buses" box on p.25) gets you to the area direct from Sydney airport.

The fit and intrepid can get here by **bike**: from Manly, head up the northern beaches and hop on a ferry service from Palm Beach (see p.140) to **Ettalong** (departs Palm Beach daily 6.30am, 7.30am, 9am, 10.30am, noon, 2pm, 3.30pm & 5pm, except Sat from 7.30am, Sun from 9am; departs Ettalong daily 6am, 7am, 8am, 9.40am, 11.10am, 12.40pm, 4.10pm, 5.40pm, except Sat from 8am, Sun from 9.40am; $7.50 one-way; ☎02/9918 2747, ⓦwww.palmbeachferry.com.au), then continue up through Woy Woy and Gosford to the coast.

You can also reach **Patonga** by **ferry** with Palm Beach and Hawkesbury River Ferries (☎02/9997 4815, ⓦwww.sydneyseniccruises.com), departing from Palm Beach daily at 11am (also 9am & 3.45pm hols & weekends; $6.50 one-way) and returning from Patonga at 4.15pm (also 9.30am & 3pm hols & weekends); Hawkesbury River Ferries (see box on p.274) also run a service from Brooklyn. Walkers can alight from the ferry and hike to Pearl Beach (see opposite).

Within the Central Coast area, a well-developed **bus service** is run by a collection of operators: Busways Central Coast (☎02/4368 2277), Busways Peninsula (☎02/4392 6666), Gosford Bus Service (☎02/4325 1781) and The Entrance Red Bus Services (☎02/4332 8655). For **taxis**, call Central Coast Taxis ☎13 10 08.

(Mon–Fri 10am–4pm, Sat 10am–12.30pm; ☎02/4385 4074, ⓦwww
.cctourism.com.au) – there's not much incentive to stay. Gosford's main appeal
is as a gateway to a couple of excellent wildlife reserves, two wonderful national
parks and beyond them a pair of idyllic beach retreats.

Calga Springs Sanctuary

Fifteen minutes' drive west of Gosford, **Calga Springs Sanctuary**, just off
the F3 freeway, at Peats Ridge Road, Calga (daily 10am–5pm; $14; ⓦwww
.calgasanctuary.com), was set up by the former Federal Minister for the
Environment, Barry Cohen, and his son in an attempt to save Australian
wildlife from introduced species; entry fees to the 170-acre site, with its huge
variety of native plants, birds and animals, include a knowledgeable guided tour
along the 2km of walking trails past Aboriginal rock engravings.

Australian Reptile Park

A similar distance west of Gosford, just off the Pacific Highway, the **Australian
Reptile Park** (daily 9am–5pm; $18; ⓦwww.reptilepark.com.au; Peninsula Bus
Lines #38 from Gosford) has a long history of providing snake and funnel web
spider venom for the Commonwealth Serum Laboratories, and you can watch
both kinds of creatures being milked. Spider World and The Lost World of
Reptiles are fun, interactive exhibitions and visitors can pat Eric, the giant
crocodile, touch a python, or hand-feed kangaroos.

Brisbane Waters and Bouddi national parks

Brisbane Waters National Park, immediately south of Gosford, is the site of
the **Bulgandry Aboriginal engravings**, which are of a style unique to the
Sydney region, with figurative outlines scratched boldly into sandstone. The
site, no longer frequented by the Guringgai people – whose territory ranged
south as far as Sydney Harbour and north to Lake Macquarie – is 7km southwest of Gosford off the Woy Woy Road.

Tiny **Bouddi National Park** is 20km southeast along the coast, at the
mouth of Broken Bay, and is a great spot for bushwalking, with **camping** facilities at Putty Beach, Little Beach and Tallow Beach: book through the NPWS
office at 207 Albury St, Gosford (☎02/4324 4911), which also has information
on both parks.

You can visit the rock art sites with Coastal Eco-Tours (☎02/4344 3392,
ⓦwww.coastalecotours.com.au), who offer excellent small-group expert-led
bushwalking tours in both national parks, focusing on bush medicine (the
operator is a qualified pharmacologist), bush tucker and bush skills ($110 includes
picnic lunch and Woy Woy station pick-ups). A two-day one-night bush survival
course ($380) teaches bush skills and includes kayaking and camping.

Pearl Beach and Patonga

Surrounded by Brisbane Waters National Park, friendly, undeveloped **PEARL
BEACH**, just over a 25-kilometre drive from Gosford via Woy Woy and Umina,
is a small community which expands at weekends. There are holiday houses to
rent, but no other accommodation. Besides the popular *Sit 'n' Chats Beach Cafe*
(live jazz Sun noon–4pm) and a restaurant, *Pearls on the Beach* (licensed and BYO;
bookings ☎02/4342 4400; closed Mon–Wed, no dinner Sun), there's a general store (daily 8am–6pm) also selling petrol, a real estate agent which can
arrange holiday lets (☎02/4341 7555, ⓦwww.pearlbeachrealestate.com.au;

from $700 per week in peak season), and some tennis courts. The very pretty, sheltered beach, popular with families, has a relaxing open-access saltwater pool at one end.

You can walk from the end of Crystal Avenue to the neighbouring beach set-tlement of **PATONGA**, visiting a lookout and the **Crommelin Native Arboretum** en route (by road from Pearl Beach, Patonga is 2km southwest). The 45-minute walk is best undertaken on the last Sunday of the month when the **Patonga Beach market** is held (8am–4pm). Ocean Planet, 25 Broken Bay Rd, Ettalong Beach (℡02/4342 2222, @www.oceanplanet.com.au; kayak hire from $30 half-day), offers **kayaking trips** on Patonga Creek (8km; 7hr; $92.50), with pick-ups from Woy Woy station.

To get to Pearl Beach or Patonga, take the Busways Peninsula **bus** (℡02/4392 6666) from Woy Woy station or the **ferry** to Patonga from Palm Beach or Brooklyn (see box on p.274).

Terrigal

Twelve kilometres southeast of Gosford, beautiful **TERRIGAL**, backed by bush-covered hills, is one of the liveliest spots on the Central Coast, a thriving beach resort with a strong café culture. The big curve of beach has a pictur-esque sandstone headland, and the sheltered eastern end, The Haven, where the boats moor, is popular with families. With rocketing house prices all along the Central Coast, Terrigal's main street has been invaded by real estate agents and the town has taken a decidedly upmarket turn. Much of the social life revolves around the five-star *Crowne Plaza Hotel*, with its grand marble lobby and pricey boutiques, which dominates one end of **The Esplanade**.

Central Coast Tourism at Rotary Park, Terrigal Drive (daily 9am–5pm, May–Sept closed Sun; ℡02/4385 4430, @www.cctourism.com.au), is a good source of information on the whole region, and can make free accommoda-tion bookings. Terrigal is a popular spot for **water-based activities**, and oper-ators include Erina Sail 'n' Ski (℡02/4365 2355; sailboarding lessons and hire); Learn To Surf (℡02/4332 0523; 1hr lesson $20); Central Coast Charters (℡0427 665 544; ocean and river cruises, deep sea and game fishing); Kincumber Water-ski School (℡0414 685 005; first-timer sessions $50); and the long-running, well-respected Terrigal Dive School (℡02/4384 1219; five-day diving courses $385, shore or boat dives $60/80).

To get to Terrigal, take Busways #80, #81 or #82 from Gosford; #81 also links Terrigal to Avoca Beach (see opposite).

Accommodation and eating

Crowne Plaza Terrigal, the swanky resort **hotel** on the corner of Pine Tree Lane (℡02/4384 9111, @www.crowneplaza.com; ❻), has three restaurants, two bars, a nightclub, a pool, gym and tennis courts; all this costs from $285 per night, including buffet breakfast and champagne. The pleasant YHA-affiliated *Terrigal Beach Backpackers Lodge*, 12 Campbell Crescent ℡02/4385 3330, @www.terrigalbeachlodge.com.au; rooms ❷, dorms $24), is only one minute's walk from the beach; boogie-boards are provided free. *Terrigal Beachhouse Motel*, 7 Painters Lane, off the northern end of The Esplanade (℡02/4385 9564, @www.accommodationterrigal.com; share bathroom ❷–❸, en suite ❸–❹), feels like a cross between a motel and a backpackers; the seriously old motel has been brightly painted and has a comfortable feel, with a common room downstairs (but no kitchen). Rooms are small and old-fashioned but very clean; the cheapest share bathroom. The same outfit also runs the more upmarket motel *Tiarri* (all rooms with own courtyard ❻), and rents apartments ($350–895). If you're after a holiday unit (from around $400 weekly), contact Hunters Real Estate, 104 Terrigal Esplanade (☎02/4384 1444, ✉hunters @ozemail.com.au).

Terrigal has a great **café** scene: *Louvres*, 60 The Esplanade, is beachy but sophisticated with a lovely plant-filled courtyard, and serves all the café favourites (daily 8am–9pm); *Aromas on Sea* has the best café position (and great coffee, or drinks from the hotel bar with your food), on the breezy terrace of the *Crowne Plaza* looking right over the beach (daily 8am–5pm, Fri & Sat to 9pm); while the local favourite is the tiny *Patcinos*, a block back from the beach at 17 Church St, near the hostel. The best fish and chips comes from *Fish Bonez,* 90 The Esplanade (takeaway or eat-in), while *The Break*, on Pinetree Lane behind the *Crowne Plaza*, specializes in gourmet pizzas; its fun, intimate **bar** is a good alternative to the *Crowne*'s packed beer garden – the *Florida Beach Bar* – or its posh *Lord Ashley Lounge* upstairs. The **restaurant** scene is dominated by Thai eateries: two of the best are the stylish *A-Oi Thai*, near the *Crowne Plaza* at 3 Kurrawyba Ave (☎02/4385 6611), and the cheap and cheerful *N Thai Sing*, 84 The Esplanade (☎02/4385 9700).

Avoca Beach

Six kilometres to the south of Terrigal, and altogether quieter, **AVOCA BEACH** is especially popular with surfers. A large, crescent-shaped and sandy beach between two headlands, it has its own surf life-saving club and a safe children's rock pool. West of the beach are the still waters of **Avoca Lake**. Avoca's pleasant small-town atmosphere is enhanced by the Avoca Beach Theatre (☎02/4382 2156), a little-changed early-1950s cinema near the beach on Avoca Drive. You can **learn to surf** with Central Coast Surf School (☎02/4382 1020; 1hr lesson $25); Aquamuse (☎02/4368 4172), by the bridge in Heazlett Park, hire out pedal-boats, pedal-bikes, kayaks and surf skis to use on the lake.

To **get to Avoca**, take Busways #79 from Gosford or #81 from Terrigal.

Accommodation and eating

Limited overnight **accommodation** in Avoca includes the self-contained cabins and villas of *The Palms*, Carolina Park, off The Round Drive (☎02/4382 1227, ✇www.palmsavoca.com.au; ❹), an upmarket, garden-set holiday resort which has swimming pools, spa, and games room. Otherwise, the best bet is to rent a holiday unit (from $450 per week) – call George Brand Real Estate (☎02/4382 1311) for listings.

For **eating**, grab fish and chips, gourmet and veggie burgers and Turkish bread sandwiches from the groovy, colourful *Prawn Star Seafood Cafe*, at the end of the main set of shops at 168 Avoca Drive (8.30am–9.30pm, closed Tues & Wed, daily school hols), or there's fine dining at the expensive French-run *Feast* at Shop 3, 85 Avoca Drive (☎02/4381 0707), at the end of the beach near the SLSC, with an open deck right over the beach; adjacent *Mad-Caf* at Shop 2, is a great place for a coffee with its own beachfront terrace.

The Entrance

Further north, Tuggerah and Munmorah lakes meet the sea at **THE ENTRANCE**, a beautiful place with water extending as far as the eye can see. It's a favourite fishing spot with anglers – and with swarms of **pelicans**, which turn up for the afternoon fish-feeds (daily 3.30pm; free) at Memorial Park, near the visitor centre (see below).

The beaches and lakes along the coast from here to Newcastle are crowded with caravan parks, motels and outfits offering the opportunity to fish, wind-surf, sail or waterski; although less attractive than places further north, they make a great day-trip or weekend escape from Sydney. Pro Dive Central Coast, 96 The Entrance Rd (☎02/4334 1559), arranges **scuba-diving** lessons and daily boat dives, and rents out snorkelling and dive gear.

The **Entrance Visitors Centre**, on Marine Parade (daily 9am–5pm; ☎02/4385 4074 or ☎1300 13 0708, ⓦwww.cctourism.com.au), has a free **accommodation** booking service. **By bus**, get to The Entrance with The Entrance Red Bus Services: #21, #22, #23 from Gosford station; #24, #25, #26 from Tuggerah or Wyong train stations.

The Hunter Valley

I n Australia (and, increasingly, worldwide) the **Hunter Valley** is synonymous with fine **wine**. The first vines were planted 150 years ago and are mainly the two classic white-wine varieties of Semillon and Chardonnay, with Pinot Noir and Shiraz dominating the reds. In what seems a bizarre juxtaposition, this is also a very important **coal-mining region**: in the upper part of the valley especially, the two often go hand-in-hand. By far the best-known area, however, is in the Lower Hunter Valley around the main town of Cessnock – even the town's jail has its own vineyard, and the prisoners have produced some prizewinning wines. One of the most appealing aspects of the Hunter Valley wine country is the bush and farming feel of the place, with the vast plantings of vineyards seemingly lost among bushland, forested ridges, red-soiled dirt tracks, and paddocks with grazing cattle.

Lower Hunter Valley

CESSNOCK, two hours' drive north of Sydney, is uninteresting in itself, and surprisingly unsophisticated given the wine culture surrounding it, though at the time of writing the rather ugly main drag, Vincent Street, was being landscaped in an attempt to improve things. Its big old country pubs are probably its best feature and staying in one provides a taste of Australian rural life. Most of the **wine-tasting** is around the area called **Pokolbin** (no town to speak of), spread over three kilometres at the centre of the vineyards, 12–15km northwest of Cessnock and alongside some very salubrious accommodation and a fine-dining scene – all well enjoyed by weekending Sydneysiders out to pamper themselves. For overnight stays, with your own transport you'd be better off basing yourself out here, and in Cessnock only if you've come on the coach.

Information and events

Pick up the excellent, free *Hunter Valley Wine Country* guide, with a handy fold-out map in the centre, from the Sydney Visitor Centre in The Rocks (p.47), or from the brand-new circular-design **Hunter Valley Wine Country Visitor Information Centre**, Main Road, Pokolbin (Mon–Sat 9am–5pm, Sun 9am–4pm; ☎02/4990 4477, ⓦwww.winecountry.com.au), scenically sited amongst vineyards and housing the very pleasant and affordable *Wine Country Cafe*. If it's closed, the free guides are kept in a rack outside. Try to tour the

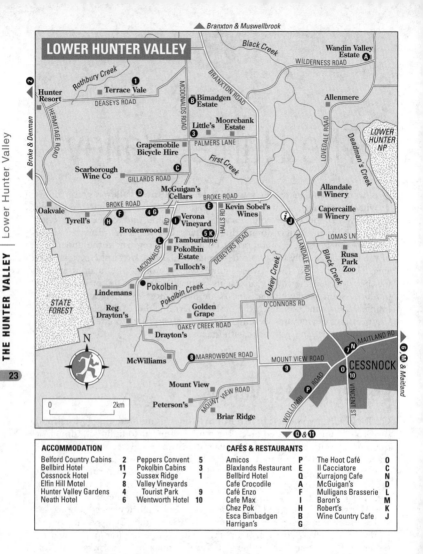

ACCOMMODATION

Belford Country Cabins	2	Peppers Convent	5
Bellbird Hotel	11	Pokolbin Cabins	3
Cessnock Hotel	7	Sussex Ridge	1
Elfin Hill Motel	8	Valley Vineyards	
Hunter Valley Gardens	4	Tourist Park	9
Neath Hotel	6	Wentworth Hotel	10

CAFÉS & RESTAURANTS

Amicos	P	The Hoot Café	O
Blaxlands Restaurant	E	Il Cacciatore	C
Bellbird Hotel	Q	Kurrajong Cafe	N
Cafe Crocodile	A	McGuigan's	D
Café Enzo	F	Mulligans Brasserie	L
Cafe Max	I	Baron's	M
Chez Pok	H	Robert's	K
Esca Bimbadgen	B	Wine Country Cafe	J
Harrigan's	G		

wineries during the week; at weekends both the number of visitors and accommodation prices go up. In February, when the place is flooded with wine-lovers enjoying the Dionysian delights of the **Hunter Valley Vintage Festival**, accommodation is impossible to find, but normally summer is a quiet time as it's so hot inland. Another lively time is **October**, when there are both opera and jazz festivals. Wyndham Estate hosts **Opera in the Vineyards** (☎02/4938 3444) in its new outdoor amphitheatre next to the Hunter River, with an accompanying food and wine fair. This is closely followed by the **Jazz in the Vines Festival** (☎02/4993 7000) held at Tyrell's Winery's Long Flat Paddock (more information on ⓦwww.jazzinthevines.com.au). For details of May's Lovedale Long Lunch, see p.286.

Getting there and tours

To get to Cessnock, catch a train from Central to Maitland or Newcastle and then a bus with Rover Motors (☎02/4991 1967). Alternatively, Keans Travel Express (Sydney ☎02/9211 3387; Muswellbrook ☎02/6543 1322) goes direct from Sydney to the Hunter Valley once daily (terminating at Scone), taking just over two hours with stops including Kurri Kurri, Neath, Cessnock, Pokolbin and Muswellbrook.

If you're without transport (there's no public transport to the wineries) – or don't want to meander unintentionally off-road after excessive wine-tasting – **vineyard tours** are a good option. Many are exhausting return trips from Sydney but several local operators offer day-trips from within the valley: Shadows Wine Tours do good-value day (7hr) tours, visiting five wineries, with pick-ups from Newcastle, Maitland, Cessnock and Pokolbin included ($40, or $60 with restaurant lunch; ☎02/4990 7002); Hunter Vineyard Tours runs small-group bus tours visiting five well-chosen wineries over six hours, all offering tastings ($45 including pick-up from Cessnock; Newcastle or Maitland pick-ups $5 extra; restaurant lunch $20 extra or BYO; ☎02/4991 1659, ⓦwww.huntervineyardtours.com.au). The more expensive Hunter Valley Day Tours have a small-group wine-and-cheese-tasting tour ($80 for pick-ups from Cessnock, Pokolbin and Maitland; $95 for Newcastle pick-ups; ☎02/4938 5031, ⓦwww.huntertourism.com/daytours). Pedal power is also popular: **rent bikes** from Grapemobile, on the corner of McDonalds Road and Palmers Lane, Pokolbin (☎0500 804 039, ⓦwww.grapemobile.com.au; $30 per day, $22 half-day). For a **taxi** call: Cessnock RadioCabs (☎02/4990 1111).

Accommodation

Since the Hunter Valley is a popular weekend trip for Sydneysiders, accommodation **prices** invariably rise on Friday and Saturday nights when most places only offer two-night deals. We have specified in the listings below the cost of the cheapest available double in high season both during the week and also at weekends. If you're going to be here at a weekend, or during the February vintage festival, advance **booking** is essential. Most of the accommodation is around Pokolbin.

Belford Country Cabins 659 Hermitage Rd, Pokolbin ☎02/6574 7100, ⓦwww.belfordcabins.com.au. Family-run, fully equipped two- and four-bedroom wooden bungalows (sleeping up to four or eight). Great bushland location, small pool and playground. Min 2-night stay at weekends. ⑤, weekend ⑤–⑥

Bellbird Hotel 388 Wollombi Rd, Bellbird, 5km southwest of Cessnock ☎02/4990 1094, ⓕ4991 5475. Great classic country pub, circa 1908, with wide iron-lace. Public bar is often full of country characters. Eat inexpensive no-frills bistro food in the very pleasant vine-covered and flower-filled beer garden; adjacent children's playground. All rooms share bathrooms. Midweek rates include a light breakfast ②, generous cooked one at weekends ④

Cessnock Hotel 234 Wollombi Rd, Cessnock ☎02/4990 1002, ⓦwww.huntervalleyhotels.com.au. Right in the centre of town, this recently renovated pub is now very much city-style, with a great bistro-cum-bar, the *Kurrajong Cafe*, taking over most of downstairs (breakfast to dinner; modern Australian plus meaty pub favourites; mains average $14; couple of vegetarian options). Rooms all share bathroom but are huge with high ceilings, fans and very comfy beds. Big verandah for guests to hang out on; cooked breakfast served in the café. ④, weekend ⑤

Elfin Hill Motel Marrowbone Rd, Pokolbin

Hunter Valley wineries

More than sixty **wineries** cluster around the Hunter Valley, almost all of them offering tastings. The most-visited are in the lower part of the valley, near Pokolbin, but there are also a few gems in the upper valley, around Wybong and Denman, west of Muswellbrook. Below are a few of our favourites or those that offer tours.

Lower Hunter

Allandale Winery Lovedale Rd, Pokolbin ☎02/4990 4526. Picturesque, small winery established in 1978. Set on a hill, with great views overlooking the vineyard and the Brokenback Range. They're happy for you to visit during vintage time, when you can see the small operation in action; try their prizewinning Chardonnay. One of the best. Mon–Sat 9am–5pm, Sun 10am–5pm.

Drayton's Family Wines Oakey Creek Rd, Pokolbin ☎02/4998 7513. Friendly, family winery, established for over 150 years and well known for their ports. BBQ and picnic facilities; children's play area. Tours Mon–Fri 11am. Mon–Fri 8am–5pm, Sat & Sun 10am–5pm.

Hermitage Road Cellars and Winery Hunter Resort, Hermitage Rd, Pokolbin ☎02/4998 7777. The largest commercial winery, lacking in atmosphere but offering informative wine tours (9am, 11am & 2pm; $5.50 which is refunded if you buy a bottle of wine; booking essential) or a two-hour "Wine School" tutorial (daily 9am; $25). Daily 9am–5pm.

Kevin Sobel's Wines Cnr Broke and Halls roads, Pokolbin ☎02/4998 7766. The welcome at this small, simple winery is wonderfully down-to-earth, and includes a greeting by Joe, the resident St Bernard. The circular timber-and-glass building itself is a real treat, with a home-made, wonky feel. Picnic tables outside. Daily 9am–5pm.

Lindemans McDonalds Rd, Pokolbin ☎02/4998 7684. One of the Hunter's best-known names; Dr Lindeman first planted vines in the valley in 1842. The museum here has a collection of winemaking paraphernalia. Daily 10am–5pm.

Scarborough Wine Co Gilliards Rd, Pokolbin ☎02/4998 7563. Small, friendly winery specializing in Chardonnay and Pinot Noir. Pleasantly relaxed sit-down tastings are held in a small cottage on Hungerford Hill with wonderful valley views. Daily 9am–5pm.

☎02/4998 7543, ⓔelfinhill@hunterlink.com.au. Friendly, family-run hilltop motel with extensive views. Comfortable air-con units in timber cabins, plus a saltwater pool and BBQ area. ❺, weekend ❻

Hunter Valley Gardens Broke Rd, Pokolbin ☎02/4998 7854, ⓦwww.hvg.com.au. Modern combined motel and hotel complex overlooking the vineyards, complete with an Irish pub, *Harrigan's*, bistro, pool, spa, tennis courts and three standards of accommodation: four-and-a-half-star in *The Lodge* ($215, weekend $240); motel-style in *Harrigan's* (❼, weekend ❽); or in self-contained one- and two-bedroom cabins at *Grapeview Villas* (from ❸, weekend from ❺, 2-day minimum at weekends). One room is accessible to disabled guests.

Neath Hotel Cessnock Rd, Neath, 6km east of Cessnock ☎02/4930 4270, ⓦwww.huntervalleyhotels.com.au. B&B in a nicely furnished big old country pub, listed by the National Trust; all rooms share bath. Fri and Sat night rates include a cooked breakfast and a three-course meal in *Baron's*, the antique-filled restaurant. Restaurant Sat nights only; cheaper bistro rest of week. Midweek rates include a light breakfast ❹, weekend ❻

Peppers Convent Halls Rd, Pokolbin ☎02/4998 7764, ⓦwww.peppers.com.au. The swankiest place to stay in the Hunter Valley, with a price to match (from $310 per night). The guesthouse, converted from an old convent, is very cosy, with fireplaces and low beams, and is part of the Peppertree winery. Attached fine-dining

Small Winemakers Centre Verona Vineyard, McDonalds Rd, Pokolbin ☎02/4998 7668. Sells wines produced by several other small vineyards; the tasting charge levied on some wines is usually refunded on purchases. Excellent *Harry's Sandwich Bar* downstairs, or try the BYO *Cafe Max* upstairs, with balcony views of vineyards and far-off hills and an eclectic menu to team with your wine (Wed–Sun 11am–4pm). Winery daily 10am–5pm.

Tamburlaine Wines McDonalds Rd, Pokolbin ☎02/4998 7570. The jasmine-scented garden outside gives a hint of the flowery, elegant wines within. Only a small range of wines – too small even for the domestic market, so you must buy here. Tastings are well orchestrated and delivered with a heap of experience. Daily 9.30am–5pm.

Tyrrell's Family Vineyard Broke Rd, Pokolbin ☎02/4998 7509. The oldest independent family vineyards, producing consistently good wines. The tiny ironbark slab hut, where Edward Tyrrell lived when he began the winery in 1858, is still in the grounds, and the old winery with its cool earth floor is much as it was. Beautiful setting against the Brokenback Range. Mon–Sat 8am–5pm, with free tour 1.30pm.

Wandin Valley Estate Cnr Wilderness and Lovedale roads ☎02/4930 7317. One of the most picturesquely sited wineries, set on a hundred acres of vineyards with a creek and magnificent views across the Watego and Brokenback ranges, shared by the great little *Cafe Crocodile* (weekend brunch, lunch Wed–Sun, dinner Fri & Sat; wine at cellar door prices and by the glass). Very friendly, relaxed cellar door and tours 11am Sat & Sun. Daily 10am–5pm.

Upper Hunter

Cruikshank Callatoota Estate Wybong Rd, Wybong, Upper Hunter Valley, 18km north of Denman ☎02/6547 8149. Winemaker John Cruikshank is a real character who has been making red wine here since 1974. Vineyard BBQ and picnic facilities, or light lunch available. Daily 9am–5pm.

Rosemount Estate Rosemount Rd, Denman, Upper Hunter ☎02/6549 6400. Producer of some of Australia's best-known, award-winning wines, and with an excellent vineyard brasserie (Tues–Sun 10am–3pm). Winery daily 10am–4pm.

restaurant, *Robert's* (☎02/4998 7330; licensed) in a charming 1876 wooden farmhouse filled with flowers; French rustic-style food emerges from wood-fired ovens. ❽

Pokolbin Cabins Palmers Lane, Pokolbin ☎02/4998 7611, ℱ4998 7873. In the midst of the wineries, this extensive complex has two- and three-bedroom log cabins and six-bedroom homesteads, fully equipped with everything from linen and CD-player to firewood. Swimming pool and tennis court in the shady grounds. ❹, weekend ❻

Sussex Ridge Off Deaseys Rd, Pokolbin ☎02/4998 7753, ℗www.sussexridge.com.au. Guesthouse in a classic two-storey, tin-roofed homestead among extensive bushland, with great views from the balcony. En-suite rooms. Two communal lounge areas with open fires; outdoor BBQ area; swimming pool. Cooked breakfast included. ❻, weekend ❼

Valley Vineyards Tourist Park Mount View Rd, 2km northwest of Cessnock ☎02/4990 2573, ℗www.valleyvineyard.com.au. High-standard campsite with camp kitchen, portable BBQs and pool. Cabins have external en suites, cottages internal. Cabins ❷, cottages ❹

Wentworth Hotel 36 Vincent St, Cessnock ☎02/4990 1364, ℗www.wentworthhotelcessnock.com.au. Large old country hotel transformed into the town's Irish-theme pub. Rooms are tasteful, well furnished in "colonial" style, clean and spacious with washbasin, ceiling fan and heating; light breakfast included. ❸, weekend ❺

Eating and drinking

Most of the many excellent (and pricey) Hunter Valley restaurants are attached to the various wineries or are among the vineyards, rather than in the towns, while the Hunter's large old pubs (some detailed in accommodation on p.283) dish out less fancy but more affordable grub. Every year over a mid-May weekend eight wineries along and around the very scenic Lovedale and Wilderness roads team up with local restaurants to host the **Lovedale Long Lunch** (℡02/4930 7611, Ⓦwww.lovedalelonglunch.com.au), with wine and gourmet food served amongst the vines. You can taste free samples of The Hunter Valley Cheese Company's handmade wares, or buy some to accompany a picnic, at the McGuigan Bros Winery, Broke Road, Pokolbin. Other places to eat or drink than those listed below are included in the "Hunter Valley wineries" box on pp.284–285.

Amicos 138 Wollombi Rd, Cessnock ℡02/4991 1995. A few kilometres from the town centre, this is a very popular cheap eat with the locals. Serves Italian and Mexican food (including pizza, pasta and salads), in a lively, colourful atmosphere. Licensed & BYO. Daily from 6pm.

Blaxlands Restaurant Broke Rd, Pokolbin ℡02/4998 7550. More than a hundred wines from the Hunter Valley are available at this well-regarded restaurant in an 1829 sandstone cottage. You can eat outside on the verandah. Expensive. Booking advised.

Café Enzo Peppers Creek Antiques, Broke Rd, Pokolbin ℡02/4998 7233. Courtyard café with a light Mediterranean menu and excellent Italian-style coffee. Wed–Sun 10am–5pm.

Chez Pok *Pepper's Guesthouse*, Ekerts Rd, Pokolbin ℡02/4998 7596. Highly regarded restaurant stylishly using local produce including fresh-picked herbs. The views overlooking vineyards are very pretty as is the antique-filled cottage interior. Expensive. Daily from 7am to dinner.

Esca Bimbadgen Lot 21, McDonalds Rd, Pokolbin ℡02/4998 4666. With a squint, this winery, complete with bell tower, could be in Europe. Its modern restaurant, however, is all timber and glass, reached via the working winery, and with wonderful vineyard views from the balcony. Food (mains around the $30 mark) is contemporary European, with veal, spatchcock and roast duck on the menu. Licensed. Lunch daily, dinner Wed–Sat.

The Hoot Café 115 Vincent St, Cessnock. Bright and airy café with whirring ceiling fans and a soul music soundtrack. Gourmet sandwiches, filo pastries, samosas, nachos, delicious stuffed potatoes, tasty cakes, and good coffee. Mon–Fri 8am–4pm, Sat 8am–1pm.

Il Cacciatore Hermitage Lodge, cnr McDonalds and Gilliards roads, Pokolbin ℡02/4998 7639. Excellent upmarket Northern Italian restaurant with a wide choice, including fish dishes. Desserts such as chocolate pasta ensure that the place is packed. Dinner nightly plus lunch Sat & Sun. Licensed & BYO.

Mulligans Brasserie Cypress Lakes Resort, McDonalds Rd, Pokolbin ℡02/4993 1555. Gourmet sandwiches, salads, tortillas and burgers accompanied by pleasant courtyard views looking out over the resort's pool and verdant golf course. Licensed. Daily 6.30am–10pm.

Around Cessnock

Cessnock lies more or less due west of Newcastle, in an area of small creeks and tributaries of the Hunter River. Even in the main valley of the Hunter, however, where the New England Highway heads up towards the mountains of the Great Dividing Range and the New England Plateau, the impression is overwhelmingly rural, with green meadows and pastures interspersed with cornfields, vegetable patches and, of course, vineyards. Old mansions and sleepy hamlets, dating back to colonial times, complete the seemingly idyllic pastoral scene – though coal is extracted nearby from several enormous open-cast mines to feed Newcastle's power stations. The area is dotted with interesting old country towns: even **Maitland** and **Singleton**, two of the main centres of the coal industry, boast historic buildings that help retain a beguilingly colonial flavour.

WOLLOMBI, a homesteading settlement some 30km south of Cessnock, is the gateway to the Hunter Valley on the scenic inland route from Sydney, which involves leaving the freeway at Calga and heading north via Mangrove and Bucketty. The **Wollombi Tavern**, known for its peculiar Dr Jurd's Jungle Juice (a free taste is offered), makes a fine refreshment stop – sitting out on the wooden verandah looking over the creek to trees, fields and hills. There are **Aboriginal rock carvings** and cave paintings throughout the area, some of which can be visited on horseback with the Wollombi Horse Riding Centre (1hr 30min–2hr; $30; ☎02/4998 3221), 4km past the *Wollombi Tavern* on the Singleton Road; there is also fully equipped barnstay accommodation (❸) and riverside camping at the horse-riding centre. The **New Gokula Farm**, halfway between Cessnock and Wollombi on the Wollombi Road (☎02/4998 1800), is a Hare Krishna community that puts on a free vegetarian feast at 12.30pm on Sunday; call in advance about staying in their guesthouse (BYO linen and bedding; by donation) – a very peaceful spot flanked by bush-covered hills.

The Blue Mountains region

he section of the Great Dividing Range nearest Sydney gets its name from the blue mist that rises from millions of eucalyptus trees and hangs in the mountain air, tinting the sky and the range alike. In the early days of the colony, the **Blue Mountains** were believed to be an insur-mountable barrier to the west. The first expeditions followed the streams in the valleys until they were defeated by cliff faces rising vertically above them. Only in 1813, when the explorers Wentworth, Blaxland and Lawson followed the

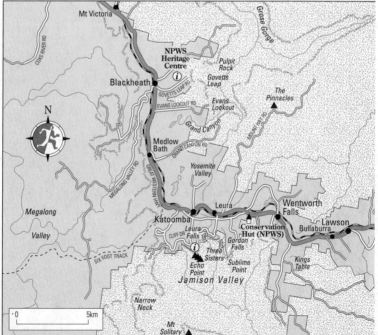

ridges instead of the valleys, were the mountains finally conquered, allowing the western plains to be opened up for settlement. The range is surmounted by a plateau at an altitude of more than 1000m where, over millions of years, rivers have carved deep valleys into the sandstone, and winds and driving rain have helped to deepen the ravines, creating a spectacular scenery of sheer precipices and walled canyons. Before white settlement, the Daruk Aborigines lived here, dressed in animal-skin cloaks to ward off the cold. An early coal-mining industry, based in Katoomba, was followed by tourism which snowballed after the arrival of the railway in 1868; by 1900 the first three mountain stations of Wentworth Falls, Katoomba and Mount Victoria had been established as fashionable resorts, extolling the health-giving benefits of eucalyptus-tinged mountain air. In 2000 the Blue Mountains became a **World Heritage Listed** site, joining the Great Barrier Reef; the listing came after abseiling was finally banned on the mountains' most famous scenic wonder, the **Three Sisters**, after forty years of clambering had caused significant erosion. The Blue Mountains stand out from other Australian forests, in particular for the recently discovered **Wollemi Pine** (see p.301), a "living fossil" which dates back to the dinosaur era.

All the villages and towns of the romantically dubbed "**City of the Blue Mountains**" – Glenbrook, Springwood, Wentworth Falls, Katoomba and Blackheath – lie on a ridge, connected by the Great Western Highway. Around them is the **Blue Mountains National Park**, the fourth-largest national park in the state and to many minds the best. The region makes a great weekend break from the city, with stunning views and clean air complemented by a wide range of accommodation, cafés and restaurants. But be warned: at weekends,

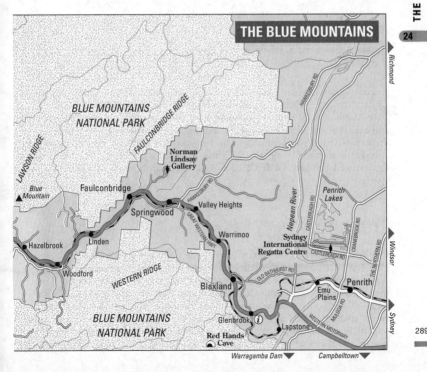

THE BLUE MOUNTAINS

BLUE MOUNTAINS NATIONAL PARK

FAULCONBRIDGE RIDGE

LAWSON RIDGE

Norman Lindsay Gallery

Blue Mountain

Faulconbridge

Valley Heights

Springwood

Warrimoo

Hazelbrook

Linden

Woodford

WESTERN RIDGE

Blaxland

BLUE MOUNTAINS NATIONAL PARK

Glenbrook

Red Hands Cave

Lapstone

HAWKESBURY RD

GREAT WESTERN HWY

Nepean River

CASTLEREAGH RD

CRANEBROOK RD

Penrith Lakes

Sydney International Regatta Centre

CASTLEREAGH RD

OLD BATHURST RD

THE NORTHERN RD

Emu Plains

Penrith

MULGOA RD

WESTERN MOTORWAY

Richmond

Windsor

Sydney

Warragamba Dam

Campbelltown

Blue Mountains tours

From Katoomba

Trolley Tours (☎1800 801 577, ⓦwww.trolleytours.com.au) is a minibus decked out like a tram that takes the scenic route from Katoomba to Leura around Cliff Drive, and continues to the Three Sisters and the Skyway cable car (8 daily, roughly 9.30am–4.15pm to coordinate with Katoomba train arrival times; $12 all-day pass includes travel on the ordinary Mountainlink bus service, p.291). The Trolley Tour and Mountainlink buses leave from the bus stands outside the *Carrington Hotel* on Katoomba Street, just near the train station.

Fantastic Aussie Tours, 283 Main St, Katoomba, by the train station (☎02/4782 1866 or 1300 300 915, ⓦwww.fantastic-aussie-tours.com.au), operate the Blue Mountains Explorer Bus which links Katoomba and Leura with all attractions, including the Edge Maxvision Cinema, Three Sisters, the Skyway, Wentworth Falls, Narrow Neck and other lookouts over thirty stops, in a red double-decker bus (departs Katoomba half-hourly 9.30am–4.30pm, last return 5.15pm; $25 all-day pass). Although the Explorer Bus is pricier, it is more frequent, has a wider route with more stops, and comes with a 32-page guidebook which gives substantial discounts on entry fees to other attractions. Fantastic Aussie Tours also do large-group coach tours: there's a day-tour to the Jenolan Caves (daily from $75) and a combined bushwalk and cave visit ($105), plus adventure caving ($130). A small-group half-day 4WD tour takes in the Blue Mountains National Park ($92); all prices include entry fees. Also see p.308 for details of Fantastic Aussie Tours' three-day guided Six Foot Track walks and its daily transfer service to the start of the walk.

Tread Lightly Eco Tours (☎02/4788 1229 ⓦwww.treadlightly.com.au) offer recommended small-group expert-guided off-the-beaten-track half-day and full-day bushwalk and 4WD tours from Katoomba; the popular two-hour morning Wilderness Walk ($25) takes in some of the Six Foot Track.

From Sydney

Several operators run day-tours from Sydney; we've listed a range of recom-

and during the summer holidays, Katoomba is thronged with escapees from the city, and prices escalate accordingly. Even at their most crowded, though, the Blue Mountains always offer somewhere where you can find peace and quiet, and even solitude – the deep gorges and high rocks make much of the terrain inaccessible except to bushwalkers and mountaineers. Climbing schools offer courses in rock-climbing, abseiling and canyoning for both beginners and experienced climbers, while Glenbrook is a popular mountain-biking spot.

Transport

Public transport to the mountains is quite good but your own vehicle will give you much greater flexibility once you've arrived, allowing you to take detours to old mansions, cottage gardens and the lookout points scattered along the ridge. **Trains** leave from Central Station to Mount Victoria and follow the highway, stopping at all the major towns en route (frequent departures until about midnight; 2hr; $11.40 one-way to Katoomba, $13.60 off-peak day return). If you're dependent on public transport, Katoomba makes the best base: facilities and services are concentrated here, and there are **local buses** to mended outfits below. Some operators also package up accommodation and activity deals.

Blue Mountains Canyon Tours (℡ & ℻02/9371 5859, ⓦwww.canyontours.com.au) explore the Blue Mountains' deep canyons, combining a thrilling mix of abseiling down waterfalls, swimming through cave slots, bushwalking and rock-climbing. Wet canyoning is offered October to April, dry canyoning is available all year. Depending on the area or the number of abseils, trips range from $150 to $210. The most popular wet-canyoning trip is to Fortress Creek (grade 2; $150), near Leura, picking up from Sydney at 7am and returning 7pm.

Oz Trek (℡02/9666 4662, ⓦwww.oztrek.com.au) are a recommended outfit with active full-day tours to the Blue Mountains ($54), with a choice of three bushwalks (30min–1hr 30min) in small groups (max 21). The trip can be extended to overnight packages with either horse riding ($209), abseiling ($209), or a Jenolan Caves visit ($179–199). Coogee, Bondi, Kings Cross, Central and Glebe pick-ups.

Wildframe Ecotours (℡02/9314 0658, ⓦwww.wildframe.com) provide two full-day tours to the Blue Mountains. The Grand Canyon Ecotour ($76) is for fit walkers, as it includes a small-group bushwalk (max 16) through the Grand Canyon (5km; 3hr); BYO lunch in Katoomba. The Blue Mountains Bush Tour ($86) is more relaxed with short bushwalks and lunch at a mountain lodge. Kangaroo spotting and boomerang-throwing practice promised on both trips. Kings Cross and city pick-ups.

WonderBus (℡02/9555 9800 or 1800 669 800, ⓦwww.wonderbus.com.au) have three good-value day-tours to the Blue Mountains. The Eco Tour includes wildlife-watching and a two- to three-hour bushwalk ($70), while the Discovery Tour includes Featherdale Wildlife Park and lunch ($95). The unique Walkabout Aboriginal Tour is an all-day off-the-beaten-track bush roam (around 10km) between Faulconbridge and Springwood led by an Aboriginal guide; expect to look at Aboriginal rock carvings, swim in waterholes in summer, and eat a bushtucker lunch ($95; own train journey to Faulconbridge and ex-Springwood).

attractions in the vicinity and to other centres. Mountainlink (℡02/4782 3333) have five commuter routes from Katoomba: to Medlow Bath, Blackheath and Mount Victoria; to Echo Point; to Leura and Gordon Falls; to North Katoomba; and to the Katoomba Aquatic Centre, the scenic railway, Leura, Wentworth Falls, Bullaburra, Lawson, Hazelbrook and Woodford. Buses run daily between about 7am and 6pm, roughly half-hourly. It costs $2.20, for example, to get to Echo Point, while an all-day bus pass, valid on all routes, including the Trolley Tour minibus detailed on p.290, costs $12. All buses leave town from Katoomba Street outside the *Carrington Hotel*.

Information and accommodation

The **Blue Mountains Information Centre** (Mon–Fri 9am–5pm, Sat & Sun 8.30am–4.30pm; ℡1300 653 408, ⓦwww.bluemts.com.au) is on the Great Western Highway at Glenbrook (see p.296), the gateway to the Blue Mountains. The centre has a huge amount of information on the area, including a couple of useful free publications: the *Blue Mountains Wonderland Visitors Guide*, which has several detailed colour maps, and *This Month in the Blue Mountains*. The other

△ Rock-climbing

official tourist information centre is at **Echo Point**, near Katoomba (see p.301); both offices have vacancy listings and can **book accommodation**.

Accommodation rates rise on Friday and Saturday nights, so you might choose to visit on weekdays when it's quieter and cheaper. Apart from the caravan parks and rental agency mentioned here, we have listed accommodation in the relevant town accounts; prices given are for a double room available in high season and the price range indicates midweek to weekend rates. **Katoomba** (see p.298) is the obvious choice if arriving by train, particularly for those on a budget since it has several **hostels** to choose from, but if you have your own transport you can indulge in some of the more unusual and characterful guesthouses in **Blackheath** (see p.304) and **Mount Victoria** (see p.305), and there's five-star luxury at Leura (see p.298). Blue Mountains Budget Accommodation Group (☏02/4782 2652, ⓦwww.pnc.com.au/~ivanhoe) offer a range of good-value self-catering holiday homes and cabins in Katoomba and Blackheath. There are also lots of pricier bush-set cabins and retreat-style places to stay on Evans Lookout Road just beyond Blackheath, backing onto the national park including *Jemby-Rinjah* (see p.304).

Blue Mountains directory

Bookshops There are several interesting secondhand bookshops on Katoomba Street, Katoomba, and in Blackheath (see p.304) and Mount Victoria (p.305). New books can be bought at the very literary Megalong Books, 183 The Mall, Leura ☏02/4784 1302.

Bus services Mountainlink ☏02/4782 4213.

Camping equipment If you haven't got your own gear, you must rent it in Sydney before you come up (see Sydney "Directory", p.265). Alternatively, Paddy Pallin, 166 Katoomba St (☏02/4782 4466), sells camping gear and a good range of topographic maps and bushwalking guides, as does Katoomba Adventure Centre (see p.294), or for cheap gear go to K-Mart (next door to Coles supermarket, see below).

Car rental Thrifty, 19 Edward St, Katoomba ☏02/4782 9488.

Hospital Blue Mountains District Anzac Memorial, Katoomba ☏02/4782 2111.

Internet access *Barcode 6ix*, 6 Katoomba St, Katoomba, opposite the station, has 12 terminals ($2.50 15min, $5.50 1hr); it's also a cheap Thai eat.

Laundry The Washing Well, K-Mart car park, Katoomba. Daily 7am–7pm.

Pharmacies, late-night Blooms Springwood Pharmacy, 161 Macquarie Rd, Springwood ☏02/4751 2963; Mon–Fri 8.30am–9pm, Sat 8.30am–7pm, Sun 9am–7pm. Greenwell & Thomas, 145 Katoomba St, Katoomba ☏02/4782 1066; Mon–Fri 8.30am–7pm, Sat & Sun 8.30am–6pm. Deliveries available from both Mon–Fri.

Post office Katoomba Post Office, Pioneer Place opposite Coles supermarket, off Katoomba St, Katoomba, NSW 2780.

Supermarket Coles, Pioneer Place off Katoomba St, Katoomba (daily 6am–midnight).

Taxis Taxis wait outside the main Blue Mountains train stations to meet arrivals; otherwise call Katoomba Radio Cabs ☏02/4782 1311, or Blue Mountains Taxi Cab ☏02/4759 3000.

Trains Katoomba Station general enquiries ☏02/4782 1902. Transport Infoline ☏13 15 00.

Travel Agents Backpackers Travel Centre, 283 Main St, Katoomba ☏02/4782 5342, ⓦwww.backpackerstravel.net.au. Bookings for domestic buses, trains, flights and tours.

To get even closer to nature, you can **camp** in the bush at several NPWS sites. The **NPWS** has ranger stations at Wentworth Falls (see p.297) and Blackheath (see p.304) where you can get comprehensive walking and camping information. There are NPWS camping and picnic sites reached by car near Glenbrook, Woodford, Wentworth Falls, Blackheath and Oberon, and backpack camping is allowed in most areas; contact the NPWS for details. The only point where vehicle entry must be paid is at Glenbrook ($6).

Or for more comfort, there are two **caravan parks**: *Katoomba Falls Caravan Park*, at Katoomba Falls Rd (T & F 02/4782 1835; en-suite cabins ❹) and *Blackheath Caravan Park* at Prince Edward St (T 02/4787 8101; en-suite cabins ❸, cabins ❷) by a big park and swimming pool. You can also camp in the grounds of *Blue Mountains Backpackers* (p.300).

Mountain activities

There's heaps to do in the mountains, from bushwalking to canyoning, meditation and yoga.

Adventure activities

The **Australian School of Mountaineering** at Paddy Pallin, 166 Katoomba St (T 02/4782 2014, W www.asmguides.com or www.canyons.com.au) is Katoomba's original abseiling outfit, offering daily day-long courses ($119 including lunch), plus canyoning (daily Oct–May; lunch included $135), rock-climbing and bush-survival courses. Canyoning is the big thing with **Katoomba Adventure Centre**, 1 Katoomba St, opposite the station (T 02/4782 4009 or 1800 824 009, W www.kacadventures.com), with beginners' full-day canyoning and abseiling trips in the Grand Canyon or Empress Canyon ($139, includes lunch), rock-climbing and mountain-biking and serious off-track adventure walks and camping trips. **High 'n' Wild Mountain Adventures**, 3/5 Katoomba St (T 02/4782 6224, W www.high-n-wild.com.au), has a consistently good reputation for its beginners' courses in abseiling (full day $119 including lunch, half-day $75), canyoning (full day $139, half-day $85) and rock-climbing (2 days; $259) and half-day mountain biking ($99). If the weather is bad, you can train at **Blackheath Climb Centre**, Shed 4, 134 Station St, Blackheath (Mon & Tues 4–8pm, Wed–Fri 1–8pm, Sat & Sun 1–6pm; $10; T 02/4787 5771).

Bike rental

Cycle Tech, 182 Katoomba St, Katoomba (T 02/4782 2800), has mountain bikes from $27.50 half-day, $49.50 full day.

Cinemas

The **Edge Maxvision Cinema** shows *The Edge – The Movie* (see p.301), as well as new-release feature films on a giant screen ($11.50; cheap tickets $8.50 all day Tues). **Mount Vic Flicks**, Harley Ave, off Station St, Mount Victoria (T 02/4787 1577), is a quaint local cinema in an old hall showing a fine programme of prestige new releases and independent films (Thurs–Sun, daily during school holidays; cheap tickets Thurs). **Glenbrook Cinema**, cnr Ross Street and Great Western Highway, is a quality, family-run cinema with cheap tickets for all sessions (T 02/4739 4433, W www.glenbrookcinema.com.au).

Festivals

The **Blue Mountains Music Festival** (W www.bmff.org.au) is a three-day mid-March bash featuring folk, roots and blues from Australian and international musicians on

The foothills: Penrith

At the foot of the Blue Mountains in a curve of the Nepean River, **PEN-RITH** is the most westerly of Sydney's satellite towns. Penrith has an old-fashioned Aussie feel about it – a tight community that is immensely proud of the Panthers, its boisterous rugby league team and the huge Panthers Leagues Club, on Mulgoa Road (T02/4720 5555), is the town's eating, drinking, entertainment – and gambling – hub (visitors are welcome).

From Penrith Station, you can't miss the huge lettering announcing the **Museum of Fire** on Castlereagh Road in a former power station (daily 10am–3pm, closed last fortnight Dec; $7; Wwww.museumoffire.com.au), which focuses on one of Australia's greatest and recently most widespread perils, with a serious message about fire safety. The museum has an extensive

several indoor and outdoor stages; it includes food and craft stalls and kids' entertainment. A ticket for the whole weekend costs $110 or $75 for a day ticket. **Winter Magic** is a day-long, pagan-feeling fancy dress celebration of the Southern Hemisphere winter soltice in mid-June. Katoomba Street is closed to traffic and lined with market and food stalls and half the public is dressed up in witchy-looking fantasy gear – kids especially. There are music stages dotted around town, a morning street parade complete with African-style drumming, and another parade as darkness falls, followed by a fireworks' display; check at the tourist office for details.

Horse riding
Blue Mountains Horse Riding Adventures (T02/4787 8688, Wwww.megalong.cc) have a variety of escorted trail rides in the Megalong Valley and along the Coxs River, from a beginners' one-hour Wilderness Ride ($35) to an experienced riders' all-day adventure ride, helping to drive cattle along the river ($165). Pick-ups from Blackheath. **Werriberri Trail Rides** (T02/4787 9171) offers horse riding for all abilities and pony rides for children in the Megalong Valley. Their two-hour ride, including pick-up from Katoomba, costs $55.

Massage
Crystal Lodge, 19 Abbotsford Rd, Katoomba (T02/4782 5122, Wwww.crystallodge .com.au), offers a wide range of holistic therapies, including aromatherapy massage (1hr 30min; $80), therapeutic massage (1hr; $60) and foot reflexology (1hr; $60).

Meditation
Australian Buddhist Vihara, 43 Cliff Drive, Katoomba (T02/4782 2704), host free meditation sessions Sunday 8–11am and one-hour sessions daily 8am & 6pm.

Swimming
Aquatic Centre, Gates Ave, Katoomba (Mon–Fri 6am–8pm, Sat & Sun 8am–8pm, winter weekends to 6.30pm; T02/4782 1748), has outdoor, heated Olympic-sized and children's pools, plus an attached complex which is open all year with heated indoor pool, sauna, spa and gym. Entry is $3.80 (plus sauna and spa $7; plus gym $8; plus gym, sauna and spa $11).

Yoga
At the **Blue Mountains Yoga Studio**, 4/118 Main St, Katoomba (T02/4782 6718) you can join in casual yoga classes for beginners to advanced and also yoga retreats.

collection of fire-fighting vehicles (fifty in all) – which kids especially love – and memorabilia, and also a gift shop stocked with fire-fighting souvenirs.

Penrith is also the home of the extensive International Regatta Centre on Penrith Lakes, spreading between Castlereagh and Cranebrook roads north of the town centre, which was used in the Olympics; **Penrith Whitewater Stadium** here was the competition venue for the canoe/kayak-slalom events. You can go on a thrilling, one-hour beginners' **white-water rafting** session, completing five to eight circuits of the 320-metre-long, grade-three course ($60.50, $49.50 May–Sept; bookings ☏02/4730 4333, ⊛www.penrithwhitewater.com.au).

You can take in the splendour of the spectacular **Nepean Gorge** from the decks of the paddle steamer *Nepean Belle* (range of cruises from $13 for 1hr 30min, morning or afternoon tea $5 extra; bookings ☏02/4733 1274) or head 24km south to the **Warragamba Dam**. The dam has created the huge reservoir of **Lake Burragorang**, a popular picnic spot with barbecues and a kiosk, and some easy walking trails through the bush.

Glenbrook to Faulconbridge

Once you're off the busy highway and away from the information centre (see p.291), **GLENBROOK**, 10km on from Penrith, is a pleasant village arranged around the train station, with a great cinema and lots of cafés and adventure shops; the section of the **Blue Mountains National Park** here is popular for **mountain biking** along the **Oaks Fire Trail** (it's best to start the thirty-kilometre trail higher up the mountain in **WOODFORD** and head downhill, ending up at the cafés of Glenbrook; bike rental is only available at Katoomba, see p.300). The park entrance (cars $6) is just over a kilometre from the train station following Burfitt Parade then Bruce Road alongside the railway line as it heads back towards Sydney; about 200m before the entrance you'll cross a railway bridge. There are two bushwalks to two swimmable waterholes, **Blue Pool** and **Jellybean Pool**, not far from the entrance to the park, while several walking trails start from the Causeway, just under a kilometre into the park via a winding hilly road, which isn't too pleasant to walk (there's plenty of parking at the Causeway). One of the best walks is to see the Aboriginal hand stencils on the walls of **Red Hands Cave** (3hr return; medium difficulty). You can also drive or cycle to the cave and on to the grassy creekside Euroka picnic ground (camping available), where there are lots of eastern grey kangaroos.

Eleven kilometres northwest of Glenbrook, **SPRINGWOOD** is home to many of the artists who have settled in the mountains, and there are numerous shops selling antiques and arts and crafts, and it's a good starting point for bushwalks in Sassafras Gully. You can turn off here onto Hawkesbury Road to take a scenic drive down to Richmond (see p.275). Further west is **FAULCONBRIDGE**, where it's well worth visiting the exhibition of paintings and drawings at the **Norman Lindsay Gallery**, a National Trust property set amongst extensive gardens at 14 Norman Lindsay Crescent (daily 10am–4pm; $8). The controversial artist and poet (1879–1969), whose nude studies scandalized Australia in the 1930s and whose story was told in the 1994 film *Sirens* (with Elle McPherson as one of the life models), spent the last part of his life here. He is also famous for his humorous children's tale, *The Magic Pudding*, made into a film in 2001; some of the streets around the gallery, such as Bill Barnacle Avenue, are named after its characters.

Wentworth Falls

The small village of **WENTWORTH FALLS**, 18km further along the Great
Western Highway from Faulconbridge, was named after William Wentworth,
one of the famous trio who conquered the mountains in 1813. A signposted
road leads from the highway to the **Wentworth Falls Reserve**, with superb
views of the waterfall tumbling down into the Jamison Valley. You can reach this
picnic area from Wentworth train station by following **Darwin's Walk** – the
route followed by the famous naturalist in 1836. Of the view, which has
changed little, Charles Darwin wrote, "If we imagine a winding harbour, with
its deep water surrounded by bold cliff-like shores, laid dry, and a forest sprung
up on its sandy bottom, we should then have the appearance and structure here
exhibited. This kind of view was to me quite novel, and extremely magnificent."
   Most of the other bushwalks in the area start from the NPWS **Valley of the
Waters Conservation Hut** (daily 9am–5pm; ☏02/4757 3827), about 3km
from the station at the end of Fletcher Street. Neither tour bus service drops
off here, and Mountain Link bus services (☏02/4782 3333 for times; see p.291)
are infrequent; you could take a taxi from the rank outside the train station
rather than walking. The hut is in a fantastic location overlooking the Jamison
Valley, and from its wonderful *Conservation Hut Cafe* you can take full advantage of the stupendous views through the big windows or from the deck outside; in winter an open fire crackles in the grate. A wide selection of bushwalks,
detailed on boards outside, ranges from the two-hour **Valley of the Waters
track**, which descends into the valley, to an extended two-day walk to **Mount
Solitary**. One of the most rewarding is the quite strenuous, six-kilometre
National Pass, a one-way walk which will conveniently get you back to the
train station and takes in Wentworth Falls en route.
   A great place to **eat** in Wentworth Falls is the relaxed BYO café *Il Postino*, at
13 Station St, opposite the train station (daily 8.30am–6pm; plus dinner Fri &
Sat bookings essential ☏02/4757 1615). Housed in the original old post office,
the cracked walls have become part of an artfully distressed, light and airy interior. There are outside tables on a street-facing courtyard and the menu is
Mediterranean- and Thai-slanted – Turkish bread melts, pasta, Thai fish cakes,
salads and gourmet burgers – with plenty for vegetarians; nothing costs over
$14. They also offer an excellent all-day breakfast featuring lots of different
kinds of pancakes. *Conditorei Patisserie Schwarz*, Renae Arcade, 30 Station St
(Mon & Wed–Sun 7.30am–5.30pm), does scrumptious German-style pastries
to eat in or take away, which are ideal to replenish your energies after a bushwalk. It has an old-fashioned, cosy coffee-house atmosphere and is popular
with older locals and visitors.

Leura

Just two kilometres east of Katoomba (see p.298), the more upmarket
LEURA, packed with great cafés, art galleries and small boutiques, retains its
own distinct identity and a real village atmosphere. It helps that the main street
– The Mall – is quite secluded from the highway and its green median strip
practically qualifies as a small park. Even the flower-filled station manages to
look pretty, and indeed Leura is renowned for its beautiful **gardens**, some of

24

which are open to the public during the **Leura Gardens Festival** (early to mid-Oct; $12 for visits to around 8 gardens, or $3 per garden; more details from the tourist office).

One garden that opens all year round is the beautiful National Trust-listed **Everglades Gardens** (daily 9am–sunset; $6), situated in the grounds of an elegant mansion at 37 Everglades Ave. There are enjoyable views from its formal terraces, with a colourful display of azaleas and rhododendrons, an aboretum, and peacocks strutting among it all.

Not far from the village, the flowers give way to the bush: less tame scenery, such as **Leura Cascades**, can be viewed from the picnic area on Cliff Drive; to see it at closer quarters, take the two- to three-hour walk to the base and back. Other waterfalls in the area include the much-photographed **Bridal Veil Falls**, accessible from the Cascades picnic area, and **Gordon Falls**, which you can walk to from Lone Pine Avenue. To the east of Gordon Falls, Sublime Point Road leads to the aptly named **Sublime Point** lookout, with panoramic views of the Jamison Valley. A popular walking track from Leura Falls is the Federal Pass, which skirts the cliffs between here and **Katoomba Falls** (6km one-way; 2hr 30min).

You can **stay** near the village at the impressive *Peppers Fairmont Resort*, 1 Sublime Point Rd, 2km southeast of Leura (T02/4782 5222, Wwww.peppers .com.au; ◉), a huge four-and-a-half-star resort (over 200 rooms) in peaceful grounds with fantastic recreational facilities. There's a large indoor pool and spa, but a wintry swim in the heated outdoor pool and a dip in the steaming spa is quite magical. There's also a gym, and squash and tennis courts.

There are a number of options in Leura if you're looking for something to **eat**. *Cafe Bon Ton*, 192 The Mall (Mon–Fri 11.30am–5pm, Sat & Sun 8am–5pm, plus dinner nightly except Tues), an upmarket, BYO corner café with an extensive and inviting garden terrace out front, shaded by some impressive old trees, makes a very pleasant spot for good coffee, fresh cakes or lunch or weekend breakfast on a fine day. Food ranges from filled baguettes through pasta and salads to interesting modern Australian main meals (average $17). *Landseers*, 178 The Mall (daily 7.30am–5pm), is a tiny café with a very striking, cosily dark interior – or you can sit outside in the courtyard. Substantial sandwiches, soups and lasagne are available, plus delicious home-made cakes and puddings. A big range of food at reasonable prices makes *The Mountain Deli*, 134 The Mall (Mon–Fri & Sun 9am–6pm, Sat 8am–6pm), a popular choice with the locals. It serves good-value sandwiches, delicious home-baked cakes, and has friendly staff.

Katoomba and around

KATOOMBA, the biggest town in the Blue Mountains and the area's commercial heart, is also the best located for the major sights of Echo Point and the Three Sisters. It has a lively café culture on the main drag, **Katoomba Street**, which runs downhill from the train station; the street is also full of vintage and retro clothes, secondhand bookstores, antique dealers and gift shops. When the town was first discovered by fashionable city dwellers in the late nineteenth century, the grandiose **Carrington Hotel**, prominently located at the top of Katoomba Street, was the height of elegance, with its lead lighting and wood panelling (an in-house historian gives 1hr tours of the hotel; $7.50 on demand). It's recently been returned to its former glory, with elegant sloping

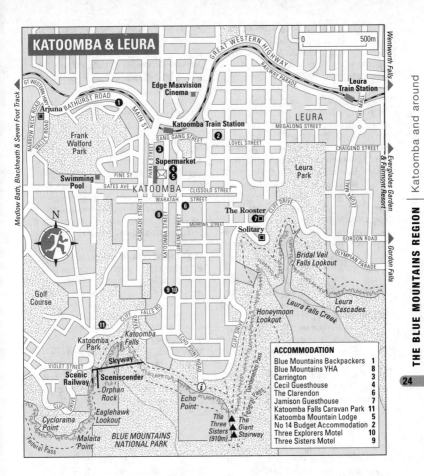

KATOOMBA & LEURA

0   500m

GREAT WESTERN HIGHWAY

RAILWAY PARADE

Edge Maxvision Cinema

Leura Train Station

THE MALL

Katoomba Train Station **❷**

LEURA

MEGALONG STREET

❶ GT WESTERN HWY

NARROW NECK ROAD

VALLEY ROAD

BATHURST ROAD

Arjuna ■

MAIN ST

Frank Walford Park

LOVEL STREET

CRAIGEND STREET

GANG GANG STREET

PARKE STREET

❸

Supermarket

❹
❺

Leura Park

Swimming Pool

PINE ST

GATES AVE

K A T O O M B A

CLISSOLD STREET

LEURA MALL

WARATAH   STREET

N

CASCADE STREET

KATOOMBA STREET

LURLINE STREET

❽   **❻**

The Rooster **❼**■

MERRIWA STREET

Solitary ■

CLIFF DRIVE

GORDON ROAD

OLYMPIAN PARADE

TURING

Bridal Veil Falls Lookout

Leura Falls Creek

Leura Cascades

❾❿

Golf Course

CLIFF FALLS RD

ECHO POINT ROAD

CLIFF DRIVE

Honeymoon Lookout

Dardanelles Pass

⓫

Katoomba Park

Katoomba Falls

VIOLET STREET

Skyway

Scenic Railway

Sceniscender

Orphan Rock

CLIFF DRIVE

Eaglehawk Lookout

Cyclorama Point

Malaita Point

Federal Pass

Federal Pass

Echo Point

ℹ

The Three Sisters (910m)

The Giant Stairway

BLUE MOUNTAINS NATIONAL PARK

ACCOMMODATION

Blue Mountains Backpackers	**1**
Blue Mountains YHA	**8**
Carrington	**3**
Cecil Guesthouse	**4**
The Clarendon	**6**
Jamison Guesthouse	**7**
Katoomba Falls Caravan Park	**11**
Katoomba Mountain Lodge	**5**
No 14 Budget Accommodation	**2**
Three Explorers Motel	**10**
Three Sisters Motel	**9**

lawns running down to the new **town square** which was finished in early 2003; the old high-school site next door is set to include a cultural centre as well as an upmarket shopping centre. Katoomba also boomed during the era of **Art Deco** and lots of cafés and restaurants feature the style, notably the **Paragon Cafe** at 65 Katoomba St (see p.303).

Accommodation

Katoomba has the greatest concentration of accommodation in the mountains, and a wide range, from grand hotels to characterful guesthouses and a stash of backpackers' hostels.

Hotels and guesthouses

Carrington Hotel 15–47 Katoomba St
☎ 02/4782 1111, ⓦ www.thecarrington.com.au.
When it opened in 1882, the *Carrington*

was one of the region's finest hotels and it has been fully restored. Original features include stained-glass windows and open fireplaces, a splendid dining room and ball-room, cocktail bar, a snooker and games room, library and guest lounges. The spacious rooms are beautifully decorated in rich Heritage colours. Budget rooms – sharing bathrooms – are very good value as they are just as nicely decorated and come with kettle, phone and TV, plus masses of very private bathrooms (with baths) to use. ❺ , en suite ❻–❽

Cecil Guesthouse 108 Katoomba St ☎02/4782 1411, ⓦwww.ourguest.com.au. Very central choice, peacefully set back from the main drag and surrounded by greenery, and with great views over the town and Jamison Valley from the common areas and some bedrooms (these ones go first). Shabby but charming – an old-fashioned 1940s atmosphere with log fires, games room and tennis courts, plus modern touches such as the spa (and the sometimes surly service). Most rooms share bathrooms. Good single rates. Cooked breakfast included; dinner served if booked in advance. ❺

The Clarendon Cnr Lurline and Waratah streets ☎02/4782 1322, ⓦwww.clarendonguesthouse.com.au. Classic 1920s guesthouse with its own cocktail bar and restaurant, and cabaret weekends. Also swimming pool, sauna, gym, open fires, games room and garden. The guesthouse rooms are best – avoid the fairly unattractive, 1970s-style

Hostels

Blue Mountains Backpackers 190 Bathurst Rd ☎02/4782 4226 or 1800 624 226, ⓦwww.kacadventures.com/bmb. Colourfully painted, very homy and comfortable bungalow near the station, with dorms sleeping six to ten and doubles. Separate TV/video rooms, games to play, a small kitchen, free tea and coffee and lots of info on and lifts to bushwalks. Linen included for doubles and twins only. They also have tent and van sites for $13. Dorms $19, rooms ❷

Blue Mountains YHA 207 Katoomba St ☎02/4782 1416, ⓔbluemountains@yhansw.org.au. Huge 200-bed YHA hostel right in the town centre. The former 1930s guesthouse has been modernized but retains its beautiful leaded windows, Art Deco decor, huge ballroom and an old-fashioned mountain retreat ambience, with an open fire in the reading room, a separate games room

motel rooms. Mostly en suites but budget rooms without bathroom also available. ❹–❻

Jamison Guesthouse 48 Merriwa St, cnr Cliff Drive ☎02/4782 1206. Built as a guesthouse in 1903 and still going strong, this is a seriously charming place in a great spot giving it amazing, unimpeded views across the Jamison Valley. The feel is very much that of a small European hotel, added to by the French restaurant downstairs, *The Rooster*, in a gorgeous dining room full of original fixtures (dinner nightly, lunch Sat & Sun; set-price menus $52/$64) and with big picture windows. Upstairs, a breakfast room gives splendid views – provisions (and an egg cooker) come with the room – and there's a sitting room with a fireplace. All rooms en suite. ❻

Three Explorers Motel 197 Lurline St ☎02/4782 1733, ⓦwww.bluemts.com.au/3explorers. Well-run, three-star place, a cut above the usual charmless motel, on two levels with tastefully decorated units. Spa rooms plus large family suites. Great spot near Echo Point. Minimum two-night stay at weekends. ❻

Three Sisters Motel 348 Katoomba St ☎02/4782 2911, ⓕ4782 6263. Small, old-style red-brick motel units, but clean, well-equipped and run by an amiable couple. Excellent location near Echo Point. ❸

(with pool table), Internet access and a very pleasant courtyard. Most rooms and some of the four-bed dorms are en suite (also eight-share dorms). Mountain-bike rental for guests and abseiling and Jenolan Caves trips and other tours can be booked. A dedicated information room comes complete with topographic maps and the friendly staff on reception are very helpful. Dorms $19–23, rooms ❸

Katoomba Mountain Lodge Church Lane, off 31 Lurline St ☎ & ⓕ02/4782 3933, ⓦwww.bluemts.com.au/kmtlodge. Central budget accommodation with great views over the town from its verandah, TV room and some bedrooms. Four- and six-bed dorms and attractive doubles (all share bathrooms) with window seats. Small kitchen, and large dining room with free tea and coffee. Cheap breakfast and dinner available. Dorms $16–20, rooms ❷

No 14 Budget Accommodation 14 Lovel St ☎02/4782 7104, ⓦwww.bluemts.com.au/No14. This relaxed hostel in a charming restored former guesthouse – polished floors, cosy fire, and original features – is like a home away from home, run by an informative, friendly young couple. Mostly twin and double rooms, some en suite, plus four-share dorms with comfy beds instead of bunks; all centrally heated. Peaceful veran-dah surrounded by pretty plants and valley views. Dorms $20, rooms ❸

The Edge Maxvision Cinema

Across the railway line (use the foot-tunnel under the station), a stunning introduction to the ecology of the Blue Mountains can be explored at the **Edge Maxvision Cinema**, at 225–237 Great Western Highway (☎02/4782 8928, ⓦwww.maxvision.com.au), a huge six-storey cinema screen created as a venue to show *The Edge – The Movie* (daily 10.20am, 11.05am, 12.10pm, 1.30pm, 2.15pm & 5.30pm; $13.50). The highlight of the forty-minute film is the segment about the "dinosaur trees", a stand of thirty-metre-high **Wollemi Pine**, previously known only from fossil material over sixty million years old. The trees – miraculously still existing – survive deep within a sheltered rain-forest gully in the **Wollemi National Park**, north of Katoomba, and made headlines when they were first discovered in 1994 by a group of canyoners. To film the pines, whose exact location is kept secret, it was necessary to work closely with the NPWS; there is an informative NPWS display in the cinema lobby. You can see a Wollemi Pine seedling in the Blue Mountains at the Mount Tomah Botanic Garden (see p.305).

Echo Point

A 25-minute walk south from the train station down Katoomba Street and along Lurline Street and Echo Point Road (or by Mountainlink or tour bus from outside the Savoy Theatre will bring you to **Echo Point**, the location of the **information centre** (daily 9am–5pm; ☎1300 653 408). From here you have breathtaking vistas that take in the Blue Mountains' most famous landmark, the **Three Sisters** (910m). These three gnarled rocky points take their name from an Aboriginal Dreamtime story which relates how the Katoomba people were losing a battle against the rival Nepean people: the Katoomba leader, fearing that his three beautiful daughters would be carried off by the enemy, turned them to stone, but was tragically killed before he could reverse his spell. They have stood here ever since, subjected to the indig-nities of thousands of tourist cameras and kept awake at night by spectacular floodlighting.

The Three Sisters are at the top of the **Giant Stairway**, the beginning of the very steep stairs into the three-hundred-metre-deep **Jamison Valley** below, where there are several walking tracks to places with such intriguing names as **Orphan Rock** and **Ruined Castle**. There's a popular walking route, taking about two hours and graded medium, down the stairway and partway along the **Federal Pass** to the **Landslide**, and then on to the Scenic Railway and Sceniscender (see below), either of which you can take back up to the ridge.

Scenic World

If you want to spare yourself the trek down into the Jamison Valley – or the walk back up – head for the tacky **Scenic World complex** at the end of Violet Street, where you can choose between two equally thrilling modes of transport. The **Scenic Railway** (daily 9am–5pm; every 10min; last train up leaves at 4.50pm; $6 one-way; ⓦ www.scenicworld.com.au), originally built in the 1880s to carry coal, is a funicular that glides down an impossibly steep gorge to the valley floor. Even more vertiginous, but not as nail-biting, is **Sceniscender** (same price and hours), an $8 million high-tech cable car (wheelchair accessible), opened in late 2000. With floor-to-ceiling windows, the views as the car drops 545m are really spectacular. At the base, there's a 330-metre elevated boardwalk through forest to the base of the Scenic Railway via the entrance to the **old coal mine**, where an audiovisual display tells the story of the mine at the time when the funicular railway still hauled coal.

Back up on the ridge, you can get your legs trembling again with **Skyway** (daily 9am–5pm; $10), a rickety-looking cable-car contraption that starts inside the Scenic World complex next to the Scenic Railway and travels 350m across to the other side of the gorge and back again – you can't actually get off – giving those who can bear to look a bird's-eye view of Orphan Rock, Katoomba Falls and the Jamison Valley. The Scenic World complex also features a **Scenic Cinema** which shows a seventeen-minute film, *Rapture in Blue* ($4.40), of the mountain sights, designed to satisfy visitors who have missed the fabulous views on wet and misty days. There are more views at the complex's overpriced cafeteria-style **revolving restaurant** (9am–5pm daily), with a souvenir shop next door.

Medlow Bath

One train stop beyond Katoomba, the quiet village **MEDLOW BATH** is based around the distinctively domed **Hydro Majestic Hotel** (on the Great Western Highway) which was built as an exclusive health resort in 1904 on an escarpment overlooking the **Megalong Valley**. The hotel had a meticulous make-over by the Mercure hotel chain in 2000, and the public areas in particular have been restored to their Edwardian and Art Deco former glory. It's worth a stopoff to gaze at the interiors and the stunning bush views from the balcony beer garden – walk through the Megalong Room to get outside; you can take a drink out there anytime. The Megalong Room has the same view from its windows, but the buffet-style café is overpriced.

Eating and drinking

Cuisine in the Blue Mountains has gone way beyond the ubiquitous "Devonshire teas", with some well-regarded restaurants, and a real **café culture** in Katoomba in particular. A huge amount of cafés line thriving Katoomba Street with several popular new ones at the bottom of the hill.

Cafés and light meals

Blues Café 57 Katoomba St. Bakery and cosy (mostly) vegetarian café – this place has been going for years. Daily 9am–5pm.
Cafe 123 123 Katoomba St. White, bright modern place with a couple of outside tables and a counter with stools indoors, which does simple, inexpensive food that's as fresh and healthy as the decor: really good cleansing juices, organic wheat-grass shots, sandwiches, focaccia and muffins.

Coffee is freshly roasted too and comes from a truly cute espresso machine. Daily 8.30pm–6pm.
Cafe Zuppa 36 Katoomba St ☎ 02/4782 9247. Amiable staff, an Art Deco interior, generous servings and affordable prices for the simple food – from sandwiches to steaks. BYO. Daily 7am–10pm.
Hominy Bakery 185 Katoomba St. *Hominy* bakes divine sourdough to take home, as

well as gorgeous wholefood cakes, plus pies and pizza by the slice. It has no eating area of its own, but the street's picnic tables are just outside.

House of Penang 183 Katoomba St. Popular Chinese and Malaysian fast-food joint with a few eat-in tables. Delicious laksa noodle soups for $6–10 and even cheaper lunch specials. Separate, extensive vegetarian menu. Daily 10am–10pm.

The Paragon Café 65 Katoomba St. Known for its fabulous handmade chocolates and sweets – check out the window and the counter display – and its wonderful National Trust-listed Art Deco interior complete with cocktail bar. They do meals, but you're better off buying chocolate or having a coffee and a gawk. Licensed. Tues–Sun 10am–4pm.

Parakeet Café 195B Katoomba St. Eclectic, colourful café, its walls covered with paintings by mountains' artists is a big favourite with the locals for the simple, inexpensive food, hearty soups and down-to-earth atmosphere. Daily 8am–9pm, later Sat night when there's live music, usually blues.

Restaurants

There's also French provincial cuisine at *Jamison Guesthouse's* restaurant *The Rooster* (see p.300).

Arjuna 16 Valley Rd, just off the Great Western Highway ☎02/4782 4662. Excellent, authentic Indian restaurant. A bit out of the way – think taxi or own car – but positioned for spectacular sunset views, so get there early. Good veggie choices too. BYO. Evenings from 6pm; closed Tues & Wed.

Avalon Restaurant 18 Katoomba St ☎02/4782 5532. Stylish restaurant with the ambience of a quirky café, located in the dress circle of the old Savoy Theatre, with many Art Deco features intact. Beautiful views down the valley too – coming here for lunch should be high on the agenda. Moderately expensive menu, but generous servings and to-die-for desserts. Separate bar, so you can come here just for a drink and soak up the atmosphere. BYO & licensed. Lunch & dinner Wed–Sun.

Cozzi Nostri 189 Katoomba St ☎02/4782 3445. Stylish and congenial little place with lots of fish and a lighter, less meaty menu than most Italian restaurants. Pasta ranges from $14 to $16, and mains are around the $20 mark. Dinner Wed–Sun. BYO.

Siam Cuisine 172 Katoomba St ☎02/4782 5671. Popular, inexpensive Thai restaurant with cheap lunch-time specials. BYO. Tues–Sun 11.30am–2.30pm & 5.30–10pm.

Solitary 90 Cliff Drive, Leura Falls ☎02/4782 1164. Perched on a hairpin bend on the mountains' scenic cliff-hugging road, the views of the Jamison Valley and Mount Solitary from this former Kiosk, now modern Australian restaurant are sublime. Expect beautifully laid tables, eager service, a well-chosen and reasonably priced wine list, jazz soundtrack, and fine food. There's a fireplace in the back room, and picnic tables outside that are popular for the weekend breakfast. Moderate to expensive. Licensed. Lunch Sat & Sun, dinner Tues-Sat.

Treis-ilies Greek Cypriot Taverna Katoomba St ☎02/4782 1217. This open-fronted tile-floored place has a very lively authentic taverna feel and serves all the Greek favourites, plus pizza and pasta (lunch Wed–Sun, dinner nightly). Servings are meagre, food and drinks are overpriced and the wine list is mediocre, but the atmosphere makes this and the related nightclub across the road (see p.304) fun spots to go out.

Bars and nightlife

Carrington Hotel 15–47 Katoomba St ☎02/4782 1111. The *Carrington Hotel* (see also p.299) has a host of bars, in and around the grand old building on Katoomba Street. Within the old hotel, *Champagne Charlies Cocktail Bar* has a decorative glass ceiling dome and chandeliers. You can order an understandably pricey drink and take it into one of the classic Kentia-palm filled lounges or out onto the wonderful front verandah overlooking the lawns. The really splendid *Grand Dining Room* has columns and decorative inlaid ceilings; the high tea buffet here is a treat (3–5pm;

$12.50). Cheaper drinks and a more lively atmosphere are found in the modern annexe next door, the *Carrington Bar* (jazz on Sat nights), and the more down-to-earth public bar, *The Sporters*, has a separate entrance on Main Street opposite the train station; there's a nightclub above, *The Attic* (Fri & Sat 10am–3am; $5).

The Clarendon Cnr Lurline and Waratah streets ☏ 02/4782 1322, ⓦ www.clarendonguesthouse .com.au. The salubrious little cocktail bar of the *Clarendon Guesthouse* (see p.300) hosts live music – often great jazz and folk acts – or cabaret/comedy every Sat night (also often Thurs & Fri nights). You can come for dinner and a show, or show only.

Bar opens at 6pm, food is served from 7pm. There's also a regular Wed night Irish music session. No smoking.

Gearins Hotel 273 Great Western Highway ☏ 02/4782 4395. On the other side of the railway line, this huge hotel is a hive of activity, with several bars where you can play pool and see bands; it stays open very late and is lively, sometimes getting a little rough.

TrisElies Nightclub Katoomba St ☏ 02/4782 4026, ⓦ www.triselies.com.au. Live music – world, blues, rock – and DJs Thurs–Sat (cover charge $5–10) are on offer here; food focus is steaks and shareable meze. Thurs–Sun 7pm–3am.

Blackheath

North of Katoomba, there are more lookout points at **BLACKHEATH** – just as impressive as Echo Point and much less busy. One of the best is **Govetts Leap**, near the NPWS **Blackheath Heritage Centre** (daily 9am–4.30pm; ☏ 02/4787 8877). The centre has good interpretive material on history, flora and fauna, as well as practical information (with plenty on the adjacent Wollemi and Kanangra Boyd parks too). The two-kilometre **Fairfax Heritage Track** from the NPWS Centre is wheelchair- and pram-accessible and takes in the Govetts Leap Lookout with its marvellous panorama of the Grose Valley and Bridal Veil Falls. Although many walks start from the centre, one of the most popular, **The Grand Canyon**, begins from Evans Lookout Road at the south end of town, west of the Great Western Highway. The village of Blackheath itself looks dull from the highway, but **Govetts Leap Road**, and shady, tree-lined Wentworth Street that crosses it, have lots of antique and craft shops – there's excellent browsing among the thirty stalls of the **Victory Theatre Antique Centre**, 17 Govetts Leap Rd (daily 10am–5pm) – and there are also great cafés and restaurants. Southwest of Blackheath, the beautiful **Megalong Valley** is popular for **horse riding** (see "Mountain activities" box, p.295).

Accommodation and eating

Blackheath has some great **accommodation** options. *Glenella*, 56 Govett's Leap Rd (☏ 02/4787 8352, ⓕ 4787 6114; ❺ en suite ❻), is a charming guesthouse in a 1905 homestead with a well-regarded restaurant (dinner Fri & Sat; licensed). Rooms are furnished with antiques and rates vary with size of room. Most are en suite, but there are a few cheaper share-bathroom options. *Jemby-Rinjah Lodge*, 336 Evans Lookout Rd, (☏ 02/4787 7622, ⓦ www.jembyrinjahlodge .com.au; ❻), has distinctive one- and two-bedroom timber cabins (sleeping two to six people with own wood fires) in bushland near the Grose Valley. There's also a large licensed common area whose focal point is the huge circular "fire pit", where a restaurant also operates on Friday and Saturday nights (Fri Italian buffet $29, Sat two-course meal $40). The lodge has good links with National Park rangers, and bushwalks are organized for guests. There is a minimum two-night stay at weekends. *Kanangra Lodge*, 9 Belvedere Ave

(☎02/4787 8715, ⓦwww.kanangralodge.com; ❼) is a spacious, elegant and peaceful B&B with four large en-suite guest rooms decorated in warm, inviting colours. There are open fireplaces in its cosy lounges and all rooms overlook the beautiful garden.

Govetts Leap Road and Wentworth Street have the pick of places to **eat**. *Bakehouse on Wentworth*, 105 Wentworth St, is a cottage-like bakery selling European-style and organic bread and yummy pies and pastries plus excellent coffee. Seating is in the front courtyard. The BYO *Victory Cafe*, 17 Govetts Leap Rd (daily 8.30am–5pm, plus dinner Fri & Sat; ☎02/4787 6777), occupies a very pleasant space in the front of an old Art Deco theatre, now converted into an antiques centre, and also houses a book stall. The menu offers standard café fare with an interesting spin, as well as mains such as Greek-style fish, all-day breakfasts, and plenty for vegetarians. Dinner (bookings essential) goes Asian – Indian, Thai, Indonesian and Malaysian all feature. Diners rave about the sensational, seasonal food and fantastic desserts at *Vulcan's*, 33 Govetts Leap Rd, (lunch & dinner Fri–Sun; bookings essential ☎02/4787 6899; BYO), housed in an early-twentieth-century bakery.

Mount Victoria and around

Secluded and peaceful **MOUNT VICTORIA**, 6km from Blackheath, is the last mountain settlement proper, and the only one with an authentic, unspoilt village feel. There's a great old pub, and a tiny cinema in the public hall (see p.294), where the patron introduces the varied films and defends his choice. Worth a browse are several antique shops and secondhand book stores. Some short **walks** start from the Fairy Bower Picnic area, a ten-minute walk from the Great Western Highway via Mount Piddington Road: get details from any Blue Mountains tourist office, or ask at the *Victoria and Albert Guesthouse* (see p.306).

The Hartley Historic Site

The **Hartley Historic Site** (daily 10am–1pm & 2–4.30pm; ⓦwww.npws .nsw.gov.au) lies at the foot of the scenic Victoria Pass in the small valley of the River Lett, 11km from Mount Victoria on the Great Western Highway. It's also close to the town of Lithgow – 12km northwest on the highway – which can make a good base from which to visit (see p.306). It cannot be reached by public transport.

The site is a well-preserved nineteenth-century village, which began to develop as settlers headed west and forged roads through the mountains. The need for a police centre led to the building of a courthouse here in 1837, and the village of Hartley developed around it until it was bypassed by the Great Western Highway in 1887. It's free to look at the site, and a map is provided in the NPWS information centre and shop (daily 10am–4.30pm) but to enter the buildings – only the courthouse is currently visitable – you have to take a guided tour (10am, 11am, noon, 2pm & 3pm; 30min; $4.40).

Mount Tomah Botanic Garden

Beyond Mount Victoria, drivers can circle back towards Sydney via the scenic **Bells Line of Road**, which heads east through the fruit- and vegetable-growing areas of Bilpin and Kurrajong to Richmond, with growers selling their produce at roadside stalls. On the way you'll pass **Mount Tomah Botanic Garden** (daily: April–Sept 10am–4pm, Oct–March 10am–5pm; $4.40; ☎02/4567 2154 for details of free guided tours; ⓦwww.rbgsyd.gov.au), an outpost of Sydney's Royal Botanic Gardens since 1987. There's a rhododendron garden, a display of conifers and a collection of southern hemisphere cool-climate species. The popular *Garden Restaurant* at the visitors centre (lunch daily; licensed; ☎02/4567 2060) has fantastic north-facing views over the gardens, Wollemi National Park and the orchards of Bilbin. Main courses – contemporary Australian – are a pricey $30 but the views make it worthwhile; book for a balcony table at weekends. Cheaper light lunches (sandwiches, pies) are also available and there's a kiosk. There is no public transport to the gardens. By car, you can continue west along the Bells Line of Road to the Zig Zag Railway at Clarence, just over 35km away (see below).

Mount Victoria accommodation and eating

For somewhere to **stay** in the village try the *Hotel Imperial*, Station St, (☎02/4787 1233, ⓦwww.bluemts.com.au/hotelimperial; B&B ④–⑤, en suite ⑦–⑧), a restored country-style pub with beautiful lead lighting. Good-value, filling and tasty bistro meals can be eaten in the foyer, ballroom, on the verandah or in the garden, and the dining-room restaurant is open on Saturday for dinner. Built in 1914, the traditional *Victoria and Albert Guesthouse*, 19 Station St, (☎02/4787 1241, ⓦwww.ourguest.com.au/victoria.albert.html; ③–④, en suite ⑤–⑥), has lovely original fixtures. Rooms are large though a little run-down and cheaper rooms share bathroom. A cooked breakfast is included, served in the café at the back that overlooks the lovely garden with pool, spa and sauna. There is also a bar and restaurant. The *Bay Tree Tea Shop*, 26 Station St (10am–5pm; closed Mon & Tues outside of school holidays), is a family-run **café** in a cute weatherboard cottage with tables on the front verandah for a sunny day, or cosy ones inside. Excellent scones with jam and cream ($4.50) and good coffee and pots of tea are served.

The Zig Zag Railway

LITHGOW, on the Great Western Highway, 12km northwest of Hartley, is a charming coal-mining town nestled under bush-clad hills, with wide leafy streets and some imposing old buildings. Situated about 13km east of the town on the Bells Line of Road, by the small settlement of Clarence, is the **Zig Zag Railway**. In the 1860s engineers were faced with the problem of how to get the main western railway line from the top of the Blue Mountains down the steep drop to the Lithgow Valley, so they came up with a series of zigzag ramps. These fell into disuse in the early twentieth century, but tracks were relaid by rail enthusiasts in the 1970s. Served by old steam trains, the picturesque line passes through two tunnels and over three viaducts. You can stop at points along the way and rejoin a later train.

The Zig Zag Railway can be reached by ordinary State Rail train on the regular service between Sydney and Lithgow, by requesting the guard in advance to stop at the Zig Zag platform; you then walk across the line to Bottom Point platform at the base of the Lithgow Valley. To catch the Zig Zag Railway from Clarence, which is at the top of the valley, you'll need to have your own transport, or take the Fantastic Aussie Tours (see p.290). Zig Zag trains depart from Clarence daily (11am, 1pm & 3pm; from the Zig Zag platform add 40min to these times; $17; ⓦwww.zigzagrailway.com.au).

There are plenty of **motels** in and around Lithgow – and the helpful **Lithgow Visitor Information Centre**, 1 Cooerwull Rd (daily 9am–5pm; ⓣ02/6353 1859; ⓦwww.tourism.lithgow.com) can advise on accommodation.

The Jenolan Caves and Kanangra Boyd National Park

Kanangra Boyd National Park shares a boundary with the Blue Mountains National Park. Further south than the latter, much of it is inaccessible but you can explore the rugged beauty of **Kanangra Walls**, where the Boyd Plateau falls away to reveal a wilderness area of creeks, deep gorges and rivers below. Reached via the **Jenolan Caves**, three **walks** leave from the car park at Kanangra Walls: a short lookout walk, a waterfall stroll and a longer plateau walk – contact the NPWS in Oberon for details (ⓣ02/6336 1972; $6 car entry). Boyd River and Dingo Dell camping grounds, both off Kanangra Walls Road, have **free bush camping**; (pit toilets; no drinking water at Dingo Dell). You can get to **Oberon**, a timber-milling town and the closest settlement to Kanangra, by Countrylink bus from Mount Victoria (3 weekly).

The Jenolan Caves

The **Jenolan Caves** lie 30km southwest across the mountains from Katoomba on the far edge of the Kanangra Boyd National Park – over 80km by road – and contain New South Wales' most spectacular limestone formations. There are nine "show" caves with prices for a guided tour of each cave ranging from $15 to $27.50 depending on the cave (guided tours various times daily 10am–5pm; 1hr 30min–2hr). If you're coming for just a day, plan to see one or two caves: the best general cave is the Lucas Cave ($15; 1hr 30min), and a more spectacular one is the Temple of Baal ($22; 1hr 30min) while the extensive River Cave, with its tranquil Pool of Reflection, is the longest and priciest ($27.50; 2hr). Buying a ticket for two more caves works out to be a better deal; for example, the Lucas combined with the Temple of Baal is $29.50. The system of caves is surrounded by the **Jenolan Karst Conservation Reserve**, a fauna and flora sanctuary with picnic facilities and walking trails to small waterfalls and lookout points. It and the caves are looked after by The Jenolan Caves Trust (ⓣ02/6359 3311, ⓦwww.jenolancaves.org.au), who also offer **adventure caving** in various other caves (from a $60.50, 3hr tour to a $187.50, 7hr tour). There's no public transport to the caves but you can get here from Katoomba with Fantastic Aussie Tours (see p.290) or many other tours are available from Sydney (see box, pp.290–291).

Six Foot Track

You can actually **walk** from Katoomba to the Jenolan Caves; the 42-kilometre-long **Six Foot Track** through the bush begins at the Explorers Tree next to the Great Western Highway about 2.5km west of Katoomba train station; you'll need to allow two to three days for the walk, and you're advised to carry plenty of water. The track, which finishes near *Jenolan Caves House* (see below), was originally cut as a bridle path in 1884 to provide access to the caves from Katoomba. There are four basic **campsites** along the way, plus well-equipped cabins at Binda Flats, *Jenolan Cottages*, reached by car from Jenolan Caves Road, sleeping six to eight people, with a minimum two-night stay at weekends (❹–❺; BYO linen). Book the cabins through Jenolan Caves Trust (see p.307), who will also supply details and **information** on the walk. Wentworth Falls NPWS information centre (see p.297) can provide more information on camping.

Fantastic Aussie Tours (see p.290) offer good-value three-day, two-night fully catered and supported **guided walks** along the Six Foot Track ($315; departs 9.30am first and third Wed of month; tent camping). If you're going it alone, the same company provides a daily transfer service for bushwalkers to the start of the track and then a return service a few days later from the Jenolan Caves ($47); you can leave your car in their depot. The same service will get you from Katoomba to the Jenolan Caves (2hr 15min; departs Katoomba 10.30am; departs Jenolan Caves 3.45pm), designed as an overnight rather than a day-return service; otherwise the same company offers day-tours from Katoomba, as do several other operators (see "Directory", p.267).

A more unusual way to do the track is to enter the annual **Six Foot Track Marathon**, held in March, Australia's largest off-road marathon (around 600 entrants), which is a fundraiser for the Rural Fire Service (details from ⓦ www.sixfoot.com).

Accommodation

The Jenolan Karst Conservation Reserve (see p.307) has a spacious simple **campsite** (no powered sites), in a rural and secluded spot 1.6km from the caves along the Jenolan River from where you can walk back to the caves. *Jenolan Caves House* (ⓣ 02/6359 3322, ⓦ www.jenolancaves.com), the focus for the area, apart from the caves themselves, is a rather romantic, charming old hotel which found fame as a honeymoon destination in the 1920s and is now part of the *Jenolan Caves Resort*. In the old hotel, which also has a good restaurant, there are recently refurbished en-suite rooms (❼–❽), and cheaper share-bathroom versions (❺–❼). The newer annexe, the *Mountain Lodge*, has motel-style rooms and two- to three-bedroom units without the character (❻–❽); family rooms sleep four to six in the *Gatehouse* (❹–❺; BYO linen), which has shared communal areas, including a kitchen. *Jenolan Cabins*, 42 Edith Road, 4km west of Jenolan Caves on Porcupine Hill (ⓣ 02/6335 6239, ⓦ www.bluemts.com.au /jenolancabins; ❻, min 2-night stay at weekends), are very reasonably priced, well-equipped, modern, two-bedroom timber cabins with wood fires that accommodate six (BYO linen). All have magnificent views over the Blue Mountains National Park, Kanangra Boyd National Park and the Jenolan Caves Reserve.

Royal National Park and beyond

T he Princes Highway and the Illawarra railway hug the edge of the **Royal National Park**, a huge nature reserve right on Sydney's doorstep, for more than 20km. The park is only 32km from the city, but marks Sydney's southern extent, separating it from the gradual suburban sprawl of Wollongong, a working class industrial centre 85km south of Sydney. A stunning **coastal route** heads through the Royal National Park to **Thirroul**, outside Wollongong, where D.H. Lawrence famously wrote most of his novel *Kangaroo*. Eight kilometres south of Wollongong, Australia's largest **Buddhist temple**, **Nan Tien**, rewards a visit.

The Royal National Park

Established in 1879, the **Royal National Park** was the second national park in the world (after Yellowstone in the USA). On the eastern side, from Jibbon Head to Garie Beach, the park falls away abruptly to the ocean, creating a spectacular coastline of steep cliffs broken here and there by creeks cascading into the seas and little coves with fine sandy beaches; the remains of **Aboriginal rock carvings** are the only traces of the original Dharawal people.

Transport, information and accommodation

The railway between Sydney and Wollongong marks the Royal National Park's western border, and from the train the scenery is fantastic – streams, waterfalls,

---

Surfing trips to the park

Waves Surf School offers a different way to get to and see the Royal National Park on their one- or two-day "Learn To Surf" trips (℡ 0414 682 228 or 1800 851 101, ⓦ www.wavessurfschool.com.au). As well as transport, surfing gear and tuition, the one-day trip includes lunch ($65), while the two-day version gets you meals, guided bushwalking and camping or a sleep-on-board bus ($169). There are pick-ups at Bondi, Coogee, Kings Cross and the city centre.

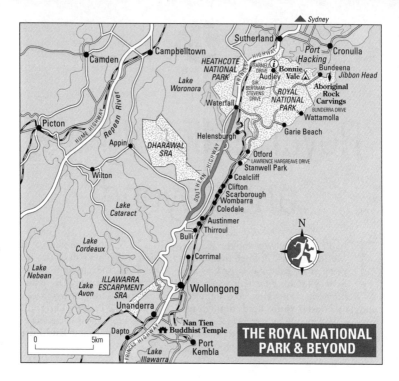

rock formations and rainforest flora fly past the window. If you want to explore more closely, get off at one of the **train stations** along the way: Loftus, Engadine, Heathcote, Waterfall or Otford – all starting points for walking trails into the park. The Sydney Tramway Museum at Loftus (see p.312) provides a Parklink service on an old Sydney **tram** (Sun & public holidays hourly 9.15am–4.15pm; Wed on demand 10.15am–2.15pm; 30min; $3 one-way, $5 return) to the NPWS visitor centre (see opposite).

An interesting way to get to the park is by **ferry** from the southern beachside suburb of Cronulla (see p.144) at the Tonkin Street wharf just below the train station: Cronulla and National Park Ferries take 25 minutes to cross Port Hacking to the small town of **Bundeena** (see opposite) at the park's northeast tip (Mon–Fri hourly 5.30am–6.30pm except 12.30pm but continuous during school hols; Sat & Sun Sept–March 8.30am–6.30pm, April–Oct to 5.30pm; returns from Bundeena hourly: Mon–Fri 6am–7pm, except 1pm; Sat & Sun Sept–March 9am–7pm, April–Oct to 6pm; $3.30. Narrated cruises: Sept–May daily 10.30am; June–Aug Mon, Wed, Fri & Sun 10.30am; 3hr; $15; cruise bookings ☎02/9523 2990, ⓦwww.cronullaandnationalparkferrycruises .com).

Finally, you can **drive** into the park at various points ($10 car entry; gates open 24hr except the Garie Beach gates which close at 8.30pm). Cars are allowed right through the park, exiting at **Waterfall** on the Princes Highway or **Stanwell Park** on Lawrence Hargrave Drive; if you are just driving through the park and not stopping, tell the National Parks officer in the pay-booth and the entry fee will be waived.

Information

The free fold-out *Royal National Park* **brochure** is excellent, and detailed enough to use for bushwalks and camping, but a more comprehensive *Royal National Park Tourist Map* ($6) is also available. A good book to buy is *Discovering Royal National Park on Foot* by Alan Fairley ($10.95). All are available from the **NPWS Visitor Centre** (daily 8.30am–4.30pm; ☎02/9542 0648, ⓦwww.npws.nsw.gov.au), which lies 2km south of Loftus train station, or from the National Parks Centre, 102 George St, The Rocks (☎02/9253 4600).

Accommodation

There's a small, very basic but secluded YHA **youth hostel** inside the park 1km from Garie Beach (book in advance at any YHA hostel; key must be collected in advance; rooms ❶, dorms $11), with no electricity or showers. Just west of Bundeena on the shores of the Hacking River is an NPWS **campsite**, the *Bonnie Vale Camping Ground* (no powered sites), but for more comfort, try *Bundeena Caravan Park*, south of Bundeena's wharf on Scarborough Street (☎02/9523 9520; cabins ❷, en suite ❸). There is also a **bushcamp** at North Era which requires a permit from the visitor centre. This site can get booked out weeks in advance at weekends, so book well ahead; the permit can be posted out to you (which can take up to five days), or you can purchase it before leaving from the National Parks Centre in Sydney (see p.19).

The park

The ultimate trek is the spectacular 26-kilometre **Coastal Walk**, taking in the entire coastal length of the park. Give yourself two days to complete it, beginning at either Bundeena (see below) or Otford, and camping overnight at the officially designated bush camp at North Era (several other campsites were closed at the time of writing). The walk is gruelling, as you have to carry your own water supplies for most of the walk; water is available at Wattamolla and Garie but it must be purified. En route you'll pass **Wattamolla** and **Garie beaches**, both with good surfing waves, and kiosks. An easier but still satisfying option is to hike just part of the route, such as the popular trail from **Otford** down to beachfront **Burning Palms** (2hr one-way; no camping).

In the north of the park, via Farnell Ave, the **Royal National Park Visitor Centre** (daily 8.30am–4.30pm; ☎02/9542 0648) is at **Audley**, a picturesque picnic ground (with kiosk) on the Hacking River, where you can rent a boat or canoe for a leisurely paddle. From the visitor centre an easy wheelchair-accessible one-kilometre track heads to the **Bungoona Lookout**, which boasts panoramic views.

Bundeena

To begin the Coastal Walk (see above) from Bundeena, follow The Avenue and Lambeth Walk for 1km to the national park gate. A shorter option is the pleasant half-day walk to pretty sheltered **Little Marley Beach** for a swim and a picnic (2hr one-way) – or head down a pathway to **Jibbons Beach**, a thirty-minute stroll which will take you past some Dharawal rock engravings, where faint outlines of a kangaroo, stingrays, whales and a six-fingered man can be seen (pick up the *Jibbon Aboriginal Rock Engravings Walk* map and leaflet from the café near the wharf). There are a couple of great cafés and a sheltered little beach immediately by the ferry wharf.

Sydney Tramway Museum

Trams operated in Sydney for a century, until 1961, and examples of the old Sydney fleet, including a Bondi tram, as well as trams from around the world, are on display at the **Sydney Tramway Museum** (Wed 9.30am–3.30pm, Sun 10am–5pm; last entry 1hr before closing; $14 includes Parklink and unlimited tram rides; ⓦwww.sydneytramwaymuseum.com.au), right next to Loftus train station. You can ride a tram on the 3.5-kilometre line which heads via bushland towards Sutherland, or take the two-kilometre Parklink track to the NPWS visitor centre at Audley (see p.311). There's a kiosk and picnic facilities at the museum.

Heathcote National Park

Heathcote National Park, across the Princes Highway from the Royal National Park, is much smaller and quieter. This is a serious bushwalkers' park with no roads and a ban on trail bikes. The best **train** station for the park is Waterfall, from where you can follow a twelve-kilometre trail through the park, before catching a train back from Heathcote. On the way you pass through a variety of vegetation and alongside several swimmable pools – the carved sandstone of the **Kingfisher Pool** is the most picturesque. There is a small, very basic six-site **camping ground** here (no drinking water; $3 per adult), and another one at Mirang Pool. Camping permits are available from the Royal National Park NPWS Visitor Centre (see p.311) or the Rocks NPWS office (see p.47). By **car**, you can reach the picnic area at Woronora Dam on the western edge of the park: turn east off the Princes Highway onto Woronora Road (free entry).

The scenic route south of the national parks

For a scenic excursion south from Sydney, the **coastal drive** from the Royal National Park to **Thirroul**, just outside Wollongong, is stunning. The route runs between rugged sandstone coastal cliffs on one side and bush-covered escarpment on the other, with beautiful beaches and great pubs and cafés en route.

Follow the Princes Highway south out of Sydney, exiting into the Royal National Park after Loftus onto Farnell Drive; the entry fee at the gate is waived if you are just driving through without stopping. The road through the park emerges above the cliffs at **Otford**, beyond which follow **Lawrence Hargreave Drive** (Route 68) to Thirroul. A few kilometres from Otford is the impressive clifftop lookout on Bald Hill above **Stanwell Park**, where you're likely to see the breathtaking sight of **hang-gliders** taking off and soaring down. You can join in with the Sydney Hang Gliding Centre (☎02/4294 4294, ⓦwww.hanggliding.com.au), which offers tandem flights with an instructor for around $180 during the week, $195 at weekends (available daily depending on the weather); the centre also runs courses from $195 per day. At **Clifton**, 5km south of Stanwell Park, the *Imperial Hotel*, sitting right on the

△ The Royal National Park

cliff's edge, is a must for an en-route drink. There's more impressive cliff scenery as you pass through **Scarborough** (best seen from the historic *Scarborough Hotel*), just over 2km south, and nearby **Wombarra**, another kilometre on.

Austinmer

By the time you get to **AUSTINMER**, 4km on from Wombarra, you've come to a break in the stunning cliffs and into some heavy surf territory. The down-to-earth town has a popular, very clean, patrolled surf beach that gets packed out on summer weekends. Across the road from the beach, there's delicious fish and chips at *Ann's Quality Foods* (but expect long weekend waits), or good coffee and more upmarket eats at the big and airy BYO bakery-café, *Cov*, next door.

Thirroul

Just 2km south of Austinmer, **THIRROUL** is the spot where the English novelist D.H. Lawrence wrote *Kangaroo* during his short Australian interlude; the town and the surrounding area are a substantial part of the novel, though he renamed the then-sleepy village Mullumbimby. Today, Thirroul is gradually being swallowed up by the suburban sprawl of Wollongong.

At the southern end of Thirroul's beach, **Sandford Point** (labelled Bulli Point on maps) is a famous surfing break. A sixty-kilometre cycle track runs from Thirroul south along the coast through Wollongong to Lake Illawarra.

Thirroul is busy, with plenty of shops and **cafés**, including the excellent and appropriately literary *Oskar's Wild Bookstore & Coffee Bar* at 289 Lawrence Hargrave Drive. If you want a **place to stay**, *The Beaches Hotel*, 272 Lawrence Hargrave Drive (℡02/4267 2288, ℱ4268 2255, rooms ❷, apartment ❺), is a modern, stylish pub complex that has one good-value and spacious two-bedroom apartment, plus cheaper share-bathroom **rooms**. You can barbecue your own steaks in the popular beer garden or eat in the bistro; weekend bands and pool tables provide entertainment, though the former can make accommodation noisy.

The Illawarra Escarpment

A kilometre south of Thirroul, Lawrence Hargrave Drive joins up with the Princes Highway, which heads south to Wollongong (Route 60) or northwest, up to a section of the forested **Illawarra Escarpment** and the **Bulli Pass**. There are fantastic views from the Bulli Lookout, which has its own café, and a couple of kilometres further north heading back towards Sydney is the appropriately named **Sublime Point Lookout**. You can explore the escarpment using the **walking tracks** which start from the lookouts. Another extensive part of the **Illawarra Escarpment State Recreation Area**, with several walking tracks, is about 10km west of Wollongong's city centre on Mount Kembla and Mount Keira.

The Nan Tien Temple

Eight kilometres south of Wollongong the vast **Nan Tien Temple**, on Berkeley Road in Berkeley, is the largest Buddhist temple in Australia. It's reached by car via the F6 Expressway, turning left at the Five Islands Road exit then following the signs, or by train from Central Station to Unanderra station, followed by a twenty-minute walk.

The Fo Guang Shan Buddhists welcome visitors to the temple (Tues–Sun & public holiday Mon 9am–5pm) and offer a good-value $7 vegetarian lunch, monthly two-day meditation retreats and peaceful and surprisingly upmarket **guesthouse** accommodation (℡02/4272 0600, Ⓦwww.ozemail.com .au/~nantien; ❹). Their weekend-long annual cultural festival in December provides a good antidote to the commercial frenzy of Christmas; check their website for details.

Contexts

Contexts

History

The first European settlers who arrived at Botany Bay in 1788 saw Australia as **terra nullius** – empty land – on the principle that Aborigines didn't "use" the country in an agricultural sense. However, decades of archeological work, the reports of early settlers and oral tradition have established a minimum date of forty thousand years for human occupation, and evidence that Aboriginal peoples shaped and controlled their land as surely as any farmer.

The early history of Sydney is very much that of white Australia, right from its founding as a **penal colony** amid brutality, deprivation and despair. The first **free settlers** began to arrive in 1793 and were able to avail themselves of convict labour, as prisoners worked as bonded domestics and labourers. Despite living under a harsh system of punishment, the convicts' good behaviour was rewarded with the opportunity to become self-employed and own their own land. Indeed, those with total pardons or whose sentences had expired, the "emancipists", eventually became some of the most influential citizens, such as architect Francis Greenway.

The opening up of the western plains to development after a trio of **explorers** successfully traversed the Blue Mountains saw more white settlers arrive, and the long era of transportation to the colony of New South Wales ended in the 1840s. Soon the **goldrushes** of the 1850s brought many more free settlers from all corners of the world, some of them **Chinese**, whose descendents still operate businesses in Haymarket today. However, the notorious **White Australia policy** was developed after a goldrush-induced xenophobia, and it wasn't until the period after World War II, when Australia desperately needed workers and a larger population, that waves of culturally varied migrants began to arrive, transforming Sydney into the cosmopolitan city it is today.

Prehistory and Aboriginal occupation

In the area around Sydney, there were about three thousand Aboriginal inhabitants at the time of colonization, divided into two tribes organized and related according to complex kinship systems, and with two different languages and several dialects: the **Eora**, whom settlers called the "coast tribe", and the **Dharug**, who lived further inland. Common to the two tribes was a belief that land, wildlife and people were an interdependent whole, engendering a sympathy for the natural processes, and maintaining a balance between population and natural resources. Legends about the mythical **Dreamtime**, when creative forces roamed the land, provided **verbal maps** of tribal territory and linked natural features to the actions of these Dreamtime ancestors.

The early records of the colony mainly describe the lifestyle and habits of the **Eora people**, who, because there staple diet was fish and seafood, made temporary camps close to the shore, usually sleeping in the open by fires. Even in the winter they went naked. Shaping canoes from a single piece of bark, they would fish on the harbour using fish-hooks made from shells attached to fishing lines of bark fibre or spear-fish from rocks with multipronged wooden spears spiked with kangaroo teeth. The fish diet was supplemented by the hunting of kangaroo and other game and gathering plants such as yams. Besides story-telling and ceremonial dancing, other cultural expression was through **rock engraving**, usually of outlines of creatures such as kangaroo and fish.

The first Europeans

Although earlier attempts had been made to locate and map the continent by the Dutch, Spanish and French, it was only with the *Endeavour* expedition headed by Captain **James Cook** that a concerted effort was made. Cook had headed to Tahiti (where scientists observed the movements of the planet Venus), then mapped New Zealand's coastline before sailing west in 1770 to search for the Great Southern Land.

The British arrived at **Botany Bay** in April 1770; Cook commented on the Aborigines' initial indifference to seeing the *Endeavour* but when a party of forty sailors attempted to land, two Aborigines attacked them with spears and were driven off by musket fire. The party set up camp for eight days, while botanist **Sir Joseph Banks** studied, collected and recorded specimens of the unique plant and animal life. They continued up the Queensland coast, entered the treacherous passages of the Great Barrier Reef, ran aground and stopped for six weeks to repair the *Endeavour*. When they set off again Cook successfully managed to navigate the rest of the reef, and claimed Australia's eastern seaboard – which he named **New South Wales** – on August 21, 1770.

Founding of the colony of New South Wales

The outcome of the American War of Independence in 1783 saw Britain deprived of anywhere to transport convicted criminals; they were temporarily housed in prison ships or "hulks", moored on the Thames in London, while the government tried to solve the problem. Sir Joseph Banks advocated Botany Bay as an ideal location for a **penal colony** that could soon become self-sufficient. The government agreed and on May 13, 1787 the **First Fleet**, carrying over a thousand people, 736 of them convicts, set sail on eleven ships – two of them navy vessels, the *Sirius* and the *Supply* – under the command of Captain **Arthur Phillip**. Reaching Botany Bay on January 18, 1788, they expected the "fine meadows" that Captain Cook had described. What greeted them was mostly swamp, scrub and sand dunes which Phillip deemed unsuitable for his purposes, moving the fleet north, to the well-wooded **Port Jackson** on **January 26**, a date marked nationwide as Australia Day (see p.250).

Camp was set up on what was named **Sydney Cove** (after Viscount Sydney, then secretary of state in Great Britain) beside the all-important freshwater source, the **Tank Stream**, which now runs under the city streets. Government officials camped on the eastern side of the stream while the marines and convicts were relegated to the west. The **convicts** ranged from a boy of 9 to a woman of 82 and were a multicultural bunch, including English, Scots, black and white Americans, Germans and Norwegians; 188 of them were female. (Convict ships from Ireland began arriving in 1791; ninety percent of those on board were Catholic, many of them were political prisoners and the Irish went on to have an important influence on the city.)

Once Phillip had read the Act of Parliament founding the new colony of New South Wales and was commissioned as **governor**, he gave a speech enjoining the assembled convicts to be industrious, decent and righteous. Directed by the marines, they were used as labour to build the city or became bonded servants, but unless they were found guilty of further crimes, they were not imprisoned or shackled and were free to marry (fourteen convict marriages occurred in the first weeks of settlement alone). Aged mostly between 15 and 25, the convicts had youth on their side. Phillip's method of "the gallows and the lash" and chain-gang justice deterred most from committing more crime, and there was also nowhere really to escape to; the lure of a "ticket of leave", which rewarded good behaviour and meant self-employment and the opportunity to own land, proved a strong incentive to reforming, though not necessarily refining, this former underclass of people.

In the first three years of settlement, the colonists and convicts suffered erratic weather and **starvation**, soil which appeared to be agriculturally worthless, and Aboriginal hostility. The Eora's land had been invaded, half of their numbers wiped out by smallpox, and they were also starving as the settlers shot at their game. When supply ships did arrive, they usually came with hundreds more convicts to further burden the colony.

It was not until 1790, when land was successfully farmed further west at **Parramatta**, that the hunger began to abate. Phillip returned to Britain in 1792 and the first **free settlers** arrived in 1793, while war with France reduced the numbers of convicts being transported to the colony.

The rum corps and Governor Macquarie

After Phillip's departure, the military, known as the **New South Wales Corps** (or more familiarly as the "rum corps"), soon became the supreme political force in the colony. Headed by **John Macarthur**, the 500-strong corps soon manipulated the temporary governor, Major Francis Grose, into serving their interests. Grose gave out land grants and allowed the officers liberal use of convict labour to develop their holdings. Exploiting their access to free land and cheap labour, the corrupt corps' members became rich farmowners and virtually established a currency based on their monopoly, rum. Events culminated in the **Rum Rebellion** of 1808, when merchant and pastoral factions, supported by the military, ousted mutiny-plagued Governor **William Bligh**, formerly of the *Bounty*, who had attempted to restore order. Britain finally took notice of the colony's anarchic state, and resolved matters by appointing the firm-handed Colonel **Lachlan Macquarie**, backed by the 73rd Regiment, as Bligh's replacement in 1810. Macquarie settled the various disputes – Macarthur had already fled to Britain – and brought the colony eleven years of disciplined progress.

Macquarie has been labelled the "Father of Australia" for his vision of a country that could rise above its convict origins; he implemented enlightened policies towards former convicts or **emancipists**, enrolling them in public offices. The most famous of these was **Francis Greenway**, the convicted forger who he appointed civil architect, and with whom Macquarie set about an ambitious programme of public buildings and parks. But he offended those who regarded the colony's prime purpose as a place of punishment.

In 1813, the **explorers** Wentworth, Blaxland and Lawson were the first white men to successfully cross the Blue Mountains, opening up the western plains to agricultural development (the mountains' original Aboriginal inhabitants had been familiar with the area's seemingly insurmountable streams, forested valleys and cliff faces for thousands of years). More white settlers arrived with the opening up of the west, and in 1821 Macquarie's successor Sir Thomas Brisbane was instructed to segregate, not integrate, convicts. To this end, New South Wales officially graduated from being a penal settlement to a new **British colony** in 1823, and convicts were used to colonize newly explored regions – Western Australia, Tasmania and Queensland – as far away from Sydney's free settlers as possible. By the 1840s the transportation of convicts to New South Wales had ended (the last shipment of convicts arrived in Van Dieman's Land in 1853).

The Victorian era

Australia's first **goldrush** occurred in 1851 near Bathurst, west of Sydney. Between 1850 and 1890 Sydney's population jumped from 60,000 to 400,000; terraced houses were jammed together, and with their decorative cast-iron railings and balconies, they remain one of Sydney's most distinctive heritage features. The first railway line, to Granville near Parramatta, was built in 1855. However, until the 1880s tramway system most people preferred living in the city centre within walking distance of work.

During the Victorian era, Sydney's population became even more starkly divided into the haves and the have-nots: self-consciously replicating life in the mother country, the genteel classes took tea on their verandahs and erected grandiloquent monuments such as the Town Hall, the Strand Arcade and the Queen Victoria Building in homage to English architecture of the time. Meanwhile, the poor lived in slums where disease, crime, prostitution and alcoholism were rife. An outbreak of the plague in The Rocks in 1900 made wholesale **slum clearances** unavoidable, and with the demolitions came a change in attitudes. Strict new vice laws meant the end of the bad old days of drunken taverns and rowdy brothels.

Federation, World War I and World War II

With **federation** in 1901, the separate colonies came under one central government and a nation was created. Unhappily for Sydney, Melbourne was the capital of the **Commonwealth of Australia** until Canberra was built in 1927 – exactly halfway between the two rival cities. The **Immigration Act** was the first piece of legislation to be passed by the new parliament, reflecting the nationalist drive behind federation. The act heralded the

White Australia policy – greatly restricting non-European immigration right up until 1958.

With the outbreak of **World War I** in 1914, Australia promised to support Britain to "the last man and the last shilling", and there was a patriotic rush to enlist in the army. This enthusiasm tapered with the slaughter at **Gallipoli** – when 11,000 **Anzacs** (Australian and New Zealand Army Corps) died in the eight-month battle in Turkey – and began the first serious questioning of Anglo-Australian relationships. The aftermath of Gallipoli is considered to be the true birth of Australian national identity.

As the **Great Depression** set in, in 1929, Australia faced collapsing economic and political systems; pressed for a loan, the Bank of England forced a restructuring of the Australian economy. This scenario, of Australia still financially dependent on Britain but clearly regarded as an upstart nation, came to a head as a result of the 1932 controversy over England's "**Bodyline**" bowling technique at an international cricket series at the **Sydney Cricket Ground**. The loan was virtually made conditional on Australian cricket authorities dropping their allegations that British bowlers were deliberately trying to injure Australian batsmen during the tour. In the midst of this troubled scenario, it was a miracle that construction continued on the **Sydney Harbour Bridge**, which opened in 1932.

During **World War II**, Labor Prime Minister **John Curtin**, concerned about Australia's vulnerability after the Japanese attack on Pearl Harbor, made the radical decision of shifting the country's commitment in the war from defending Britain and Europe to fighting off an invasion of Australia from Asia. In February the Japanese unexpectedly bombed Darwin, launched **submarine raids** against Sydney and Newcastle, and invaded New Guinea. Feeling abandoned by Britain, Curtin appealed to the USA, who quickly adopted Australia as a base for coordinating Pacific operations under **General Douglas MacArthur**, who made his headquarters in Sydney at the Grace Building, on York Street (now the *Grace Hotel*).

The postwar generation

Australia came out of World War II realizing that the country was closer to Asia than Europe, and it began to look to the USA and the Pacific, as well as Britain, for direction. **Immigration** was speeded up, fuelled by Australia's recent vulnerability. Under the slogan "Populate or Perish", the government reintroduced assisted passages from Britain – the "ten-pound-poms" – also accepting substantial numbers of European refugees. The new European migrant populations ("New Australian"), a substantial number of Italians, Greeks and Eastern Europeans among them, colonized the inner city, giving it a more cosmopolitan face.

Anglo-Australians took on board postwar prosperity during the conservative **Menzies era** – Robert Menzies remained prime minister from 1949 until 1966 – and headed for the suburbs and the now affordable dream of their own home on a plot of land. Over the next few decades, Sydney settled into comfortable suburban living as the redbrick, fibro and weatherboard bungalows sprawled west and southwards into the new suburbs, while the comfy parochialism of the Menzies years saw Australian writers, artists and intellectuals leave the country in droves.

CONTEXTS | History

Modern Sydney

Immigration continued in waves, with a large influx of people from postwar Vietnam and Southeast Asia aided by Gough Whitlam's tolerant Labor government (before it was famously sacked by the governor general in 1975). Concentrated ethnic enclaves include a vibrant Vietnamese community at Cabramatta, a Filippino focus in Blacktown and an emerging Chinese community in Ashfield, resulting from the thousands of Chinese students whom the prime minister **Bob Hawke** allowed to remain in Australia on humanitarian grounds after the Tian'anmen Square massacre in 1989.

Other developments were more concrete. When the restrictions limiting the height of buildings was lifted in 1957, the development of Sydney's high-rise skyline really took off. Notably tall office blocks include the 183-metre Australia Square Tower (1961–67), and the 244-metre MLC Centre (1975–78) designed by Sydney's most prominent architect, **Harry Seidler**. The Sydney Tower (1981) is – at 259m – the tallest and most recognizable structure in the skyline. But it's the **Sydney Opera House** which can claim to be both the most striking and controversial of Sydney's postwar buildings, originally designed by the Danish architect Jørn Utzon in 1957 and finally opening in 1973.

This building boom saw many Heritage buildings unthinkingly demolished. The New South Wales premier, Robin Askin (1965–74), was keen for many residential areas of the inner city to make way for new office blocks and hotels. People began protesting against developments and a radical union, the Builders' Labourers Federation (BLF) put might behind the dissent. The BLF secretary, Jack Mundey, coined the term **Green Ban**, meaning the withdrawal of union labour for projects opposed by the community and potentially damaging to the environment. In November 1971 a Green Ban was placed on demolition of The Rocks: two-thirds of the city's most historic area would have been redeveloped if the Sydney Cove Redevelopment Authority had had its way. In October 1973, non-union workers poised for demolition were stopped by eighty members of the Rocks Resident Action Group. A compromise in 1975 saw some development but the residential areas were extended and historic buildings restored.

Askin's development schemes were set aside by Labor Premier **Neville Wran** in 1976, but pressure for a bicentennial project saw a fortune spent on the controversial **Darling Harbour redevelopment**, which opened in 1988, a commercial extravaganza of shops, restaurants, a casino and tourist attractions. Environmentalists were particularly opposed to the ugly monorail trundling above the city streets and providing little more than a tourist link.

When Sydney beat Beijing in 1993 for the 2000 Olympics, the city rejoiced. But in January 1994 the world watched stunned as the future Olympic city went up in flames: front-page images of the two icons of Australia, the Opera House and the Harbour Bridge were silhouetted against an orange, smoke-filled sky during the **Black Friday** bush fires, which destroyed 250 homes and cost four lives.

In 1995 a New South Wales Labor government was elected under the leadership of the outspoken ex-journalist **Premier Bob Carr**. Labor were re-elected for a third term in the 2003 state elections, and Carr seems intent on staying in office indefinitely. In preparation for the Olympics, Carr's unenviable task had been to coordinate the city's biggest infrastructure project since the construction of the Sydney Harbour Bridge. More than $2.5 billion of public money was spent on major road and rail projects, including a $630 million rail link from the airport to the city, and a $93 million rail link to Olympic venues at the $470 million Homebush Bay site.

The 2000 Sydney Olympics (see p.254) turned out to be a big success, sending the city's confidence in itself skyrocketing and the city **post-Olympics** is still exuberant. Development continues apace, with ever more freeways and a cross-city tunnel in development. Real-estate prices are at record highs, with a generation now effectively priced out of the market, and more and more luxury apartments overtaking characterful old waterfront wharves. Apartment living has finally come to the Central Business District too, with an injection of residential life and everyday facilities such as supermarkets into an area that used to be quiet at weekends once the workers had cleared out. The gap between rich and poor in Sydney continues to increase and as the upwardly mobile move closer to the centre and remain in the eastern suburbs and the North Shore, the less affluent renters are forced towards the increasingly troubled, poorly serviced western suburbs. Sydney is changing rapidly and in its rush to be declared an "international city", it perhaps risks a substantial part of its unique charm and vigour.

Books

Many of the best books by Australian writers or about Australia are not available overseas, so you may be surprised at the range of local titles available in Australian **bookshops**; we have reviewed several favourite Sydney stores on pp.236–237 and have included websites where available for online sales. A good website to check is ⓦwww.gleebooks.com.au, one of Australia's best literary booksellers, with a whole host of recent reviews; you can order books online, to be posted overseas. Titles marked with ⊡ are especially recommended.

History and politics

Robyn Annear *Nothing But Gold.* With an eye for interestingly obscure details and managing to convey a sense of irony without becoming cynical, this is a wonderfully readable account of the goldrushes of the nineteenth century, a period in Australia's history which perhaps did more than any other to shape the country's national character.

⊡ **John Birmingham** *Leviathan: the Unauthorised Biography of Sydney.* Birmingham's 1999 tome casts a contemporary eye on the dark side of Sydney's history, from nauseating accounts of Rocks' slum life and the 1900 plague outbreak, through the 1970s traumas of Vietnamese boat people, to scandals of police corruption.

Meredith and Verity Burgmann *Green Bans, Red Union.* The full political ins and outs of the Green Bans of the 1970s – when the radical New South Wales Builders' Labourers union, led by Jack Mundey, resisted developers' plans for The Rocks and other areas of Sydney.

Manning Clark *A Short History of Australia.* A condensed version of this leading historian's multivolumed tome, focusing on dreary successions of political administrations over two centuries, and cynically concluding with the "Age of Ruins".

Ann Coombs *Sex and Anarchy: The Life and Death of the Sydney Push.*

The Sydney Push are part of the Sydney legend, a network of anarchists and bohemians who met up at pubs through the conservative 1950s and 1960s, experiencing the sexual revolution a generation before mainstream society and influencing everyone from Germaine Greer to Robert Hughes.

David Day *Claiming A Continent: A New History of Australia.* A good general and easily readable history of the whole country, looking at Australia's history from a contemporary point of view, with the possession, dispossession and ownership of the land – and thus issues of race – central to the narrative.

Michael Duffy, David Foster et al *Crossing the Blue Mountains: Journeys Through Two Centuries.* Eleven personal accounts of crossing the Blue Mountains, including Gregory Blaxland's famous expedition with Wentworth and Lawson in 1813 when they found a route across; Charles Darwin's visit in 1836 as part of his five-year world trip on the *Beagle*; and contemporary novelist David Foster's reflections on wilderness, solitude and eucalyptus as he walks from Mittagong to Katoomba.

Jack Egan *Buried Alive, Sydney 1788–92: Eyewitness accounts of the making of a nation.* A fascinatingly detailed and almost day-by-day view of the first five years of the

Australian writing and writers

Australian writing came into its own in the **1890s**, when a strong nationalistic movement, leading up to eventual federation in 1901, produced writers such as Henry Lawson and the balladeer A.B. "Banjo" Paterson, who romanticized the bush and glorified the mateship ethos. Outstanding women writers, such as Miles Franklin and Barbara Baynton, gave a feminine slant to the bush tale and set the trend for a strong female authorship.

In the **twentieth and twenty-first centuries**, Australian novelists came to be recognized in the international arena: Patrick White was awarded a Nobel Prize in 1973, Peter Carey won the Booker Prize in 1988 and again in 2001, and Kate Grenville scored the 2001 Orange Prize for Fiction. Other writers who have made a name for themselves within Australia, such as David Malouf, Julia Leigh, Tim Winton, Thomas Keneally, Richard Flanagan, Chloe Hooper and Robyn Davidson, have aroused curiosity further afield. Some of the best were recently collected together in the international literary magazine, *Granta*, in *Granta 70: Australia: The New New World*. Literary journals such as *Meanjin*, *Southerly*, *Westerly* and *Heat* provide a forum and exposure for short fiction, essays, reviews and new and established writers. The big prizes in Australian fiction include the **Vogel Prize** for the best unpublished novel written by an author under the age of 35, and the country's most coveted literary prize, the **Miles Franklin Award**.

Many British and multinational **publishers** have setups in Australia, publishing an Australian list of books which are never seen overseas. As booksellers usually have separate Australian fiction and nonfiction sections you can easily zero in on the local stuff. There are also several newer small, independent publishers with an interesting output: anything by Text (@www.textpublishing.com.au), Giramondo (@www .giramondopublishing.com), Duffy & Snellgrove (@www.duffyandsnellgrove.com.au) and Brandl & Schlesinger (@www.brandl.com.au) is worth a look.

For the latest information on the **Australian literary scene**, get hold of a copy of the Australian Book Review (ten issues per year; @home.vicnet.net.au/~abr) or read it at the State Library (see p.65), and grab the "Spectrum" section of the Saturday edition of *The Sydney Morning Herald* or the "Review" section of *The Australian*'s excellent weekend supplement. Gleebooks (see p.237), Ariel (p.236) and Dymocks (p.237) as well as other booksellers hold readings and literary events, but the best chance to see a host of Australian (and international) writers read and talk their work is at the Sydney Writers Festival in May (see p.251). Also check out the Writers' Walk at Circular Quay (p.55).

city's settlement, culled from diaries and letters, and connected by Egan's narrative.

Bruce Elder *Blood on the Wattle: Massacres and Maltreatment of Aboriginal Australians Since 1788*. A heart-rending account of the horrors inflicted on the continent's indigenous peoples, covering infamous nineteenth-century massacres as well as more recent mid-twentieth-century scandals of the Stolen Generation children.

⬛★ **Tim Flannery** (ed) *Watkin Trench 1788*. A reissue of two accounts – "A Narrative of the Expedition to Botany Bay" and "A Complete Account of the Settlement of Port Jackson" – written by Trench, a captain of the marines who came ashore with the First Fleet. Trench, a natural storyteller and fine writer, was a young man in his twenties, and the accounts brim with youthful curiosity. *The Birth of Sydney* (ed) is an anthology of writings from the 1770s to the 1850s, including accounts by Captain Cook, Charles Darwin, Anthony Trollope and Mark Twain, as well as lesser-known voices. It also includes a fantastic forty-page essay by Flannery, "The Sandstone City", drawing connections between ecology, Aboriginal history and present-day Sydney.

Alan Frost *Botany Bay Mirages: Illusions of Australia's Convict Beginnings.* Historian Frost's well-argued attempt to overturn many long-cherished notions about European settlement.

Donald Horne *The Lucky Country.* Although nearly thirty years old, this seminal analysis of Australian society, written in 1976, has yet to be matched and is still often quoted.

★ **Robert Hughes** *The Fatal Shore.* A minutely detailed epic of the origins of transportation and the brutal beginnings of white Australia.

Grace Karskens *The Rocks: Life in Early Sydney.* Karskens' detailed social history draws a vivid picture of Australia's earliest neighbourhood from 1788 until the 1830s.

Rosemary Neill *White Out: How Politics is Killing Black Australia.* Published in 2003, Journalist Neill asserts in this outspoken book that the rhetoric of self-determination and empowerment excuses the wider society from doing anything to reduce the disparity between black and white Australian populations. Busting taboos about indigenous affairs, she criticizes both left and right ideologies.

Portia Robinson *The Women of Botany Bay.* After painstaking research into the records of every woman transported from Britain between 1787 and 1828, as well as the wives of convicts who settled in Australia, Robinson is able to tell us just who the women of Botany Bay really were.

Peter Spearitt *Sydney's Century: a History.* A very readable academic history, following Sydney's social and physical development in the twentieth century. Archival photographs, maps, cartoons, advertisements and snippets from novels and magazines help flesh out a fascinating portrait.

Larry Writer *Razor.* A satisfyingly lurid account of the mean streets of inner-city Sydney of the 1930s, with its vicious gang wars and rule by two blood-enemy vice queens, Tilly Devine and Kate Leigh. The two women oversaw empires based on prostitution, gambling, alcohol, drugs and extortion. Engrossing photos and crims' mugshots accompany the text.

Biography and autobiography

John Dale *Huckstepp: a Dangerous Life.* The still-unsolved 1986 murder of Sallie-Anne Huckstepp, herself steeped in Sydney's criminal underworld of drugs and prostitution, continues to capture the public imagination. When her drug-dealing boyfriend, Lanfranchi, was shot dead in 1981 by detective Roger Rogerson, later proved to be one of New South Wales' most corrupt officers, the young, beautiful and articulate Huckstepp went to the national media to accuse the police force of cold-blooded murder. This investigation by Dale, also a writer of detective fiction, is as engrossing as any thriller.

Robin Dalton *Aunts Up the Cross.* Dalton, a prominent London literary agent, spent her childhood in the 1920s and 1930s in Kings Cross, in a huge mansion peopled by the eccentric aunts (and uncles) of the title.

Dulcie Deamer *The Queen of Bohemia.* Dulcie Deamer, Kings Cross resident for half a century, wrote this memoir in her seventies, attempting to capture the bohemian literary and artistic community of

Sydney in the Roaring Twenties. Deamer, a standout with her theatrical outfits, dancing and imaginative rituals, reigned undisputed queen of all the other eccentrics of the period.

★ **Clive James** *Unreliable Memoirs*. The expat satirist humorously recalls his postwar childhood and adolescence in Sydney's southern suburbs.

Jill Ker Conway *The Road from Coorain*. Conway's childhood, on a drought-stricken Outback station during the 1940s, is movingly told, as is her battle to establish herself as a young historian in sexist, provincial 1950s Sydney.

Hazel Rowley *Christina Stead: a Biography*. Stead (1902–83) has been acclaimed as Australia's greatest novelist. After spending years in Paris, London and New York with her American husband, she returned to her native Sydney in her old age.

Travel writing

Bill Bryson *Down Under* (published in the US as *In a Sunburnt Country*). Famously funny travel writer Bill Bryson devotes a chapter of his Australia book, published in 2000, to "the frappaccino heaven that is modern Sydney".

★ **Peter Carey** *30 Days in Sydney*. This is part of Bloomsbury Publishers' "The Writer and the City" project, where "some of the finest writers of our time reveal the secrets of a city they know best"; the first book in the series was Edmund White's Paris tribute, *The Flaneur*. Based in New York, famous Australian writer Carey set himself a thirty-day time frame and subtitled his book "A wildly distorted account", to defuse ideas that it might be a comprehensive guide. As he hangs out with old friends, it is their lives, the tales they tell and the often nostalgic trips around Sydney form the basis of this vivid city portrait.

Louis-Claude Desaulses de Freycinet *Reflections on New South Wales*. The fascinating journals of the French explorer – who first visited Port Jackson in 1802 as Baudin's cartographer, and again in 1819 as the commander of the *Uranie* – describing the time he spent six weeks travelling around New South Wales with his wife; translated for the first time into English in 2001.

Richard Hall (ed) *The Oxford Book of Sydney*. Oxford University Press's contribution to the deluge of books on Sydney which came out in time for the Olympics: this wide-ranging collection of writing – including journalism, letters, poems and novel excerpts – spans 1788 to 1997.

Geoffrey Moorhouse *Sydney*. The internationally renowned British historian and travel writer has made Sydney the subject of his nineteenth book. All the latest developments – from the Gay Mardi Gras to police corruption and inner-city Aboriginal poverty – are analysed, and their roots traced back to the city's beginnings.

★ **Jan Morris** *Sydney*. An insightful and informative account of Australia's favourite city by one of the world's most respected travel writers; written in the early 1990s, so now a little dated but nevertheless set to become a classic.

Ruth Park *Ruth Park's Sydney*. By one of Australia's most loved storytellers, author of *The Harp in the South* trilogy (see p.330), Park's impressionistic and personal look takes the form of a walking guide full of anecdotes and literary quotations; written in 1973, and long out of print, it was revised and expanded in 1999 by Rafe Champion.

Sydney in fiction

Peter Corris *The Empty Beach*. Australia's answer to Raymond Chandler. This is one of a series of Cliff Hardy detective stories, all set in a glittering but seedy Sydney. Private eye Hardy investigates murder and exploitation in a Bondi old people's home.

Eleanor Dark *The Timeless Land*. A historical novel which recounts the beginnings of Australia.

Tom Gilling *Miles McGinty*. Gilling is known for his colourful historical fables. Nineteenth-century Sydney comes alive in this riotous, entertaining love story of Miles, who becomes a levitator's assistant and begins to float on air, and Isabel, who wants to fly.

Kate Grenville *Lilian's Story*. The tragicomic tale of Lilian Singer is loosely based on the life of Bea Miles, the eccentric, Shakespeare-spouting, tram-stopping, taxi-hijacking Sydney bag lady. *The Idea of Perfection*, set in the tiny, fictional New South Wales town of Karakarook, and about two unlikely characters who fall in love, won the UK's 2001 Orange Prize for Fiction.

Linda Jaivin *Eat Me*. A successful first novel billed as an "erotic feast"; opens with a memorable fruit-squeezing scene as three trendy women (fashion editor, academic and writer) hang out in Darlinghurst cafés and swap stories of sexual exploits – though we never quite know who is telling the truth.

★ **Malcolm Knox** *Summerland*. The "summerland" of the title is Palm Beach, Sydney's playground for the wealthy, where narrator Richard has been coming every year to stay with friend and golden boy Hugh Bowman, and now, in adulthood, their partners. Richard's telling of the disintegration of a friendship and the downfall of Hugh gives a critical insight into an exclusive, less-than-perfect social milieu.

★ **Roger McDonald** *Mr Darwin's Shooter*. The shooter of the title is Syms Covington, Charles Darwin's servant on the famous *Beagle* expedition. He eventually settled in Sydney's Watsons Bay, and is captured here in the 1850s as, now middle-aged and troubled by the theory of evolution he helped to evolve, he awaits with trepidation the publication of *The Origin of the Species*. Finely written and immaculately researched.

Ruth Park *The Harp in the South*. First published in 1948, this first book of the trilogy is a well-loved tale of inner-Sydney slum life in 1940s Surry Hills. The spirited Darcy family's battle against poverty provides memorable characters, not least the Darcy grandmother with her fierce Irish humour.

Dorothy Porter *The Monkey's Mask*. This novel in verse is a detective thriller and a fine piece of erotica. A tough lesbian private investigator trawls through the Sydney literary scene on the hunt for a murderer of a young student. Disturbing, full of suspense – and very witty. Recently made into a film.

Mandy Sayer and Louis Nowra (eds) *In The Gutter... Looking At The Stars*. Subtitled "A literary adventure through Kings Cross", this anthology – combining fiction, poetry and memoir from a cast of well-known Australian writers past and present – portrays Sydney's red light district as Australia's great bohemian quarter.

★ **Christina Stead** *For Love Alone*. Set largely around Sydney Harbour in the 1920s, where the late author grew up, this novel follows the obsessive Teresa Hawkins, a poor but artistic girl from an unconventional family, who scrounges and saves to head for London and love.

Kylie Tennant *Ride on Stranger*. First published in 1943, this is a humorous portrait of Sydney between the two world wars, seen through the eyes of a newcomer.

Food and wine

Jean-Paul Bruneteau *Tukka: Real Australian Food*. This chef, who arrived in Australia in 1967 as a child from France, is passionate about the use and understanding of native Australian foods. More than just a cookbook, this is a wide-ranging combination of well-researched history and botany too.

★ **Ben Canaider and Greg Duncan Powell** *Drink Drank Drunk*. Fun, no-nonsense 2003 guide to Australian wine by an irreverent duo.

★ **Bill Granger** *Sydney Food*. The self-taught chef Granger runs the very popular *bills* (see p.177) in Darlinghurst. His cooking style is based on using the freshest ingredients in simple combinations. Although he is originally from Melbourne, this book is something of a homage to Sydney, and includes gorgeous pictures of city settings that makes it a great souvenir.

Huon Hooke and Ralph Kyte-Powell *The Penguin Good Australian Wine Guide*. Released every year in Australia, this is a handy book for a wine buff to buy on the ground, with the best wines and prices detailed to help navigate you around the bottle shop.

Kylie Kwong *Kylie Kwong: Recipes & Stories*. Sydney chef Kylie Kwong cooks contemporary Chinese at her stylish restaurant *Billy Kwong* (see p.187). Her cookbook not only provides some great recipes but gives an insight into Chinese-Australian culture, from shopping in Chinatown to memorable family meals.

Tim Low *Bush Tucker: Australia's Wild Food Harvest* and *Wild Food Plants of Australia*. Guides to the bountiful supply of bushtucker that was once the mainstay of the Aboriginal diet; the latter is pocket-sized and contains clear photographs of over 180 plants, describing their uses.

Art and architecture

Wally Caruana *Aboriginal Art*. An excellent illustrated paperback introduction to all styles of Aboriginal art.

Philip Drewe and Jørn Utzon *Sydney Opera House*. A study of one of the world's most striking pieces of contemporary architecture, designed by Jørn Utzon, with detailed photographs and notes.

Robert Hughes *The Art of Australia*. The internationally acclaimed art historian, author of *The Shock of the New*, cut his teeth on this seminal dissection of Australian art up to the 1960s.

Alice Spigelman *Almost Full Circle: Harry Seidler*. Biography of Sydney's (and Australia's) most notable architect, the Viennese-born Seidler, who migrated to Australia in 1948 after a wartime internment in Canada. He went on to build Sydney's first skyscraper, the fifty-storey Australia Square on George Street, in 1963, and has continued to revolutionize the skyline.

Specialist guides

Alan Fairley *Sydney's Best Bushland Walks.* The "Top 30" walks detailed – which include nature notes and maps – are all accessible by public transport.

Tim Flannery *The Future Eaters.* Palaeontologist Flannery here poses that as the first human beings migrated down to Australasia, the Aborigines, Maoris and other Polynesian peoples changed the region's flora and fauna in startling ways, and began consuming the resources needed for their own future; the Europeans made an even greater impact on the environment, continuing this "future eating" of natural resources.

Kangaroo Press Publish a useful series of special interest guides including *Seeing Sydney By Bicycle* by Julia Thorn and *Sydney by Ferry and Foot* by John Gunter.

Greg Pritchard *Climbing Australia: the Essential Guide.* The most up-to-date, comprehensive guide for rock-climbers. Covers everything from the major climbing sites to the best websites, with easy-to-understand route descriptions.

Tyrone Thomas *100 Walks in NSW.* Forty-six of the walks cover the area detailed in this book, with tracks on the Central Coast, in the Royal National Park and the Blue Mountains.

Mark Warren *Atlas of Australian Surfing.* A comprehensive guide to riding the best of Australia's waves.

Mary White *The Greening of Gondwana.* Classic work on the evolution of Australia's flora and geography.

Index

and small print

Index

Entries in colour indicate a map

A rough guide to Rough Guides

In the summer of 1981, Mark Ellingham, a recent graduate from Bristol University, was travelling round Greece and couldn't find a guidebook that really met his needs. On the one hand there were the student guides, insistent on saving every last cent, and on the other the heavyweight cultural tomes whose authors seemed to have spent more time in a research library than lounging away the afternoon at a taverna or on the beach.

In a bid to avoid getting a job, Mark and a small group of writers set about creating their own guidebook. It was a guide to Greece that aimed to combine a journalistic approach to description with a thoroughly practical approach to travellers' needs – a guide that would incorporate culture, history and contemporary insights with a critical edge, together with up-to-date, value-for-money listings. Back in London, Mark and the team finished their Rough Guide, as they called it, and talked Routledge into publishing the book.

That first *Rough Guide to Greece*, published in 1982, was a student scheme that became a publishing phenomenon. The immediate success of the book – with numerous reprints and a Thomas Cook Prize shortlisting – spawned a series that rapidly covered dozens of destinations. Rough Guides had a ready market among low-budget backpackers, but soon also acquired a much broader and older readership that relished Rough Guides' wit and inquisitiveness as much as their enthusiastic, critical approach. Everyone wants value for money, but not at any price.

Rough Guides soon began supplementing the "rougher" information about hostels and low-budget listings with the kind of detail on restaurants and quality hotels that independent-minded visitors on any budget might expect, whether on business in New York or trekking in Thailand.

These days the guides – distributed worldwide by the Penguin Group – offer recommendations from shoestring to luxury and cover more than 200 destinations around the globe, including almost every country in the Americas and Europe, more than half of Africa, and most of Asia and Australasia. Our ever-growing team of authors and photographers is spread all over the world, particularly in Europe, the USA and Australia.

In 1994, we published the *Rough Guide to World Music* and *Rough Guide to Classical Music*, and a year later the *Rough Guide to the Internet*. All three books have become benchmark titles in their fields – which encouraged us to expand into other areas of publishing, mainly around popular culture. Rough Guides now publish:

- Travel guides to more than 200 destinations worldwide
- Dictionary phrasebooks for 22 major languages
- History guides ranging from Ireland to Islam
- Maps printed on rip-proof and waterproof Polyart™ paper
- Music guides running the gamut from Opera to Elvis
- Restaurant guides to London, New York and San Francisco
- Reference books on topics as diverse as the Weather and Shakespeare
- Sports guides from Formula 1 to Man Utd
- Pop culture books from Lord of the Rings to Cult TV
- World Music CDs in association with World Music Network.

Visit **www.roughguides.com** to see our latest publications.

Rough Guide credits

Text editor: Sally Schafer
Managing director: Kevin Fitzgerald
Series editor: Mark Ellingham
Editorial: Martin Dunford, Jonathan Buckley, Kate Berens, Ann-Marie Shaw, Helena Smith, Olivia Swift, Ruth Blackmore, Geoff Howard, Claire Saunders, Gavin Thomas, Alexander Mark Rogers, Polly Thomas, Joe Staines, Richard Lim, Duncan Clark, Peter Buckley, Lucy Ratcliffe, Alison Murchie, Matthew Teller, Andrew Dickson, Fran Sandham, Matthew Milton, Karoline Densley (UK); Andrew Rosenberg, Yuki Takagaki, Richard Koss, Hunter Slaton (US)
Design & Layout: Link Hall, Helen Prior, Julia Bovis, Katie Pringle, Rachel Holmes, Andy Turner, Dan May, Tanya Hall, John McKay, Sophie Hewat (UK); Madhulita Mohapatra,

Umesh Aggarwal, Sunil Sharma (India)
Cartography: Maxine Repath, Ed Wright, Katie Lloyd-Jones (UK); Manish Chandra, Rajesh Chhibber, Jai Prakash Mishra (India)
Cover art direction: Louise Boulton
Picture research: Sharon Martins, Mark Thomas
Online: Kelly Martinez, Anja Mutic-Blessing, Jennifer Gold, Audra Epstein, Suzanne Welles, Cree Lawson (US); Manik Chauhan, Amarjyoti Dutta, Narender Kumar (India)
Finance: Gary Singh
Marketing & Publicity: Richard Trillo, Niki Smith, David Wearn, Chloë Roberts, Demelza Dallow, Claire Southern (UK); Geoff Colquitt, David Wechsler, Megan Kennedy (US)
Administration: Julie Sanderson
RG India: Punita Singh

Publishing information

This third edition published November 2003 by **Rough Guides Ltd**,
80 Strand, London WC2R 0RL
345 Hudson St, 4th Floor,
New York, NY 10014, USA.
Distributed by the Penguin Group
Penguin Books Ltd,
80 Strand, London WC2R 0RL
Penguin Putnam, Inc.
375 Hudson St, NY 10014, USA
Penguin Books Australia Ltd,
487 Maroondah Highway, PO Box 257,
Ringwood, Victoria 3134, Australia
Penguin Books Canada Ltd,
10 Alcorn Avenue, Toronto ON,
M4V 1E4 Canada
Penguin Books (NZ) Ltd,
182–190 Wairau Road, Auckland 10,
New Zealand
Typeset in Bembo and Helvetica to an original design by Henry Iles.
Printed in Italy by LegoPrint S.p.A.

352pp includes index.
A catalogue record for this book is available from the British Library.

ISBN 1-84353-116-X

The publishers and authors have done their best to ensure the accuracy and currency of all the information in **The Rough Guide to Sydney**; however, they can accept no responsibility for any loss, injury or inconvenience sustained by any traveller as a result of information or advice contained in the guide.

1   3   5   7   9   8   6   4   2

Help us update

We've gone to a lot of effort to ensure that the fifth edition of **The Rough Guide to Sydney** is accurate and up to date. However, things change – places get "discovered", opening hours are notoriously fickle, restaurants and rooms raise prices or lower standards. If you feel we've got it wrong or left something out, we'd like to know, and if you can remember the address, the price, the time, the phone number, so much the better.

We'll credit all contributions, and send a copy of the next edition (or any other Rough Guide if you prefer) for the best letters. Everyone who writes to us and isn't already a subscriber will receive a copy of our full-colour thrice-yearly newsletter. Please mark letters: "**Rough Guide Sydney Update**" and send to: Rough Guides, 80 Strand, London WC2R 0RL, or Rough Guides, 4th Floor, 345 Hudson St, New York, NY 10014. Or send an email to **mail@roughguides.com**.

Have your questions answered and tell others about your trip at **www.roughguides.atinfopop.com**.

Acknowledgements

The author would like to thank Adrian Proszenko for bars, clubs and music research. Thanks to Linden Hyatt for Blue Mountains hospitality, Janine Daly for kindness, support and extra research, Michael Schofield for tips on sport, Caroline Nesbitt, Franca Morelli and Margaret and Arthur Daly for fabulous help with childcare, and special thanks to my little companion Lila. Thanks also to Sally Schafer and Claire Saunders for Herculean editing efforts and the wonderful cartography team who deciphered all those maps.

In addition the editor would like to thank all those involved in producing this book, including Umesh Aggarwal for expert typesetting and layout; Mark Thomas for excellent picture research; Katie Lloyd-Jones, Stratigraphics and Miles Irving for their cartographic expertise; Louise Boulton for the superb cover; David Price for proofreading; Claire Saunders, Helena Smith and Alison Murchie for additional editing; and special thanks to Clifton Wilkinson and Claire Saunders for all their advice and to Jinny Uppington for last-minute help.

Readers' letters

Many thanks to the readers of the last edition who took the time to write in with their comments and suggestions:

Sally Attwood, Tim Burford, Julie Clayton, Richard Crighton, Tom Crow, Chris Davis, Ian T. Farley, Suzanne Genever, Sam Griggs, Elizabeth Hogan, Jo Hunt, Susan Jackson, Ingrid K. Lund, Tracy Lynch, Sally Martin, Mike Mordue, Katherine Moxhay, Moyra Pierce, Sally Robbins, Theresa Tuke, Barbara and Beverly Tyler.

SMALL PRINT

Photo credits

SMALL PRINT

Rough Guides publishes new books every month:

Rough Guides music & reference

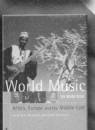

NOTES

Present this voucher at Sydney Aquarium and receive **25% off** each adult & child* ticket purchased

The No.1 attraction in Australia,
The most extensive display of Australian
aquatic life in the world,
The biggest collection of sharks in captivity
The largest Great Barrier Reef
complex in the world

SYDNEY AQUARIUM

Sydney Aquarium
Darling Harbour
Open 9am to 10pm

*This offer is for single admission type tickets only. Cannot be used in conjunction with any
other combined ticket or offer. This coupon must be presented to the cashier on arrival.
Discount is not valid on Family admission rates. VALID TO 31st October 2004

0000043

**Don't miss the experience of a lifetime... Visit the Oceanworld
website to find out more, at www.sharkdive.oceanworld.com.au**

25% discount **NOT** valid on Shark Dive Xtreme

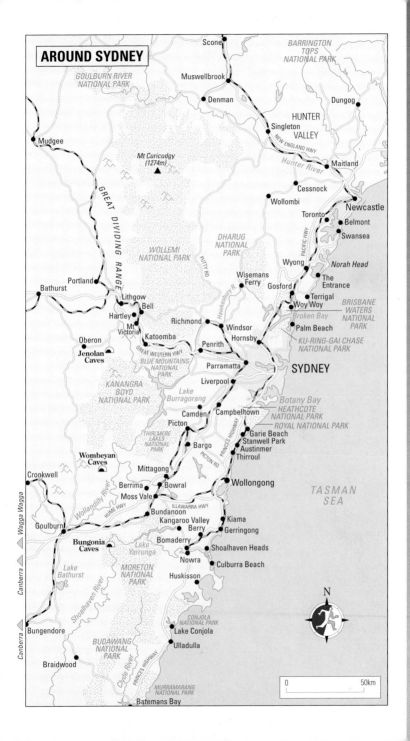

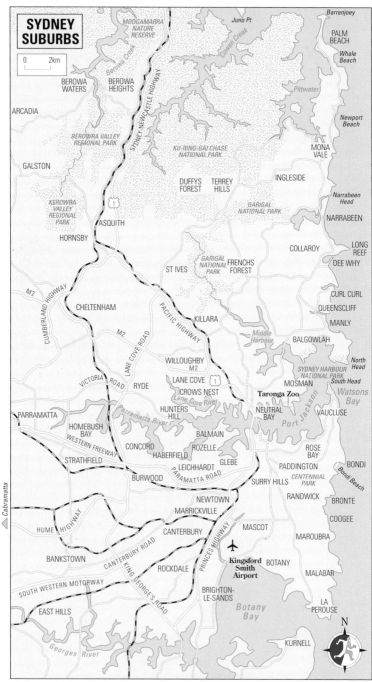

SYDNEY SUBURBS

0   2km

Barrenjoey
PALM BEACH
Whale Beach
Juno Pt
Cowan Creek
MOOGAMARRA NATURE RESERVE
Berowra Creek
BEROWA WATERS
BEROWA HEIGHTS
SYDNEY-NEWCASTLE HIGHWAY
Pittwater
ARCADIA
BEROWRA VALLEY REGIONAL PARK
KU-RING-GAI CHASE NATIONAL PARK
Newport Beach
GALSTON
MONA VALE
KERONRA VALLEY REGIONAL PARK
DUFFYS FOREST
TERREY HILLS
INGLESIDE
ASQUITH
BARIGAL NATIONAL PARK
Narrabeen Head
NARRABEEN
HORNSBY
GARIGAL NATIONAL PARK
FRENCHS FOREST
COLLAROY
LONG REEF
DEE WHY
M2
CUMBERLAND HIGHWAY
ST IVES
CURL CURL
QUEENSCLIFF
CHELTENHAM
PACIFIC HIGHWAY
KILLARA
MANLY
M2
LANE COVE ROAD
Middle Harbour
BALGOWLAH
North Head
VICTORIA ROAD
WILLOUGHBY
M2
SYDNEY HARBOUR NATIONAL PARK
LANE COVE
CROWS NEST
MOSMAN
South Head
Watsons Bay
RYDE
Lane Cove River
Taronga Zoo
PARRAMATTA
HUNTERS HILL
NEUTRAL BAY
VAUCLUSE
Parramatta River
Port Jackson
HOMEBUSH BAY
BALMAIN
WESTERN FREEWAY
CONCORD
ROZELLE
ROSE BAY
STRATHFIELD
HABERFIELD
GLEBE
PADDINGTON
BONDI
LEICHHARDT
PARRAMATTA ROAD
CENTENNIAL PARK
Bondi Beach
BURWOOD
SURRY HILLS
Cabramatta
NEWTOWN
RANDWICK
BRONTE
MARRICKVILLE
MASCOT
COOGEE
HUME HIGHWAY
CANTERBURY
MAROUBRA
BANKSTOWN
CANTERBURY ROAD
PRINCES HIGHWAY
ROCKDALE
Kingsford Smith Airport
BOTANY
MALABAR
SOUTH WESTERN MOTORWAY
KING GEORGE'S ROAD
BRIGHTON-LE-SANDS
LA PEROUSE
EAST HILLS
Botany Bay
Georges River
KURNELL

N

Cronulla

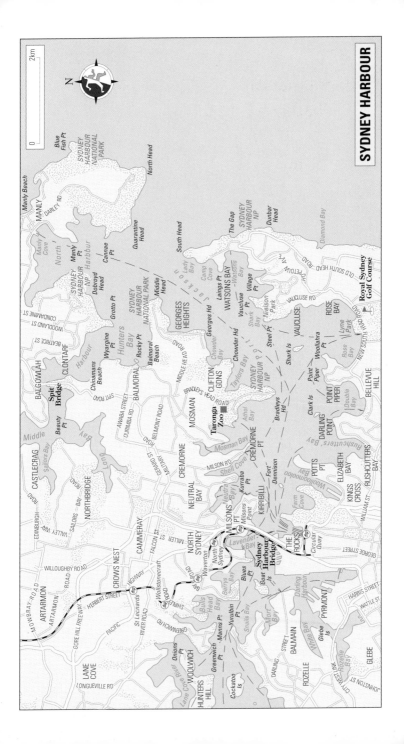

SYDNEY HARBOUR

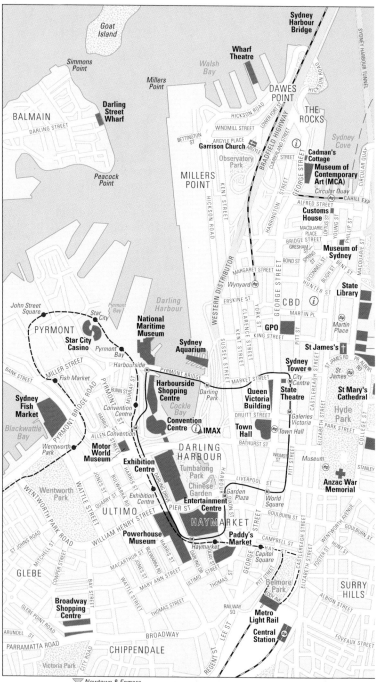

Goat
Island

Simmons
Point

Millers
Point

Walsh
Bay

**Wharf
Theatre**

**Sydney
Harbour
Bridge**

BALMAIN

**Darling
Street
Wharf**

DARLING STREET

HICKSON ROAD

WINDMILL STREET

BETTINGTON
ST

ARGYLE PLACE

Garrison Church

Observatory
Park

ARGYLE
STREET

CUMBERLAND STREET

DAWES
POINT

THE
ROCKS

Sydney
Cove

**Cadman's
Cottage**

**Museum of
Contemporary
Art (MCA)**

GEORGE STREET

Circular Quay

CIRCULAR QUAY

CAHILL EXP

Peacock
Point

MILLERS
POINT

KENT STREET

HICKSON ROAD

ALFRED STREET

**Customs
House**

YOUNG ST

PHILLIP ST

MACQUARIE
PLACE

BRIDGE STREET

GRESHAM ST

**Museum of
Sydney**

MACQUARIE STREET

BOND ST

SPRING
ST

LOFTUS ST

BENT ST

BLIGH ST

O'CONNELL ST

**State
Library**

Darling
Harbour

Pyrmont
Bay

Star
City

John Street
Square

PYRMONT

**Star City
Casino**

Pyrmont
Bay

MARGARET STREET

ERSKINE STREET

Wynyard

CBD

GEORGE STREET

YORK STREET

CLARENCE STREET

KENT STREET

HUNTER ST

MARTIN PL

GPO

KING STREET

**Martin
Place**

**National
Maritime
Museum**

**Sydney
Aquarium**

Harbourside

PYRMONT BRIDGE

SUSSEX STREET

MARKET STREET

St James's

**Sydney
Tower**

City
Centre

St James

PR ALBERT
RD

ST JAMES RD

BANK STREET

MILLER STREET

Fish Market

**Harbourside
Shopping
Centre**

Darling
Park

**Queen
Victoria
Building**

**State
Theatre**

CASTLEREAGH STREET

PITT ST

**St Mary's
Cathedral**

**Sydney
Fish
Market**

Blackwattle
Bay

Cockle
Bay

**Convention
Centre** **IMAX**

DRUITT STREET

Galeries
Victoria

**Town
Hall**

BATHURST ST

Town Hall

ELIZABETH STREET

PARK STREET

**Hyde
Park**

Convention
Centre

BUNN ST

MURRAY ST

HARRIS ST

ALLEN
Convention

**Motor
World
Museum**

Wentworth
Park

**DARLING
HARBOUR**

WILMOT
ST

Museum

STANLEY

**Exhibition
Centre**

**Tumbalong
Park**

LIVERPOOL ST

Garden
Plaza

World
Square

**Anzac War
Memorial**

JONES ST

BULWARRA RD

QUARRY ST

CARLING DRIVE

Exhibition
Centre

**Chinese
Garden**

**Entertainment
Centre**

PIER ST

ULTIMO

WILLIAM HENRY STREET

WENTWORTH PARK ROAD

WATTLE STREET

HAYMARKET

HARBOUR STREET

GEORGE STREET

GOULBURN ST

WENTWORTH AVENUE

GOULBURN ST

HUNT ST

FOSTER STREET

CASTLEREAGH STREET

ELIZABETH STREET

**SURRY
HILLS**

ST JOHNS ROAD

MITCHELLS ST

GLEBE

COWPER STREET

BAY STREET

**Powerhouse
Museum**

MACARTHUR ST

BULWARRA RD

JONES ST

MARY ANN STREET

DARLING DR

ULTIMO STREET

Haymarket

**Paddy's
Market**

HAY ST

**Capitol
Square**

CAMPBELL ST

ALBION STREET

**Broadway
Shopping
Centre**

GLEBE POINT ROAD

THOMAS STREET

**Belmore
Park**

KETTY AVE

**Metro
Light Rail**

FOVEAUX STREET

ARUNDEL
ST

PARRAMATTA ROAD

CITY ROAD

BROADWAY

RAILWAY
SQ

LEE ST

REGENT ST

PITT ST

ELIZABETH STREET

**Central
Station**

CHIPPENDALE

Victoria Park

Newtown & Enmore

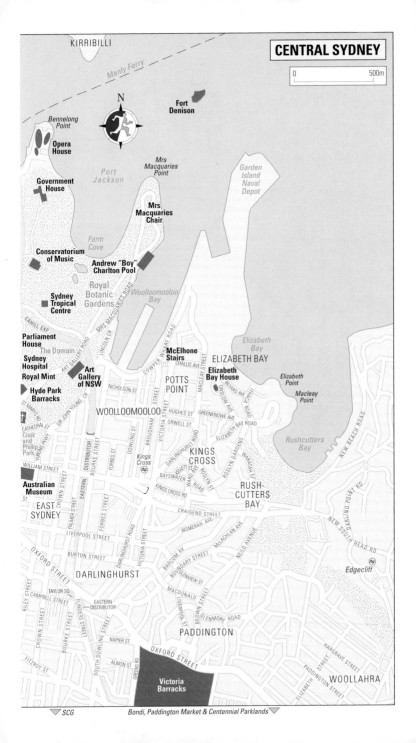

CENTRAL SYDNEY

0   500m

KIRRIBILLI

Manly Ferry

N

Fort
Denison

Bennelong
Point

Opera
House

Government
House

Port
Jackson

Mrs
Macquaries
Point

Garden
Island
Naval
Depot

Mrs
Macquaries
Chair

Farm
Cove

Conservatorium
of Music

Andrew "Boy"
Charlton Pool

Royal
Botanic
Gardens

Woolloomooloo
Bay

Sydney
Tropical
Centre

CAHILL EXP

Elizabeth
Bay

Parliament
House

The Domain

McElhone
Stairs

CHALLIS AVE

ELIZABETH BAY

Elizabeth
Point

Sydney
Hospital

Royal Mint

Art
Gallery
of NSW

POTTS
POINT

Elizabeth
Bay House

Macleay
Point

Hyde Park
Barracks

NICHOLSON ST

HUGHES ST

GREENKNOWE AVE

Rushcutters
Bay

WOOLLOOMOOLOO

ORWELL ST

Cook
and
Phillip
Park

DISTRIBUTOR

BROUGHAM STREET

VICTORIA STREET

DARLINGHURST ROAD

ELIZABETH BAY ROAD

WILLIAM STREET

BOURKE STREET

FORBES ST

Kings
Cross

KINGS
CROSS

ROSLYN GARDENS

WARATAH ST

NEW BEACH ROAD

Australian
Museum

EASTERN

BAYSWATER

KINGS CROSS RD

RUSH-
CUTTERS
BAY

EAST
SYDNEY

CROWN STREET

PALMER STREET

FORBES STREET

DARLINGHURST ROAD

CRAIGEND STREET

LIVERPOOL STREET

VICTORIA STREET

WOMERAH AVE

MCLACHLAN AVE

NEILD AVENUE

NEW SOUTH HEAD RD

OXFORD STREET

BURTON STREET

DARLINGHURST

BARCOM AV

BOUNDARY STREET

GLENVIEW ST

Edgecliff

RILEY STREET

TAYLOR SQ

CAMPBELL STREET

FLINDERS STREET

EASTERN
DISTRIBUTOR

MACDONALD ST

LIVERPOOL ST

BROWN STREET

GLENMORE ROAD

CROWN STREET

BOURKE STREET

NAPIER ST

SOUTH DOWLING STREET

PADDINGTON

HARGRAVE STREET

FITZROY ST

ALBION RD

GREENS RD

OXFORD STREET

Victoria
Barracks

PADDINGTON STREET

WOOLLAHRA

ELIZABETH STREET

▽ SCG   Bondi, Paddington Market & Centennial Parklands ▽

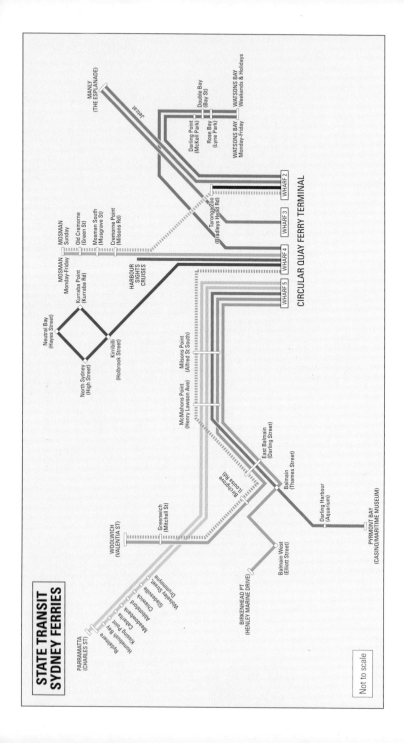

STATE TRANSIT SYDNEY FERRIES

Not to scale

CIRCULAR QUAY FERRY TERMINAL

WHARF 2
WHARF 3
WHARF 4
WHARF 5

MANLY (THE ESPLANADE)

JetCat

Double Bay (Bay St)
Darling Point (McKell Park)
Rose Bay (Lyne Park)
WATSONS BAY Weekends & Holidays
WATSONS BAY Monday-Friday

Taronga Zoo (Bradleys Head Rd)

MOSMAN Sunday
MOSMAN Monday-Friday
Old Cremorne (Green St)
Mosman South (Musgrave St)
Cremorne Point (Milsons Rd)
Kurraba Point (Kurraba Rd)

HARBOUR SIGHTS CRUISES

Neutral Bay (Hayes Street)
Kirribilli (Holbrook Street)
North Sydney (High Street)

Milsons Point (Alfred St South)
McMahons Point (Henry Lawson Ave)

East Balmain (Darling Street)
Balmain (Thames Street)
Birchgrove (Louisa Rd)

Darling Harbour (Aquarium)

PYRMONT BAY (CASINO/MARITIME MUSEUM)

Balmain West (Elliott Street)
BIRKENHEAD PT (HENLEY MARINE DRIVE)

WOOLWICH (VALENTIA ST)
Greenwich (Mitchell St)

PARRAMATTA (CHARLES ST)
Rydalmere
Homebush Bay
Kissing Point
Cabarita
Meadowbank
Abbotsford
Gladesville
Chiswick
Wolseley Street
Drummoyne

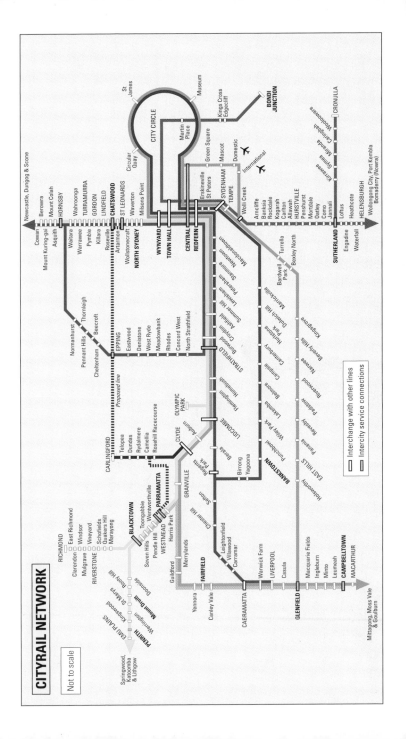

CITYRAIL NETWORK

Not to scale

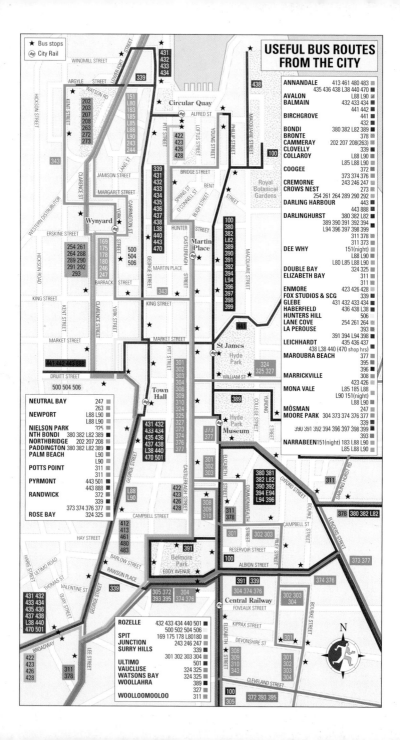